MANAGERIAL FINANCE: ESSENTIALS

MANAGERIAL FINANCE: ESSENTIALS

CHARLES O. KRONCKE
The University of Wisconsin

ERWIN ESSER NEMMERS
Northwestern University

ALAN E. GRUNEWALD
Michigan State University

HG
4026
K76
1976

West Publishing Company

St. Paul • New York • Boston

Los Angeles • San Francisco

Kroncke, Charles
  Managerial finance.

  Bibliography: p.
  Includes index.
    1.   Corporations—Finance.   2.   Business enter-
prises—Finance.   I.   Nemmers, Erwin Esser,
1916–   joint author.   II.   Grunewald,
Alan E. joint author.   III.   Title.
HG 4026 p. K76   658.1'5   76-2048

ISBN 0-8299-0098-5

PREFACE

The financial decisions in a firm center on the planning, raising, and investing of funds. In this book, the financial manger is identified as performing these functions with the avowed objective of maximizing the value of the firm. *Managerial Finance: Essentials* is designed to equip the financial manager with the necessary tools to achieve that objective.

As an "essentials" version, this book is intended for an introductory course in business finance. Analytical, institutional, and theoretical materials are combined for a comprehensive presentation of financial management. We strive to present our ideas in a clear, simple yet rigorous manner. A background in accounting and economics serves as a useful prerequisite for any study of business finance. No other preparation is necessary to read and understand this text.

Several related publications enhance the effectiveness of the textbook. The *Instructor's Manual* includes answers to the questions and problems at the end of each chapter and has extensive examination materials. The *Programmed Study Guide* is for student use and includes an outline of the text, a graduated set of problems for each chapter with many step-by-step solutions, and self-exercise examination and review questions and answers. The student using the *Programmed Study Guide* can work from the problems with solutions to the problems at the end of each chapter of the text. The text problems will in turn prepare the student to solve the remaining problems in the *Guide*. A casebook is currently being prepared.

Acknowledgement is due to those who did a very effective reviewing of our manuscript: Eugene Drzycimski, Ramon Johnson, George Pinches, Jerry Poe, Malcolm Richards, Dale Singh, and Charles Wade. A special debt is owed Professor Stephen L. Hawk for his suggestions on the structure and organization of the capital budgeting section and specifically for his exposition of cash flows which appears as Chapter 11.

The typing assistance of Mrs. Ann Anderson of The University of Wisconsin-Madison is acknowledged with pleasure and sincere thanks.

Madison, Wisconsin   C. O. K.

Chicago, Illinois   E. E. N.

East Lansing, Michigan   A. E. G.

January, 1976

TABLE OF CONTENTS

Part One

THE FINANCE FUNCTION—AN OVERVIEW

Part Two

THE MANAGEMENT OF WORKING CAPITAL

Part Three

THE MANAGEMENT OF FIXED ASSETS

Part Four

INTERMEDIATE AND LONG-TERM FINANCING

Part Five

THEORY OF FINANCE

Part Six

MANAGEMENT PROBLEMS IN LONG-TERM FINANCING

MANAGERIAL FINANCE: ESSENTIALS

part one
THE FINANCE FUNCTION— AN OVERVIEW

1

THE FINANCIAL MANAGER
AND THE FIRM

The financial manager is the focus of this text. As we forge the tools of finance, such as the techniques of analysis, financial planning, forecasting, and monitoring the firm's activities, we take the viewpoint of the financial manager. But at appropriate times we view the firm through the eyes of its sources of funds—the lenders, trade creditors, and owners.

To present a realistic view of financial decision making we begin by characterizing the firm as a system described in terms of a model that shows how the financial elements of the firm fit together. The objective of the financial manager, and thus of the model, is the maximization of the market value of the firm.

THE FINANCIAL MANAGER AND THE ECONOMY

The financial manager is a key member of the top management team. Observation of the real world shows that the effects of his decisions are felt throughout the firm. Though the final decision on all financial matters rests with the owners—the board of directors in the case of a corporation—the financial manager has a major role in planning and raising the funds needed by the firm and then putting those funds to work profitably. The decisions he makes directly affect the fortunes of the firm and have an impact on the welfare of the economy.

Because business firms are responsible for the allocation of the largest portion of our nation's labor, raw materials, and capital resources, the more efficient the performance of the financial manager, the more prosperous both the firm and the economy will be. Thus we study problems such as whether to expand plant capacity or increase inventories as well as methods used to compare the profitability of various investment proposals. New developments of recent years in the field of financial management suggest that further improvements will come rapidly.

Over the years many forms of organization have been developed. Of all these the business firm remains the most efficient allocator of human and natural resources because it must meet the test of survival in the marketplace. Firms strive to survive, and in the process, to make a profit. While profit maximization as a goal has guided both economists and businessmen for decades, the firm should look beyond immediate profits and be involved in social issues such as clean air and water, nondiscriminatory hiring practices, fair wages to its employees, education, and consumer confidence in its products. This commitment is in the long-run interest of both the firm and society.

THE FIRM AS A SYSTEM

In Figure 1.1 we view the firm as a system operating in an environment and having three subsystems—production, distribution, and finance. If we think of this system as a "black box," we realize that inputs to this box are controllable variables, such as the levels of receivables and inventory to carry, and noncontrollable variables, such as the levels of interest rates and the rate of inflation. The outputs are the results of the system which then feed back acting upon the input variables.

In our study of the firm as an allocator of resources, we are concerned with what goes on inside that black box in relation to the finance subsystem —its organization, its function, and its contribution to the prosperity of the firm and the welfare of society. We seek optimal values for controllable variables and study the impact of noncontrollable variables on possible solutions.

The finance function within this function concentrates on decisions involving investment, financing, and dividend policy.

Investment. This decision concerns allocation of resources among new projects. The returns from these projects lie in the *future,* but their costs must be paid *today.* Further, the return over cost expected in the future must be measured against the risk assumed in reaching for that profit. Meanwhile funds for the proposed projects may be diverted from what the

Figure 1.1. Model of a firm.

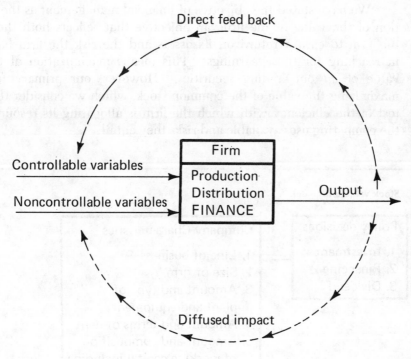

firm is presently doing with these funds or may be raised by the sale of new securities.

Financing. This decision involves the capital structure of the firm—the percentage of the firm's financing obtained through debt (long or short term), preferred stock, common stock, and retained earnings.

Dividend. This decision involves the timing and the percentage of earnings to be paid out in dividends to preferred and common stockholders. The portion not paid out is retained earnings, an important source of further financing.

MAXIMIZATION OF THE MARKET VALUE OF THE FIRM

The test of the firm's "stewardship," or efficient use, of funds under its control is value of the firm—how much people are willing to pay for the company as measured by the prices they bid for its securities. The more efficiently a firm allocates its resources, the higher the earnings available to security holders in relation to risk.

We have stated the objective of financial management as the maximization of the value of the firm, an objective that reflects both the ability of the firm to earn a return on its assets and the risk the firm has assumed in reaching for those earnings. This means maximization of the market value of *all* outstanding securities. However, our primary focus is on maximizing the value of the common stock, which we consider the ultimate test of the efficiency with which the firm is allocating its resources among the competing uses available and risks they entail.

Figure 1.2. Stock valuation model.

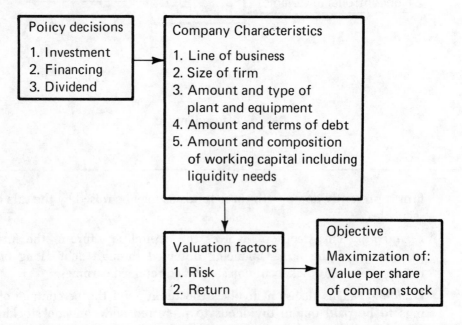

The value of the firm depends on how well the management performs its production, distribution, and finance functions. Management decisions in these areas will determine the risk-return profile of the firm. Investors place a value on this risk–return package by the prices they are willing to pay for the firm's securities. Figure 1.2 illustrates the role of the finance function in the valuation process of common stock.

Maximization versus Satisficing

Firms are organized to produce and distribute goods and services in anticipation of generating *earnings*—sales minus costs, including taxes. The profit motive is the engine that drives the economy. Funds flow to industries where earnings expectations are high, and the individual firm allocates its available funds to projects that promise the best rate of return, always considering the risk involved.

A necessary condition for all this to take place is that the firm survive through time. Survival requires an organization that is capable of cooperative effort, that has an awareness that the firm exists in an ongoing society and economy, that operates in a changing technological environment, and that generates the profits necessary to cover the risks of doing business in an uncertain environment. People are unwilling to expose their capital to a chance of loss unless there is a proportionate prospect of a return. Thus risk taking is a genuine cost of business operations, one that must be covered if the firm is to continue to fulfill its function of supplying society with desirable goods and services at fair prices. There is no conflict between the goals of maximizing market value of the firm and satisficing. Those who say they seek satisficing simply have a greater risk aversion than those who say they seek maximization. Those satisficing simply maximize at a lower level of risk.

Management Goals versus Stockholder Goals

The intermediate goals of management and stockholders frequently are at variance, though their long-run objectives usually coincide. In a firm whose stock is widely distributed an outside stockholder (not part of management) generally can have little direct influence on a given decision. Ownership and control are separated. This often gives rise to a conflict of goals.

Stockholders may prefer that the firm assume more risk by financing with debt to increase earnings; management may prefer to play it safe by using retained earnings. The stockholder can diversify his portfolio, but it is harder for management to diversify its job security risk. Stockholders may prefer a higher cash dividend to provide more spendable income; management may prefer a larger cash balance to give it greater maneuverability. These conflicts are almost always resolved in favor of management's views. Stockholder revolts are rare, and even more rarely do they succeed.

Though a separation of ownership and management functions exists, the conflict of their views can be overemphasized. The interests of both groups are reasonably similar. The stockholdings of top management of major companies such as GM, IBM, du Pont, and so on, are larger than commonly supposed. A considerable portion of top management's compensation is provided by stock options in lieu of salary. In fact, in many cases stock compensation, dividends, bonuses, and capital gains outweigh the compensation received in the form of salary.

Liquidity versus Profitability

Another basic conflict facing the financial manager is liquidity versus profitability. A firm may be highly profitable and yet encounter serious financial difficulties because it is unable to meet commitments when due. With the urge to reach for earnings the firm may leave itself with insufficient liquid reserves to meet an unexpectedly heavy drain of cash: an uninsured catastrophe may occur and require funds; payments on accounts receivable may decline sharply, thus depriving the firm of a substantial inflow; or a planned loan from a bank may not materialize.

The financial manager can drive down the risk of a shortage of liquid funds by increasing the percentage of the firm's assets held in cash or near cash items. But this result can be achieved only at the expense of the profitability of the firm, that is, through reducing the percentage of assets that are "earning" assets such as plant and equipment.

ORGANIZATIONAL FRAMEWORK FOR FINANCIAL MANAGEMENT

The finance function is not a standardized operation. It varies from firm to firm, depending on the size of the company and industry. In small firms the owner generally handles the acquisition of funds and management of its capital. He arranges for needed loans, extends credit, collects receivables, draws up a cash budget, and manages the cash account. Little delegation of functions exists.

In medium-sized firms specialization becomes apparent. The top financial officer may be called treasurer, controller, or vice-president of finance. His role varies with the policy of the firm and his own abilities. He may be responsible for the credit and collection department, the accounting department, the annual reports, or the capital budgeting program.

In a large firm the top financial manager is likely to be a vice-president of finance, reporting directly to the president, and frequently he is on the board of directors. He has the responsibility for financial policy and planning. Under him may be the treasurer and controller. The treasurer is responsible for arranging to meet the liquidity needs of the firm, and the controller serves as the chief monitor of the overall performance of the firm. In some large firms all financial responsibilities are divided between a treasurer and controller.

Important among the responsibilities of the financial executive is long-range planning: estimating industry trends, forecasting revenues and costs, evaluating ways of raising needed capital, and budgeting. The financial manager participates in decisions involving dividend policy, the acquisition of other firms, the refinancing of maturing debt, and the introduction of a major new product. Managing the firm's working capital (such as arranging for short-term loans), supervising the extension of credit and the collection of receivables, preparing the cash budget, and disbursing funds occupy much of the financial manager's time. Thus to fulfill his position competently, he needs a good background in accounting, a thorough understanding of financial management, and an intimate knowledge of the operations of the firm whose activities he is guiding.

Summary

The welfare of society requires efficient allocation of resources. The business firm generally does this job well. The value of the firm is measured by the prices investors are willing to pay for its securities, and these prices indicate how well a particular firm is doing its job.

The goal of the financial manager is maximization of the value of the firm. Achievement of this goal requires the financial manager to integrate financing, investment, and dividend decisions. In his daily activities the financial manager, whether his title is treasurer, controller, or vice-president of finance, must provide for the liquidity needs of the firm and be concerned with its profitability. The financial manager's reach for profits is constrained by the firm's need for liquidity. Also in reaching for profits he must consider the element of risk. Risk and return are the major elements influencing the value of the firm.

Study Questions

1. Why must each of us be concerned with the efficient allocation of economic resources?
2. Discuss risk taking as a cost of doing business.
3. Contrast the activities of planning, organizing, executing, and controlling in the small and the large firm.

4. Discuss some of the implications of a firm's financial decisions upon the economy.
5. The establishment of a standard set of solutions to financial problems which is operational and will lead to good results is not possible. Discuss.
6. Give the three major decisions into which all the decisions related to the finance function can be classified. Describe each.
7. Why do we take maximization of the market value of the firm as the objective of our financial management model, and what is the significance of this objective to society?
8. At what points are the intermediate goals of management and stockholders frequently at variance?
9. Generally it is not possible for an industrial organization to be highly liquid and highly profitable at the same time. Discuss. Is the same true for an individual managing his own investment assets? What exists in the economy that prevents liquidity and profitability from being jointly available?

Problems

1. Study the histories of several well-known firms that have failed, such as Penn Central, Four Seasons Nursing Homes, or Viatron Computer Systems Corporation, and ascertain the extent to which the failure can be ascribed to financial decisions.
2. Examine a random sample of annual reports of industrial and public utility firms that indicate the occupation of each of its directors. Note the number and position of those representing the finance area.

Selected References

Anthony, R. N., "The Trouble with Profit Maximization," *Harvard Business Review*, 38 (Nov.–Dec. 1960), pp. 126–134.

Branch, B., "Corporate Objectives and Market Performance," *Financial Management*, 2 (Summer 1973), pp. 24–29.

Dewing, A. S., *The Financial Policy of Corporations*, vol. 1, 5th ed. New York: Ronald Press, 1953, chap. 1.

Donaldson, G., "Financial Goals: Management vs. Stockholders," *Harvard Business Review*, 41 (May–June 1963), pp. 116–129.

Drucker, P. F., "Business Objectives and Survival Needs," *Journal of Business*, 31 (Apr. 1958), pp. 81–90.

Forrester, J. W., *Industrial Dynamics*. Cambridge, Mass.: M. I. T. Press, 1962, chap. 1 and 2.

Krum, J. R., "Who Controls Finance in the Giants?" *Financial Executive*, 38 (Mar. 1970), pp. 20–29.

Lewellen, W. G., "Management and Ownership in the Large Firm," *Journal of Finance*, 24 (May 1969), pp. 299–322.

Moag, J. S., W. T. Carleton, and E. M. Lerner, "Defining the Finance Function: A Model-Systems Approach," *Journal of Finance*, 22 (Dec. 1967), pp. 543–555.

Weston, J. F., *The Scope and Methodology of Finance*. Englewood Cliffs, N. J.: Prentice-Hall, 1966.

——, "New Themes in Finance," *Journal of Finance*, 29 (Mar. 1974), pp. 237–243.

2

THE FLOW OF FUNDS IN A FIRM

FLOW OF FUNDS SYSTEM

A firm may be likened to a living organism and characterized as a system. Each major activity of the firm, such as production, distribution, or finance, may be compared to a vital organ. The flow of funds through the firm may be thought of as the life blood of the organism. Figure 2.1 shows the flow of the firm.

Funds enter the firm in the form of cash and credit, are converted into goods and services, and then are reconverted into cash through the sale of goods and services. The process is then repeated and is continuous.

Cash: The Focal Point of the Flow of Funds

Generally the first cash available to the firm is provided by the owners—proprietor, partners, or original stockholders. Once the firm is established, credit is obtained from suppliers, additional cash may be obtained through a bank loan, and needed equipment may be leased.

If the firm is a manufacturer, cash and credit are applied to the purchase of raw materials, labor, supplies, heat, light, and so on. Through manufacturing, the raw materials are converted into work-in-process and then into finished goods. With the sale of the merchandise on credit, the finished goods are converted into accounts receivable, and collection of the receivables reinstates the cash to begin a new cycle. As the process continues and if no losses occur, the value of the firm will be higher at the end of the period than at the beginning. The increase in value represents the profit the firm earned through its goods-creating activities.

Figure 2.1.   The flow of funds through a firm.

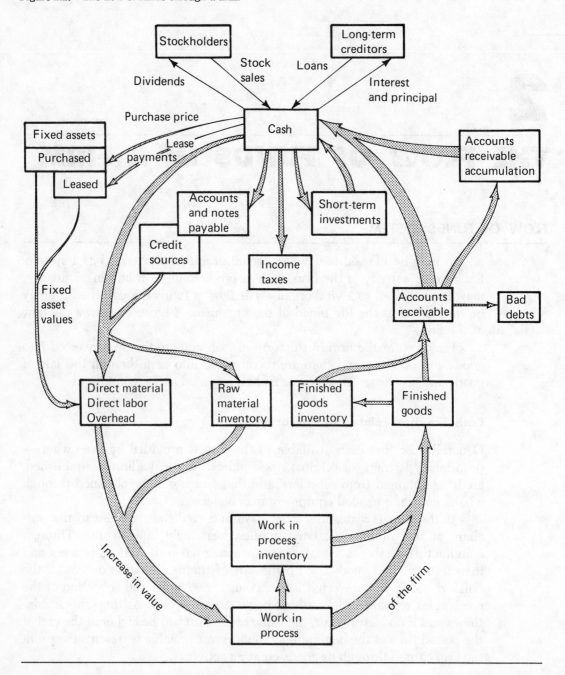

However, the cash position of the firm may be higher or lower at the end of the period than at the beginning, regardless of the profit. The firm's cash balance will rise if the cash inflows of the period exceed the cash outflows. If the reverse is true, the cash balance will fall. On the other hand, profit or loss, and hence the increase or decrease in the total value of the firm, depends on whether sales (both cash and credit sales) plus other revenue for the period exceed the cost of operation.

As the flow of funds proceeds from one stage to another, a portion of the flow may be to work-in-process inventory, finished goods inventory, or accounts receivable. If the production, distribution, and collection flows were fully synchronized, there would be no need for reservoirs of raw materials, work-in-process, or finished goods. However, purchasing of materials, sale of the merchandise, and collection of receivables usually occur at different rates. It may be cheaper to purchase in large quantities and store raw materials to meet future production needs rather than gearing purchasing to production. Or, it may be more economical to produce in long production runs and build up finished goods inventory to meet future sales than to vary production at the same rate as the sale of goods is varying. Collection policies may be relaxed or trade terms lengthened to meet competition, causing receivables to increase. Consequently, there are reservoirs of raw materials, work-in-process, finished goods, and accounts receivable to permit the activities of purchasing, production, sales, and collection to be carried on at different rates. The levels in each reservoir (funds invested) are like water in a bathtub. When the flows from the faucet into the bathtub and the flow out through the waste pipe are altered, the level of the water in the bathtub changes. A change in the amount of funds invested in a particular asset may depend on either outside economic forces, such as a change in raw material prices, or inside decisions, such as a decision to increase production or change credit terms.

When the goods and services are reconverted to cash, they can be used to pay trade creditors, make interest and principal payments, pay income taxes, declare dividends, purchase plant and equipment, and begin the process all over again. If more cash is available than required to continue the purchasing–manufacturing–sale process, the excess can be invested temporarily in short-term securities. If a greater amount of funds is needed than can be withdrawn from the cash account, additional funds can be obtained through the sale of short-term investments, through a bank loan, or through the sale of bonds or stock.

The mainstream of the flow consists of cash and credit through inventory to receivables, and back into cash. There are two subsidiary flows: (1)

the two-way flow from long-term creditors and owners to the firm and back again, and (2) the flow of funds into plant and equipment and their recapture through a noncash charge of depreciation against cost of goods sold. A glance back at Figure 2.1 will reveal a difference between these two subsidiary flows. The first is completely separate from the mainstream. The second, though outside the mainstream, is still part of it. The funds invested in plant and equipment are eventually converted into the value of the final product.

Depreciation as a Funds Generator

Plant and equipment purchases are usually paid for in cash shortly after delivery. These fixed assets are used up over a period of time known as their useful life. The accounting charge made in any period for the use of fixed assets is called *depreciation expense*. It is a noncash charge—the cash went out at the time of purchase. When combined with the cash costs of operation, such as materials, labor, heat, light, and administration, this noncash charge determines the total cost of producing the goods. When the merchandise is sold, the difference between the selling price and the total cash cost represents the net *inflow* of cash due to operations for the period. The amount of net cash inflow will exceed the profit by the amount of the depreciation charge. It is in this sense that depreciation expense is referred to as a source of funds.

Funds flow into the firm through cash resulting from sales. When the selling price is higher than the cash costs of producing the goods, the result is a net inflow of funds; when cash costs exceed the selling price, the result is a net outflow of funds. It is only through the successful operation of the firm, therefore, that depreciation is a generator of funds. If plant and equipment remain idle, no goods being produced and sold, depreciation can be charged, but no funds will flow into the firm except through income tax refund due to a loss.

The relation among cash, funds, depreciation, and economic values can be illustrated by an example. Assume Opec, Inc., has just completed its first refinery at a cost of $1 million. The plant's useful life is ten years. The depreciation charge is, therefore, $100,000 per year under straight-line depreciation. Table 2.1 is the income statement at the close of the first year's operation.

With all sales on a cash basis, the total *funds inflow* is $400,000 for the year. Costs total $280,000, leaving a profit of $120,000. For simplicity assume no income taxes. Of the $280,000 only $180,000 represents *cash out-*

lays. The other $100,000 is a noncash charge representing *depreciation* on the plant and equipment. The funds for these assets were paid out earlier and are now being recouped.

If we examine the company balance sheets at the start and at the end of the year (Table 2.2), the balance sheet footings increase by $120,000, the amount of the profit for the period.

The profit represents the additional value that flowed into the firm from customers buying the product. This increase in the *value* of the firm is specifically recognized by the $120,000 retained earnings entry. In addition

Table 2.1. **Opec, Inc., Income Statement**
January 1–December 31, 1976

Sales		$400,000
Less cost of:		
Labor, materials, overhead	$180,000	
Depreciation	100,000	280,000
Profit before taxes		$120,000

to this net inflow of values there is a rearrangement of values on the asset side of the balance sheet.

Since no reinvestment took place in plant and equipment or inventory expansion, the net inflow accumulated in the cash account, which rose from $50,000 to $270,000, is the amount of profit plus depreciation expense.

Table 2.2. **Opec, Inc., Comparative Balance Sheet**

Assets	December 31 1976	December 31 1975	Liabilities and Net Worth	December 31 1976	December 31 1975
Cash	$ 270,000	$ 50,000	Accounts payable	$ 100,000	$ 100,000
Inventory	150,000	150,000	Common stock	1,100,000	1,100,000
Plant and equipment	1,000,000	1,000,000	Retained earnings	120,000	0
Less accumulated depreciation	100,000	0	Total liabilities and net worth	$1,320,000	$1,200,000
Net plant and equipment	900,000	1,000,000			
Total assets	$1,320,000	1,200,000			

PREPARING THE STATEMENT OF CHANGES IN FINANCIAL POSITION

The *statement of changes in financial position*, also known as a *sources and application of funds statement*, shows the net amount of funds generated and the use to which the funds were put. To prepare this statement, first calculate the balance sheet changes that took place in the asset, liability, and net worth items. Then classify and sort the net changes in each account according to whether it is a source or use of funds. Among the uses of funds are (1) increases in assets, (2) decreases in liabilities, and (3) decreases in net worth. The sources of funds are those that provide the firm with the power of purchase. On the balance sheet they are (1) decreases in assets, (2) increases in liabilities, and (3) increases in net worth. *A decrease in cash is a source of funds.* In addition, we need certain items from the income statement, such as depreciation (source), earnings (source), and dividends (use). The statement of Opec, Inc., is given in Table 2.3.

Table 2.3. Opec, Inc., Statement of Changes in Financial Position
For Year 1976

Source of Funds	
Net earnings for year	$120,000
Depreciation	100,000
	$220,000
Application of Funds	
Increase in cash	$220,000
Cash Reconciliation	
Cash, January 1, 1975	$ 50,000
Profit	120,000
Depreciation	100,000
Cash, January 1, 1976	$270,000

Sales produced $400,000, cash expenses were $180,000, and, since no additional investments are made, the entire amount of the net funds inflow of $220,000 is lodged in the cash account.

IMPACT OF THE DEPRECIATION CHARGE ON THE FLOW OF FUNDS

When sales take place, funds flow into the firm. The amount of depreciation charged affects the amount of taxable profit and hence the amount of income tax due. The net amount of funds generated during the period is reduced by the taxes paid. Since depreciation is a cost, it qualifies as a deduction from income but does not require a cash outlay. Thus a firm is able through depreciation to influence the timing of its income tax liability and therefore the time pattern of its cash outlays over a span of years.

The firm is interested in deferring income taxes because present dollars are more valuable than future dollars. Present money is more valuable than future money because a dollar invested today will earn interest. Consequently, a dollar to be received in one year is worth something less than a dollar today. A firm's depreciation policy can be an effective instrument for increasing present funds at the expense of future funds by reducing present income taxes but increasing future income taxes. Thus the gain in deferring income taxes is the interest earned during the period of deferral. There is no reduction of income taxes over the whole life of the investment by the deferral process if income tax rates do not change.

Straight-Line versus Accelerated Depreciation

Management has a choice of depreciation methods at the time of purchase of an asset. We compare two methods, *straight-line depreciation* and *sum-of-the-years'-digits method*. Under the straight-line method the depreciation charge for each year is the same and is computed by dividing the cost of equipment, reduced by the salvage value, by the life in years of the asset. Under the sum-of-the-years'-digits method the annual depreciation charge declines each year and is computed by multiplying the cost of the equipment, reduced by the salvage value, by a fraction whose numerator is the remaining years of life of the equipment at the start of each year and whose denominator is the sum of the number of years of life of the asset at the time the asset was acquired.[1]

Following straight-line depreciation (SLD) in our Opec, Inc., example, $100,000 of depreciation would be charged each year for 10 years. With the sum-of-the-years'-digits method (SOYD) the charge the first year would be 10/55 of $1 million, or $181,818. Considering only these two depreciation alternatives, we trace the effect on profits and the flow of funds in the first year of operation in Table 2.4. Note that even though profits after income taxes would be significantly *reduced* in the first year through the

---

[1] For example, an asset with a life of four years is acquired. To determine the denominator, we sum the years 1 to 4, which equals 10. The numerator is the remaining years of life of the asset at the start of each year. The first year depreciation would be 4/10, the second year 3/10, the third year 2/10, and the fourth year 1/10 times the cost of the asset less the salvage value. But for the straight-line method, depreciation would be 1/4 each year.

Table 2.4. Opec, Inc., Comparative Funds Statements under SOYD and SLD Depreciation Alternatives*

	SOYD		SLD	
Sales		$400,000		$400,000
Less cost of				
Labor, materials, overhead	$180,000		$180,000	
Depreciation	182,000**		100,000	
Operating expense		362,000		280,000
Operating income		38,000		120,000
Less income tax (40%)		15,200		48,000
Profits after taxes		22,800		72,000
Add back depreciation		182,000		100,000
Net cash inflow		$204,800		$172,000

* Based on Tables 2.1 and 2.2.
** Rounded; first year's depreciation.

charging of accelerated depreciation, the flow of cash would be *increased* because the income tax outflow is reduced.

Depreciation as a Tax Shield

Depreciation is a tax shield for a profitable firm since depreciation charges against income do not affect the net inflow of funds from operations before income taxes but can be taken as a deduction to reduce income taxes. Table 2.4 shows SOYD reduced income taxes in the first year by $32,800 (from $48,000 to $15,200), which results in an increase of *net* cash inflow by $32,800 (from $172,000 to $204,800). By the same token, SOYD *reduced* after-tax profits by $49,200 (from $72,000 to $22,800), which is the result of the increase in depreciation of $82,000 (from $100,000 to $182,000), less the tax saving of $32,800 ($48,000 to $15,200). The net inflow of funds at the end of the period before income taxes will be the same regardless of the amount charged for depreciation. But the amount remaining after income taxes will be affected by the amount of depreciation charged. The higher the depreciation charged, the greater the total operating expense and the lower the income tax liability. Since funds not paid out in taxes remain with the firm, depreciation serves to shield the firm's cash.

The use of any accelerated depreciation method only postpones the tax liability and the accompanying necessary cash outflow. In later years when the depreciation charge is low, the income tax liability and the cash outflow will rise. In the interval the firm—assuming corporate tax rates do not rise —has the equivalent of an interest-free loan and an improved liquidity position.

If the firm is growing rapidly and new assets are acquired faster than the old ones are being retired, the firm is able to defer income taxes for as long as it grows. If the firm can grow indefinitely, then accelerated depreciation results in a permanent interest-free loan by the government to the firm in the amount of the difference between the tax liabilities under the straight-line and the accelerated methods.

Summary

Cash is the focal point of the flow of funds through the system. The funds flow from cash through raw material purchases, work-in-process, finished goods inventory, accounts receivable, and back to cash. Inventories are maintained to permit purchasing, production, and sales to be carried on at different rates. Changes in the levels of cash, inventories, receivables, and payables will depend upon the relative rates of purchasing, production, distribution, collection from customers of the firm, and payment to creditors of the firm.

Sales (or other revenues) are the source of funds inflow. When cash costs of production and income taxes are deducted, the balance represents the net inflow of funds. The same figure may be obtained by starting with net profit and adding back depreciation. Depreciation is sometimes referred to as a source of funds.

The method of depreciation adopted influences the reported earnings figure and the flow of funds. Accelerated depreciation will result in high charges in the early years, with profits reduced but cash inflow increased. The increased "costs" reduce the tax liability. Under straight-line depreciation "costs" would be less, taxable profits higher, the tax liability higher, and net cash inflow would be reduced in the early years. Firms adopt accelerated depreciation to obtain the larger net funds inflow in the early years, which is an interest-free "loan" by the government against future tax liability that may become due.

Study Questions

1. Why is cash important to a firm?
2. Distinguish between cash and profit.
3. What are the advantages and disadvantages to a toy manufacturer, the bulk of whose sales occur shortly before the Christmas holidays, of following a level

production plant compared to producing just prior to the anticipated arrival of orders?

4. Under what conditions can depreciation be referred to as a source of funds?
5. Explain in detail why small changes in sales volume frequently cause major changes in the production rate.
6. A rapidly growing but profitable firm is frequently in poor financial condition. Explain this phenomenon.
7. A barely profitable firm in a declining industry may currently be in excellent financial health. Explain this phenomenon.
8. How does depreciation serve as a tax shield? How is it possible to increase the charge for depreciation, reduce net income, and increase the inflow of funds?
9. Why do we say cash is the focal point of the flow of funds? What are the subsidiary flows?

Problems

1. Two firms of reasonably similar quality in the same industry both report earnings of $1 per share and are selling at $20 per share. Company Fast uses accelerated depreciation and Company Slow uses straight-line depreciation.

   Develop illustrative figures for the two companies and demonstrate which company would be the more attractive investment.

2. Show by example that the higher the tax rate, the more desirable the adoption of some method of accelerated depreciation over straight-line depreciation.

3. The president of Mercury, Inc., is puzzled. Profit last year was $300,000 and yet cash rose by $500,000 from $100,000 to $600,000. He asks you to explain. Mercury only buys and sells for cash. Books are kept on a cash basis but depreciation is recognized. Examining the books of the firm you obtain the following information:

   Sales amounted to $2.9 million.

   Cash expenses were $2.4 million.

   Inventory, plant, and equipment remained unchanged.

   Cash at the beginning of the year January 1, 1975, was $100,000.

   Depreciation charge for the year was $200,000.

   To explain the situation to the president, draw up a funds statement and a cash reconciliation.

4. Suppose that in December, Mercury (Problem 3) had purchased $100,000 worth of equipment for cash. Would the funds-generated and the funds-applied totals be affected by this transaction? Which numbers on your funds statement and cash reconciliation would be affected?

Selected References

Bodenhorn, D., "A Cash-Flow Concept of Profit," *Journal of Finance*, 19 (Mar. 1964), pp. 16–31.

Bonini, C. P., R. K. Jaedicke, and H. M. Wagner, *Management Controls*. New York: McGraw-Hill, 1964.

Dearden, J., "Can Management Information Be Automated?" *Harvard Business Review*, 42 (Mar.–Apr. 1964), pp. 128–135.

Englemann, K., "The 'Internal-Cash-Generation' Phenomenon," *Financial Analysts Journal*, 17 (Sept.–Oct. 1961), pp. 37–40.

Helfert, E. A., *Techniques of Financial Analysis*, 3d ed. Homewood, Ill.: Richard D. Irwin, 1972, chap. 1.

McDonough, A. M., and L. J. Garrett, *Management Systems*. Homewood, Ill.: Richard D. Irwin, 1965.

McLean, J. H., "Depreciation: Its Relationship to Funds," *Financial Analysts Journal*, 19 (May–June 1963), pp. 73–78.

Paton, W. A., "The 'Cash-Flow' Illusion," *Accounting Review*, 38 (Apr. 1963), pp. 243–251.

Rayman, R. A., "An Extension of the System of Accounts: The Segregation of Funds and Value," *Journal of Accounting Research*, 7 (Spring 1969), pp. 53–89.

Staubus, G. J., "Alternative Asset Flow Concepts," *Accounting Review*, 41 (July 1966), pp. 397–412.

3
FINANCIAL RATIO ANALYSIS

Conditions change and with them a firm's bill-paying ability and profitability. To plan the firm's future, the financial manager must be able (1) to assess the firm's current position and (2) to understand the impact of changing economic conditions. The purpose of these opening chapters is to develop these twin capabilities.

FINANCIAL STATEMENTS

The basic documents used in analyzing the financial condition of a business are the balance sheet and income statement. We study these financial statements because the quantitative data contained therein are helpful in making decisions that are economic rather than emotional. The balance sheet tells us the current financial position of the firm, while the income statement measures the success of an enterprise over a given period of time. Through the study of a series of financial statements, clues as to future financial statements can be developed.

The Balance Sheet: A "Snapshot" of the Firm

The balance sheet is a "snapshot" of the firm at a given point in time. The drawing up of a balance sheet is one way to convey the financial characteristics of a firm and to provide a basis for analyzing its strengths and weaknesses.

It is essential that the financial analyst understand the accounting principles underlying the balance sheet, and since much analysis involves comparison of a series of balance sheets, it is vital that consistency be maintained in the accounting from one balance sheet to the next.

Distinguishing between Cash and Profit

When a dollar is started on its way through the firm's system, it is anticipated that when it returns to the cash account it will bring with it an added amount. If only the dollar returns, the firm will be covering its out-of-pocket costs but will be running at a deficit to the extent of the noncash charges such as depreciation. If the dollar returns carrying with it an amount sufficient to cover the firm's cash and noncash costs, the firm will be just breaking even. If the dollar comes back with an amount beyond this, the excess is profit.

One feature that distinguishes the cash flow and profit is that cash is a readily identifiable money unit, whereas profit is an accounting number representing the excess of revenue over all of the firm's cash and noncash costs that may be properly allocated to that period. The task of the accountant is to determine the expenses to be charged to the period. Cash expenses are usually easily allocated. It is the noncash charges that cause difficulty.

Noncash charges include depreciation, the bad-debt charge, and the charging of prepaid expense. A five-year insurance policy, for example, may be purchased and paid for in cash, with one fifth of the cost of the policy charged against income each year.

A number of cash flows do not affect the income statement. These flows include dividend disbursements, payments for materials and supplies previously purchased on credit, and collection of receivables. The receipt of funds from a loan or sale of securities would swell the inflow of cash but would not represent profit. The payment for supplies would cause a large outflow of cash but also would not affect profit. Frequently the payment date disrupts the correspondence between cash flow and profit, a good example being the payment of wages and salaries at year end. In determining the profit for a year, the cost of the labor inputs is properly allocated to that year, but if workers are paid every two weeks, the cash may actually not be paid out until 10 days after the close of the year. The cash would flow out on pay day, but the costs for the first few days of the pay period would be reflected on the income statement for the previous year.

FINANCIAL RATIO ANALYSIS

One aspect of financial analysis lies in easily computed ratios relating various items of the balance sheet and income statement. The financial manager seeks to draw meaning from these financial ratios. He needs experience, insight, and imagination.

Before proceeding with a discussion of ratios several comments are in order. Even casual observation reveals that financial ratio analysis is a skill widely practiced by financial managers, creditors of all kinds, and investors. Thus the topic merits the considerable attention we accord it. But financial ratio analysis also has many deficiencies. In this regard the student is urged to consider with particular care the following remarks and the discussion later in this chapter on the hazards in the use of ratios.

First, though ratio analysis may be used with some confidence to evaluate the financial position of a firm in relation to similar firms and to measure the progress of a firm toward particular goals such as improved liquidity and higher income relative to sales, the predictive powers of ratio analysis are open to serious question. Predicting the future earnings of a firm and its financial condition (solid, weak, bankrupt) some years hence using ratios is a hazardous activity. And yet it is precisely the future that is of greatest concern to those analyzing the financial statements of a firm: the financial manager trying to decide whether to build a new plant, the creditor trying to decide whether to extend a loan, the investor trying to decide whether to buy a block of stock.

Second, the arithmetic precision with which a particular ratio can be computed may blind the analyst to the weakness of the input data used for the ratio computation. This may cause the analyst to place undue reliance on the ratio result. Worse yet, the analyst may become enamored with ratio computation and lose sight of the purpose of the analysis. Ratio computation may become an end in itself.

Third, no ratio standing alone has any particular meaning. Only groups of ratios computed at various points in time can, in conjunction with numerous related qualitative factors such as the honesty and shrewdness of management, provide an analyst with insight into a firm's current and potential earning and financial condition.

Below we group ratios into four classifications. The purpose is to help the student remember the ratios, nothing more. We dislike, as do others, such a classification. It is artificial and does not in itself aid the analyst in selecting the proper ratios to evaluate a particular situation. But it is a convenient device.

Classification of Ratios

Financial ratios may be grouped into four classifications:
1. *Liquidity:* to measure ability of the firm to meet obligations maturing within a year.
2. *Activity:* to measure the intensity of the firm's resource utilization.

3. *Leverage:* to measure the firm's use of fixed-charge financing obligations (bonds, leases, preferred stock).
4. *Profitability:* to measure management's ability to generate profits.

Illustrative Analysis

To illustrate the analysis a financial manager would conduct to determine the financial strength and earning power of his firm and gain insight into developing trends, we use the firm BTE, Inc., a manufacturer of electrical distribution equipment. We begin with the analysis of the comparative balance sheet (Table 3.1).

LIQUIDITY RATIOS

The working capital position of a firm (its current assets and current liabilities) is evaluated through the use of several ratios that measure liquidity. Current assets in the normal course of business are converted into cash within one year; current liabilities are debts of the firm payable within one year.

Current Ratio

The current ratio is the ratio of current assets to current liabilities. Current assets (CA) include cash, bank balances, marketable securities being held as a short-term substitute for cash, accounts receivable, and inventories. Current liabilities (CL) include accounts payable, notes payable, bank loans, that portion of long-term debt that will mature within one year, and various accrued items. The comparative balance sheet for BTE, Inc. (Table 3.1) shows the following current ratios:

$$\text{current ratio} = \frac{\text{CA}}{\text{CL}} = \begin{cases} \dfrac{\$10,966,000}{\$5,819,000} = 1.9 & \quad 1976 \\[3ex] \dfrac{\$6,940,000}{\$3,388,000} = 2.0 & \quad 1975 \end{cases}$$

A current ratio of 1.9 means that for every $1 of current liabilities the firm has $1.90 of current assets.

The current ratio is widely used, but it is only a rough measure and can be misleading. For example, BTE, Inc., seeking to improve its current ratio

Table 3.1. BTE, Inc., Comparative Balance Sheet

Assets	December 31 1976	December 31 1975
Current assets		
Cash	$ 155,000	$ 400,000
Accounts receivable (net)	3,113,000	1,780,000
Inventories	7,698,000	4,760,000
Total current assets	$10,966,000	$6,940,000
Plant and equipment	4,317,000	3,711,000
Less depreciation	1,462,000	1,164,000
Net fixed assets	$ 2,855,000	$2,547,000
Total assets	$13,821,000	$9,487,000

Liabilities and Stockholders' Investment	December 31 1976	December 31 1975
Current liabilities		
Accounts payable	$ 1,432,000	$ 685,000
Notes payable	2,389,000	1,600,000
Accrued items	813,000	567,000
Federal and state income taxes	1,065,000	416,000
Installments due within one year on long-term promissory notes payable	120,000	120,000
Total current liabilities	$ 5,819,000	$3,388,000
Long-term promissory notes	2,160,000	2,280,000
Stockholders' investment, common stock par value $1	832,000	761,000
Additional paid-in capital	1,036,000	194,000
Retained earnings	3,974,000	2,864,000
Total net worth	5,842,000	3,819,000
Total liabilities and net worth	$13,821,000	$9,487,000

in 1975, might just before the balance sheet date pay off $300,000 of current liabilities with cash. Though this action might temporarily leave the firm short of cash, its current ratio would rise to 2.1.

Since the current ratio includes inventory and receivables, there exist other possibilities for misjudging the liquidity position of the firm. The inventory may not be easily salable. If it consists of toys and the balance sheet date is August 31, the inventory is probably highly salable because most toys are sold in the months just before Christmas. An acceptable current ratio would indicate a favorable liquidity position. With the firm carrying a large inventory of toys on December 31, the same ratio would indicate a poorer working capital position. In judging the liquidity position of his firm the financial manager must estimate the salability of the inventory. Receivables, while not normally causing difficulty because of their nearness to cash, also deserve some attention. At times some accounts become uncollectible. A firm with many small accounts is less vulnerable to large losses than a firm with a few very large accounts. It is customary to show a bad-debt reserve against receivables, but not a reserve against inventory because this is more difficult to determine.

A low current ratio indicates a weak liquidity position. The firm may experience difficulty in meeting its maturing obligations. The low ratio may be due to heavy losses, excessive financing on a short-term basis, or the practice of using current funds to finance fixed assets. A current ratio that is too high might indicate that management is overly concerned with liquidity and sacrificing earnings for short-term safety.

Quick Ratio

The quick ratio is the ratio of current assets minus inventory to current liabilities. This is a more stringent test than the current ratio. The focus is on the cash and near-cash coverage of the current liabilities. The BTE, Inc., comparative balance sheet (Table 3.1) shows the following quick ratios:

$$\text{quick ratio} = \frac{\text{CA} - \text{inventory}}{\text{CL}} \begin{cases} \dfrac{\$10,966,000 - \$7,698,000}{\$5,819,000} = & \overset{\textit{1976}}{0.56} \\[2em] \dfrac{\$6,940,000 - \$4,760,000}{\$3,388,000} = & \underset{\textit{1975}}{0.64} \end{cases}$$

A quick ratio of 0.56 means that in 1976 for every dollar of current liabilities the firm has 56 cents of near-cash items.

The farther removed an asset is from cash, the less liquid. The nearness of inventory to receivables (and then cash) depends on its salability. The range of liquidity for inventory is wider than for receivables. In receivables the firm has a claim to cash that it can legally press—the customer is under obligation to pay. In inventory the firm has a claim only to the ownership of the merchandise. It has the right to sell the goods for whatever the market will pay; if the market will pay nothing, the firm does not have a right to collect anything.

Percentage Composition of the Working Capital

This is the percentage each component of the current assets bears to the total. Since some current assets are more liquid than others, determination of the percentage each bears to the total will provide some insight into the firm's liquidity position, as shown in Table 3.2.

Table 3.2. BTE, Inc., Comparative Analysis of Working Capital*

Current Assets	December 31 1976	December 31 1975
Cash	1.4%	5.8%
Accounts receivable	28.4	25.6
Inventory	70.2	68.6
	100.0%	100.0%

* Based on Table 3.1.

BTE's current and quick ratios for 1976 and 1975 indicate a declining liquidity situation. But there is more. The current and quick ratios, while showing relatively little change from 1975 to 1976, hide the drop in cash and the increase in receivables and inventory.

Cash to Average-Daily-Purchase Ratio

This is the ratio of cash and near-cash items to the average daily purchases. The ratio is calculated in two steps. First, we calculate daily purchases. For computational ease, we assume BTE's purchases represent 60 percent of cost of goods sold (COGS) and 360 days in a year. Daily purchases are

$$\frac{\text{COGS} \times 0.6}{360}^{*} = \begin{cases} \dfrac{\$15,158,000 \times 0.6}{360} = \$25,000 & 1976 \quad 1975 \\[2em] \dfrac{\$10,780,000 \times 0.6}{360} = & \$18,000 \end{cases}$$

* Based on Table 3.3

Then, the ratio of cash to average daily purchases is

$$\frac{\text{cash}}{\text{daily purchases}} = \begin{cases} \dfrac{\$155,000}{\$\ 25,000} = 6.2 \text{ days} & 1976 \quad 1975 \\[2em] \dfrac{\$400,000}{\$\ 18,000} = & 22.2 \text{ days} \end{cases}$$

The deteriorating liquidity position is evident as cash in 1976 represents 6.2 days purchases as opposed to 22.2 days purchases the year previous. We are further interested in relating daily purchases to accounts payable. In 1976 we see that BTE is taking over 57 days on the average to pay its supplier. This is up from 38 days in 1975. The calculations are

$$\frac{\text{accounts payable}}{\text{daily purchases}} \qquad \begin{cases} \dfrac{\$1,432,000}{\$\ \ \ 25,000} = 57 \text{ days} & 1976 \quad 1975 \\[2em] \dfrac{\$\ 685,000}{\$\ \ \ 18,000} = & 38 \text{ days} \end{cases}$$

Summarizing the 1976 working capital position of BTE, we find that the quick ratio of 0.56, the low percentage of cash to total current assets and average daily purchases, and the large amount of payables on the books indicate that the firm is in a poorer liquidity position than indicated by the current ratio of 1.9.

In evaluating the liquidity position of a firm, the sophisticated financial manager will also consider the firm's reserve borrowing power and financial strength of the insiders. If these sources are strong, the firm can operate with a lower cash balance relative to its daily requirements than other firms.

ACTIVITY RATIOS

Activity ratios measure how effectively the firm manages its assets. For example, the inventory-turnover ratio gives clues as to the salability of the inventory. It is a measure of the work the firm is getting out of the funds invested in inventory.

Inventory Turnover

This ratio represents the relation of cost of goods sold (COGS) to inventory (either ending inventory or average of beginning and ending inventory). The inventory turnover of BTE, Inc., using ending inventory is as follows:

$$\text{inventory turnover} = \frac{\text{COGS}}{\text{inventory}} = \begin{cases} \dfrac{\$15,158,000}{\$\ 7,698,000} = 2.0 \times & 1976 \\[3ex] \dfrac{\$10,780,000}{\$\ 4,760,000} = \quad 2.3 \times & 1975 \end{cases}$$

The COGS figures are obtained from Table 3.3, the ending inventory figures from Table 3.1. An inventory-turnover ratio of 2.0 times means

---

Table 3.3. BTE, Inc., Comparative Income Statement

	Year Ending December 31	
	1976	1975
Net sales	$21,425,000	$15,007,000
Costs and expenses		
Cost of goods sold	15,158,000	10,780,000
Selling and administrative expenses	2,825,000	2,204,000
Interest expense	242,000	153,000
Total cost and expenses	18,225,000	13,137,000
Profit before income taxes	3,200,000	1,870,000
Income taxes		
Federal	1,440,000	807,000
State	170,000	93,000
Net profit	$ 1,590,000	$ 970,000

each dollar of inventory is converted to sales 2.0 times per year. The higher the turnover ratio, the greater the profit, provided gross margin does not change.

The inventory-turnover ratio can help us evaluate the significance of a rise or decline in the percentage of inventory to total current assets. A sharp increase in inventory as a percent of current assets with sales rising rapidly presents a different picture than a rise in inventory as a percent of current assets with sales declining. In the first case the firm with a growing demand for its product is shifting cash and near-cash resources into inventory to meet the rising sales volume. True, the firm is becoming less liquid— it has less cash on hand to meet its short-term obligations. But its inventory is selling rapidly and there need be little concern for large inventory losses. The firm can count on converting merchandise to cash through sales in the normal course of business. In the second case the firm also is becoming less liquid. But the factors accompanying that increasing illiquidity are different. Cash and near-cash resources are being locked into inventory that is becoming less marketable. The ability of the firm to meet its short-term debts is deteriorating as sales drop and inventory mounts. Should this trend continue, the earnings of the firm will decline as it is forced to liquidate inventory at reduced prices to obtain cash.

To modify the uniqueness that may result from basing calculations on a single balance sheet date, inventory turnover is often calculated by taking the average of the inventory at the beginning and at the end of the year:

$$\text{inventory turnover} = \frac{\text{COGS}}{(\text{Inv } 12/31/76 + \text{Inv } 12/31/75)/2}$$

$$= \frac{\$15,158,000}{\$7,698,000 + \$4,760,000/2} = 2.4 \times$$

Average Collection Period

The ratio of receivables to average daily credit sales is the average collection period. This is a measure of the relative size of the receivables account, the collectibility of the receivables, and the firm's credit policy enforcement standard. *Credit policy* refers to the terms of sale the vendor extends to customers. With a credit policy of net 30 days (meaning the vendor's customer must pay his bill without discount within 30 days) we would probably inquire into the operation of the credit department and its enforcement of the firm's credit standards if receivables outstanding represent 60 days credit sales.

The average collection period is calculated in two steps. First, we calculate the average daily credit sales. Assume that 80 percent of BTE's sales are on credit. In 1976 sales were $21,425,000 and in 1975 sales were $15,007,000. We use a 360-day year for ease of computation:

$$\text{daily credit sales} = \begin{cases} \dfrac{\$17,140,000}{360} = \$48,000 & 1976 \\[2em] \dfrac{\$12,006,000}{360} = & \quad \$33,000 \quad 1975 \end{cases}$$

Second, divide the average daily credit sales into the year-end receivables:

$$\begin{array}{l} \text{days credit sales} \\ \text{outstanding} \\ \text{as receivables} \end{array} = \dfrac{\text{receivables}}{\begin{array}{c}\text{average daily}\\\text{credit sales}\end{array}} = \begin{cases} \dfrac{\$3,113,000}{\$48,000} = 65 \text{ days} & 1976 \\[2em] \dfrac{\$1,780,000}{\$33,000} = & \quad 54 \text{ days} \quad 1975 \end{cases}$$

At year end 1976 BTE had receivables equivalent to 65 days credit sales, up from 54 days in 1975. As the firm increased its sales from 1975 to 1976, it also became more liberal in its credit and collection policies. Receivables rose faster than sales. Paralleling this situation, inventory turnover declined. Assuming that BTE credit sales are on the basis of net 30 days, then the level of receivables outstanding is significantly above its appropriate level.

Another activity ratio is total asset turnover, the ratio of sales to assets. We discuss this ratio in conjunction with profitability measures later in this chapter.

LEVERAGE RATIOS

One set of ratios is available to measure the protection that the firm offers long-term creditors. These ratios consist of two subsets: one measures protection of assets, the other measures protection of earnings. Both measure the extent to which leverage has been used.

Debt Coverage

Debt coverage is shown in the ratio of debt to total assets. This *debt-to-assets ratio* measures the relative use made of creditor funds to finance the firm and is of interest to both creditors and owners.

For large firms where current liabilities are a small percent of total assets, short-term debt and current liabilities can be omitted in the calculation of the debt-to-assets ratio. For smaller firms where the current liabilities account is relatively large the debt-to-assets ratio is calculated on the basis of total debt to total assets. For BTE,

$$\frac{\text{percentage of}}{\text{debt financing}} = \frac{\text{total debt}}{\text{total assets}} = \begin{cases} \dfrac{\$5,819,000 + \$2,160,000}{\$13,821,000} = 57.7\% & 1976 \\[2em] \dfrac{\$3,388,000 + \$2,280,000}{\$9,487,000} = & 59.7\% \quad 1975 \end{cases}$$

In 1976 creditors supplied 57.7 percent of the funds, a decline from 59.7 percent for 1975. The working capital position of the firm had deteriorated, but its long-term financing position improved.

A widely used ratio calculated to measure the relative proportions of creditor and equity funds is the *debt-to-equity ratio* which shows the creditor funds in terms of the stockholder equity funds—preferred stock, common stock, capital surplus, and retained earnings:

$$\text{debt-to-equity relationship} = \frac{\text{total debt}}{\text{equity funds}} = \begin{cases} \dfrac{\$7,979,000}{\$5,842,000} = 1.37 & 1976 \\[2em] \dfrac{\$5,668,000}{\$3,819,000} = & 1.48 \quad 1975 \end{cases}$$

These figures tell us that in 1976 creditors supplied $1.37 for every dollar supplied by stockholders and that in 1975, they supplied $1.48 for every dollar supplied by stockholders.

For creditors the lower the percent of creditor funds, the better because the equity funds, or net worth, serve as a cushion to absorb any shrinkage in the value of the assets. Any increase in the value of the assets increases the cushion for the creditors. Creditors want prompt payment, and if they are bondholders, they want to receive punctually the promised interest and the repayment of principal at maturity. For example, with creditor funds representing 20 percent of the value of the assets it would be possible for the assets to shrink by 80 percent before the creditors would begin to suffer a loss of principal (assuming the assets are worth their book value). In contrast, if creditors supplied 70 percent of the funds employed, the value of the assets could shrink by but 30 percent before the claims of the creditors against the firm would begin to be impaired.

Whether a given debt-to-equity relationship depicts a favorable or unfavorable condition depends on the industry, the stability of earnings, the trend, and the investment interests of the analyst. A low percentage of debt to equity is favorable from the creditor's position. A large margin of protection provides safety. The same low percentage of debt, however, may be viewed as quite unsatisfactory by shareholders. They may see a neglected opportunity for using low-cost debt to acquire capital equipment that could earn a high return.

Times Interest Earned

The ratio of earnings before interest and taxes (EBIT) to interest charges measures the protection earnings afford the bondholders. If, for example, times interest earned is 5, this means interest charges have been earned 5 times over and earnings could decline 80 percent and still be sufficient to meet interest charges. Lease payments also constitute a fixed charge and should be included in the calculation if the firm has leased assets and the lease contract is not subject to cancellation by the firm. The ratio then is known as *times fixed charges earned*.

The BTE example (Table 3.3) shows the following:

$$\text{times fixed charges earned} = \frac{\text{EBIT}}{\text{fixed charges}} = \begin{cases} \dfrac{\$3,442,000}{\$242,000} = 14 \times \\[2em] \dfrac{\$2,023,000}{\$153,000} = \qquad 13 \times \end{cases}$$

$$\begin{array}{cc} 1976 & 1975 \end{array}$$

In 1976 BTE earned its fixed charges 14 times and in 1975, 13 times. EBIT could drop by roughly 93 percent from the 1976 level before the firm would not be covering charges.

Where two or more debt issues are outstanding, the correct procedure to follow in computing the times interest earned figure on the junior issue is the *overall* method. Divide total interest charges on all issues into the earnings available either before or after deduction of federal income taxes. Though total earnings before taxes is available for the payment of interest charges, some analysts prefer deducting income taxes from the earnings available for the payment of fixed charges before computing times fixed charges. They believe this method yields a more conservative figure, which it does. Others do not deduct federal income taxes, and we also recommend not deducting income taxes. However, firms may also have preferred stock outstanding, and preferred dividends are not a tax-deductible expense. The financial manager seeking to obtain comparable figures of different firms—some with only debt outstanding, others with debt and preferred stock, and still others with only preferred stock—must deduct income taxes before calculating times interest and preferred dividends earned to make the ratios for all firms comparable, as is done in Table 3.4.

Table 3.4. **Total Interest and Preferred Dividend Coverage Calculation**

EBIT		$100,000
Interest on bonds	$40,000	
Net after interest	60,000	
Federal income tax (50 percent rate)		30,000
Total after taxes available for interest and dividends		70,000
Preferred dividends	10,000	
Total interest and preferred dividend charges		50,000
Total interest and preferred dividend charge, coverage after taxes $= \dfrac{\$70,000}{\$50,000} =$		1.4×

Initially the ability of a firm to meet its interest charges is dependent upon its cash position. Earnings might not cover charges and the firm could still meet its obligations with a substantial cash balance. However, losses mean a net outflow of economic values, and the firm will find it increasingly difficult to meet its interest payments under continuing deficits. This drain will ultimately exhaust the cash balance. The fundamental support for the fixed charges is earnings. Therefore when a firm is not earning its fixed charges, though interest payments continue, the market value of all outstanding issues of the firm declines.

PROFITABILITY RATIOS

Earning power or return on investment is the ability of the firm to earn a return on its operating assets.

Return on Investment (ROI)

Return on operating asset investment, which we shorten to return on investment (ROI), is the measure of the firm's annual net operating income to the investment committed to generate this income. We define *net operating income* (NOI) as earnings before interest and income taxes produced by operating assets. Excluded are nonoperating income items such as rent on a leased warehouse or interest on long-term investments. We wish to focus on the income generated by our operating assets undistorted by the manner in which the firm is financed or taxed, and so defined NOI = EBIT. We define *operating assets* as the total of those assets—net of depreciation and bad debts—employed in the ordinary course of business. Excluded are securities held as long-term investment, vacant land held for speculative purposes, leased property no longer directly employed in operations, and so on. For BTE we have (from Tables 3.1 and 3.3)

$$\frac{\text{return on investment}}{\text{(based on year-end assets)}} = \frac{\text{net operating income}}{\text{operating assets}}$$

$$= \begin{cases} \dfrac{\$3,442,000}{\$13,821,000} = 24.9\% \\[2em] \dfrac{\$2,023,000}{\$9,487,000} = 21.3\% \end{cases} \quad \begin{matrix} 1976 & 1975 \end{matrix}$$

In 1976 BTE earned 24.9 percent on its invested capital and in 1975, 21.3 percent. Now let us examine the factors that influence the return on investment figures. The larger the spread between sales and costs, the greater the profit. The ratio of NOI to sales is the operating margin. For BTE the computation is (from Table 3.3)

$$\text{operating margin} = \frac{\text{net operating income}}{\text{sales}} = \begin{cases} \dfrac{\$3,442,000}{\$21,425,000} = 16.1\% \\[2em] \dfrac{\$2,023,000}{\$15,007,000} = 13.5\% \end{cases} \quad \begin{matrix} 1976 & 1975 \end{matrix}$$

For every dollar of sales BTE generated in 1976, an income of 16.1 cents was attained. This is an increase of 2.6 cents per dollar of sales over the previous year. ROI depends not only on income but also on the efficiency with which management utilizes the firm's assets. The smaller the asset investment necessary to generate a given level of sales, the more desirable it is. The ratio of sales to operating assets is known as *asset turnover*. For BTE we have

$$\text{asset turnover} = \frac{\text{sales}}{\text{operating assets}} = \begin{cases} \dfrac{\$21,425,000}{\$13,821,000} = 1.55 \times & \quad \textit{1976} \quad \textit{1975} \\[2em] \dfrac{\$15,007,000}{\$9,487,000} = & \qquad \qquad 1.58 \times \end{cases}$$

Combining operating margin and the asset turnover ratio, we have ROI:

$$\begin{aligned} \frac{\text{return on}}{\text{investment}} &= \frac{\text{net operating income}}{\text{sales}} \times \frac{\text{sales}}{\text{operating assets}} \\[1em] &= \frac{\text{net operating income}}{\text{operating assets}} \end{aligned}$$

The relationship of margin times asset turnover, though yielding the same figure as ROI calculated directly, highlights the elements comprising the final figure. In Figure 3.1 these elements are grouped along two analytic streams that depict the earnings-generating mechanism of a firm.

Earning Power of BTE and Methods of Increasing ROI

The ROI for BTE was higher in 1976 than in 1975—24.9 percent versus 21.3 percent. The higher 1976 return is due to a wider margin. Asset turnover slowed, but the margin widened sufficiently to compensate and thus raise ROI. If the margin had remained the same, the ROI would have dropped because of the reduced asset turnover.

Figure 3.1 suggests five actions that lead to an increase in ROI. Starting at the top of the figure, one action is to reduce the cost of sales or the selling and administrative expenses and thereby increase NOI. A second action is to increase the selling price, but not so high that the drop in volume offsets the wider spread between selling price and cost. The result will be an increase in NOI as long as the wider margin is more than sufficient to offset any reduced asset turnover. Third, we can reduce the selling price to gain a larger volume. If the increase in volume and asset turnover is more

Figure 3.1. Relation of elements that determine return on investment. The figures are those of the BTE example for 1976.

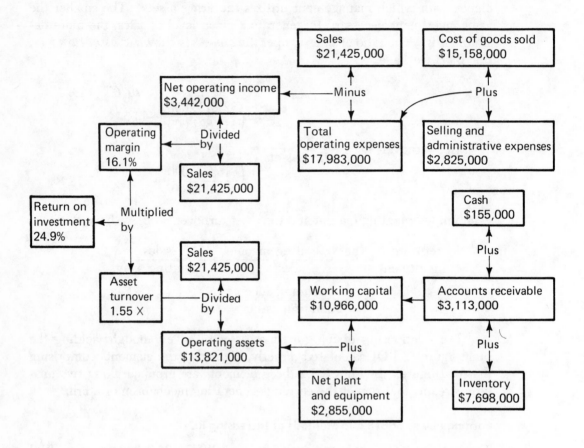

than sufficient to compensate for the narrower margin, ROI will rise. A fourth action is to reduce the investment in working capital and fixed assets. Generating the same sales and net operating income with a smaller capital investment will raise ROI. Fifth, increasing the sales volume without a change in prices while keeping the total investment constant will increase NOI and ROI.

Return on Common Stock

Increasing the productivity of a firm's assets is one way to increase the returns on common stock. Another way is to finance the firm by using debt, preferred stock, common stock, and retained earnings in such a combination that the common stockholder's equity earns as high a return as possible without assuming undue risk. The usual measure of return on common stock relates net profit available to the common stock to the common equity (net worth minus any preferred outstanding). For BTE, which has no preferred, the computation is

$$\begin{aligned} &\text{return on common stock equity} \\ &\text{(based on year-end net worth)} \end{aligned} = \frac{\text{net profit}}{\text{net worth}}$$

$$= \begin{cases} \dfrac{\$1,590,000}{\$5,842,000} = 27.2\% & \\[2em] \dfrac{\$970,000}{\$3,819,000} = & 25.4\% \end{cases}$$

$$\begin{array}{cc} 1976 & 1975 \end{array}$$

USE AND HAZARDS IN THE USE OF RATIOS

Many items appear on the balance sheet and income statement, and the computation of many ratios is possible. The analyst should have a reason for computing whatever ratios he selects. Too many ratios are apt to be confusing; a few well-chosen ones will be enlightening.

When analyzing a firm, the trend is important as well as the current condition. Evaluation of trend requires that the same ratio be compared at different points in time. A financially weak firm growing stronger presents an entirely different picture than a financially strong firm declining in strength. But watch for turning points. For much of the time it is safe to predict the continuation of a trend. But the big money is made and lost at the turns.

Note that a ratio is made up of two numbers, the numerator and the denominator. A change in the ratio from one period to the next can be caused by a change in the numerator, the denominator, or both, and the cause of the change in the ratio will affect the significance of the change. For example, if a firm has a current ratio greater than 1:1, the current ratio can be improved by increasing current assets or by decreasing current liabilities. An increase in current assets relative to current liabilities as a result of highly profitable operations in the last year is indicative of a real improvement in the working capital position of the firm. But if just before the balance sheet date management pays off overdue creditors, with the intention of allowing current liabilities to again accumulate after the balance sheet date, the improved current ratio will not be reflecting solid improvement. The quick

Table 3.5. Summary of Financial Ratios

Liquidity ratios

1. Current ratio = $\dfrac{\text{current assets}}{\text{current liabilities}}$.

2. Quick ratio = $\dfrac{\text{current assets} - \text{inventory}}{\text{current liabilities}}$.

3. Cash to average daily purchases ratio = $\dfrac{\text{cash}}{\text{annual purchases}/360}$.

Activity ratios

4. Inventory turnover = $\dfrac{\text{cost of goods sold}}{(\text{beginning inventory} + \text{ending inventory})/2}$

   or $\dfrac{\text{cost of goods sold}}{\text{ending inventory}}$.

5. Average collection period = $\dfrac{\text{receivables}}{\text{credit sales}/360}$.

6. Asset turnover = $\dfrac{\text{sales}}{\text{operating assets}}$.

Leverage ratios

7. Percentage of debt financing = $\dfrac{\text{total debt}}{\text{total assets}}$.

8. Debt-to-equity relationship = $\dfrac{\text{total debt}}{\text{equity funds}}$.

9. Times fixed charges earned = $\dfrac{\text{earnings before interest and taxes}}{\text{fixed charges}}$.

Profitability ratios

10. Return on investment = $\dfrac{\text{net operating income}}{\text{operating assets}}$.

11. Operating margin = $\dfrac{\text{net operating income}}{\text{sales}}$.

12. Return on common = $\dfrac{\text{net profit}}{\text{net worth}}$.

ratio, however, will reflect the cash disbursement. If the current ratio is less than 1:1, management can improve the current ratio through increasing current liabilities by the same amount as current assets, for example, by buying inventory on credit. The quick ratio though would point up the real change that had taken place. The working capital position of the firm as reflected in the current and quick ratios is also substantially affected by changes in fixed assets and in long-term debt and equity. The use of working capital to finance fixed asset acquisitions will reduce the current and quick ratios, while the sale of bonds and stock will improve them. Table 3.5 gives a summary of financial ratios.

Summary

Ratios are tools of analysis. The basic statements normally analyzed are the balance sheet and income statement. The short-term creditor, since his loan will be repaid from accounts receivable and through conversion of inventory to cash in the normal course of business, looks primarily to the current and quick ratios, the percentage that cash, receivables, and inventory bear to total working capital, the amount of cash in terms of average daily purchases, inventory turnover, and day's credit sales outstanding. He looks for liquidity.

Long-term suppliers of funds are interested in the return the firm is earning on its total invested capital. They look primarily to the debt-to-equity relationship, times charges earned, and the prospects for long-term earnings. A good working capital position can be quickly dissipated through large losses.

Return on investment is a function of operating margin times asset turnover and is a measure of management's ability to operate the firm. By studying the components of return on investment we can understand how a firm generates earnings.

The concerns of holders of common stock are earnings and dividends. They are interested in both the return on total capital of the firm and the return on common equity.

Study Questions

1. To eliminate the wide variability in accounting treatment, would it be reasonable for the Securities and Exchange Commission to impose a uniform standard of financial statements on all industrial firms? Discuss.
2. Why does management place such emphasis on the earnings figures? Why do stockholders also focus on the earnings figure?
3. How would the analysis of a firm's financial statements differ if conducted by a short-term creditor? a long-term creditor? or a stockholder?
4. What are the ratios that measure the liquidity position of the firm? Can one "poor" ratio be offset by another "good" ratio?
5. What are the dangers indicated by weak liquidity ratios?

6. How can increasing a firm's inventory turnover improve its profitability? Its working capital position?

7. Enterprise return on investment is frequently employed as one test of the quality of management. Discuss. What other measures would you use to obtain a fair appraisal of management?

8. Would return on net worth be a better test of management efficiency than return on investment?

9. What factors or conditions would you seek to change if you wished to improve the operating margin of your firm, the asset turnover? Which factors would you most likely be able to influence? Does your answer depend upon the industry you have in mind? How?

10. What factors or conditions would you seek to change if you wished to improve the return on net worth? What factors would you most likely be able to influence? Does your answer depend upon the industry you have in mind? How?

Problems

1. The Soglin Lumber Company at the beginning of the heavy building season on April 30 has current assets of $300,000 and current liabilities of $600,000. Compute the current ratio after giving effect to each of the following transactions. Cumulate the transactions.
   a. $50,000 of additional inventory was purchased on credit.
   b. An additional $200,000 of cash was borrowed on a short-term loan from the friendly banker.
      What do you notice about the current ratio? Through increasing short-term financing do you think management can ever make it reach 1? surpass 1? Why not?
      On August 31 the firm has current assets of $500,000 and current liabilities of $500,000. Compute the current ratio after giving effect to each of the following transactions. Cumulate the transactions.
   c. A $100,000 bank loan is paid off with cash.
   d. $200,000 of inventory is acquired on credit.
   e. Income taxes of $50,000 are paid.
      What do you notice about the current ratio? What is the mathematical principle involved?
      On December 31 the firm has current assets of $200,000 and current liabilities of $100,000. Compute the current ratio after giving effect to each of the following transactions. Cumulate the transactions.
   f. $400,000 of cash is borrowed from the friendly banker.
   g. $200,000 of additional inventory is acquired on credit.
      What do you notice about the current ratio? Through increasing short-term financing would it ever reach 1? Why not? What are the implications of the mechanics for computing the current ratio to the financial executive in the management of working capital?

2. Using the December 31 Soglin Lumber Company figures of current assets ($400,000) and current liabilities ($200,000), compute the current ratio and net working capital after giving effect to each of the following transactions. *Do not* cumulate.

a. Several new trucks are purchased for $20,000 cash.

b. $40,000 of new machinery is purchased on a short-term note.

c. A dividend of $10,000 is paid (assume accrued dividends on the balance sheet).

d. $5,000 of accounts receivable is collected.

e. $15,000 of short-term Treasury securities is purchased.

f. A $50,000 mortage is taken out on the building to increase cash.

g. $20,000 of accounts payable is paid off.

h. Old machinery is sold for $10,000 cash.

i. A long-term note of $20,000 is paid off.

Contrast the answers to g and i. What is the reason for the disparity? What implications for working capital management do you see?

3. The balance sheet and income statement for 1976 and 1975 of the Reynolds Machine Company appear in Table 3.6 and Table 3.7.

a. From the Reynolds Machine Company financial statements compute the following for the years 1976 and 1975: (1) current ratio, (2) quick ratio, (3) percentage composition of current assets, (4) cash in terms of average daily purchases (materials are 60% of cost of goods sold), (5) inventory turnover using ending inventory), (6) days credit sales outstanding, (7) long-term debt-to-equity ratio, (8) times interest charges earned, (9) earnings per

Table 3.6. Reynolds Machine Company Balance Sheet

| | December 31 | | | December 31 | |
	1976	1975		1976	1975
Current assets			Current liabilities		
Cash	$ 437,000	$ 396,000	Accounts payable	$ 705,000	$ 598,000
Marketable			Loans	195,000	174,000
securities	377,000	570,000	Accrued items	279,000	296,000
Accounts					
receivable (net)	803,000	574,000			
Inventories	390,000	297,000			
Prepaid					
insurance, etc.	46,000	93,000			
Total current assets	2,053,000	1,930,000	Total current		
			liabilities	1,179,000	1,068,000
Fixed assets			Long-tem debt	659,000	599,000
Land	65,000	57,000	Capital stock		
Building and			530,000 shares		
equipment	5,742,000	4,495,000	outstanding	1,311,000	—
	5,807,000	4,552,000	356,000 shares		
Less depreciation	2,708,000	2,248,000	outstanding	—	862,000
Net fixed assets	3,099,000	2,304,000	Retained earnings	2,011,000	1,716,000
Goodwill less			Net worth	3,322,000	2,578,000
amortization	8,000	11,000	Total liabilities and		
Total assets	$5,160,000	$4,245,000	net worth	$5,160,000	$4,245,000

Table 3.7. Reynolds Machine Company Income Statement

	Year Ending December 31 1976	1975
Sales	$4,348,000	$3,673,000
Costs and expenses		
Costs of goods sold	2,742,000	2,205,000
Depreciation	460,000	423,000
Operating costs	3,202,000	2,628,000
Operating profit	1,146,000	1,045,000
Amortization of goodwill	3,000	3,000
Interest expense	24,000	18,000
Total operating and nonoperating expenses	3,229,000	2,649,000
	1,119,000	1,024,000
Other income	35,000	36,000
Net before income tax	1,154,000	1,060,000
Income tax	528,000	483,000
Net profit	$ 626,000	$ 577,000
Other information		
Earnings per share	$ 1.18	$ 1.62
Dividends per share	0.625	0.46
Market price per share	$40.00	$30.00

All sales are made on credit.

Note: A rights offering resulting in the increase in stock outstanding was made in early 1976. All per share figures are adjusted.

    share (verify the figures), (10) price–earnings ratio, and (11) dividend yield.

    b. What does your analysis regarding the financial condition of this company reveal?

    c. Compute the long-term debt-to-equity ratio using the market value of the equity (number of shares of stock outstanding times market price) instead of book equity. What does this tell you about "cost" and "value"? What can you surmise from the market's valuation of this company?

4. Prepare a funds statement for Reynolds Machine Company for 1976.

5. The financial manager of the Puzzle Corporation, upon hearing that the firm's president just completed a course in financial management, submitted to him a year-end balance sheet (Table 3.8) and additional items of information with a note suggesting that the completion of the balance sheet would be a good opportunity for him to demonstrate his knowledge and at the same time to get in some practice.

Table 3.8. Puzzle Corporation Balance Sheet
December 31, 1976

Assets		Liabilities and Net Worth	
Cash		Accounts payable	
Accounts receivable		Long-term debt	
Inventory		Common stock	$250,000
Plant and equipment	$800,000	Surplus	550,000

Additional Information: Days credit sales outstanding, 30, based on a 360-day year; interest at the rate of 5 percent, or $5,000, was paid on the long-term debt; debt-to-equity ratio 0.75:1;   operating asset turnover (sales to operating assets) 2;   quick ratio 1:1;   current ratio 1.2:1;   all sales are on credit.

Unfortunately the president did not do his lessons well and asks you as his assistant to complete the balance sheet.

Table 3.9. Elixir Drug Company Balance Sheet
December 31, 1976

Cash	$ 96,000	Accounts payable	$ 42,000
Receivables	74,000	Notes payable	5,000
Inventory	90,000	Other current liabilities	30,000
Total current assets	260,000	Total current liabilities	77,000
Fixed assets (net)	104,000	Long-term debt	23,000
		Net worth	264,000
Total assets	$364,000	Total liabilities and net worth	$364,000

Table 3.10. Elixir Drug Company Income Statement
For Year Ended December 31, 1976

Sales		$450,000
Costs		
Cost of sales	$124,000	
Distribution and marketing	146,000	
Research	25,000	
Administrative and other	45,000	340,000
Profit before income tax		110,000
Income tax		50,000
Net profit		$ 60,000

Table 3.11. Ratios and Averages for Drug Industry

	Elixir	*Industry Average*
Current ratio		2.2×
Sales to inventory		6.0×
Days credit sales outstanding as receivables		55 days
Total debt to net worth		54.9%
Sales to total assets		1.3×
Sales to net worth		2.1×
Net profit to sales		4.8%
Net profit to total assets		8.4%
Net profit to net worth		13.0%

6. Analyze the financial data in Tables 3.9 and 3.10 taken from the 1976 statements of the Elixir Drug Company. Industry averages for the drug industry are given below for purposes of comparison (Table 3.11).
   a. Compute the indicated ratios for Elixir.
   b. Compare your ratio results with the industry averages to detect possible management policy errors.

Selected References

Altman, E. I., "Financial Ratios, Discriminant Analysis and the Prediction of Corporate Bankruptcy," *Journal of Finance,* 23 (Sept. 1968), pp. 589–609.

Bierman, H., Jr., "Measuring Financial Liquidity," *Accounting Review,* 35 (Oct. 1960), pp. 628–632.

Foulke, R. A., *Practical Financial Statement Analysis,* 6th ed. New York: McGraw-Hill, 1968.

Grunewald, A. E., "Computer-Assisted Investment Analysis," *Business Topics* (Spring 1967), pp. 11–19.

Helfert, E. A., *Techniques of Financial Analysis,* 3d ed. Homewood, Ill.: Richard D. Irwin, 1972.

Hobgood, G., "Increased Disclosure in 1969 Annual Reports," *Financial Executive,* 38 (Aug. 1970), pp. 24–33.

Horrigan, J. O., "A Short History of Financial Ratio Analysis," *Accounting Review,* 43 (Apr. 1968), pp. 284–294.

Jaedicke, R. K., and R. T. Sprouse, *Accounting Flows: Income, Funds, and Cash.* Englewood Cliffs, N. J.: Prentice-Hall, 1965.

Mason, P., "Cash Flow Analysis and Funds Statements," *Journal of Accountancy,* 111 (Mar. 1961), pp. 59–72.

McFarland, W. B., "Review of Funds Flow Analysis," *Harvard Business Review,* 41 (Sept.–Oct. 1963), pp. 162 ff.

Murray, R., "Lessons for Financial Analysis," *Journal of Finance,* 26 (May 1971), pp. 327–332.

Spacek, L., "The Merger Accounting Dilemma," *Financial Executive,* 38 (Feb. 1970), pp. 38 ff.

Spencer, C. H., and T. S. Barnhisel, "A Decade of Price-Level Changes—The Effect on the Financial Statements of Cummins Engine Company," *Accounting Review,* 40 (Jan. 1965), pp. 144–153.

4

BREAK-EVEN ANALYSIS AND LEVERAGE

In previous chapters we studied how the flow of funds of a firm is affected by changing economic conditions and learned how to evaluate a firm's financial position. In this chapter we will study how earnings fluctuate with revenue and how both the level and the volatility of earnings are affected by the extent to which the firm is levered.

Leverage may be defined as earning more by the use of assets than the firm pays as fixed costs and as earning more by the use of borrowed funds than the firm pays as a fixed charge. The former is known as *operating* leverage; the latter as *financial* leverage. A study of leverage traditionally begins with a break-even analysis—a study of the relationships between revenue, fixed and variable costs, and profits.

BREAK-EVEN ANALYSIS

The operating costs of every firm may be classified into fixed and variable to determine the break-even point. Fixed costs are assumed not to change with the *level* of production but with production *capacity*. Depreciation charges, property taxes, insurance, and officers' salaries are examples. Variable costs are assumed to change in direct proportion to the level of production. Should the level of output rise by 10 percent, variable costs will also rise 10 percent. Raw materials, direct wages, and some supplies are examples.

Relation between Fixed and Variable Costs

Since fixed costs are assumed not to vary with output, the amount allocated to each unit produced varies inversely (but not linearly) with the volume of output. In contrast, variable costs per unit tend to remain constant, although in economic theory variable unit costs at first decline and then rise. Thus since the fixed cost per unit falls as output rises, whereas variable cost per unit remains constant, the total cost per unit falls, at least over a considerable range.

Table 4.1 shows changes in output and total and unit costs, both fixed and variable, where variable cost per unit is constant.

Table 4.1. Brady Company Linear Relationship among Changes in Volume, Output Total, and Unit Costs of Product Produced and Sold*

Sales (Units)	Fixed Costs		Variable Costs		Combined Costs	
	Total	Per Unit	Total	Per Unit	Total	Per Unit
10,000	$60,000	$6.00	$ 4,000	$0.40	$ 64,000	$6.40
50,000	60,000	1.20	20,000	0.40	80,000	1.60
100,000	60,000	0.60	40,000	0.40	100,000	1.00
150,000	60,000	0.40	60,000	0.40	120,000	0.80
200,000	60,000	0.30	80,000	0.40	140,000	0.70

* Everything produced is immediately sold.

The movement of these three costs may be presented mathematically and graphically. Let F equal the fixed cost for any level of production, v the variable cost per unit, and x the number of units produced. Then the total cost C_t is expressed as

$$C_t = F + vx$$
$$C_t = \$60,000 + 0.40x$$

Determination of the Break-Even Point

For each dollar of revenue, a portion must be applied to cover variable cost. The balance is applied to cover fixed cost. After fixed and variable costs are covered, the remainder is net operating income (NOI). Should the margin of revenue be just sufficient at a given level of sales in units to cover fixed and variable costs, the firm will be operating at the break-even point. For example, suppose the firm in Table 4.1 sells its product for $1 per unit. The total revenue function R is then price per unit times x, the number of units sold, or

$$R = px$$
$$= \$1x$$

The volume required to achieve the break-even point is determined by the amount of fixed cost to be recovered and the margin over variable cost. The rate at which the fixed cost will be recovered is determined by the percent that variable cost represents of each dollar of revenue. In our example variable cost represents 40 cents of each dollar of revenue. Fixed cost would be recovered at the rate of 60 cents for each dollar of revenue.

Once the break-even point is reached, profits will climb more quickly than costs with a further rise in sales. But should revenue decline, profits will also fall more precipitously.

The *break-even point in units* may be computed directly. At break-even

$$\text{total revenue} = \text{total costs}$$
$$px = F + vx$$
$$\$1x = \$60,000 + 0.40x$$
$$x = 100,000 \text{ units}$$

The *break-even point* in dollars is equal to fixed cost divided by the profit contribution per dollar of revenue. In our example,

$$\text{break-even in dollars} = \frac{\text{fixed cost}}{1 - \text{variable cost per dollar of revenue}}$$
$$= \frac{\$60,000}{1 - 0.40} = \$100,000$$

These cost and revenue relationships are shown graphically in Figure 4.1.

Limitations of Break-Even Analysis

Break-even analysis suffers from six limitations.

1. It generally assumes an unlimited demand for the firm's product at a fixed price and constant returns to scale.
2. It requires a strict classification of all costs into fixed and variable.

Figure 4.1. Break-even chart for cost data of Table 4.1.

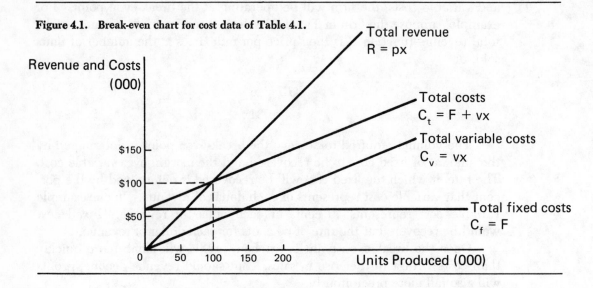

3. It assumes either a single product or an invariant product mix in the case of a multiple product firm.
4. In a dynamic environment major reliance must be placed on judgment in determining the necessary information inputs to the break-even analysis.
5. The planning horizon of the analysis is short and reflects the status quo.
6. Profits are not a simple residual but controllable to a considerable degree by management.

The test of a method or technique is whether it leads to correct decisions. Where the probability is good that the break-even analysis will lead to correct decisions, it should be applied.

Nonlinear Break-Even Analysis

Relationships in the business world are frequently nonlinear. Because of economies and diseconomies of scale, variable cost per unit may at first fall and then rise over some range of output. Thus in many cases it is necessary to abandon the linear assumption in break-even analysis and to work with nonlinear relationships, as shown in Figure 4.2.

Profit is maximized at the volume where marginal revenue equals marginal cost. Marginal revenue is the slope of the total revenue curve and marginal cost is the slope of the total cost curve. If we have at least one nonlinear relation (either total revenue or total cost), we will have an upper and a lower break-even point.

Figure 4.2. Nonlinear break-even chart.

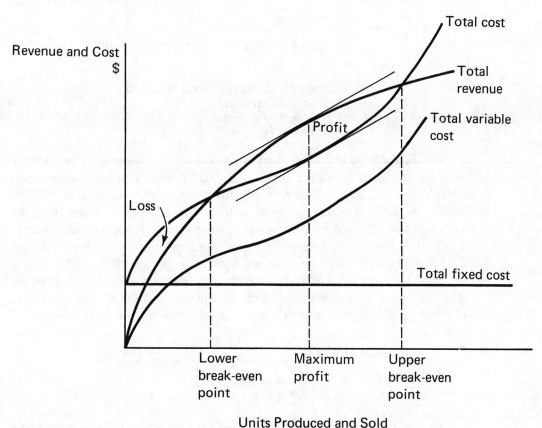

OPERATING LEVERAGE: IMPACT ON NET OPERATING INCOME (NOI)

Up to this point we have concentrated on the level of the break-even point. A useful way to extend this analysis is through an examination of the rate of change that occurs in NOI when output changes. The fluctuation in NOI is known as *business risk*. The relationship between changes in output and changes in NOI is formalized in the concept of the degree of operating leverage (DOL). By definition,

$$\frac{\text{degree of operating leverage}}{\text{at sale of } x \text{ units}} = \frac{\text{percent change in NOI}}{\text{percent change in revenue or output}}$$

The degree of operating leverage at a point can also be calculated directly by the formula

$$\text{degree of operating leverage at sale of } x \text{ units} = \frac{x(p - v)}{x(p - v) - F}$$

where

x = number of units produced and sold
p = selling price per unit
v = variable cost per unit
F = total fixed cost.

To illustrate how this concept is used, assume the Brady Company in Table 4.1 forecasts an output level of 150,000 units. The break-even point is 100,000 units, so the firm is expecting to generate an NOI of $30,000 (50,000 × 0.6). Unfortunately it is truly the exception rather than the rule when the sales forecast turns out to be correct. It seems reasonable to assume that the Brady Company management would be interested in the effect that errors in the sales forecast have on expected NOI. DOL is one technique that can be used to investigate this question. Since 150,000 units is the sales forecast, this is the most obvious point at which to compute DOL. Substituting the appropriate values in our equation for the DOL, we get

$$\text{DOL } 150,000 = \frac{150,000(\$1 - 0.40)}{150,000(\$1 - 0.40) - \$60,000}$$

$$= \frac{\$90,000}{\$30,000} = 3$$

The degree of operating leverage may also be computed when we know the break-even point:

$$\text{degree of operating leverage at sale of } x \text{ units} = \frac{x}{x - (\text{break-even point in units})}$$

For the Brady Company;

$$\text{degree of operating leverage at sale of 150,000 units} = \frac{150,000}{150,000 - 100,000} = 3$$

Once management has obtained the value of the DOL, they have an understanding of the volatility which is inherent in the firm's NOI. In the present case they would know that if output were increased by 10% *from its forecast level,* then NOI would increase by a factor of 3 times the increase in output, or by 30%. Unfortunately this leveraging factor works in both directions. If output fell short of the forecast level by 10%, then NOI would be 30% lower than anticipated. The DOL varies for each level of output. In our example we computed DOL at 150,000 units equal to 3.0. As the point at which we compute the DOL moves closer to the break-even point, the DOL increases and becomes very large as the break-even point is approached. Conversely, when we move away from the break-even point, the DOL decreases.

FINANCIAL LEVERAGE: IMPACT ON EARNINGS PER SHARE (EPS)

Financial leverage is introduced into the capital structure (total of long-term debt, preferred stock, and common stock accounts) when funds are obtained on a fixed-return basis. Then any variation in NOI (also defined as earnings before interest and taxes) is magnified on EPS. The greater the degree of financial leverage, the wider the fluctuations in EPS for any variation in NOI. This variation in EPS is known as *financial risk*.

Continuing our example of the Brady Company, let us observe the impact of variations in NOI on EPS. In an effort to enhance earnings per share when the outlook appears bleak, the company decides to refinance, going from all common stock to a capital structure that is 60% bonds. The details are given in Table 4.2.

Table 4.2. Brady Company Balance Sheets before and after Refinancing

	Before	
Assets:		Liabilities and equity:
$100,000		$100,000 common stock (25,000 shares @ $4)
	After	
Assets:		Liabilities and equity:
		$ 60,000 bonds—5%
		40,000 common stock (10,000 shares @ $4)
$100,000		$100,000

Assume that the earnings of the Brady Company decline after this capital structure change. As can be seen from Table 4.3, EPS declines faster than NOI.

A 16.7 percent drop in NOI results in an 18.5% drop in EPS; a 20 percent drop in NOI from $25,000 to $20,000 results in a 22.7 percent drop in EPS. Using the same figures, except postulating a rising earnings trend going from $20,000 NOI to $25,000 NOI, we have a 25 percent increase in NOI resulting in a 29.4 percent increase in EPS.

Had Brady Company continued with 100 percent common stock financ-

Table 4.3. **Brady Company Earnings in Three Successive Years**

	1st Year	2nd Year 16.7% Drop in NOI	3rd Year Additional 20% Drop in NOI
NOI	$30,000	$25,000	$20,000
Bond interest	3,000	3,000	3,000
Earnings before taxes	27,000	22,000	17,000
Taxes (50 percent rate)	13,500	11,000	8,500
Earnings after taxes	$13,500	$11,000	$ 8,500
EPS	$ 1.35	$ 1.10	$ 0.85
Change in NOI*	—	−16.7%	−20.0%
Change in EPS*	—	−18.5%	−22.7%

* Change is from the first to the second year and the second to the third year.

ing, 25,000 shares of $4 par stock outstanding, the respective EPS would be 60, 50, and 20 cents for the three years as shown in Table 4.4. The EPS decline is in direct proportion to the drop in NOI. While EPS declines, the remaining stockholders are better with the capital structure change than they would have been without it.

Table 4.4. **Brady Company EPS if Refinancing Did Not Occur**

	1st Year	2nd Year 16% Drop in NOI	3rd Year Additional 20% Drop in NOI
NOI	$30,000	$25,000	$20,000
Bond interest	—	—	—
Earnings before taxes	30,000	25,000	20,000
Taxes (50 percent rate)	15,000	12,500	10,000
Earnings after taxes	$15,000	$12,500	$10,000
EPS	$ 0.60	$ 0.50	$ 0.40
Change in EBIT*	—	−16.7%	−20%
Change in EPS*	—	−16.7%	−20%

* Change is from the first to the second year and the second to the third year.

Computing Financial Leverage

Similar to the operating leverage, the degree of financial leverage (DFL) can also be computed as a point measure. The measure describes the relationship of a percentage change in earnings per share (EPS) at a given NOI for any percentage change in NOI. From Table 4.3 we can compute the DFL at an NOI of $30,000 by using the expression

$$\text{degree of financial leverage at an NOI of \$30,000} = \frac{\text{percent change in EPS}}{\text{percent change in NOI}} = \frac{18.5\%}{16.7\%} = 1.11$$

The degree of financial leverage can be determined directly knowing only the specified level of NOI and interest by using the expression

$$\text{degree of financial leverage at specified level of NOI} = \frac{\text{NOI}}{\text{NOI} - I}$$

where I is the interest on debt in dollars.

For the Brady Company, Table 4.3, we have

$$\text{degree of financial leverage at an NOI of \$30,000} = \frac{\$30,000}{\$30,000 - \$3,000} = \frac{\$30,000}{\$27,000} = 1.11$$

Having obtained the value of the DFL, the Brady Company has a measure of the volatility of earnings per share. At an NOI level of $30,000, earnings per share will rise or fall 1.11 times faster than a change in NOI. Other things equal, increasing the interest charge will raise the degree of financial leverage and vice versa.

OPERATING AND FINANCIAL LEVERAGE TOGETHER

Financial and operating leverage combine to produce a wider percentage change in earnings for a given percentage change in revenue. The example of the Brady Company (Table 4.5) indicates how a 10 percent increase in revenue is magnified to a 30 percent increase in NOI by operating leverage, and further magnified to 33⅓ percent increase in earnings available to the common stock by financial leverage. The same variability holds on the down side.

Normally it would not seem desirable to finance a high operating leverage firm with large amounts of debt, but the controlling factor is variability

Table 4.5. Brady Company Effect of a 10 Percent Increase in Revenues on Earnings Available to the Common Stock

			Increase (%)
Sales, units	150,000	165,000	10
Revenues, $1/unit	$150,000	$165,000	
Variable costs, $0.40/unit	60,000	66,000	
Fixed costs	60,000	60,000	
Net operating income	30,000	39,000	30
Interest	3,000	3,000	
	27,000	36,000	
Taxes (50%)	13,500	18,000	
Net available to the common stock	$ 13,500	$ 18,000	33⅓

of revenue. A stable firm, such as an electric utility, can advantageously combine high operating and financial leverage. Producing above the break-even point with little probability of falling below it, the risk assumed by the firm is small. The absence of substantial revenue variation means that the net available for the common stock will not fluctuate widely and will not impart a speculative character to the common stock.

The degree of operating leverage can be combined with the degree of financial leverage to compute the total leverage effect on earnings available to the common stock for a given change in sales, that is,

$$\text{combined degree of leverage at sale of } x \text{ units} = \frac{x(p - v)}{x(p - v) - F - I}$$

For the Brady Company, Table 4.5, we have

$$\text{combined degree of leverage at sale of 150,000 units} = \frac{150,000(\$1.00 - \$0.40)}{150,000(\$1.00 - \$0.40) - \$60,000 - \$3,000}$$

$$= \frac{\$90,000}{\$27,000} = 3\frac{1}{3}$$

At the 150,000 unit level of sales, a 10 percent change in sales will cause a 33⅓ percent change in earnings available to the common stock; that is, the change in earnings available to the common stock will be 3.3⅓ times as great as the change in sales.

Summary

Break-even analysis is a study of the relationships between revenue, fixed and variable costs, and profits. At break-even, total revenue equals total cost and profit is zero. Once the break-even point is reached, profits rise faster than costs with increased sales. Break-even can be expressed in terms of units of production or dollars. Usually break-even analysis assumes linear relationships between revenue and costs, but this assumption can be abandoned when nonlinear conditions prevail.

Operating leverage results from the presence of fixed costs that magnify net operating income fluctuations flowing from small variations in revenue. The larger the fixed costs relative to the variable costs, the greater the degree of operating leverage. The closer we are to the break-even point, that point where the excess of revenue over variable cost is just sufficient to cover fixed costs, the greater the degree of operating leverage.

The return to shareholders can be raised through financing a portion of the asset requirements with debt. Financial leverage is favorable when the firm is able to earn more on its assets than it is paying for borrowed funds, and unfavorable when the converse is true. Generally it is undesirable to finance a firm with high operating leverage by means of high financial leverage. The main consideration is the stability of revenues.

Study Questions

1. What is the relation between fixed costs and operating leverage? Develop a simple example illustrating the operating leverage phenomenon. Introduce the dynamic dimension into your illustration by postulating given changes in sales.
2. What data would you as a financial manager require to develop a break-even chart? What information would you hope to gain from your break-even analysis? How would this help you in reaching sound financial decisions?
3. Assuming other things equal, what will be the effect of the following decisions on a firm's break-even point and on its degree of operating leverage?
   a. Selling prices are increased.
   b. a new plant is purchased that will increase depreciation charges by $50,000.
   c. A new materials flow system is introduced that will reduce variable costs by 1 cent per unit.
4. What is the relation between debt financing and financial leverage? Develop a simple example illustrating the financial leverage phenomenon. Introduce the dynamic dimension into your illustration by postulating given changes in NOI.

5. What are the circumstances under which a firm's total costs will vary in direct proportion to changes in output? What industries seem to have such cost characteristics? Do they tend to have a high or low break-even point?
6. Referring to Question 5, answer the same questions for firms whose total costs vary hardly at all with changes in output.

Problems

1. Classify the following costs as fixed (F), variable (V), and partially fixed and partially variable (F/V). Be sure you can support your answer. (a) Raw materials, (b) electric power, (c) president's salary, (d) heat, (e) direct wages, (f) wages of supervisory plant personnel, (g) property taxes, (h) fire insurance, (i) obsolescence, (j) cleaning and janitor supplies.
2. Melody Milk, Inc., organized to manufacture and sell a new dietary drink known as DD, has just completed its first year of operation. The financial statements are presented in Tables 4.6 and 4.7.

Table 4.6. Melody Milk Inc., Balance Sheet (Year End)

Assets		Liabilities	
Cash	$ 2,000	Accounts payable	$10,000
Accounts receivable	10,000	Notes payable (6%)	5,000
Inventory	6,000	Long-term debt (6%)	5,000
Plant and equipment (net)	22,000	Common stock, $6 par	6,000
		Retained earnings	14,000
Total assets	$40,000	Total liabilities and net worth	$40,000

Table 4.7. Melody Milk, Inc., Other Information

Selling price of DD	$2.50 per package
Fixed cost (total) other than interest and taxes	$50,000
Variable cost other than interest and income taxes	$1.50 per package

a. Using the formula $px = F + vx$ compute the break-even point in units. Determine the break-even point in dollars.
b. Compute NOI at the 60,000 package level. Assume sales rise by 50 percent to 90,000 packages. Now recompute NOI. What is the percentage increase in NOI? Assume sales rise 100 percent to 120,000 packages. Recompute NOI. What is the percentage rise in NOI?

c. Using the formula (degree of operating leverage at sale of x units) = $\%\triangle NOI/\%\triangle$ sales, compute the degree of operating leverage at the 60,000 package level for a 50 percent and a 100 percent increase in sales.

d. Draw a break-even chart of the firm.

e. The management of Melody Milk plans to expand. Determine the new break-even point in units and dollars if fixed costs rise from $50,000 to $54,000 and variable costs fall from $1.50 to $1.30 per package.

f. Calculate earnings per share at $0, $10,000, and $20,000 debt levels for combinations of $1000, $5000, and $10,000 NOI. Assume an interest rate of 6%, an income tax rate of 50 percent, and that additional shares could be sold or repurchased at $40 per share net to the firm to replace dollars of debt.

3. Wilco Corporation recently released the following income statement:

Sales (100,000 units @ $1)	$100,000
Variable cost	40,000
Profit margin	60,000
Fixed cost	20,000
NOI	40,000
Interest	15,000
Net income	$ 25,000

Calculate the following.

a. The degree of operating leverage at the current sales level.

b. The degree of financial leverage.

c. The combined degree of leverage.

Selected References

Hobbs, J. B., "Volume-Mix-Price/Cost Budget Variance Analysis: A Proper Approach," *Accounting Review,* 39 (Oct. 1967), pp. 905–913.

Hugon, J. H., "Breakeven Analysis in Three Dimensions," *Financial Executive,* 33 (Dec. 1965), pp. 22–26.

Jaedicke, R. K., and A. A. Robichek, "Cost-Volume-Profit Analysis under Conditions of Uncertainty," *Accounting Review,* 39 (Oct. 1964), pp. 917–926.

Kelvie, W. E., and J. M. Sinclair, "New Technique for Breakeven Charts," *Financial Executive,* 36 (June 1968), pp. 31–43.

Morrison, T. A., and E. Kaczka, "A New Application of Calculus and Risk Analysis to Cost-Volume-Profit Changes," *Accounting Review,* 44 (Apr. 1969), pp. 330–343.

Pfahl, J. K., D. T. Crary, and R. H. Howard, "The Limits of Leverage," *Financial Executive,* 38 (May 1970), pp. 48–56.

Raun, D. L., "The Limitations of Profit Graphs, Breakeven Analysis, and Budgets," *Accounting Review,* 39 (Oct. 1964), pp. 927–945.

——, "Product-Mix Analysis by Linear Programming," *NAA—Management Accounting,* 47 (Sept. 1965–Aug. 1966), pp. 3–13.

Reinhardt, V. E., "Break Even Analysis for Lockheed's Tri-Star: An Application of Financial Theory," *Journal of Finance,* 28 (Sept. 1973), pp. 821–838.

Robbins, S., and E. Foster, Jr., "Profit-Planning and the Finance Function," *Journal of Finance,* 12 (Dec. 1957), pp. 451–467.

5

PROFIT PLANNING AND CONTROL

Planning for profit requires that we forecast sales. We must know the various possible levels of sales and the resultant profitability to determine the level of plant operation that will earn an optimal profit. A tool frequently applied in profit planning, given a sales forecast, is break-even analysis. In Chapter 4 we introduced break-even analysis to examine the concepts of operating and financial leverage. Now we use break-even analysis to decide on the price and the number of units of each product to offer for sale.

Actively planning for profits means aggressively adjusting the activities of the firm, such as shifting the product mix to meet anticipated external factors. Establishment of sales targets and cost limits is essential. These provide the guidelines for action and a control of performance. If actual sales and costs vary widely from the target figures, management must inquire into the reasons. Significant variations do occur and may be justified. To provide control and permit the information feedback mechanism to operate, it is important to reconcile promptly the budgeted with the actual figures. Reports must flow back to the decision makers who are then in a position to make new decisions based on more current information.

To produce the variety of products and the different quantities of each to satisfy the anticipated sales demand requires a particular level and mix of assets—cash, receivables, inventory, and fixed assets. This asset need must be financed. Proceeding from the sales and profit forecasts, the financing needs of the firm can be planned. With such a forecast the financial manager can arrange both the amounts and the sources to supply the needed funds. Forward planning of this type reduces the risk of the firm, raises investor confidence, and should lead to increases in the market value of the firm.

SALES FORECASTING—TREND EXTRAPOLATION

The sales forecast is crucial to budgeting. From the sales forecast follows the estimate of cost of goods sold and decisions concerning inventory levels, purchases of raw materials, employment level, distribution and selling expenses, administrative and general expenses, and financial requirements. These activities of purchasing, producing, selling, and administering are separate but must be planned as a system in relation to the sales forecast.

To illustrate trend extrapolation—the use of a sales forecast to estimate future financial requirements—consider the data in Table 5.1 concerning

Table 5.1. Optics, Inc., Relation between Inventory and Sales

Year	Sales	Inventory	Inventory as a Percent of Sales
1971	$100,000	$35,000	35%
1972	130,000	36,500	28
1973	160,000	38,400	24
1974	200,000	40,000	20
1975	250,000	42,500	17
1976	—	—	—
1977	—	—	—
1978	—	—	—
1979	—	—	—
1980 (estimated)	600,000	60,000	10

actual sales, inventory, and inventory as a percent of sales figures for the period of 1971–1975 and the target inventory requirement for 1980.

In Figure 5.1 the data of Table 5.1 are plotted on a scatter diagram and a free-hand line is fitted. Reading the vertical axis we obtain the estimated level of $60,000 inventory for 1980 estimated sales of $600,000. This is extrapolation of the historical pattern into the future. Trend extrapolation is the simplest forecasting practice.

More sophisticated sales forecasting methods are available. They include naive techniques such as moving average and exponential smoothing which are similar to trend extrapolation in that sales are forecast from a

Figure 5.1. Optics, Inc., scatter diagram illustrating relation between sales and inventory.

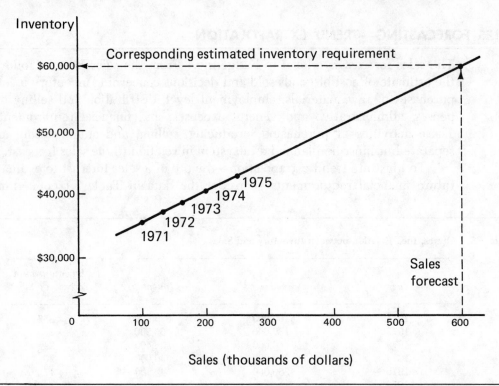

series of past sales. Also available are regression analysis and simultaneous equation models which identify external variables useful for forecasting sales.

PROFIT PLANNING THROUGH BREAK-EVEN ANALYSIS

Break-even analysis rests on the fact that some costs vary with production, while others remain fixed. When fixed costs are present, a firm will incur losses up to that minimum unit volume of sales that covers fixed costs. We seek a plan for operation above the break-even point.

To illustrate the use of break-even analysis, consider the firm of Optics, Inc., which manufactures a special-effects bulb that sells for $2. The firm normally sells 100,000 of these bulbs per year and earns a net operating income (NOI) of $30,000. Evidence of price cutting in Optics' industry abounds. We are asked to estimate the combinations of selling price and volume necessary to maintain the existing NOI level.

Table 5.2. Optics, Inc., Sales, Cost, and Profit Estimates

Basic Data	Price Decrease		Current Price	Price Increase	
	20%	10%		10%	20%
Sales, units	166,667	125,000	100,000	83,333	71,429
Unit price	$1.60	$1.80	$2.00	$2.20	$2.40
Sales, dollars	$266,667	$225,000	$200,000	$183,333	$171,429
Variable costs, $1 per unit	166,667	125,000	100,000	83,333	71,429
Fixed costs	70,000	70,000	70,000	70,000	70,000
Total costs	$236,667	$195,000	$170,000	$153,000	$141,429
Target net operating income	$ 30,000	$ 30,000	$ 30,000	$ 30,000	$ 30,000

This is a break-even problem with one exception. Instead of seeking a sales level at which total revenues equal total cost, we seek the levels where total revenues equal total costs plus our target NOI, or

$$px = F + vx + \$30{,}000$$

Utilizing the equation we create Table 5.2. This table shows the sales necessary to earn the target NOI should increasing competition dictate price reductions of 10 or 20 percent. Table 5.2 also indicates how much less need be sold if prices could be raised and certain sections of the market abandoned. Starting with these data, recommendations can be made regarding production levels, financing requirements, sales campaigns, and advertising budgets.

In Chapter 4 we noted the limitations of break-even analysis. Review of these limitations is a good first step when applying this technique as a method of predicting profit.

FLEXIBLE (VARIABLE) BUDGETS

A budget is a formalized quantitative plan for allocating the firm's resources in a future period. A *fixed budget* is a plan containing revenue, production, and cost figures designed to meet a target level of output, say 100,000 units. A *flexible budget* is prepared for a range of activities and focuses on efficiency of operation. For a given level of operations, the flexible budget tells management what the costs will be. The actual performance of the firm will be influenced by external events over which management has little control and by the efficiency with which the firm operates.

Preparation of a flexible budget requires a sales forecast, a classification of all costs, their separation into fixed and variable, and the establishment of responsibility (cost) centers. The centers permit grouping of costs and the assignment of each center to a manager for control. After assignment to a center, the controllable expenses are related to some measure of productive activity. Various yardsticks used include machine hours, direct labor hours, direct material costs, and units of output. With costs separated into fixed and variable, total costs for a given volume within the range budgeted by management may be computed.

Large firms have extended the idea of responsibility accounting by establishing investment centers that correspond to the divisions of the firm. For example, a large firm with a truck division, a farm equipment division, and a construction equipment division may designate each of these as an investment center. Each division has its own invested capital, is responsible for revenue and expenses, and its performance is measured by relating its net operating income to its invested capital. At the end of the period the budgeted amount is compared with the actual. If wide variations occur, reasons are sought. *The variation may have resulted because actual production differed widely from what had been budgeted.*

Knowing why less was expended than budgeted is as important as knowing why more was spent. Perhaps savings are being accomplished at the expense of future operations through skimpy maintenance or inadequate staffing. The individual responsible for the center could be mistakenly rewarded if bonuses are based solely on currently measured efficiency, for his department performance would be overstated.

Prompt feedback of information is necessary to make the flexible budgeting system work. The objective is to keep the actual in line with the budgeted. Once the actual is determined, the process of interpreting the variance from the actual should begin. When the cause of the variance is determined, the information should flow back to those responsible for planning operations. The budget for the succeeding period may then incorporate the new information. The financial manager must take care not to overreact to every discrepancy between the actual and the budgeted. Only significant discrepancies should result in budget changes. Separation of significant from random discrepancies is an art and difficult at best.

CONTROL

One important part of financial management is review. In Chapter 3 we discussed financial ratios and showed how they could be used to analyze the firm so that no aspect of its operation gets out of balance. When using the flexible budget as an instrument of planning and control, additional controls are available.

After the budget is established, review and control are in order. Departure of actual costs from those budgeted will occur. Management requires some system for determining whether the departures warrant inquiry. The extremes are to investigate all departures or to investigate none. Some departures are too small; others are so large that they command inquiry. Thus some limit on deviations is usually selected, and any deviation below the limit is not investigated. The limit may be either in terms of absolute size or in terms of relative magnitude.

To illustrate, assume that Optics, Inc., has budgeted $100,000 for the quarter for direct labor. This budgeted amount is a forecast. The actual amount spent will depart from this amount. The discrepancy may be caused by a shift in basic conditions (either internal to the firm or external) or by random events. If we estimate that there is a 50–50 chance that departures attributable to random events will approximate $10,000 or less, we might then set $10,000 as the limit of random deviations that we choose not to investigate.

There is a danger in this type of decision rule. For example, a deviation under $10,000 might be the sum of two significant deviations in opposite directions: a favorable deviation of $30,000 and an unfavorable deviation of $20,000, both of which would call for study. For example, the net deviation of $10,000 might have resulted from a 30 percent increase in output per manhour and a 40 percent increase in overtime, assuming overtime is paid a 50 percent premium. The production manager achieved a $10,000 reduction in costs by firing a large part of the work force and going overtime with the balance of the force.

PRO FORMA FINANCIAL STATEMENTS

Pro forma income statements and balance sheets provide management with a picture of the firm's profitability over the coming period and its financial condition at the end of the period, given certain assumptions. Management may also wish to plan operations over multiple periods of time, say five years. Pro forma statements involve estimating sales, expenses, profits, capital expenditures, and other activities over each period and drawing up an income statement for the period and an ending balance sheet.

The creation of pro forma statements involves a two-step process. Step 1 requires that a sales forecast be made and step 2 involves identifying those balance sheet and income statement items that vary directly with sales. To illustrate this process, consider the Rainbow Tea Company (Table 5.3), a new firm.

Table 5.3. Rainbow Tea Company Opening Balance Sheet
January 1, 1976

Assets		Liabilities and Net Worth	
Cash	$ 350	Accounts payable	$ 150
Inventory	150	Current liabilities	150
Total current assets	500	Common stock	1350
Plant and equipment	1000		
Total assets	$1500	Total liabilities and net worth	$1500

Short-Term Planning

The financial manager of the Rainbow Tea Company wishes to estimate what the balance sheet will look like at the end of the year. He estimates sales, expenses, and profits for the coming year, as shown in Table 5.4. In addition he identifies those balance sheet items that he expects will vary with sales and expresses them as a percent of sales (Table 5.5).

Table 5.5. Rainbow Tea Company Balance Sheet Items as a Percent of Sales

Assets		Liabilities and Net Worth	
Cash	3%	Accounts payable	8%
Receivables	8%		
Inventory	13%		

Armed with the information in Tables 5.4 and 5.5, we are ready to generate a pro forma balance sheet. We will use the item "Bank Loan" to balance assets and liabilities. In constructing Table 5.6 we further assume that all profits are retained and that the depreciation expense for the year was $50.

The pro forma financial statements provide us with a picture of the impact of the expected production level during the coming period on the firm's financial requirements. As Table 5.3 shows, at the beginning of the period Rainbow Tea's assets totaled $1500, payables $150, and common stock

Table 5.6. Rainbow Tea Company Pro Forma Balance Sheet
December 31, 1976

Current assets			Current liabilities	
Cash		$ 150	Accounts payable	$ 400
Receivables		400	Bank loan (balance item)	250
Inventory		650	Common stock	1350
Plant and equipment	$1000		Retained earnings	150
Depreciation	50	950		
Total assets		$2150		$2150

$1350 with no bank loan. To support the $5000 sales expected of Table 5.4, we would have total (asset) financial requirements of $2150. Since we have common stock of $1350 and payables of $150, we must raise $650. But

Table 5.4. Rainbow Tea Company Pro Forma Profit and Loss Statement
January 1–December 31, 1976

Sales	$5000	100%
Cost of goods sold	4000	80
Gross profit	1000	20
Operating expenses	700	14
Profit before taxes	300	6
Taxes (50 percent rate)	150	3
Net profit	$ 150	3%

$150 will be generated from retained earnings, hence we must raise $500 externally by either an increase in the balance of payables during the period, a bank loan, or both.

Long-Term Planning

Suppose also that the financial manager is interested in looking five years ahead. The detailing of all expenditures to obtain a rough idea of the profitability and financial condition of the firm through estimating sales, profits, and plant and equipment requirements over the period is unnecessary. A simpler procedure is available.

Assume we expect sales to double in five years, plant and equipment purchases to keep pace with production output, net profits to continue at 3

Table 5.7. Rainbow Tea Company Five-Year Growth Pattern

Year	Sales	Net Profit at 3 Percent of Sales	Plant and Equipment at Cost	Depreciation Charged at 5 Percent per Annum
2	$ 6000	$ 180	$1200	$ 60
3	7000	210	1400	70
4	8000	240	1600	80
5	9000	270	1800	90
6	10,000	300	2000	100
Total		$1200		$400

percent of sales, and depreciation to be charged at 5 percent per annum. The five-year growth pattern of the firm appears in Table 5.7.

Assuming that the balance sheet relationships of Table 5.5 are constant, the pro forma balance sheet of Rainbow Tea five years hence might appear

Table 5.8. Rainbow Tea Company Pro Forma Balance Sheet Five Years Hence

Current assets			Current liabilities	
Cash		$ 300	Accounts payable	$ 800
Accounts receivable		800	Bank loan	450
Inventory		1300		1250
		2400	Common stock plus prior	
Plant and equipment	$2000		retained earnings	1500*
Depreciation	450	1550	New retained earnings	1200
Total assets		$3950	Total liabilities and net worth	$3950

* From Table 5.6.

as in Table 5.8. The expected retained earnings plus depreciation expense turn out to be almost enough to finance the expected growth. The bank loan need be increased only $200. The funds flow statement of Table 5.9 shows the detail.

Table 5.9. Rainbow Tea Company Pro Forma Funds Flow Statement for Five More Years

Additional Funds Required		Additional Funds Provided	
Cash	$ 150	Accounts payable	$ 400
Accounts receivable	400	Bank loan	200
Inventory	650	Retained earnings	1200
Plant and equipment	1000	Depreciation	400
Total funds required	$2200	Total funds provided	$2200

Summary

Planning and control are vital to the firm's long-run survival. A key to successful planning is the sales forecast. Utilizing such a forecast, break-even analysis can be employed to estimate the sales volume necessary to earn the planned net operating income.

Budgets provide management with a map of the road and serve as a standard of performance. Management can check the performance of the firm, evaluate the efficiency of operation, and modify its plans accordingly.

Using pro forma financial statements management can estimate the profitability over the next period and the financial condition of the firm at the end of that period. If management is satisfied, the plans can be formalized and put into effect. Otherwise new plans can be laid and the effect of the plans evaluated from a new set of pro forma statements.

Study Questions

1. In the absence of adequate and reliable data, profit planning cannot be successful. Explain. In the absence of a mass of data in centuries past can we conclude that businessmen did not plan?
2. Why is it sometimes possible for a large firm to plan more successfully than a small firm? If a large firm were sufficiently influential to be able to modify its environment, how would its planning be improved?
3. The sales figure is the key figure in every forecast of operations level and profit. What guides would you use to estimate next year's sales for the following products: (a) baby carriage, (b) engagement rings, (c) automobiles, (d) mink coats, (e) earth-moving equipment?
4. How can break-even analysis assist in profit planning? Does the nature of the firm's operation influence its measure of profit planning success? How? Would

lack of success invalidate the use of the break-even analysis in profit planning? Explain.

5. A budget provides the firm not only with a glimpse of the future but also with a standard against which the firm's performance can be measured. Explain. Why is the prompt feedback of information regarding performance necessary for good control and improved decisions?

6. How do projected income and balance sheet statements assist in financial planning? What do they provide that the budget does not? What are the dangers of relaxed control over accounts receivable and inventory?

Problems

1. For the glamorous hostess the Party Supply Company markets a disposable paper dress and napkins to match. The set is currently priced at $10 and Party is selling 10,000 sets annually. Normal profit on the item before taxes is $10,000. Variable costs are $7 a set and fixed costs are $20,000. The possibility exists that competitive products may enter the market. The competition may fail, however.

a. Determine the sales volume required to maintain normal profit if the price were forced down to $7.50 a set; the sales volume required to maintain normal profit if prices could be raised to $13 a set. Supply the necessary figures in Table 5.10.

Table 5.10. Party Supply Company Sales, Cost, and Profit Estimates

Basic Data	Price Drop	Current Price	Price Increase
Unit price	$ 7.50	$ 10	$ 13
Required unit sales	—	10,000	—
Required dollar sales	—	$100,000	—
Variable costs of $7 per unit	—	$ 70,000	—
Fixed costs	$20,000	$ 20,000	$20,000
Total costs	—	$ 90,000	—
Normal profit	$10,000	$ 10,000	$10,000

b. After examining the data, how would you evaluate the significance of a forced price reduction to $7.50?

2. The sales of Molasses, Inc., last year were $100,000. Sales for the current year are expected to rise 20 percent, to $120,000. The financial manager is asked to estimate the additional financing required to support the higher sales volume.

The recent balance sheet of the firm appears in Table 5.11.

Table 5.11. Molasses, Inc., Balance Sheet
December 31, 1976

Cash	$ 5,000	Accounts payable	$ 6,000
Accounts receivable	8,000	Notes payable	5,000
Inventory	15,000	Bonds	10,000
Fixed assets (net)	32,000	Common stock	15,000
		Retained earnings	24,000
Total assets	$60,000	Total liabilities and net worth	$60,000

a. Observing that except for bonds, common stock, and retained earnings, the balance sheet items vary directly with sales, the financial manager asks that you express each such balance sheet item as a percent of last year's sales.

b. Estimate the total additional financing Molasses will require if sales go from $100,000 to $120,000.

c. Molasses earns a profit after income tax of 5 percent on sales and pays out 40 percent of its earnings in dividends. Income taxes are to be ignored. Determine the amount of additional external financing the firm will require to support sales of $120,000.

d. Construct a pro forma balance sheet as of December 31, 1977, based on sales of $120,000 for the year. As balancing items use "additional external financing needed" and "additional internal funds" under "retained earnings."

3. (Problem 2 continued.) Fiscal 1977 proves to be a good year. Sales of Molasses, Inc., reach $125,000. The balance sheet of the firm at the close of the year appears in Table 5.12.

Table 5.12. Molasses, Inc., Balance Sheet
December 31, 1977

Cash	$ 5,000	Accounts payable	$10,000
Accounts receivable	12,500	Notes payable	15,500
Inventory	25,000	Bonds	10,000
Fixed assets (net)	35,000	Common stock	15,000
		Retained earnings	27,000
Total assets	$77,500	Total liabilities and net worth	$77,500

a. Using the actual December 31, 1976, and December 31, 1977, balance sheets, compute each of the above balance sheet items as a percent of 1976 and 1977 sales, $100,000 and $125,000, respectively.

b. Given the estimated and actual 1977 sales figures, the pro forma and the actual December 31, 1977, balance sheets, and your answer to Problem 3a, discuss the appropriateness of the percent-of-sales method of forecasting financial requirements.

Selected References

Chambers, J. C., S. K. Mullick, and D. D. Smith, "How to Choose the Right Forecasting Technique," *Harvard Business Review*, 49 (July–Aug. 1971), pp. 45–74.

Chisholm, R. K., and G. R. Whitaker, Jr., *Forecasting Methods*. Homewood, Ill.: Richard D. Irwin, 1971.

Dapuch, N., J. G. Birnberg, and J. Demski, "An Extension of Standard Cash Variance Analysis," *Accounting Review*, 42 (July 1967), pp. 526–536.

Jaedicke, R. K., and A. R. Robichek, "Cost-Volume-Profit Analysis under Conditions of Uncertainty," *Accounting Review*, 39 (Oct. 1964), pp. 917–926.

Jensen, R. E., "A Multiple Regression Model for Cost Control—Assumptions and Limitations," *Accounting Review*, 42 (Apr. 1967), pp. 265–273.

Morrison, T. A., and E. Kaczke, "A New Application of Calculus and Risk Analysis to Cost-Volume-Profit Changes," *Accounting Review*, 44 (Apr. 1969), pp. 330–343.

Parker, G. C., and E. L. Segura, "How to Get a Better Forecast," *Harvard Business Review*, 49 (Mar.–Apr. 1971), pp. 99–109.

part two
THE MANAGEMENT OF WORKING CAPITAL

6

THE MONEY MANAGEMENT SYSTEM

A firm requires cash to pay its bills in order to continue production. The financial manager cannot time cash inflows to coincide with required cash outflows. Thus the firm must hold liquid balances—cash and assets readily convertible into cash—to absorb the drain of a cash outflow greater than the cash inflow over some period of time. But holding cash and short-term securities is costly; cash does not produce goods and services, and the return on short-term securities is low. Thus if the financial manager is to maximize the value of the firm he must (1) weigh the need for liquid balances against their opportunity cost (the rate that could be earned on the funds in the best alternative use), and (2) fix the proportion of these liquid balances that should be held in the form of cash and the proportion that should be held in short-term securities. This is what the management of money is all about.

MOTIVES FOR HOLDING CASH

A firm has the same motives as an individual for holding cash—transactions, precautionary, and speculative motives.

Transactions Motive

The transactions motive describes cash held to carry on its routine activities. Were inflows and outflows perfectly synchronized, the firm would need only a small cash balance; but this does not occur in the real world.

By analyzing its activities the firm can isolate the causes for normal discrepancies between the outflow and inflow of cash. One cause may be that the firm requires customers to pay by the 10th of the month following purchase but pays its own suppliers at the end of the month of purchase. Another may be extraordinary outflows, such as real estate, income taxes, and machinery purchases, and extraordinary inflows, such as the sale of securities, of unneeded machinery and equipment, and of surplus inventory.

Precautionary Motive

Unpredictable discrepancies are met (in part) with precautionary cash reserves. Floods, strikes, and the failure of important customers are events that can interrupt the best-laid financial plans. Providing for the unpredictable is difficult. The amount provided is a function of the firm's willingness to assume this risk and of its reserve borrowing power. A firm wishing to avoid this risk holds large cash balances and maintains good banking relationships as a second line of defense. A somewhat less cautious or less affluent firm may activate most of its cash resources and depend on its line of credit for any unusual demands.[1] The firm willing to assume high risk or one in tight straits has most of its resources committed to productive activities, including a good portion of its borrowing power. Such a management's forecast and hope are that no sudden demand for funds will arise during a period of tight financial conditions. Once these conditions have passed and larger earnings have been generated, the firm will have taken the risk and won. It is now affluent and can maintain a solid working capital position. Most financial managers seek a middle course, maintaining some cash to meet the precautionary motive and keeping the firm's credit lines open to meet any large, unexpected demands for cash.

Speculative Motive

The speculative motive for holding cash is a result of seeking opportunities, such as buying inventory at favorable prices, either at depressed prices or at normal prices just before an anticipated rise. Generally it is assumed that firms do not speculate on inventory purchases. It is not easy, however, to draw the line between shrewd buying of large quantities of inventory at what in retrospect are favorable prices and speculating on future inventory

---

[1] A line of credit involves a commitment by the bank to lend to the firm funds as needed up to a predetermined limit. To obtain a line of credit the firm must usually pay a commitment fee.

prices. It sounds good to say the financial manager should be primarily concerned with the profitable operations of the firm and not seek speculative opportunities. Yet the cost of raw materials inventory is such an important item in the cost structure of most firms that the acquisition of large inventory lots at favorable prices may mean the difference between profit and loss.

THE FIRM'S INVESTMENT IN CASH

To some extent cash and inventory management pose similar problems. The financial manager holds the minimum cash necessary to keep operations flowing smoothly so maximum funds can be invested in the plant or used to reduce indebtedness. There is, however, an important difference between cash and inventory. The outflow of cash is more controllable, and expenditures are planned, but the inflow is partially noncontrollable and subject to more variation. With inventory the reverse is true. The inflow is largely planned and controllable, but the outflow (finished goods) is dependent upon the desires of the customer and is more uncontrollable.

Balancing the Need for Cash and Its Cost

Cash is a strange asset. A firm seeks to receive it in the shortest possible time but hold as little of it as possible. The more cash a firm has available, the less need there is for recourse to the banks in the event of unexpected expenditures or a slowdown in collections. But then the firm will experience a lower rate of return on investment since a portion of these funds could be invested in plant and equipment that would yield expected profits. This is the opportunity cost of holding idle cash balances. We speak in terms of expected profit since no guarantee exists that the funds if invested will return a profit. On the other hand, if the firm commits the maximum amount of funds to fixed assets, its debt-paying ability may be low and the dependence on banks high. Then, when the firm is under financial strain and the economic outlook cloudy, banks may refuse to lend. At a minimum, the inability to borrow would cause financial embarrassment to the firm and perhaps losses since then it must liquidate assets in an effort to raise the funds.

It is more profitable to maintain good credit sources than to hold extra cash or short-term securities against unexpected use. But the maintenance of rapidly available credit sources is not without cost. The size of the firm's bank balance determines the strength of the banking relationship. Deposits are crucial to a bank, and the larger and less active the account, the greater the value to the bank. But demand deposits do not earn a return for the firm. As compensation for deposits, the banker can offer an active interest in the credit needs of the firm. During periods when banks have more funds than loan opportunities, the banker's interest will be of modest value to the firm. The banker can offer other services—tangible (credit information) and intangible (financial advice and business contacts). When banks have more oportunities than funds, they favor the applications of firms that maintain satisfactory balances. The customer's deposit balance is a major credit-rationing standard of banks. Since firms value their banking relationship and desire access to credit on short notice, profitable and well-established firms maintain substantial balances. The cost in lost income is felt to be worth the accommodation provided by the banker.

A minimum level of cash is necessary to carry on business activities. Operating expenses normally must be paid before the product is sold and the proceeds are collected. Cash should be available to take trade discounts. Missing discounts is expensive short-term financing. A good credit rating and the availability and cost of credit are dependent upon an adequate cash position. Lending institutions and suppliers set financial standards they expect firms to meet. Ratios are the measuring technique and cash is the object measured. Finally, cash is a completely liquid asset, which can be given in exchange immediately. No uncertainty exists regarding acceptability. Cash also offers the ability to take advantage of special purchases of raw materials, to finance expansion, or even to acquire a subsidiary.

Cash as a Working Asset

To this point we have described cash as contributing to the liquidity position of the firm and other assets as being the real producers of earnings. But in planning for the long-run survival of the firm we must seek to maintain adequate funds for each asset group to carry on efficient production and meet future requirements. All assets must be working assets and contribute to the maximization of the value of the firm. Hence excess cash should be employed elsewhere.

CASH PLANNING THROUGH THE CASH BUDGET

Every firm must plan and control its use of cash. Failure to do so will at a minimum result in a reduced return on investment; at the extreme lies bankruptcy. The firm's cash balance at the end of any given period is the result of numerous interrelated activities. Planning is required, and the cash budget is the planning instrument. For efficient operation, management must know in advance when and how much cash will be needed to carry on the firm's activities. If more cash is needed than will be generated from operations, plans must be made to obtain the needed funds from either short-term creditors or long-term investors. If a surplus of cash is expected, decisions must be made concerning the period for which the funds are to be invested and the kinds of securities to be purchased—Treasury bills, certificates of deposit, commercial paper, and so on. As the firm becomes more sophisticated in planning and controlling cash, the amount necessary to support any given level of operations is reduced.

The cash budget is a formal statement showing estimated cash income and cash expenditures over the firm's planning horizon. The net cash position (excess or deficiency) of the firm as it moves from one budgeting subperiod to another is highlighted. The period of time covered by the cash budget may be one year, six months, three months, or some other period. The subperiods may be a day, a week, a month, or a quarter, depending upon the needs of the firm. If the firm's flow of funds is dependable, a cash budget covering a period of a year divided into quarterly intervals may be appropriate. Where substantial uncertainty is associated with the flow of funds, a quarterly cash budget broken into monthly or weekly intervals may be necessary.

The cash budget is the key to arranging needed funds on the most favorable terms available or to investing excess funds. With adequate time to study his firm's needs, the financial manager can afford to be selective. Contrast this situation with that of a firm that has not forecast its cash requirements. Suddenly it finds itself short of funds. With the need pressing and little time to explore alternative avenues of financing, the financial manager must accept the best terms offered in a crisis situation. These terms will not be as favorable, since the lack of planning indicates to the lender that there is an organizational deficiency. The firm, therefore, represents a higher risk.

The cash budget includes only cash flows—in and out. Noncash items, such as depreciation, are excluded. But the effect of depreciation in reducing income taxes will be there. A classification of cash flows is given in Table 6.1. The direction of the flow is the basis of the classification.

The cash budget can be used to develop pro forma financial statements. In the forthcoming example the financial manager is concerned about the amount of future financial needs and uses the cash budget to forecast them.

Table 6.1. **Typical Cash Flows**

Cash Outflows	Cash Inflows
Direct labor	Cash Sales
Material and supplies	Collection of receivables
Administrative expenses	Interest income
Accounts payable	Dividend income
Repayment of bank loans	Tax refund
Retirement of loans outstanding	Bank loan
Repurchase of common and preferred stock	Sales of bonds and preferred or common stock
Interest payments	Sale of plant and equipment
Dividend payments	
Purchase of plant and equipment	
Tax payments	

Assume that the Tourist Gift Shop is planning for the coming tourist season, which begins April 1 and closes September 30. The financial manager must estimate the monthly cash flows and arrange for an adequate loan but does not wish to borrow excessively, knowing that the banker will be impressed with an orderly loan request supported by concrete estimates that will make the terms of the loan more favorable. Accordingly, the financial manager, beginning with the balance sheet of March 31 shown in Table 6.2, prepares a cash budget.

Table 6.2. **Tourist Gift Shop Balance Sheet**
March 31

Assets			Liabilities and Net Worth		
Cash		$ 3000	Accrued salaries		$ 500
Inventory*		8000	Other liabilities	2500	$ 3000
Equipment	$70,000				
Depreciation	13,000	57,000	Capital		65,000
Total assets		$68,000	Total liabilities and net worth		$68,000

* Composed of $2000 minimum inventory plus $6000 of inventory scheduled to be sold next month.

After consulting with the marketing manager, the financial manager estimates sales, as given in Table 6.3. After reviewing salaries and other

Table 6.3. Sales Forecast

April	$10,000
May	20,000
June	30,000
July	50,000
August	40,000
September	20,000

Table 6.4. Salary Expense Budget

April	$1500
May	2000
June	2500
July	4000
August	3000
September	2000

major operating expenses in previous years and relating these to the sales volume, he estimates salary costs, as given in Table 6.4. He estimates the other expenses will approximate 12 percent of sales. Depreciation is calculated at the rate of 1 percent per month on original cost. The Shop is expected to operate along the following lines.

1. Sales (scheduled in Table 6.5) will be 80 percent cash and 20 percent credit. The credit sales will all be collected in the following month, and no bad debts are expected.
2. The gross profit margin on sales will average 40 percent.
3. All inventory purchases will be paid for during the month in which they are made.
4. A basic inventory of $2000 (at cost) will be maintained. The Shop will follow a policy of purchasing enough additional inventory each month to cover the following month's sales.
5. A minimum cash balance of $3000 will be maintained.
6. New equipment orders of $20,000, scheduled for May 1 delivery, and $10,000 for June 1 delivery, have been made. Payment will be made at the time of delivery. All equipment is depreciated at the rate of 1 percent per month.
7. Accrued salaries and other liabilities will remain unchanged.
8. No taxes are due till after the close of the tourist season.

After gathering these figures together, the financial manager organizes them according to the direction of cash flow, as shown in Table 6.5 The difference between cash inflow and outflow is the net monthly cash gain or loss. Adding the beginning cash balance to this figure gives him the amount of cash available at the end of each month. Since he decided on a minimum cash balance of $3000, this amount must be accounted for in the loan request.

Total cash needs peak in June when $49,200 must be borrowed. Inflows exceed outflows in July, August, and September. As a result the Tourist Gift Shop will have $4600 of excess cash by the end of the season.

From the initial data and the cash budget figures we can now estimate the profitability of the coming tourist season by drawing up the pro forma

Table 6.5. Tourist Gift Shop Cash Budget

	April	May	June	July	August	September
Sales	$10,000	$20,000	$30,000	$50,000	$40,000	$20,000
Inflows						
Cash sales	8,000	16,000	24,000	40,000	32,000	16,000
Collection of accounts						
receivable		2,000	4,000	6,000	10,000	8,000
Total	$ 8,000	$18,000	$28,000	$46,000	$42,000	$24,000
Outflows						
Inventory	$12,000	$18,000	$30,000	$24,000	$12,000	
Salary	1,500	2,000	2,500	4,000	3,000	$ 2,000
Expense	1,200	2,400	3,600	6,000	4,800	2,400
Equipment		20,000	10,000			
Total	$14,700	$42,400	$46,100	$34,000	$19,800	$ 4,400
Net monthly cash gain or (loss)*	($6,700)	($24,400)	($18,100)	$12,000	$22,200	$19,600
Plus beginning cash balance	3,000	(3,700)	(28,100)	(46,200)	(34,200)	(12,000)
Cumulative cash balance end of month	($3,700)	($28,100)	($46,200)	($34,200)	($12,000)	$ 7,600
Less required minimum cash balance	3,000	3,000	3,000	3,000	3,000	3,000
Cumulative borrowing necessary to maintain $3000 balance	$6,700	$31,100	$49,200	$37,200	$15,000	—
Cash above minimum needs	—	—	—	—	—	$ 4,600

* Amounts in parentheses are cash losses or negative cash balances.

Table 6.6. Tourist Gift Shop Pro Forma Income Statement
April 1–September 30

Costs		Sales	$170,000
Cost of goods sold	$102,000		
Salaries	15,000		
Expenses	20,400		
Depreciation*	5,600		
Profit (pre tax)	27,000		
	$170,000		$170,000

* Composed of depreciation charged at the rate of 1 percent per month on $70,000 for 6 months, 1 percent per month on $20,000 for 5 months, and 1 percent per month on $10,000 for 4 months.

income statement shown in Table 6.6 using the data above. The balancing figure is profit before income taxes.

Next we draw up the pro forma balance sheet as of the close of the tourist season, as shown in Table 6.7. The cash on hand on September 30 is the sum of the beginning cash balance of $3000, and the cumulative cash gain of $4600, that is, $7600. Receivables will be 20 percent of September sales of $20,000; inventory will be the amount purchased during September plus the opening inventory of $2000; equipment will be the $70,000 plus the $30,000 purchased, minus the beginning depreciation of $13,000 and the accumulated depreciation of $5600. Accrued expenses, other liabilities, and capital are assumed to remain constant.

Table 6.7. Tourist Gift Shop Pro Forma Balance Sheet
September 30

Assets			Liabilities and Net Worth		
Cash		$ 7600	Accrued expenses	$ 500	
Accounts receivable		4000	Other liabilities	2500	$ 3000
Inventory		2000	Capital	65,000	
Equipment	$100,000		Retained earnings	27,000	92,000
Depreciation	18,600	81,400	Total liabilities and		
Total assets		$95,000	net worth		$95,000

A pretax profit of $27,000 is anticipated. At current corporate tax rates (22 percent on first $25,000 and 48 percent on the excess over $25,000), the Tourist Gift Shop has a future tax liability of $6460. Since this amount is almost equal to the cash balance as of September 30, the financial manager must plan ahead for this payment.

THE MEANS OF MANAGING THE CASH FLOWS

In monitoring the money management system the financial manager must be alert to discover ways of accelerating inflows and delaying outflows. More avenues are open in the former area.

Speeding the Inflow: A Network of Banking Connections and a Concentration Bank

Firms seek ways to speed up the collection of checks to make funds available sooner. Higher profitability per investment dollar results from reduced interest payments because of less borrowing, diminished reliance on bank lending, and perhaps even lower interest rates.

Commercial banks are interconnected through a series of correspondent banking relationships. Funds are transferred by wire among major banks. Federal Reserve banks, through which most commercial banks clear their checks, are also linked by a wire transfer system. A small firm may deal with only one bank located in its home community, where it deposits checks for collection. A national firm may have several hundred accounts in as many banks throughout the country to expedite check collection. One bank in each area is selected to service the needs of one or several of the firm's branches. Funds are maintained there up to a certain point, and when the balance rises above this limit, the excess is transferred to a concentration bank located in a large city. The concentration banks are in turn linked to a control bank in the city of the home office. The control bank works closely with the firm in meeting its liquidity requirements, in investing its temporarily idle balances, and in maintaining control of the firm's entire banking network.

The more banking relationships a firm establishes, the shorter the time span from mailing of the checks by the customer to deposit in a company account. However, since minimum balances must be maintained in each bank, the more bank accounts, the larger the total minimum balance maintained. The objective of control is to maintain balances at each bank sufficient to cover bank service charges and meet the operating needs of the division in that area. With daily information on current balances the financial manager shifts funds quickly by wire to any section of the country or the world or invests the balances not immediately needed. The overall time required to convert customers' checks to spendable cash depends on the extensiveness of the banking network, the methods by which funds are shifted, and the frequency with which they are shifted. The financial manager must judge the point at which the availability of the funds outweighs the cost of transferring them from one bank to another.

Lock-Box Banking

Firms wishing to speed the cash inflow and relieve themselves of clerical tasks have adopted the simple system of lock-box banking. The firm rents a post office lock box in every city where it has a servicing bank, designates the bank as its collection agent for that region, and notifies customers to mail payment to the lock box. The bank picks up the mail each day, deposits the checks, and sends the firm the deposit slip listing the checks deposited. Prearranged procedures are followed for nonconforming items, such as checks for incorrect amounts. Lock-box banking is recommended in an area where the firm has no regional office but desires a check collection point.

Regulating the Outflow

The lock-box system that speeds the inflow of funds can also speed the outflow. But far fewer firms use multiple disbursing points. With a network of banks, the disbursing officer can transfer funds from one region to another as needed to cover checks presented for payment, thus reducing the total idle cash balances. Speeding the outflow reduces the firm's own funds by making them available more quickly to suppliers, but this can produce valuable goodwill.

A firm short of funds and wishing to maintain its float will not seek to speed payment. There are cases in which firms have maintained balances in distant banks in order to slow the payment process.

MANAGING CASH IN EXCESS OF REQUIREMENTS

Temporarily excess cash may arise from many factors, such as a seasonal downswing, a spurt in the collection of receivables, or an improvement in inventory management. Or the firm may be accumulating funds in anticipation of some major outlay such as the initial payment on a new project, dividend payments, or partial debt retirement. Holding these funds as demand deposits would guarantee their availability when needed. However, the funds can earn income in short-term obligations that offer safety of principal. Although firms may invest idle funds for only short periods of time, the amounts available for investment can be large enough to warrant investing them. Thus $10 million invested at 9 percent for 4 days, say over a long weekend, will earn over $9000. This income is generated with a small amount of additional administrative cost. The guides should be marketability *and* safety of principal, for exposure to risk for the sake of a slightly higher yield is a poor tradeoff.

The safety of principal policy eliminates from consideration the purchase of common and preferred stock and long-term bonds. The value of long-term government securities presents little risk if held to maturity, but even a small increase in the current interest rate will cause a significant drop in the market prices of the issue.

Treasury Securities—Outlet for Temporarily Excess Cash

Treasury securities are popular instruments for the investment of temporarily idle corporate funds. Their appeal derives from safety, liquidity, and a wide range of maturities. The principal types of Treasury securities are bills, tax anticipation bills, certificates of indebtedness, notes, and bonds.

Treasury bills are customarily issued each week and fall due in 91 days, but they are also offered as due in 182 days, and occasionally 1-year bills are issued. Tax anticipation bills mature approximately 1 week after the April, June, September, and December quarterly income tax due dates. Since they may be used to pay taxes on these dates at face value, the holder gains about 1 week's extra interest. All bills are sold at a discount and mature at face value, the yield being determined by the spread between the purchase price and the maturity value. Normally there are large amounts of bills outstanding and regular offerings. The bill market is active, resulting in a narrow spread between bid and offer.

Longer-term investments offering a higher yield are certificates of indebtedness, which mature in one year or less; notes with an original maturity of seven years; and bonds which have a maturity of over seven years. Certificates of indebtedness may be issued on a discount basis or carry a coupon. Both bills and certificates have been employed by the Treasury to raise funds in anticipation of tax receipts and may be used in the payment of federal income taxes. Because these obligations generally mature a few days after the income tax payment date, they afford the owner a few days' extra interest, since they may be tendered in payment of taxes on the due date. Though government notes and bonds are not ordinarily of interest to the financial manager, with the passage of time they enter the short-term class (maturity of 1 year or less) and sell on a yield basis approximately comparable to other short-term Treasury securities.

Commercial Paper

For the firm desiring a yield above Treasury bills of the same maturity an alternative is high-grade commercial paper.[2] In recent years commercial paper has carried yields equal to the prime rate on commercial bank loans.

Repurchase Agreements

Under a repurchase agreement the firm arranges to purchase a substantial amount of Treasury obligations from a dealer who agrees to repurchase them at an agreed-upon price at a later date. Through this arrangement the firm earns a relatively good return on its funds, though ordinarily not as high as on commercial paper, has collateral for its "loan" to the dealer, and helps the dealer carry his government security inventory. These repurchase agreements are tailored to the specific needs of the firm. Agreements may cover a period as short as overnight or some longer time span. Corporations have found repurchase agreements a desirable outlet for temporarily idle funds, and a large portion of the inventory of government securities dealers is financed through these money market instruments.

Certificates of Deposit (CD)

Certificates of deposit represent time deposits in commercial banks for periods from 30 to 360 days that are interest bearing, negotiable, and marketable. The yield varies according to maturity and the general level of interest rates. At the time of original issue there is a maximum rate that banks can pay, regulated by the Federal Reserve System. Though they are of recent origin, CDs are now issued by banks across the nation. They are popular with financial managers because they offer a higher yield than do government securities, commercial paper, or repurchase agreements. The certificates compete directly with commercial paper and the rates are approximately equal. When a disparity arises due to market factors, funds

[2] See Chapter 11 for a discussion of the characteristics and market for commercial paper.

flow from the lower yielding to the higher yielding instruments. But when interest rates rise and the Federal Reserve does not raise the maximum allowable rates on CDs, new issues of CDs are not competitive.

Many financial managers prefer the certificates of the larger banks because of their presumed greater safety and better marketability. As a result, the rates obtainable on the certificates of the smaller banks run to about one fourth of 1 percent higher than those paid by the major banks in the financial centers. The rates are publicized by the banks and changed only infrequently to keep in step with money market conditions. Certificates are offered by some banks only in denominations of $1 million, but others offer them in denominations of as low as $1000.

Summary

Cash is held for transaction, precautionary, and speculative motives. The carrying of excess cash balances is costly since earnings on them are lost. Crisis borrowing is also costly; favorable terms can seldom be arranged under pressure. The cash budget provides a procedure for estimating cash flows and determining in advance the cash needs or surplus funds available.

Excess cash balances should be invested. Temporarily idle funds should be invested in short-term high-grade securities. Safety of principal and liquidity are the leading guidelines. Appropriate issues are Treasury bills and notes, certificates of deposit, and commercial paper.

Study Questions

1. Why do we say that cash is a strange asset? How does improvement in the speed of communications influence our thinking regarding cash?
2. Why is borrowing to meet short-term financial needs an economic use of resources? How is this activity assisted by a well-developed financial system?
3. Why is it desirable for a firm to invest its temporarily idle short-term funds? Would this be possible without a well-developed financial system? What forms of investment might a firm select? Is it in the national interest for firms to invest their temporarily idle funds? Should the government encourage it by legislation or otherwise?
4. Since cash does not "earn," can we still call it a working asset? Why? What are the motives for holding cash? How do they relate to cash as a working asset?
5. How does the cash budget assist the financial manager in employing the resources of the firm in an optimum manner? How does this relate to arranging for timely borrowing or investing temporarily idle balances?

Problems

1. As financial manager of Sky Rocket, Inc., a part of your responsibility is planning for the financial requirements during the peak season of January 1 to June 30. A cash budget and pro forma income statement and balance sheet are normally prepared. The current balance sheet appears in Table 6.8.

Table 6.8. Sky Rocket, Inc., Balance Sheet
December 31

Cash		$ 160,000		
Accounts receivable		100,000		
Inventory		490,000		
Fixed assets	$300,000		Common stock	$ 100,000
Depreciation	50,000	250,000	Retained earnings	900,000
Total assets		$1,000,000	Total liabilities and net worth	$1,000,000

The sales forecast prepared by the marketing vice-president appears in Table 6.9.

Table 6.9. Sky Rocket, Inc., Sales Forecast

January	$200,000
February	400,000
March	500,000
April	600,000
May	900,000
June	500,000
July	100,000

The operating department provided the estimates given in Table 6.10.

Table 6.10. Sky Rocket, Inc., Monthly Salary Expenses

January	$30,000
February	50,000
March	70,000
April	90,000
May	110,000
June	60,000

Monthly selling and administrative expenses are expected to be 10 percent of sales. Depreciation charges are 1 percent per month. Sky Rocket operates on the following terms.

1. Sales are on a net 30-day basis. The firm's customers seek to economize the use of cash, so sales made in one month are never collected until the next month.
2. Sky Rocket's suppliers demand cash for purchases.
3. The firm purchases enough inventory each month to cover the following month's sales.
4. The cost of goods sold is 60 percent of sales.
5. A basic inventory of $370,000 is maintained at all times to give customers prompt service.
6. A minimum cash balance of $100,000 is maintained.
   Additional Information:
7. New equipment purchases of $50,000 are scheduled for March 1 delivery. Payment is made at the time of delivery.
8. Interest charged by the bank is at the rate of 1 percent per month. The amount needed as indicated by the cash budget is borrowed at the beginning of that month. Repayment is made at the end of the month. The interest is payable at the end of June when it is anticipated that the firm will have a net cash inflow. Borrowing is in $1000 units.
9. The income tax rate is at 50 percent and payable in July on the profit earned during the period January 1 to June 30. Recognize accrued income tax in the financial statements.
   a. Prepare a cash budget for the period January 1 to June 30.
   b. Prepare a pro forma income statement for the same period.
   c. Prepare a pro forma balance sheet as of June 30.
   d. Financial analysis:
      (i) What is the month of peak borrowing needs?
      (ii) Why do the borrowing requirements mount so rapidly?
      (iii) If Sky Rocket's level of operation next year is approximately the same as this year's, what do you estimate its borrowing requirements to be?
      (iv) Would you recommend that Sky Rocket sell stock to eliminate the seasonal borrowing at the high interest cost?

2. The Coordinate Instrument Company is studying the desirability of establishing a lock-box system in Texas to speed the inflow of spendable cash. Annual credit sales in that area currently total $18 million. Use of a lock-box system would reduce the dead float from 10 to 3 days. The bank in Houston would require a $60,000 minimum balance to service the account. Ignore administrative costs.
   a. Assuming a 360-day year, calculate the net amount of funds freed through the establishment of the lock-box system.
   b. If these freed funds would now be permanent excess working capital, would it "pay" the firm to install the system? On what factors would it depend?
   c. If these funds would be only temporarily idle funds, would it be desirable to install the system now or wait until the funds are needed for the capital expansion program? Study a current issue of the *Wall Street Journal* and the *Federal Reserve Bulletin* and determine how much you could earn on these funds in a short period of time, say 90 days, 180 days, 6 months, 1 year.

Selected References

Anderson, P. F., and R. D. B. Harman, "The Management of Excess Corporate Cash," *Financial Executive*, 32 (Oct. 1964), pp. 26–30 ff.

Anderton, F. N., "Centralized Cash Management for a Decentralized Company," *N.A.A. Management Accounting*, 47 (Sept. 1965–Aug. 1966), pp. 51–59.

Baxter, N. D., "Marketability, Default Risk, and Yields on Money Market Instruments," *Journal of Financial and Quantitative Analysis*, 3 (Mar. 1968), pp. 75–85.

Bloch, E., "Short Cycles in Corporate Demand for Government Securities and Cash," *American Economic Review*, 53 (Dec. 1963), pp. 1058–1077.

Griswold, J. A., "How to Lose Money with Cash," *Financial Executive*, 34 (Aug. 1966), pp. 28–34.

Horn, F. E., "Managing Cash," *Journal of Accountancy*, 117 (Apr. 1964), pp. 56–62.

Jacobs, D. P., "The Marketable Security Portfolios of Non-Financial Corporations, Investment Practices and Trends," *Journal of Finance*, 15 (Sept. 1969), pp. 341–352.

Jeffers, J. R., and J. Kwon, "A Portfolio Approach to Corporate Demands for Government Securities," *Journal of Finance*, 24 (Dec. 1969), pp. 905–919.

Kraus, A., C. Janssen, and A. McAdams, "The Lock Box Location Problem," *Journal of Bank Research*, 1 (Autumn 1970), pp. 50–58.

Law, W. A., and M. C. Crum, "New Trend in Finance: The Negotiable C. D.," *Harvard Business Review*, 41 (Jan.–Feb. 1963), pp. 115–126.

Reed, W. L., Jr., "Profits from Better Cash Management," *Financial Executive*, 40 (May 1972), pp. 40–42 ff.

Ross-Skinner, J., "The Profitable Art of Handling Corporate Cash," *Dun's Review and Modern Industry*, 79 (May 1962), pp. 38–41 ff.

Sprenkle, C. M., "Is the Precautionary Demand for Money Negative?" *Journal of Finance*, 22 (Mar. 1967), pp. 77–82.

Stancill, J. M., *The Management of Working Capital*. Scranton, Pa.: Intext Educational Publishers, 1971.

7

THE RECEIVABLES
MANAGEMENT SYSTEM

In selling goods and services the firm extends *trade credit* to its customers. Because the vendor is usually well acquainted with the business of his customers and because it is profitable, he extends generous credit as compared to suppliers of other types of funds.

The level of receivables at any moment is determined by the volume of credit sales, terms of sales, standards for extension of credit, and collection pressure. Our objective is to optimize the firm's investment in receivables.

The principle of trade credit is to stimulate sales and contribute to the overall profitability of the firm, not to eliminate all credit losses. If the latter were the best policy, the firm would extend no credit. We seek to balance the cost of extending credit and bad-debt losses against the additional profit generated from extending credit to obtain the highest overall profit. Such a credit policy will contribute most to maximizing the value of the firm.

A FIRM'S INVESTMENT IN RECEIVABLES

Selling on Account

Receivables arise when merchandise is sold and payment deferred. The seller, in effect, offers the purchaser a loan for a limited time such as 30 days. The seller may offer to discount the price 1 percent if payment is made within a shorter period.

The majority of credit sales are on open-book account, that is, the customer orders and the seller ships and invoices the buyer for the amount due but does not require a signed statement from the customer acknowledging his debt other than the buyer's original purchase order.

Our remarks regarding the management of receivables are directed toward the firm extending credit to other firms. However, many retail sales are made on credit, as evidenced by the familiar revolving 30-day charge and the installment account. Smaller retail items are generally sold on open-book account, but major durable goods such as automobiles are generally sold on the basis of an installment sales contract.

For the selling firm, trade credit means that the flow of funds from cash back to cash does not cycle as rapidly as if credit were not offered. Inventory is converted into receivables instead of cash when a credit sale takes place. The total assets of the firm are larger by the amount of the receivables carried than if the firm sold on cash terms, assuming the firm must obtain additional funds to finance its carrying of receivables.

As a first approximation, the cost of these funds might be viewed as the cost of borrowing from a bank at a rate such as 10 percent. However, financing is a continuous process. It is not possible to say which source of funds has financed which group of assets. The firm has some of its wealth tied up in receivables, and the cost of holding those receivables is the opportunity cost of earnings that might be generated if those funds were invested in other assets such as plant and equipment.

Four other costs are incurred when extending trade credit—the expense of investigating the credit worthiness of the customer, the expenses of collecting the funds owed, lossed incurred when some customers fail to pay, and any cash discount offered. Though particular nonpaying customers cannot be identified with certainty before credit is extended, the percentage that the aggregate of bad debts bears to aggregate credit sales can be predicted with fair accuracy.

Benefits of Extending Trade Credit

Credit extension boosts sales volume that is expected to add to total earnings. Though the return per unit of sales may decline due to the added costs of credit extension, total earnings may rise. The shift from a cash on delivery (COD) basis to the extension of 30-day terms will result in increased sales, but will the increased sales volume be sufficient to offset the reduced profit per unit? Yes, if credit is carefully managed and the firm is not yet at economic capacity.

Trade Credit as a Positive Policy—An Example

Omega can sell for cash or extend credit for 30 or 60 days. Goods are currently being sold COD with Omega selling 100 electronic components a month at $10 each. The present cost is $8 per unit and profit per month is $200. The manager seeks to stimulate sales by trade terms of 30 days. Sales jump to 160 units generating revenue of $1600.

Production costs remain at $8 per unit (assuming the spreading of fixed costs is offset by other costs), and gross profit climbs to $320. However, this figure is not clear profit. The adoption of credit terms requires the firm to establish a new procedure to screen the credit worthiness of applicants and a collection procedure to watch the accounts and stimulate laggards into paying. In carrying out these activities, Omega incurs an additional cost of 50 cents per unit. Further, some of the accounts, despite the best efforts at collection, remain uncollectible. These amount to ¼ of 1 percent of sales. Despite the added costs, net earnings rise from $200 to $326, as shown in Table 7.1.

Table 7.1. Omega Company Influence of Trade Terms on Sales and Profits

| | Trade Term Options | | |
	COD	30 Days	60 Days
Sales, units	100	160	200
Sales, dollars	$1000	$1600	$2000
Cost of sales	800	1280	1600
Collection expense	—	80	160
Bad-debt expense	—	4	20
Profit	$ 200	$ 236	$ 220

The manager, flushed with success at what 30 days of credit does, decides to go all the way and adopts credit terms of 60 days. If a little credit is a good thing, a lot of credit is better. True to expectations, sales again jump sharply. This time, however, the percentage increase in sales is not as great, and costs rise more than proportionately. Net earnings decline. The manager has overshot the mark. The tasks of investigating credit applicants and collecting become substantially more costly, since many marginal firms can now meet the more liberal trade terms and become heavily indebted before the collection process swings into action. Because of the higher proportion of marginal firms, the uncollectible receivables rise. Sales climb to

200 units, yielding a gross revenue of $2000, as appears in Table 7.1. Let us assume production costs remain at $8 per unit. But the collection expense rises from 50 cents to 80 cents per unit, whereas the bad-debt expense jumps from ¼ of 1 percent of sales to 1 percent. The resulting profit falls to $220, as shown in Table 7.1.

The managers at Omego can further refine their analysis of credit terms. Suppose all sales generated under the 30-day option now become credit sales. Then the firm would have a new asset, accounts receivable, listed at $1600, in which they have invested $1280 of the firm's funds.

The firm requires a rate of return on its investments in accounts receivable just as it requires a rate of return on any other asset it invests in. If Omega requires an annual rate of return of 20 percent (1.66 percent per month), then the expected profitability of Table 7.1 should be reduced from $236 to $214.67 ($1280 × 0.0166 = $21.33).

The investment in accounts receivable under the 60-day option is $3200 ($1600 per month × 2 months). The profitability of this option declines from the $220 of Table 7.1 to $166.69 ($3200 × 0.0166 = $53.31). Thus extension of 30-day terms is preferable to the more liberal 60-day option.

TRADE CREDIT TRENDS AND PRACTICES

Trade credit can be used in various situations to stimulate sales and expand profits. Some firms when introducing a new product grant especially liberal terms. The availability of excess capacity influences the extension of trade credit by some firms to high-risk customers. For other firms it is a high profit margin on the item sold that affects the credit extended to these customers. But the greatest pressure to liberalize credit comes from trade terms offered by competitors.

Trade Terms

When a firm sells merchandise on credit it is offering the purchaser a package consisting of two parts, the goods plus limited financing. The seller can also offer a discount for early payment. The purchaser then has the option of obtaining his own financing in order to receive the discount or to let the seller carry the credit.

Trade terms commonly found in industry are 2/10/net 30, that is, a 2 percent discount is permitted on the price if payment is made within 10 days, with the full amount due at the end of 30 days. The discount period may start with the date of shipping, the date of the invoice, or the date of receipt of goods (ROG).

It is cheaper for the purchaser to take the 2 percent discount and borrow at say 10 percent to effect payment by the 10th. The reasoning is as follows. The 2 percent discount is lost if the bill is not paid by the 10th, but in any event it should be paid by the 30th. The buyer exchanges the 2 percent discount for the use of the money for an additional 20 days. Since there are approximately eighteen 20-day periods in a year, the effective annual rate approaches 36 percent.

Extending cash discounts for early payment tends to increase sales, since the firm is, in fact, offering the goods at a reduced price. Under 2/10/net 30 terms the seller would carry the receivable for 10 days instead of 30 days. If the amount of the cash discount just offsets the savings from not having to carry the receivables the extra 20 days, the seller earns the normal margin between sales price and cost. If the discount exceeds the savings, the seller's margin of profit is reduced. In setting the trade terms we must be careful not to grant excessive discounts for early payment in order to capture a larger sales volume. The net result may be a reduction in total profit. Terms of 1/10/net 30 are equivalent to 18 percent per year and 2/10/net 30 to 36 percent per year. Some firms may earn 18 percent on their total assets, but few are able to earn 36 percent.

MANAGING THE FLOW OF RECEIVABLES

The three control points regulating the flow and level of receivables through the system after credit terms have been set are analysis of the customer's credit worthiness, matching his credit worthiness against the firm's standard, and collection procedure. The determinants of a firm's credit standard are trade practices in the industry, the firm's attitude toward credit risks, and the financial status of most of the firm's customers.

Analyzing the Customer's Credit Worthiness

To evaluate the credit worthiness of a potential customer we consider character (the willingness of the customer to do his best to pay), capacity (the financial ability of the buyer, particularly liquidity), and current economic conditions. There are many sources of credit information. Perhaps the best known is Dun & Bradstreet, Inc., which makes available to its subscribers a reference book and written credit reports. The reference book rates about three million businesses of all types based on Dun & Bradstreet's credit appraisal of the firms and their estimated financial strength. The rating system is composed of a combination of letters and numbers. The estimated financial strength (net worth) of the firm is rated by letter. A number indicates Dun & Bradstreet's composite credit analysis of the firm. For example, a BA 2 rating indicates a firm with an estimated net worth of between $300,000 and $500,000 and a credit standing estimated as good. A rating of FF 4 indicates a firm with an estimated net worth of between $10,000 and $20,000 and a limited credit standing, as shown in Figure 7.1.

If additional information is desired, Dun & Bradstreet will supply a credit report that provides background on the history of the firm, its location, the nature of the business, and financial information, as shown in Figure 7.2. The report also shows the amount of credit some suppliers have extended, the amount currently owed these suppliers, whether discounts are taken, and whether payment is prompt or slow.

The weakness of the Dun & Bradstreet service is that, except for payment information furnished by suppliers of the firm and a few matters such as public records of judgments against the firm, Dun & Bradstreet passes on information furnished by the firm itself. The firm is hardly an unbiased source. In fact, matters frequently get down to whether the firm can "pull the wool over the eyes" of the Dun & Bradstreet interviewer. And when the firm is in difficulty, the incentive to do so is overwhelming.

In addition to Dun & Bradstreet, information may be obtained from commercial banks, particularly the customer's bank, local credit associations, the National Association of Credit Management, financial statements, releases by the customer, the firm's own salesmen, and personal interviews. The opinion of the salesmen, though frequently helpful, may reflect a desire to make a sale rather than concern for the collectibility of the account.

Many firms when placing their first order with a new supplier volunteer as references a list of other suppliers who have extended credit.

Information-gathering activities are necessarily limited by time and cost. If in a particular industry customers demand prompt delivery, a month is not available to make a credit investigation. The customer would become impatient and place his order elsewhere, perhaps never to return. If the order is small, it would hardly pay to spend a month gathering and analyzing credit information. Therefore, small orders are decided on the basis of a brief check.

Matching a Customer's Credit Worthiness against the Firm's Standard

In judging the applicant's credit worthiness against the firm's standard we use ratio analysis and apply subjective "feel." Where the customer's credit standing is far above or below our standard the accept or reject decision is easy; where it is marginal, judgment is required. At this point the credit manager's years of experience are invaluable.

Figure 7.1. Key to Dun & Bradstreet ratings. (Courtesy of Dun & Bradstreet, Inc.)

Key to Ratings

ESTIMATED FINANCIAL STRENGTH			COMPOSITE CREDIT APPRAISAL			
			HIGH	GOOD	FAIR	LIMITED
5A	Over	$50,000,000	1	2	3	4
4A	$10,000,000 to	50,000,000	1	2	3	4
3A	1,000,000 to	10,000,000	1	2	3	4
2A	750,000 to	1,000,000	1	2	3	4
1A	500,000 to	750,000	1	2	3	4
BA	300,000 to	500,000	1	2	3	4
BB	200,000 to	300,000	1	2	3	4
CB	125,000 to	200,000	1	2	3	4
CC	75,000 to	125,000	1	2	3	4
DC	50,000 to	75,000	1	2	3	4
DD	35,000 to	50,000	1	2	3	4
EE	20,000 to	35,000	1	2	3	4
FF	10,000 to	20,000	1	2	3	4
GG	5,000 to	10,000	1	2	3	4
HH	Up to	5,000	1	2	3	4

CLASSIFICATION FOR BOTH
ESTIMATED FINANCIAL STRENGTH AND CREDIT APPRAISAL

FINANCIAL STRENGTH BRACKET	EXPLANATION
1 $125.000 and Over	When only the numeral (1 or 2) appears, it is an indication that the estimated financial strength, while not definitely classified is presumed to be within the range of the ($) figures in the corresponding bracket and that a condition is believed to exist which warrants credit in keeping with that assumption.
2 20.000 to 125.000	

ABSENCE OF RATING DESIGNATION FOLLOWING NAMES LISTED IN THE REFERENCE BOOK
The absence of a rating, expressed by two hyphens (--), is not to be construed as unfavorable but signifies circumstances difficult to classify within condensed rating symbols. It suggests the advisability of obtaining a report for additional information.

EMPLOYEE RANGE DESIGNATIONS IN REPORTS OR NAMES NOT LISTED IN THE REFERENCE BOOK

Certain businesses do not lend themselves to a Dun & Bradstreet rating and are not listed in the Reference Book. Information on these names, however, continues to be stored and updated in the D&B Business Data Bank. Reports are available on such businesses and instead of a rating they carry an Employee Range Designation (ER) which is indicative of size in terms of number of employees. No other significance should be attached.

KEY TO EMPLOYEE RANGE DESIGNATIONS

ER 1	Over 1000 Employees
ER 2	500 - 999 Employees
ER 3	100 - 499 Employees
ER 4	50 - 99 Employees
ER 5	20 - 49 Employees
ER 6	10 - 19 Employees
ER 7	5 - 9 Employees
ER 8	1 - 4 Employees
ER N	Not Available

© *Dun & Bradstreet, Inc.* **1974**
99 Church Street, New York, N.Y. 10007 18 B-7 (730801)

Figure 7.2.   Fictitious example of business information report.   (Courtesy Dun & Bradstreet.)

Dun & Bradstreet, Inc.

Please note whether name, business and street address correspond with your inquiry.

BUSINESS INFORMATION REPORT

BASE REPORT

SIC	D-U-N-S	© DUN & BRADSTREET, INC.	STARTED	RATING
34 69	04-426-3226	CD 13 APR 21 19--	1957	DD1
	ARNOLD METAL PRODUCTS CO	METAL STAMPINGS		

53 S MAIN ST
DAWSON MICH   49666
TEL 215 999-0000

SAMUEL B. ARNOLD)
GEORGE T. ARNOLD) PARTNERS

SUMMARY

PAYMENTS	DISC
SALES	$177,250
WORTH	$42,961
EMPLOYS	10
RECORD	CLEAR
CONDITION	STRONG
TREND	UP

PAYMENTS

HC	OWE	P DUE	TERMS	APR 19--	SOLD
3000	1500	1 10 30		Disc	Over 3 yrs
2500	1000	1 10 30		Disc	Over 3 yrs
2000	500	2 20 30		Disc	Old Account

FINANCE

On Apr 21 19-- S. B. Arnold, Partner, submitted the following statement dated Dec 31 19--

Cash	$ 4,870	Accts Pay	$ 6,121
Accts Rec	15,472	Notes Pay (Curr)	2,400
Mdse	14,619	Accruals	3,583
	------------		------------
Current	34,961	Current	12,104
Fixt & Equip ($4,183)	22,840	Notes Pay (Def)	5,000
CSV of Life Ins	2,264	NET WORTH	42,961
	------------		------------
Total Assets	60,065	Total	60,065

Annual sales $177,250; gross profit $47,821; net income $8,204. Fire insurance mdse $15,000; fixt $20,000. Annual rent $3,000.
Signed Apr 21 19-- ARNOLD METAL PRODUCTS CO by Samuel B. Arnold, Partner.
-----0-----

New equipment purchased last Sep was financed by bank loan. Monthly payments on loan are $200.

Arnold reported sales for the three months ended Mar 31 were up 10% compared to the same period last year. Increase was attributed by management to additional capacity provided by new equipment.

Profit is being made and retained resulting in an increase in net worth. Current debt is light in relation to worth. Inventory turnover is rapid.

BANKING

Balances average high four figures. Loans granted to low five figures, secured by equipment, now owing high four figures. Relations satisfactory.

HISTORY

Style registered Feb 1 1965 by partners. S. ARNOLD, born 1918, married. 1939 graduate of Lehigh University. 1939-50 employed by Industrial Machine Corporation, Detroit, and 1950-56 production manager with Aerial Motors Inc., Detroit. Started this business in 1957. G. ARNOLD, born 1940, single, son of Samuel. Graduated in 1963, Dawson Institute of Technology. Served U.S. Air Force 1963-1964. Admitted to partnership Feb 1965.

OPERATION

Manufactures perforated metal stampings for Industrial concerns. Sells on Net 30 day terms. Has twelve accounts. Territory greater Detroit area. Employs ten including partners. LOCATION: Rents 5,000 square feet in one story cinder block building in normal condition. Located in central business section of main street. Premises neat.
4-21 (803 77) PRA

* Source: Courtesy Dun & Bradstreet. This is a fictitious example.

[A97833]

Collection Procedure

For customers who pay promptly, no collection effort is required. But a certain percentage will be slow in paying and a smaller percentage of accounts will be noncollectible. The objective of the collection department is to speed up the slow payers and reduce the percentage of bad debts.

Extracting payment from slow-paying customers is a difficult art. The objective is to get payment without offending the customer and endangering future orders, particularly if slow payment is attributable to factors other than serious difficulty. For example, a firm may be seeking to stretch its current credit financing to the limit and thereby postpone raising new long-term capital, or a very profitable firm may be suffering from a lack of liquidity, a not uncommon phenomenon. If the collection department is too aggressive in pressing for payment, the customer may turn to other suppliers who are willing to carry this slow-paying account that promises to become a big customer in the future. Thousands of dollars of sales effort may later be required to win back an account rejected by a clerk. If the collection policy is too lenient, marginal customers will take advantage of the situation creating a substantial increase in the costs of credit extension and collection.

Customers are motivated to pay promptly, since they realize their habits will quickly become known in the industry and affect their credit standing. Furthermore, the fact that the seller can refuse to make new shipments until overdue acounts are paid exerts pressure on customers to pay promptly. Finally, if a customer refuses to pay, aggressive collection procedures, such as legal action, are in order.

If it is widely known that the customer is in serious financial difficulty, the threat of unfavorable publicity will have little effect. The creditor firm must then shift tactics. To force payment by legal action may accelerate failure of the customer, and little may be left after legal expenses to satisfy the claims of the creditors. Frequently, the best course of action is a compromise settlement of debts.

The Flow of Receivables and External Factors

Decisions on credit extension to specific customers have little influence on the flow of funds into and out of receivables. This flow is determined by the credit policies of the firm. Likewise, factors external to the firm have a greater effect on the level of receivables than do the particular credits to specific customers. General economic conditions and the intensity of competition in the industry are the controlling elements. With a prosperous economy and reduced competition, a firm may adopt a higher standard of credit acceptability. But rosy conditions cause many customers' affairs to look better than they really are. As a result receivables turnover may tend to decline.

With a decline in the economy the level of receivables will fall with the decline in sales, but not as rapidly because some buyers increase their delay in payment. The problem with receivables is the same as with inventory. Excessive receivables and inventory are easier to correct in a high-volume period than in a lower volume one when a longer time is needed to work off the excess.

Evaluating the Flow of Receivables

The ratio of credit sales to receivables is one measure of the effectiveness of credit policy and of the credit department. A corresponding measure is days credit sales outstanding as receivables. For example, if annual credit sales totaled $360,000 and today's receivables are $30,000, daily credit sales equal $1000: ($360,000/360), and receivables represent 30 days' credit sales ($30,000/$1000). Receivables turnover is 12 times, ($360,000/$30,000). These rough measures can be supplemented by an aging schedule such as Table 7.2 which summarizes receivables according to length of time outstanding.

Table 7.2. Aging Schedule of Receivables

Receivables Outstanding	Amount Outstanding	Percent
Less than 30 days	$2,800,000	70.0
30–59 days	700,000	17.5
60–89 days	400,000	10.0
Over 90 days*	100,000	2.5
	$4,000,000	100.0

* After 8 months receivables are written off as bad debts.

By computing the aging schedule of receivables at regular intervals, we detect trends toward a slowing or improvement in collection. The aging schedule is an early warning device regarding a deterioration in receivables and the increasing probability of large and unusual bad-debt losses. A significant rise in the percent of old receivables may be due to laxity in granting credit, to relaxation of past-due collections, or to external economic conditions.

An average-age-of accounts-receivable figure may be obtained by taking the mid-age point of each age category (a simplifying assumption), multiplying by the percent that that age category bears to the total, and summing, as is done in Table 7.3.

Table 7.3. Determination of Average Age of Receivables in Table 7.2

Average Age in Category	Average Age Times Percent in that Category
15 days	10.5 days
45 days	7.9
75 days	7.5
165 days*	4.1
Average age	30.0 days

* After 8 months the receivable is either collected or written off as a bad debt.

Credit Insurance

A vendor extending trade credit may maintain an efficient credit and collection department and still get hit with unusual bad-debt losses. The profits of some of the vendor's customers may fall short, their overhead may get out of hand, or they may be unable to collect from their own customers. To guard against unusual bad-debt losses the vendor may take out credit insurance.

Under credit insurance a firm can only insure against abnormal credit losses. The firm cannot insure against normal or *primary* losses. If experience shows that credit losses normally reach one half of 1 percent of sales, this is the primary loss and not insurable. To illustrate, if in a particular year we have sales of $10 million, we would then have to bear the first $50,000 of credit losses.

To contain enthusiasm for granting credit once a firm is insured, the insurance company imposes two constraints. First, the insurer restricts its coverage on individual accounts receivable. The restriction may be set in terms of a dollar limit for each account with a particular Dun & Bradstreet rating: $5000 for any account with a GG 3 rating. Second, the insurance company will require that the insured agree to coinsurance—participation in the insured credit losses. Depending on the credit risks, participation is usually from 10 to 20 percent.

The desirability of credit insurance depends on (1) the trade off between the insurance premium and the probability of unusual bad-debt losses, (2) the willingness of management to assume the risk of the unusual bad-debt losses. Most firms are willing to assume the risk, since the annual purchase of credit insurance is modest.

Firms of all sizes carry credit insurance, but most frequently the insured firms have annual sales of $1 to $50 million. The cost of insurance runs from $\frac{1}{10}$ to ¼ of 1 percent of sales. Large firms with diversified credit risks do not carry credit insurance. They self-insure, even though the cost of insurance is low, due to the small risk.

On the other hand, credit insurance protects financially weak firms or those with nondiversified credit risks. In both of these cases unusual bad-debt losses will really hurt. The likelihood is high that such losses may push the firm into bankruptcy.

Captive Finance Companies

A captive finance company is a subsidiary that serves as the finance arm of the parent firm. This subsidiary buys the accounts receivable generated by the parent's sales. Frequently these sales involve machinery and heavy equipment, such as industrial lift trucks, tractors, and highway trailers, sold on time to dealers or at retail.

Nonfinancial firms, such as Caterpillar Tractor, Clark Equipment, General Electric, ITT, Westinghouse, and White Motor, have formed captive finance companies. Many of these subsidiaries were formed in the 1950s and 1960s when sales were expanding and credit terms lengthening, thus increasing receivables beyond the abilities of firms to finance them internally. Rather than finance these burgeoning receivables through a stock issue, management decided to establish wholly owned subsidiaries to carry the receivables. The attraction of the captives is their ability to raise large amounts of debt and thereby lower the cost of raising money.

For captives, a relationship of $4 of debt to $1 of equity is not unusual. Such high debt-to-equity ratios are attainable because of the excellent collateral value of the captives' receivables. And since debt is generally cheaper than equity, the captives can raise money cheaply and that translates into a low cost of carrying the receivables.

But note, by shifting the receivables from the parent to the captive the parent loses a portion of its liquidity and thereby a portion of its own debt-bearing capacity. In part the high debt-to-equity ratio of the subsidiary is made possible at the expense of the reduced debt-carrying capacity of the parent.

Summary

The strategic matters in the receivables system are (1) credit period, (2) cash discount, (3) quality of account accepted, (4) collection efforts, (5) the seller's attitude toward this risk, and (6) the seller's cost of capital. Trade credit terms are an effective competitive instrument and rank as price concessions. Through liberalized credit terms sales can be stimulated, but added collection costs and bad-debt expense reduce profit.

The in-and-out flow of funds from the receivables account is controlled by investigation of the credit worthiness of the customer, matching the customer's financial standing with the standards of the firm and collection procedure. During prosperity these controls may fail because customers' affairs look better than they are and receivables rise faster than sales. In a declining economy, sales fall faster than receivables.

A vendor may use credit insurance to guard against unusual bad-debt losses. Coverage is restricted to rated receivables and the vendor must agree to share in the losses.

A captive finance company buys the receivables generated by the parent's sales. Captives carry a high debt-to-equity ratio and have a low cost of capital.

Study Questions

1. Why does the extension of credit slow the flow of funds from cash back to cash? How can changing the credit terms affect the speed of the cycle?
2. Explain the complaint by a credit manager that when credit is being extended too cautiously the marketing department calls, when it is granted too liberally the treasurer calls, and when it is just right no one calls.
3. Why is it easier to pursue a credit policy that seeks to minimize bad-debt losses than one that seeks to make the greatest contribution to profits? Why are these goals incompatible?
4. What are the costs of extending trade credit?
5. Under what conditions might a firm make a rather intensive credit analysis? a token credit analysis? Is there a difference between the credit analysis undertaken by an industrial firm and that conducted by a bank? Explain.
6. Would a firm in the following circumstances tend to have generous or restrictive

credit terms, and why: (a) has a high margin of profit, (b) is introducing a new product, (c) is short of working capital, (d) has a monopoly position in the market, (e) is in a period of declining economic activity?

7. How do the analysis of the customer's credit worthiness, the matching of the analysis against the financial standard required by the firm, and the collection procedure influence the inflow and outflow of receivables? How can these controls be adjusted to correspond with the level of economic activity? Is this a good idea?

8. Determine whether the cash discount a company offers its customers is likely to be increased, decreased, remain unchanged, or be indeterminate as a result of the following situations; explain your answer in each case: (a) new competition enters the field, (b) economic activity reaches capacity levels, (c) the price of raw materials increases, (d) the firm achieves a monopoly position, (e) a new credit manager is hired.

Problems

1. The Pine Company has annual credit sales of $720,000. At year end accounts receivable outstanding were $180,000. Pine sells on net 30-day terms. Using the following formulas,

$$\text{average credit sales per day} = \frac{\text{annual credit sales}}{360}$$

$$\frac{\text{days credit sales outstanding}}{\text{as accounts receivable}} = \frac{\text{accounts receivable outstanding}}{\text{average credit sales per day}}$$

   a. Determine the number of days credit sales outstanding as accounts receivable. Use a 360-day year.
   b. Compare this with the credit terms of Pine. What can you say about the firm's collection policy?
   c. If the firm were to sell on net 45-day terms and hold to them, what would be the level of receivables? How much working capital would be freed for other uses?

2. Credit managers often claim the bad-debt losses come straight out of profit. The marginal cost of credit losses is considered to be the amount of the written off bad debt. The credit manager of the Firefly Candle Company thinks this way. Last year the firm had $1 million in sales, $700,000 in cost of goods sold, and $200,000 in selling and administrative expenses. Sales included a sale with a potential bad-debt loss of $2000.
   a. Following the credit manager's line of reasoning, calculate earnings before income taxes on a before and after bad-debt loss basis. What is the apparent marginal cost of the sale? Does this appear to be a fair way of presenting the cost of the bad-debt loss?
   b. Suppose that analysis revealed the following about the $2000 bad-debt sale: variable costs on the shipment totaled $1400, the manufacturing cost of goods sold was $1200, and selling and administrative expenses were $200. The sale contributed $600 to profit.

Draw up the corrected camparative income statements showing the earnings before taxes on the basis of the sale not being made and on the basis of the sale being made, but with the account uncollectible. What is the apparent marginal cost of the sale? Does this appear to be a reasonable way of presenting the bad-debt loss? Why?

c. Suppose that when the sale is made there exists a 50 percent chance that the customer will pay. What would be the expected value of the bad-debt expense? Calculate the income before taxes on the basis of the sale being made and the expected value of the bed-debt loss. What is the apparent marginal cost of the sale? Does this appear to be a more reasonable way of representing the bad-debt loss? Why? What would have to be the expected value of the bad-debt loss before it would pay Firefly to ship the $2000 worth of candles to the customer?

3. The Y. Askum Company has annual credit sales of $144,000. Terms are net 30 days. Because of the firm's lax collection policy accounts are paid in 70 days on the average.

a. How much does the firm have tied up in receivables? Use a 360-day year.

b. What should the firm's investment in receivables be?

c. If the firm has an opportunity cost of investment in receivables of 10 percent, what would be the effect on profits of reducing receivables to a level corresponding to the firm's trade terms of net 30 days (other things equal)?

4. Shakey, Inc., sells to a limited number of customers. To protect itself against financial ruin the firm carries credit insurance. The cost of the insurance is ¼ of 1 percent of the firm's annual sales of $1 million. The insurance policy excludes the first $30,000 of loss per year and carries a 20 percent coinsurance clause on Dun & Bradstreet rated accounts. Coverage on each account, based on the customer's rating, is limited as follows:

BB	$50,000
CB	45,000
CC	30,000
DC	20,000
DD	15,000

a. What is the dollar cost of the credit insurance?

b. How large a credit loss in a single year must the firm incur before the insurance policy begins to pay off?

c. During the year, four of Shakey's customers stumble into bankruptcy. Credit losses on these four accounts and the Dun & Bradstreet rating on each at the time the goods were shipped are as follows:

CB	$25,000
CC	5,000
DC	15,000
DD	20,000

How much will Shakey collect on its credit insurance policy?

Selected References

Bursk, E. C., "View Your Customers as Investment," *Harvard Business Review,* 44 (May–June 1966), pp. 91–94.

Davis, P. M., "Marginal Analysis of Credit Sales," *Accounting Review,* 41 (Jan. 1966), pp. 121–166.

Griswold, J. A., "How to Lose Money with Cash," *Financial Executive,* 34 (Aug. 1966), pp. 28–30 ff.

Kaplan, R. M., "Credit Risks and Opportunities," *Harvard Business Review,* 45 (Mar.–Apr. 1967), pp. 83–88.

Lane, S., "Submarginal Credit Risk Classification," *Journal of Financial and Quantitative Analysis,* 7 (Jan. 1972), pp. 379–85.

Lewellen, W. G., "Finance Subsidiaries and Corporate Borrowing Capacity," *Financial Management,* 1 (Spring 1972), pp. 21–31.

——, and R. W. Johnson, "Better Way to Monitor Accounts Receivable," *Harvard Business Review,* 50 (May–June 1972), pp. 101–109.

Marrah, G. L., "Managing Receivables," *Financial Executive,* 38 (July 1970), pp. 40–44.

Schiff, M., and Z. Lieber, "A Model for the Integration of Credit and Inventory Management," *Journal of Finance,* 29 (Mar. 1974), pp. 133–140.

Smith, D. W., "Efficient Credit Management with Time Sharing," *Financial Executive,* 39 (Mar. 1971), pp. 26–30.

Welshans, M. T., "Using Credit for Profit Making," *Harvard Business Review,* 45 (Jan.–Feb. 1967), pp. 141–156.

Wrightsman, D., "Optimal Credit Terms for Accounts Receivable," *Quarterly Review of Economics and Business,* 9 (Summer 1969), pp. 59–66.

Zelnick, J., "Credit Analysis by Computer," *Financial Executive,* 34 (June 1966), pp. 26ff.

8

THE INVENTORY MANAGEMENT SYSTEM

In the flow of funds from cash back to cash, inventories (and receivables) represent an intermediate stage in the cycle. Every manufacturer must acquire input material to make its products; every wholesaler and retailer must purchase finished goods to sell. And since purchases, production, and sale are seldom completely in step, firms generally are required to maintain stocks of inventory.

Inventory management is important both for short-run liquidity and long-term profitability. Overstocking of some items will result in excessive investment and costs. Understocking of other items will mean lost sales or production time. Either imbalance will adversely affect profits. Overstocking will decrease liquidity since funds will be in the form of inventory rather than cash. Investors will place a lower value on the firm than if its inventory is well managed.

Some costs are incurred by a firm in maintaining its inventory while other costs that would be incurred if no inventory were carried can be avoided by carrying inventory. *Optimal inventory policy* maximizes the value of the firm since it balances these costs to produce the lowest total cost of inventory.

THE FIRM'S INVESTMENT IN INVENTORY

It is not unusual for a firm to carry thousands of different types of items in inventory ranging from those widely used to those that turn over slowly. We will examine those inventory items of sufficient volume to warrant the application of sophisticated inventory control methods aimed at providing the best customer service at the least cost.

The Uncertain Value of Inventory

Unlike receivables and cash, inventory may have no easily determinable value. A dollar in cash can command a dollar's worth of goods and services. With receivables, the firm has a legal right to collect cash. Inventory, however, has value only to the extent that it can be sold, and the amount for which the goods can be sold varies from day to day. Consider a department store stocking its toy inventory. Some days before Christmas the toys have considerable value; the day after Christmas, half their value has disappeared. They are the same toys, but with the season over they can only be sold at reduced prices.

Maintaining the Right Amount of Inventory

A firm must have the right inventory at the right time to meet demand so that it can earn a profit. The flow of funds aspect is also important. The faster the inventory flows through sales into receivables, the less the dollar investment of inventory relative to sales. With the same dollar profit being earned on a reduced inventory, the rate of return on investment is increased. Further, inventory carrying costs (storage, handling, obsolescence, and spoilage) are reduced with a high turnover. Driving inventory too low has undesirable results such as additional setup costs for more frequent production runs, an increased number of raw material orders, underutilization of capital and labor when a shortage of a particular raw material halts production, and the loss of sales as a result of not being able to meet delivery schedules.

The sales manager is oriented toward sales volume and customer satisfaction, and these are promoted by prompt delivery. Insufficient inventory is felt directly while a reduced return on investment due to carrying too much inventory is felt indirectly. The production manager wants long production runs to reduce the number of times fixed setup costs are incurred, thereby reducing per unit costs, but this raises the average level of inventory. The financial manager must establish policies leading to an optimum inventory, that is, he strives to balance low unit production and ordering costs through long production runs against increased carrying costs for larger inventory. Similarly, the stock of finished goods carried should be high enough to meet the demands of most customers, but not the demand of all customers for all items at all times. At some point the added profit to be generated from the added sales is more than offset by the marginal cost of carrying additional inventory.

FUNCTION AND COST OF CARRYING INVENTORY

The holding of inventory is costly. What function does inventory serve? Unavoidably, while production continues, some "goods-in-process" inventory exists. Inventory will be in transit, moving from one machine to another. For example, automobiles moving down the line are goods in process from the moment the chassis is hooked to the assembling line to the time the finished unit is driven off. But what of the raw material and finished goods inventory?

Raw materials inventory is maintained to assure the flow of production. A guaranteed flow of raw materials from our supplier at the rate it is being used in production would greatly reduce the need for a raw materials inventory. Similarly, if we could sell our finished products at the rate they are being produced, there would be need to carry only a small finished-goods inventory. But the firm usually has little control over the rate at which its products are sold. A firm usually finds it more economical to order at one rate, produce at a second, and sell at a third. The carrying of inventories at each of these three stages enables us to uncouple the buying, producing, and selling functions to engage in each activity at its economic rate.

Fixed and variable costs influence the economic inventory level. Costs such as handling, taxes, insurance, record keeping, obsolescence, and spoilage are variable as is the cost of capital of the funds invested in the inventory. Depreciation, most of the cost of storing the inventory, and the cost of the capital invested in the inventory-handling equipment are fixed. These fixed and variable costs can be measured. But the different risks specifically associated with different kinds of inventory are difficult to measure.

DETERMINING THE OPTIMUM INVENTORY LEVEL— DEMAND A RANDOM VARIABLE

A firm operating under certainty would experience little difficulty in determining the proper inventory level. Demand would be known in advance and likewise the profit—sales price per unit minus cost per unit times the number of items sold. Although occasionally demand is known with certainty—the number of diplomas at graduation—usually it is not and sales must be estimated. In the following discussion we assume that sales are not influenced by any systematic causes but can be described by a random variable function.

An Example

To illustrate, the demand of red roses sold by the Campus Florist may fluctuate within the limits of 7 to 10 dozen. The probability of selling roses on any particular day is given in Table 8.1.

Table 8.1. Campus Florist Probability Distribution of Demand for Red Roses

Probability p_i	0.1	0.2	0.4	0.3
Daily demand x_i	7	8	9	10

The roses are long-stemmed, cost $5, and sell for $10 per dozen. They must be sold in one day or they become worthless. The florist can carry an inventory of 7, 8, 9, or 10 dozen roses. If an inventory of 7 dozen roses is carried, the sale of more than 7 dozen is impossible. It is quite probable, however, that calls for more than 7 dozen will occur; in fact, there is a 0.9 probability.

Stocking 7 dozen roses costs $35, yields revenue of $70 when all are sold and a gross profit of $35. This profit will be earned with a probability of 1.0 or certainty. The results of the other inventory strategies are given in Table 8.2.

Table 8.2. Expected Profit Calculations of the Campus Florist Using Probabilities and Demand, Shown in Table 8.1

Inventory Strategy	Stock in Dozens	Calculations	Expected Profit
1	7	1.0($35)	= $35
2	8	0.1($30) + 0.9($40)	= 39
3	9	0.1($25) + 0.2($35) + 0.7($45)	= 41
4	10	0.1($20) + 0.2($30) + 0.4($40) + 0.3($50)	= 39

The expected profit for each inventory strategy is determined by the profit to be earned at each sales level multiplied by the probability of that level of sales occurring, and summing. For example, if we stock 8 dozen roses, there is a 0.1 probability that sales will reach 7 dozen and a 0.9 probability that sales will reach 8 dozen (or higher if we have the inventory). The profit on 7 dozen roses when 8 dozen are stocked is $(7 \times \$10) - (8 \times \$5) = \$30$. The profit on 8 dozen roses when 8 dozen are stocked is $(8 \times \$10) - (8 \times \$5) = \$40$. Multiplying by the respective probabilities, we have $0.1(\$30) + 0.09(\$40) = \$39$ expected profit from stocking 8 dozen roses.

Following our analysis, we would stock 9 dozen roses daily. Strategy 3 will lead to the best average daily profit—$41.

The expected value of a probability distribution need not, as in this case, correspond to an actual outcome, nor does it necessarily represent the most likely event. It is simply a weighted average of the outcomes.

Note that we are assuming a 1-day lead time in order to get roses for our inventory. The problem would become more complicated if we were able to procure roses on a half-day's notice at a premium, say $6 a dozen.

DETERMINING THE ECONOMIC ORDER QUANTITY (EOQ)— DEMAND KNOWN

Determining the right inventory level necessitates the resolution of conflicting goals. A large inventory will assure continuous production and guard against stock-outs. But, associated with it are high carrying costs. A low inventory minimizes carrying cost but increases stock-out costs, whether due to lost sales or to lost production. Buying or producing in large quantities reduces the order costs and setup costs per period but raises the average inventory level and carrying costs. Smaller orders or shorter production runs reduce the carrying costs through reducing the average inventory level, but raise the per-period reordering costs or setup costs and increase the peril of stock-outs through bringing the inventory level more frequently to the action point. The benefits derived from inventory availability must be balanced against the costs of carrying that amount of inventory. This requires an analysis of the economic order quantity (EOQ) in the case of a merchandiser or the economic production run in the case of a manufacturer.

The Inventory Cycle

The situation facing a merchandiser is shown graphically in Figure 8.1. Plotting inventory on the vertical axis and time in months on the horizontal axis, we have inventory I as a function of time t. Starting at time zero we

Figure 8.1. Inventory levels over time assuming two different order quantities *A* and *B*.

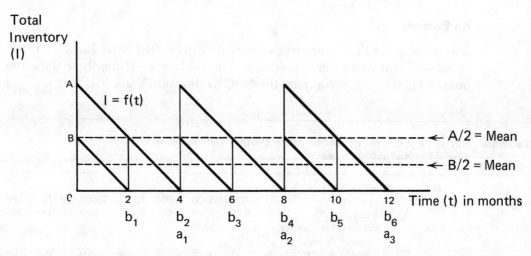

assume a new order is placed and delivery immediately received. We also assume usage of the inventory is at a constant rate and continuous. If each time we order amount *A*, which is twice amount *B*, we must place an order every four months, three orders per year. If we order amount *B* each time, we order every two months, or six times a year, and we incur twice the ordering costs that we would by ordering *A* three times a year. If we order amount *A* we will on the average carry twice as high an inventory as if we order amount *B* each time. The average inventory for the order quantity *A* is $(A/2)$; for the order quantity *B* it is $(B/2)$. There is an optimum point

Table 8.3. Stevens Paint Company—Kwik Kote Product
Symbols for annual demand, item cost, ordering cost, carrying cost, order size, and economic order quantity

		Formula Symbols
Demand per year	3000 items	D
Cost per unit other than carrying and order cost	$1.00	b
Carrying costs per item for one year	$0.20	k
Cost of placing each order	$12.00	s
Number of items ordered each time		x
Economic order quantity		x_q

between frequency of ordering and the carrying of inventory where the marginal cost of ordering just equals the marginal carrying cost.

An Example

Assume Stevens Paint introduces a new product called Kwik Kote. The demand and cost factors are summarized in Table 8.3. Using these data, the financial manager can compute the EOQ as shown in Table 8.4.

Table 8.4. Stevens Paint Company Economic Order Quantity Determination
Annual Demand at 3000 Items

Db	Cost of items purchased per year	$3000	$3000	$3000	$3000	$3000	$3000	$3000
x	Order size	3000	1500	1000	600	500	300	100
D/x	Number of orders per year = demand per year/order size	1	2	3	5	6	10	30
$x/2$	Average inventory = order size/2	1500	750	500	300	250	150	50
$kx/2$	Carrying costs = cost of carrying each unit for one year × average inventory	$ 300	$ 150	$ 100	$ 60	$ 50	$ 30	$ 10
$s(D/x)$	Ordering costs = cost per order × number of orders	$ 12	$ 24	$ 36	$ 60	$ 72	$ 120	$ 360
$kx/2 + s(D/x)$	Total carrying and ordering costs	$ 312	$ 174	$ 136	$ 120	$ 122	$ 150	$ 370
$Db + kx/2 + s(D/x)$	Total cost	$3312	$3174	$3136	$3120	$3122	$3150	$3370

The graphic solution in Figure 8.2 shows the EOQ to be 600 items. Stevens should place five orders per year (3000/600), incurring an annual combined inventory-ordering and carrying cost of $120. This cost would be less than any other ordering strategy.

The same result can be attained through a mathematical solution. The formula for the EOQ is

$$x_q = \sqrt{\frac{2sD}{k}}$$

where s, D, and k are as defined in Table 8.3. Substituting in the formula we arrive at the same answer as in Table 8.4:

$$x_q = \sqrt{\frac{2 \times \$12 \times 3000}{\$0.20}}$$

$$x_q = \sqrt{\frac{\$72,000}{\$0.20}}$$

$$x_q = 600 \text{ units}$$

Figure 8.2. Stevens Paint Company. Graphic determination of economic order quantity based on Table 8.4.

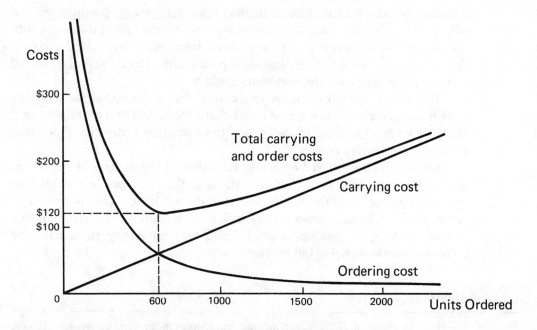

SAFETY STOCK—WHY CARRY?

Up to this point we have assumed that when inventory is exhausted, a new order is placed and delivery is received immediately. In practice a lead time must be established to cover the span between the time an order is placed or production initiated and the time of scheduled arrival of the inventory. Hence a safety cushion of inventory, or *safety stock*, is needed to absorb the demand between the time the old inventory actually runs out and the new inventory is available. Further delay in the actual receipt of the inventory may result because of strikes, floods, transportation delays, and so on. Or we may have unusually high demand between the order point and the actual delivery of the new inventory. The challenge is to estimate the *optimum safety stock level*—the point where the advantages obtained from carrying additional safety stocks just balance the cost of carrying this stock. To determine this level requires that we balance the stock-out costs and their probability of occurring against the costs of carrying the *additional* inventory.[1]

Summary

Holding inventory is necessary to uncouple purchasing, production, and selling, but it is also costly. The pressures to increase inventories are substantial and efforts must be made to keep inventories low. Under conditions of uncertainty we can make use of probabilities to establish the level of inventory that will yield the maximum profit.

The EOQ inventory model recognizes that some costs rise with the level of inventory (carrying cost) and that others decline (ordering cost). The EOQ model is used to determine the inventory order size that minimizes total inventory cost.

Some inventory must be carried to cushion irregularities in shipments or absorb increased demand between the time the inventory is scheduled to run out and the time the goods are actually received. This is known as safety stock. The economic safety-stock level is found by determining the cost of carrying various safety-stock levels and comparing them with the costs resulting from being out of stock.

Study Questions

1. How do speed of communications and transportation affect the inventory level a firm must carry? Is this in the national interest? In what way?
2. How is proper inventory management linked (a) to the short-run liquidity of the firm? (b) to the long-run profitability of the firm?
3. How might a firm requiring scrap copper differ in its policy concerning its raw materials inventory from a firm requiring bicycle tires? Which firm might be tempted to speculate on its inventory? Why? Would you agree that the wider the fluctuation in the price of the inventory, the smaller the stock of inventory that should be maintained and the smaller each purchase order? Explain.
4. With demand constant, why is the average inventory carried always one half that ordered for the period? Would this also be true if the firm faced a seasonal demand?

[1] For an illustration of the safety stock problem, see E. E. Nemmers and A. E. Grunewald, *Basic Managerial Finance*, 2nd ed. St. Paul, Minn.: West Publishing, 1975, pp. 142–145.

5. What data are necessary for determining the EOQ? Why is the EOQ always at the point where the slopes of carrying costs and order costs are equal but of opposite sign? Is the same true for the carrying costs and setup costs for a manufacturer seeking to determine the economic production run? Why?

6. What is the purpose of safety stock? Will the size of the safety stock be influenced by the firm's attitude toward risk? Why should this be so?

7. What tests can a firm apply to determine if its inventory position is in line with that of its competitors? What is to be gained and what are the dangers of applying such tests? Would they on balance be worthwhile?

8. As a firm grows in size, will it tend to carry a larger or a smaller proportionate amount of inventory? Why? Would the variety of inventory items increase or decrease? Does the number of different inventory items a firm must carry affect the total size of the inventory? How?

Problems

1. The Beloit Novelty Company carries a wide assortment of items for its customers. One item, the matchless match, is particularly popular. Wishing to keep its inventory under control, management selects this item to initiate its new program of ordering only the economic quantity each time. You are given the following information. Help them solve their problem.

Annual demand   160,000 units
Price per unit $4
Carrying cost   40 cents per unit, or 10 percent per dollar of inventory value
Cost per order $5 per order

a. Fill in the blanks. Identify the economic order quantity.

Size of order						
Number of orders	1	10	20	40	80	100
Average inventory						
Carrying cost						
Order cost						
Total cost						

b. Determine the economic order quantity by use of the mathematical formula.

2. The Bridal Shop stocks rolls of flowered ribbon. The annual demand reaches 8000 for these rolls. Each roll costs $10 and the order cost is $40 per order. Carrying

costs are 10 percent, or $1 per roll. The Bridal Shop is currently ordering on an optimum basis.

Ribbon Wholesalers, in an effort to shift some of its inventory to the Bridal Shop, points to the high ordering cost of $40 and suggests that orders be placed only once a year. As an inducement they offer the management a 4 percent discount if the annual ordering policy is adopted.

a. Evaluate this offer and make a recommendation to accept or reject it. Show the calculations upon which you base your recommendation. Ignore interest on any borrowing that may be necessary to accept the offer.

b. If you reject the offer, what reasonable counteroffer might you make?

3. The economic order quantity formula, a method for controlling investment in inventory, is sometimes referred to as an inventory model. In order to build such a model we must first specify all inventory-associated costs that rise and that decline with higher levels of inventory. All such costs can be classified into three categories.

a. Costs associated with carrying inventory.

b. Costs associated with ordering and receiving inventory.

c. Costs associated with running short of inventory.

Give as many inventory-associated costs that fall into each of the above three categories as you can.

4. The management of cash can be viewed as an inventory problem involving the determination of the optimum cash balance. Note that in our cash budgeting discussion we did not consider how to find an optimum cash balance. The similarity between the cash management problem and the inventory problem can be seen by correctly matching the statements in columns I and II.

I. *Inventory Problem*	II. *Cash Management Problem*
a. Carrying cost	i. Brokerage costs of buying and selling securities
b. Order cost	
c. Inflows of inventory (orders)	ii. Cash revenue, borrowing, sale of securities
d. Outflows of inventory	iii. Cash purchases and expenses
e. Safety stocks	iv. Opportunity cost of having funds tied up in low- or nonearning assets
	v. Minimum cash balance

Selected References

Arnold, R. W., "Inventory Management," *The Woman C.P.A.*, 22 (Feb. 1969), pp. 3–5 ff.

Crankshaw, C. D., and R. J. Corlett, "Stock Inventory Control with Data Bases and Analysis," *Management Accounting* (May 1970), pp. 26–28.

Eilon, S., and J. Elmaleh, "Adaptive Limits in Inventory Control," *Management Science*, 16 (Apr. 1970), pp. B533–B548.

Gross, D., and A. Soriano, "The Effect of Reducing Leadtime on Inventory Levels—Simulation Analysis," *Management Science,* 16 (Oct. 1969), pp. B61–B76.

Hofer, C. F., "Analysis of Fixed Costs in Inventory," *Management Accounting* (Sept. 1970), pp. 15–17.

Magee, J. F., "Guides to Inventory Policy: Functions and Lot Size," *Harvard Business Review,* 34 (Jan.–Feb. 1956), pp. 49–60.

——, "Guides to Inventory Policy: Problems of Uncertainty," *Harvard Business Review,* 34 (Mar.–Apr. 1956), pp. 103–116.

——, "Guides to Inventory Policy: Anticipating Future Needs," *Harvard Business Review,* 34 (May–June 1956), pp. 57–70.

Mao, J. C. T., *Quantitative Analysis of Financial Decisions.* New York: Macmillan, 1969, pp. 121–127.

Morgan, J. I., "Questions for Solving the Inventory Problem," *Harvard Business Review,* 41 (July–Aug. 1963), pp. 95–110.

Schussel, G., and S. Price, "A Case History in Optimum Inventory Scheduling," *Operations Research,* 18 (Jan.–Feb. 1970), pp. 1–23.

Shapiro, A., "Optimal Inventory and Credit-Granting Strategies under Inflation and Devaluation," *Journal of Financial and Quantitative Analysis,* 7 (Jan. 1973), pp. 37–46.

Snyder, A., "Principles of Inventory Management," *Financial Executive,* 32 (Apr. 1964), pp. 13–21.

Thurston, P. H., "Requirements Planning for Inventory Control," *Harvard Business Review,* 50 (Mar.–Apr. 1972), pp. 67–71.

9

SOURCES AND FORMS OF SHORT-TERM FINANCING

Short-term credit is defined as debt that is to be repaid within one year. It may be either secured or unsecured. In this chapter we first consider those sources of short-term financing that do not require collateral. We discuss the availability, cost, and risk of trade credit, commercial bank loans, and commercial paper. Then we examine secured short-term loans and discuss collateral loans, factoring accounts receivable, and warehousing of inventories.

UNSECURED SHORT-TERM SOURCES OF FUNDS

TRADE CREDIT

Recurring purchases of material by a firm are seldom paid by cash on delivery (COD). Trade credit is extended by the seller to the purchaser. The longer the credit period and the larger the volume of purchases, the larger the amount of credit received.

Trade credit arises in a simple manner. The purchaser sends an order to the supplier for the goods desired. The supplier checks the firm's credit and if good, sends the merchandise, entering on his books the amount of the shipment and sending an invoice covering the items to be delivered, the cost, and terms of sale. This system is simple and flexible. The major portion of trade credit is extended on this "open-book" account basis.

The Cash Discount

Trade credit terms may extend a cash discount for payment within a specified period, but full payment is due thereafter. Cash discounts should be distinguished from quantity discounts for the size of the order, and from trade discounts granted only to certain members of an industry group. The interest rates implicit in various credit terms are shown in Table 9.1.[1]

Table 9.1. Selected Trade Credit Terms and Their Respective Costs Computed Using the Formula

$$\text{Annualized interest cost} = \frac{\text{percent discount}}{1.00 - \text{percent discount}} \times \frac{360 \text{ days}}{\text{credit period} - \text{discount period}}$$

(payment is assumed made on the due date)

	Trade Terms	Implicit Annual Interest Cost
a.	1/10, n/30	18.18%
f.	1/10, n/60	7.27
g.	2/10, n/30	36.72
b.	2/10, n/40	24.48
d.	2/10, n/60	14.69
c.	3/15, n/60	24.72
e.	6/10, n/90	28.71

Delaying payment beyond the due date may not involve any immediate added cost to the purchaser but will result in a damaged credit reputation, reduced ability to obtain trade credit in the future, and worst of all, difficulty in obtaining inventory during periods of high demand. Suppliers will favor their better paying customers. But delaying payment may not produce these consequences. It depends on the customs in the industry, the supplier, and the level of economic activity.

Stretching Payment beyond the Due Date

Though payment is due, in practice payment may be stretched beyond the due date. Some suppliers regard trade terms casually. When extending

---

[1] See Chapter 7 for a discussion of the interest cost implied in the cash discount.

say 2/10, n/30 based on the invoice date they stiffly require payment by the 10th if the discount is to be taken, but do not enforce payment by the 30th. The supplier may permit accounts to become overdue without getting excited. When the account is 10 days overdue he may send a friendly notice requesting payment, and at the end of 20 days he may send a stronger notice. Only after 30 days may the supplier press for payment. Knowing this policy, a buyer could plan his payments for the 50th day after purchase (20 days overdue). This would leave him with a little margin before the supplier hits the boiling point. Stretching payment in this manner will bring the cost of trade credit down substantially—in this case to approximately 18 percent. The principle is, if one cannot take the cash discount, the farther the payment can be pushed into the future, the lower the implicit cost of the trade credit.

Management of Trade Credit

Frequently trade credit is mismanaged because it is easy to obtain, requires few formalities, and is flexible, expanding as inventory rises and contracting as purchases are reduced. Should the firm be a little late in paying a bill, no immediate harm may be apparent. If discounts are taken, the use of trade credit provides "cost-free" financing. Weighing the profit margin on the sale against the cost of reviewing the financial condition of each customer leads some manufacturers to be liberal in extending trade credit. After continued dealings with a customer the supplier develops experience regarding the firm's bill-paying habits. The customer in turn also acquires a feel for the collection policies of his suppliers. But the best strategy for the purchaser is to take discounts. The credit information exchange network operates efficiently and fast enough to make a firm's payment record widely known. A record of prompt payment lifts the firm's reputation and enhances its ability to obtain credit from banks and other lenders.

A firm relying heavily on trade credit because its financing ability is limited must engage in a difficult balancing act. Payment may be pushed as far into the future as suppliers will tolerate. Periodic cleanup on a rotating basis of all accounts due will tend to keep suppliers somewhat calm. The placement of orders with suppliers who are lax in collections will stretch the amount of trade credit obtainable. The other end of the balancing act is that suppliers may call a halt to further credit extension and force a long-term debt or equity issue at an inopportune time.

FINANCING BY COMMERCIAL BANK CREDIT

Commercial banks and finance companies are the principal sources of short-term negotiated credit. Since finance companies seldom make unsecured loans, discussion of them is deferred to later in this chapter. Banks in the aggregate are a smaller source of short-term financing than is trade credit. Notes payable to banks on the balance sheet of a firm usually indicate commercial bank borrowing.

The Bank as a Lending Organization

The availability of bank credit is important to the success of a firm whether the firm is currently borrowing or not. A short-term loan can usually be arranged quickly with but a few more formalities than trade credit. Flexibility in the form of tailoring to the borrower's needs is an important advantage of bank borrowing. To the nonborrowing firm the bank can serve as a reserve source of funds.

A firm with a good credit reputation will be able to borrow from some bank when the need arises. The word "some" is emphasized because not all banks have the same loan policies. Some are cautious and conservative, others aggressive and anxious to build new business; hence, the firm may be turned down by one bank but not by another. The financial manager should choose his banking connections so his firm's needs are met.

For a firm to hold idle reserve balances to meet every sudden unexpected cash drain is uneconomic. Both the firm's deposits and borrowing are valuable to the bank. The bank can use a portion of the deposit to loan to other firms or to purchase income-yielding securities. Borrowing by the firm generates income for the bank.

All financial managers are interested in obtaining bank credit to meet short-term needs. The more aggressive firms and many small firms are interested in obtaining as much bank credit as possible. Though the purpose of a bank is to make loans, it cannot assume much risk. While a bank is interested in earnings, its focus must be on safety of principal because the bank's assets must be sufficiently liquid to meet depositors' demands. In contrast, a firm is primarily concerned with profitability and is willing to take risks to achieve this goal. Thus the borrowing firm and the lending banker do not see eye to eye—and the banker is in the stronger position because he has numerous alternatives for putting his money to work, such as, for example, municipal bonds that give a satisfactory tax-free return, or government bonds. Since municipal and government bonds involve little risk, the banker must consider the tradeoff between the risk–return of bonds against commercial loans.

The financial manager, in contrast, is often in urgent need of bank credit but with few alternative sources of cheap funds. Inventory purchasing may be necessary to meet a major selling season, receivables collection may be slowing, the purchase of new machinery or equipment may suddenly become desirable, or any one of a dozen needs for cash may arise. Accommodating these needs may mean profit while failure to accommodate them may result in losses. The banker does not find himself in this position.

Selection of the Bank and Banker

Banks vary widely in their view of risk and their role in the community. Some follow a cautious lending policy, others are more liberal, and still others are quite aggressive. One bank may be stockholder oriented, seeking a good rate of earnings growth. Another may seek to establish itself as one of the "big" banks in the community, be willing to pay high rates on certificates of deposit to increase its pool of loanable funds, and to make liberal loans at low rates to get customers and build volume to obtain larger profits later. Immediate profits may be secondary.

Several bankers within an institution may evaluate a loan application with reasonable care and yet not reach the same conclusion regarding the risk. Further, some bankers may emphasize service to the community and stimulation of its growth and prosperity; others may not be so motivated.

Size of the Bank. For the firm, as both depositor and borrower, size of the bank is important. Among banks size and safety often go together, and the firm as depositor is interested in safety. Demand deposits are insured by the Federal Deposit Insurance Corporation (FDIC) to $40,000, but the bank balance of even a modest-sized firm would exceed this amount. Further, the size of a loan a bank may grant to a single borrower is limited by the bank's capital and surplus. National banks cannot make a loan to any one borrower in excess of 10 percent of capital stock and surplus. State banks have similar restrictions. This limit is 25 percent if the loan is secured by livestock, goods in storage, or government securities. Therefore, the firm as a borrower would also tend to favor a bank large enough to be able to accommodate its growing loan demands; yet in a smaller bank, the firm may get more personal attention. The loan may be arranged by the bank president himself. If the firm is satisfied with the safety of the bank, and the best loan accommodation can be obtained there, then that may be the bank to choose. Size alone is not a determining factor. The bank may have correspondents in other parts of the country who will take the amount by which the loan exceeds the legal limit of the bank's lending power.

A large bank may have a specialist in the firm's particular line of business. Being closer to the field the specialist may be more knowledgeable as to loan requests. Also, the specialist may be a source of information and extend expert advice on many aspects of the business.

Bank Lending Policy. Some insight into the lending policies of a bank and its ability to make additional loans can be obtained by analyzing its financial position. A bank with a high deposit (that is, liability) to capital ratio has a thin equity position and must be cautious since it has little cushion to absorb losses and therefore should make only low-risk loans. Another measure of a bank's financial position is the loan-to-deposit ratio. Loans normally yield a higher return than securities but are less liquid. A high loan-to-deposit ratio may mean a bank is "loaned up"; a new loan would be hard to get. But it will also indicate the bank's policy of preferring loans. A low ratio may mean that the bank could safely make additional loans or that the banker may be ultraconservative and interested only in prime risk-free loans; the slightest hint of risk may mean refusal. Finally, to meet sudden withdrawals of demand depositors, banks carry a substantial percentage of cash and government obligations. An abnormally high ratio of reserves indicates the bank is preoccupied with safety rather than earnings, but a low ratio indicates earnings are important and the bank is aggressively making loans, particularly if the bank also has a high loan-to-deposit ratio.

The financial manager might favor the "middle of the road" bank. Obtaining even a low-risk loan from an illiquid bank is difficult. And the firm as a depositor avoids an illiquid bank because of concern with the safety of the firm's funds. But it may be equally difficult to obtain a loan that represents a fair amount of risk from a liquid bank unless the bank has a specialist in the firm's area of business or the financial manager makes contact with a skilled loan officer. A great deal may depend on the personalities involved. In any event, as depositor of a highly liquid bank, the financial manager would be able to sleep comfortably nights. Unless the firm is an old and valued customer (that is, carries large bank balances), illiquid, loaned-up banks should be avoided. The firm should prefer the bank that provides good protection for its depositors and follows a fairly aggressive loan policy.

Other Factors to be Considered in Selecting a Bank. The interest rate on a prospective loan is one element to consider. Even though the anticipated profitability of the project is the major factor, the cost of a loan in these high-interest times is important. Furthermore, all banks may not charge the same rate for a given loan for many reasons. One bank may feel that a certain firm is a better risk than other banks. Another bank may be loaned up but willing to make room at a high price. Though it is usually not good practice to shop around for the lowest rate for a particular loan, it does make sense to do so before establishing banking connections. The firm that establishes a banking connection, but still keeps abreast of developments in the money and capital markets and makes broad contact with the banking community, provides good insurance that poor loan service by the present bank will be detected, indicating that it is time for a change of banks.

Shopping for a rate on each loan, however, is usually poor practice for the same reasons that changing doctors for every illness would be; the benefits of prior analysis are lost, the possibility of misdiagnosis increases, and so on.

The firm should also consider the charges levied for check handling, collection, and the availability and quality of services, such as the collection of notes and bills of exchange, the handling of foreign exchange, trust department services, and credit and business information services. All large banks are able to render good service at competitive rates in each of these areas. In the smaller banks not all these services are available directly but are obtainable indirectly through a correspondent bank. Where the services are provided directly, such as the management of securities under trust agreement, the quality of the service may depend largely on the skill of one or a few individuals rather than on the organization itself.

Finally, there is convenience of the bank's location. A firm in a small community will likely carry its account with the local bank. Even if the firm is large, it will carry one account there. A firm located in a large metropolitan area containing many banks will select that institution with which it can work out a mutually satisfactory arrangement, and convenience of location may be one factor.

Uses of Short-Term Bank Credit

Seasonal Financing. Bank credit is excellent for financing seasonal bulges in inventory and receivables. These "self-liquidating" loans please the banker and most firms can expect to obtain bank credit for seasonal needs. The repayment proceeds are generated from the sale of the merchandise or the collection of the receivables and do not depend on the profitability of the firm.

For a stable firm any seasonal borrowing requirement can be readily established. But the expanding firm with a *growing* basic level of receivables and inventory will have more than a seasonal borrowing requirement. Here bank credit may be employed, either by design or inadvertently, to finance a part of the firm's permanent capital needs. This may go on until the bank realizes the situation and forces the firm to seek other financing. Besides its ready availability in the short run, bank credit is usually cheaper than long-term debt. But recently rising interest rates show that it would have been cheaper to finance by long term at an earlier period rather than to finance continually by short term.

Other Needs for Short-Term Loans. A weak firm or one employing its assets to the maximum may borrow monthly to take advantage of trade discounts—say, at the beginning of the month—and repay during the month as the receivables are collected. Though attractive to the firm, a loan arrangement of this kind might be difficult to obtain as the banker may feel that the firm is operating too close to the line. He may either refuse to lend or demand higher rates or even security. Since the passing of trade discounts put additional pressure on the weak firm, such a bank loan, though costly, would still be desirable.

The financially strong and tightly run organization can weigh the cost of bank credit against long-term financing. Here bank credit may be strategically employed as interim financing while the firm is awaiting a more favorable period to undertake long-term financing. A typical example would be a firm that, for competitive reasons, must launch a major expansion project immediately but finds that rates for long-term financing are currently prohibitive.

Borrowing Arrangements for Short-Term Bank Credit

Single Loan. Occasional bank borrowing is done by signing a promissory note. Each borrowing requires a fresh analysis and a new negotiation. The note may be for 30 days to 1 year, but most notes are for 30 to 90 days, although they may be renewed at maturity. Such a short maturity gives borrower and lender the opportunity to adjust the interest rate to new money market conditions. In today's world of erratic interest rates, many notes provide that the rate will change automatically and on the same date as any change in the *prime rate*, which is the lowest rate a bank charges to its most credit-worthy customers. The loan may be repayable in a lump sum or in installments and may provide for payment before due date (prepayment) at no penalty or at a penalty.

Line of Credit. A firm with periodic borrowing requirements can eliminate negotiation each time a new loan becomes necessary by arranging for a *line of credit* with the bank, which is a formal (written) or informal (oral) arrangement providing the bank will lend up to a predetermined limit as long as agreed conditions are maintained. The firm may "draw down" varying amounts as needed against the line up to the limit specified. A promissory note for the amount, showing interest and date of maturity, is drawn up each time a loan is made against the line of credit, which is usually renegotiated once a year.

The line of credit is a sound financial planning arrangement. The firm can rely on it and can plan without having to know the exact amount of funds needed each month. The bank will provide the requested funds as long as the agreed conditions are maintained, which usually include maintenance of a minimum working capital.

Revolving Credit. This is a formal line of credit secured by receivables or inventory. The term *revolving credit* implies that each new loan involves new receivables or inventory.

Cost of Short-Term Bank Credit

Interest rates vary by size of firm, industry, and section of the country. The bank's rate to the small firm is higher than to large firms, although less than could be obtained elsewhere. The reason is that the costs of loaning to a small firm are larger *per loan dollar* because of the fixed costs of a loan. Furthermore, the risks are higher than for a larger firm. Public utilities, because of their stability, and large finance companies, because of their asset liquidity, receive favorable rates. Construction firms, because of their high risk, tend to pay the highest rates. Banks in the northern and eastern sections of the country charge lower rates than those in the South and West because the supply of funds is greater and lending opportunities less in the northern and eastern sections.

Industry, size of firm, and location are factors management must recognize when seeking a loan. Timing often cannot be greatly altered. The funds must be obtained when needed, whether money is tight or loose. Consequently, to keep the interest cost down, the borrower must work to keep his firm healthy and maintain good banking relations by seeing that the bank is kept up to date on the progress of the firm.

Other Provisions Attached to Short-Term Bank Credit

Compensating Balance. Banks usually require their business customers to maintain a checking account balance or compensating balance of 15 to 20 percent of the loan. The bank and the customer, when agreeing on the loan terms, settle on the compensating balance, which provides several advantages to the bank. First the compensating balance increases the effective interest rate. A 20 percent compensating balance raises the effective rate up to 25 percent. A customer requiring $10,000 must borrow $12,500. At simple interest, 5 percent on the $12,500 equals $625 interest, but since the firm can only use $10,000, the effective rate is 6¼ percent. However, the firm ordinarily has funds in its checking account and these funds count in the computation.

Through right of offset the bank reduces its risk by compensating balances if the firm should fail. The amount the firm has on deposit at the time of failure may be applied by the bank against the loan, thus reducing the amount of its unsecured claim against the firm. The bank's *reduced* claim will then rank as unsecured if the bank has no collateral and will participate proportionately with other unsecured creditors.

Bankers argue that the maintenance of a compensating balance is in the firm's best interest as well as the bank's. A firm should follow conservative practices. For the bank this is so; for the risk-taking firm the matter is not so clear-cut. The bank is not interested in making risky loans, but the firm may quite properly assume risk to attain profits and a more competitive level of operations.

Annual Cleanup. The requirement that the firm be "out of the bank" a minimum of 1 month each year at least superficially demonstrates that the firm is not using bank credit to finance long-term needs. Bank credit is extended to finance seasonal needs, and the annual cleanup provides some evidence that the loan is being used for its intended purpose.

Brief borrowing from another bank is one method of negating the annual cleanup provision, but this is difficult where the second bank is alert. Another dodge is to permit accounts payable to expand and after the cleanup period to pay them quickly with newly borrowed funds. Banks stop this by requiring the cleanup period to be a longer period like 75 days. Accounts payable usually cannot be stretched an *additional* 75 days by the borrowing firms. Borrowers have an institutionalized advantage in that banks are afraid of being caught alone with a loan that goes sour. Consequently, if another bank extended a firm credit, the bank is reassured of the firm's credit worthiness and will lend even though the firm finances the annual cleanup through the second bank.

Protective Provisions. For smaller and weak firms a bank may set minimum working capital ratios, impose restrictions on dividends and salaries, and prohibit the repayment of insider shareholder loans. Though the risk associated with a short-term loan is substantially less than that attached to a long-term loan, the management of a sinking firm may try to salvage as much as possible before all is lost. Thus the bank sets these restrictions to prevent the firm's assets from flowing out the back door.

COMMERCIAL PAPER AS A SHORT-TERM SOURCE OF FUNDS

Short-term corporate unsecured promissory notes sold at a discount on the open market are known as *commercial paper*. These negotiable notes are in even amounts such as $10,000 (the minimum) and go to the millions. The total issue by one firm often runs into the millions of dollars and is seldom less than $100,000. Maturities are 20–270 days. Commercial paper is an important source of credit to commercial, industrial, and sales finance firms, although it totals only about one fifth the amount of commercial loans by banks.

The Commercial Paper Market

The commercial paper market is well organized and restricted to firms with top-quality credit. Major sales finance companies such as Associates Investment Company and General Motors Acceptance Corporation sell their paper directly to investors. Other firms typically sell theirs through middlemen called *dealers*. Dealers are granted a marketing spread of ¼ to ½ or 1 percent. Purchasers of commercial paper include nonfinancial institutions, pension funds, and universities. Commercial paper provides these organizations with a low-risk, short-term moderate return investment. The rate is higher than that on short-term Treasury securities but typically below the prime rate. The risk of loss is negligible.[2]

Firms issuing commercial paper are ordinarily willing to tailor maturity to the needs of the buyer who seeks to have the necessary funds available to meet dividend, tax, or other obligations falling due. Further, finance companies usually issue commercial paper whenever there is a demand, thus permitting corporate investors to place their temporarily idle funds as they accumulate. The finance companies control the volume of paper issued by

---

[2] The rapid expansion of the commercial paper market started in the latter part of the 1960s and was accompanied by a deterioration in the quality of the paper issued. This deterioration went unnoticed by some until mid-1970 when Penn Central Transportation Company defaulted on its outstanding paper. Penn Central went into receivership with $87 million of commercial paper in trusting hands. Panic developed in the commercial paper market and Chrysler Financial Corporation was almost tipped over. *New York Times*, July 7, 1970, section 3, pp. 1, 11; F. C. Schadrack and F. S. Breimyer, "Recent Developments in the Commercial Paper Market," *Federal Reserve Bank of New York—Monthly Review*, 52 (Dec. 1970), pp. 280–291.

modifying the terms rather than by restricting the offerings. Generally, commercial paper is held to maturity by the purchaser. No secondary market for the paper exists. However, the major finance companies will usually repurchase the paper if requested, or, if the paper was originally purchased from a dealer, repurchase arrangements with that dealer can be negotiated.

An advantage of commercial paper is that large amounts of funds can be raised hourly without having to deal with a number of banks. The main disadvantage is that the commercial paper market is an impersonal market. Investors look solely for the best yield at the lowest risk. No extensions at maturity are possible; new paper must be sold or other sources of financing sought.

SECURED SHORT-TERM SOURCES OF FUNDS

A lender normally does not extend credit if the risk of default by the borrower is high, nor does he demand security if the risk of default is low. The lender is concerned with safety of principal and a fair return. With collateral the lender has both the cash-generating ability of the firm and the collateral of the pledged asset as sources of loan repayment. Should the borrower fail, the lender has a prior claim over other creditors to the collateral and the lender can force sale of the asset to repay the loan.

COLLATERAL LOANS

Businesses prefer to borrow on an unsecured basis. Pledging of security restricts further borrowing and is bothersome and costly. Firms are more anxious to pledge security if they receive a reduction in interest rate, but this seldom occurs. A weak borrower usually must either provide collateral and agree to a stiff rate of interest or not receive the loan.

Many firms are not of sufficient financial stature to obtain unsecured credit from commercial banks. One study reported two thirds of the outstanding business loans of national banks and one half of the dollar volume represented were guaranteed by a third party or secured. Though commercial banks are the most important source of secured loans, *finance companies* also grant secured business loans.

Characteristics of Good Collateral

The two most important characteristics of good collateral are legality of claim to the asset in event the borrower defaults and probable recovery value on the asset. Government securities left with the lender rank high on both counts. Should the borrower default, the lender simply sells the securities in his possession. Recovery value is high as "governments" are stable in price, have a ready market, and a large block can be disposed of quickly without affecting price. The common stocks of listed corporations also make good collateral, but their wider price fluctuations result in lower loan value of these securities—typically 80 percent against 90 percent on governments. At the other end of the spectrum are the shares of closely held companies. Such securities adequately fill the ownership protection requirement but not that of predictable recovery value. Lack of a market makes determination of their value difficult.

Working Capital Assets as Collateral

Inventories of raw materials such as grain or steel are marketable collateral, have durability, and their value is quickly ascertainable. But because they are portable and fungible (one specimen may be used in place of another in satisfaction of an obligation), they suffer from title or ownership protection weakness. Other inventory items, such as fresh fish or produce, while quite marketable, remain in that state for only a short time. Their lack of durability makes them poor collateral.

The title protection problem arises partly because the borrower may require the raw material in production, whereas the lender wants the inventory stored and controlled. Since the raw material cannot be in both places at once, a number of devices have been established to safeguard the title of the lender but permit release of the inventory when needed in production.

Work in process is infrequently pledged as collateral because it changes in form, lacks marketability, has uncertain recovery value, and has weak title protection. As the raw material is fed into the production stream, it is difficult to separate the pledged parts from those claimed by the general creditors. When financial difficulty occurs, the general creditors want to find as many of a firm's assets unpledged as possible. The secured creditor, therefore, must make certain that no defect exists in his claim to a particular group of assets. The lender can avoid this difficulty by obtaining a security agreement that provides for a "floating" lien on the shifting stock, that is, one that shifts from one batch of raw material to the next. Even so, great reliance must be placed on the honesty of the borrower. The goods remain in his control and are not clearly identifiable. Commercial finance companies are the primary lenders in this area.

Finished goods such as appliances or automobiles serve as good collateral. Their durability, marketability, and predictable recovery value rank high, and they offer title protection. But the lender must be confident of the integrity of the borrower. The goods to be sold may be in the borrower's showroom. The borrower has control over the merchandise, and when this is sold also has control over the proceeds of the sale. The lender, therefore, must spot check the dealer's showroom to determine whether the goods are still on the floor. If sold, the funds should be flowing to the lender to repay the loan made against that particular unit.

Receivables have good collateral qualities and are frequently pledged, but there are difficulties. Keeping track of many receivables is costly. The borrower may pledge nonexistent accounts. Confusion may arise in identifying the pledged accounts in the event of the borrower's financial difficulty. Still worse, the customer owing the receivable may have counterclaims for defective merchandise, incomplete shipment, or may return the merchandise.

ACCOUNTS RECEIVABLE FINANCING

Borrowing

Borrowing against receivables is based on an agreement, including a promissory note, setting forth the terms and procedures and sometimes providing for pledging of all or only specified receivables. A stack of invoices is placed with the lender for review and appraisal. Those that do not meet the lender's credit standards are rejected. Credit may be extended on the basis of an acceptable pool of receivables. Payment by customers of their accounts, returned merchandise and allowances for defects, and bad debts reduce the pool of credit available. The pool is expanded through replenishment with newly generated receivables. To protect against loss, the lender sets a prudent margin between the face value of the receivables and the amount of the loan, selects only sound receivables, and establishes a claim against the receivables pledged. To perfect his security interest the lender files a copy of the security agreement in one or more offices of the state, including the secretary of state of the state where the collateral is located.

The legal form used to borrow against receivables is standard. Thus it pays for the borrower to shop for the most attractive package of percentage amount advanced and interest rate. Lenders extend from 50 to 90 percent of the value of the receivables pledged. The average is 75 to 80 percent. Such characteristics as the financial position of the borrower, the credit standing of the customer, and the proportion of returns and allowances determine the actual proportion advanced. Commercial banks lend somewhat less on the average than finance companies such as Commercial Credit and CIT but charge lower rates. Commercial bank interest charges average 1 to 6 percent over the prime rate. Some banks levy an additional annual service charge of 1 percent on the balance outstanding. Finance company charges run from a daily rate of $\frac{1}{40}$ of 1 percent or 9 percent annually for large accounts to $\frac{1}{15}$ of 1 percent or 24 percent annually.

Most receivables financing is done on the *nonnotification plan*. The customer is not notified that the receivable has been pledged by the seller, but the receivables are pledged with recourse, that is, should the customer not pay, the lender can look to the seller for payment. Under the *notification plan* the customer is informed by the seller that the account has been pledged and directed to make payment to the lender. Again, recourse is applicable. If the customer does not pay, the borrower must still pay the lender.

To prevent fraud and establish its claim to the collateral, the lender usually requests copies of the invoices, requires the borrowing firm to mark its receivables ledger to show the assigned accounts, and reserves the right to inspect the books. The borrower may also be required to deposit all customer payments in the form they are received, thus enabling the lender to verify the receivables, note defective merchandise claims, and make certain the borrower is paying immediately.

Factoring

Factoring involves the sale (not mere assignment) of receivables to a financial institution such as a commercial finance company or one of a few commercial banks who recently entered the field. The sale is usually without recourse; if the customer does not pay, the factor takes the loss. Consequently, the factor selects carefully the receivables purchased. Before shipping goods the firm can get the factor's approval of the credit of any customer whose receivable the firm expects to "factor." If the factor approves, the goods are shipped and the factor buys the receivable. Should the factor not approve, the firm can still ship and assume the credit risk. When the receivables are sold, the customer is notified and instructed to make payment directly to the factor. The receivables when sold no longer appear on the firm's balance sheet. A firm borrowing against receivables carries them on the balance sheet and footnotes their pledged status.

The factor performs a number of services for its client firm in addition to the lending service. This makes it difficult to compare the costs of factoring with borrowing against receivables. The factor serves as a credit department for the client firm, checking the financial condition of its customers.

The factor also relieves the client of collection efforts. When the factor purchases the receivables, he assumes the risk that the customer will not pay. Only the last service is unique to the factor. The other services may or may not be furnished as part of ordinary accounts receivable financing.

Factors charge service fees (commission) of from 1 to 3 percent of the receivables purchased, the rate depending on the risk of the paper bought, the amount of business, and the size and maturity of the receivables. These charges cover the cost of credit examination, collection expense, and bad-debt losses (risk taking). A firm in the 1 percent category that turns its receivables 12 times a year is paying 12 percent of the average dollar volume for having its receivables serviced. Interest at the rate of about 3 percent above prime is charged for funds withdrawn ahead of the normal collection or average due date, that is, from the date of the sale of the receivables to the average customer due date. Any funds not drawn by the firm before the customer's due date bear no interest charge, and funds earn interest when collected by the factor but left with the factor after the customer due date.

The factoring agreement is renewable on an annual basis but may be canceled on short notice. When the process of factoring is continuous (as new receivables arise, they are regularly sold to the factor), then the factor provides not only credit for temporary or peak needs but is also financing a portion of the firm's permanent working capital.

Finance Companies

Finance companies engage in many secured lending activities. Sales finance companies handle both wholesale and retail financing. They make loans to finance a dealer's inventory of automobiles or appliances and purchase the "paper" of the customers buying the merchandise on the installment plan. Commercial finance companies make loans to businesses that commercial banks cannot accept because of risk. These loans may be secured by any acceptable asset, receivables and inventory being most frequently pledged. Factors specialize in financing accounts receivables either by making secured loans or by purchasing the receivables.

When making a loan, commercial finance companies and factors rely for safety primarily upon the collateral offered by the borrower and may lend many times his net worth or working capital. Often the firm is small or moderate sized or was recently established and is growing rapidly. Further, its management may be relatively inexperienced. To keep losses tolerable, these financial institutions have developed complex procedures whose high cost is borne by the borrower in the form of interest and service charges.

INVENTORY FINANCING

Terms

Much business credit is secured by a pledge of inventory, and commercial banks are the primary lenders. Approximately 10 percent of all secured loans by banks are backed by inventories. Large and medium-sized firms are the major clients. Small firms with less than $50,000 in assets obtain relatively little credit via this financing option.

A wide variety of products may be pledged as collateral for a loan. Raw materials and finished goods have the highest collateral value. Next come certain standard purchased parts that can be returned to the supplier at a discount. Finally, and almost without collateral value, is work in process.

The inventory may be on the borrower's site, in storage, or in transit. It may remain in the possession of the borrower or be stored with a third party. Title (ownership) of goods in transit is evidenced by a *bill of lading;* title to those stored in a warehouse is covered by a *warehouse receipt.* Grains and vegetable oils are examples of inventory secured by warehouse receipts. Title is the basis on which much inventory financing is done.

If inventory is the security, the lender considers the durability, the ability to identify, the salability, and the validity of his lien against the assets. When making the loan, the lender takes a margin of safety to protect against a decline in the value of the merchandise. Perishability, stability of market price, and cost of liquidation are the risks considered. The amount loaned ranges from 50 to 80 percent of the book value of the inventory. The exact percentage is a matter of judgment, bargaining, and trade-off against other terms of the loan, particularly the interest rate. One lender might be willing to grant a higher amount but also charge a higher rate; another a lower amount but at a lower rate.

Although interest rates on inventory-backed loans made by commercial banks are lower than rates charged by commercial finance companies, bank lenders may require a compensating balance of 15 to 20 percent which will increase the "effective interest rate." Other lenders may impose service charges to cover the cost of checking the inventory on the borrower's premises. If the inventory is placed in a public or terminal warehouse, that is, a warehouse that rents space to all comers, there will be charges to cover "in and out" handling costs. If a field warehouse (used by the borrower only) is set up on the premises of the borrower, fixed or variable costs will be incurred. Generally the rates on the borrowed funds do not vary significantly, the major variation being the service charges that arise from the costs of checking and handling the merchandise and the length of time it is in storage.

Who Holds the Collateralized Inventory?

Having reached an agreement with the lender on the terms of the loan to be secured by inventory, the firm is asked to sign a promissory note covering the loan of funds and a document evidencing title to the inventory serving as the collateral. These are the two basic pieces of paper underlying the deal. Because of the fixed costs of setting up such an arrangement, the loan is usually for a substantial sum and regularly renewed.

Inventory in Borrower's Possession. Appliances and automobiles are identifiable by serial number, and their presence on the showroom floor is necessary for their sale. Hence they are usually left in possession of the borrower. Protection of the lender is through a *security agreement* under which the borrower agrees to hold the units and the sale proceeds for the lender. The proceeds must be forwarded to the lender immediately upon sale of a unit. The lender protects himself against unsecured creditors by filing the security agreement in the county where the borrower's office is and in the state capitol and by requiring the borrower to keep the units properly insured. The lender makes periodic unannounced inspections to ascertain that the borrower still has the pledged units for which the lender has not yet received sale proceeds as repayment of the loan.

This *floor-plan arrangement* serves the firm by keeping paper work to a minimum and permitting display of the merchandise. The major disadvantage to the lender is dependence on the honesty of the dealer. If it is not imperative that the inventory remain in the borrower's possession, the lender can obtain greater safety by requiring the borrower to store the inventory in a warehouse.

Inventory in Warehouseman's Possession. Upon receipt of the goods the warehouseman issues a warehouse receipt and releases the goods only upon presentation of this piece of paper. The lender is protected against the claims of unsecured creditors since the goods are segregated, and against the dishonesty of the borrower since the goods are no longer in his hands.

But loss may still be sustained. The warehouse receipt is subject to fraudulent use; an innocent holder of the receipt can claim the goods. The receipt does not warrant the quality or value of the goods nor provide for insurance. If the borrower does not have good title to the goods (as with stolen goods), the lender gets no title. Furthermore, the lender must satisfy himself that the goods are what they are purported to be—perhaps by opening the boxes to see that they actually contain cans of cherries and not applesauce. Through the years some spectacular frauds running to millions of dollars have been based on fake warehouse receipts and nonexistent inventory. Yet warehousing, and particularly field warehousing, remains a popular method for facilitating loans secured by inventory.

Table 9.2. Provisions of Secured Short-Term Financing Arrangements

Type of Financing Arrangement	Funds Obtainable as a Percent of Value of Asset	Interest Rate	Other Typical Provisions
Receivables loan (bank)	50–90%	1 to 6% over prime rate	Service charge, compensating balance
Receivables loan (finance company)	50–90%	9–24%	Service charge
Factoring	97–99%	3% above prime	Interest earned on funds left with factor
Inventory loan	50–80%	1 to 6% over prime rate	Service charge, banks may require compensating balance

---

To carry out *field warehousing*, the premises of the borrower are used as a warehouse for the collateral pledged. The field warehouse may be a simple fenced-in area containing lumber, scrap iron, or coal awaiting use in the production process or sale. Or it may be a building containing stored cotton, cases of canned goods, or tanks of salad oil. Signs are posted around the segregated area stating who has control. If the area is in control of a separate company which is bonded and has its own employees, it is a true warehouse. However, "field warehousing" may not involve a separate warehouse company and may use employees of the borrower.

A summary of types of secured short-term financing appears in Table 9.2.

Summary

Trade credit is the most widely used form of unsecured short-term financing. Trade credit can be an expensive form of short-term financing if cash discounts are missed and full payment is made a short time later.

Bank credit is a frequent source of short-term funds, but not as widely used as is trade credit. Self-liquidating loans, whether secured or not, are the specialty of the commercial banker. The firm's banking connection should be chosen carefully. The bank's lending policies, services available, experience, size, and location should be compatible with the firm's deposit, borrowing, and collection requirements.

Commercial paper are corporate unsecured short-term promissory notes sold in the open market. The selling firms are large with high credit ratings. The notes must be paid at maturity. Financial institutions and firms with temporarily surplus funds purchase commercial paper. The rates are higher than those on short-term Treasury securities and the risk is small. As a result, they are attractive short-term investments.

A pledge of assets may be required when there is substantial risk as to ability to repay. Both the borrower and the lender prefer an unsecured loan since the pledging of assets is costly and cumbersome. Receivables and inventory are the assets most frequently pledged by business firms for short-term loans.

The purpose of collateral is to minimize the lender's risk of loss. To achieve this the lender's claim to the pledged assets must be valid, the recovery value of the assets stable and ascertainable, and an adequate margin must exist between the value of the assets and the loan principal. Government securities make excellent collateral with a loan value of 90 percent. Listed common stocks carry a loan value of 80 percent. Loans against receivables run from 50 to 90 percent and against raw material or finished goods from 50 to 80 percent. Work in process carries little loan value.

Receivables may be factored (sold) as well as pledged, usually with recourse. The factor examines the credit position of the firm's customers and decides which receivables to purchase. The firm selling the goods can withdraw the funds immediately or wait until the receivables' due date. When receivables are purchased, the factor incurs less risk of title imperfection than when receivables are pledged. In the latter case the lender must be sure that the pledge of receivables is noted on the borrower's books and that all receivables are genuine.

Raw materials, such as grains or metals, serve as excellent loan collateral. Market prices can be checked daily against the loan amount. Similarly, automobiles and appliances are readily acceptable. Some problems arise in assuring a valid claim by the lender to these assets. Raw material is frequently needed in production; the appliances and automobiles must be on the showroom floor. The lender retains title and control over the raw materials required in the borrower's production process by having them placed in a field warehouse. The loan is secured by the inventory in the field warehouse, and the lender releases it to the firm as the firm makes payment on its loan. Automobiles and appliances are normally floor planned. The dealer borrows against the units, holds them in trust for the lender, displays them for sale, and when sold remits the amount of the loan to the lender. The lender is trusting the borrower because at one moment in time the borrower has both the funds of the lender and of the customer who bought the goods. Lenders make frequent checks to be sure either the unit is on the floor or the funds are on the way to the bank.

Study Questions

1. Passing cash discounts results in a high cost of short-term trade credit financing if payment is required shortly after the discount date. How may the implicit interest cost be reduced? How does this method operate?

2. What major factors influence a firm's use of trade credit? Is the state of the economy one of these? If so, how do economic conditions influence the use of trade credit? On balance do you think a firm would have a larger accounts payable balance during a period of economic boom or during one of recession? Explain.

3. Suppliers generally extend trade credit more quickly and more easily than bankers. Explain the reasons for the difference. How is it possible for a firm to obtain trade credit and be refused bank credit?

4. What are the rates charged on trade credit, bank credit, and commercial paper? How do you account for the differences? How do these rates relate to the bank prime rate? To the short-term Treasury bill rate?

5. What factors should be considered in selecting a bank? Why is shopping around for the best terms on a loan generally to be avoided by a firm? How can an alert financial manager sensitive to money market conditions save his firm the necessity of shopping around for the best terms?

6. What do compensating balances offer the bank in the event the firm is forced into bankruptcy?

7. What is the annual cleanup and what purpose does it serve? How may this requirement be avoided? Why may a bank tolerate and even encourage this maneuver?

8. What are the characteristics of good collateral? Give examples of good and "bad" collateral and show how each possesses or does not possess these characteristics.

9. Distinguish between borrowing against and factoring accounts receivable. Com-

pare the effect each will have on the firm's balance sheet as measured by familiar ratios.

10. What difficulties may arise in accepting raw material inventory as collateral for a loan? How may these difficulties be avoided?

11. What are warehouse receipts? How may they be used as collateral for a loan? What risks are present for a lender loaning against a pledge of warehouse receipts and how may the risk be minimized?

12. What services does a factor perform? Why may some of these services be particularly advantageous to a small firm just getting started?

Problems

1. You have just been married and are purchasing your major appliances from Castle Stores. The terms are 3/10, n/90.
   a. Should you not be able to pay by the 10th, what would be the rate you are paying for credit, on an annual basis, if you paid by
      (i) the 20th day after purchase,
      (ii) the 70th day after purchase,
      (iii) the 90th day after purchase?
   b. Examination of your financial condition reveals that you will not be able to pay for the appliances until one year from today. The banker, eager to help, offers a loan of the necessary funds at 6 percent a year. You accept the offer, make the purchase, and resolve not to pay anyone more than 6 percent for the use of credit. From the date of purchase, for how many days must you delay payment to equal the bank loan rate? *Corollary:* The loan from the banker must be for how many days? At 6 percent, what would be the interest cost on a loan of $3000 from the banker? Use a 360-day year.

2. Cold Cereals, Inc., signs a one-year $20,000 note. Annual interest is 6 percent, discounted.
   a. How much will the bank credit to the firm's account?
   b. What is the effective rate of interest being paid on the loan?

3. The following year Cold Cereals, Inc., decides to switch banks. The bank does not discount its loans but requires a 20 percent compensating balance. Interest is at 5 percent.
   a. How much will the firm have to borrow to have available the required amount as calculated in Question 2a?
   b. Compute the annual dollar interest cost of borrowing this amount for one year at 5 percent. Remember that the loan is not discounted. Also compute the effective rate of interest.
   c. Was it smart to switch banks? What savings, if any, were realized?

4. Cold Cereals, Inc., fails and is forced to liquidate. The balance sheet upon liquidation is given in Table 9.3.

   The assets in liquidation bring the stated balance sheet figures. One advantage to banks of compensating balances is the right of offset; should a firm fail, the amount it has on deposit with the bank can be used to offset the bank loan. It need not be thrown into the pot to help satisfy the claims of all the creditors.

Table 9.3. Cold Cereals, Inc., Balance Sheet

Cash on deposit	$ 20,000	Accounts payable	$120,000
Other assets	90,000	Bank loan	50,000
Deficit	110,000	Capital	50,000
Total assets	$220,000	Total liabilities and net worth	$220,000

    a. How many cents on the dollar would the creditors receive if the bank did not have the right of offset?

    b. How many cents on the dollar would the general accounts payable creditors receive if the bank has the right of offset?

    c. With the right of offset, how much in absolute dollars will the bank receive?

    d. With the right of offset, what is the percentage recovery that the bank makes? How does this compare with the other creditors?

5. The working capital of the Devon Company has deteriorated in recent years and now stands as shown in Table 9.4.

Table 9.4. Devon Company Working Capital Position

Current Assets		Current Liabilities	
Cash	$ 20,000	Trade payables	$ 70,000
Receivables	50,000	Notes payable	30,000
Inventory	80,000		
Total current assets	$150,000	Total current liabilities	$100,000

Note: Since only the working capital portion of the balance sheet is presented, the statement need not "balance."

    a. Compute the current and quick ratios.

    b. A $30,000 short-term bank loan backed by a pledge of receivables is contemplated. Compute the liquidity ratios assuming the loan is made.

    c. A sale of $30,000 of receivables to a factor is contemplated. Compute the liquidity ratios assuming the receivables are factored, the funds withdrawn immediately, and the notes paid off.

6. Nevada Machine Company has experienced a rapid growth of sales in recent years. Control, however, has been lax and profits have not kept pace. The result has been a tightened financial condition. Further growth in sales is anticipated, and additional financing required. The financial condition of Nevada Machine Company appears in Table 9.5.

Table 9.5. Nevada Machine Company Balance Sheet
December 31, 1976

Cash		$ 60,000	Accounts payable	$150,000
Accounts receivable		200,000	Bank notes	350,000
Inventory		240,000	Common stock	200,000
Plant and equipment	$400,000		Retained earnings	100,000
Depreciation	100,000	300,000		
Total assets		$800,000	Total liabilities and net worth	$800,000

Other pertinent data are

1. Sales during the past year totaled $1,200,000. Sales are made evenly throughout the year.
2. Purchases are normally 50 percent of sales.
3. The inventory cost is 80 percent of sales.
4. The machines are sold on a net 30-day basis. All sales are on credit.
5. Inventory should equal a 45-day supply.
6. Purchases are also on a net 30-day basis.
    a. Compute the liquidity ratios, the excess receivables and inventory being carried, and the extent to which Nevada is not paying its suppliers promptly.
    b. Nevada Machine plans to factor $150,000 of receivables, pay off its suppliers to the net 30-day level, and with the remaining portion pay off part of the unsecured notes payable. The banker has been exerting pressure for some payment. Compute the effect this plan will have on the liquidity ratios. How much of the bank loan can be repaid if the deal goes through? Do you see any difficulty in Nevada Machine arranging this deal?
    c. The factoring deal falls through. The bank reluctantly decides to go along for one more year, provided management agrees to have the firm's working capital position at year's end in a satisfactory condition—receivables, inventory and payables at the above indicated normal levels. Sales are expected to be $1,500,000, profit after income taxes 10 percent of sales, no dividends will be paid, replacements are to equal depreciation charges, and cash should be 5 percent of sales. Draw up the pro forma balance sheet and determine the extent of the bank's loan to Nevada Machine. By what amount would the bank's loan be decreased or increased?
    d. Draw up a source and application of funds statement to show the anticipated flow of funds.
    e. Calculate the firm's liquidity ratios and comment on the anticipated working capital position.
    f. Sales and earnings develop as anticipated, plant and equipment and depreciation remain the same, but cash drops to $50,000, receivables stand at 45 days, inventory at 90 days, and payables at 60 days. The bank has financed the

expansion. Draw up the pro forma balance sheet showing the amount of bank loan now outstanding.

g. The bank now calls a halt and demands that by the end of the year its entire loan be paid off. In addition, $100,000 of new equipment must be purchased. Disregard depreciation. You are called in to recommend a plan of action to meet the bank's demand. Draw up a source and application of funds statement to highlight your recommendations.

Selected References

Abraham, A. B., "Factoring—The New Frontier for Commercial Banks," *The Journal of Commercial Bank Lending,* 53 (Apr. 1971), pp. 32–43.

Addison, E. T., "Factoring: A Case History," *Financial Executive,* 31 (Nov. 1963), pp. 32–33.

Adler, M., "Administration of Inventory Loans under the Uniform Commercial Code," *The Journal of Commercial Bank Lending,* 52 (Apr. 1970), pp. 55–60.

Agemian, C. A., "Maintaining an Effective Bank Relationship," *Financial Executive,* 32 (Jan. 1964), pp. 24–28.

Benson, G. J., "Commercial Bank Price Discrimination against Small Loans: An Empirical Study," *Journal of Finance,* 19 (Dec. 1964), pp. 631–643.

Brosky, J. J., *The Implicit Cost of Trade Credit and Theory of Optimal Terms of Sale.* New York: Credit Research Foundation, 1969.

Cates, D. C., and J. R. Olson, "Do Corporations Properly Analyze Banks," *Financial Executive,* 34 (Sept. 1966), pp. 22–24 ff.

Christe, R. A., "New Developments in the Commercial Paper Market," *Industrial Banker,* 35 (Aug. 1969), pp. 10–13 ff.

Daniels, F. L., S. C. Legg, and E. C. Yuille, "Accounts Receivable and Related Inventory Financing," *Journal of Commercial Bank Lending,* 52 (July 1970), pp. 38–53.

Edwards, R. E., "Finance Companies and Their Creditors," *Journal of Commercial Bank Lending,* 54 (Oct. 1971), pp. 2–10.

Fisher, D. J., "Factoring—An Industry on the Move," *The Conference Board Record,* 9 (Apr. 1972), pp. 42–45.

Flechig, T. G., "The Effects of Concentration on Bank Loan Rates," *Journal of Finance,* 20 (May 1965), pp. 298–311.

Gibson, W. E., "Compensating Balance Requirements," *National Banking Review,* 2 (Mar. 1965), pp. 298–311.

Gordon, R. L., "Talking Business with a Banker," *Financial Executive,* 35 (Feb. 1967), pp. 10 ff.

Harris, D. G., "Rationing Credit to Business: More than Interest Rates," *Business Review— Federal Reserve Bank of Philadelphia* (Aug. 1970), pp. 3–14.

————, "Some Evidence on Differential Lending Practices at Commercial Banks," *Journal of Finance,* 28 (Dec. 1973), pp. 1303–1311.

Hayes, D. A., *Bank Lending Policies: Issues and Practices.* Ann Arbor, Mich.: University of Michigan Press, 1964.

Holmes, W., "Market Values of Inventories—Perils and Pitfalls," *Journal of Commercial Bank Lending,* 55 (Apr. 1973), pp. 30–36.

Levenson, A. M., "Interest Rate and Cost Differentials in Bank Lending to Small and Large Businesses," *Review of Economics and Statistics,* 44 (May 1962), pp. 190–197.

Nadler, P. S., "Compensating Balances and the Prime at Twilight," *Harvard Business Review,* 50 (Jan.–Feb. 1972), pp. 112–130.

Popma, J., "A Behind-the-Scenes Look at Factoring," *Credit and Financial Management*, 65 (May 1963), pp. 31–33.

Robinson, R. I., *The Management of Bank Funds*, 2d ed. New York: McGraw-Hill, 1962.

Schadrack, F. C., Jr., "Demand and Supply in the Commercial Paper Market," *Journal of Finance*, 25 (Sept. 1970), pp. 837–852.

Seiler, J., "Commercial Financing Risks Outlined for Bankers," *Burroughs Clearing House*, 56 (Jan. 1972), pp. 22 ff.

Stone, B., "How Secure is Secured Financing under the Code?" *Burroughs Clearing House*, 50 (Apr. 1966), pp. 46 ff.

Stone, B. K., "The Cost of Bank Loans," *Journal of Financial and Quantitative Analysis*, 7 (Dec. 1972), pp. 2077–2086.

Wellman, M. T., "Field Warehousing—Protective Measures!" *Robert Morris Associates Bulletin*, 47 (Mar. 1965), pp. 302–312.

part three
THE MANAGEMENT
OF FIXED ASSETS

10

THE TECHNIQUES OF CAPITAL BUDGETING

AN OVERVIEW OF CAPITAL BUDGETING

Capital budgeting involves evaluating investment alternatives and ranking them in order of descending attractiveness. Once ranked, the question is whether all, none, or only a limited number of projects should be accepted. As the number of projects accepted increases, so does the firm's need for capital.

For a firm, the list of proposed investments traces out its demand curve for funds. Since all proposed investments are likely to differ in terms of their economic attractiveness, management will seek capital for the most attractive investment first and then seek to finance the purchase of the less attractive alternatives. Finally, at some point they decide that the remaining proposals are not sufficiently attractive to justify investment.

Investors following somewhat the same procedure trace out the firm's supply curve of funds. An individual firm represents only one of a large number of alternatives which they consider when making a decision as to where their capital should be allocated. They will not increase the flow of capital to a firm unless they can expect a larger return on their investment than can be earned on other alternatives. Therefore if an increasing allocation of funds is to be supplied to a firm, these funds will be associated with an increasing rate of return expectation on the part of investors. The interaction of these supply and demand curves is illustrated in Figure 10.1.

Underlying the construction of this diagram is the assumption that for a capital investment to be economically justified, the revenue flows from the

Figure 10.1. The supply and demand for capital by the firm.

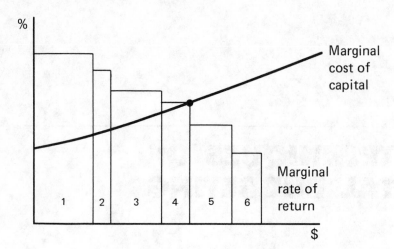

project must be sufficient to cover not only all its direct and indirect operating costs, but also the rate of return requirements of investors. The costs of capital are as much a real cost of doing business as are the more familiar costs of the other factors of production. Economists have concluded that the optimal investment policy for a firm is to invest in projects in order of decreasing attractiveness until the marginal rate of return (MRR) on the last project is equal to the marginal cost of the last dollar of capital supplied to the firm (MCC). Following this maxim, the firm in Figure 10.1 would accept projects 1, 2, 3, 4 and reject projects 5 and 6.

Capital budgeting introduces the most important theoretical concept to be covered in this book—the theory of valuation. The concept underlying this theory is that all business assets derive their value from the services they are expected to provide over future periods of time. Valuation theory, then, has two features. First, it specifies that current value is a function of future events which can never be known with certainty. Second, it requires that this series of future events be processed so that they can be evaluated at a single point of time, usually the present. The theory which can be concisely and simply stated in one or two sentences actually is very complex in application.

To the businessman, the two most important applications deal with capital assets and the firm's securities. This chapter discusses capital assets and Chapter 18 discusses securities.

PROCEDURES FOR RANKING INVESTMENT PROPOSALS

Table 10.1 presents a set of six projects which are proposed for investment. In addition to the information included in this table, several assumptions are made. First, all the projects are of equivalent risk. Thus the differences which may appear among the projects will be the result of differences in the way in which they are evaluated. The inclusion of risk into capital budgeting analysis is the topic of Chapter 12.

Table 10.1. The Cost and Expected Revenue Projections for Six Proposed Investments

| Investment | Cost | Expected Revenue Flow in Year | | | |
		1	2	3	4
A	$20,000	$20,000	$0	$0	$ 0
B	20,000	8,000	8,000	8,000	8,000
C	20,000	20,000	8,000	7,000	6,000
D	20,000	15,000	7,000	6,000	6,000
E	20,000	6,000	6,000	6,000	20,000
F	20,000	7,500	7,500	8,000	9,000

Second, cash outflows (costs) occur at the beginning of the year and cash inflows (revenues) occur at the end of the year. This assumption is a departure from reality but serves to simplify the analysis.

Third, all six projects have the same initial cost. As with the other assumptions, this assumption is made so that attention may be concentrated on the techniques used in capital budgeting analysis.

Fourth, the revenue flows shown in Table 10.1 are defined as the net income from the investment plus the annual depreciation taken on the investment. The discussion of the reasons underlying this specific definition has been deferred until the next chapter.

Ranking Projects by Inspection

The problem which confronts us in Table 10.1 is one which businessmen have had to confront for years. Probably the first and most frequently used approach is to examine the characteristics of the projects and make the decision as to their relative desirability on the basis of intuition. Given that businessmen are not generally known for their stupidity, we suspect many good decisions have been made using this approach.

How much progress could be made using this technique? A visual examination of the six projects in Table 10.1 indicates some easy conclusions. First, compare project A and project C. As far as cost and the expected revenue flow in the first year are concerned, the projects are identical. However, project C has a positive revenue flow in years 2, 3, and 4, and project A has no revenue flow in these years; thus it appears that project C is more desirable than project A. As a second step, compare project B with project F. Over the four years of their economic life, both projects promise to return a total of $32,000 in expected benefits. However, in the first two years project B returns $500 more per year than project F, and as intuition might indicate, a preference for receiving the same return earlier rather than later, project B would probably be rated higher than project F.

A comparison of project C with the other five projects indicates that it is the most desirable proposal of the six. Project C has the largest total revenue flow and, in addition, receives the greatest proportion of its revenue flow in the early rather than the later years. Thus we see that a reasonable amount of progress can be made in evaluating these investment proposals just through intuitive reasoning. Unfortunately this is not always the case, and further analysis indicates the nature of the problems which remain.

A comparison of project D with project E illustrates one of these problems. Project D promises a total revenue flow of $34,000, of which a substantial proportion is expected to be received in the first two years. On the other hand, project E promises a larger revenue flow, $38,000. The problem is that the largest part of the revenue flow of project E does not occur until the last year of its economic life. Intuition does not provide a quick easy answer to the question of whether it is better to have a larger revenue flow which has to be waited for or a somewhat smaller revenue flow that occurs quicker.

Actually a fundamental problem remains to be solved. Assume the firm had $20,000 available to invest and that it could not obtain any additional capital. While intuition indicates that project C is the best of the six projects, it does not indicate if the project is sufficiently attractive to justify investment. This raises another but equally important aspect of the capital budgeting problem. Not only must we be able to rank investment projects in order of their relative attractiveness, we must also have some standard of performance which enables us to decide whether all, none, or only some of the projects should be undertaken. And while an individual may in some instances be willing to state that a certain project is so obviously profitable that it should be accepted, this is hardly precise or rigorous enough to be applied to a large number of proposals. Therefore, while some progress can be made by the process of inspection, a number of problems exist which remain to be solved.

Ranking Projects by Payback

Another technique in widespread use is the ranking of investment proposals by the payback period. The payback period is the number of years which it takes the project to recover its original cost. In terms of ranking projects then, the shorter the payback period, the better the project.

For example, applying the payback period to project B and project D yields the following results. In the case of project B, because the revenue flow is expected to be constant over the project's economic life, the payback period can be calculated by dividing the annual revenue flow into the cost of the asset. Therefore, the payback period for project B (PB_B) is

$$PB_B = \frac{\$20,000}{\$8,000} = 2\frac{1}{2} \text{ years}$$

However, when dealing with project D where the revenue flow is not constant from year to year, the payback period must be computed in a step-by-step fashion. To recover the $20,000 cost of project D, payback requires the use of the entire $15,000 revenue flow in the first year plus $5000 of the $7000 from the second year. By convention, the payback period for project D would be expressed as $1\frac{5}{7}$ years, even though this violates the previous assumption that revenue flows occur at the end of the year:

Year	Remaining Cost Balance	Annual Revenue Flow Needed
1	$20,000	$15,000
2	5,000	$ 5,000 of $7,000
3	0	0
4	0	0

Table 10.2 presents a summary of the payback computation along with the ranking accorded each project by this criterion. When a comparison is made between the ranking assigned by the payback criterion and some of the conclusions we might arrive at through the process of inspection, some interesting problems appear. First, Table 10.2 shows that payback ranks

project *A* as equivalent to project *C*. However, an intuitive analysis of the two projects indicated that project *C* was superior to project *A*. This conclusion was arrived at by noting that while the revenue flows from the two projects are equivalent in the first year, project *C* continues to provide benefits in the remaining 3 years and project *A* does not. This example illustrates an important characteristic of payback. When this criterion is mechanically applied to proposed investments, all benefits that are expected to be received after the payback period are ignored in the analysis.

Table 10.2. Proposed Investments Ranked by Payback Period

Project	Payback Period	Ranking
A	1 year	1
B	2½ years	4
C	1 year	1
D	1⅝ years	3
E	3¹⁄₁₀ years	6
F	2⅝ years	5

However, only the most extreme proponent of this approach would ever suggest that it be interpreted in this manner. In practice, revenue flows occurring after the payback period are in some undefined way included in the analysis and, at the least, are used to make decisions when only small marginal differences in payback exist between competing projects. Actually the treatment of these "benefits after the payback period" varies widely from firm to firm. This is precisely the problem with this criterion. If in fact these benefits after the payback period can be forecast and if the firm has devoted valuable managerial time and effort to develop these figures, they should be considered in the analysis in some consistent and rational way.

A further characteristic of payback is that it ignores the *timing* of the receipt of benefits expected to be received *prior* to the end of the payback period. Like payback's lack of consideration of benefits which occur after the payback period, the problems caused by this characteristic depend on the way in which payback is used. If the criterion is blindly applied to the forecast data, some bad decisions are bound to be made.

To this point the discussion has been limited to some of the major issues involved in the ranking of projects. As indicated in the introductory comments to this chapter, ranking is only part of the investment decision. A complete solution requires a decision rule that enables the financial manager to determine which, if any, of the projects should be accepted. Without the existence of such a rule, investment might be made in projects that are simply the best out of a number of bad alternatives.

The payback criterion does not provide this decision rule. In practice, a capital budget review committee might specify the maximum payback period that is acceptable. For instance, if the firm in the present example had specified the maximum payback period as three years, then projects A, B, C, D, and F would be accepted for investment whereas project E would be rejected. Is this a reasonable procedure? The answer depends on what factors are considered in setting the maximum acceptable payback period. Many factors could enter into this decision, but probably the more important would be the liquidity requirements of the firm, the average or normal life of the products produced by the company, the nature of the new investments in relation to existing products, and risk. Suffice it to say that the more thought and analysis given to the specification of the maximum allowable payback period, the better the results.

Ranking Projects by Average Rate of Return

Another procedure for the ranking of investment proposals is the average rate of return (ARR). Unlike the payback period, this procedure produces a familiar percentage rate of return figure which is then used to rank the alternative investments. The precise definition of terms used varies considerably from user to user, but most definitions are similar in form to that previously discussed for profitability ratios:

$$\text{average rate of return} = \frac{\text{income concept}}{\text{asset concept}}$$

The ARR technique generally uses an accounting definition for income rather than the definition used for the benefits as specified for the other techniques. Consequently, to arrive at the net income figures to be used in this computation, the appropriate depreciation figure has to be subtracted from each of the values given in Table 10.1. For example, using straight-line depreciation, the annual depreciation expense for project C is $5000. Subtracting depreciation from each of the values for project C produces the following net income figures: year 1, $15,000; year 2, $3000; Year 3, $2000; and Year 4, $1000.

Given this definition of income, a commonly used definition of the ARR is

$$\text{ARR} = \frac{\text{average annual income}}{\text{average investment}}$$

The numerator is computed by arithmetically averaging the annual net income figures. Thus for project C the average annual net income is

$$\frac{\$15,000 + \$3000 + \$2000 + \$1000}{4} = \$5250$$

The denominator, average investment, is intended to reflect the average amount of capital committed to the investment over its economic life. Therefore, like the numerator, the denominator is computed by averaging the depreciated asset values of the investment. At each point in time, project C's depreciated asset value assuming straight-line depreciation would be as follows:

End of Year	Depreciated Asset Value
0	$20,000
1	15,000
2	10,000
3	5,000
4	0

Using these values, the denominator is computed as

$$\frac{\$20,000 + \$15,000 + \$10,000 + \$5000 + \$0}{5} = \$10,000[1]$$

Then the ARR for project C is

$$\text{ARR}_c = \frac{\$5250}{\$10,000} = 52.5 \text{ percent}$$

[1] A shorthand method of computing average investment is possible when the asset is depreciated using the straight-line method. In this case, depreciation is a linear function, and average investment can be obtained by adding together the beginning and ending depreciated asset values and dividing by two ($20,000 + 0/2 = $10,000).

Table 10.3 summarizes the results of the ARR computation for all six projects and repeats the payback rankings for comparison purposes. As would be expected, using the ARR criterion, projects are ranked from highest to lowest based on the magnitude of the ARR.

Table 10.3. Proposed Investments Ranked by ARR and Payback

Project	ARR	ARR Ranking	Payback Ranking
A	0%*	6	1
B	30.0	4	4
C	52.5	1	1
D	35.0	3	3
E	45.0	2	6
F	30.0	4	5

* The ARR for project A is 0 because with only a 1-year life, the depreciation taken on the asset in the first year is $20,000. Net income is therefore 0.

The characteristics of ARR can best be illustrated by discussing the relationship between the rankings assigned to payback and those assigned by ARR. A substantial difference in ranking exists between the two techniques for project A. The fact that ARR ranks project A as the worst project of the six whereas payback ranks it in a tie as the best is a result of the ARR criterion taking into account all the benefit flows from the projects, not just those up to the payback period. In this sense, the ARR criterion is a more sophisticated form of analysis than is the payback criterion.

A further examination of Table 10.3 shows that ARR ranks project B and project F as being equivalent. The reason for the equivalency in ranking of the two projects is that ARR treats every dollar of benefit flow as equivalent, no matter when it is expected to be received. Thus while ARR does consider all the benefits expected to be received on the project, the averaging process used in its computation assumes the benefits are distributed equally over every year during the life of the project. As pointed out in the discussion of ranking by inspection, there is reason to believe that a better solution is possible.

The ARR criterion is like payback in that once the projects have been ranked, a decision rule must be determined through some additional form of analysis. The ARR criterion, by itself, does not provide a standard against which the expected performance of the new projects may be evaluated. On the surface it might seem as if the ARR criterion is preferable in that its computation produces a rate of return measure which is familiar to most businessmen. Care must be taken that familiarity is not interpreted as meaning better, because a standard can be set for the ARR criterion just as arbitrarily as for any other form of analysis.

PROJECT EVALUATION BY DISCOUNTED CASH FLOW TECHNIQUES

The Meaning of the Time Value of Money

The preceding discussion has shown that both the payback criterion and the ARR criterion have certain limitations which must be accounted for by the analyst if these criteria are to be used intelligently. The search for a form of analysis that did not require as much supplemental analysis resulted in the discounted cash flow approach to valuation. As a technique, the discounted cash flow approaches are conceptually superior to the other approaches that have been discussed in that they (1) take into account all future benefits, (2) account for the timing of when the benefits are received, and (3) provide an accept–reject decision rule in addition to ranking projects.

The premise underlying the discounted cash flow models is that the value of an asset is equal to the present value of all the expected benefits to be received from that asset in the future. These approaches explicitly recognize that money has a time value, that is, a dollar today is worth more than one dollar to be received one year from now. There are at least two reasons why a current sum of money might be valued more highly than a future sum of money.

Uncertainty. The first is the existence of uncertainty. Any decision which has been made on the basis of a forecast of future events has the potential of being incorrect. Consequently, when given a choice between the receipt of $1 today versus one year from today, most individuals would prefer the current dollar. This preference would exist because of the large number of events which could occur between today and one year from today that might put receipt of the future dollar in jeopardy. These events might be of the nature of a change in the economy in the case of a capital investment or they might take the form of a broken promise by an individual. Whatever the nature of these events, a future promise or expectation must be regarded as being uncertain relative to the occurrence of a current event.

Because of uncertainty, a common practice is to regard the receipt of a future sum of money as being less valuable than a current sum of money. Consequently, adjustments are often made to the value of dollars to be received at different points in time to reflect differences in the likelihood that these dollars will actually be received. The most common way in which this type of an adjustment is made is through an increase in the rate of return demanded on an investment.

Alternative Uses. A second reason why the time value of money needs to be accounted for is that capital has alternative uses. As discussed in the introduction to this chapter, capital is allocated to a firm only after it has been determined that the uses to which the firm will put the capital are at least as good as other alternative uses. Thus capital has an "opportunity cost" defined as the rate of return that could be earned on the next best alternative investment. However, to be able to make decisions about the entire capital budget of the firm, the opportunity cost concept must be more general than defining it on a project by project basis. For capital budgeting purposes the opportunity cost concept is generalized to apply to all the funds provided by investors and is measured by the rate of return which they demand on their investment. This rate of return is referred to as the cost of capital.

The Mathematics of the Time Value of Money

The concept of opportunity cost leads to the discounted cash flow approach to capital budgeting. To understand this approach we must familiarize ourselves with the mathematics of compound interest and discount. As the formulas for compound discount are derived from the law of compound interest, we first develop the case of compound interest. Assume an investor currently has P dollars of capital which he can invest at a compound rate of interest i and desires to know how much he will have at the end of a certain number of years n. The ending amount of money A_n can be determined by constructing a schedule similar to that shown in Table 10.4.

Table 10.4. The Mechanics of Compound Interest

P = beginning principal
iP = amount of interest earned during year 1
$A_1 = P + iP = P(1 + i)$
= principal plus interest at end of year 1
$iP(1 + i)$ = interest during year 2
$A_2 = P(1 + i) + iP(1 + i) = P(1 + i)(1 + i) = P(1 + i)^2$
= principal plus interest at end of year 2

This procedure can be carried out for any number of years desired and can be generalized by the equation

$$A_n = P(1 + i)^n$$

For example, at 10 percent interest, $1 invested today would be worth $1.10 at the end of the first year. Then, if this $1.10 is reinvested at 10 percent interest for a second year, the total amount of money available at the end of the second year is $1.21. The critical point which distinguishes compound interest from simple interest is that in compound interest, all interest which is earned is assumed to be reinvested and therefore interest is earned on interest. This point can be illustrated symbolically by carrying out the multiplication in the two-period case. From the general rule of compound interest the amount of money available at the end of the second year is equal to

$$A_2 = P(1 + i)^2$$
$$= P(1 + 2i + i^2)$$
$$= P + 2(iP) + i(Pi)$$

Thus the ending amount of money has three components, (1) the beginning principal P, (2) two years of simple interest $2(iP)$, and (3) the interest earned during the second year on the first year's interest $i(Pi)$. In our example, the dollar figures corresponding to these components would be (1) the $1 of orignal principal, (2) two times the simple interest of $0.10 per year, and (3) the interest earned at 10 percent on the $0.10 simple interest in the first year or $0.1 \times \$0.10 = \$0.01$. As before, the sum of these components is $1.21.

The law of compound interest can be expanded to cover the case where a certain amount is expected to be invested at the beginning of each year over a period of time. For instance, in the preceding example we assumed $1.00 was invested today and wanted to find out what it would be worth at 10 percent interest in two years. The problem we are now addressing is what would be the total amount of money at the end of the second year if we invested $1.00 today and an additional $1.00 one year from now. As we saw, the terminal value of the first dollar was

$$A_2 = \$1.00(1.10)^2 = \$1.21$$

Now an additional dollar is invested at the beginning of the second year. As this dollar will only be invested for one year, it will have a terminal value of

$$A_2{}^1 = \$1.00(1.10)^1 = \$1.10$$

Thus the terminal value of this sequence of investments will simply be the sum of the two individual terminal values. This can be expressed as

$$
\begin{aligned}
\text{total terminal value} &= A_2 + A_2{}^1 \\
&= \$1.00(1.10)^2 + \$1.00(1.10)^1 \\
&= \$1.21 + \$1.10 \\
&= \$2.31
\end{aligned}
$$

In a more general form, this is simply

$$
\begin{aligned}
\text{total terminal value} &= A_2 + A_2{}^1 \\
&= P(1 + i)^2 + P(1 + i) \\
&= P[(1 + i)^2 + (1 + i)^1] \\
&= P \sum_{t=1}^{2} (1 + i)^t
\end{aligned}
$$

where

$$\sum_{t=1}^{2}(1 + i)^t = (1 + i)^1 + (1 + i)^2$$

This situation is referred to as the value of an annuity, and as the above discussion indicates, is simply the summation of the values of a series of single investments. For computational convenience, compound interest factors are provided in Tables A.3 and A.4 of the Appendix at the back of the book. Table A.3 gives the compound interest factors for a current investment of $1. Table A.4 gives the compound interest factors for a series or annuity of $1 investments. Table A.4 is simply the summation of the factors in Table A.3.

In capital budgeting, the financial manager is dealing with a different but highly related problem. Rather than being interested in the amount of money he will have at the end of a certain number of years, his problem is one of forecasting future revenue flows for a number of projects and then evaluating the different projects at a common point in time, usually the present. Therefore, the problem of concern to the financial manager is the reverse of the problem considered by compound interest, that is, management wants to know what is the value today of a series of benefit flows to be received at various points in time during the future. The answer to this question is obtained by solving the compound interest equation for P, the present sum of money, rather than for A_n, the sum of money at some future point in time. Thus

$$P = A_n \left(\frac{1}{1+t} \right)^n$$

is the general form of compound discount. The term $[1/(1+i)]^n$ is generally referred to as the compound discount factor, or for short, simply the discount factor. Thus in our example the present value of a dollar to be received one year from now, discounted at 10 percent, is

$$P = \$1.00 \left(\frac{1}{1.10} \right)^1$$
$$= \$1.00(0.909)$$
$$= \$0.909$$

As with the terminal value of an annuity, this analysis can be extended to cover the case of the present value of a series (or annuity) of future revenue flows. The formula for the present value of a series of investments is simply the summation of the present values of a series of individual investments. Assume we expect to receive \$1 at the end of each of the next two years.

$$\text{present value of 1st dollar} = \$1.00 \left(\frac{1}{1.10} \right)^1 = \$1.00(0.909) = \$0.909$$

$$\text{present value of 2nd dollar} = \$1.00 \left(\frac{1}{1.10} \right)^2 = \$1.00(0.826) = \$0.826$$

$$\text{total present value} = \$1.00 \left(\frac{1}{1.10} \right)^1 + \$1.00 \left(\frac{1}{1.10} \right)^2 = \$0.909 + \$0.826$$
$$= \$1.735$$
$$= \$1.00 \sum_{t=1}^{2} \frac{1}{(1+0.10)^t} = \$1.735$$

The general formula for the present value of a series (or annuity) of expected receipts is

$$\text{present value} = \sum_{t=1}^{n} \frac{A_N}{(1+i)^t}$$

Tables A.1 and A.2 in the Appendix at the back of the book present compound discount factors. Table A.1 presents the discount factors for $1 to be received at the end of the nth year. Table A.2 summarizes the factors in Table A.1 and therefore presents the discount factors for an annuity of $1 to be received for n years.

The Net Present Value Model

Within the context of discounted cash flow, there are two general models in use for capital budgeting decisions, the net present value model and the internal rate of return model. The net present value (NPV) of a project is defined as the present value of the cash benefits minus the present value of the cash outflows, with both flows being discounted at the cost of capital. The decision rule used with the net present value model is to accept all projects whose NPV ≥ 0 and to reject those projects for which NPV < 0. In the context of a capital budgeting problem, the cash outflows are usually identified as simply the cost of the investment, which for computational purposes is assumed to take place at time zero. Therefore, in symbolic terms the net present value of a project is

$$\text{NPV} = \sum_{t=1}^{n} \frac{\text{CF}_t}{(1+k)^t} - I$$

where

$$\text{CF}_t = \text{cash flow at end of year } t$$
$$I = \text{cost of project}$$
$$k = \text{cost of capital}$$

For example, the NPV for project B, using 8 percent as the cost of capital is

$$\text{NPV}_B = \sum_{t=1}^{4} \frac{\$8000}{(1+0.08)^t} - \$20{,}000$$
$$= \$8000(3.312) - \$20{,}000$$
$$= \$26{,}496 - \$20{,}000$$
$$= \$6496$$

For project C, NPV is

$$\text{NPV}_C = \frac{\$20,000}{(1.08)^1} + \frac{\$8000}{(1.08)^2} + \frac{\$7000}{(1.08)^3} + \frac{\$6000}{(1.08)^4} - \$20,000$$

$$= \$20,000(0.926) + \$8000(0.857) + \$7000(0.794) + \$6000(0.735)$$
$$- \$20,000$$

$$= \$18,520 + \$6856 + \$5558 + \$4410 - \$20,000$$

$$= \$35,344 - \$20,000$$

$$= \$15,344$$

Thus project C has a higher NPV than project B and consequently would be ranked as a better project. At the same time, both projects have positive NPVs, and therefore both would be accepted by the firm. Table 10.5 summarizes the NPVs and the corresponding NPV ranking for each project in addition to showing the payback and ARR rankings for comparison purposes.

Table 10.5. Proposed Investments Ranked by Payback, ARR and NPV

Investment	Payback Rank	ARR Rank	NPV	NPV Rank
A	1	6	−$ 1480	6
B	4	4	+$ 6496	4
C	1	1	+$15,344	1
D	3	3	+$ 9063	3
E	6	2	+$10,162	2
F	5	4	+$ 6340	5

An analysis of the results in Table 10.5 shows that the NPV approach successfully handles the ranking inconsistencies that occurred in payback and ARR. NPV shows the clear distinction which exists between project A and project C, which was ignored by the strict application of payback. It also accounts for the differences in the timing of the cash flows between project B and project F, which were ignored by ARR. Finally, the NPV approach yields the decision that projects B through F should be accepted whereas project A should be rejected. As the previous discussion pointed out, this decision cannot be provided by the other techniques without supplementary analysis.

The Internal Rate of Return Model

The internal rate of return (IRR) approach, as contrasted to NPV, does not solve the present value formula for the excess present value but rather is that rate of return which makes the present value of the cash inflows equal to the present value of the cash outflows. Once this rate of return is obtained, it is compared to the cost of capital, and the accept–reject decision is made according to the following rule. If IRR $\geq$ cost of capital, then the project should be accepted. If IRR $<$ cost of capital, then the project is rejected. This approach is stated symbolically as

$$I = \sum_{t=1}^{n} \frac{CF_t}{(1 + IRR)^t}$$

where IRR is the solution internal rate of return.

A comparison of the IRR equation with the NPV equation shows that they are the same but are solved for different values:

$$\text{net present value} \quad NPV = \sum_{t=1}^{n} \frac{CF_t}{(1 + k)^t} - I$$

$$\text{internal rate of return} \quad 0 = \sum_{t=1}^{n} \frac{CF_t}{(1 + IRR)^t} - I$$

If IRR is equal to k, then the project would have an NPV equal to zero. If IRR $> k$, then the NPV must be greater than 0. And finally, if IRR $< k$, then NPV < 0.

A minor inconvenience is that the IRR cannot be solved without going through a trial and error process. This inconvenience is serious if a large number of projects have to be ranked and the computations done by hand. The procedure can be programmed if a computer is available.

In the case of project B a trial-and-error process is not necessary because the cash flows of the project are forecast to be an annuity. If we substitute the values for project B into the IRR equation, the solution is obtained directly:

$$I = \sum_{t=1}^{n} \frac{CF_t}{(1 + IRR)^t}$$

$$\$20,000 = \$8000 \sum_{t=1}^{4} \frac{1}{(1 + IRR)^t}$$

$$\frac{\$20,000}{\$ \ 8000} = \sum_{t=1}^{4} \frac{1}{(1 + IRR)^t} = 2.5$$

As shown in this computation, since the benefit flow is an annuity, the equation can be solved for the discount factor that equates a flow of $8000 for 4 years with the $20,000 cost.   Having determined that the discount factor is 2.5, it is necessary to consult the annuity tables to determine what discount rate corresponds to a discount factor of 2.5 for four years.   The IRR for project B turns out to be 22 percent.

For project C the solution is not this simple and a trial-and-error process must be used.   Assume that the first guess for the IRR is 20 percent. Obtaining the discount factors from the present value table and multiplying produces the following result:

Year	Benefit Flow	Discount Factor	Present Value
1	$20,000	0.833	$16,660
2	8,000	0.694	5,552
3	7,000	0.579	4,053
4	6,000	0.482	2,892
Present value of benefits			$29,157

Remembering that the IRR is defined as the discount rate at which the present value of the benefits is equal to the present value of the cost, a comparison with the $20,000 cost indicates that further computations will be necessary.   In this case the 20 percent discount rate results in the present value of the benefits being $9157 larger than the present value of the cost. Since an inverse relationship exists between the magnitude of the discount rate and that of the discount factor, the discount rate must be raised to lower the present value of the benefits.   Unfortunately it is very difficult to intuitively estimate how much the discount rate must be raised in order to obtain the correct solution.   If we assume our next guess was 40 percent, the following solution is obtained:

Year	Benefit Flow	Discount Factor	Present Value
1	$20,000	0.714	$14,280
2	8,000	0.510	4,080
3	7,000	0.364	2,548
4	6,000	0.260	1,560
Present value of benefits			$22,468

As before, the present value of the benefits is larger than the present value of the cost, indicating that the 40 percent discount rate is not high enough. Raising the discount rate to 50 percent yields a present value of $20,152 and at 55 percent the present value is $19,149. It is reasonable to guesstimate that the IRR is approximately equal to 52 percent.[2]

Table 10.6 presents a summary of the IRR computations in addition to the results of the previous analysis. Having completed the ranking of the projects, the next step is to apply the IRR decision rule to determine the projects that would be accepted for investment and those that would be rejected. Using the previously assumed cost of capital of 8 percent, a comparison of this rate with the computed IRRs indicates that project A would be rejected and projects B through F would be accepted. Note that this is exactly the same set of conclusions as we arrived at by the use of the NPV approach. In fact, as is shown in the next section of this chapter, the NPV

Table 10.6. Proposed Investments Ranked by Payback, ARR, NPV, and IRR

Investment	Payback Rank	ARR Rank	NPV Rank	IRR	IRR Rank
A	1	6	6	0%	6
B	4	4	4	22%	4
C	1	1	1	52%	1
D	3	3	3	32%	2
E	6	2	2	25%	3
F	5	4	5	21%	5

[2] A suggested approach to attempting to arrive quickly at a solution for the IRR is to try and bracket the IRR with the second rate used. After present values are obtained that are both larger and smaller than cost, it is usually easier to estimate which rate the IRR is closer to. This approach was used in the solution presented here for project C but failed because we did not bracket the IRR on either the second or third guess.

and IRR approaches will always yield the same *accept or reject* decision for any given project.

Further analysis of Table 10.6, however, yields the somewhat disturbing result that the NPV and IRR criteria do not necessarily *rank* the projects in the same order. This point is highlighted by the dashed rectangle in Table 10.6 which shows that while NPV ranks project *E* ahead of project *D*, IRR ranks project *D* ahead of project *E*. The next section analyzes why this difference in rankings occurs.

The Reinvestment Rate Problem

As just noted, it is possible for two discounted cash flow approaches to produce differences in the ranking of projects. It might seem that exact rankings of projects are not of overwhelming importance because if the projects are profitable in an IRR or NPV sense, they will be accepted. This, however, is a misleading impression, as profitable projects are not always accepted. For example, if a firm is buying a machine to produce a new product, it will consider several machines produced by different manufacturers. Since only one machine is required, the proposed alternatives are referred to as being mutually exclusive, that is, when one is accepted, the other alternatives are automatically rejected. Consequently, the firm's concern is to purchase the most profitable machine, and the rankings assigned are of the utmost importance.

Another case where otherwise profitable projects are rejected is when a firm is faced with capital rationing. *Capital rationing* exists when the firm does not obtain and invest as much capital as would be consistent under the MRR=MCC analysis. This impediment to the proper functioning of the theory can and does occur in the real world for reasons that can be internal or external to the firm. For instance, some firms specify the amount of capital available for new investment prior to an analysis of the proposed projects. When the specified amount of capital has been exhausted during any one planning period, all remaining projects are postponed to some later period. Some projects which are profitable are foregone by such a policy. While the reasons for capital rationing are varied, the fact remains that often decisions must be made in this context. Thus the difference in the ranking of projects by NPV and IRR is very important and must be analyzed further.

In general there are two situations under which the NPV and IRR techniques produce different rankings. First, differences in rankings can occur if there are large differences in the *timing of the receipt of the cash flows* on alternative projects. Second, if the alternative projects have substantially *different costs*, then differences in rankings can also occur. Both of these possibilities will be discussed, but since the differences in rankings between project D and project E are caused by the differences in the timing of the cash flows, this point will be discussed first.

For the moment assume that project D and project E are the only investments currently being considered by the firm and that they are mutually exclusive. Table 10.7 summarizes the relevant data for these projects. As the previous discussion has pointed out, if the analyst were using the IRR criterion, project D would be accepted over project E. However, were the NPV criterion used, the opposite decision would be arrived at; project E would be preferred over project D because it has a higher NPV. Looking further into this problem, it is apparent that the timing of the cash flows is substantially different for the two projects. Project D receives its largest cash flow in the first year, whereas project E receives the largest cash flow in the last year. This difference together with the fact that the IRRs on both projects are substantially larger than the cost of capital combine to produce the differences in rankings.

Table 10.7. An Illustration of Two Projects Whose Costs Are Equal, Yet Have Conflicting Rankings

Project	Cost	1	2	3	4	IRR	NPV at 8%
D	$20,000	$15,000	$7,000	$6,000	$ 6,000	32%	$ 9,063
E	20,000	6,000	6,000	6,000	20,000	25%	10,162

To address the question, "Which of the two criteria yields the better answer?", it is useful to change perspective. Assume that the projects are evaluated at the end of their economic life rather than at the beginning. The project producing the largest amount of terminal wealth at the end of the four years becomes the better choice. Then from this perspective, the question becomes, "Which project will provide the highest terminal wealth, project D or project E?"

The answer depends on what the firm does with the cash flows it will receive from project D and project E over the intervening years. If the firm did nothing with the cash flows except to put them in a stagnant noninterest yielding bank account, the terminal wealth for the two projects would be the summation of their cash flows, or

terminal wealth: project D = $34,000 = $15,000 + $7000 + $6000 + $6000
terminal wealth: project E = $38,000 = $6000 + $6000 + $6000 + $20,000

This situation is the same as assuming that the cash flows are reinvested at a 0 percent rate of return, and under this assumption project E would be preferred as it produces the highest terminal value.

Extending this analysis further, assume that the firm could reinvest the cash flows at a rate of return equal to 8 percent, the cost of capital. Using this assumption, the terminal value of the two projects is computed as follows:

project D:

$$\begin{aligned}
\$15,000(1.08)^3 &= \$15,000(1.2597) = \$18,896 \\
7000(1.08)^2 &= 7000(1.1664) = 8165 \\
6000(1.08)^1 &= 6000(1.0800) = 6480 \\
6000(1.08)^0 &= 6000(1.0000) = 6000 \\
\text{total terminal value} & \qquad\qquad = \$39,541
\end{aligned}$$

project E:

$$\begin{aligned}
\$6000(1.08)^3 &= \$\ 6000(1.2597) = \$\ 7558 \\
6000(1.08)^2 &= 6000(1.1664) = 6998 \\
6000(1.08)^1 &= 6000(1.0800) = 6480 \\
2000(1.08)^0 &= 20,000(1.0000) = 20,000 \\
\text{total terminal value} & \qquad\qquad = \$41,036
\end{aligned}$$

In making this computation the cash flows are assumed to be received at the end of each period. Thus for an investment with a four-year life, when computing terminal values there are really only three reinvestment periods. This point is illustrated in Figure 10.2 which uses project D as an example.

The $15,000 received at the end of the first year is assumed to be reinvested at the beginning of the second year. Having selected the end of the fourth year as the point at which the terminal value is to be computed, Figure 10.2 shows that the $15,000 can be invested during the second, third, and fourth years, or for a total of three years. The terminal value of the $15,000 is therefore $\$15,000(1.08)^3 = \$18,896$.

As these computations indicate, when the cash flows of the two projects are assumed to be reinvested at a rate equal to the cost of capital of 8 percent, project E still has a higher terminal value than project D and therefore would be the preferred project. Note that this conclusion is the same conclusion arrived at by use of the NPV model.

Below we present two more computations of the terminal values of the two projects, one using a reinvestment rate of 13 percent and the other using a reinvestment rate of 20 percent.

Figure 10.2. The reinvestment of Project D's cash flows.

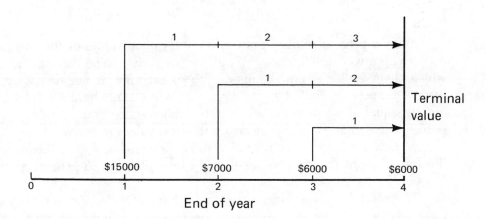

Reinvestment rate 13 percent:
project D:

$$\$15,000(1.13)^3 = \$15,000(1.4429) = \$21,644$$
$$7000(1.13)^2 = 7000(1.2769) = 8938$$
$$6000(1.13)^1 = 6000(1.13) = 6780$$
$$6000(1.13)^0 = 6000(1.0000) = 6000$$
$$\text{total terminal value} = \$43,362$$

project E:

$$\$\ 6000(1.13)^3 = \$\ 6000(1.4429) = \$\ 8657$$
$$6000(1.13)^2 = 6000(1.2769) = 7661$$
$$6000(1.13)^1 = 6000(1.1300) = 6780$$
$$20,000(1.13)^0 = 20,000(1.0000) = 20,000$$
$$\text{total terminal value} = \$43,098$$

Reinvestment rate 20 percent:
project D:

$$\$15,000(1.20)^3 = \$15,000(1.7280) = \$25,920$$
$$7000(1.20)^2 = 7000(1.4400) = 10,080$$
$$6000(1.20)^1 = 6000(1.2000) = 7200$$
$$6000(1.20)^0 = 6000(1.0000) = 6000$$
$$\text{total terminal value} = \$49,200$$

project E:

$$
\begin{aligned}
\$\ 6000(1.20)^3 &= \$\ 6000(1.7280) = \$10{,}368 \\
6000(1.20)^2 &= 6000(1.4400) = 8640 \\
6000(1.20)^1 &= 6000(1.2000) = 7200 \\
20{,}000(1.20)^0 &= 20{,}000(1.0000) = 20{,}000 \\
\text{total terminal value} &\qquad\qquad = \$46{,}208
\end{aligned}
$$

At a 13 percent reinvestment rate the terminal values of the two projects are approximately equal. (While we could determine the exact rate at which they would be equal, this degree of precision is not necessary for present purposes. The following discussion will assume terminal values are exactly equal at 13 percent.) When the reinvestment rate is raised to 20 percent, the ranking of the projects by terminal values reverses. At this rate project D has a larger terminal value than does project E, and therefore, if the firm thought that reinvestment could take place at 20 percent, project D would be the more attractive.

These relationships are illustrated in Figure 10.3. For reinvestment rates less than 13 percent, project E always yields a higher terminal value than does project D. And note that it is in this range that NPV computed using a cost of capital of 8 percent ranks project E above project D. However, for reinvestment rates above 13 percent project D yields a higher terminal value than project E and consequently would be the preferred investment. Notice also that the IRRs of project D and project E are both greater than 13 percent and that the ranking of the two projects by IRR is the same as the ranking of the two projects by terminal values when reinvestment rates greater than 13 percent are used.

This result should not be surprising when one reconsiders the power of compound interest and the difference in the timing of the cash flows on the two projects. Since project D has its largest cash flow at the beginning of the project's life, as the reinvestment rate is increased, the terminal value increases by having this large flow compounded for three years at higher and higher rates of interest. Conversely, since the largest cash flow in project E occurs at the end of the project's life, the terminal value of this project does not receive any benefit from an increase in the reinvestment rate, because this cash flow is never reinvested. In this situation, 13 percent is the "critical reinvestment rate" above which the early cash flows in project D receive a sufficient benefit from being compounded that the terminal value of project D becomes larger than that for project E.

This discussion shows that given a cost of capital of 8 percent, the NPV criterion will always yield the correct decision if actual reinvestment rates turn out to be less than 13 percent. However, if reinvestment rates were greater than 13 percent, then the IRR criterion would have yielded the better decision. Thus a correct decision not only depends on the character-

Figure 10.3. The terminal values of Projects D and E at selected reinvestment rates.

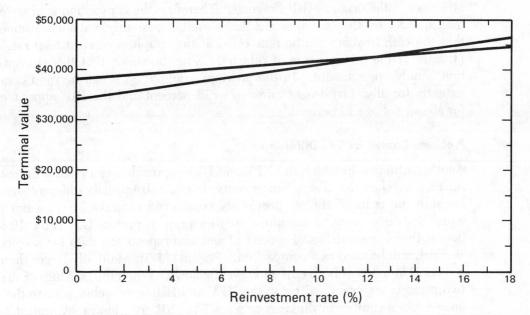

istics of the individual projects themselves, but also on the level of forecast reinvestment rates. This brings up the question of where forecast reinvestment rates come from. The answer is difficult as it is highly dependent on the nature of the business the firm is in and on the characteristics of the investment opportunities that will be available in those years. In our example, if the firm thought it would have highly profitable investment opportunities during the next year, it should follow the decision indicated by the IRR criterion. However, if management felt only average opportunities would be available (by average we mean an IRR in the 8–10 percent range), then the decision indicated by NPV would be the better.

A Note on Terminology

In the finance literature a convention has arisen over the use of the phrase "implied reinvestment rate." In the NPV approach, if we *assume* that the cash benefits can be reinvested at the cost of capital, then the terminal values of any number of competing investment projects will always bear the same relationship (ranking) to each other as did their net present values. Thus consistency in ranking is maintained between present values and terminal values when the NPV approach is used *if* we *assume* the existence of this "implied investment rate." Likewise, when using the IRR approach, if we *assume* that the cash benefits can be reinvested at the internal rate of return, then terminal value rankings will bear the same relationship to each other as did the original IRR rankings. Therefore the convention is to state that in order for the IRR approach to be used consistently, we must assume that the cash benefits can be reinvested at the "implied reinvestment rate" (that is, at the internal rate of return). Note, however, that this convention is only approximate. In the previous example NPV can be used consistently for all reinvestment rates up to 13 percent and the IRR approach for all rates above 13 percent.

Problems Caused by Size Differences

Another situation in which the NPV and IRR approaches can yield different rankings is when the alternative projects are of a substantially different size. Because the costs of the six previously considered projects were assumed equal, it is necessary to introduce another project, project G. Table 10.8 details the characteristics of project G and also repeats the data for project B which will be used as a comparison. Project G is substantially larger than project B in terms of both cost and revenue flows. When the rankings of the two projects are examined using the NPV and IRR approaches, we see that once again a conflict in rankings arises. The IRR criterion ranks project B ahead of project G, whereas the NPV criterion produces the reverse ranking. A large project might produce a larger NPV than a small project simply because of the magnitude of the numbers involved. This can occur even if the larger project is less profitable than the smaller project.

Table 10.8. An Illustration of Two Projects with Unequal Cost and Conflicting Rankings.

Project	Cost	Benefit Flow				IRR	8% NPV	PI
		1	2	3	4			
B	$20,000	$ 8,000	$ 8,000	$ 8,000	$ 8,000	22%	$6,496	1.32
G	40,000	15,000	15,000	15,000	15,000	18%	9,680	1.24

Such a discrepancy in ranking is caused by the fact that the NPV is expressed in absolute values. To remedy this problem, the usual approach is to compute the profitability index (PI). The PI is defined as the present value of the benefits divided by the present value of cost, or in equation form,

$$PI = \frac{\sum_{t=1}^{n} \dfrac{CF_t}{(1+k)^t}}{I}$$

The decision rule for this approach is to accept those projects whose $PI \geq 1.0$ and reject those projects for which $PI < 1.0$. Thus for the two projects in this example

$$PI_B = \frac{\sum_{t=1}^{4} \dfrac{\$8000}{(1.08)^t}}{\$20,000} = \frac{\$26,496}{\$20,000} = 1.32$$

and

$$PI_G = \frac{\sum_{t=1}^{4} \dfrac{\$15,000}{(1.08)^t}}{\$40,000} = \frac{\$49,680}{\$40,000} = 1.24$$

Thus the PI is an attempt to normalize the size differences between the two projects by determining how many dollars of present value are produced for each dollar of investment. In the present case both projects would be accepted if they were independent, but if they were mutually exclusive, project B would be chosen over project G because of its higher PI.

The problem with the PI approach is that it can oversimplify the investment problem. Assume that the two projects are mutually exclusive. If the financial manager is seriously considering these two projects with costs of $20,000 and $40,000, this implies that he either has sufficient capital already available in the company's coffers to purchase the $40,000 project should it be selected, or he is willing to go to the capital market and obtain twice the capital that would be necessary to finance the $20,000 project.

For exposition purposes assume that the financial manager has $40,000 in cash available for investment. The question then becomes, if project B is selected rather than project G, what is done with the left over $20,000? One way in which this problem can be analyzed is to more closely examine the difference between the two projects. Table 10.9 presents what the excess of project G would be over project B. As shown in this table, the excess of project G over project B would itself be a profitable investment. This excess has a positive NPV at an 8 percent cost of capital and a 14 percent IRR. Given this information, management must determine what it would do with the excess $20,000 were project B selected because of its higher IRR and PI. While there are many possible uses for these funds, one approach would be to determine if the firm had another investment opportunity available that promised to be at least as profitable as this hypothetical excess of project G over project B. If it does not, then project G might be the better decision, even though the previous analysis indicated otherwise.

Table 10.9. The Excess of Project G Over B

Project	Cost	1	2	3	4	IRR	8% NPV
G	$40,000	$15,000	$15,000	$15,000	$15,000	18%	$9,680
B	20,000	8,000	8,000	8,000	8,000	22%	6,496
Difference	$20,000	$ 7,000	$ 7,000	$ 7,000	$ 7,000	14%	$3,184

To make this point clearer, assume the firm decided to purchase project B. What would be the combined result if management then invested the remaining $20,000 in a project that had an expected revenue flow of $6500 for four years? Even though this new project would be profitable, the combined total of project B plus this new project would not be as profitable as project G taken by itself. Thus considering project B and project G in isolation from all other possible investments would lead to a nonoptimal decision. Furthermore, the opposite would be true if the firm had had another investment available that was better than the excess of project G over project B. In this case the better decision would be to accept project B plus the new project because the combination would be better than project G by itself.

A firm is a combination of assets, and investment decisions should not be made in a vacuum. As we just observed, a combination of smaller projects may be more profitable than a single large project. Consequently, the financial manager must be concerned with the profitability of packages or portfolios of assets rather than with single projects. Further, this portfolio problem becomes more complex when we realize that the cash flows from several projects are often interrelated or dependent upon each other. When considering investment in one project, the analyst must also be concerned with the effects (if any) that acceptance of this project might have on the cash flows of other projects.

PROJECT CONTROL

The last steps in the capital budgeting process are control of the expenditure of funds and audit of the performance of the project after completion. Detailed cost records showing the data of the approved project, the authorized expenditures, the amount expended, the percentage of the project completed, and the estimated completion date are essential. If the project costs more than originally authorized, the additional expenditures must be included. These reports may be compiled monthly or quarterly, depending in part on the size of the project and the reliability of the original cost estimates. They aid us in cash planning, serving as an early warning system of possible difficulties, and providing a guide to the accuracy of estimates of project costs. If the reports reveal that substantial overexpenditures may be anticipated, we will usually have the project reviewed. If warranted, additional funds can be requested or the project can be terminated.

Frequently a firm will establish a deviation standard such as 10 percent that requires the submission of a report to obtain additional funds when expenditures exceed the originally budgeted funds. When the project is finished, a completion report is drawn up. This report permits an evaluation of the cost-estimating accuracy of the capital budgeting system and will make suggestions for avoiding similar errors in the future. As a further check, some firms also require a report on the performance of a project after it has been in operation for several years.

Areas of interest in reviewing project audits are the generation of project proposals, development of cost and revenue estimates, evaluation of the attractiveness of the projects, and actual attractiveness of projects after completion and operation. Management might find, for example, that revenues are conservatively estimated, that is, projects are generating a higher yield than anticipated. Such information can be fed back to those responsible for developing the revenue estimates with a view to raising their level of optimism. Management itself might take a more liberal attitude in approving capital expenditure projects. Additional outside funds might even be raised to take advantage of the stream of projects that had previously been viewed too conservatively.

Summary

Capital budgeting focuses on the evaluation and selection of investment proposals. Underlying the procedures of capital budgeting is a theory of valuation that states that assets have value to the extent that they produce future income.

Of the various ranking systems, payback (number of years required to recapture the cost of the investment) is widely used. It is easy to calculate, can serve as a coarse screen for selecting attractive projects, tells a firm how long it will have its money tied up, and weeds out longer term paybacks. A disadvantage is that it does not consider the flows of a project after the cost of the investment has been recovered. The average rate of return system relates the expected earnings (accounting definition) of the project to the required investment. This system considers the earnings over the life of the project but does not adjust for the time value of money nor, usually, for depreciation.

The IRR and the NPV systems consider depreciation and the time value of money. The IRR system requires the determination of the discount rate that causes the summed present values of the annual cash inflows to equal the cost of the project. The NPV system requires selecting a discount rate to use in evaluating projects, summing the present values of cash inflows at that rate, and subtracting the cost of the project. The profitability index (PI) is found by computing the ratio of the sum of the present values of the cash inflows (discounted at the required rate of return) to the cost of the project.

NPV, IRR, and PI are discounted cash flow techniques. They are conceptually correct methods of evaluating investments, and they always give the same accept–reject decision. However, when the timing of cash inflows of one project is quite different from the receipt of another or when projects differ in initial cost, these "correct" methods may rank the projects in different order. The difference in ranking is the result of different reinvestment assumptions. The cost of capital is the implied reinvestment rate in the NPV method, whereas the solution internal rate is the implied reinvestment rate in IRR. Techniques are available to resolve this ranking problem.

Study Questions

1. How is the value of an asset determined?
2. What are the advantages and disadvantages of the payback method? Of the average rate of return method?
3. Explain what is meant by the time value of money. Which capital budgeting techniques take this concept into consideration? How is it possible for the capital budgeting techniques that do not take it into consideration to lead to wrong decisions?
4. Contrast the IRR and the NPV systems. Under what circumstances may they lead to comparable recommendations? To conflicting recommendations? Where these two systems lead to conflicting recommendations, what criteria should be used to select the project?

5. What is capital rationing? Why does it exist?
6. Why is project control an important stage in any capital expenditure system? How can detailed records lead to improved capital budgeting decisions?

Problems

1. Compute the following.
   a. The present value of $8000 to be received at the end of 15 years when discounted at 20 percent.
   b. The present value of $8000 to be received at the end of 5 years when discounted at 20 percent.
   c. The present value of $8000 to be received at the end of 15 years when discounted at 15 percent.
   d. The present value of $8000 to be received at the end of 5 years when discounted at 5 percent.
   e. The present value of $2000 per year for 5 years discounted at 10 percent.
   f. The present value of $2000 per year for 15 years discounted at 10 percent.
   g. The present value of $1000 per year for 9 years discounted at 10 percent plus the present value of $5000 to be received at the end of the tenth year discounted at 10 percent.

2. How much would an investor be willing to pay for a $1000 ten-year bond which pays $50 interest semiannually and is sold to yield 8 percent, compounded semiannually?

3. How much would be paid for a $1000 ten-year bond that pays $30 interest semiannually and is sold to yield 12 percent, compounded semiannually?

4. The Tart Foundation, a tax-exempt organization, owns various investment projects. One project is doing poorly and is being considered for replacement. Three projects have been proposed, but funds are available for only one project. Management asks for your recommendation. The projects are coded Maple, Peach, and Rose. The projects are expected each to require a $30,000 outlay, have an estimated life of five years, three years, and four years, respectively. The foundation's required rate of return is 12 percent. The anticipated cash inflows for the three projects are given in Table 10.10.

Table 10.10. Tart Foundation Cash Inflows of Proposed Capital Expenditure Projects

Year	Project Maple	Project Peach	Project Rose
1	$10,000	$17,000	$10,000
2	10,000	17,000	10,000
3	10,000	10,000	10,000
4	10,000	—	5,000
5	10,000	—	—

    a. Determine the payback period for each project.

    b. Determine the average return on average investment for each project. Remember to deduct the required depreciation charge from each cash inflow figure to obtain the necessary net income figure. To simplify calculations use straight-line depreciation.

    c. Determine the internal rate of return for each project.

    d. Determine the present value of each project and its profitability index. Recall that the required rate of return is 12 percent.

    e. Rank each project applying the methods of payback, average return on investment, internal rate of return, and profitability index.

    f. Explain why the five capital budgeting systems yield conflicting answers.

5. A firm can purchase a machine by paying $1000 down and another $1000 one year from today. The installation of the machine promises cash flows of $800 annually for a period of four years. The cost of funds employed by the firm is 12 percent.

    a. What is the rate of return on this proposal?

    b. What is its net present value?

6. Evaluate each pair of conflicting proposals for which data are shown, using net present value and internal rate of return. Cost of capital is 8 percent.

	Project	Initial Outlay	Annual Cash Benefits 1	2	3	4
a.	1	$ 8,000	$3,000	$3,000	$3,000	$3,000
	2	14,000	5,200	5,200	4,800	4,800
b.	X	$ 6,000	$ 0	$8,100	$ 0	$ 0
	Y	6,000	0	0	0	9,600

7. Music World, Inc., is contemplating the introduction of a new instrument called the Rhythmette. The cost of the project, the required rate of return, and other pertinent data appear in Table 10.11.

Table 10.11. Music World, Inc., Rhythmette Project

Year	0	1	2	3	4	5
Outflow at year end	$10,000	—	—	$10,000	—	—
Cash inflow at year end	—	$5,000	$5,000	—	$10,000	$20,000
Required rate of return on investment, 10%						

Management asks that you determine the profitability index.

8. A Las Vegas Casino has been put up for sale. The owner is asking $3,600,000 in cash or $6,000,000 with nothing down. The $6,000,000 is to be paid in five equal installments due at the end of each year.
   a. What is your implicit rate of interest if you buy and do not pay cash?
   b. Suppose you have the $3,600,000 in cash and also another investment opportunity that promises a 25 percent annual return over the next five years. Just on the basis of the data given, which is more attractive—pay cash for the casino or buy it "on the installment plan" and invest the $3,600,000 in the available opportunity? What other factor(s) might you consider in reaching this decision?

9. The Greenhouse, a large nursery, is considering a new watering machine that will cost $25,000. The machine is expected to generate net cash benefits after taxes for six years. These benefits are expected to be the same amount each year and no salvage value is anticipated. The expected present value arising from purchase of the machine is $43,500 and the company's cost of capital is 10 percent.
   a. Calculate the net cash benefits after taxes in each of the six years.
   b. Compute the profitability index.
   c. Compute the payback period.

10. If in Problem 9, the net cash benefits were $8000 in each of the six years, calculate (a) the net present value, (b) the internal rate of return.

11. Refer to Table A.2 in the Appendix and graph the present value of an annuity of $1 per year. Use discount rates of 1, 5, 10, and 20 percent.
    a. Graph the points at five-year intervals from 0 to 25 on Figure 10.4.
    b. With reference to Figure 10.4 how do you explain the almost linear relationship between the number of years $1 is to be received per year and the

Figure 10.4. Present worth of a $1 per year annuity at various rates of discount.

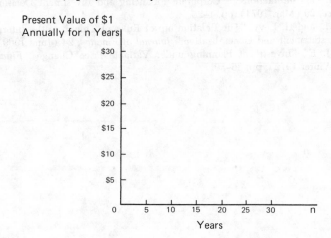

value of that stream of income when discounted at 1 percent? How do you explain the very pronounced curvature of the 20 percent curve and the rapid approach to a horizontal position?

Selected References

Bernhard, R. H., "Mathematical Programming Models for Capital Budgeting—A Survey, Generalization, and Critique," *Journal of Financial and Quantitative Analysis,* 4 (June 1969), pp. 111–158.

Bierman, H., Jr., and S. Smidt, *The Capital Budgeting Decision,* 3d ed. New York: Macmillan, 1971.

Boulder, J. B., and E. S. Buffa, "Corporate Models: On-Line Real Time Systems," *Harvard Business Review,* 48 (July–Aug. 1970), pp. 65–83.

Cheng, P. L., and J. P. Shelton, "A Contribution to the Theory of Capital Budgeting—The Multi-investment Case," *Journal of Finance,* 18 (Dec. 1963), pp. 622–636.

Donaldson, G., "Strategic Hurdle Rates for Capital Investment," *Harvard Business Review,* 50 (Mar.–Apr. 1972), pp. 50–58.

Elton, E. J., "Capital Rationing and External Discount Rates," *Journal of Finance,* 25 (June 1970), pp. 573–584.

Gershefski, G. W., "Building a Corporate Financial Model," *Harvard Business Review,* 47 (July–Aug. 1968), pp. 61–72.

Grunewald, A. E., "Capital Budgeting Strategy," *Management International Review,* 2–3 (1967), pp. 103–130.

Haynes, W. W., and M. B. Solomon, "A Misplaced Emphasis in Capital Budgeting," *Quarterly Review of Economics and Business,* 2 (Feb. 1962), pp. 39–46.

Klammer, T., "Empirical Evidence of the Adoption of Sophisticated Capital Budgeting Techniques," *Journal of Business,* 45 (July 1972), pp. 387–397.

Lewellen, W. G., H. P. Lanser, and J. J. McConnell, "Payback Substitutes for Discounted Cash Flow," *Financial Management,* 2 (Summer 1973), pp. 17–25.

Mao, J. C. T., "Survey of Capital Budgeting: Theory and Practice," *Journal of Finance,* 25 (May 1970), pp. 349–360.

Myers, S. C., "Interactions of Corporate Financing and Investment Decisions," *Journal of Finance,* 29 (Mar. 1974), pp. 1–25.

Sarnat, M., and H. Levy, "The Relationship of Rules of Thumb to the Internal Rate of Return: A Restatement and Generalization," *Journal of Finance,* 24 (June 1969), pp. 479–489.

Walter, J. E., "Investment Planning under Variable Price Change," *Financial Management,* 2 (Winter 1972), pp. 36–50.

11

THE CASH FLOWS
OF CAPITAL BUDGETING

In the previous chapter we concentrated on the different decision techniques that can be employed in the purchase of capital assets. We assumed certain values for the cash flows but did not discuss their derivation. In this chapter we discuss the nature and derivation of those cash flows.

From the point of view of the practitioner the generation or derivation of the cash flows is by far the most time consuming and possibly the most important part of the capital budgeting process. Analyzing an investment proposal requires two steps. First, management must make forecasts of the costs and benefits associated with it. Second, these costs and benefits must be organized in a consistent logical framework and evaluated to determine if the investment should be undertaken. Step 1 consists of the generation of the data to be analyzed, and step 2 consists of the techniques that are used in the analysis.

Even if management is aware of the correct techniques for evaluating an investment proposal, these techniques will not ensure that a correct decision is made if the data which they use have been improperly generated. However, it is conceivable that if management has good input data, a correct decision could be made even if a theoretically correct way of evaluating the data were not used. Such was the case with investment C in Chapter 10 which was ranked as the best investment simply by a process of inspection. Consequently, the importance of this aspect of the capital budgeting process cannot be overemphasized.

THE BASIC NATURE OF THE CASH FLOWS

Most capital budgeting problems are concerned with both cash inflows and cash outflows. Cash inflows can be viewed either as positive revenue inflows which occur through an increase in sales or as benefits which occur because some investment which is made today results in a reduction in costs which otherwise would have to be paid in the future. These benefits occur at various points in time in the future. The pattern of cash outflows is different in that there is usually an immediate outflow for the purchase of the asset and, in addition, outflows at various future points in time as other costs are incurred. These flows are schematically illustrated in Figure 11.1.

Figure 11.1. The cash flow pattern of typical investments.

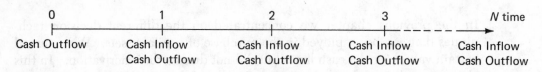

Two characteristics of these flows should be noted. First, in the usual case, the cash outflow takes place at time 0 and is large relative to all other cash flows. Second, the cash inflows must on balance be larger than the cash outflows, although it is not necessary that this be the case in each and every year. In fact, it is not uncommon to find situations where the cash outflows are greater than the cash inflows in the early years. However, the investment would not be made unless this situation were ultimately reversed.

Given these characteristics of the cash flows, we next consider which ones are relevant for a capital budgeting analysis. To decide the relevancy of a particular cash flow, a general principle can be used. *A cash flow (inflow or outflow) which occurs because the decision was made to invest in a particular project must be included in the analysis in some form.* We are considering investing a certain amount of dollars today. Why? Because we expect to obtain some benefits in the future. Which benefits? Only those that occur because we made the investment and no others. This will be particularly important to remember when we consider the replacement decision.

The Investment (Costs Occurring at Time $t = 0$)

When using annual discounting we usually consider the cost or investment to take place at time zero. This is not strictly true because a certain delay is usually experienced in obtaining the asset and getting it into operation. It is also common to undertake an investment which will require a number of capital outlays spread over various future points in time. No matter what the time pattern of the capital outlays, they are all important and must be included in the analysis at the point in time at which they occur.

The investment or cost for capital budgeting purposes is not simply the invoice cost of the asset. All costs that must be incurred to put the asset into the use for which it was purchased should be considered as part of its capital cost. For instance, in the purchase of a machine, freight charges are often negotiated and must be paid by the buyer. If so, they become part of the investment. Once the machine has been purchased, a number of additional costs will usually be incurred. Any costs to install the machine, such as building modifications, required alterations to other machines, redesign of the production line, removal of old asset, are all relevant costs and should be included in the investment or cost of the asset.

Several other flows can occur at time $t = 0$ which are viewed as adjustments to the cost of the asset. Some of these flows are not part of the capital cost of the asset, but because they occur at time $t = 0$ they are often classified as such. For example, in the decision to replace an asset, the old asset may be sold or scrapped. The salvage or resale value of the old asset is a positive cash inflow that occurred because of the replacement decision; it reduces the cost of the new asset. Conversely, in a situation where someone is paid to remove an old asset, this flow increases the cost of the new asset. The book value of the old asset is a sunk cost and any gain or loss on disposition of this asset should not enter into the analysis except for its tax effects. If we dispose of the old asset at a book gain, then we will have to pay a tax on this gain which will increase our *cash* tax payment to the government this year. Likewise, if we incur a loss on the disposition of the old asset, the reduction in our cash tax outflow should be included in the analysis. By convention, this change in the tax liability is considered an adjustment to the cost for capital budgeting purposes.

Another adjustment to the cost for capital budgeting analysis is any added investment in working capital balances. The two most common situations which require an investment in working capital in addition to the cost of the asset occur when the firm is undertaking a new venture or when it is expanding the volume of some previously produced product. Each dollar invested in fixed assets requires a certain dollar investment in cash, accounts receivable, and inventory. These additional requirements for investment in working capital are not trivial in that the fixed asset cannot be used without it, and in certain types of industries it can be substantial. Consequently, since this additional capital investment is required for the firm to use the fixed asset, it must be considered as part of the cost of the investment.

The usual procedure for handling investment in working capital is to assume that it is recovered at the end of the life of the asset. Thus we add the working capital to the cash inflows from the asset in the last year of its life and discount this to the present. There are two reasons for assuming the working capital investment is recovered in this manner. First, it corresponds to a cash flow that the firm could in fact receive if, at the end of the asset's life, it chose to allocate capital to other productive uses. Second, if recovery of this working capital were not assumed at the end of the asset's life, then for the project to have a positive net present value (or an internal rate of return greater than the cost of capital) it would have to be sufficiently profitable to recover the working capital investment plus a rate of return on this investment. Since the capital invested in working capital is available for recovery and is not being used up in an economic sense, requiring projects to recover this investment would result in too high a profitability requirement and therefore the rejection of investments that are economically justified.

The Annual Cash Flows

The annual cash flows that are discounted in the capital budgeting analysis are defined as earnings after tax plus depreciation. The financial manager must construct a pro forma or forecast income statement for the particular project being analyzed for each year in the future in which cash flows are expected to occur. Thus sales and all expenses must be forecast in much the same way as pro forma income statements are constructed in the budgeting process. In the end we wind up using a single summary figure to represent the net flow for any particular year. Thus this figure has many sources of potential error.

To compute the annual cash flows, one of the two alternatives presented in Table 11.1 can be used. Table 11.1 should be viewed as an abbreviated version of the working papers that would be used to generate the forecast cash flows. While it depends on the specific project being analyzed, the financial manager would have a more detailed breakdown of the ex-

Table 11.1. The Computation of Annual Cash Flows.

Sales	$30,000
Direct cash expenses	5,000
Depreciation	10,000
Earnings before tax	15,000
Tax at 50%	7,500
Earnings after tax	7,500
Depreciation	10,000
Earnings after tax plus depreciation	$17,500

or alternatively,

	Accounting Flow	Cash Flow
Sales	$30,000	$30,000
Direct cash expenses	5,000	5,000
Depreciation	10,000	
Earnings before tax	15,000	
Tax	7,500	7,500
Earnings after tax	$ 7,500	
Cash inflow		$17,500

penses associated with the project. For instance, it might be useful to include a breakdown of the expenses into direct labor expense, raw materials, and maintenance. In practice the degree to which these expenses will be broken down depends on the ability of the financial manager to obtain sufficient information to make these estimates. Often when an entirely new project is being considered, both the estimates for sales and expenses must be made in a very gross aggregate fashion.

Cash Flows

The flows generated in Table 11.1 are cash flows and are not the more familiar net income. The actual amount of funds generated by any particular project for reinvestment will be the cash flows as computed in Table 11.1 and will not be the net income flow. Consequently, cash flows must be used rather than net income.

Depreciation and Taxes

Depreciation affects the cash flow computation of Table 11.1 through its impact on the tax liability of the firm. In computing the correct expected tax liability associated with an investment, depreciation is deducted in arriving at taxable income. Table 11.1 shows two alternative ways of making this computation.

Interest

The purchase of a specific asset often is associated with the creation of some debt obligation (for instance a bank loan), and because the source of funds seems to be tied directly to the investment, there is a strong impulse to deduct the interest charges from the cash flows of the project. We stress that such a procedure is fundamentally wrong for the following two reasons.

To begin with, the decision of how the *firm* should be financed is essentially independent of the decision to accept a specific *project* for investment. As will be discussed in Chapter 19, management should finance the firm with the capital structure which minimizes the firm's overall capital costs. Thus the relevant question is how the firm as a whole should be financed and not how a specific asset should be financed. In a sense every asset of the firm can be viewed as being financed with the same proportions of the various sources of capital that are used to finance the firm as a whole.

The fallacy of identifying specific sources of funds with individual investments can be illustrated. Because of the differences in risk characteristics between debt and equity securities from the point of view of the investor, the cost of debt capital is usually lower than the cost of equity capital. Assume for the moment that the after tax cost of debt is 5 percent and the after tax cost of equity is 12 percent. Now further assume that management had decided to raise $100,000 by issuing debt and using the proceeds to invest in some project. If the proposed projects offered a potential after tax return of 10 percent and a comparison of this return was made with the after tax debt cost of 5 percent, it would appear that a wise decision was being made. However, suppose this investment was being considered and the firm decided to satisfy its immediate need for funds by selling stock. Then a comparison of the cost of the immediate sources of funds with the return on the investment would indicate that the project should not be undertaken. If such comparisons were made, management could change its investment decisions back and forth from accept to reject simply by obtaining funds from alternative sources. The basic economic decision of whether a particular project should be undertaken or not should not be influenced because it is currently more convenient to obtain funds from one source rather than another.

The second reason why interest is not deducted from the cash flows is found in the mathematics of discounting. Assume the cost of funds to be 6 percent, and that we have the opportunity to invest \$10,000 in a savings and loan for one year at a 6 percent return. Assuming interest is paid annually, the equation for the internal rate of return of this investment is

$$\$10,000 = \frac{\$10,600}{(1 + k)^1}$$

and

$$k = 0.06$$

In this case, the return we earn on the investment (\$600 or 6 percent) is equal to our cost of funds and the MRR = MCC requirement would be satisfied. By discounting the revenue flow from the investment we reduce its present value to exactly \$10,000, which was the original amount of capital. Now assume we subtracted an expense equal to the cost of funds from the revenue flow. The numerator of the right-hand side of the equation would be \$10,600 − 600 or \$10,000. If we then discounted \$10,000 to the present at 6 percent, the net present value of the investment would be \$9439, which would indicate that the investment did not return the required 6 percent. However, we know this conclusion is in error because the example was constructed to earn 6 percent. In effect, if we both subtracted the \$600 from the revenue flow and discounted at 6 percent, then we would be double counting the expenses for the cost of funds. If it is remembered that the purpose for discounting was to ensure that the revenue flows on accepted projects were sufficient to cover the cost of funds, then it is easy to realize that subtracting these costs would result in double counting. We may conclude that in a capital budgeting procedure, *all financing costs and their associated tax implications are accounted for in the discounting mechanism and that it is incorrect to make any deductions from the revenue flows to account for these costs.*

The Concept of Incremental Cash Flows

The reason a firm purchases a new asset is because it is either more efficient and therefore will reduce costs, or it is capable of higher volume, or both. Thus it is the incremental cash flow from the new asset over and above the old asset that is the relevant cash flow in a capital budgeting analysis. To illustrate this point, Table 11.2 shows the incremental concept using forecast income statements for both the old and new assets one year in the future. The objective of the financial manager is to arrive at the value of $CF_n - CF_o$.

Table 11.2. Computation of Incremental Cash Flows Forecast Income Statements— Old and New Assets—End of Year 1

	Old Asset	New Asset	Incremental Cash Flow	
Sales S	S_o	S_n	$S_n - S_o$	
Cash expenses C	C_o	C_n	$-(C_n - C_o)$	
Depreciation D	D_o	D_n	$-(D_n - D_o)$	
Taxable income TI	TI_o	TI_n	$TI_n - TI_o$	
Tax T	T_o	T_n	$-(T_n - T_o)$	
Earnings after tax E	E_o	E_n	$E_n - E_o$	
Depreciation	D_o	D_n	$+ D_n - D_o$	
Cash flow CF	CF_o	CF_n	$CF_n - CF_o$	
Sales	$10,000	$20,000	$+10,000	(1)
Cash expenses	4,000	3,500	$+ 500	(2)
Depreciation	2,000	5,000	− 3,000	(3)
Taxable income	$ 4,000	$11,500	$ 7,500	(4)
Tax	2,000	5,750	3,750	(5)
Earnings after tax	$ 2,000	$ 5,750	$ 3,750	(6)
Depreciation	2,000	5,000	3,000	(7)
Cash flow	$ 4,000	$10,750	$ 6,750	(8)

Line 1 indicates that the new asset which is being considered has the capacity to at least double the sales volume of the old machine. Using the incremental concept, the relevant increase in sales is the difference between $20,000 and $10,000 or $10,000. Line 2 indicates a decrease in the cash expenses from $4000 on the old machine to $3500 on the new machine. While this may seem somewhat unusual because of the higher volume on the new machine, it could easily be the result of substantially lower labor costs on the new machine. The effect of this cost decrease is shown in line 2 of the incremental column, where the $500 difference in cost is added rather than subtracted in arriving at taxable income. While a decrease in cost is of benefit to the firm, it will result in a higher taxable income. Line 3 is used to compute the incremental depreciation of $3000 and line 4 shows the incremental taxable income to be $7500. Finally line 8 indicates that the forecast cash flow for the first year is $6750. This same process would have to be carried out in each year of the new asset's economic life.

In general the incremental concept must be applied in all situations involving a capital budgeting analysis. If management is considering purchase of an asset which involves the production of an entirely new product, then the entire cash flow from the new asset is an increment from zero and therefore the relevant cash flow. Whether or not a replacement decision is being considered, the incremental concept should be applied in determining all cash flows from the asset.

A FRAMEWORK FOR ORGANIZING CASH FLOW FORECASTS

The examples used in these two chapters have employed single estimates of the cash flows in each period, and these might be thought of as management's best estimate of the cash flow. However, many events other than the ones which are forecast are possible. To get a better picture of the potential profitability of a particular asset, the alternative possible outcomes should somehow be considered in the analysis. The purpose of this section is to present a general framework that can be used to help organize alternative forecasts in a consistent manner. The suggested framework helps the financial manager enumerate the relevant alternative outcomes in a manner which enables him to obtain a better picture of the potential for success or failure inherent in any given investment. This approach can be viewed as a first stage in a process of attempting to account for uncertainty in investment decisions.

The field of decision sciences has for years used an analytical framework, referred to as a tree diagram, which is extremely useful for enumerating and analyzing alternative outcomes. An example of a decision tree is Figure 11.2, which is intended to be illustrative and can easily be modified to account for many other possibilities. This example is set in the context of the decision about whether a new machine should be purchased to take advantage of estimated additional demand for an existing product. Underlying Figure 11.2 are several assumptions concerning the estimates of the magnitude of this additional demand. The example assumes that the investment has a four-year life and that total additional demand can range from a low of approximately $106,000 to a high of approximately $133,000. Two initial levels of demand, $100,000 and $60,000, have been estimated.

Given the above assumptions, Figure 11.2 was constructed as follows. Using one or a combination of sales forecasting techniques, management has estimated four final levels of demand which they feel are relevant to the problem: $67,500, $80,000, $106,000, and $122,500. In this case the $122,500 figure was arrived at by assuming the initial sales of the product were high and that demand would continue to grow at a rate of 7 percent over the life of the project ($100,000 \times (1.07)^3 = $122,500$). Further, man-

Figure 11.2. Decision Tree Enumeration of Alternative Cash Flows.

Initial Sales	Subsequent Demand Growth	Cost Conditions	Branch Number	Net Present Value at 6%
High $100,000	7% High	High VC = 0.8(S)	(1)	$13,252
		Normal VC = 0.7(S)	2	$36,214
	Low 2%	High VC = 0.8(S)	3	$10,107
		Normal VC = 0.7(S)	4	$31,498
Low $60,000	10% High	High VC = 0.8(S)	5	$-3,930
		Normal VC = 0.7(S)	6	$10,444
	Low 4%	High VC = 0.8(S)	7	$-6,265
		Normal VC = 0.7(S)	8	$6,935

agement also wanted to account for the possibility of an initially strong ex-ploitation of additional demand ($100,000) followed by a period of slow growth, 2 percent. This results in the estimate of $106,000 ($100,000 × $(1.02)^3 = \$106,000$). The third estimate was made by assuming some diffi-culties in getting the project on stream with the result that the initial pene-tration was only $60,000, but was followed by reasonably good growth of 10 percent. The combination of these factors produces fourth-year demand of $60,000 × $(1.10)^3 = \$80,000$. Finally, assuming an initial low sales level, management also wanted to account for competitive pressures holding down the growth rate to 4 percent, which results in a fourth-year sales estimate of $67,500. Many alternative possibilities exist other than those included in this example. As always, judgment is required on the part of management, not only to formulate the possible alternative outcomes, but also to restrict the analysis to those which realistically should be considered. When management uses a framework for the analysis like the tree diagram, the fact that alternatives are required forces consideration of a number of possibilities that would otherwise likely be ignored.

As discussed previously, expenses as well as revenues must be estimated to arrive at the cash flows. In this example we have chosen to reflect different cost conditions by assuming normal costs to be 70 percent of sales and high costs at 80 percent of sales. These estimates would be arrived at by drawing on management's knowledge of conditions in the raw materials and labor markets that impact on this particular project as well as from inputs from the production department.

Having arrived at these estimates, the next step requires that the cash flows be computed. Table 11.3 presents the entire income statements for one branch of the tree diagram and the final cash flow values for the other five branches. The computations in Table 11.3 assume a cost for capital budgeting purposes of $50,000 and a cost of capital of 6 percent. Both Figure 11.2 and Table 11.3 show the NPV for each branch in the tree diagram.

Having completed the computations for the tree diagram, the next step is interpretation. We have quite a different picture of this proposed project than would be the case if we restricted our analysis to only our best estimates. We can now view the wide range of potential profitability from this project which varies from a high of NPV = $36,214 (branch 2) to a low of NPV = $-6265 (branch 7). Further, the tree diagram shows that in six of the eight branches, the project has a positive NPV and therefore would be profitable.

Perhaps the most important part of the interpretation involves an investigation of the sensitivity of NPV to the various assumptions we have made. The following points can be determined from a more detailed analysis of Figure 11.2 and Table 11.3. First, the two cases where the project would produce a negative NPV occur when the firm is experiencing high cost conditions (VC = 0.80 sales). Second, the importance of costs to the degree of profitability is further underscored when we compare the pairs of NPVs which are the same except for costs: branch 1 versus branch 2, branch 3 versus branch 4, etc. In the branch 1 versus branch 2 comparison, incurring high versus normal costs causes NPV to drop by approximately 64 percent, ($36,214 − $13,252)/$36,214. In the branch 3 versus branch 4 comparison, NPV drops by 68 percent due to high costs. Third, within the initial high and low sales categories, the subsequent growth in sales does not appear to be critically important to acceptance or rejection of the project. The appropriate comparisons here are branch 1 with branch 3, branch 2 with branch 4, and branch 5 with branch 7, branch 6 with branch 8. The per-

Table 11.3. Cash Flow Computations for Figure 11.2

Branch		1	2	3	4	Net Present Value at 6%
			Year			
1	Sales	$100,000	$107,000	$114,490	$122,504	
	Variable cost	80,000	85,600	91,592	98,003	
	Depreciation*	12,500	12,500	12,500	12,500	
	Earnings before tax	7,500	8,900	10,398	12,001	
	Tax at 40%	3,000	3,560	4,159	4,800	
	Earnings after tax	4,500	5,340	6,239	7,201	
	Depreciation	12,500	12,500	12,500	12,500	
	Cash flow	$ 17,000	$ 17,840	$ 18,739	$ 19,701	$+13,252
2	Cash Flow	$ 23,000	$ 24,260	$ 25,608	$ 27,050	$+36,214
3	Cash Flow	$ 17,000	$ 17,240	$ 17,484	$ 17,735	$+10,107
4	Cash Flow	$ 23,000	$ 23,360	$ 23,727	$ 24,100	$+31,498
5	Cash Flow	$ 12,200	$ 12,920	$ 13,712	$ 14,583	$− 3,930
6	Cash Flow	$ 15,800	$ 16,880	$ 18,068	$ 19,375	$+10,444
7	Cash Flow	$ 12,200	$ 12,488	$ 12,788	$ 13,099	$− 6,265
8	Cash Flow	$ 15,800	$ 16,232	$ 16,681	$ 17,149	$+ 6,935

* Cost = $50,000, straight-line depreciation.

centage decreases in NPV caused by low versus high growth are much smaller than those caused by high costs. Fourth, if the firm decides to undertake the project it can attempt to ensure its profitability in one of two ways. It can expend serious effort to assure an initial high sales level. If our other assumptions are reasonably accurate, success with an initial sales level of around $100,000 will guarantee the profitability of the project. On the other hand, the firm could concentrate its efforts on controlling project cost because if it can keep costs in the estimated normal range, project profitability can be assured no matter what combinations of the other factors that have been considered occur. Actually, good management would not view this as an either/or situation. Strict attention would be paid to both aspects of the project should it be undertaken.

We believe that the tree diagram has given management a substantially better picture of the characteristics of the project than would be the case if they simply used single best estimates of each of the components of cash flow. The sensitivity of NPV to each of the estimates is particularly useful information in making a final decision. Before making that final decision, management would be well advised to return to the beginning of the analysis and recheck two critical points. First, are the alternatives considered in the tree diagram the relevant alternatives. Second, the actual estimates should be rechecked for realism.

Conducting a thorough investigation of the project does not guarantee the success of the investment. Whenever we are dealing with the future, a high degree of uncertainty exists, and our estimates may turn out to be incorrect or unanticipated events may occur and cause the investment to be unprofitable. Nevertheless, decisions must be made and they have to be made using information that is available to us at the time we make the decision. This is why it is imperative that we make the best use possible of the information we do have access to.

Summary

A correct computation of cash flows is essential for a successful capital budgeting system. To do this, management must forecast the costs and benefits of all proposals. All cash flows resulting from the investment decision must be accounted for.

Cash flow is defined as earnings after tax plus depreciation. Depreciation affects the cash flow because it lowers the firm's tax liability. Interest and other financial charges should be omitted from the cash flow computation of a project, since they are already accounted for in the discounting mechanism.

Incremental cash flows are the relevant flows in a capital budgeting analysis. Many factors will enter into the estimation of these incremental cash flows. A device such as a tree diagram will help the financial manager enumerate the many alternatives so that he obtains a clearer picture of the potential success or failure of a given investment.

Study Questions

1. Define the term cash inflow. What are the major sources of cash inflows in a capital budgeting context?
2. Does the book value for an old asset affect the cost of a new asset in a replacement decision?
3. How is working capital accounted for in a decision to acquire a new machine?
4. How can the method of depreciation affect the profitability of the project?
5. Why are all financial charges excluded from the cash flow calculations?
6. What is the meaning of the term "incremental cash flow"?

Problems

1. The Ham Bone Packing Company is planning a modernization of its production line, which is expected to result in savings before depreciation and taxes of $7000 per year. The cost of the equipment is $15,000. Ham Bone requires a 15 percent return on investment. Income taxes are at a 50 percent rate (Table 11.4).

Table 11.4. Ham Bone Packing Company Modernization Program Data

	Year				
	1	2	3	4	5
Savings before depreciation and taxes	$7,000	$7,000	$7,000	$7,000	$7,000
Depreciation, sum-of-years' digits method	5,000	4,000	3,000	2,000	1,000
Taxable income	2,000	3,000	4,000	5,000	6,000
Income tax (50%)	1,000	1,500	2,000	2,500	3,000
Cash flow from operations	6,000	5,500	5,000	4,500	4,000
Cost of equipment, $15,000					
Required return on investment, 15%					

a. Determine the profitability index.
b. Determine the internal rate of return.
c. Determine the profitability index and the internal rate of return if straight-line depreciation were required by tax law.
d. Compare your answers in parts (a), (b), and (c). How do you explain that the project appears less attractive when using straight-line depreciation than when the sum-of-the-years' digits method is employed? Why is the difference so small?
2. Two conflicting proposals of equal risk have been made for the purchase of new equipment. The data on each are given below:

	A	B
Net cash outlay	$8,400	$6,000
Salvage value	0	0
Estimated life	6 years	6 years
Net earnings before depreciation and taxes:		
1–3 years	$2,600	$1,600
4–6 years	2,000	1,600

Assume straight-line depreciation and a corporate tax rate of 40 percent. Cost of capital is 8 percent. Provide the necessary computations to rank each project in terms of:

a. internal rate of return
b. net present value
c. profitability index
d. payback
e. average rate of return.

3. We are considering purchasing a new machine to replace an existing old machine. The new machine has an invoice cost of $34,000, an estimated economic life of six years, a tax life of four years, and $1000 salvage value at the end of its useful life. Furthermore, if we purchase the new machine we will have to invest an additional $6000 in working capital. The old machine has a book value of $8000 and a current market value of $3300. If we replace the old machine with the new machine, we will incur a net cost of $300. The company has a cost of capital of 0.10 and an income tax rate of 0.60. Schedules for revenues and expenses on the new and old machines are given below.

In computing the revelant cash flows assume the following.

1. The working capital is recovered at the end of the machine's useful life.
2. Use straight-line depreciation.
3. A zero salvage in calculating the depreciation charge.
4. The tax savings on the sale of the old machine and the benefits of the investment tax credit accrue to the firm one year hence.
5. Only one third of the tax credit is allowed due to the short tax life of the machine.

			Year			
	1	2	3	4	5	6
Old machine						
Revenues	$ 9,000	$ 9,000	$ 9,000	$ 9,000	0	0
Operating costs	2,000	2,000	2,000	2,000		
New machine						
Revenues	60,000	50,000	40,000	30,000	25,000	20,000
Operating costs	18,000	18,000	18,000	18,000	18,000	18,000

    a.   Calculate the net cash outlay of this investment.

    b.   Compute the incremental net cash benefits of the new machine.

    c.   Compute the net present value of the new machine.

4. K-D Manufacturing Company is beginning full production this month and is acquiring a new machine for a price of $18,000 cash. Freight charges will be $700 and installation expense will be $1300. The new machine will replace an old worn model with a depreciated book value of $6000 that can be sold for $2000 cash. The new machine is expected to have a useful life of ten years, straight-line depreciation is used, and no salvage value is expected. After tax net cash benefits before depreciation of $3000 per year are expected.

    Assume a cost of capital of 10 percent and a 50 percent tax rate on earned income.

    a.   What is the net cash outlay of this investment?

    b.   What is the profitability index?

    c.   What is the internal rate of return?

5. K-D Manufacturing purchased another machine for $12,000 which was expected to generate incremental cash gains before depreciation of $4000 per year. The estimated life of the machine is six years and straight-line depreciation is used. Use the same tax rates as in Problem 4. There are no freight or installation costs involved in this purchase.

    a.   What are the net cash benefits expected annually from the new machine?

    b.   What is the internal rate of return?

Selected References

See citations at the end of Chapter 10.

12

CAPITAL BUDGETING UNDER UNCERTAINTY

In the previous two chapters the discussion assumed away differences in risk between projects. While risk differences may have been intuitively recognized, they were not explicitly accounted for. Using discounted cash flow procedures and not distinguishing risk differences between projects implicitly makes an asumption about risk. The discount rate used in these procedures, the cost of capital, reflects the compensation that the suppliers of capital demand for exposing themselves to the risk of the firm. Thus this discount rate already reflects a certain level of risk. If we apply this discount rate to all proposed investments, we are making three assumptions about the riskiness of the projects.

1. All proposed investments have equivalent risk.
2. All proposed investments have the same risk characteristics as the firm as a whole.
3. The acceptance of any one project, or for that matter, any series of investments, will not change the overall risk characteristics of the firm as a whole.

These assumptions are implicit in the mechanics of both NPV and IRR. When these risk assumptions do not correspond with the nature of the projects being evaluated, specific adjustments are necessary. The purpose of this chapter is to discuss some of the techniques that have been proposed to measure risk and to show how the concept of risk can be integrated into a capital budgeting analysis.

RISK DEFINED

The risk of an investment is defined as the potential variability in its rate of return. To make this concept clear, think in terms of the difference between *ex ante* (before the fact) and *ex post* (after the fact) rates of return. Assume an investment made several years ago just completed its useful economic life. At this point we could compute an ex post rate of return on the project to analyze how efficient the initial decision to invest was. The computation would be a single rate of return computed using known ex post data.

This is quite a different situation from the one we faced when the investment was originally proposed. At that time we computed an expected rate of return for the project (or, as we suggested in the previous chapter, a number of rates of return by using the decision tree), and we recognized that this rate of return was not the only possible outcome from the investment. This point is the essence of the concept of risk. In an ex ante sense, any investment that is undertaken has many possible outcomes. The outcome that is finally realized in an ex post sense is only one of these many possibilities. Thus the risk of a single investment project is defined as the existence of multiple possible outcomes from the project.

Consider the following illustration. Assume you wish to predict the profitability of a new product. You know that costs will be between 50 and 60 percent of sales and that sales are sensitive to economic conditions. Management estimates the most likely outcomes to be a normal economy and a cost level of 50 percent of sales. Using these estimates in Table 12.1, the most likely estimate of profit is seen to be $400. However, if we assume

Table 12.1. The Possible Profit Outcomes of a New Product

State of Economy	Sales	Cost	Possible Profit Outcomes
Boom	$1,000	$600 500	$400 500
Normal	800	480 400	320 400
Recession	600	360 300	240 300

three possible states of the economy, the actual profitability could be one of several possible outcomes.

The point of the illustration is that while we think one certain outcome may be most likely, the possibility exists that the actual outcome will be substantially different from what we expected. What we want to develop is a technique that will reflect these uncertainties by accounting for multiple possible outcomes.

THE CONCEPT OF PROBABILITY

Before discussing techniques, we must first explain the concept of probability. Modern statistics allows for the existence of two types of probabilities, classical and subjective. Classical probability is the frequency of occurrence of a specific event produced in a controlled experiment repeated a large number of times. The critical components of this definition are as follows.

1. Specific event—the outcome or event must be capable of being rigorously defined.
2. Controlled experiment—the event is produced by an operation that can be controlled in a manner which assures that the experiment may be exactly repeated.
3. Repetition—the situation must be one in which the experiment may be repeated a large number of times under exactly the same circumstances.

Note the interpretation of classical probability. Knowing the probability does not enable us to state that the next outcome will be a certain event X. Rather, it enables us to state that if we performed the experiment N times, then X would be expected to occur a certain number of times. The percentage of times X would be expected to occur is written $\Pr(X)$, and therefore the number of times X would occur out of N trials is equal to $[\Pr(X)]N$. The classical probability concept cannot be applied to all or even many business decisions. Some cases, such as those associated with production, are amenable to treatment with classical probability concepts; however, many other problems are not.

Of more relevance to business decision making is the use of subjective probability concepts. A subjective probability is a statement of belief or opinion by an analyst about the likelihood that a given event will occur. The word *subjective* means that the estimate is made by an individual. Different people will very likely arrive at different probability estimates. The statement of the belief in the form of a probability is intended to quantify that belief so a decision can be made that will be consistent with it.

The interpretation of subjective probabilities is quite different from that of classical probabilities. With subjective probabilities we rarely consider the possibility of repeated events. We are usually concerned with a one-shot decision. Therefore in the following situation:

Possible Outcome	Probability
$300	0.25
500	0.50
700	0.25
	1.00

we do not mean that 25 percent of the time the outcome will be $300 and 50 percent of the time the outcome will be $500. Rather we mean for the one outcome that will occur, the $500 outcome is twice as likely as either the $300 or $700 outcome.

THE PROBABILITY DISTRIBUTION

The two characteristics of a probability distribution that are of immediate interest are the mean and the standard deviation. These characteristics are measures of the central tendency and the dispersion of the probability distribution, that is, the mean is the most likely outcome and the standard deviation measures how much different outcomes might vary from the most likely outcome. Consider the following two investments:

	A			B	
P_i		Outcome = R_i	P_i		Outcome = R_i
0.20		$300	0.30		$200
0.60		500	0.40		500
0.20		700	0.30		800
1.00			1.00		

The mean outcome R is defined as

$$R = \sum_{i=1}^{N} P_i R_i$$

where

R_i = return associated with i^{th} outcome
P_i = probability of ith outcome
N = number of possible outcomes
R = mean or expected value.

For project A the mean is

$$
\begin{aligned}
R_A &= 0.20(\$300) + 0.60(\$500) + 0.20(\$700) \\
&= \$60 + \$300 + \$140 \\
&= \$500
\end{aligned}
$$

For project B,

$$
\begin{aligned}
R_B &= 0.30(\$200) + 0.40(\$500) + 0.30(\$800) \\
&= \$60 + \$200 + \$240 \\
&= \$500
\end{aligned}
$$

The standard deviation σ is calculated using the equation

$$\sigma = \sqrt{\sum_{i=1}^{N} (R_i - R)^2 P_i}$$

For project A the standard deviation is

$$
\begin{aligned}
\sigma_A &= \sqrt{0.20(\$300 - \$500)^2 + 0.60(\$500 - \$500)^2 + 0.20(\$700 - \$500)^2} \\
&= \$126.5
\end{aligned}
$$

For project B

$$
\begin{aligned}
\sigma_B &= \sqrt{0.30(\$200 - \$500)^2 + 0.40(\$500 - \$500)^2 + 0.30(\$800 - \$500)^2} \\
&= \$232.5
\end{aligned}
$$

To summarize,

$$
\begin{aligned}
R_A &= \$500 & \sigma_A &= \$126.50 \\
R_B &= \$500 & \sigma_B &= \$232.50
\end{aligned}
$$

If we were to illustrate the outcome probabilities of projects A and B, they would appear as shown in Figures 12.1 and 12.2.

Figure 12.1. Outcome probabilities of project A.

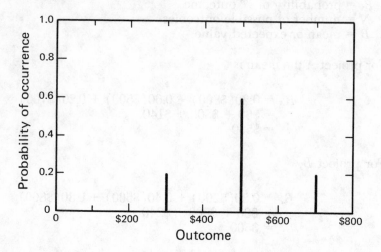

Figure 12.2. Outcome probabilities of project B.

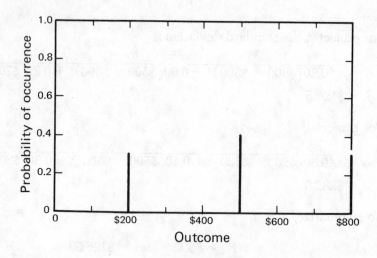

Both project A and project B have the same expected revenue flows. However, as is illustrated, the possible outcomes for project B have more dispersion than the outcomes for project A. As a result, project B is said to expose the company to more risk than does project A. In effect, we are equating the concept of variability with risk.

The standard deviation is a good measure of risk in the case of projects A and B because their expected returns were identical. When the expected returns differ, the coefficient of variation—the ratio of the project's standard deviation to its expected return—is used. For each project the coefficient of variation CV is

project A:

$$CV = \frac{\sigma_A}{R_A} = \frac{\$126.5}{\$500} = 0.253$$

project B:

$$CV = \frac{\sigma_B}{R_B} = \frac{\$232.5}{\$500} = 0.465$$

Assuming that investors are averse to risk, project A would be preferred to project B because it promises the same expected return for a lower amount of risk. A more difficult problem exists when the expected return and the risk of one project are higher than the expected return and risk of another. For example, if the expected return of project C is $600 and the coefficient of variation is 0.30, is the project more or less preferable to project A with an expected return of $500 and a coefficient of variation of 0.253? To answer this question it is necessary to turn to utility theory.

UTILITY THEORY

In economic theory a common assumption is that individuals attempt to maximize utility or satisfaction from their economic activities. While there are references in literature and history to individuals who derive satisfaction from having wealth for its own sake, most people desire wealth because it enables them to increase their level of consumption. Thus theorists hold that an individual's satisfaction is a function of his wealth.

Maximization of wealth is consistent with the more theoretical construct of maximization of utility. In a certain world wealth would be sub-stituted for utility and maximized. In investments this would be accom-plished by the purchase of those assets with the highest rate of return. In an uncertain world it is no longer possible to maximize utility; rather we must maximize *expected* utility. As our previous discussion of multiple pos-sible outcomes noted, it is no longer sufficient to consider only the return from an investment, we must also consider the variability of the return. Thus expected utility becomes a function of both the return and the risk (variability) of the investment.

The usual procedure is to assume that investors are risk averse, that is, other things being equal, they prefer to be exposed to less risk rather than more risk. In terms of the language of utility theory, we assume that inves-tors have a diminishing marginal utility of money. This means that an ad-ditional quantity of money yields the investor less satisfaction (utility) than the loss of a similar sum will cost in lost satisfaction. This concept can be seen in Figure 12.3, where utility is measured in units which are referred to as "utils."

Utility curve *AB* exhibits diminishing marginal utility for money. If the businessman has an income of $600, he has 6.25 utils of satisfaction. The

Figure 12.3. The diminishing marginal utility of money.

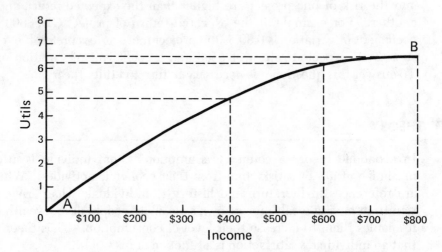

receipt of an additional $200 increases his utility to 6.5 utils, whereas a loss of $200 decreases his utility to 4.75 utils. Since he stands to gain 0.25 utils or lose 1.50 utils, this businessman would not be willing to make a 50–50 bet on the chance of winning or losing $200.

The assumption of diminishing marginal utility of money is based on empirical observations of individual behavior. These observations suggest that most people are risk averse. This is important because it means that equal positive and negative increments to wealth have different effects on the individual's perceived level of utility. This differential effect from gains and losses substantially increases the importance of a consideration of the risk (variability) associated with any decision.

To show how utility theory, the diminishing marginal utility of money, and risk can all be incorporated in the capital budgeting decision, assume we are considering investing $400 in either project A or project B. In addition, assume we have the alternative of putting the $400 in a federally insured savings account at 5 percent interest. The utility analysis could take the following form.

	1 P_i	2 R_i	3 Utils	4 1×3 Expected Utility
Project A	0.20	$300	5.25	1.05
	0.60	500	7.00	4.20
	0.20	700	7.75	1.55
				6.80 utils
Project B	0.30	$200	4.00	1.2
	0.40	500	7.00	2.8
	0.30	800	7.875	2.3625
				6.3625 utils
Savings	1.0	420	6.4	6.4 utils

Project A has a higher expected utility than the savings alternative, which in turn has a higher expected utility than project B—6.8 utils > 6.4 utils > 6.3625 utils. Therefore an investor who makes decisions on the basis of expected utility would prefer project A.

Despite its theoretical appeal, there has been little direct use of utility theory in decison making. Its use requires that we empirically determine the shape of the utility function. This has proven to be an extremely difficult task. At this point its primary use is as a theoretical construct to help analyze our motives when making a decision. To the extent it helps us gain insight into our behavior patterns, it should improve the quality of our decision making.

TECHNIQUES TO A DECISION

Payback

One of the reasons for the popularity of the payback period is that it can be viewed as a way of accounting for risk. The logic for this view is based on the assumption that time is the factor that causes risk to exist. The feeling is that the farther one must forecast into the fuure, the more likely is the forecast to be in error. Since the payback criterion ignores forecasted revenue flows which are expected to occur after the payback period, the "riskiest" flows are excluded from the computation. Using this logic we would have to conclude that the longer the payback period, the "riskier" the project.

However, there are some problems. Such an approach would not protect against unforeseen poor outcomes in the early years; it will only protect against poor results subsequent to the payback period. Using payback as a method for handling risk has all the defects cited earlier (Chapter 10). One possible result of using this approach is that highly risky short-lived projects could be accepted and a virtually risk-free long-lived project could be rejected.

Using the Decision Tree to Estimate the Return and
Risk Characteristics of a Project

In the previous chapter we noted that a tree diagram is a useful technique for enumerating the relevant potential outcomes from a project. It is possible to integrate subjective probabilities into the tree diagram. The example we used in Chapter 11 provided estimates of the initial and total levels of demand and of possible cost conditions that could exist. This example is summarized in the restated tree diagram presented in Figure 12.4.

Figure 12.4. Decision tree.

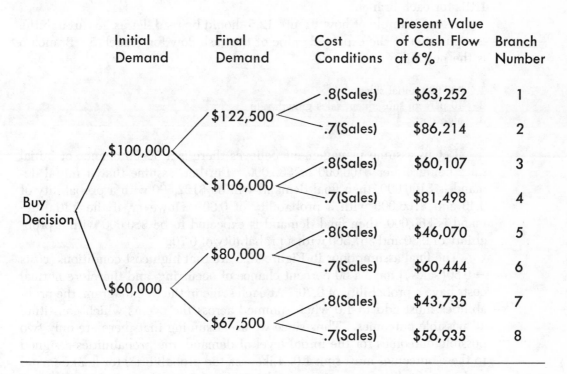

Initial Demand	Final Demand	Cost Conditions	Present Value of Cash Flow at 6%	Branch Number
		.8(Sales)	$63,252	1
	$122,500	.7(Sales)	$86,214	2
$100,000		.8(Sales)	$60,107	3
	$106,000	.7(Sales)	$81,498	4
		.8(Sales)	$46,070	5
	$80,000	.7(Sales)	$60,444	6
$60,000		.8(Sales)	$43,735	7
	$67,500	.7(Sales)	$56,935	8

(Buy Decision)

The conclusions we were able to reach from this diagram were the following.

1. Six of the eight possibilities will prove profitable. Branch 2 is most profitable while branch 7 is most unprofitable. Remember, the machine costs $50,000, so the NPV of branch 7 is − $6265.
2. The percentage profitability decrease caused by low versus high sales growth rates is much smaller than the profitability decrease caused by high costs, that is, profit is more sensitive to cost than to demand conditions.

If we are able to make some judgment about the likelihood that certain future levels of demand and cost will exist, we can utilize the decision tree diagram above to calculate the expected value of investing in this machine. The advantage of calculating expected values in this manner is that we are explicitly including all possibilities that management is aware of and our estimates of the likelihood of their occurrence. Figure 12.5 is a restated

Figure 12.4, but this time we have added management's subjective probability estimates of each outcome. In addition, Figure 12.5 also presents the IRRs for each branch.

As an example of how Figure 12.5 should be read, let us go through the computation of the expected value of the cash flow for branch 5. Branch 5 is the possibility of

1. $60,000 initial sales
2. 10 percent subsequent sales growth rate
3. high cost.

Let us assume management believes there is a 50–50 chance of initial sales being either $100,000 or $60,000. Further, assume that if initial demand is $100,000, then final demand will be $122,500 with a probability of 0.40 and $106,000 with a probability of 0.60. However, if the initial demand is $60,000, then final demand is expected to be $80,000 with a probability of 0.30 and $67,500 with a probability of 0.70.

The final assumptions in Figure 12.5 are that high cost conditions [costs = 0.80(sales)] have a 30 percent chance of occurring, and therefore normal costs have a probability of 0.70. At each stage in the tree diagram, the probabilities must add to 1.0 when summed across the events which constitute all possible outcomes. Thus since we are assuming that there are only two possible outcomes for the initial level of demand, the probabilities assigned to these outcomes must sum 1.0. Likewise the probabilities for final demand and cost conditions must also each sum to 1.0 at any branch in the tree diagram.

Once the probabilities have been assigned to each of the expected outcomes, the next step involves computing the probability of each branch. To proceed along branch 5 we would have to have a low initial level of demand (Pr = 0.50), followed by an $80,000 level of final demand (Pr = 0.30) in addition to a high level of costs (Pr = 0.30). The probability of all these events occurring is (0.50)(0.30)(0.30) = 0.045. Column 5 in Figure 12.5 carries out this computation for all eight branches in the tree diagram. Since the eight branches are assumed to encompass all possible outcomes, the probabilities in column 5 must also sum to 1.0.

From this point we may take one of two approaches. If we wish, we can compute the present value of the cash flows. These computations are carried out and the results presented in column 4. We then combine column 4 with column 5 to obtain the expected value and the standard deviation of the cash flows (column 6). Thus we would have

Figure 12.5. Decision tree with subjective probability.

(1) Initial Demand	(2) Final Demand	(3) Cost Conditions	(4) Present Value of Cash Flows @ 6%	(5) Probability	(6) Expected Value Cash Flow	(7) IRR	(8) Expected Value IRR	(9) Branch
		.80 (Sales)	$63,252	.06	$3,795.12	.17	.0102	1
	$122,500	.70 (Sales)	$86,214	.14	$12,069.96	.33	.0462	2
$100,000		.80 (Sales)	$60,107	.09	$5,409.63	.14	.0126	3
	$106,000	.70 (Sales)	$81,498	.21	$17,114.58	.31	.0651	4
		.80 (Sales)	$46,070	.045	$2,073.50	.03	.00135	5
	$80,000	.70 (Sales)	$60,444	.105	$6,346.62	.14	.0147	6
$60,000		.80 (Sales)	$43,735	.105	$4,592.18	.005	.000525	7
	$67,500	.70 (Sales)	$56,935	.245	$13,949.00	.11	.02695	8
				1.0				

Buy Decision

Initial Demand branches: .5 and .5
Final Demand branches from $100,000: .4 → $122,500, .6 → $106,000
Final Demand branches from $60,000: .30 → $80,000, .70 → $67,500
Cost Conditions branches: .3 and .7

$$E(CF) = \$65,350.67$$
$$-Cost = \$50,000.00$$
$$E(NPV) = \$15,350.67$$
$$\sigma NPV = \$14,286$$

$$E(IRR) = .178$$
$$\sigma IRR = .112$$

$$E(\text{cash flow}) = 0.06(\$63,252) + 0.14(\$86,214) + \cdots + 0.245(\$56,935)$$
$$= \$65,350.67$$

Subtracting the assumed cost of the project from the expected value of the cash flows produces the expected net present value $E(\text{NPV})$ for the project. Symbolically this is

$$E(\text{CF}) - \text{cost} = E(\text{NPV})$$
$$\$65,350.67 - \$50,000 = \$15,350.67$$

Finally, to make the most use of our available information, we would also compute the standard deviation of the NPVs, $\sigma(\text{NPV})$, which is \$14,286.

A second approach we could take would be to concentrate on the internal rates of return rather than the NPVs. Column 7 in Figure 12.5 presents the IRRs for each branch in the tree diagram. To compute the expected value and standard deviation of the IRRs we would proceed in the same fashion as was used when dealing with NPVs. These computations are carried out in column 8. As is summarized at the bottom of column 8,

$$E(\text{IRR}) = 0.178$$
$$\sigma(\text{IRR}) = 0.112$$

As a result, either in terms of NPVs or IRRs we now have a measure of both the magnitude of the expected return and of the potential variability (risk) of the return. We have used the tree diagram to estimate the expected return and its standard deviation, but we are still faced with the problem of making the final decision about whether to accept or reject the project. Is an expected return of 17.8 percent sufficiently high to offset the risk in the project as measured by its standard deviation? To answer this question, the risk–return information generated in this section must be combined with utility theory.

RISK-ADJUSTED DISCOUNT RATES

Another technique for handling uncertainty in capital budgeting is the risk-adjusted discount rate. This procedure involves making an estimate of the risk associated with a proposed investment and then adjusting the discount rate to reflect this risk. This approach requires that a discount rate be tailored to fit the characteristics of each project.

If we define a riskless rate of return as the rate earned on an asset whose returns may be determined with certainty, then a risk premium commensurate with the risk of the project must be added to the risk-free rate when investing in a risky project. Following the IRR system, the hurdle rate would be raised by this premium amount for projects carrying risk, and under the NPV system the cost of capital would be increased. For example, with the rate on short-term government bonds at 6 percent, a firm may require as adequate risk compensation a 15 percent return on additions to productive capacity, 25 percent on new products, and 40 percent on investments in developing countries.

Subjective adjustments have proved workable, and it is not possible to say that more sophisticated systems yield superior results.

Summary

Our purpose in this chapter has been to explore briefly some of the techniques that have been proposed for dealing with risk. While this chapter is far from a complete survey of the entire field, most of the major concepts have been covered. It should be obvious from our discussion that risk or uncertainty is a very difficult thing to contend with and that, especially in terms of practical application, much work remains to be done. However, saying that risk is a difficult topic does not make it go away. Businessmen everywhere must contend with it on a daily basis. Even though currently available techniques leave much to be desired, we believe that there is much to be gained by studying them despite their limitations. The more insight we can obtain into the ways decisions are made and the factors that are important in any decision, the better will be the improvements in the future.

Study Questions

1. What assumptions concerning risk are built into the discount rate used in capital budgeting analysis?
2. What is the meaning of risk? What are the most popular statistical measures of risk?
3. Why may the use of the standard deviation as a risk measure lead to wrong decisions? What modifications can be made to obtain an improved measure?
4. Differentiate between classical and subjective probabilities. Which are more relevant to the businessman?
5. Explain the term "diminishing marginal utility of money."
6. Why might the utility of an additional dollar of income not be as high to a prosperous firm as to a marginal firm?

7. How does willingness to risk a certain sum of money on a project relate to the size of the firm? Is this a rational attitude? Why?
8. What are the dangers of using payback as a technique for coping with risk?
9. What are risk-adjusted discount rates?

Problems

1. Waco, Inc., is considering two mutually exclusive projects, A and B. Project A's investment is $10,000, project B's is $12,000. Table 12.2 presents the net present value probability distribution for each project.

Table 12.2. NPV Probability Distribution of Projects A and B

Project A		Project B	
Probability	NPV Estimate	Probability	NPV Estimate
0.1	$1,000	0.2	$1,000
0.4	2,000	0.3	2,000
0.4	4,000	0.3	4,000
0.1	5,000	0.2	5,000

a. Compute the expected net present value of projects A and B.
b. Compute the standard deviation of each probability distribution.
c. Compute the coefficient of variation for each project.
d. Rank projects A and B according to expected net present value and risk.

2. The Peer Gynt Music Company is considering expanding its present downtown location. The project cost is $20,000. Table 12.3 gives appropriate net present value estimates and their probabilities.

a. Determine the expected return of the project and the risk (standard deviation).

Before any action can be taken, the opportunity arises to establish a second store in the new Red Mill suburban shopping center. The project cost is $30,000.

Table 12.3. Peer Gynt Music Company Net Present Value Estimates of Expansion Project

NPV Estimate	Probability
$3,000	0.2
4,000	0.6
5,000	0.2
	1.0

Table 12.4 presents the net present value estimates for the project and their probabilities.

Table 12.4. Peer Gynt Music Company Net Present Value Estimates of Red Mill Shopping Center Project

NPV Estimate	Probability
$11,000	0.3
12,000	0.4
13,000	0.3
	1.0

    b.   Determine the expected return of the shopping center project and the risk.

    c.   Comparing the expansion and Red Mill shopping center projects, which promises to be more profitable? Which carries the least risk? How would you decide which project to select?

3.   Joe Go-Go, an energetic young businessman, is interested in determining his utility function and turns to you for help. After some close questioning you determine the following facts.

Figure 12.6. Joe Go-Go's utility curve for money.

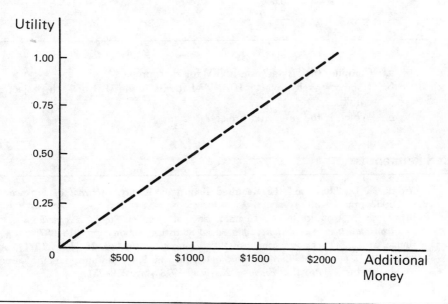

a. Offered the opportunity to gamble $1000 with 50–50 odds of doubling his money or losing it, Go-Go would refuse to gamble. He would hold onto his $1000.

b. Offered the opportunity to gamble $500 with 50–50 odds of winning $1000 or losing the $500, he would gamble.

c. Offered the opportunity to gamble $700 with 50–50 odds of winning $1000 or losing the $700, he would be indifferent as to whether he gambled or not. The $700 certain would be equally attractive to him as the gamble with 50–50 odds.

You conclude that $2000 has a utility of 1.00 to Go-Go. No money, of course, has a zero utility. The $700 has a utility of 0.50, since Go-Go would be willing to accept 50–50 odds of doubling his $1000 fortune or losing $700 or not gambling at all and keeping the $700 safe. Given these three points, trace Go-Go's utility curve on the graph in Figure 12.6. If the relationship between utility and money were linear, the curve would be a straight line, as indicated in the graph. Does the curve indicate that Go-Go is a risk taker or a risk avoider?

4. The Fauerbach Company uses risk-adjusted discount rates. Under consideration are two mutually exclusive projects. Each costs $7500 and has an expected life of three years.

Project A is believed to be riskier and management requires a risk premium of 5 percent. Projects B requires a risk premium of 3 percent. The risk-free rate is 6 percent. The net cash flows of each project are

A		B
$1,500	Year 1	$4,500
3,500	Year 2	3,500
7,500	Year 3	2,500

a. Compute the risk-adjusted NPV for each project.

b. Compute each project's IRR. What rate is the IRR of each project compared with?

c. Which is the preferred project?

Selected References

Arditti, F. D., "Risk and the Required Return on Equity," *Journal of Finance,* 22 (Mar. 1967), pp. 14–36.

Benishay, H. "Attitudes toward Characteristics of Common Stock," *Proceedings of the American Statistical Association* (1968 Social Statistics Section), pp. 318–337.

Blume, M. E., "On the Assessment of Risk," *Journal of Finance,* 26 (Mar. 1971), pp. 95–117.

Breen, W. J., and E. M. Lerner, "Corporate Financial Strategies and Market Measures of Risk and Return," *Journal of Finance,* 28 (May 1973), pp. 339–351.

Brown, R., "Do Managers Find Decision Theory Useful?" *Harvard Business Review,* 48 (May-June 1970), pp. 78–89.

Fisher, I. M., and R. G. Hall, "Risk and Corporate Rates of Return," *Quarterly Journal of Economics,* 83 (Feb. 1969), pp. 79–92.

Gentry, J., and J. Pike, "An Empirical Study of the Risk-Return Hypothesis Using Common Stock Portfolios of Life Insurance Companies," *Journal of Financial and Quantitative Analysis,* 5 (June 1970), pp. 179–186.

Hakansson, N. H., "Friedman—Savage Utility Functions Consistent with Risk Aversion," *Quarterly Journal of Economics,* 86 (Aug. 1970), pp. 472–487.

Hertz, D. B., "Risk Analysis in Capital Investments," *Harvard Business Review,* 42 (Jan.–Feb. 1964), pp. 95–106.

Hirshleifer, J., "Investment Decision under Uncertainty: Applications of the State-Preference Approach," *Quarterly Journal of Economics,* 80 (May 1966), pp. 252–277.

Lerner, E. M., and R. E. Machol, "Risk, Ruin and Investment Analysis," *Journal of Financial and Quantitative Analysis,* 4 (Dec. 1969), pp. 473–492.

Lintner, J., "Security Prices, Risk, and Maximal Gains from Diversification," *Journal of Finance,* 20 (Dec. 1965), pp. 587–615.

Litzenberger, R. H., and A. P. Budd, "Corporate Investment Criteria and the Valuation of Risk Assets," *Journal of Financial and Quantitative Analysis,* 5 (Dec. 1970), pp. 395–419.

Magee, J. F., "How to Use Decision Trees in Capital Budgeting," *Harvard Business Review,* 42 (Sept.–Oct. 1964), pp. 79–95.

Markowitz, H., "Portfolio Selection," *Journal of Finance,* 7(Mar. 1952), pp. 77–91.

Morton, W. A., "Risk and Return: Instability of Earnings as a Measure of Risk," *Land Economics,* 45 (May 1969), pp. 229–261.

Näsland, B., "A Model of Capital Budgeting under Risk," *Journal of Business,* 39 (Apr. 1966), pp. 257–271.

Richardson, L. K., "Do High Risks Lead to High Returns?" *Financial Analysts Journal,* 26 (Mar.–Apr. 1970), pp. 88–99.

Rubenstein, M. E., "A Mean-Variance Synthesis of Corporate Financial Theory," *Journal of Finance,* 28 (Mar. 1973), pp. 167–181.

Stapleton, R. C., "Portfolio Analysis, Stock Valuation and Capital Budgeting Decision Rules for Risky Projects," *Journal of Finance,* 26 (Mar. 1971), pp. 95–117.

Swalm, R. O., "Utility Theory—Insights into Risk Taking," *Harvard Business Review,* 44 (Nov.–Dec. 1966), pp. 123–136.

Virts, J. R., "Weighing Risk in Capacity Expansion," *Harvard Business Review,* 48 (May–June 1970), pp. 132–141.

Wood, D. H., "Improving Estimates that Involve Uncertainty," *Harvard Business Review,* 44 (July–Aug. 1966), pp. 91–98.

Appendix 1

Evaluating Return and Risk of an Asset Portfolio

Up to now we have assumed that projects are independent of each other. Seldom can one project, however, be considered apart from the other projects a firm adopts. Adopting one group of projects will represent a different composite return and degree of risk than commitment of the same total capital to a different project mix.

Return and Risk of a Group of Projects. The return from an asset portfolio may be considered the weighted average of the percentage of total funds invested in each project times the expected (mean) return from the project. But the risk of the portfolio is not simply a weighted average of the risk estimated to be associated with the individual projects. This is true only if the returns of the individual projects are perfectly positively correlated with each other. To the extent risks of individual projects offset each other, we can select an asset portfolio that yields the optimum risk–return combination.

If variation is our measure of risk, then the higher the variation, the greater the risk of a portfolio. The variation of the portfolio is determined in part by the variability of the individual projects, in part by the extent to which the variabilities of individual projects tend to offset each other, and by the percent of total capital invested in each project. The variability of one project associated with the variability of another is called the *covariance*. For a project portfolio that may contain either one, the other, or both projects the net variation may range from zero, where equal amounts of funds are committed to two perfectly negatively correlated projects, to the variation of the highest risk project if all the funds are invested in that one project.

Perfectly Positively Correlated Projects. Assume that the Pine Box Casket Company has a given sum to invest in either or both of two projects, new hand tools or additional advertising, in any amounts desired. If proportionately the returns on both projects rise and fall together, the projects are perfectly positively correlated. Then any combination of the two has the same expected return and carries the same risk. Suppose, for example, that each project has the cash flow estimates and corresponding probabilities shown in Table 12.5.

Table 12.5. Pine Box Casket Company Expected Return, Hand Tools or Additional Advertising

Probabilities P_i	Cash Flow Estimates R_i	
0.2	$2,000	$R_i = \$3,000$
0.6	$3,000	
0.2	$4,000	$\sigma = \$633$

Since the returns of the two projects are perfectly positively correlated, their total may be treated as a single project. Regardless of the percentage of a fixed sum—say M—committed to the projects, the portfolio will yield the same expected rate of return and carry the same risk, provided the entire amount is invested. Should we have available $2M$ funds and decide to undertake fully both projects, we will have the figures found in Table 12.6. Doubling the amount invested doubles the expected return and the standard deviation.

Perfectly Negatively Correlated Projects. Suppose we have two perfectly negatively correlated projects. They are a new hearse and a new ambulance for the Friendly Funeral Home.[1] The cost of each vehicle is the same, namely $10,800, and each vehicle is to be in service for four years and then junked at no salvage value. Three economic conditions may prevail, as shown in Table 12.7. If the first economic condition prevails (many deaths by suicide require a hearse but no ambulance), the hearse is expected to yield $6000 of revenue and the ambulance $2000; if the second condition prevails, the hearse and the ambulance can each be expected to earn $4000; and if the third condition prevails, the hearse can be expected to yield $2000 and the

[1] In this community faster ambulance service means fewer hearse passengers.

ambulance $6000. The expected return of this asset portfolio with an equal amount of funds invested in each project is $8000. The standard deviation of the portfolio is zero because the portfolio always returns $8000. Though each project individually involves some variation, the two risks perfectly offset each other.

Table 12.6. Pine Box Casket Company Expected Return, Hand Tools and Additional Advertising, Investment Doubled

Probabilities P_i	Cash Flow Estimates R_i	
0.2	$4,000	$R_i = \$6,000$
0.6	$6,000	
0.2	$8,000	$\sigma = \$1,267$

Table 12.7. Friendly Funeral Home Hearse and Ambulance Investment Estimated Cash Flows and Probabilities under Three Possible Economic Conditions

Possible Economic Condition w_i	Estimated Probability P_i	Estimated Return on Individual Projects		Estimated Return, Combined Projects
		Ambulance	Hearse	
w_1	0.2	$2,000	$6,000	$8,000
w_2	0.6	$4,000	$4,000	$8,000
w_3	0.2	$6,000	$2,000	$8,000

Optimum Combination of Projects. Most asset portfolios consist of projects falling somewhere between being perfectly positively correlated and perfectly negatively correlated. Let us see how the percentage amounts invested in two projects affect the expected return and the risk from the portfolio.

Boothill Memorial Company has the opportunity to acquire additional quarrying rights for granite and marble. Based on historical data, the expected return for the granite project is $3000 and for the marble project $3300. The expected return $E(Q)$ of the total quarry operation is given by

$$E(Q) = aE(b) + (1 - a)E(M) \tag{12-1}$$
$$= a(\$3000) + 1 - a(\$3300)$$

where a equals the percentage invested in the granite quarry and $(1 - a)$ the percentage invested in the marble quarry.

Table 12.8. Boothill Memorial Company Expected Returns and Variance for Different Mixes of Projects G and M

Proportions of G	M	Expected Return from Total Quarry Operations*	Variance** (Risk of Quarrying)
1.0	0.0	$3,000	$ 800.0
0.9	0.1	3,030	536.1
0.8	0.2	3,060	334.4
0.7	0.3	3,090	224.9
0.6	0.4	3,120	177.6
0.5	0.5	3,150	202.5
0.4	0.6	3,180	299.6
0.3	0.7	3,210	468.9
0.2	0.8	3,240	710.4
0.1	0.9	3,270	1,024.1
0.0	1.0	3,300	1,410.0

* Computed by use of Eq. (12-1) where $E(G)$ is $3000 and $E(M)$ is $3300.
** Computed by use of Eq. (12-2).

To determine the risk attached to any combination of the two projects, we need the variance of each project and the covariance of the projects. The risk, var Q, of the total quarry is determined by

$$\text{var}(Q) = a^2 \, \text{var}(G) + (1 - a)^2 \, \text{var}(M) + 2a(1 - a) \, \text{cov}(G,M) \qquad (12\text{-}2)$$

Based on historical data, the variances and the covariance were determined to be:

$$\text{var}(G) = \quad \$ \, 800$$
$$\text{var}(M) = \quad \$1410$$
$$\text{cov}(G,M) = -\$ \, 700$$

binations of the granite and marble quarry projects. We give the calculations for one Using Eqs. (12-1) and (12-2) we can calculate the expected return and risk for various com- combination:

$$G = a = 0.6$$
$$M = (1 - a) = 0.4$$
$$E(Q) = 0.6(\$3000) + 0.4(\$3300)$$
$$= \$3120$$
$$\text{var}(Q) = (0.6)^2\$800 + (0.4)^2\$1410 + 0.2(0.6)(0.4)(-\$700)$$
$$= \$288 + \$255 - \$336$$
$$= \$177$$

Figure 12.7. Boothill Memorial Company risk and expected return associated with different mixes of the granite and marble projects. Based on Table 12.8.

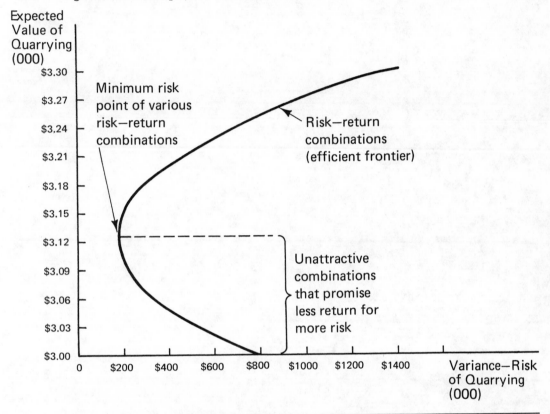

Note that whereas the expected return from quarrying is a simple weighted average of the returns from granite and marble, the risk of a combined granite–marble quarry can be less than the least risky project. This reduction in risk by diversifying between projects is called the *portfolio effect*. Other risk–return points are presented in Table 12.8. The expected return from quarrying varies from $3000 to $3300; the variance from $177.60 to $1410. The least risk occurs when 60 percent of the available funds are invested in the granite project and 40 percent in the marble project. The data of Table 12.8 are graphed in Figure 12.7.

part four
INTERMEDIATE AND LONG-TERM FINANCING

13

TERM LOANS AND LEASE FINANCING

All intermediate financing involves maturities beyond one year, but the line on the other end is not drawn on a time basis but on the type of arrangements for the loan and its repayment. Intermediate financing generally provides for periodic, payments whereas long-term financing usually is repaid in a lump sum at maturity. Three major forms of intermediate financing exist—term loans, installment financing, and leasing.

Liquidity is the key to a short-term loan. With intermediate financing the emphasis shifts to profitability. The longer loan span makes preoccupation with liquidity hazardous. Extended periods of unprofitable operation dissipate liquid assets, but if the firm is profitable, it generates funds that may be used to repay the loan.

TERM LOANS

Term loans are normally paid off in regular installments covering principal and interest and are privately placed with banks or insurance companies. This arrangement neatly fits the financing of a permanent increase in working capital or the acquisition of a specific asset such as equipment. Maturity is tailored to the firm's expected earning power and cash-generating abilities. Funds are not raised for a longer period of time than needed, and idle funds need not be temporarily reinvested. Also, term funds may be obtainable at a lower rate than long-term debt funds, thus widening the leverage gain, and are usually cheaper and more quickly obtained than the selling of stock.

Term financing is well suited to meeting the needs of smaller and growing firms.

There are also disadvantages. Financing a permanent need with term funds requires that the expected level of earnings be realized to repay the loan as projected. The two time schedules (loan repayment and increased earnings) must mesh. Committing the firm to a sizable annual payment for a number of years is risky, but the risk is lessened if the firm has a good margin of safety between expected earnings and annual payments and if future earnings can be accurately predicted.

Lenders

Commercial banks and insurance companies are the leading sources of term loan funds. Bank term loans are generally 1 to 5 years and are given mostly to small firms that have $10 million or less in assets. Insurance company loans are frequently 5 to 15 years and are made to large firms. Many term loans involve the bank taking the short maturities of the loan and an insurance company the long maturities. Government agencies, such as the Small Business Administration (SBA), also lend to firms on a term loan basis where other financial institutions are unwilling to lend. Banks frequently participate in loans made by the SBA by making all or part of the loan subject to the guarantee of the SBA as to interest and principal repayment, with the borrower paying a fee to the SBA for this guarantee.

Provisions

A note or a series of notes is executed by the borrower with staggered maturity dates for the several repayments. To reduce the risk arising from longer maturity and uncertainty of future earnings, the lender makes a thorough financial analysis of the firm, requires the submission of future periodic financial statements, may or may not require collateral, but will impose protective covenants. The collateral taken is mainly stock, bonds, machinery and equipment, or other long-term assets. The protective covenants include provisions such as the maintenance of specified amounts of working capital and net worth, "key" man insurance on the lives of the top management, and prohibitions (unless the lender consents) against sale of assets, acquisition of further debt, repayment of existing debt (particularly loans by officers), the payment of dividends, increases in officer's salaries, or the reacquisition of the firm's stock. Most of these so-called negative limitations are designed to prevent taking assets "out the back door" and leaving the lender with a corporate shell.

Besides these protective provisions, the loan contract will contain the *acceleration clause,* which provides that in the event of any default (in payment or of any other provision of the loan) the entire note may be declared due and payable immediately. In the absence of this clause the firm is liable only for the installment currently due.

Computing Payments

Term loans are typically repayable in equal installments covering both interest and principal. Where these installments do not fully repay the loan at maturity, the last payment is larger and called a *balloon* payment. Balloons are not popular with lenders. Most term loans may be repaid ahead of schedule but with a prepayment penalty (usually one year's interest on the prepayment).

To illustrate the determination of a term loan amortization (repayment) schedule assume a firm borrows $1000 for five years with interest at 8 percent. The $1000 is really the present value of a stream of annual payments for five years discounted at 8 percent. We want to find the amount of each of these annual payments. From Chapter 10 we know that the present value PV of a stream of uniform payments equals the annual payment A_n times the discount factor DF (Table A.2 at end of this book), or $PV = A_n(DF)$. Solving for A_n we have $A_n = PV/DF$. Thus $1000/3.993 \cong 250 where 3.993 is the DF for five annual payments at 8 percent. The $250 annual payment includes principal and interest. The first year's interest is $80 ($1000 × 8%) and principal repayment $170 ($250 − $80). The complete schedule for the five years is shown in Table 13.1

Table 13.1. Computation of Term Loan Repayments per $1000 over Five Equal Annual Installments at 8 Percent

Year	(1) Annual Payment $(A_n = PV/DF)$	(2) Interest	(3) Principal (1) − (2)	(4) Remaining Balance at End of Year $1000 − (3) Cumulated
1	$ 250 or ($1000/3.993)	$80 or ($1000 × 0.08)	$170 or ($250 − $80)	$830
2	250	66 or [(1000 − 170) × 0.08]	184 or (250 − 66)	646
3	250	52 or [(1000 − 354) × 0.08]	198 or (250 − 52)	448
4	250	36 or [(1000 − 552) × 0.08]	214 or (250 − 36)	234
5	250	19 or [(1000 − 766) × 0.08]	231 or (250 − 19)	0*
Total	$1250			

* Rounding error.

Cost

The rate on term loan financing averages 1 percent higher than for short-term credit lent the same borrower. The financial standing of the borrower, the size of the loan, and the condition of the capital market determine the exact rate charged. A financially strong firm borrowing a large amount may pay only slightly more than the prime rate. A small firm might pay 4 or 5 percent over prime. On larger term loans the rate may change over the life of the loan with variations in the prime rate. This practice is growing. Likewise lenders are currently seeking part of their compensation in the form of options to buy common stock at a price fixed over some agreed upon period. If the firm prospers and its stock rises above the option price, the lender can take capital gains.

INSTALLMENT EQUIPMENT FINANCING

The purchase of income-producing machinery or equipment on a plan providing for an initial down payment and installment payments amortizing the remaining balance is known as *installment equipment financing*. Commercial finance companies (sometimes the subsidiaries of the equipment manufacturer) are the primary sources of this type of credit. Commercial banks are entering this area. The field has grown rapidly due to increasing mechanization of all phases of production, but is still small relative to other intermediate term financing.

The cost of this financing is high. Small firms or those with weak credit ratings are forced to follow a policy of pay-as-you-earn and, thus, use the collateral of the purchased equipment and the down payment to induce the borrower to lend. The weaker the credit rating, the larger the down payment required. Acquisition of equipment on the installment plan enables the firm to obtain a greater amount of credit than otherwise possible, and is attractive to the firm if substantially improved future revenues can be expected from the new asset.

The reasons for the high cost of installment equipment financing are the risk borne by the lender, the administrative cost of servicing the loan, and the poor bargaining power and limited alternatives of the borrower. The down payment on a piece of equipment—factory, farm, medical, bowling, hotel or restaurant, and so on—may range from 20 to 35 percent of the purchase price with the balance amortized over three to five years. The payments include principal and interest and are set to recover the amount of the loan substantially in advance of the estimated decline in the value of the equipment.

The lender looks to the recovery value of the equipment as protection for his loan and to the pressure on the borrower to meet the payment schedule in order to keep the equipment. The situation is analogous to the equipment trust certificate in railroading which is issued to finance rolling stock. Even when issued by a weak railroad, these securities are of high quality since without a locomotive, the railroad stops. If the resale value of the pledged asset fails to cover the outstanding portion of the loan at any time, the lender can seldom find other unmortgaged assets of the borrower to recover the difference. The repayment schedule may provide for uniform payments over the stipulated term or may follow the anticipated decline in market value of the asset.

Installment financing may be arranged either with the manufacturer or dealer selling the equipment or directly with a finance company. The basic document is a contract that retains title to the equipment in the lender until payment is completed. The manufacturer or the dealer arranging financing may either retain the paper himself or in turn may discount it with a finance company. Usually when the manufacturer or dealer sells the paper to a finance company, it is stipulated that in the event of default the lender may repossess the equipment and return it to the manufacturer or dealer in order to recover full payment of the balance due. Then the manufacturer or dealer reconditions and sells the equipment, retaining any gain and absorbing any loss.

LEASING

A lease is a contractual arrangement whereby the lessor (property owner) grants the lessee (user) the right to the services of the property for a specified time period in return for periodic payments. The lessee may be given an option to renew the lease or an option to purchase, exercisable during the term of the lease or at its end.

The leasing of real property has long been a method of obtaining the use of this asset. During the past 20 years, the popularity of leasing has spread to other assets and grown rapidly, attracting many firms as lessors offering a wide variety of deals—so diverse that the topic must be considered largely in general terms. The specific lease agreement is usually tailored to the requirements and bargaining position of the lessee vis-à-vis the lessor.

LEASE ARRANGEMENTS

Leases may be classified as operating leases and financial leases. An *operating lease* involves some period less than the normal life of the asset and hence recovery from the first lessee of less than the asset's cost. A *financial lease* involves recovery of the full cost from the lessee. One variation of the financial lease is the *sale and lease-back arrangement* in which the present owner sells the asset to the leasing firm and immediately leases it back for some specified term.

Although our main concern is with financial leases, operating leases have become so important, they deserve comment.

Operating Leases

An example of an operating lease is a contract for a jet plane to ferry the firm's executive team. The lease may give the firm the right to cancel before the lease expiration date. The lease will also provide for maintenance by the lessor.

Computers, trucks, automobiles, and specialized equipment are typical assets involved in operating leases.

Financial Leases

A financial lease is not cancelable and commits the lessee to make a series of payments whose sum is greater than the cost of the asset because a return on the investment is included. Maintenance is usually the obligation of the lessee.

Equipment and real estate are typical assets involved in financial leases. Specialized leasing companies are active in the equipment leasing field as are commercial banks since a 1963 Comptroller of the Currency ruling permitting national banks to acquire and lease assets to customers.

The customer selects the equipment, negotiates the terms with the manufacturer, arranges for the bank or specialized leasing company to purchase the equipment and immediately leases. The many different kinds of assets and the competitiveness of leasing have led to considerable specialization. Some firms specialize in the leasing of vehicles, others in office equipment and computers, and still others in industrial equipment. Life insurance companies dominate the long-term real estate leasing market.

Leasing is not merely an alternative financing plan for the user but a sales tool for the manufacturer of the asset. Cash-short customers cause a manufacturer to form a leasing subsidiary which buys the equipment from the manufacturer for lease to customers, thus promoting the sale of the manufacturer's equipment. The major profit is made on the sale of the equipment. The leasing operation is subservient to this objective.

The principal financial difference between an installment purchase and a financial lease lies in the length of time over which payments are made—

the cost is paid in a much shorter period of time in installment purchasing. Other important differences are that the installment purchaser owns any residual value and likewise can resell while the lessee in a financial lease does not own the residual value at the end of the lease and cannot alter his situation as in a resale.

The Financial Lease as a Form of Debt Financing

The financial lease creates long-term contractual obligations similar to debt financing. Term of the lease is not the determinative factor. By signing a lease, the lessee agrees to pay fixed rental fees, service the property, and maintain financial standards. A debtor–creditor relationship runs between lessee and lessor.

The rental payments and protective provisions of a lease must be met as promptly and as fully as bond issue covenants, but the consequences of defaulting on a realty lease differ from defaulting on debt. Under a lease the lessor may take possession of his property by a prompt court order in the event the lessee does not fulfill the terms of the agreement. The lessor's claim to damages is limited to one year's rent for realty in the event of bankruptcy and liquidation. If the firm is reorganized and the trustee in reorganization rejects the lease, the lessor is limited to a maximum of three years' rent for realty. A bondholder, on the other hand, has a claim against the firm for the entire principal and unpaid interest. Even when his claim is secured by a mortgage, a creditor cannot upon default simply come in and take possession. A court order after a hearing is needed to foreclose a mortgage for the debt and the creditor collects only his debt; any surplus on a sale goes to the debtor or other creditors.

Avoidance of the Risks of Ownership through the Insurance Principle

Leasing avoids the risks of ownership and substitutes a fee for the risks of obsolescence and the possible decline in the value of the asset through time. Leasing real estate is desirable in an area subject to an erosion of value due to market, traffic, or population shifts. Similarly, leasing is desirable for the acquisition of high-technology equipment subject to rapid and sudden obsolescence. The lessor is usually more knowledgeable than the lessee regarding risk of obsolescence and includes in the rental payments a premium for bearing this risk.

The lessee gains from the insurance principle. Particularly as to specialized assets, the lessee might suffer a large loss due to technological change if he bought and owned. The lease enables him to shift this risk to the lessor. The lessor can spread the loss of a sudden technological change as to one piece of equipment over the many pieces that he has leased, provided these pieces are not all exposed to the same technological risk.

Flexibility

If equipment becomes obsolete and is returned to the lessor before expiration of the lease, the lessee can substitute new equipment under a new lease for the obsolete equipment of the old lease.

The leasing of real estate for terms running from 20 to 100 years provides little if any flexibility over ownership. We have a heavy commitment in the property in either event. In fact, leasing may be less flexible unless the lease is transferable. But if the lessee owned the property, he could terminate the situation by selling the asset. If the utility of leased property to the lessee declines, the firm must still make rental payments. Subleasing by the lessee is usually not prohibited as long as the original lessee remains secondarily liable, that is, the original lessee is liable to pay if the new lessee defaults.

Many business properties not earning a profit—a particular theater, for example—can seldom be made profitable simply by a change of ownership. Downward valuation of the property and wiping out some claims in bankruptcy usually is necessary before unprofitable property can again show a satisfactory return on investment.

Outright ownership of the property in a case such as the theater might provide more flexibility. Assuming we own a chain of theaters and one of these is no longer profitable, we can demolish it and construct a parking ramp. Leasing would tie us to the theater operation.

Tax Advantage

A firm owning real estate can depreciate the building but not the land. But if the firm enters a sale and lease-back arrangement, it can deduct the entire rental payment for federal income tax purposes, thus including amortization of the cost of the land as well as buildings over the term of the lease. This maneuver is particularly attractive where the land component constitutes a high percentage of the total value of the real estate or where the building is already fully depreciated on the books of the owner who sells and leases back. Any gain on the sale of real estate in the sale and lease-back is subject to capital gains tax. But this rate is 30 percent, while the rental payments are offset against income taxed at a rate of 48 percent.

Leasing May Be the Only Alternative

We have assumed the firm has a choice. But a small or weak firm unable to secure the necessary funds for purchase may be forced to lease. Competitive pressures to expand may leave the firm little alternative when earnings are poor, credit sources dried up, and the debt market closed to the firm.

Sometimes the owner of the asset refuses to sell. A computer manufacturer or shoe machinery producer wishing to retain ultimate control over the equipment may insist on lease terms. Or the owners of land may desire to hold the land for capital appreciation. But they may be willing to sell the timber or mineral rights, or permit the erection of a building. Furthermore, purchase of the asset may not be feasible considering the business of the firm. For an arts and crafts shop in midtown Manhattan, leasing space on the ground floor is the viable alternative to purchasing the skyscraper.

COST OF LEASING VERSUS OWNING

The final decision between leasing and owning rests on comparative costs. Interest cost and income tax deductions are two factors in the comparison. The implicit interest cost of lease funds can run from ½ to 2 percent higher than on comparable term loans. This differential can be partly attributed to an imperfect market situation and partly to the insurance principle where the lessor is expert at specific risks and seeks compensation for this service. Lessors may not adjust the implied interest rate on the lease for the residual value of the asset at the end of the lease, resulting in a higher lease cost. Under competitive pressures, the interest rate implied in a lease can approach that of comparable term loans. Much depends on the bargaining power of the respective parties and the residual value of the asset.

Implied Interest Rate in Leasing

Under highly simplified assumptions, the interest rate implied in leasing can be calculated by equating the present value of the after-tax lease payments and the estimated after-tax residual value of the equipment with its cost. The interest rate that does this is the internal rate of return. Comparisons must be made over a specific time period because at different time cutoff points, the same terms will produce opposite decisions.

To illustrate, assume Suds, Inc., requires a new pretzel machine. The cost of the machine is $13,896. The firm can lease the machine at a rental of $3000 a year for six years. Consulting the present value tables at the end of the text we find that the before tax cost of leasing is 8 percent, assuming zero residual value.[1] Should there be a residual value of $3000, the effective gross cost of the lease financing would jump to 12 percent.

The Residual Value Factor

Residual value considerations are important in all cases. Suppose that in the case of Suds the lessor estimates $2500 residual value for the equipment and sets the rental payments at $2500 per year to earn a 6 percent return on investment. If subsequently the actual residual value of the equipment drops to $1000, the lessor earns 4 percent.

Residual values in real estate leasing are frequently in the distant future and, hence, their present value is of less consequence. But major swings upward occur in real estate values and offset the futurity dimension. Equipment normally declines in value. The guessing concerns the rate of decline, the chances and timing of a technological breakthrough that will render the present equipment obsolete. But real estate values not only may decline substantially, but also appreciate tremendously. The range within which the residual value of the real estate may fluctuate is wider.

For example, a firm may find a lease or loan equally attractive to secure a shopping center location, given the estimated residual value. The actual residual value likely will *in retrospect* make either the lease or the loan the superior arrangement. A substantially high residual value will favor ownership. If the property were leased, upon termination of the lease the firm must seek another location at high cost or remain at the same location at increased rental. On the other hand, a substantially lower residual value would favor leasing. At termination the firm returns the property to the owner and seeks another, more desirable location or pays a lower rental.

Because of the wider range within which real estate residual values may fall, the risk element is prominent in such lease or own decisions. One way to analyze the risk element is to cast the estimates of residual value as a probability distribution and to use the concept of expected value and its standard deviation to measure the confidence to place in the computations.

Calculating the Cost of Leasing versus Buying

The most meaningful method of comparing leasing to borrowing is on an after-tax basis, but in practice comparisons are difficult because the required assumptions affect leasing and owning differently.

---

[1] $13,896/$3000 = 4.632. Refer to Table A.2 at the end of the text and run your finger across the six-year row until you hit 4.6229 (4.632 $\simeq$ 4.6229). Look to the top of the table and find 8 percent. This is the implicit interest cost.

An Example: Assume Alpine Ski, Inc., wants to build new facilities. The financial position of the firm is good. Borrowing on a 6 percent term-loan basis is possible. The facilities cost $252,340—$200,000 building and $52,340 land. The owner will sell the land for $52,340 and let the firm construct the building, or will construct the building and lease the facility to Alpine Ski at a rental of $22,000 a year for 20 years. Assuming zero residual value of both land and building, the rental is sufficient to amortize the total cost of the property over the 20-year period and provide the lessor with a 6 percent return on investment.[2] With income taxes at 50 percent, the net after-tax outflow on the firm will be $11,000. The $22,000 annual lease payment creates a tax shield of $11,000.

Compiling a schedule of after-tax cash outflows under the borrowing alternative is more difficult. The entire annual payment cannot be tax deducted as an expense, only the interest on the loan and the allowable depreciation on the building. The after-tax cash outflow under the borrowing alternative, to be compared with the after-tax lease payments, is calculated by deducting from the annual loan payments the tax shield created by the interest and allowable depreciation charge. The remainder is our net out of pocket cash cost. The calculations for the first three years are computed on Table 13.2.

Table 13.2. Alpine Ski, Inc., Net After-Tax Cash Outflow under the Term Loan Arrangement and Lease for the First Three Years

	First Year	*Second Year*	*Third Year*
Term loan			
Loan amortization			
Principal	$6,860	$ 7,271	$ 7,707
Interest	15,140	14,729	14,293
	$22,000	$22,000	$22,000
Depreciation	$10,000	$10,000	$10,000
Interest	15,140	14,729	14,293
Total expense	25,140	24,729	24,293
Tax shield (50 percent)	12,570	12,365	12,147
Before-tax loan payment	22,000	22,000	22,000
After-tax cash outflow	$ 9,430	$ 9,635	$ 9,853
Lease			
After-tax cash outflow	$11,000	$11,000	$11,000

---

[2] $252,340/$22,000 = 11.47. From Table A.2 for 20 years, this represents an interest return of 6 percent.

A loan of $252,340 is necessary to acquire the property. The first year's interest payment at 6 percent is $15,140. We know $22,000 per year for 20 years will amortize a loan of $252,340 and provide a yield of 6 percent. Thus deducting from the $22,000 the $15,140 first year's interest payment, we find $6860 is return of principal. Only the $15,140 is tax deductible. To calculate the total tax shield, we also need the depreciation charges. Alpine Ski charges depreciation on a straight-line basis. For simplicity, assume the life of the building is 20 years.

Depreciation charges in the first and subsequent years are $10,000 ($200,000/20) per year. The total tax-deductible expense is $25,140 ($15,140 + 10,000). The tax shield is $12,570 (income tax rate of 50 percent). The before-tax payment on the term loan is $22,000. Deducting the tax shield, the after-tax payment is $9430 ($22,000 − $12,570). This figure compares with an after-tax payment of $11,000 under the lease arrangement.

Table 13.3. Lease versus Buy Analysis

	(1)	(2)	(3)	(4) $(1) \times (3)$	(5) $(2) \times (3)$
	After Tax Cash Outflow		11% PV	Discounted Cash Outflows	
Year	Lease	Loan	Factor	Lease	Loan
1	$ 11,000	$ 9,430	0.90090	$ 9,910	$ 8,495
2	11,000	9,635	0,81162	8,928	7,820
3	11,000	9,853	0.73119	8,043	7,204
4	11,000	10,085	0.65873	7,246	6,643
5	11,000	10,330	0.59345	6,528	6,130
6	11,000	10,590	0.53464	5,881	5,662
7	11,000	10,865	0.48166	5,298	5,233
8	11,000	11,157	0.43393	4,773	4,841
9	11,000	11,468	0.39092	4,300	4,483
10	11,000	11,794	0.35218	3,874	4,154
11	11,000	12,142	0.31728	3,490	3,852
12	11,000	12,510	0.28584	3,144	3,576
13	11,000	12,901	0.25751	2,833	3,322
14	11,000	13,315	0.23199	2,552	3,089
15	11,000	13,754	0.20900	2,299	2,875
16	11,000	14,219	0.18829	2,071	2,677
17	11,000	14,713	0.16963	1,866	2,496
18	11,000	15,244	0.15282	1,681	2,330
19	11,000	15,799	0.13768	1,514	2,175
20	11,000	16,386	0.12403	1,364	2,032
	$220,000	$246,190		$87,595	$89,089

In Table 13.3 the after-tax cash outflows for the 20-year period for both the lease and the loan are recorded. After year 7, the annual after-tax cash outflow for the loan exceeds that of the lease. Since the outflows for the loan payments are greater in later years, a present value analysis is necessary to determine which financing method is more costly.

The total after-tax dollar outflow of the lease is $220,000 as opposed to $246,190 for the loan—a differential of $26,190 in favor of leasing. Using 11 percent[3] as the appropriate discount rate, leasing is still favored although the differential now is only $1494 ($89,089 − $87,595).

To Lease or to Borrow? Is it more attractive to lease the property for 20 years, committing ourselves to pay $22,000 ($11,000 out of pocket) each year for a cumulative total on a time-adjusted basis of $87,595 and losing the property at the end of the period, or to take the term loan, also committing ourselves to paying $22,000 each year for a cumulative time-adjusted after-tax total of $89,089 and owning the property?

The land is currently worth $52,340 and the building $200,000. Assume after 20 years that the building is worthless, the land worth $52,340, and that the firm requires at least an 11 percent return on its projects. Then looking back, borrowing to buy would have been more attractive than leasing since $52,340 discounted at 11 percent yields $6490, which is greater than the prior $1494 difference between leasing and borrowing.

In the example we used straight-line depreciation and found the 11 percent time-adjusted net after-tax cash outflows were less for the lease than for owning when terminal value is zero. If we used accelerated depreciation, the taxes in the early years would be lower for a loan due to the higher depreciation charges (higher tax shield), thus decreasing the net after-tax cash outflows in these years. Since the lease outflows are unaffected, the result would be to change the time adjusted net after-tax cash outflow differential between leasing and owning to favor owning.

LEASE FINANCING TRAPS

The drafting of lease agreements is no job for amateurs. In a lease title to the property remains in the lessor's name and the entire amount of the lease payment may be deducted by the lessee for income tax purposes. Consequently, every lease agreement has two attackers—creditors and tax col-

---

[3] The appropriate discount factor is the weighted marginal cost of capital, a concept we will discuss in Chapter 19.

lectors. Creditors are only an intermittent threat; tax collectors are a constant threat. When a firm runs into financial difficulty, creditors of the lessee will take a hard look at the lease agreements, since the other assets are seldom sufficient to cover all the creditor claims. Consequently, to bolster their position creditors prefer to have the leased assets declared the property of the lessee rather than have the lessor simply repossess his property. Tax collectors would like to see the lease payments as payments on an installment sales contract. This would permit the lessee firm to deduct only an imputed interest payment plus depreciation rather than all the rental payment. The remainder would be considered a payment of principal. The result would be higher annual income tax payments for the lessee firm.

If an option in the lease permitting the lessee to buy and have prior lease payments credited to the purchase price exists, the lessee is in effect free to decide whether he has a lease or an installment sales contract. Such freedom, the tax collector argues, is intended only to avoid taxes. If the option to buy exists, but without credit against the purchase price for prior lease payments, some of the tax collector's argument is negated. The way to reduce the risk that the transaction will be classified as an installment purchase is to have the option price implicitly allow for rental payments through a declining option price over time. However, the option price cannot be reset every year, or it will be easy for the tax collector to show what is really going on.

Summary

Term loans and installment financing of equipment are forms of intermediate-term borrowing. This type of lending focuses on profitability. Term and installment loans are usually paid off in installments over the life of the loan. Term loans may be secured, and usually carry protective provisions designed to maintain the financial condition of the firm. Interest is charged on the unpaid balance. Small firms may find secured installment financing the only form of financing available. The cost is high. Interest charged is usually on the original balance and a large down payment is required as well as installment payments.

Leasing is an alternative to ownership for a firm to obtain the use of physical assets and has long been used in real estate. An early use in the equipment financing field is found in rolling stock leasing by railroads. Now leasing has spread to a wide variety of assets. The terms of the lease are tailored to the needs of the lessee.

The charges levied by the lessor are frequently higher than costs to borrow and buy, but leasing may provide other advantages. Restrictive bond covenants may be avoided; a higher percentage of the asset acquisition price may be financed; the risk of obsolescence is avoided and maintenance burdens may be shifted (both at a cost); and the problem of disposing of old equipment is eliminated.

The effective cost of leasing can be substantially affected by the residual value of the asset. Though not high when standardized equipment such as automobiles is involved, that risk rises rapidly for specialized equipment such as computers subject to rapid obsolescence or real estate where terminal values can rise significantly. Should a more rapid degree of obsolescence take place than contemplated in the lease payment schedule, the leasing option would be more attractive. When considering real estate, should a substantial and unforeseen appreciation in property value take place, ownership would be more attractive.

Lease rental payments are a fixed obligation. Failure to meet the lease provisions brings financial difficulties. The lessor has an advantage over the lessee's creditors, secured or unsecured. Upon default the lessor repossesses his property by a prompt court order. The secured creditor must wait longer for a court action before he can force the sale of the property in satisfaction of the debt, and then he gets none of the surplus if the property brings more than the debt. Thus financial institutions are willing to lease equipment to small and weak firms but not to lend to these firms.

Study Questions

1. Distinguish between a term loan and an installment financing loan. Which is more likely to be unavailable to the smaller firm? Why?
2. Despite the fact that the cost of installment equipment financing is high, why may it still be advantageous for some firms to finance their equipment needs by this method?
3. What are some of the protective covenants in a term loan and what is their purpose? How does the acceleration clause protect the lender? Whom does the balloon payment provision benefit? How?
4. Total lease payments normally exceed the lessor's cost of the property. What factors explain this differential? Since the lessor over the term of the lease is expected to recover at least his cost of the property, why should the credit worthiness of the lessee be of concern?
5. Why does the residual value element impart a greater risk to the borrow-and-buy versus lease decision when real estate is involved rather than automobiles? Would the decision be tipped one way or the other if the financial manager anticipated

a stepped up rate of inflation if the firm were contemplating leasing real estate? automobiles?

6. Why may a firm find it possible to lease equipment and yet not be able to borrow at the bank? In what way can we say a lessor may be better protected than a secured creditor in the event of default? in what way less well protected?

7. Leasing lost part of its competitive advantage when accelerated depreciation was allowed for tax purposes. Explain.

8. What reasons exist for leasing?

9. The credit worthiness of the lessee is of greater importance to the lessor when specialized equipment such as a special-purpose machine is leased than when standardized equipment such as rolling stock is leased. Explain. Equipment trust certificates secured by rolling stock will be of the highest financial quality even if issued by a weak railroad. How does your answer to the first part of this question help explain this phenomenon?

10. The financial ratios will be different depending upon whether a firm leases or borrows and buys. Which ratios will be affected and how?

11. Borrowing agreements frequently carry provisions against the firm incurring additional indebtedness. What device comes to mind for avoiding such provisions? How can lenders protect themselves against such a maneuver?

Problems

1. Sarong Textiles, Inc., is planning to lease a piece of new equipment which sells in the market for $73,600. Lease payments are $10,000 per year, payable at the end of the year. The lease agreement runs for 10 years and is a net lease, that is, the lessee bears all maintenance, property taxes, and so forth.
   a. If the equipment were worthless at the end of 10 years, what would be the effective rate of interest?
   b. Sarong Textiles signs the lease and pays $10,000 per year rental for 10 years. The value of the equipment at the expiration of the lease is $53,100. What is the effective rate of interest that Leasing, Inc., earned on its investment?

2. Sarong Textiles, now convinced of the high cost of leasing, decides to borrow at 6 percent and purchase land and buildings costing $815,100. Leasing, Inc., offers to buy the real estate and lease it back to Sarong Textiles for 50 years at an annual rental of $50,000. Leasing, Inc., says it would be satisfied with a 6 percent return on its investment.
   a. What is the residual value of the property that Leasing, Inc., is anticipating? (The present value factors corresponding to 6 percent and 50 years are 0.054 and 15.762 in terms of Tables A.1 and A.2 at the end of the text.)
   b. Should the value of the property decline to zero at the end of 50 years, would the effective rate of return earned by Leasing, Inc., be materially affected? Give your reasons. (The present value of $1 to be received every year for 50 years discounted at 5 percent is 18.256.)
   c. The residual value of the property at the end of 50 years rises to approximately $10 million. What is the effective earnings rate generated by the stream of

payments of $50,000 per year for 50 years and a terminal value of $10 million in exchange for a present outlay of $815,100? Would borrowing at 6 percent have been a good use of leverage? Ignore capital gains tax adjustment. (The present value factors corresponding to 8 percent and 50 years are 0.021 and 12.233 in terms of Tables A.1 and A.2 at the end of the text.)

d. Sarong Textiles, Inc., can normally earn 10 percent on capital invested in its operating activities. Would purchase of the facilities with the 6 percent borrowed funds, in restrospect, have been a wise decision if the funds could have been invested in regular operations?

e. Would it have been attractive for Sarong Textiles to borrow at 6 percent and use the funds in operations and lease the real estate, even if the residual value of the real estate were $10 million?

3. Green-Wood Timber, Inc., has been caught in a working capital squeeze at a time when its short-term borrowing power is exhausted. Demand for its products is rising and additional working capital is needed. The latest financial statement of the firm appears in Table 13.4.

Table 13.4. Green-Wood Timber, Inc., Balance Sheet

Cash	$ 2,000,000	Accounts payable	$ 4,000,000
Accounts receivable	3,000,000	Notes payable	6,000,000
Inventory	5,000,000		
Total current assets	10,000,000	Total current liabilities	10,000,000
Land, plant, and equipment		Long-term debt	10,000,000
(net)	15,000,000	Common stock and surplus	5,000,000
Total assets	$25,000,000	Total liabilities and net worth	$25,000,000

a. Compute the current, quick, and long-term debt-to-equity ratios. How does the financial condition of the firm appear?

b. Green-Wood Timber plans to sell and lease back $10 million of its timber lands. The $10 million is to be used to pay off $2 million of accounts payable, $3 million of notes payable, and $5 million of long-term debt to ease the pressure being exerted by its creditors. Prepare a pro forma balance sheet giving effect to this transaction and calculate the current, quick, and debt-to-equity ratios. Does the financial position of the firm seem improved?

c. The timber lands, valued at $10 million, are being leased at an annual rental of $1,100,000 for 25 years. The general opinion is that the residual value of the land after the timber has been cleared is marginal. No reforestation is planned. What is the interest rate being charged on the lease, assuming the terminal value is zero?

d. The leasing firm, however, anticipates a 15 percent return on its investment on this deal. What is the residual value of the land being anticipated by the leasing firm?

Selected References

Alexson, A. S., "Needed: A Generally Accepted Method for Measuring Lease Commitments," *Financial Executive*, 39 (July 1971), pp. 40 ff.

Alsobrook, G. H., "Small Business Term Loans by Banks," *Robert Morris Associates Bulletin*, 48 (Oct. 1965), pp. 61–77.

Bierman, H., Jr., "Accounting for Capitalized Leases: Tax Considerations," *Accounting Review*, 48 (Apr. 1973), pp. 421–424.

Bower, R. S., F. C. Herringer, and J. P. Williamson, "Lease Evaluation," *Accounting Review*, 41 (Apr. 1966), pp. 257–265.

Budzeika, G., "Term Lending by New York City Banks," *Monthly Review Federal Reserve Bank of New York*, 43 (Feb. 1961), pp. 27–31.

Clark, D. C., "Leases as Loan Security," *Journal of Commercial Bank Lending*, 54 (Apr. 1972), pp. 25–30.

Cook, D. C., "The Case against Capitalizing Leases," *Harvard Business Review*, 41 (Jan.–Feb.), pp. 145–150 ff.

Gordon, M. J., "A General Solution to the Buy or Lease Decision: A Pedagogical Note," *Journal of Finance*, 29 (Mar. 1974), pp. 245–250.

Jenkins, D. O., "Purchase or Cancellable Lease: Which is Better?" *Financial Executive*, 38 (Apr. 1970), pp. 26–31.

Johnson, R. W., and W. Lewellen, "Analysis of the Lease-or-Buy Decision," *Journal of Finance*, 27 (Sept. 1972), pp. 815–823.

Roenfeldt, R. L., and J. S. Osteryoung, "Analysis of Financial Leases," *Financial Management* 2 (Spring 1973), pp. 74–87.

Shapiro, H. D., "Just Because You Like Beer, Why Buy a Brewery?" *Corporate Financing*, 4 (Mar.–Apr. 1972), pp. 37–39 ff.

Simon, S. J., "The Lease-Option Plan—Its Tax and Accounting Implications," *Journal of Accountancy*, 113 (Apr. 1962), pp. 34–45.

Vancil, R. F., "Lease or Borrow—New Method of Analysis," *Harvard Business Review*, 39 (Sept.–Oct. 1961), pp. 122–136.

———, "Lease or Borrow—Steps in Negotiation," *Harvard Business Review*, 39 (Nov.–Dec. 1961), pp. 138–159.

———, and R. N. Anthony, "The Financial Community Looks at Leasing," *Harvard Business Review*, 37 (Nov.–Dec. 1959), pp. 110–130.

Weeks, P. A., J. C. Chambers, and S. K. Mullick, "Lease–Buy Planning Decisions," *Management Science*, 15 (Feb. 1969), pp. B295–B307.

Wilhelm, M. F., Jr., "Purchase or Lease: That Is the Question," *Management Accounting*, 51 (July 1969), pp. 43–46.

Zeher, L. A., Jr., "Investor Leasing Programs," *Financial Executive*, 38 (July 1970), pp. 62–64.

Zises, A., "Law and Order in Lease Accounting," *Financial Executive*, 38 (July 1970), pp. 46–54.

14

SOURCES OF
LONG-TERM FINANCING

Organized security exchanges play a vital role in the functioning of the capital market. The New York Stock Exchange (the Big Board) overshadows all other exchanges with the American Stock Exchange, also located in New York City, outstripping the remainder.

There were 3377 corporations with 3923 stock issues and 2165 bond issues listed on these exchanges on June 30, 1973.[1] The majority of companies with issues listed on any exchange (52 percent of issuers and 90 percent of listed bond issues) were listed on the New York Stock Exchange. In market value of listed shares traded, the New York Stock Exchange led in 1972 with 78 percent of the total volume of $204 billion, followed by the American Stock Exchange with 10 percent. The other 12 exchanges had a total of only 12 percent in volume of shares traded. These 12 exchanges serve companies with regional interest and also duplicate some listings on the two New York exchanges.

Stock exchanges are important to the corporate financial manager for a variety of reasons.

1. An exchange is an efficient and relatively inexpensive way of carrying on transactions in securities. Self-regulation and government regulation of the exchange guard against fraud and a host of other practices that would shake confidence.

[1] Securities and Exchange Commission, *39th Annual Report*, year ended June 30, 1973, pp. 154 ff.

The practice of the members of the exchange in making good on any defalcation of a member adds to the functioning of the exchange.[2]

2. Information on prices and trading volume is quickly and accurately transmitted, and the availability of such information is a stabilizing force. Price changes are smaller and more frequent on a continuously functioning exchange than would be true otherwise.

3. The improved marketability offered by an exchange creates higher collateral values for securities.

LISTING

The advantage of marketability gained by listing on an exchange can be overstated. Ultimately, marketability of a security depends more on the size of the issue, its distribution, and the character of its holders than on the listing on an exchange. Some over-the-counter issues have a larger volume of trading than many listed issues. All exchanges maintain minimum listing requirements, which vary from time to time. These requirements are designed to ensure that the security will have a sufficient volume of trading. Listing also involves a commitment by the corporation to release information regularly and to respond promptly to special inquiries by the exchange.

There are potential dangers in listing. Wide distribution of a security may increase the possibility of loss of control of a corporation. It is possible for speculators to acquire control through corralling the smaller number of shares needed for control than would be necessary if ownership were more concentrated. Listing may also increase management's concern with security prices and thereby divert energies from regular business activities. Or management may become unduly concerned with the short-term effect of a decision on the price of its securities rather than with the long-run consequences of the decision.

Listing Requirements

To be eligible for listing on the New York Stock Exchange, a company must currently (1975) have

1. At least 2000 stockholders with 100 shares or more
2. At least 1 million shares publicly held

---

[2] Mention should be made of the 1970 insolvency guarantee fund set up by the New York Stock Exchange after the Haupt failure following the salad oil swindle. Under federal legislation passed in 1970, individual accounts are insured up to $60,000 against defalcation by brokers.

3. A minimum market value of $16 million for publicly held shares
4. Net tangible assets of $16 million
5. Pretax annual earnings of $2.5 million in most recent year and $2 million in the two preceding years.

Bond and preferred stock issues do not have to show as wide a distribution, and the American and regional exchanges set less stringent standards for all types of securities. The requirements (1975) for listing in the American Stock Exchange are

1. Net worth of $3 million
2. Net earnings in the last year of at least $300,000 and pretax earnings of $500,000
3. A minimum of 300,000 publicly owned shares (excluding shares owned by officers and directors and family-held shares)
4. A minimum of 900 public stockholders, including 600 with lots of 100 shares or more
5. A minimum aggregate market value of $2 million for publicly held shares
6. Shares selling at a minimum of $5 a share for a reasonable period of time prior to filing the listing application.

The listing committee will not approve nonvoting common or preferred stock that does not provide for voting rights after more than two years of default in dividend payment. The listing committee will also examine conflicts of interests in an applying company.

In addition to meeting the eligibility requirements, the company must furnish the exchange with much of the same material as would appear in an SEC registration statement, for example, the charter and bylaws, so that information concerning the number of shares and classes of stock issued, the rights of classes of stockholders, and voting and annual meeting requirements is readily available. The company's financial history must be set out and information must be given concerning the firm's growth record, properties held, product lines, personnel, and like matters. Subsidiary and affiliated companies must be identified. Independently certified balance sheets and income statements must be furnished, and the company must agree to furnish financial statements to stockholders. The distribution among holders of the issue must be set out in detail so the exchange can satisfy itself that a substantial part of the issue is widely held and a free market will exist in the issue. If too large a part of the issue is closely held, it would be possible for manipulation to occur. Also, the company must maintain independent stock transfer facilities in the city of the exchange to facilitate transfers and to reduce the chances of fraudulent certificates. Engraving of certificates is required in order to reduce the possibilities of forgeries.

The SEC receives a duplicate of the listing application and must consent to the listing. Once the common stock of a company is listed, the New York Stock Exchange will list any other security of that company, preferred stock or bond, regardless of how small the distribution of that security.

Delisting by an exchange requires SEC approval and can occur for a number of reasons. The New York Stock Exchange will delist a company if any of the following occurs:

1. Average net earnings for the past three years fall below $600,000.
2. Market value of common shares falls below $8 million or holdings by noninsiders fall below $5 million in market value.
3. Number of round lot shareholders falls below 1200.
4. Number of publicly owned shares drops below 600,000.

In 1974, 44 companies were delisted by the New York Stock Exchange. This number includes bankruptcies and mergers.

Secondary Distributions and Exchange Distributions

An important function of the organized exchanges is to handle the sale of large blocks of stock that otherwise might upset the price performance on an issue and trigger violent, although temporary, price action. A *secondary* is the sale of a large block of stock that originates with a security holder, not with the issuing corporation. The use of the secondary is an alternative to disposing of a large block of stock in small lots over a long time. In the case of a secondary, buying orders are solicited after the close of the market on one day in an effort to dispose of the entire lot before the opening the next morning. The consent of the exchange is necessary for such activity. The offering is usually at the closing price or slightly below. The buyer pays no commission, which is a bit of an incentive to purchase, but the seller pays a commission, ordinarily larger than the regular exchange commission, to compensate for the special effort. A group of buyers may purchase all or part of the block for redistribution at their risk. Securities dealers who are not members of the exchange may participate.

The secondary may require SEC or state blue sky registration. Thus if the block is being sold by one in control of the issue (any holder of more than 10 percent of the issue), the seller is limited in a 6-month period to the sale of no more than 1 percent of the total issue or the average daily trading volume in the most recent 3-week period, whichever is less. If the seller wants to sell a block larger than this, the issue must be registered with the SEC.

An *exchange distribution* is a technique that has been available since SEC approval in 1942. This is the offering of a block of stock smaller than a secondary and made during regular trading hours. It requires the consent of the exchange and is offered at a fixed price, with only the seller paying the special commission. The minimum size of a special offering is 1000 shares and $25,000 in market value.

The Specialist

The role of the *specialist* is important to the smooth functioning of an organized exchange. Each listed security is assigned to at least one specialist, and more active issues have more than one specialist. Members of the exchange with buy or sell orders in a security go to the post of a specialist in that security who then executes or matches buy and sell orders. The specialist is responsible for maintaining an orderly market in that security.[3] In doing so, he frequently trades for his own account, making profits or losses, but he must execute customers' orders before his own. He maintains files of all open orders (orders away from the market price) arranged in the sequence in which he received them. It is apparent that there must be an objective set of rules governing the sequence in which orders are filled, since the price of the security may move before all who want to do business at a stated price are taken care of. The simplest rule would be to handle all orders at a given price in the order in which they are received, regardless of the type of order. This is the rule but only within categories of types of orders. Without listing the complete rules governing priority of orders, we can cite some examples. A regular-way order (in which payment and delivery of the stock are due on the fifth business day following the transaction) takes precedence over a next-day order (in which payment and delivery are due on the next business day) at the same price. Or the larger of two orders received at the same time will be filled first. Or, in the case of identically sized orders received simultaneously, the flip of a coin will determine which is to be executed when both cannot be executed.

---

[3] Failure to do so may result in disciplinary action by the Exchange. The specialist in General Motors stock was censured for permitting the price to fluctuate widely on October 14, 1971— traded as high as $83¾ and closed at $81⅛.

The Odd Lot Dealer

In addition to a specialist, there is the *odd lot dealer*. With some exceptions for high-priced stocks, an *odd lot* is an order for less than 100 shares of a stock. To illustrate the handling of an odd lot, assume an odd lot sale order. When the price of a stock moves up, all of the odd lot orders at the *old* price will be filled. This is so because, in order to receive a given price for the sale of an odd lot, the market price must reach *more* than the desired price. The price is ⅛ of a point *more* for stocks selling under $55 and ¼ *more* for those selling at $55 and more. Then, even though the odd lot dealer has no matching buy order, he must execute the sell order by buying for his own account. The extra ⅛ or ¼ compensates him for the risk he takes as well as the higher unit cost of executing the order compared to the round 100 shares.

THE OVER-THE-COUNTER MARKETS

The over-the-counter markets are best described as all activities of trading securities through brokers that do not occur on organized exchanges. The over-the-counter markets handle the great bulk of security issues in number but not dollar volume. Although federal government bonds are listed, most of the trading in them is over-the-counter. Only a few state and municipal issues are listed, and the great bulk of them are traded over-the-counter. Almost all bank and insurance shares are traded over-the-counter, as well as about half of the corporate bond and preferred stock sales. Thus listed securities predominate only in railroads, utilities, and industrial common stocks. Most new issues by corporations are by those whose securities are traded over-the-counter.

Quotations of the over-the-counter markets are published as representative bid and ask figures rather than as the price of actual transactions. These figures, along with volume of trading of some issues, appear daily in metropolitan newspapers for securities of local interest. *The Wall Street Journal* publishes daily bid and ask figures for a large list of over-the-counter stocks. Currently the requirement for appearing in this list is 1500 or more stockholders. On Mondays this newspaper also publishes bid and ask figures regionally in several editions for securities that have a more limited distribution. All of these quotations originate with members of the National Association of Security Dealers and, specifically, with an investment banker making a market in the security. Ordinarily this is the investment banker who was the manager of the last public offering of that security.

In addition, the National Quotation Bureau publishes the *National*

Daily Quotation Service in regional editions containing security quotations together with the names of brokers who are interested in each issue.

State and municipal bonds offered for sale appear daily in *The Blue List*.

In the over-the-counter markets, brokers act not only as agents but also as principals, buying and selling for their own account. Thus their profit may inculde not only the commission, which follows the rates of the Big Board, but also some spread where they have bought the security at a somewhat lower price.

While the SEC has jurisdiction over the over-the-counter markets, the actual policing is done by the National Association of Security Dealers with more than 3000 member firms under a system of self-regulation made possible by the Maloney Act of 1938. The most effective tool in this policing is the practice of limiting to members the price concessions from wholesalers to retailers at the time of a public offering. These concessions are vital to the profits of a broker.

In 1965 the SEC extended its jurisdiction over securities traded over-the-counter. Previously only public offerings of over-the-counter securities came under the SEC. Now the requirements of a proxy statement and the limitations on insiders, which had previously applied only to listed securities, are extended to all issues with 500 stockholders traded over-the-counter. An *insider* is defined as an officer, director, or one holding 10 percent of the security. Insiders are prohibited from profiting by selling and buying within 6 months thereafter, or vice versa. Any profit from such an insider transaction is payable to the company. All transactions by insiders must be reported monthly to the SEC and are published monthly by the SEC in the *Official Summary of Security Transaction and Holdings* and appear in *The Wall Street Journal*. In the case of a listed security, insiders are also barred from selling short.

THE THIRD AND FOURTH MARKETS

The term *third market* has been applied to "off-board" trading through brokers of securities listed on the New York and/or American stock exchanges. Recently the term *fourth market* has been applied to direct trading between buyer and seller without the use of a broker.[4] There is no law requiring that transactions in listed securities go through an exchange,

---

[4] The "first market" is trading of listed securities on the stock exchanges. The "second market" is the trading of unlisted securities through brokers on the over-the-counter market.

although Exchange rules require members to do so. This activity is not solely directed at eliminating or reducing commissions, but also at securing better prices for larger blocks of stocks. In essence the third market seeks to locate "potential" buyers and sellers, namely, those who might be willing to buy or sell but who do not presently have open orders on the exchange at prices for which they would be willing to do business. More than three quarters of the third market sales are of securities that are principally traded on the New York Stock Exchange. In particular issues at particular times the trading in the third market exceeds that on the exchanges.

TRADITIONAL INVESTMENT BANKING

Investment banking is concerned with the merchandising of securities. Sometimes a distinction is drawn between investment banking and broker-age. The term "investment banking" is then restricted to the primary market—the underwriting of new security issues, that is, the investment banker buys a new issue of securities for his own account with the expectation of reselling quickly. The term "brokerage" covers the secondary market with the investment banker (broker) serving as an agent on a commission basis in buying or selling securities for the account of another.

A third category falls between underwriting and brokerage, namely, the investment banker acting as a dealer who functions in the secondary market. In this case the investment banker buys shares of an existing issue of securities in the open market for his own account for later resale. A dealer is seeking a profit greater than just a commission because he expects to sell at a higher price than he paid. The expected profit rewards him for the risk he takes that the price may fall rather than rise.

Investment Counseling

An important role of the investment banker is investment counseling. This service has many forms.

First, the investment banker may act as a financial adviser to corporations whose securities he has underwritten. Sometimes the investment banker carries out this role by being on the board of directors of the client corporation. Holding such a directorship may be questionable because it may give rise to a suspicion that dealings between the corporation and the investment banker are not at arm's length. Furthermore, the presence of the investment banker on the board makes that individual an "insider" with special access to information about the corporation. At the same time that person may be dealing for his own account in the securities of the corporation. Thus the question of a conflict of interests arises (particularly in the case of a corporation whose securities are traded over-the-counter) between the role of the investment banker in maintaining the after market and his interest in turning a profit based on his evaluation of the future of the corporation, which depends in part on his information.

Second, the investment banker offers counseling services to individual and institutional investors. He may furnish a wide spectrum of services, ranging from merely offering special reports and analyses of industries or of specific companies to agreeing to assume complete management of the investment account of the client.

Third, the investment banker may enter a long-term agreement with a mutual fund to act as manager of the fund's assets. With the great growth of mutual funds after World War II some investment bankers have been attracted to this field and have "sponsored" funds, benefiting not only from the management fee but also from the commissions generated by the funds' transactions.

The investment banker offers a wide range of services, including management of an investment fund, record-keeping for tax and other purposes, custodial care of the securities, income collection, and disposition of rights or warrants. At the one extreme is the management contract with a mutual fund and at the other are limited services for accounts as small as $100,000 to $200,000.

In general, fees for such service start at ½ of 1 percent per year and ultimately slide down to ¼ of 1 percent as the size of the fund increases. Fees vary not only with the size of the fund and with the type of service, but also with the type of client; whether the account is individual or corporate, a pension or profit-sharing fund, a charitable or educational institution.

THE UNDERWRITING OPERATION

The heart of investment banking is the underwriting of an original issue of securities by a corporation or an offering of a block of stock by large stockholders in a transaction called a secondary issue. The issue may be offered by a corporation that already has a publicly held issue or by one that is going public for the first time. This distinction is more important than that of whether or not the corporation's securities are listed on an exchange.

Whether the new issue is by a corporation already publicly owned or by one going public for the first time, the process and documents used are the same. The type of investment banker involved, however, is often different. Few corporations go public for the first time through the services of a "national" house; most go public through a regional investment banker. Then as the corporation grows, additional issues usually are managed by a national house.

Planning for Underwriting and Timing the Offering

Before an underwriting occurs there is considerable planning and numerous conferences between the seller and investment banker. One of the most important matters to be settled is the timing of the offering. To achieve an optimum price for the issue, both the firm and conditions in the capital market must be healthy.

The underwriting may involve objectives beyond the raising of funds for the firm, the most frequent being the establishment of a market for the firm's securities. In the absence of a market value for the firm's securities, all the owners of the firm's securities are exposed to serious risks as to the fair market value that will be set by tax authorities in cases of gift, inheritance, and estate taxes. In addition, establishing a market for the firm's securities under favorable circumstances will bring benefits at a later date for other offerings. The market value of a security depends in part on the amount of seasoning that the firm's securities have had.

During the preunderwriting period extensive investigations are carried on by accounting, legal, financial, and engineering experts to satisfy the investment banker as to the quality of the securities to be offered. In the case of a company going public for the first time, the underwriter may offer a set price before the registration process begins. That commitment would be subject only to major and unforeseen changes in either the capital market or the condition of the corporation. In the case of securities of a company that is already publicly held, the price will not be set until shortly before the offering. Often this time will be the close of business the day before the offering. What the price will be involves a phenomenon called *underpricing*. For the issue to be successful there must be an inducement to the public to buy the securities to be offered rather than the same securities in the open market. There is considerable variation in the amount of underpricing. In the case of stocks traded over-the-counter, the underpricing may be no more than to offer the stock at the bid price rather than at the average of the bid and ask prices. In the case of stocks listed on an exchange, a set differential from the closing price on the day preceding the offering may be used.

During the preliminary negotiations between the investment banker and the issuer an *upset price* may be agreed upon. An upset price is that price below which the issuer has the option not to proceed with the offering should the market price drop during the registration process.

The Registration Process

The preliminary activities of underwriting, which may have extended over a period as long as several years (but seldom as short as several months), culminate in the registration process. The *Securities Act of 1933* requires the registration with the Securities and Exchange Commission (SEC) of all publicly offered securities in amounts over $500,000, either offered interstate or through the U.S. mails.[5]

The federal act does not involve any qualitative judgment by the SEC. Rather, the federal act is directed solely at truthful and adequate disclosure of facts relevant to the proposed issue. This is in contrast to the so-called *blue sky* legislation of some states, which purports to examine the quality of the issue and the fairness of the offering price. In recent years states have simplified the matter of compliance with state laws by permitting the filing of duplicate federal registration papers.

In the registration process a prospectus is prepared for distribution to prospective brokers and buyers. The prospectus covers such matters as

1. The history of the company
2. The use of the proceeds of the proposed offering
3. The recent price range of the security (if previously traded)
4. The capitalization of the company before and after the proposed issue
5. The dividend history of the company
6. The profit and loss statement for at least the most recent five years and quarters of a year
7. The business activities of the company
8. The properties owned by the company
9. Management personnel of the company and their compensation
10. Any stock option plans, employee stock purchase, deferred compensation, profit sharing, and similar plans
11. The principal holders of securities
12. The security proposed
13. The underwriting agreement proposed
14. Identification of those passing on legal and accounting questions
15. Financial statements, including a recent balance sheet, the profit and loss statements for the last five years, statement of retained earnings for the last three

---

[5] Even amounts under $500,000 are subject to the requirement of a prospectus (called an "offering circular") conforming to Regulation A if the U.S. mails are used or if the offering crosses state lines.

years, and supporting schedules covering depreciation, taxes, rents, and royalties, and special items

16. The participating underwriters and the share of each

The preliminary prospectus is called a "red herring" because on it is printed vertically in red ink a statement indicating that while the prospectus has been filed with the SEC, it has not yet become effective. This serves to warn anyone receiving it that there may be changes in it or additions to it before it becomes effective.[6]

In addition to the prospectus, the issuer files a registration statement, which contains among other items

1. The proposed agreement among underwriters, the underwriting (or purchase) agreement, and any dealer agreements
2. The articles of incorporation and by-laws of the issuer
3. Any loan agreements of the issuer
4. Any stock option, profit-sharing, retirement, or other plans of the issuer
5. Any contracts with related persons

This registration statement (in most cases Form S–1) becomes effective 20 days after it is filed, unless the SEC acts during this time. Invariably the SEC notes some items requiring clarification or amplification. In this case an amended registration statement is prepared and another 20-day waiting period is begun. The second waiting period can be accelerated.

While the SEC registration is in progress, the issuer proceeds with the process of filing under the laws of each state in which the issue will be offered for sale so that both federal and state clearances will arrive at the same time.

Formation of the Underwriting Syndicate

After the registration statement is filed with the SEC, the managing underwriter organizes the underwriting syndicate. The latter may have previously engaged in informal discussions concerning the proposed issue with other prospective underwriters, but the filing of the registration statement (which is reported in newspapers) sets the wheels in motion.

The *underwriting syndicate* consists of the managing underwriter and

---

[6] Where there are serious changes between the "red herring" and the final prospectus, the SEC may require that a second "red herring" be circulated. In any event, every ultimate purchaser of the security must receive a copy of the final prospectus.

as many other underwriters as are needed to account for the entire offering. The agreement among underwriters may provide for a divided or an undivided syndicate. The *divided syndicate* is the most common and specifies the maximum number of shares for which each underwriter is liable. Most commonly there is a provision that, in addition to the participation of each underwriter as stated in the prospectus, each will be liable for an additional amount, often 10 percent, of his participation if fellow underwriters are unable to sell their agreed-upon share. In the *undivided syndicate* each underwriter is liable for any unsold securities in proportion to his participation, regardless of how many he may have sold.

The underwriting syndicate is concerned with three basic documents:

1. The *agreement among underwriters,* which states the rights and liabilities of the underwriters among themselves.
2. The *purchase* or *underwriting agreement,* which states the terms of sale by the issuer to the underwriting syndicate. This includes the price to be paid to the issuer and the price at which the securities will be sold to the public. This price difference is called the "*spread.*"
3. The *selling group agreement,* which covers the purchase of securities by brokers in smaller quantities from the underwriting syndicate.

Function of the Selling Group and Stabilization

The underwriters are, in effect, wholesalers who may retail part of their participation directly to the public and wholesale another part to brokers in smaller quantities. These brokers, called the *selling group,* then retail to the public. The subscription of each broker is made in a document that commits him not to sell to the public below the stated price; if securities sold by the broker are repurchased by the underwriters in the market in order to achieve stabilization prior to the termination of the syndicate, the broker is bound to sell again the securities or be liable for the costs of the underwriters in repurchasing and reselling.

Stabilization involves the maintenance by the managing underwriter during the period of the syndicate of such a bid price for the securities as will stabilize the market price no lower than the offering price for the issue. This prevents any cumulative downward movement of the price of the security during the selling or syndicate period.

Typically there is a distinction between brokers who enter the selling group and sign the document just described, called the *selected dealers agreement,* and other brokers who simply buy shares as agents of the public. The selected dealers receive a larger commission from the underwriters.

Setting the Price, the Sale, and Stabilization

The price of the stock to be offered is usually set by the managing under-writer after the close of business the day before the proposed offering. The price is usually set at or slightly under the "bid side of the market" at the close.

The night before many things happen. The attorneys complete a price amendment to be filed with the SEC the next morning and a courier leaves by night plane to Washington, D. C., for the filing. High-speed presses grind out thousands of copies of the final prospectus, which move out by special delivery air mail or courier to be on hand the following morning around the country. Then as dawn is breaking in California, with Hawaii and Alaska still asleep, a telegram leaves the SEC declaring that registration has become effective. Similar telegrams are awaited from all the states where the offering is to be made. With the receipt of these telegrams, tele-phones start to jingle and selling of the securities commences all over the country.

Most offerings are subject to stabilization. This is usually carried out by *overselling* the issue. That is, if 100,000 shares are being offered, the managing underwriter authorizes the sale of say 105,000 shares or even more, depending on market conditions and the strength of the offering. Then, in order to deliver the extra 5000 shares, the managing underwriter enters the market as a buyer and in so doing supports the price. If the manager mis-judged, he may have to pay more than the issue price. Profits or losses from stabilization are shared pro rata by the underwriting syndicate. Once the manager judges the market for the issue stabilized, he declares the syndicate ended. For a successful issue this is usually the second or third day after the offering; for a "sticky" issue the time may be a week or ten days. Even if all the issue is not sold, the syndicate would then be declared terminated and each underwriter would be left with his pro rata share of unsold securities.

ALTERNATIVES TO UNDERWRITING

Instead of the underwriting procedure just discussed, three alternatives are available to an issuer of securities:

1. A best-efforts or agency sale
2. Direct sale to the public by the issuer
3. Private placement

Best-Efforts Sales, or Agency Sales, and Direct Sales to the Public

The *best-efforts sale* employs the services of the investment banker as a selling agent. Thus the full risk is on the issuer, and the unsold securities may be turned back to the issuer by the investment banker. The commission for best-efforts selling is higher than for underwriting because the effort in selling is greater.

Oddly enough, issuers at both ends of the quality spectrum tend to use the best-efforts procedure. Issuers of high quality appear prepared to take the negligible risk of some unsold securities. On the other hand, very speculative small concerns cannot get an underwriter and are forced to use the best-efforts or agency basis.

The same situation exists for the alternative of direct selling by the issuer to the public without the use of any investment banker. Here high-quality issuers may proceed by a rights or warrant offering,[7] giving each stockholder the right to subscribe to the new issue at a price significantly below the current market price. This has been done by American Telephone and Telegraph Company. Such rights can be sold by the stockholders to others who wish to exercise them. At the other extreme a small concern occasionally will attempt to sell some of its securities by advertising in local newspapers. To avoid SEC registration such offers are limited to residents of one state and require the buyer to sign a statement that he is purchasing for investment and not for resale.

In connection with the rights offering just described, a "stand-by" underwriting agreement may be entered into by the issuer. Such an agreement provides that the underwriter will pick up all or some agreed maximum of the issue not sold by the exercise of rights.

The After-Market

One matter of prime interest to the issuer if the securities are not listed on an exchange but are traded over-the-counter is what happens to the price of the securities after they have been issued. This will vitally affect the next issue of the corporation.

The managing underwriter should "make the after-market" in the security. Other investment bankers and brokers will turn to him for information about the affairs of the issuer and for a bid and ask quotation. In making the after-market an investment banker forms an estimate of what

[7] Rights are discussed more fully in Chapter 17.

the security is worth in the current market and goes long or short in an effort to approximate that price. If he does not do this but merely acts as an agent, the price of the security will fluctuate more widely. Weakness on the part of the investment banker making the after-market will soon be detected by others and the security will be shunned.

Private Placement

The most important alternative to underwriting is private placement of securities with one or a few large buyers, often insurance companies and pension funds. Corporate officers give four principal reasons for the shift from underwritten public offerings to private placement. First, they cite that the long waiting periods for registration with the SEC create a hazard that the market may shift in this period. The underwriting agreement is usually not signed until the day before the public offering, and this risk of change in the market falls on the issuer.

Second, private placement avoids the costs of registration and the underwriting spread, as well as potential criminal and civil liabilities for the officers and directors for statements in the prospectus that may later be held to be false or misleading. There is liability not only for statements made but for failure to make statements about matters that later appear to have been significant. However, not all the costs of underwriting are saved. First, there are costs in a private placement and, second, the buyer of the private placement may succeed in capturing a part of the cost saving by slightly adjusting the yield or price he offers.

The third reason advanced by the issuer in favor of private placement is the great increase in funds available in the hands of institutional investors which not only creates pressure but also enables such institutions to buy larger parts of issues without violating the rule of investment diversification.

The fourth reason is that private placement permits modification of the terms of the loan during the period of the loan because of the small number of security holders whose consent is required. This cannot be done when there are thousands of bondholders except through the expensive process of calling the issue.

There is a sticky point in private placement: When does a private placement cease to be private and become public (and hence subject to registration) because of the number of buyers of the security? Most state "blue sky laws" answer this problem by setting the maximum number of buyers for a situation entitled to exemption. Federal legislation and administrative practice have not done this but have permitted the question to be resolved on the basis of the number of buyers involved, the financial knowledge of the buyers, and other factors. The counsel's office of the SEC examines each case submitted and gives the issuer a statement that, if the question is raised, it will render an opinion to the SEC recommending that the transaction be or not be recognized as private or public, depending on the facts of each case.

The vast growth in private placements has presented a challenge as well as an opportunity to investment bankers. Many investment bankers have turned to serving the new development as agents, brokers, or "finders," collecting a fee for bringing buyer and seller together.

COST OF UNDERWRITING

Our discussion has indicated that considerable attention is focused on the costs of floating an issue of corporate securities. These costs to the issuer are easily classified into the underwriter's spread and the expenses of flotation.

Three generalizations are possible:

1. The costs of issuing common stock are substantially higher than those of issuing preferred stock, and the latter in turn is more expensive to issue than bonds. This reflects the differences in underwriting risk.
2. The costs of issuing are in inverse proportion to the size of the issue.
3. The expenses of an issue (other than the underwriting fee) fall more in proportion to the size of the issue than underwriting commissions fall.

The expenses (other than the underwriting spread) are primarily printing costs, legal fees, and accounting costs. These expenses are more fixed than variable with the size of the issue. Hence they decline as a percentage of proceeds. The other expenses are engineering investigation costs in the case of some issues, the filing fee of the SEC, the transfer agent's fees, the costs of qualifying under state blue sky laws, and miscellaneous expenses such as telephone and telegraph.

Summary

Securities are traded either on the stock exchanges or on the over-the-counter market. By far the largest of the 14 organized securities is the New York

Stock Exchange. Each exchange is made up of member firms who act for themselves and for customers.

Listing on an exchange requires the application of the issuer. The various exchanges have minimum standards for listing in order to reduce fraud and to assure the listing of only such securities as have a sufficiently broad interest among investors.

Much of the work of the exchange is carried on by the specialist who handles the transactions in a particular security and is responsible for maintaining an orderly market in that security. To do this the specialist will trade for his own account. Another important function is performed by the odd lot dealer, who handles less than round lots. In most cases a round lot is 100 shares.

The over-the-counter market handles the great bulk of security issues, including most of the volume in federal and municipal bonds, almost all the bank and insurance shares, and half of the corporate bond and preferred stock sales, as well as smaller common stock issues.

The third market involves "off-board" trading in listed issues and involves searching out buyers or sellers of large blocks of stock to be handled in a single transaction.

Investment banking is the merchandising of securities. It includes both underwriting new issues and trading in previously issued securities. The investment banker deals for his own account and also acts as agent in buying and selling securities for his customers. The issuance of new securities is subject to SEC regulation under the Securities Act of 1933, and trading on the stock exchanges is subject to the Securities Exchange Act of 1934.

Private placement is direct dealing between the issuer of the securities and the buyer and is not subject to regulation. Investment bankers assist in private placements and also furnish investment counseling service.

In the underwriting process the investment banker uses a prospectus of the issue, which must make full disclosure of all relevant facts concerning the issuer and the issue. The issuing company is required to file a registration statement with the SEC which includes much more detail than the prospectus. Underwriting is carried out by a syndicate of underwriters brought together to handle the particular issue. The underwriters organize a selling group to assist in the sale.

The costs of underwriting are classified into two categories, (1) the underwriting commission and (2) other costs, such as printing, legal, and accounting expenses. Both kinds of costs decline as a percentage of proceeds as the size of the issue increases. The costs of handling common stock are higher than those for handling preferred stock, and the costs for the latter, in turn, are higher than for bonds.

Study Questions

1. The role of the specialist in a listed security has been frequently criticized. Do you think specialists should be eliminated as part of the exchange picture? If so, what device would you recommend to perform the matching of buy and sell orders?
2. Should the third market be subject to regulation such as applies to the organized exchange?
3. Does regulation of the securities markets increase or decrease the volatility of the price of securities? Before you leap to an answer, consider the argument that increased certainty about the absence of fraud, manipulation, and so on encourages people to take risks they otherwise might not take.
4. In the income tax laws of England and Canada, capital gains are not taxed on the grounds that they are not income but rather, are changes in one's capital account. On the other hand, some states (such as Wisconsin) tax capital gains at the same rate as ordinary income. Would a change in the federal income tax law (which taxes capital gains) to either English–Canadian position of no tax on capital gains or to the full tax position of some states have a substantial effect on the prices of securities? In this connection, remember that a large part of the volume of present security transactions is accounted for by pension funds and other institutions that are not subject to income tax.
5. As the financial officer of a company going public, would you recommend that the company invite a number of investment bankers to make bids and proposals or would you advise the company to concentrate on a single investment banker?
6. Would you recommend that a company pursue a policy of obtaining its debt financing through private placement but its equity financing through public offerings?
7. Some states under blue sky laws limit the maximum price–earnings ratio at which common stock may be offered. Do you think this is a sound proposition or would you favor limiting the underwriter's commission to a maximum percentage of the offering price as a more effective means of achieving the same objective?
8. In some public offerings of securities the prospectus reveals that the underwriters as part of their compensation will receive options to purchase a stated number of additional shares for a stated period (often one year) at the net price to be received by the issuer for the shares presently offered for sale. Would you favor such a provision if you were the officer of the issuer? if you were considering purchasing the shares? If such a provision were not granted the underwriters, what might the alternatives be?
9. Will the underwriting commission be larger for the first offering of the common stock of a closely held corporation than for the same size offering of a publicly owned corporation, assuming that the two companies are identical in all respects, that is, are in the same industry, have the same product lines and records and the same debt leverage, and so on? Would there be any difference if the offering were for bonds rather than for common stock?

Problems

1. Secure a recent prospectus from a broker or directly from an underwriter (whose name can be obtained from advertisements in *The Wall Street Journal* or on the

financial pages of a metropolitan newspaper). From the prospectus and the use of investment manuals such as Moody's or Standard & Poor's determine the following.

a. Is this an initial public offering or have the company's securities been publicly traded previously?

b. Is the offering by the company only, by selling stockholders, or jointly by the company and selling stockholders?

c. What is the relationship of the offering price to prior prices for the security (if this is not a first issue) or to prices of securities of comparable and competing companies (if it is a first issue)?

d. What is the pattern of the price of the security after the public offering (paying attention to the movement of the general securities market as measured by the Dow-Jones Industrial Average or some similar index)?

e. What is the underwriting commission as a percentage of gross proceeds?

f. What is the number of underwriters and the dollar amount and percentage of the issue that each underwriter assumed as well as the provision (if stated in the prospectus) covering the situation in which one of the underwriters may be unable to sell his amount and seeks to turn it back to the other underwriters?

2. On November 21, 1966, RTE Corporation of Waukesha, Wisconsin, sold an offering of 70,000 shares of common stock at $14.50 per share at a commission of $1.20 per share through a firm (not agency) underwriting syndicate of 14 firms whose home offices are in New York, Chicago, Milwaukee, Denver, Cleveland, Los Angeles, Kansas City, Des Moines, Philadelphia, New Orleans, and Fayetteville,

Table 14.1. RTE Corporation Stock Record, 1958–1967

Year*	Sales (millions)	Earnings (thousands)	Earnings per Share	Dividends per Share	Bid** per Share High	Low
1958	$ 4.3	$ 311	$0.41	$0.08	$ 8	$ 6
1959	5.1	305	0.40	0.17	9½	6
1960	5.7	233	0.31	0.17	6	5
1961	6.6	309	0.41	0.17	5½	4½
1962	7.8	337	0.44	0.19	9½	4
1963†	7.3	195	0.26	0.15	6¾	3½
1964	9.4	603	0.79	0.23	11½	6½
1965	12.7	952	1.25	0.31	17¾	10
1966	15.0	970	1.27	0.50	16⅜	12
1967	21.4	1,590	2.03	0.60	55	13

* Fiscal year ended March 31.
** This information is on a calendar year basis.
† In this year industry prices collapsed as a result of the antitrust proceedings begun in 1960 involving most manufacturers in the electric power industry but not RTE.

N. C. (several firms had home offices in New York and Chicago). Two of the firms (Walston & Company, Inc., and Dempsey, Tegeler & Company, Inc.) were "national wire houses" with offices in cities throughout the country. The proceeds of the offering were applied to working capital.

In 1966 RTE was the fifth largest manufacturer of distribution transformers (after General Electric, Westinghouse, McGraw-Edison, and Allis-Chalmers). The firm produces only that product. A distribution transformer is the familiar small tank on the electric pole near residences and serves to step down electric power from thousands of volts to the 110 and 220 volts used by customers.

RTE went public in October 1958, by the offering of approximately 100,000 shares (adjusted for stock dividends) by selling stockholders through a single underwriter, Loewi & Company, Inc., of Milwaukee, at $6 per share. This was a firm underwriting with a commission of $57,000. Before this offering RTE had 60 stockholders and after it 400 stockholders. Between 1958 and 1966 the list of stockholders grew to 1200 (of whom more than 900 were located in Wisconsin) by sales of the original 60 stockholders. The 1966 offering increased the number of stockholders to 1700. The stock was traded over-the-counter, and after the 1966 offering there were 831,467 shares outstanding. The 10-year record of RTE appears in Table 14.1.

Table 14.2. Industry Record of Sales

	Sales (millions)	Transformer Price Index (1949 = 100)
1950	$138	102
1951	230	115
1952	167	111
1953	183	116
1954	178	128
1955	222	128
1956	250	132
1957	230	141
1958	205	138
1959	234	132
1960	211	129
1961	210	126
1962	213	118
1963	186	96
1964	222	96
1965	257	96
1966	312	99

Source: National Electric Manufacturers Association.

Additional information is available in Moody's *Industrials* or Standard & Poor's *Manuals.* The only comparable companies (manufacturing electric powertype transformers only) were Central Transformer Company and Moloney Electric Company, both publicly owned during this period. These companies merged in October 1965. RTE stock was split 3 for 1 in August, 1968.

The industry record of sales of the product manufactured by RTE and of the pricing of this product appears in Table 14.2.

a. Why was a single underwriter used for the initial offering in October 1958?
b. How was the initial offering price probably determined?
c. Why was a syndicate of 14 underwriters used in November 1966?
d. How was the price determined in the second offering?
e. Why do you think the 1966 underwriting commission (as a percentage of gross proceeds) did not differ much from that in 1958?
f. Is the stock qualified for listing on the New York Stock Exchange? on the American Stock Exchange? on the Midwest Exchange?
g. Why do you think the stock is not listed?
h. Why did the price of the stock advance so sharply after the November 1966 offering?

Selected References

Blume, M. E., and F. Husic, "Price, Beta, and Exchange Listing," *Journal of Finance,* 28 (May 1973), pp. 283–299.

Cohan, A. B., *Private Placements and Public Offerings: Market Shares Since 1945.* Chapel Hill, N.C.: University of North Carolina Press, 1961.

Commission on Money and Credit, *Private Financial Institutions.* Englewood Cliffs, N. J.: Prentice-Hall, 1963.

Cooke, G. W., *The Stock Markets.* New York: Simmons-Boardman Publishing Company, 1964.

Corey, E. R., *Direct Placement of Corporate Securities.* Cambridge, Mass.: Harvard University Press, 1961.

Eiteman, D. K., "The SEC Special Study and the Exchange Markets," *Journal of Finance* 21 (May 1966), pp. 311–323.

Eiteman, W. J., C. A. Dice, and D. K. Eiteman, *The Stock Market,* 4th ed. New York: McGraw-Hill, 1966.

Fredman, A. J., and C. C. Johnson, "Effect of New NYSE Fee Structure on the Third Market," *Financial Executive,* 38 (Oct. 1970), pp. 18–23.

Friend, I., and M. E. Blume, "Competitive Commissions on the New York Stock Exchange," *Journal of Finance,* 28 (Sept. 1973), pp. 795–819.

Friend, I., G. W. Hoffman, W. J. Winn, M. Hamburg, and S. Schorr. *The Over-the-Counter Securities Markets.* New York: McGraw-Hill, 1958.

Friend, L., H. P. Minsky, and V. L. Andrews, *Private Capital Markets.* Englewood Cliffs, N. J.: Prentice-Hall, 1964.

Hayes, III, S. L., "Investment Banking: Power Structure in Flux," *Harvard Business Review,* 49 (Mar.–Apr. 1971), pp. 136–152.

Howell, P. C., "Competition in the Capital Markets," *Harvard Business Review,* 31 (May–June 1963), pp. 88–93.

Investment Bankers Association of America, *Investment Banking.* Englewood Cliffs, N.J.: Prentice-Hall, 1949.

Leffler, G. L., and L. G. Farwell, *The Stock Market,* 3d ed. New York: Ronald Press, 1963.

Life Insurance Companies of America, *Life Insurance Companies as Financial Institutions.* Englewood Cliffs, N.J.: Prentice-Hall, 1962.

Logue, D. E., "On the Pricing of Unseasoned Equity Issues: 1965–1969," *Journal of Financial and Quantitative Analysis,* 8 (Jan. 1973), pp. 91–104.

Loll, L. M., Jr., and J. G. Buckley, *The Over-the-Counter Securities Markets: A Review Guide,* 2d ed. Englewod Cliffs, N. J.: Prentice-Hall, 1967.

McKinley, G. W., "Life Insurance Company Lending to Small Business," *Journal of Finance,* 16 (May 1961), pp. 280–290.

Robinson, R. I., *Money and Capital Markets.* New York: McGraw-Hill, 1964.

Schultz, B. E., *The Securities Market,* rev. ed. New York: Harper & Row, 1963.

Sears, G. A., "Public Offerings for Smaller Companies," *Harvard Business Review,* 46 (Sept.–Oct. 1968), pp. 112–120.

Securities and Exchange Commission, *Cost of Flotation of Corporate Securities 1951–1955.* Washington, D. C.: Government Printing Office, 1957.

——, *Cost of Flotation of Registered Equity Issues, 1963–1965.* Washington, D. C.: Government Printing Office, 1970.

——, *Privately Placed Securities: Cost of Flotation.* Washington, D. C. Government Printing Office, 1952.

——, *Special Study of Securities Markets.* Washington, D. C.: Government Printing Office, 1963.

Soldofsky, R. M., "The Size and Maturity of Direct Placement Loans," *Journal of Finance,* 15 (Mar. 1960), pp. 32–44.

Stoll, H. R., and A. J. Curley, "Small Business and the New Issues Market for Equities," *Journal of Financial and Quantitative Analysis,* 5 (Sept. 1970), pp. 309–322.

Taft, R. W., "The Greening of the Red Herring Prospectus," *Financial Executive,* 39 (Nov. 1971), pp. 73–76.

Van Horne, J. C., "New Listings and Their Price Behavior," *Journal of Finance,* 25 (Sept. 1970), pp. 783–794.

Walter, J. E., *The Role of Regional Security Exchanges.* Berkeley, Calif.: University of California Press, 1957.

Waterman, M. H., *Investment Banking Functions.* Ann Arbor, Mich.: University of Michigan Press, 1958.

Williams, B. S., and M. Letwat, "Underwritten Calls of Industrial Convertible Securities, 1950–61," *Quarterly Review of Economics and Business,* 3 (Winter 1963), pp. 71–77.

15

LONG-TERM DEBT FINANCING

In this chapter we examine corporate long-term financing. After examining the terminology of long-term debt we proceed to the basic device of the indenture and the trustee, the key questions of priority, security, additional borrowing, and other rights, and the arguments for and against long-term debt. We then focus on specialized areas such as convertible debt, warrants, and income bonds. Finally, we consider planning for maturity with the alternatives of retirement or refunding of the debt.

TERMINOLOGY

If a debt issue over $1 million is offered publicly, there must be a trust agreement, called an *indenture,* between the borrowing corporation and a trustee who serves as a representative of all the buyers of the debt securities. The key points of the trust agreement are usually summarized in the debt security itself. The debt security issued under the indenture may be called a *bond* or a *debenture.* The word "debenture" is usually used to identify a general obligation of the borrower that is not secured by a mortgage. If there is a mortgage as security, the document is called a bond. But unsecured debt securities are also called bonds. A debenture is a bond, but not all bonds are debentures. If the debt instrument matures in less than one year from the time of issue, the security is called a *note.* All debt maturing in more than one year is called *funded debt.* This does not mean that there is a cash fund linked with the debt; rather "funded" is a financial term to describe debt with a maturity over one year.

A *mortgage* is a grant, by the borrower to one class of creditors, of preference or priority in a specific asset. In the event of any default by the borrower or violation of any other condition, the creditor holding the mortgage is entitled to force the sale of the specific asset and to receive full payment of his claim from the proceeds of the sale of the specific asset before any other creditors receive anything from such proceeds. The legal procedure by which the creditor forces the sale of the asset when the debtor defaults is called *foreclosure*. This is a proceeding for the protection of the debtor in which the creditor must prove in court that there is a debt, that there has been default in its terms, and that the debt is secured by a mortgage. Finally, the creditor asks the court to order the sale of the mortgaged asset, with the proceeds to be used to pay the lender's claim.

The Indenture and the Trustee

Once bonds are issued (and many issues are in bearer form[1]), it will be impossible to assemble the bondholders to rewrite the agreement should some unusual developments occur. Thus to set the specific terms of the loan agreement, the indenture will usually run hundreds of pages. The indenture specifies the duties and compensations of the trustee, the form of bonds to be issued, the number, amount, interest rate, maturity, a description of the property mortgaged if any, call or redemption provisions, the terms upon which additional bonds may be issued, the percentage of bondholders needed to cause amendments of the agreements, conversion rights if any, sinking fund provisions if any, and remedies of bondholders in the event of default. Protective provisions cover items such as payment of taxes, maintenance of insurance, limitation on other mortgaging, and condition under which the borrower may pay dividends.

The standard unit for a bond is $1000 or multiples thereof and the price is quoted as a percentage of par (but without a percentage sign). Thus if the bond quotation is 120, it means $1200 for a bond of $1000 par value. The bond is negotiable[2] and may be in (1) full bearer form, that is, the bond and its attached interest coupons can be sold by whomever has possession of it, (2) registered form as to principal and bearer form as to interest coupons, or (3) fully registered form as to principal and interest. By registered we mean that the owner's name apears on the bond and that a register of owners

---

[1] An instrument is in bearer form when it reads "payable to bearer," or if payable to a stated person, has been endorsed in blank by that person, that is, the person to whom payable has simply signed his name with nothing more.

[2] This means that in law the buyer of the bond who receives it in good faith, having paid value for it before maturity and with no notice of any defect, will prevail over others who claim rights to it. A negotiable instrument can be recovered from a thief but not from one who bought it for fair value from a thief with no knowledge of the theft and prior to any default of the bond.

is maintained by the trustee (or a separate institution acting as a registrar). Registered as to interest means there are no coupons attached but the owner receives the interest by check.

The trustee's main duties are (1) to certify, that is, vouch for the authenticity of the bonds at the time they are issued, (2) to verify that all the commitments of the borrower are carried out, and (3) to assert the rights of the bondholders in the event of default, such as to bring foreclosure. As a result of the laxness of trustees of bond issues in the Great Depression, bondholders frequently did not receive the benefits specified in the indenture. As a result, the Trust Indenture Act of 1939 gave the SEC jurisdiction over indentures so that the trustee must be independent of the borrower, have sufficient power to act for the bondholders, and can be held liable for his actions.

Classification of Bonds

Bonds can be classified in many ways. For our purposes we can identify the key bases of classification as (1) what the priority position of the bond is, (2) what the security for the bond is, (3) what the rights of the borrower regarding the issuance of more debt are, and (4) what unusual rights the bondholder has. Many categories of bonds involve merely an identification of the situation leading to the issuance of the bond rather than the substantive rights of the bondholder. Thus a refunding bond may simply indicate that it replaces a previously issued but now expired bond, or it may replace a bond that has been called in for payment before maturity.

Bond priority and security provisions affect the interest rate of the bond both directly as to what the underwriter of the bonds will seek and indirectly because of their effect on the bond rating (AAA, AA, A, and so on) which the issue will receive from Moody's or Standard & Poor's.

Priority. As to priority, the question always is, prior to what? Even unsecured bonds may have priority over some other debt, such as a subordinated debenture that has been subordinated to the bond and hence will be paid only after the bond is paid. If no contrary provision exists, all debt has equal priority, particularly over all ownership or equity interests. Most priority is concerned with specific property mortgaged as security for the particular bond issue. Such property may be real estate, leases, other securities, or any property. To the extent that the specific property is inadequate to pay off the bonds in full, the unpaid balance of the bonds qualifies as a general or unsecured debt.

Security.   It is apparent that the security for the bond issue may be linked to the priority of the issue.   The security may be identified as certain parcels of real estate or it may include all real estate owned by the corporation. The bond may include a so-called *after-acquired property clause.*   Under this provision all future property that the corporation may acquire automatically becomes subject to the mortgage.   The benefit of such a clause to the bondholder is dubious.   The clause tends to be used to bolster what otherwise would be a weak issue, but as soon as the issue containing the clause has been sold, the first order of business for the borrower is to develop means to avoid the effect of the clause in hampering further financing.

Right of Borrower to Issue More Debt.   The bond indenture may contain various provisions covering the right of the borrower to issue more debt. The first question is whether more bonds may be issued against the same security and with equal rank.   If this is true, the issue is called an *open-end mortgage bond.*   Even in this case there will be a limit provided as to the total additional bonds that may be so issued.   If at the time of the first issue no more bonds may be issued against the security, the bonds are *closed-end mortgage bonds.*   The right of the borrower to issue more bonds, whether or not against the particular security, may also be limited.   There are many ways of achieving this objective.   The obvious method, placing a specific dollar limit, is seldom used in public offerings because the bond issuer will object to the inflexibility.

In private placements, however, the provision is common that no other bonds may be issued.   This provision is paired with another stating that when additional bond money is sought by the borrowing corporation, the lender will be given the first opportunity to purchase any new proposed bonds.   Then if the lender is not interested, the borrower may solicit the additional money elsewhere on the same terms as were offered the lender.   If the borrower can find a second lender on this basis, the first bond indenture contains specific provisions providing, for example, that the new bond issue will pay off the first bond issue (usually at some premium).

In addition to the control over the right of the borrower to issue additional bonds, the bond indenture can, at least indirectly, control the amount of short-term borrowing or trade credit that the bond issuer can obtain.   This is done by provisions covering the maintenance of a minimum current ratio, minimum working capital, dividend conditions, and so on.   These provisions will not only affect the right of the borrower to additional long- or short-term funds, but it also will specify the balance the borrower must maintain between current assets and fixed assets and the ratio of current assets to current liabilities.

Additional Rights of the Bondholder. Here we are concerned with the rights the bondholder may receive over and above the myriad provisions seeking to protect him against default. The earliest of these rights to develop was the provision for voting in the event of default either in payment due or in any covenant of the agreement. There are many provisions possible, ranging from a provision for complete control of voting by the bondholders to some type of pro rata participation in voting with stockholders. One technical provision that should be mentioned is the *acceleration clause*, which provides that as soon as any default occurs, all the obligations under the particular issue of the borrower become due immediately, particularly the payment of the principal.

Particularly since the end of World War II, a movement has developed to offer bondholders additional rights under the assumption that the borrower will prosper. These rights focus on conversion privileges and warrants to buy common stock and have become so prominent as to justify separate consideration later in this chapter.

ARGUMENTS FOR AND AGAINST LONG-TERM DEBT

Having examined the institutional framework of long-term debt commitments, we are in a position to evaluate the arguments for and against long-term debt.

From the viewpoint of the lender (the bondholder), it has been customary to speak of risk, income, and control as dominant factors, but this classification omits some matters of grave concern to the bondholder. Risk is often thought to include only two items, the risk of loss of principal or interest and the risk of call. Default has been discussed and the bondholder is more secure than other security holders, both as to earnings and in the event of liquidation. There is also the risk that he may lose a favorable investment by call before maturity, thus presenting him with the problem of reinvesting his money. But these are only two of the classical risks of investment. The others are (1) the liquidity risk, (2) the risk of change in the interest rate, and (3) the risk of change in the purchasing power of money. It is the last that has dominated the scene (particularly for bondholders) since the end of World War II. Bondholders' concern with this risk has led to the increasing use of convertibles and warrants. As to income, the bondholder is willing to forego participation in higher earnings in return for a steady flow of income and protection against dips in earnings. The matter of control over the investment by voting rights is surrendered by the bondholder for the covenants the borrower makes. From the viewpoint of an individual bondholder, there is little tax difference between bonds and stock: both involve ordinary income taxation of earnings and both present some capital gain or loss possibilities.

If the security holder happens to be a corporation, however, preferred stock and common stock have tax advantages. The Internal Revenue Code provides for an exemption of 85 percent of the dividends paid by one taxable corporation to another. While bond interest is fully taxable, only 15 percent of preferred and common dividends are subject to tax.

From the viewpoint of the borrower (the issuer of the bonds), the cost of debt funds is lower than that of equity funds if for no other reason than because the interest is tax deductible. In addition, the borrower gains financial leverage; the swing in earnings per share with a change in income of the corporation is heightened in both directions. Leverage is not only useful in heightening earnings at some increase in risk, but it is also the basis for an issuer to diversify his risk. By passing some of the risk of the firm to creditors the issuer reduces his own funds committed to the venture and frees money for use in another venture.

However, debt has a maturity date that the issuer must provide for. Long-term debt, in particular, involves covenants that are much more extensive than those required for short-term debt. Despite the best effort to anticipate and provide for all contingencies in the indenture, events may develop that would require a change in the covenants before maturity. It is difficult to devise methods for altering covenants. The most feasible solution is to call the issue and refund.

CONVERTIBLE DEBENTURES AND CONVERTIBLE SUBORDINATED DEBENTURES

A *convertible debenture* is an unsecured obligation of a borrower carrying a rate of interest and providing the holder with the right to convert the debt into common stock of the issuer at a set price. The interest rate is lower than the rate for the same debenture without the conversion privilege because of the potential value of the privilege. The price of the common stock into which the debenture may be converted is set above the market price of the common stock at the time the debenture is issued, usually by 10 to 15 percent. A debenture usually has a call price, enabling the issuer to force conversion if the market price of the stock rises sufficiently. A *subordinated convertible debenture* usually provides that the debt will be subordinate to any other funded debt and to bank loans. Both types of convertibles may carry any of the other provisions commonly found in bonds and debentures. Convertibles have a maturity of from 10 to 30 years, with 20-year to 25-year maturities being the most common. A significant number of convertibles carry a *conversion price* step-up provision, providing for periodic increases in the conversion price.

Several factors also encourage the increasing use of convertible debentures. First is the legal restriction on insurance companies, banks, personal trusts, and some pension funds as to investment in common stocks. Also, there are large amounts of money under self-imposed restrictions of risk, for example, the restrictions imposed by the "balanced" objectives of some mutual funds. Convertible debentures offer such institutions an opportunity to participate in the capital gains afforded by common stock but with less risk than is associated with common stock.

Another factor that has encouraged the use of convertibles has to do with margin requirements. Until 1968 credit up to 90 percent could be obtained from banks for the purchase of debentures, while margin requirements on stock fluctuate and may permit as little as 30 percent credit on stock purchases. In 1968 the Federal Reserve subjected banks to the same margin rules as brokers in the case of convertibles. But convertibles have a more secure price floor than stock, thus reducing the risk of a call for additional margin.

Finally, there has been a cyclical factor at work in the case of convertibles. This was apparent in the market of 1965–1969. After the severe collapse of the speculative stock market in May 1962, many investors became wary of stocks as an investment. Convertibles attracted large sums during the period of 1965–1969 as investors saw them as a chance to have their cake and eat it too.

What happened between 1962 and 1965–1969 appears to have been a change in the risk-aversion attitude of a significant number of investors. Underwriters sensed this shift and capitalized on it by offering subordinated convertibles. Even prime credit firms were attracted to the supply of funds available in this market at this time. The use of convertible debentures has been erratic. They represented 2 percent of new total publicly issued debt in 1963, peaked at 40 percent in 1967, and then declined to 2 percent again in 1974.

Antidilution Provisions in Convertibles

Antidilution provisions are commonly found in both convertible bonds and convertible preferred stock. Because the conversion price of the common stock is fixed at the time the convertible is issued, it is necessary to provide for the adjustment of this conversion price if the issuer later (1) declares stock dividends or splits, (2) makes capital distributions to the holders of common stock, (3) grants options at less than the conversion price of the common stock stated in the convertible, or (4) sells common stock at less than the market price at the time the convertible was issued, either directly or through the use of rights. If there are no antidilution provisions, the holder of the convertible will find he has lost some of his bargain, since the capital gain on conversion will be less than it would be were there antidilution provisions.

Dual Statement of Earnings

As soon as convertible debentures are employed, the problem of the correct statement of earnings per common share arises. The Securities and Exchange Commission requires that earnings per common share be shown on both an "as is" basis, that is, with the outstanding convertible debentures figured as debt, and then on a "fully diluted basis," assuming all the convertible debentures have been converted into common stock. In the process of computing the "fully diluted basis," the interest savings, due to the fact that the outstanding convertibles are assumed converted, are added back to pre-income tax profits in order to arrive at fully diluted earnings.

This dual statement must also include not only the effects of conversion of convertible debentures but also the effects of conversion of convertible preferred stock, the exercise of warrants (to be discussed shortly), and the exercise of options.

When Will a Convertible Be Called?   Why Was It Issued?

Little evidence is available concerning the policy of corporations with respect to calling convertibles. Many policies might be adopted: call as soon as you are sure of conversion (which would be when the market price is far enough above the call price); or let the holder of the convertible decide in view of dividend increases on the common stock; or call only if necessary to present a favorable capital structure at the time when new debt is needed.

The policy on calling will most likely be related to the reason for issuing the convertible. If the issuing company needs funds but considers its stock currently undervalued by the market place, either because the entire equity market is depressed or because the market is pessimistic about this particular company, the company should resort to debt. But the company may already have exhausted its possibilities for straight debt, or the cost of debt may also be high at this time. The convertible offers a lower interest cost than straight debt (because of the tradeoff against the value of the conversion right) and presents the likelihood of the shift from debt to equity, with the corporation realizing a better price for the equity to the extent that the conversion ratio is above the market price of the common stock at the time the convertible is issued.

If the company's stock is currently overvalued in the market, the company should proceed to issue common stock for new money, but the use of a convertible would be preferable to straight debt.

These are reasons for convertibles from the company's point of view. But the relative preferences of the market place must be considered. As noted earlier, the extent of risk aversion in the market varies from time to time, as do margin requirements and the interest of restricted institutions in capital gains. As a result, the market may offer much more attractive terms for convertibles than for straight debt or equity.

The fact that the common stock of a company is selling at a certain price in the market place does not mean that underwriters would be willing to handle an offering at anywhere near that price. At the same time that the market could not stand the issue of common stock, it is quite possible for the market to have a substantial interest in convertibles. Conversely, at a time when the company wants to issue debt, the market may reject straight debt except at higher interest rates and insist on conversion rights as a sweetener.

SUBORDINATED DEBENTURES

Many convertible debentures are subordinated. In fact, any debt can be subordinated. When debt is subordinated, that debt ranks *after* the specific debt to which it is subordinated in priority on liquidation. Usually debt is subordinated only to bondholders, bank loans, and other debt to financial institutions, but not to general creditors.

Suppose that we have the situation on liquidation given in Table 15.1,

Table 15.1. Sample Subordination Situation

Proceeds		*Amount Owed*	
All assets except building	$12,500	Accounts payable	$ 15,000
Building (mortgaged)	75,000	Bank debt (unsecured)	25,000
		Mortgage loan	150,000
Total	$87,500	Subordinated debt	10,000

where the subordination agreement provides only for subordination to bank debt and where the mortgage is not held by the bank.

The proceeds in Table 15.1 are applied on liquidation of the debt as shown in Table 15.2.

Table 15.2. Application of Proceeds upon Liquidation

(1) Class of Debt	(2) Amount of Claim	(3) First Allocation	(4) Second Allocation	(5) Third Allocation	(6) Percent of Claim Paid (5)/(2)
Bank debt	$ 25,000		$ 2,500	$ 3,500	14%
Mortgage debt	150,000	$75,000	82,500	82,500	55
Accounts payable	15,000		1,500	1,500	10
Subordinated debt	10,000		1,000	0	0
Total debt	$200,000		$87,500	$87,500	43.75%

The first allocation is to pay the mortgage debt to the extent the proceeds of the mortgaged property are adequate. If the mortgage proceeds are inadequate, the unpaid mortgage debt becomes a general claim. If the mortgaged proceeds exceed the mortgage debt, the excess becomes general assets.

The second allocation takes the general assets and distributes them pro rata over all now unsatisfied debt. In Table 15.2 that debt is $75,000 of mortgage and $50,000 of other debt. With $12,500 of general assets now available, the distribution is 10 percent on each dollar. The mortgage receives an extra $7500 on its still unsatisfied $75,000.

The third allocation takes whatever the subordinated debt received in the second allocation and transfers as much of that as necessary to make whole the debt to which it is subordinated.

BONDS WITH WARRANTS, NONDEBT SECURITIES WITH WARRANTS, AND WARRANTS INITIALLY SOLD SEPARATELY

A *warrant* is a long-term option (usually for several years) to purchase a stated number of shares of a particular security (usually common stock) at a stated price (in some cases the price steps up as time goes on) for a stated period of time (some are perpetual). A warrant is not to be confused with a *stock right,* which is a short-term option, usually for 10 to 20 days, to buy stock at less than market price and is distributed to present stockholders. Warrants are used as a sweetener for long-term debt and recently even as a sweetener in deals that do not involve debt. As an option, a warrant carries no voting right, interest, or dividends.

Warrants may be detachable or nondetachable. A *detachable warrant* may be separated from the bond and sold. A *nondetachable warrant* must be passed along to the buyer when the bond is resold and can be detached only when the holder exercises the warrant to buy stock. Recently warrants have also been used with nondebt securities and even sold separately.

Warrants are an alternative to the convertible debenture as a sweetener for an issue of debt. Although detachable warrants are used on publicly offered issues and some are traded on the New York and American stock exchanges, the device is largely used in private placements. The reason is that the insurance company or other institutional long-term lender wants to continue with the debt issue. In the case of a convertible the debt issue is terminated by conversion.

As a sweetener, the warrant enables a company to sell its debt at lower rates of interest than straight debt, and in some cases a company can place debt with warrants where it otherwise could not find a lender.

The warrant differs from the convertible in this respect: cash (the option price) is paid to the corporation at the time the warrant is exercised. In the case of a convertible this is not usually the case, although a convertible can provide for the payment of additional cash as part of the conversion.

Determination of the Arbitrage Value of Warrant

The arbitrage value of a warrant at any time depends directly on (1) the difference between the market price of the common stock less the cash required by the option price of one share, times (2) the number of shares each warrant can purchase. In equation form,

$$AV_W = (MV_s - OP)S_W$$

where AV_W is the arbitrage value of the warrant, MV_s is the market value of the common stock, OP is the option price of one share of common stock, and S_W is the number of shares that can be bought with one warrant.

The market value of a detachable warrant will not drop below the arbitrage value because one could buy the warrant, exercise it, and sell the stock into which it is convertible for an immediate profit. But the market value of a detachable warrant often rides above the arbitrage value. The reason is that a warrant has great leverage—the chance for a large capital gain can be had for relatively little investment.

Leverage in Warrants

Leverage in the case of warrants can be explained by an example. Using a warrant with the right to one share of common, assume the common stock is at $20, the option price is $10, and the market price of the warrant is $10. If the common price rises to $40, the stockholder has a 100 percent gain, but if the common price rises to $40, the warrants must rise to at least $30, since the option price plus the warrant price must at least equal the common price. The gain on the warrant is 200 percent (from $10 to $30). The leverage of a warrant is greatest when the common is near the option price, which is also called the *striking price*.

If the common were to rise an additional $20 to $60, the stockholder would realize a 50 percent gain. The warrants would rise at least $20 to at least $50, but now the gain is only 66 percent. At this point the warrant holder has a greater risk on the downside (reverse leverage) plus, by the time the stock has tripled in value, the common is likely carrying a substantial dividend that the warrant holder will not receive. At this point the warrant holder must consider the financing cost of holding the warrant.

Other Factors Affecting Value of Warrants

A number of factors in addition to leverage and dividends on the common into which the warrant is convertible will affect the market value of the warrant. One of these is the margin requirement. Warrants can be bought on margin just like other listed securities, but in the case of warrants there is leverage upon leverage. First there is the leverage of the warrant itself, which we have just explained. Then there is the leverage of buying on margin. Finally, because the warrant sells for only a fraction of the price of the common, the possible loss to a warrant holder (say, in the event of bankruptcy) is far less than for the common until the common reaches a price well above the option price. Thus every time margin requirements increase (or decrease) the market interest in warrants increases (or decreases).

Warrants also offer a tax advantage over convertibles. When the warrant has a market value at the time of issuance of the debt to which it is attached, the value of the warrants can be treated as a cost of the debt, thereby reducing the principal of the debt for the issuer and creating a discount that can be amortized as a deduction for tax purposes. In turn, the gain on the sale of the warrant is a capital gain for the holder.

Three other factors affect the value of the warrant. The first is the length of time to the warrant's expiration, particularly when less than two years. The longer the period of the warrant, the greater the probability, *ceteris paribus,* that the common will at some time in the period hit a high price and give arbitrage value to the warrant. Second, if the warrant is listed on the American Exchange or the New York Stock Exchange, it has more value than if traded over-the-counter. This is due in part to the availability of margin financing and the ability to sell short offered only by listed securities. Third, the higher the dividend yield of the common stock, the lower the warrant value. This dividend effect is small but consistent. The logic is that a higher dividend causes the common price to be higher, which in turn increases the financing cost of carrying the warrant for the warrant holder, compared to a no-dividend common.

Another factor affecting the value of the warrant is the outlook for its associated common stock, particularly the volatility of the common price.

An argument is made that warrants constitute a "dilution" of ownership. Whether there is "dilution" depends on what the earnings will be on the new money paid in upon exercise of the warrants compared to the earnings on the old money. To consider that there is "dilution" just because there are more shares, without realizing that there could not be more earnings without the increase in shares, is fantasy. Yet this use of the term "dilution" frequently occurs. On the opposite side we should note that both warrants (with bonds) and convertibles are attractive compared to straight common stock financing, since the debt will enable the company to build up the new earnings so that when the exercise of the warrants or conversion takes place, there will be a minimal temporary impact on earnings per share and, hence, on the price of the common stock.

CHICAGO BOARD OPTIONS EXCHANGE

Until recently, warrants and convertibles have been the only listed options available to investors. In 1972 the new Chicago Board Options Exchange established the first organized market for puts, calls, straddles, spreads, strips, straps, and other options. Until this market was established, these functions were carried out for many years by individual securities dealers offering these agreements on an individual basis.

To define these transactions briefly, a *put* is a contract under which the holder can, for a fee, sell a given security at a fixed price in stated quantity within a stated period and the buyer will accept. A *call* is a contract under which a nonowner of a security can, for a fee, demand a security at a fixed price for a stated quantity within a stated period. A *spread* is a combination of a put and call with the owner of the spread able to demand delivery from or make delivery to the seller of the spread. The put and call are for different prices. If they are for the same price, the combination is called a *straddle*.

Since Chicago is the principal center in the United States in which "futures" of *commodities* are traded (corn, wheat, cotton, and so on, sold today at an agreed price for future delivery), it is logical that Chicago should tackle the matter of options in securities.

INCOME BONDS AND ADJUSTMENT BONDS

An *income bond* is a bond providing for the payment of interest only when it is earned. The term *adjustment bond* is a descriptive term identifying the bond as arising out of a reorganization. Income bonds may arise out of reorganization but are used by healthy corporations as well.

One attraction for issuing income bonds is the deductibility of the interest for income tax purposes. An income bond is similar to preferred stock, and if made too similar, the Internal Revenue Service will deny the tax deductibility of the "interest" payments. However, the use of provisions peculiar to bonds as opposed to preferred stock will usually satisfy tax authorities. These provisions include the use of a sinking fund, the denial of voting rights except in limited situations such as a period of nonpayment, and some type of security (mortgaged property). In addition, a bond has a maturity date, whereas a preferred stock does not. Even these provisions can be challenged. A sinking fund is similar in effect to a redemption schedule for preferred stock. Voting rights are frequently denied to preferred stock except in limited cases such as the existence of arrearage. Preferred stock can contain a commitment that there be no mortgaging by the corporation. And, finally, the maturity date of the income bonds can be thrown so far into the future as to be of little concern. This leaves one vital difference —the dividend on preferred stock need not be paid even if it is earned. Every dividend requires a decision by the board of directors, and no amount of dividend arrearage can form the basis for bankruptcy proceedings. However, under a properly drawn income bond indenture the interest if earned becomes payable and is a liability which, in turn, can be used to initiate bankruptcy proceedings if the interest is not paid.

Income bonds can provide for cumulation of an arrearage when the interest is not earned, so that whenever earnings occur the interest will be payable; or the income bond may be noncumulative in this respect.

PLANNING FOR THE MATURITY OF LONG-TERM DEBT

Any discussion of long-term debt that does not consider plans for the maturity of the debt is like a discussion of laws defining crimes that does not consider the penalties for law violation.

Planning for the future of long-term debt involves a number of alternatives:

1. Provision for a sinking fund
2. Use of serial bonds
3. Use of series bonds
4. Use of call provisions and premature retirement or refunding
5. Refunding at maturity
6. Indirect control of the situation by a specific covenant in the bonds, such as depreciation requirements, *negative pledge* clause, and dividend restriction.

Sinking Fund

A sinking fund may be defined as a segregation of funds to be applied to debt reduction, usually by the trustee under the indenture but sometimes directly by the corporation.

The sinking fund offers a wide variety of provisions designed to carry out this purpose. While a provision for periodic loan repayments may not be considered a sinking fund provision, the effect is much the same. In the case of private placements this is the form the sinking fund will take. For publicly held bonds, we can classify sinking funds into two broad classes. First, there is the type of provision requiring the company to repay some bonds pursuant to a schedule set in the indenture agreement. Thus the provision may be that annually a stated amount or percentage will be chosen by lot for repayment (with or without a premium for the bonds so chosen). Or there may be the infrequent provision that annually the corporation will set aside a stated amount of funds which will be invested in stated types of securities by a trustee for ultimate use in bond repayment.

The existence of sinking fund requirements helps maintain a market for the bonds, since the company must reacquire the necessary bonds. The use of a call provision prevents exorbitant prices in connection with the sinking fund requirements. Some indentures specify two call prices, one for general use and a lower one (by lot) to meet sinking fund requirements. Care must be taken that the sinking fund requirement, designed to protect bondholders, is not the very event that causes insolvency. Hence some provision for flexibility may exist, and this is usually tied to earnings. Termination of dividends when earnings shrink may afford as much protection to bondholders as is wise. The sinking fund is not designed to extinguish all bonds but will leave a final amount due at maturity. This amount is known as the balloon.

Serial Bonds

Instead of a sinking fund provision the entire issue may be arranged as serial bonds with varying amounts maturing each year. Such an arrangement presupposes either considerable stability of future income of the company or a readily predictable depreciation of the fixed assets to which the proceeds of the bond issue are to be applied. The principal advantage of serial bonds is interest saving, since the shorter term bonds normally carry a lower interest rate than longer term bonds. Theoretically, a parallel sinking fund provision should lower the average interest rate just as a serial bond, but the serial bond increases the size of the market by adding banks as buyers of the short-term part of the bonds. On the other hand, serial bonds do not create a market for the bonds such as results from purchases by the company to meet sinking fund requirements. And if the market rate of interest should rise compared to the rate on the bond issue, the sinking fund method would result in gains to the company through purchase of bonds at prices lower than par without invoking the call provision. Conversely, the selling bondholder suffers.

Series Bonds

Series bonds are separate issues of bonds made at different points in time and with different maturities, often under a "master" indenture. In the case of larger companies, the maturity problem can be dealt with by the series of issues so planned that there are frequent maturities but each for only a small part of the total long-term debt. In this way unfavorable market conditions at the time of individual maturities can be met with short-term funds. Such issues may be formally identified as series bonds or may simply appear under an open-end agreement as having different issue dates and different maturities.

Call Provisions and Premature Retirement or Refunding

We have already indicated that the call provision is useful in forcing conversion of convertible bonds and in protecting the company in meeting its commitments for sinking fund purposes. The call provision is also useful in accomplishing premature retirement where the company generates excess funds due to contraction in the volume of business, such as occurred after

World War II when many producers of war goods reverted to their usual peacetime production. Or the excess funds may develop as a result of good earnings and a conservative dividend policy adopted in an effort to accelerate debt retirement.

Premature refunding might occur for several reasons. A substantial drop in the market rate of interest affords a company the opportunity to refund and reduce interest costs after paying the costs of refunding.[3] Let us suppose a 40-year bond issue is entering its last 10 years. Rather than wait until maturity and assume the risk as to what the interest rate will then be, the company may seize the opportunity offered by low interest rates at this time and carry out the refunding prematurely. Or premature refunding may occur because the corporation is expanding and requires increased debt funds. In this situation, rather than "patching on" another issue, any outstanding issue would be called and the total debt requirement met by a single new issue.

Refunding at Maturity

As maturity approaches the balloon that will become due after the reduction of the issue by sinking fund payments may be handled in several ways. If during the period of the issue the corporation has prospered and the ratio of long-term debt to total capital structure has declined, the corporation may be willing to take the risk of an unfavorable long-term market for refunding at the time of the due date and will seek to cover this possibility with short-term money from banks or with a privately placed term loan. The risk in this case is really one of a sharply unfavorable interest rate rather than of default. If the company has not seen much growth in profitability during the first part of the life of the bond issue, it should move earlier on the matter of premature refunding in order to avoid the problem of an unfavorable market coinciding with the due date of the balloon.

Indirect Control by Specific Covenants

Up to this point we have been examining the problem of planning for the maturity of the debt from the point of view of the borrower. However, the lender is well advised to consider the problem. We have examined the covenants in the indenture as protection to assure timely interest payments and to control risks such as the depreciation of the mortgaged asset at a rate faster than the reduction of the debt.

---

[3] An illustration of the computation of the gains of refunding is presented in Chapter 21.

Covenants can also be used to control the risk of the situation of the borrower at maturity. Indeed, covenants can be used to induce premature refunding. Instead of the greater risk to the borrower of an unfavorable market at a single future point in time (the maturity date), we can substitute the lesser risk of an unfavorable market over a longer period by stepping up the protective requirements during the last five years of the issue. Thus the covenants can increase the liquidity requirements during this period or can raise the required ratio of net fixed assets to long-term debt. Such a situation would put pressure on the borrower to seek premature funding.

Restriction on Prepayment of Debt Issued under Tight Money Conditions

When tight money conditions develop, as they did in 1966 to 1974, lenders often seek restrictions on prepayment rather than still higher interest rates. The reason is that the lender may otherwise earn the extra 1 or 2 percent in interest for only a year or two. As money eases the borrower will refund. Accordingly, lenders may obtain provisions that the debt cannot be refunded for a minimum period of five years and thereafter only at the cost of a prepayment penalty, which might start at one year's interest and decline ½ of 1 percent per year. To sweeten this clause, the lender may agree that if the borrower seeks additional funds on any set of terms and first offers the new loan to the lender and it is rejected, the borrower may then procure the funds elsewhere on such terms and may prepay the existing loan on a much reduced penalty basis. Here we have an illustration of the greater flexibility available in private placement. It would be nearly impossible to administer such provisions in the case of a publicly offered issue.

Summary

Long-term debt financing involves bond issues with a maturity of more than 15 years. Such financing may be by a public offering of bonds or by direct placement. In either case the basic agreement is called an indenture. In the case of a public bond issue the indenture provides for a third party, designated as a trustee, to act on behalf of the bondholders to assure that the company issuing the bonds conforms to the terms of the agreement. In the event of default the trustee acts for the bondholders.

There are more than 75 different types of bonds, which vary according to the provisions of the bonds and the circumstances giving rise to their issue. Bonds are rated largely on the basis of their amount relative to equity, their priority, security, the borrower's right to issue more debt, the times interest earned, and the stability of the issuer's earnings.

Long-term debt from the point of view of the bondholder involves several risks—default, call, liquidity, change in the market rate of interest, and change in the purchasing power of money. The bondholder accepts a lower anticipated rate of earning than equity in return for improved certainty of the reduced earning and greater safety of his principal. The borrower gains financial leverage and does not part with any control.

A substantial part of the dollar volume of all bonds is in the form of convertible debentures, which give the bondholder the right to convert into common stock at a set price. If the price of the stock moves above this price, the bondholder can take a profit. In return for this option the bondholder receives a lower interest rate than would apply to straight debt of the same borrower. From the viewpoint of borrower or lender there is a trade off between a reduced interest rate and the conversion price. Convertibles appeal to a substantial part of the investing market that is legally required to invest almost entirely in bonds. Because of their attractiveness to investors, convertibles are usually subordinated to other funded debt of the borrower. Some control over the situation is maintained by the borrower's right to call the issue. If the stock is selling at or above the conversion price, the borrower can force conversion by calling a bond. A floor to the market value of the convertible is set by the bond's value as straight debt. The market price of the convertible will tend to rise above this floor as the price of the stock rises above what it was at the time the convertible was issued. The conversion value of the convertible depends on the current and expected price of the stock into which the bond is convertible.

Instead of a convertible bond, the borrower may issue bonds with detachable warrants (rights to purchase stock at a fixed price). In this case the bond is not terminated when the warrants are exercised, whereas in the case of a convertible the bond is terminated upon conversion. Detachable warrants also bring cash to the issuer when the warrant is exercised. These warrants offer great leverage and their value depends on many variables, but most important is the price of the associated common stock.

Income bonds provide for the payment of interest only during years in which the debtor earns that amount. Income bonds are similar to preferred stock but carry no voting rights and are not cumulative, although interest paid on them is tax deductible.

Planning for the future of long-term debt involves a choice of (1) sinking fund, (2) serial bonds, (3) series bonds, (4) call provisions, (5) refunding, and (6) indirect control by specific covenants.

Study Questions

1. Rank the following "protective" provisions of bonds in their order of importance to you as an investor. Then rank them from the point of view of the issuer. (a) Sinking fund provision, (b) mortgage, (c) dividend limitation, (d) minimum net working capital provision, (e) after-acquired property clause, (f) call provision, (g) limit of ratio of funded debt to total assets, (h) pledge to insure, repair, and pay taxes. Would you expect the order of your two rankings to be the same?

2. Do you think that the real reason for a mortgage is not to give priority as to the specific asset covered by the mortgage but to prevent the debtor from incurring additional indebtedness?

3. Thirty years ago and earlier industrial companies seldom had long-term debt in excess of 5 percent of their capital structure. Why is it that many industrials today have much more substantial ratios of long-term debt?

4. The use of a convertible bond results in the buyer paying more for the bond than it is worth as a straight bond and also paying more for the common stock than he would pay for it as common stock. Why then would a buyer be willing to buy a convertible?

5. The issuer of a convertible bond gets money at a lower rate than for straight debt and gets more for the common stock than an offering of common stock would realize. Why would a company issue straight debt rather than convertible bonds?

6. Do you think that the call price of a bond should be lower when the bond is called for sinking fund purposes than when it is not called for that purpose? Why?

7. Do you think that bonds should contain a provision restricting the call provision so that the bonds are not callable during an initial period (such as five or ten years)? Why?

Problems

1. Suppose a company has a mortgage debt of $4 million, general credits of $1 million, bank loans of $3 million, subordinated debentures of $1 million (which are subordinated to any bank debt), and common stock with par value of $5 million. Unmortgaged assets are $3 million and mortgaged assets $3 million. How will distribution be made in bankruptcy?

2. Suppose the bond indenture of a company specifies that the company must maintain a ratio of bond debt to the sum of subordinated debt plus net worth of 0.75:1, that subordinated debt provides that its ratio cannot exceed net worth in the ratio 0.8:1, and that the preferred stock provides that the maximum ratio to common stock be 0.5:1. What total amount of money can the company raise if $1.25 million of new common stock is sold?

3. Oscar Goodman, Inc., has an outstanding issue of 4 percent 25-year bonds sold at par and convertible into common stock at $50 a share. The bonds are callable at $108. The bonds as straight debt would have carried 5 percent at the time of issue. At the time of issue the common stock was selling at $42 and paying $1.50 dividend per year. The bonds still have 20 years to run and carry no pro-

vision for increase in conversion price, although there are the customary provisions for adjustment of conversion price in the event of stock dividends, splits, and so on. New bonds of similar quality but without conversion rights currently bear 6 percent. The stock is currently selling at $40 a share and is still paying $1.50 dividend. There is no reason to expect that the price of the stock will advance in the near future. Give your best estimate of what the market value of the bond might be.

4. Guthmann Corporation has 6 percent convertible bonds due in ten years. The present conversion price is $40 per share of common stock. In several weeks the conversion price will change to $50. The call price is $108. Nonconvertible bonds of the same type are presently yielding 6 percent. The current market price of the common stock is $50, and the shares pay an annual dividend of $2.40 per share. Will the bondholders likely convert?

5. Howard Industries has outstanding a 5 percent convertible bond issue which carries the privilege of conversion into common stock at $25 per share. The bond is callable at $105. Bonds of similar quality but without the conversion privilege are being issued on a 5 percent basis. The common stock is presently selling at $30 and the dividend rate has just been increased from $1.25 to $1.50 a share. Will the bondholders likely convert?

Selected References

Bacon, P. W., and E. L. Winn, Jr., "The Impact of Forced Conversion on Stock Prices," *Journal of Finance,* 24 (Dec. 1969), pp. 871–874.

Baumol, W. J., B. G. Malkiel, and R. E. Quandt, "The Valuation of Convertible Securities," *Quarterly Journal of Economics,* 80 (Feb. 1966), pp. 48–59.

Bladen, A., *Techniques for Investing in Convertible Bonds.* New York: Salomon Bros. & Hutzler, 1966.

Brigham, E. F., "An Analysis of Convertible Debentures," *Journal of Finance,* 21 (Mar. 1966), pp. 35–54.

Broman, K. L., "The Use of Convertible Subordinated Debentures by Industrial Firms, 1949–59," *Quarterly Review of Economics and Business,* 3 (Spring 1963), pp. 65–75.

Chen, A. H. Y., "A Model of Warrant Pricing in a Dynamic Market," *Journal of Finance,* 25 (Dec. 1970), pp. 1041–1059.

Cohan, A. B., "Yields on New Underwritten Corporate Bonds, 1935–58," *Journal of Finance,* 17 (Dec. 1962), pp. 585–605.

Frank, W. G., and Kroncke, C. O., "Classifying Conversions of Convertible Debentures Over Four Years," *Financial Management,* 3 (Summer 1974), pp. 33–39.

Halford, F. A., "Income Bonds," *Financial Analysis Journal,* 20 (Jan. 1964), pp. 73–79.

Hayes, S. L., "New Interest in Incentive Financing," *Harvard Business Review,* 44 (July–Aug. 1966), pp. 99–112.

——, and H. B. Reiling, "Sophisticated Financing Tool: the Warrant," *Harvard Business Review,* 47 (Jan.–Feb. 1969), pp. 137–150.

Jen, F. C., and J. E. Wert, "The Value of the Deferred Call Privilege," *National Banking Review,* 3 (Mar. 1966), pp. 369–378.

——, and ——, "The Effect of Call Risk on Corporate Bond Yields," *Journal of Finance,* 22 (Dec. 1967), pp. 637–651.

Johnson, R. W., "Subordinated Debentures: Debt That Serves as Equity," *Journal of Finance,* 10 (Mar. 1955) pp. 1–16.

Kassouf, S. T., "Warrant Price Behavior," *Financial Analysis Journal,* 24 (Jan.–Feb. 1968), pp. 123–126.

McKenzie, R. R., "Convertible Debentures, 1956–65," *Quarterly Review,* 6 (Winter 1966), pp. 41–51.

Poensgen, O. H., "The Valuation of Convertible Bonds: Part I: The Model," *Industrial Management Review,* 6 (Fall 1965), pp. 77–92, and "Part II: Empirical Results and Conclusions," 7 (Spring 1966), pp. 83–89.

Pye, G., "The Value of the Call Option on a Bond," *Journal of Political Economy,* 74 (Apr. 1966), pp. 200–205.

——, "The Value of Call Deferment on a Bond: Some Empirical Results," *Journal of Finance,* 22 (Dec. 1967), pp. 637–651.

Robbins, S. M., "A Bigger Role for Income Bonds," *Harvard Business Review,* 33 (Nov.–Dec. 1955), pp. 100–114.

Samuelson, P. A., and R. C. Merton, "A Complete Model of Warrant Pricing That Maximizes Utility," *The Industrial Management Review,* 10 (Winter 1969), pp. 17–46.

Shelton, J. P., "The Relations of the Price of a Warrant to the Price of Its Associated Stock," *Financial Analysts Journal,* 23 (May–June and July–August 1967), pp. 88–89 and 143–151.

Walter, J. E., and A. V. Que, "The Valuation of Convertible Bonds," *Journal of Finance,* 28 (June 1973), pp. 713–732.

Weil, R. L., Jr., J. E. Segall, and D. Green, Jr., "Premiums on Convertible Bonds," *Journal of Finance,* 23 (June 1968), pp. 445–463.

Weingartner, H. M., "Optimal Timing of Bond Refunding," *Management Science* (Mar. 1967), pp. 511–524.

Winn, W. J., and A. Hess, Jr., "The Value of the Call Privilege," *Journal of Finance,* 14 (May 1959), pp. 182–195.

16

PREFERRED STOCK FINANCING

To be considered a preferred stock, the security must represent ownership, that is, it must have no due date and must be entitled to dividends only as they are declared by the board of directors rather than as an interest payment legally enforcible on a set date. In addition, the stock must have at least some preference over common stock in the payment of dividends and may or may not have preference to assets in the event of liquidation or reorganization. Under present federal income tax law, the dividend paid on preferred stock is not deductible by the issuer, but a fully taxable corporation owning the preferred stock can claim tax deduction at 85 percent of the preferred dividend that it receives.

In the case of bonds, we found it necessary in considering priority to ask the question, prior to what? In the case of preferred stock we must ask, preferred to what? Only an examination of the specific situation can answer that question.

The provisions governing preferred stock are normally found in the corporate charter and in the resolution of the board of directors authorizing the issue. These provisions may be summarized on the stock certificate. There is no indenture or trustee such as is customary for a bond issue.

PRINCIPAL PROVISIONS ON PREFERRED STOCK

Before we consider the role of preferred stock in finance, we must examine the principal provisions associated with preferred stock.

Priority as to Some Earnings over Common Stock

Preferred stock enjoys some priority as to earnings over common stock. This priority is limited to a stated percentage or amount per share on an annual basis. If the preferred stock has par value,[1] this priority as to earnings over common stock may be a figure such as $6, or 6 percent annually in the case of a par value of $100. However, the fact that the company "earned" the amount of this priority does not assure that it will be paid. The order for payment must issue from the board of directors, and their decision rests on a number of factors, one of which is the liquidity position of the company. The board is also entitled to consider that even if cash is available, payment would work to the disadvantage of the corporation as a whole, as might be true if there were an immediate investment opportunity requiring cash.

As protection against this discretion of the board of directors, preferred stock typically carries a *cumulative* clause providing that, if the dividend is not paid, it accumulates and must be paid before any distribution to the common stockholders. Where the company experiences prolonged difficulty, these arrearages may pile up to such an extent that the firm may seek to make a compromise that would give consenting preferred stockholders a package in lieu of the arrearage. The package might include some cash, some notes, and some stock.

Participation by Preferred Stock

In general preferred stock is limited to the dividend for which it has priority over the common stock. A number of issues of preferred stock carry the right to participate in any additional dividends that may be paid by the company. The most common provision of such *participating preferred* is the right to receive an additional dividend on the same basis, share for share, as is received by the common stock after the common has received the same dividends as the initial preferred dividend.

Call, Protection, and Redemption Provisions

Most preferred stock contains a provision entitling the company to call in the preferred stock for payment. The call premium may be a set amount or may be scaled against time. Without a call provision the company may be caught when the market rate on preferred drops sharply below the rate that prevailed at the time the preferred was issued. Without a call provision the company has a problem in retrieving the preferred in order to "refund" at a

---

[1] Par value means little more than the value printed on the stock certificate and the value for the stock shown in the capital account on the balance sheet of the issuer. In the case of a bond, par can be defined as the dollar amount the corporation is obligated to repay, but in the case of a stock, the meaning of par value is less certain, particularly because of the alternative of no par stock. What "par" means as applied to stock ultimately depends on the law of the state of incorporation. How the state law defines the term has to do with the legal requirements of the state concerning what a share of stock can be sold for in terms of price and whether cash, goods, or services are permitted as payment.

lower rate. The only way for the company to do this is to repurchase the stock on the open market. However, the market will have capitalized the difference between the higher rate on the preferred and the current market rate, and the price the company would have to pay to repurchase would eliminate any gain in refunding at the then current market rates.

Preferred stock resembles debt in that earnings are limited, except in the case of participating preferred. Likewise, preferred has priority as to earnings and sometimes as to assets on liquidation. Hence, protective provisions of various kinds can be expected. In addition to the cumulative dividend provision, there often is a provision that no stock of equal or prior standing may be issued without the consent of the preferred stockholders. Otherwise the company may issue *prior preferred* carrying priority over the preferred already issued. To attempt to assure liquidity for dividends, a current ratio provision may exist. And to attempt to assure availability of earnings for dividends, a provision may be included requiring the maintenance of a minimum earned surplus before dividends may be paid on the common stock.

Redemption provisions, parallel to a sinking fund for debt, are frequently found in connection with preferred stock. These provisions may specify either the call by lot or the repurchase in the open market of a stated amount of preferred stock per year.

Voting Rights and Priority as to Assets

Preferred stock may have full voting rights (on an equal basis, share for share with the common stock), no voting rights, or limited voting rights. *Limited voting rights* typically grant all (or share for share with the common) voting rights to the preferred stock in the event of a default or arrearage for several years. Such voting rights terminate as soon as the default is cured. More often, upon default the preferred stockholders are given the right to elect some of the directors.

In recent years many state statutes have been amended to require a separate vote by *classes* of stock in order to authorize amendments of the corporate charter affecting classes differently. In such cases the law of the state of incorporation takes precedence over any contrary provisions in the stock.

Most preferred stock issues provide for priority of the par value plus unpaid arrearages over the common stock in the event of liquidation or reorganization. Sometimes liquidation preference is given to one class of common stock even though the class is not designed preferred.

Income Tax Deductibility of Intercompany Preferred Stock Dividends

One important income tax provision supports a large part of the market for preferred stock. A fully taxable corporation owning preferred stock of another (unrelated) corporation is entitled to deduct 85 percent of the preferred dividends it receives in determining its income subject to income tax.[2] Thus the owning corporation receiving 7 percent on bonds of another company will net 3.64 percent (after taxes of 48 percent), but on 7 percent preferred dividends will net 6.496 percent (after a 48 percent tax on 15 percent of the dividend). In order to be entitled to the deduction of 85 percent of the preferred dividends received, the corporation receiving the dividend must be a fully taxable corporation.

ADVANTAGES AND DISADVANTAGES OF PREFERRED STOCK FOR FINANCIAL MANAGEMENT

The advantages of preferred stock parallel those of debt. Leverage is achieved where the earning of the preferred is less than the earning of the common stock. The risks of achieving this leverage by debt include the maturity date and the fixed interest payments. Default in either respect would lead to insolvency in the case of debt. Avoiding this risk by the use of preferred stock involves the financial manager in the payment of a higher rate on preferred stock than on bonds and the tax disadvantage of the nondeductibility of preferred dividends compared to the deductibility of interest on bonds.

Lesser advantages are that preferred stock offers the opportunity of preserving assets free from mortgage and available for future financing and it may avoid parting with voting rights if the preferred is nonvoting as long as there is no arrearage. Furthermore, the use of the call provision offers the same flexibility that exists in the case of bonds. This flexibility is not available for the issuance of common stock except to a limited extent through the repurchase of common stock.

The tax disadvantage of preferred stock compared to debt severely limits the use of preferred. The after-tax cost of preferred is almost twice that of debt.[3]

---

[2] This provision is examined in Chapter 23. In the case of affiliated companies, intercompany dividends are not taxed when a consolidated return is filed.

[3] Assuming an income tax rate of approximately 50 percent and a preferred dividend rate slightly above the bond rate.

Table 16.1 illustrates the dramatic shift away from preferred stock as corporate income tax rates continued high after World War II. In the early years of the period 1931–1966, income taxes were lower than they are today, and although they were high during World War II, there was an expectation that they would ultimately revert to prewar levels. In the latter part of the period it became apparent that corporate income taxes would not fall to prewar levels. By way of explanation, bond figures point to considerable refunding during the 1930s and to a lesser extent so do the preferred stock figures. It must be remembered, too, that a high percentage of new funds for companies is retained earnings.

Table 16.1. New Corporate Security Issues by Types 1931–1951, 1960–1966, and 1968–1974* (billions)

	1931–1951		1960–1966		1968–1974	
	Amount	Percent	Amount	Percent	Amount	Percent
Bonds	$26.6	75%	$33.3	68%	$178.2	73%
Preferred stock	4.1	12	1.9	4	15.4	6
Common stock	4.5	13	13.8	28	50.9	21

* These figures exclude investment company offerings.
Sources: 1931–1951, H. C. Guthmann and H. F. Dougall, *Corporate Financial Policy,* 3d ed. Englewood Cliffs, N. J.: Prentice-Hall, 1955, p. 169; 1960–1966 and 1968–1974, Securities and Exchange Commission, *Statistical Bulletin,* monthly.

No research is available on the extent to which even the current showing of preferred stock financing rests on the 85 percent intercompany tax deduction for preferred dividends, but there are cases where "lending" corporations have been willing to buy preferred issues of companies whose bonds would not be of interest to the lender. Such purchases have been motivated by the tax deductibility of the intercompany preferred dividend to the "lender."

One factor favoring the use of preferred stock in public utility financing is that the tax disadvantage is largely removed by the legal rule that the allowable return for a public utility is determined *after* income taxes. Thus regulating commissions must increase rates charged to utility customers sufficiently so that the after-tax earning is the same whether preferred stock or debt is used, even though the use of debt would result in lower rates to customers than the use of preferred stock.

The financial manager must always consider not only the effect of the proposed financing on his company but how investors will react. Investors are attracted by the higher earnings offered by preferred stock in comparison to bonds. The fact that the market price of preferred stock fluctuates more than that of bonds and that sometimes dividend arrearages are not paid out in cash have not been important deterrents to investors.

MANAGEMENT OF PREFERRED STOCK AFTER ISSUANCE

After the preferred stock has been issued, problems of management arise that are similar to those associated with bond issues, except that the financial manager does not face the maturity problem in the case of preferred stock.

As market rates on preferred stock move downward, opportunities arise for replacing the preferred stock with another issue at lower rates, or for replacing the issue with more favorable covenants. The changing affairs of a business and of the market place may produce situations in which protective provisions of the original issue become onerous and place constraints on the firm.

For example, market conditions at the time of issuance may have forced the inclusion of a clause severely limiting the amount of debt. The company may now wish to take advantage of subordinated convertible debentures to increase the amount of common stock through conversion at prices more favorable than a direct issue of common stock. But a covenant in the preferred stock setting debt limits may stand in the way.

In computing the saving of a replacement issue it is important to compare the results after taxes. The fact that preferred stock has no maturity date simplifies the rate of return computation to a comparison of the first-year after-tax saving against the after-tax investment (some costs of replacement are tax deductible and some are not). If, however, the preferred issue has a redemption schedule, the rate of return computation for the proposed new preferred issue will involve using present value tables.

One special problem is the replacement of noncallable preferred or of an issue with a very high call premium. While noncallable preferred is not issued today, there are still some noncallable preferred issues outstanding that were issued in the 1920s. At the time of issuance, few people anticipated the severe drop in the long-term interest rate that developed in the 1930s, and fewer still anticipated the high corporate tax rates that began in the 1940s.

Except for the possibility of eliminating preferred stock afforded by a merger and the obvious case of elimination in bankruptcy reorganization, the only way to terminate a noncallable preferred stock issue is through tenders by the issuer or repurchase in the open market. Noncallable 6 and 7 percent preferred issues stood around $150 in the market place from the 1930s to the 1960s. The most important single factor that deterred repurchase by issuers was not the high premium in itself but the prospect that the long-term interest rate might rise shortly after the issuer replaced the preferred which would have permitted much less expensive replacement. Ultimately long-term interest rates did rise in late 1966 and early 1967 and many of these noncallable issues fell in the market place to the range of 100–110. In 1974 these issues fell to the range of 60–70.

RECENT USE OF CONVERTIBLE PREFERRED STOCK IN MERGERS

In recent years until an accounting change in 1970, a new phenomenon was taking place which promised to revitalize the slipping popularity of preferred stock. This was the frequent use of convertible preferred stock in mergers, particularly the conglomerate merger.

Of a total of 335 issues of preferred between 1960 and 1967 by firms that had securities listed on the New York Stock Exchange during that period, some 292 issues arose in mergers, and all of those issues were convertible.[4]

There are a number of reasons for this development. First, there was the desire of the acquiring company to use the "pooling of interests" method of accounting[5] for mergers. To qualify for this accounting treatment, the preferred had to be convertible, voting, carry no significant sinking fund provisions, and not be redeemable until after the initial conversion date. Pooling of interests could be used when the acquiring company issues common rather than convertible preferred. What was the motivation for using the convertible preferred? One important reason is to equalize the difference in dividends between the two companies. Many stockholders would oppose a merger if their dividends were altered. The easiest way to meet this problem is to create a new class of stock preserving the higher dividend

---

[4] Pinches, G. E., "Financing with Convertible Preferred Stock, 1960–1967," *Journal of Finance*, 25 (Mar. 1970), pp. 53–63.

[5] The pooling of interests method of accounting is explained in the discussion on mergers in Chapter 22. Briefly, pooling permits the acquiring company to add the earned surplus of the acquired company to its own earned surplus and to account for any excess of the purchase price over the book value of the acquired company by a charge to capital surplus. Neither of these benefits is available under the alternative "purchase" method of accounting.

for the acquired company. Furthermore, the acquired company might think itself of superior quality and thus seek the priority of a preferred both as to assets and dividends. Both of these purposes are legitimate. A third and not so legitimate a purpose may be to hide the "dilution" of earnings that may ultimately result when the preferred is converted into common stock. To deal with this abuse, the accounting profession[6] now requires that earnings per share of common stock be stated both on the basis of actually outstanding common stock and on the basis of "full dilution," assuming the conversion of all securities convertible into common stock and the exercise of all outstanding options for common stock.

The future use of convertible preferred in mergers has been hampered by the recent accounting ruling that when convertible preferred is used in a merger, the purchase method of accounting must be used.[7]

Summary

Preferred stock is ownership with no maturity but a priority as to earnings and/or liquidation rights over common stock. It carries no due date for dividends, which are payable only when the board of directors so determines, although most preferred issues provide for accrual of unpaid dividends.

Some preferred issues are participating, that is, after the stated amount per share has been paid the preferred and an equal amount per share is paid the common, then both classes participate equally in further dividends during that year. Other forms of participation may be specified.

Almost all preferred stock carries call and redemption provisions as well as various protective covenants. Some preferred stock has regular voting rights while other issues have no voting rights until dividends are in arrears. Some preferred issues are convertible into common stock at a stated price per share.

While dividends on preferred stock are not tax deductible to the issuing corporation, such dividends are 85 percent exempt from taxation when received by another taxable corporation.

[6] Accounting Principles Board Opinion No. 15, *Earnings per Share.* New York: American Institute of Certified Public Accountants, 1969; Melicher, R. W., "Financing with Convertible Preferred Stock: Comment," *Journal of Finance,* 26 (Mar. 1971), pp. 144–147; and Sprecher, C. R., "A Note on Financing Mergers with Convertible Preferred Stock," *Journal of Finance,* 26 (June 1971), pp. 683–685.

[7] Accounting Principles Board Opinions No. 16 and No. 17, *Business Combinations.* New York: American Institute of Certified Public Accountants, 1970. The purchase method of accounting is described in Chapter 22.

The advantages of preferred stock parallel those of debt with respect to leverage but without the disadvantages of a maturity date and fixed interest payments. On the other hand, preferred stock carries a higher rate and lacks tax deductibility to the issuer for dividends paid. The tax disadvantage reduces the use of preferred stock in high-tax periods compared to low-tax periods.

After issuance of the preferred stock the financial manager is faced with the question of refunding if the market rate on preferred stock falls. Because preferred has no maturity date, the computation of the profitability of refunding is simplified to a comparison of the results in the first year of refunding unless the preferred issue has a redemption schedule. If the preferred is noncallable, the refunding is carried out by repurchases in the open market or tenders to stockholders. One problem of refunding is timing. If refunding occurs too soon, the costs of a second refunding will bar taking advantage of further declines in the preferred rate.

In recent years convertible preferred stock has frequently been issued in mergers for a wide variety of reasons. The tax disadvantage of preferred stock is outweighed in the eyes of the acquiring company by the potential it sees in the acquisition. Furthermore, the acquiring company seeks to avoid using its debt capacity (or may have already exhausted it). A recent accounting rule specifying the purchase method of accounting for a merger where convertible preferred is used now limits the popularity of convertible preferred in mergers.

Study Questions

1. What factors should determine the amount of preferred stock that a company will issue?
2. Do you think that voting rights are important to preferred stockholders? Would the size of the company have a bearing on the importance you attribute to the voting rights?
3. Rank the following types of "protective" provisions found in preferred stock in the order of their importance to you as an investor. Then rank them in the reverse order of desirability to the company (that is, least desirable first, and so on). Is the order of the two rankings the same? How do you account for this?
   a. Cumulation.
   b. Limiting the ratio of debt to net worth.
   c. Limiting the earnings that can be paid to common stock as dividends and the amount of common stock that can be repurchased by the company.

    d.   Sinking fund provisions for the preferred.

    e.   Putting a lower limit on the current ratio.

    f.   Granting voting rights that expand upon arrearage.

    g.   Priority in liquidation.

4. Would your order of ranking be affected by (a) the type of industry in which the company is (for example, a public utility versus a machine tool manufacturer), (b) the amount of the preferred dividend, or (c) whether the preferred was convertible or participating? Remember there are two orders of ranking involved, yours as an investor and the issuing company's.

5. Do you think that preferred stock arrearages should appear on the company's balance sheet? in the liabilities section? in the net worth section? If you would put arrearages on the balance sheet, what account would you debit?

6. As an investor do you favor a high or a low call price on preferred stock? Why? As an issuing corporation would you favor a high or a low call price? Why?

7. What type of situations, if any, would cause a company to favor shifting from debt to preferred stock? Would the reverse of these same elements cause a company to shift from preferred stock to debt?

8. The Supreme Court has ruled that whether a security is an income bond or a preferred stock will not be decided for income tax purposes by the "label" that appears on the security. Would you apply the same principle for questions other than income taxes?

Problems

1. From Moody's or Standard & Poor's invsetment manuals or from the offering prospectus determine the following points with respect to the offering on May 18, 1965, by Control Data Corporation of 489,448 shares of 4 percent cumulative convertible preferred stock, par value $50 per share.

    a.   What is the conversion price and what is its relation to prior prices of the common stock?

    b.   What other financing was the company doing at the same time?

    c.   What use was made of the funds secured at this time?

    d.   What was the debt-to-equity ratio after these offerings?

    e.   Why did the company use expensive preferred stock (the dividends are not tax deductible) rather than secure all the funds at this time by debentures? Why did it not omit the preferred offering?

    f.   Why did the company sell a convertible preferred stock rather than common stock?

    g.   What protective provisions were offered to the preferred?

    h.   What is the call provision in the preferred?

    i.   The offer was on rights on the basis of 1 share of preferred for each 15 shares of common. The underwriters received 65 cents a share for all shares offered and an additional 55 cents for each share they acquired as a result of failure of rights to be exercised. Do you consider the underwriting commission out of line?

j. What antidilution provisions were included?

2. In 1973 Snow Products had before its board of directors the matter of a possible conversion of its preferred stock into common stock. The company began in 1965 with the production of small snow blowers.

In 1965 Snow had issued 1825 shares of $100 par preferred stock with $5 per year cumulative dividend, callable at $105. At the same time Snow sold 1125 shares of common stock with $100 par value. The first two years of operation showed a loss of $82,500. Although losses during the starting period were anticipated, the loss exceeded expectations.

The intention had been to pay preferred dividends during the starting period despite losses. As the situation developed, Snow suspended preferred dividends after the payment of $3.33 per share in 1965. In the succeeding years Snow prospered; the record appears in Table 16.2.

A temporary setback in 1972 caused the board to interrupt preferred dividends, but the resounding success in 1973 eliminated the arrearage completely. During the five-year period 1969–1973 the shortage of cash prevented Snow from paying more on the arrearage. In addition, Snow had moved from leased quarters to its own plant.

The balance sheet at year-end 1972 and 1973 is given in Table 16.3.

What do you think would be an appropriate exchange ratio of preferred for common? Who decides what the ratio will be? What factors determine the ratio?

Table 16.2. Snow Products Dividends and Earnings

	Preferred Stock			Common Stock	
Year	Paid per Share	Arrearage at Year End	Earned per Share after Preferred Dividend	Paid per Share	Book Value after Preferred Arrearage
1969	$ 0	$11.67	$57.55	0	$ 74.93
1970	5.00	11.67	73.94	0	157.00*
1971	5.00	11.67	42.96	0	201.85
1972	2.50	14.17	24.94	0	226.22
1973	19.17	0	87.54	0	314.33

* In 1969 Snow bought back $40,500 in preferred stock at par, the sellers waiving the arrearage.

Table 16.3. Snow Products Comparative Balance Sheet
December 31

	1972	1973
Assets		
Cash	$ 19,247	$ 81,026
Receivables	201,878	289,085
(Receivables reserve)	(15,000)	(15,000)
Inventory	287,866	378,891
Prepaid expenses	10,500	12,068
Total current assets	504,491	746,070
Other assets	14,351	4,752
Land and buildings	37,203	117,429
Equipment	79,636	105,734
Leasehold improvements	29,076	—
Depreciation and amortization	(31,842)	(36,593)
Net fixed and other assets	128,424	191,322
Total assets	$632,915	$937,392
Liabilities and net worth		
Notes payable	$100,640	$104,099
Accounts payable	79,398	221,396
Income taxes	23,157	71,421
Total current liabilities	203,195	396,916
Mortgage loan	13,107	44,850
Preferred stock, 1,420 shares, $100 par	142,000	142,000
Common stock, 1,125 shares, $100 par	112,500	112,500
Retained earnings	162,113	241,126
Net worth	416,613	495,626
Total liabilities and net worth	$632,915	$937,392

Selected References

Bildersee, J. S., "Some Aspects of the Performance of Non-Convertible Preferred Stocks," *Journal of Finance,* 28 (Dec. 1973), pp. 1187–1201.

Buxbaum, R. M., "Preferred Stock—Law and Draftsmanship," *California Law Review,* 42 (May 1954), pp. 243–309.

Donaldson, G., "In Defense of Preferred Stock," *Harvard Business Review,* 40 (July–Aug. 1962), pp. 123–136.

Elsaid, H. H., "Non-convertible Preferred Stock as a Financing Instrument 1950–1965: Comment," *Journal of Finance,* 24 (Dec. 1969), pp. 939–941.

Fergusson, D. A., "Preferred Stock Valuation in Reorganizations," *Journal of Finance,* 13 (Mar. 1958), pp. 48–69.

Fisch, J. H., and M. Mellman, "Pooling of Interests: The Status of the Criteria," *Journal of Accounting,* 126 (Aug. 1968), p. 43.

Fisher, D. E., and G. A. Wilt, Jr., "Nonconvertible Preferred Stock as a Financing Instrument 1950–1965," *Journal of Finance,* 23 (Sept. 1968), pp. 611–624.

———, "Recent Trends in Electric Preferred Stock Financing," *Public Utilities Fortnightly,* 78 (Sept. 15, 1966), pp. 19–31.

Melicher, R. W., "Financing with Convertible Preferred Stock: Comment," *Journal of Finance,* 26 (Mar. 1971), pp. 144–147.

Pinches, G. E., "Financing with Convertible Preferred Stock, 1960–1967," *Journal of Finance,* 25 (Mar. 1970), pp. 53–64.

———, "Financing with Convertible Preferred Stock, 1960–67: Reply," *Journal of Finance,* 26 (Mar. 1971), pp. 150–151.

Santow, L. J., "Ultimate Demise of Preferred Stock as a Source of Corporate Capital," *Financial Analysts Journal,* 18 (May–June 1962), pp. 47–50.

Sprecher, C. R., "A Note on Financing Mergers with Convertible Preferred Stock," *Journal of Finance,* 26 (June 1971), pp. 683–685.

Stevenson, R. A., "Retirement of Non-callable Preferred Stock," *Journal of Finance,* 25 (Dec. 1970), pp. 1143–1152.

Weygandt, J. J., "A Comment on Financing with Convertible Preferred Stock, 1960–67," *Journal of Finance,* 26 (Mar. 1971), pp. 148–149.

Williams, C. M., "Senior Securities—Boon for Banks?" *Harvard Business Review,* 41 (July–Aug. 1963), pp. 95–110.

17

COMMON STOCK FINANCING

THE STRUCTURE OF A CORPORATION

The ownership of a corporation is called the *equity*. Stockholders, each of whom owns one or more *shares* of the corporation, own the equity. Shares are evidenced by stock certificates stating the number and type of shares and the owner's name as it appears on the books of the corporation or its transfer agent. Partly for convenience and sometimes to shield the identity of the real owner, stock may be carried in *street name*, that is, in the name of an investment banking firm. The firm holds the stock for the benefit of the true owner. A certificate in street name makes transfer of ownership easier. If the certificate is in the name of the individual owner, transfer must be accompanied by the guarantee of a bank or broker of the owner's signature endorsing the certificate for transfer, whereas the endorsement of the investment banking firm is well known. There is some danger in the event of insolvency of the investment banking firm. Although street certificates are not the property of that firm and cannot be reached by that firm's creditors, the certificates may no longer be on hand at the time of insolvency.[1]

Stock certificates are transferable but not negotiable. Negotiability cuts off many of the claims of prior owners of a security.[2]

A brief statement of the legal status of a corporation aids understanding many of the niceties of finance. A corporation is a creature of the state of

[1] The newly established federal insurance protects individual accounts to the extent of $60,000.
[2] The requirements for negotiability are explained in Chapter 15, footnote 2.

incorporation[3] and subject to its laws. Ever since the Dartmouth College case in the early nineteenth century, corporation charters under general corporation statutes have been granted subject to the right of the state to change the applicable laws.

Corporate Charter

The *corporate charter,* also called the *articles of incorporation,* is usually kept as simple as possible because of the difficulty of procuring the required two-thirds consent of shares to amend the charter when ownership is widespread. The charter usually gives the name of the corporation; the location of its principal office (where legal papers may be served); a statement of its purposes (usually very broad) and duration (usually perpetual); a statement of the classes of stock and numbers of shares of each class that are authorized and a statement of the "preferences" of any class; and a statement of the initial number of directors and who the incorporator(s) is (are). In some states the chater must also deny certain rights or they are presumed to exist. Chief among these are the *preemptive right*[4] and voting rights for all classes. The charter may also include any other provisions not in conflict with the law of the state. One provision frequently inserted in the case of small corporations is that before the stock can be sold it must first be offered to the corporation on the terms of sale that will be proposed to others.

Bylaws

After the state corporation law and the corporate charter, the basic document is the bylaws of the corporation. The *bylaws* are the rules of operation given in sufficient detail to permit the corporation to operate effectively. Thus the bylaws specify the current number of directors; information concerning both stockholders' and directors' meetings, for example, time, place, quorum, notification procedure; the officers (to be elected by the directors) of the corporation and their duties; provisions governing the handling of cash and other assets; and many specific provisions, for example, who can authorize the purchase of fixed assets.

It is basic to corporation law that the power to manage and control rests with the *board of directors* (more strictly, with what the *majority* of the

---

[3] Only a few corporations are federally chartered. These include national banks and federal savings and loan associations. There is no federal general corporation act such as each state has.
[4] The preemptive right is the right of a stockholder to maintain his proportion of ownership in the corporation by buying his proportion of any new stock issued by the corporation.

board decides). For this reason a resolution of the board of directors is necessary for many actions. Thus the issuance of stock and debt must be authorized by resolution of the board of directors. Dividend payments can be authorized only by the board of directors.

All of this discussion identifies the scope of the stockholder whose action is limited to electing the directors and voting on those matters reserved by the state statutes to stockholders. These matters are amendment of the corporation charter, merger, consolidation, dissolution, sale of substantially all assets, reduction of the par or stated value of stock, and a few other matters that vary from state to state. The most important variation is whether stockholder consent is needed for long-term debt and mortgaging of assets.

Policy as to Choice of Directors

The management of a corporation is the responsibility of the directors. Officers administer the day-to-day affairs of a corporation, but they are legally subject to the control of directors. In many corporations the role of the board of directors is perfunctory and officers assume the role of the directors. No man can serve on many boards and do justice to his responsibility unless he is a "professional" director—one whose entire business efforts are expended in the capacity of being a director for many companies. Such a man is called a "working director," and he is paid accordingly.

These problems raise the fascinating question of what constitutes an ideal board of directors. Experience has led to the formula that one third of the board should be active managers of the company and two thirds of the board should not be active in the day-to-day affairs of the company. This has led to the expression: one third "inside" directors and two thirds "outside" directors.

The merits of this rule are apparent. The decision of the board of directors is determined by majority vote. But the "inside" directors have a biased position—their jobs are involved. Hence discretion dictates that potential control not be placed in their hands but in the hands of the outside directors. Thus in examining a corporation, the focus is placed on the qualifications and performance of the "outside" directors. A corporation without an active board of directors is little more than a legalized sole proprietorship or partnership.

Voting

There are three methods of voting—regular, common law, and cumulative. *Regular voting* accords one vote to each share of a voting class. *Common law voting* (usually limited to cooperatives and special types of corporations) accords one vote to each owner regardless of the number of shares owned. *Cumulative voting* is applicable only to the election of directors and is designed to assure minority representation on the board of directors if the minority votes its shares effectively.[5] Each share owned receives as many votes as there are directors to be elected and each shareholder can distribute those votes for such director or directors as he wishes. All directors are voted on at once, with those receiving the greatest number of votes elected.[6] Under regular voting each director is elected separately and the majority elects all directors.

Eligibility to Vote, Voting Trusts, Classified Stock

For convenience and orderly procedure the bylaws of the corporation usually provide for the establishment by the board of directors of a "record date" for determining eligibility to vote and again to determine stockholders who will receive a dividend. The record date is usually 10 to 20 days before the meeting date (or date the dividend is payable). If stock is sold after the record date but before the meeting date, the seller of the stock delivers a proxy to the buyer. This proxy is irrevocable[7] and gives the buyer the right to vote.

---

[5] Cumulative voting is highly controversial. The Illinois constitution requires it (21 other states also require it); the Wisconsin statutes (by indirection) forbid it.

[6] The formula to determine the minimum number of shares needed to elect a certain number of directors (*if* all the minority shares are cast *evenly* for only these directors and *if* the majority casts its votes *evenly* for its maximum) is

$$\frac{(\text{total } \textit{shares voting}) \times (\text{number of directors desired})}{\text{total number of directors to be elected} +1} +1$$

Any fractional share in the answer is dropped. This formula is frequently misstated. For example, some texts state total number of shares *outstanding* in the numerator. Other texts misstate the numerator in the same way but compound the error by requiring an *agreement* by factions that the formula includes only shares voted. No such agreement is needed.

It is quite possible (and it has occurred) that a minority can seize control by organizing its votes rigidly while the majority *attempts* to elect *more* directors than its votes can assure. This happens not only because the majority's votes are disorganized, but because the majority may not know how many votes the minority has. A further complication is that some votes may be cast by stockholders acting independently of the majority or the minority groups.

One method for the majority to use to avoid the result of cumulative voting is to amend the bylaws to reduce the number of directors. On this vote the majority must prevail. By reducing the board to three (the legal minimum) the majority will make minority representation impossible unless the minority controls at least 25 percent of the votes cast. It is clear that cumulative voting properly belongs in the area of game theory.

[7] Ordinary proxies are revocable despite the fact that they may contain a statement that they are irrevocable. The proxy given to the buyer of stock by one selling after the record date is an exception to this rule of law.

In many cases corporations have experienced periods when the stockholders have been divided on basic questions of policy. Sometimes the conflict has involved efforts to "raid" the corporation in which "outsiders" seek control. Because stockholders are free to change their position from one meeting to the next, a basic instability may develop. This instability can threaten the future of the corporation, mainly by creating a reluctance of groups to share the uncertainty. These groups would include the firm's executives, principal customers, suppliers, and the commercial banks and financial institutions interested in the corporation. One means of dealing with this uncertainty is the voting trust.

The *voting trust* is a device by which stockholders may surrender their right to vote by transferring their stock to the voting trustees named in the trust document. In return the stockholders receive certificates of beneficial interest in the voting trust. Only the right to vote is transferred in this process. Following a period during which the courts were somewhat hostile toward the device, most state statutes now authorize the voting trust and surround it with limitations designed to prevent abuse.

The voting trust is adaptable to resolving uncertainty and is, in addition, one basis for creating a "leverage of control" by which the majority *within* the voting trust can now control.

The voting trust is not the only device available for continuity of control. Many corporation laws authorize classified directors. Under this provision only some of the directors (usually one third) are elected each year. Thus each director holds office for three years. Since only one third is elected each year, another type of leverage of control results. Another possible provision in the corporate charter under the laws of some states is that election of a director may require more than a majority vote.

In considering the voting procedure, we must bear in mind the basic legal rule that until new directors are elected, the current directors continue to hold office. It is obvious, then, that any effort which prevents the establishment of a quorum for a meeting will continue the current control.

Another device related to voting control is the use of classified common stock. One class is created without voting rights, with this class being sold to investors. The other class with voting rights is retained by the controlling stockholders.

Proxy Fights

Despite efforts to centralize voting control and sometimes because no steps have been taken in this direction, a proxy fight may develop. A proxy is simply a written authorization to another to exercise the right to vote. Although generally one can orally appoint another to act for him, there are several areas of law where the authorization must be in writing.

The power to appoint another as agent includes the right to revoke that power before the agent has acted. Thus except in the case of stock that has been sold after the record date, the proxy is revocable. Hence the proxy signed at the later date governs in cases where more than one proxy has been signed. Likewise, the stockholder who appears personally at the meeting can revoke a proxy.

As a practical matter, in preparing for a meeting of stockholders, the disputing groups will begin by gathering proxies. The solicitation of proxies by the management of a company and by others is subject to SEC control.[8] If persons other than management seek to solicit proxies, they may rely on the required information previously furnished to stockholders. In the event no solicitation of proxies by management or any one else is undertaken, the company is still required to furnish stockholders prior to the annual meeting with the same information as would be required in a proxy statement. In addition to this information, each stockholder must receive an annual report and adequate means to register his instructions as to how his proxy should be voted on issues known in advance. If the stockholder signs but does not indicate his vote, he must be advised how the proxy will be voted. The proxy statement must include the following:

1. A statement as to revocability of the proxy.
2. Dissenter's rights as to any matter to come before the meeting.
3. A statement as to who solicits the proxy and who is paying the costs of solicitation and the name of any director who dissents if the proxy is solicited by management.
4. A statement concerning the interests of any officer or director in any matters to be acted on.
5. A statement as to the number of voting securities by class, the record date for voting, and the holders of 10 percent or more of voting securities.
6. The names of all nominees for director and their other positions with the company or principal employment for the prior five years, together with the number and class of equity securities owned by each.
7. The names of each director receiving compensation over $40,000, and the total compensation of all officers and directors as a group. The same applies for options over $10,000 to any officer or director or over $40,000 for the group.
8. A statement concerning any indebtedness over $10,000 by an officer, director, or nominee or any associate of such to the company or any material interest (over $40,000) in any transaction with the company.

---

[8] Under Regulation 14A all securities listed on organized exchanges and all over-the-counter securities which are held by more than 500 stockholders are subject to the proxy statement requirement.

9. The name and interest of any auditor to be selected at the meeting.
10. Information concerning bonus, profit sharing, pension, retirement, options, or other remuneration plans to be acted on.
11. A statement concerning securities to be authorized or issued at the meeting and the terms of any proposed transaction involving the securities.
12. Information relating to modification or exchange of securities to be acted on, any merger, consolidation, acquisition, or similar matters to be acted on, or any property acquisition or disposition or restatement of accounts to be acted on.
13. Proposed amendments to charter, bylaws, or other documents.

In the event of a proxy fight over the election or removal of directors, special rules apply.[9] Those who seek to challenge the management for proxies are required to furnish each security holder and to file with the SEC a statement listing the following:

1. The name and address of the solicitor of the proxy together with his background of residence and all occupations in the prior 10 years.
2. Any other proxy contests in which the solicitor has been involved in the prior 10 years and the outcome of such contests.
3. Any convictions or criminal proceedings in the prior 10 years.
4. The amount of securities of the company owned by the solicitor and the amounts and dates of any acquistions during the prior two years (including whether such acquisitions were financed by borrowing and how much is still owed).
5. The name, address, and holdings of anyone associated with the solicitor of the proxy.
6. The terms of any arrangements concerned with the securities of the company in which the solicitor is or was involved in the prior year.
7. Any material dealing with the company in the past year and any understandings about employment transactions with the company.
8. The amount to be contributed by the solicitor to further the solicitation of the proxy.

ADVANTAGES AND DISADVANTAGES OF COMMON STOCK FOR FINANCIAL MANAGEMENT

The prime advantage of common sotck is that it involves no fixed charges or commitments. It carries no maturity date and no obligation to pay dividends.

The increase in value of the common stock increases the credit of the business in all respects: trade credit, bank credit, and long-term credit.

The sale of common stock makes available to the company the funds of

[9] Rule 14a–11 of the Securities and Exchange Commission Regulation 14A.

that part of the money of investors which is seeking higher returns and protection against the erosion of inflation. Protection against inflation arises from the increase in the value of the real assets of the company and the increasing returns in dividends, providing profit margins are not squeezed by rising costs. Inflation protection for the common stock of a company with little debt may do little more than keep pace with the inflation. But to the extent that the company uses debt, there may be a *real* gain for the common stock. The holders of debt funds that are invested in real assets by the company will not share in the increase in money value of the assets. All of this increase in value will accrue to the common stockholders. Conversely, in times of deflation the brunt will fall on the common stock and not on the debt.

The disadvantages of the use of common stock center on the "dilution" of voting rights and the sharing of earnings with the new owners. We have already indicated that classified common stock is a device for retaining voting rights. The new common stock to be sold may be classified as nonvoting. The sharing of profits with new owners has to be weighed against the lower cost and leverage of debt as well as the risk created by debt.

Lesser disadvantages of common stock include underwriting costs that are higher than for debt or preferred stock. This higher cost follows in part from the smaller unit sales of common stock than in the case of debt or preferred stock where institutional buyers take large units. Furthermore, the risks for the underwriter both at the time of issue and the "after-market" are greater because of the greater volatility of common stock prices.

Common stock usually yields the buyer a higher return than debt and thus "costs" the company more. But with the emphasis on growth and the inflation of recent years, common stocks have been bid up to high prices, so that bond yields have actually been higher than common stock dividend yields. Thus the disadvantage of common stock relative to debt has varied considerably as far as the company seeking funds is concerned.

MANAGEMENT OF COMMON STOCK

Taking a company from the point of its inception, we shall examine various problems of managing its common stock position and the institutions that the market has developed for dealing with these problems. Since these problems do not necessarily follow a logical (or even a chronological) order, it should not be presumed that they will arise in the order in which they are presented here. The order of discussion of these problems will be (1) par, no par, and "optional" stock, (2) going public, and (3) listing on an exchange.

Par, No Par, and "Optional" or Blank Stock

The use of, or switching between, par or no par stock is largely a matter of the "cultural lag" of the laws of some states. The starting point of earlier laws was the idea that the purchase price paid by the initial stockholders was, in some sense, principal or value. However, there is an important distinction between the concept of principal as applied to debt and that of principal as applied to equity or ownership. In the case of debt, principal means the amount of money the borrower is obligated to repay at a specific point in time, namely, the maturity date. In the case of equity or ownership, principal at best can mean the amount of money that was paid to the corporation by the purchaser of common stock. There is no maturity date.

Because the law was proceeding on the premise that the amount of money paid by the initial stockholders was principal in the same sense as principal in the case of debt, the law followed the rule that additional shares could not be sold for less than par value. Otherwise the new purchasers would be taking advantage of the existing owners. The law made an initial purchaser of par stock who bought for less than par liable for the deficiency.

The law overcame its cultural lag with the first use of no par stock in New York State in 1912. The lag was closed by the legislature and not by the courts. No par stock permitted the company to sell stock at different times at different prices. As long as the price of any sale was close to the then market value and there was no bad faith or self-dealing by the directors, no liability would arise.

But the answer to this problem created new problems. No par stock created the problem of what should be shown on the balance sheet as capital stock in contrast to surplus. For a long period there was uncertainty in the law until the statutes came to incorporate definite accounting concepts. Stated value designates the amount of no par stock to be shown as capital stock on the balance sheet. Any amount received by the company in excess of stated value is reported in paid-in surplus. Stated value cannot be reduced in most states except by stockholder action but can be increased by action of the board of directors. In the case of the sale of no par stock at a price below stated value, the deficiency would be made up by a reduction in paid-in surplus and to the extent paid-in surplus is not available by a charge against earned surplus.

At the practical level, the initial decision as to par or no par common stock or the shifting of the common stock of a corporation from par to no par status or vice versa is often motivated by quirks in the franchise tax statute of the state of incorporation that discriminate in favor of either par or no par status.

Recently, many states have authorized optional or blank stock. We use the term "optional" because the statute authorizes the board of directors to vary some provisions of the stock, such as dividend rate, par or no par status, and priority or conversion privileges, from one issue to the next. Until this recent development, the articles of incorporation set out the rights of each class of stock and left no room for decision by the board of directors except as to price of the issue. The appearance of optional stock was forced by the growth of mergers and the need to tailor each stock issue to each merger.

Going Public

Chapter 14 considered the role of the underwriter but in terms more applicable to issues by companies already publicly owned. The first public offering of a company presents a different emphasis.

If sufficient time is allowed, it is possible for a company to become publicly owned without going through the process of a public offering. The term "publicly owned" does not have an exact definition. We might define public ownership as the status of being listed in the daily over-the-counter quotations in *The Wall Street Journal*. This would be too high a standard, since there are many issues sponsored by an investment banker appearing in the list quoted once weekly in the regional issue of *The Wall Street Journal*. Further, we might define public ownership as the status of appearing in the quotations published in any metropolitan newspaper, or as the status of any stock handled by any investment banker.

It is possible for the ownership of a firm's stock to spread by the natural process of large holders now and then selling off some shares. This process involves risk, since the selling stockholder might be found by regulatory bodies to be conducting a marketing or offering and therefore subject to filing requirements.

Federal Filing

We will outline the various possibilities for a smaller company to market its stock without violating state or federal laws governing the sale of securities. The federal legislation applicable to stock and administered by the SEC is found in the Securities Act of 1933. The law is based on the philosophy of full and truthful disclosure rather than any evaluation of the soundness of the stock, or of its pricing. It is not enough that what is said must be truthful; the issuer must also disclose all that is relevant. The SEC has evolved rules concerning what it considers the minimum relevant data, and it is authorized to issue a "stop order" if it finds that the information submitted is inadequate.

There are several exemptions from the federal act available to the small company. The first is the so-called private sale as opposed to the public offering. The matter of what is private and what is public is not decided on the basis of the number of buyers. Rather, the SEC places heavy emphasis on whether the buyers are knowledgeable in financial matters generally and on the reputation of the company whose stock is involved.[10] Thus 30 insurance companies buying an entire issue could easily be found to be a private placement, but a newspaper advertisement that produced only a handful of ordinary citizens as buyers would be a public offering.

The second exemption covers an offering that is intrastate only. Here the issuer avoids the use of the U.S. mails and requires each buyer to sign a statement that he is a resident of the same state as that in which the issuer is incorporated and otherwise goes to considerable lengths to make certain that no state lines are crossed.

Finally, the SEC provides for a minimum amount of filing where the offering is of an amount totaling less than $500,000 in any one year.[11] In this connection it is important that the SEC requires as part of the filing the advance submission of copies of all material to be used in solicitation and requires the issuer to furnish an offering circular to all buyers.

State Filing

In addition to federal regulation, the smaller company faces state regulatory bodies. The philosophy of most state regulation is quite different from

---

[10] This matter is normally handled by submitting a full statement of facts to the general counsel for the SEC, who then states the recommendation he would make to the commission if these facts were submitted to him. If his decision is that he would advise the commission that no illegality is involved, the letter he writes back to the company is called a "no action" letter.

[11] Such offerings are governed by Regulation A, which is discussed in detail in E. Weiss, "Regulation A under the Securities Act of 1933—Highways and Byways," *New York Law Forum*, 8 (Mar. 1962), pp. 3–131. Regulation A (Rule 257) provides for a further reduction in filing requirements if the offering is less than $50,000 in one year.

In the year ended June 30, 1973, there were 817 offerings for a total of $298 million under Regulation A, of which 444 did not use an underwriter. This figure compares with the 3285 offerings (including investment companies) totaling $59 billion that were fully registered. The fully registered figures include offerings of about $10 billion by investment companies. See *Securities and Exchange Commission*, 39th Annual Report, June 30, 1973, pp. 163, 166.

that of the federal act. These state statutes, popularly called blue sky laws, authorize the state agency to pass on the merits of the proposed transactions, namely, whether the stock represents something feasible and whether the proposed price is fair. While this might seem to be an extremely difficult assignment for the state agency, many practical working rules have been developed which aid in culling out a high percentage of proposals that have little, if any, merit. Some of these rules have been enacted by the legislature, thus leaving the agency with no discretion.

To cite a few of these rules, the lowest permissible quality of securities may be required to have clearly printed on the stock certificate and on all material of solicitation the legend, "These are speculative securities." Or limits are set concerning the maximum commission or expense that will be allowed in connection with the sale of any security. To deal with the matter of fair pricing, some states set a maximum price–earnings ratio that will be allowed even for the offering of securities of the most highly regarded corporations.

It is clear that the task of the financial manager of a small but growing business in navigating his way through regulatory problems is not easy, particularly when we consider the vulnerability of the earnings of the small company to the vicissitudes of the business cycle, the competition of established businesses in the same field, and the risks inherent in a "thin" management.

Advantages of going public accrue to both the corporation and its stockholders. For the corporation, going public means a reduction of uncertainty in future equity financing. The market place will assess the strengths and weaknesses of the company and evolve a price for the company's stock. Thus the foundation is laid for future equity financing. In the absence of the guideline furnished by even a thin market for a stock, the investment banker considering an initial issue must increase the protective margin that he seeks.

For the stockholder, going public means that his investment has marketability. In turn this has many benefits, ranging from value as collateral for loans to some certainty of valuation for gift, inheritance, and estate tax purposes.

Letter Stock

In recent years, banks, trust companies, insurance companies, and other institutions have felt pressure from their accounts for the higher earnings and inflation protection offered by common stocks. Because these institutions deal in blocks of shares, a new market has opened up for unregistered securities. If the buyer of shares is a sophisticated investor and if that buyer gives the seller (either the primary issuer or a selling stockholder) an "investment letter" stating that the purchase is for purposes of investment and not for distribution, then the sale is not subject to the requirement of registration. Such stock is called "letter stock." The buyer can resell to another who furnishes a similar letter. Under existing practice, if the buyer holds for two years he can resell without getting a new letter.

In "letter" deals, the buyer frequently protects himself by requiring the seller to agree to pay registration costs if the buyer wants to sell within the two-year period. In turn the seller may satisfy the buyer by offering a "piggy-back" registration, that is, combining the registration of the letter stock with another registered offering made by the original seller.

Listing—Advantages

Having achieved the status of a publicly held company and having grown, particularly in number of stockholders, to the point where its stock is quoted daily in *The Wall Street Journal*, the company is now ready to consider listing on one of the 14 organized exchanges.

Listing in itself will not assure active trading of a security. Ultimately trading will depend on the size of the security issue, how widely it is distributed, and the type of holder attracted to the issue. It is the last attribute that has given rise to the phrases "glamour stock," "high flyer," and "speculative stock."

Listing offers the financial manager greater marketability for the company's securities, even though new issues are not marketed on an exchange.

One specific gain of listing is the ability to engage in equity financing through the use of rights. The over-the-counter market offers no way for an underwriter to dispose of an unsold balance of rights. In this market, rights are usually limited to an amount equal to one or two years' dividends.

Listing may furnish an attraction in merger. The listed company may offer the unlisted one a better price than it could get elsewhere, because a listed company tends to have a higher market value.

To the investor, listing means that he can meet emergencies more easily by selling because of the greater liquidity of the stock. Likewise, his ability to use stock as collateral for borrowing is greatly improved if the stock is listed. The lender feels he can allow a higher percentage against the stock because of the speed with which it can be sold if that becomes necessary.

Brokers will loan the investor funds on collateral of listed securities but not on unlisted ones. Collateral value can be additionally important to the investor in enabling him to avoid the immediate payment of the capital gains tax that would follow his selling the security and later rebuying it. Furthermore, the investor avoids the risk that the market will move up during the interim.

Listing—Disadvantages

Listing also entails disadvantages. Just as listing advertises the security and its issuer more than if the company were not listed, so during adverse conditions the same spotlight focuses on the company. A collapse in the price of a security may cause a reaction on the customers of the issuer and even on its short-term credit. This reason is often given by banks (with the exception of Chase Manhattan) for their unwillingness to list. If public confidence were shaken, depositors may react by withdrawing their funds and causing a run on the bank.

Listing also presents a problem of control. The cost to outsiders of gaining control will depend on the publicly owned proportion of shares of the stock outstanding and the price per share. Speculators are attracted, particularly as the price falls. Merger becomes an increasing possibility as the firm's business slumps. There is a point before the firm reaches the reorganization or bankruptcy stage at which another, stronger company may be able to turn the situation around.

To avoid the control problem in listing, a company may shift to two classes of common stock, one voting and the other nonvoting, with only the nonvoting shares offered to the public. However, the New York Stock Exchange will not list nonvoting common stock.

Listing is also thought to increase the hazard of speculative manipulation of the stock. Many factors favor speculation on the exchange. The availability of margin transactions and improved collateral value give the speculator great leverage. Only listed securities can be sold short. This raises the question of whether speculation serves an economically useful purpose. Informed speculators are attracted by deviations from "sound" values. If a security is overpriced or underpriced, the speculator becomes interested because he expects the price to move toward the "sound" value. Uninformed speculators can accentuate the overpricing or underpricing and may exceed the actions of the informed speculators, thus causing the pricing extremes to continue and grow.

Another disadvantage of listing is that the stock may lose some of the promotional efforts of the investment bankers who were making a larger profit on each transaction when the security was traded over-the-counter because of their ability to command a price differential up to 5 percent away from the last transaction (in addition to the usual commission). This additional source of profit is removed when the stock is listed and with it the funds to pay for producing and circulating reports which the investment bankers had been sending out for the over-the-counter security.

Finally, listing may bring with it an unhealthy interest in the current price of the security. Management may become overconcerned with the immediate effect of its business decisions on the price of the security, and its judgment may be impaired. Thus major changes that are sound from a long-range point of view may be deferred for fear the current price of the security will be affected. The delay may mean that the projected change will become more costly later on or may even mean disaster for the firm.

FINANCING THROUGH RIGHTS

While bonds are underwritten and sold, common stock is frequently sold through the device of rights. A financing through rights is not done on the exchange, but the fact that a stock is listed makes it feasible to use financing with rights.

A *right* is an option to buy a given security from the issuing corporation during a stated period at a stated price. The use of the rights procedure may be required because of the existence of a preemptive right, or the right may be granted even though preemptive rights do not exist. A right is evidenced by a stock warrant or certificate issued to the stockholder and stating the number of such rights that his present ownership can claim. The warrant is distributed by the company to its stockholders and is transferable. Almost half of the number of new registered issues result from rights offerings.

An issue of rights must be registered with the SEC just as any other offering. The filing of the registration establishes the first relevant date. As already indicated, registration takes a minimum of 20 days. Hence the price of the new shares offered will be set at the effective date of the registration statement. This date is followed by the record date, used to determine what stockholders will receive the rights, which begins the trading period for rights, usually from 10 to 20 days. The trading period ends with the expiration date of the rights.

Formulas for Determining the Value of Rights

The valuation of rights has given rise to considerable theoretical speculation. The earliest approach was the development of formulas for determining the value of a right both before and after the record date. The most convenient way to develop the present discussion is by an example.

Assume a company seeks to increase its equity funds by $2 million. The firm has 500,000 shares outstanding, and the current market price is $20 per share. One might conclude that the sale of 100,000 shares at $20 per share will yield $2 million. Since there are 500,000 shares outstanding and we seek to sell 100,000 shares, it would appear that it will take five rights to buy one share. However, it is necessary to give value to the rights or there will simply be an offering of 100,000 shares at the market price, which would depress the price. In addition, we would be using a cumbersome device to carry out the offering. Thus to give them value, rights carry a subscription price for new stock that is lower than the current market price. One target may be a subscription price 20 percent under the market price, say $16 per share. Then to get $2 million we need to sell 125,000 shares ($2 million/ $16), and it will take four rights to buy one share. What will one right be worth?

Once the rights are being traded (that is, the stock is now *ex* rights) the value of one right depends on three factors, (1) the market price of a share of stock, (2) the subscription price, and (3) the number of rights needed to buy one new share:

$$R = \frac{M_e - S}{N} \qquad (17\text{--}1)$$

where R is the value of one right, M_e is the market price of the stock *ex* rights, S is the subscription price, and N is the number of rights needed to buy one new share.

It is clear that if the right has value, then the market price of the stock must drop by the amount of the value of one right on the day the stock goes *ex* rights,[12] or where M_c is the market price of the stock *cum* rights (or "rights on"):

$$M_e = M_c - R \qquad (17\text{--}2)$$

Hence we can arrive at the value of one right in terms of the market price of the stock *cum* rights by substituting Eq. (17–2) into Eq. (17–1) to get

$$R = \frac{M_c - S}{N + 1} \qquad (17\text{--}3)$$

---

[12] This will be the fifth business day before the record day, since regular delivery of stock is due on the fifth day after the sale of the stock.

Using our illustrative numbers, we get the value of one right when the stock is *cum* rights by substituting in Eq. (17–3),

$$R = \frac{\$20 - \$16}{4 + 1} = \$0.80$$

The market price of a share of stock will change over the record date [by substituting in Eq. (17–2)]:

$$M_e = \$20 - \$0.8 = \$19.20$$

Finally, the value of the right after the record date by substituting in Eq. (17–1) is

$$R = \frac{\$19.20 - 16}{4} = \$0.80$$

Why the Values Given by the Formulas Seldom Occur

One reason the values given by the formulas seldom actually occur is that the formulas are derived on false assumptions. In developing the formulas we assumed that the new money to be raised would be invested by the company and would behave in *exactly* the same manner as the total company was performing before the new money was added. Thus we assumed that the marginal earning of the new money and the marginal risk of the new money would be the same as the previous average earning and average risk. Actually, the new money may carry a higher earning (as in a growth company) or a lower earning (as in a mature company). To the extent that the market place expects above- or below-average performance by the new money, the market price of the stock *cum* rights will be disturbed immediately.

There are several other reasons the formula values seldom occur. First, many stockholders are uncertain what the evaluation of the market will be for the additional funds and investment by the company. Hence stockholders simply wait during the early part of the trading period to see what the initial reaction of the market will be. This tends to create a shortage of rights offered for sale and to drive the price up during the early days of trading; hence the well-known maxim of the market place—sell rights early in the trading period, buy them late.

A second factor is the preferential treatment accorded rights financing under the margin requirements set by the Federal Reserve System. Customarily margin requirements provide a substantially smaller margin (down payment) for rights offerings than for regular offerings. Thus the current (1975) margin is 50 percent for stock but only 25 percent for rights offerings. Prospective buyers therefore find it much easier to finance new rights offerings.

A third factor is the alternative method available for handling rights for income tax purposes. First, the income tax law permits the taxpayer to elect that rights be treated as having zero cost basis. The profit on the sale of the rights would be a capital gain. The investor can thus use the short-term capital gain to offset short-term capital losses or can report the gain as ordinary income. As an alternative the investor can allocate the cost basis of his original shares over the original shares plus the rights. This is done by dividing the market price of the right by the market price of the common stock to establish what percentage of the market price of a share of common stock is attributable to the value of a right. This percentage is then applied to the cost basis of the common stock in order to determine the cost basis of the right. The cost basis of the original shares is then adjusted by deducting the cost basis of the rights. Hence when either the original stock or the rights are sold, the capital gain of each is separately determined. This flexibility in income tax treatment is a tax advantage to the investor and accordingly an attraction for the rights method of financing.

A fourth factor is the conduct of investment bankers. Under the old pattern underwriters of a rights offering merely stabilized the price of the stock, of the rights, or of both. Any stock they acquired by virtue of their underwriting commitment would then be offered later—too late to deal with any problems of an unsuccessful offering. Modern practice involves the underwriter in taking action immediately during the trading period of the rights in order not to stabilize the price of the stock or of the rights but to assure the success of the offering and, thus, to minimize the risk that after the trading period has elapsed he will have unsold stock to market.

The fifth factor affecting rights offerings is that from 1 to 3 percent of the outstanding shares[13] on a rights offering will never act despite the fact that there would be a profit in selling the rights at any time during the offering period. This fact arises from the absence of the stockholder from home during a relatively short period of time, ignorance, or other reasons.

[13] Grimm, E. A., "The Money You Save May Be Your Own," *Exchange*, 16 (Dec. 1955), pp. 17–20.

Flexibility of Rights Offering

A rights offering presents great flexibility for the financial manager. He may schedule the offering with or without underwriting. In the event of no underwriting he may estimate the amount of rights that will not be exercised and increase the amount of the actual offering accordingly. Or he may seek a "standby" underwriting agreement under which the underwriter (for a fee) will agree to pick up any stock not purchased upon the rights offering. Standby underwriting fees are smaller than the underwriting fee that would be charged for the entire offering. *Oversubscription* rights may be used, that is, those receiving the rights may be allowed to subscribe for additional shares beyond those covered by the right. In this case, all right holders who oversubscribe will participate pro rata in any shares not taken up by the exercise of rights in the event that the oversubscription exceeds the shares unsubscribed. Or the financial manager can avoid an underwriting fee by arranging for the purchase of unsubscribed shares by employees of the offering company or some other interested group. In this case the proposed purchasing group is functioning as an underwriter.

A rights offering gives the financial manager protection against his wrong estimates of what the market reaction will be to the proposed expansion. By setting the subscription price low enough, the financial manager with no thought of a stock split achieves protection against the possibility that the market may place a lower evaluation on the expansion than he has. If the market does not agree with his estimate, the value of the right will be positive, although not as large as he expected. As long as the value of the right remains positive, the offering will be successful. Thus the financial manager has been his own underwriter. Instead of doing business for an underwriting fee, which is determined in advance by the underwriter's *estimate* of the market reaction, the financial manager is settling for what the market's actual reaction will be. That reaction may be better than the manager (or underwriter) expects or worse. In a sense, then, the use of a rights offering means that the financial manager is substituting the actual market reaction for the underwriter's estimate of the market reaction, and the financial manager can blend these two positions by using standby underwriting.

CERTIFICATES OF PARTICIPATION

Certificates of participation are expanding in usage and serve the same function as common stock but typically involve a limited partnership rather than a corporation. The certificate of participation goes under several names: a limited partnership interest, a unit of participation, or an investment contract. The certificate of participation is like common stock in that it represents ownership in the business and is a residual claimant to earnings but unlike common stock carries no voting right, it being agreed that *all* management rights reside in the general partners. Another important difference from common stock is that each holder of a certificate reports his pro rata share of profits or losses—whether distributed or not—on his personal income tax return, thus picking up depreciation and depletion allowances immediately. The tax avoidance motive is powerful.

The certificate of participation is ordinarily issued in minimum units of $5000 and, typically, the venture involves high risks such as oil and other "wildcatting," theatrical productions, real estate ventures, and breeding operations. More than 90 percent of these certificates are offered directly by firms whose assets are less than $1 million. The costs of issuance are less than for common stock because the ventures are new and have no prior accounting records to be certified, need no expensive engineering reports on reserves (if in "wildcatting"), involve reduced printing and engraving costs, and are typically not underwritten. But the issue must be registered under the Securities Act of 1933 if it exceeds $500,000 and crosses state lines. In 1963–1965 there were 146 such issues, involving $376 million, with more than 60 percent of the issues in the extractive industries. In contrast, underwritten preferred stock offerings of all industries were $598 million in this period.

Summary

Corporations exist under charters, or articles of incorporation, granted by a state and subject to the laws of the state, including future changes in the laws. Majority vote controls both stockholders' and directors' meetings. A minority may secure representation on the board in states that permit cumulative voting.

Common stock involves no fixed charge and no maturity date. Financing the needs for increased funds with common stock may involve dilution of voting rights or dilution of earnings. Dilution of voting rights can be limited by the preemptive right, which gives each common stockholder the right to his pro rata share of new stock. But the preemptive right may be denied in the corporate charter.

The management of common stock involves such questions as the use of par or no par stock and decisions concerning when to have public offerings and whether to seek listing on an exchange.

Financing through rights involves issuance to stockholders of rights to purchase new shares at a price below the current market price of the stock. This option given to existing stockholders has value and can be sold.

Certificates of participation are proportionate interests in unincorporated ventures and are similar to common stock.

Study Questions

1. If the modern tendency is to reject the preemptive right for stockholders, why are there so many rights offerings of corporate securities by companies that have denied the preemptive right to stockholders?

2. If a corporation does not provide for effective control by a stable group, it is exposed to raiding parties by those who are tempted by the prospect of acquiring control easily and then milking the assets. What devices are available to deal with this problem and under what circumstances is each device appropriate?

3. Will the ownership of common stock protect the investor against the erosion of inflation if the company makes no use of debt in its financing?

4. Is the truth and full disclosure theory of federal security legislation a better policy than the qualitative standard specified by state blue sky legislation? Are the quality and effectiveness of the agency administering the legislation more important than what the legislation is?

5. If you were employed by an investment banker to price the stock of a company going public for the first time, list in the order of importance the factors you would consider.

6. It is a fact that the offering of common stock through rights is limited to stocks listed on an exchange except that small rights offerings (limited to the amount of one or two years' dividends of that stock) occasionally are made by companies whose securities are traded over-the-counter. Is there a sound reason for the practice of investment bankers in setting such a limit to rights offerings of over-the-counter stocks?

7. Should a company seek to list its securities as soon as it can meet the minimum listing requirements of an exchange? If you think the company should wait beyond that time, what criteria should determine the ideal time for listing?

Problems

1. The term "dilution of equity" has many different meanings, but all of them refer to an effect on common stock.
   a. Dilution of equity is sometimes said to occur when the issue of additional shares results in a lower book value per share.
   b. Dilution is sometimes said to occur when the effect of an issue of additional shares reduces the market price of the shares.

c. Dilution is sometimes said to occur when conversion (of a preferred stock or of a debenture) occurs at less than the market price of a share.

What is the dilution (in the first sense above) when the company's balance sheet before an issue is as follows and the company sells 1000 shares at $60? at $100? at $500?

Current assets	$100,000	Current liabilities	$ 50,000
Fixed assets	600,000	Debt	150,000
		Capital stock, stated value	
		$100, 2,500 shares	250,000
		Surplus	250,000
Total assets	$700,000	Total liabilities and net worth	$700,000

2. What is the dilution (in the second sense given in Problem 1) when the company offers rights to stockholders to buy one added share for each ten now held at a price of $60 per new share when a share was selling at $100 before the announcement?

3. What is the dilution (in the third sense given in Problem 1) when the company sells $100,000 in convertible debentures for $98,000, convertible into common at $10 per share, the predebenture market price was $12, and the company's balance sheet has been as follows:

Current assets	$100,000	Current liabilities	$ 50,000
Fixed assets	70,000	Capital stock, $10 par,	
		10,000 shares	100,000
		Surplus	20,000
Total assets	$170,000	Total liabilities and net worth	$170,000

4. It is argued in the text that the only meaningful use of the term "dilution" is to measure whether the additional (marginal) money will earn the average of the invested money of the company. Reverting to Problem 1 and its facts, indicate whether the sale of 1000 additional shares at $60 results in dilution if the company applies the proceeds to a project that will annually earn $16,000 after taxes when the present (preissue) company is annually earning $70,000 after taxes?

Would you expect the price of the stock to rise if the project carries the same risk as the rest of the company's operations?

5. a. What is the theoretical value of a right if the stock is trading *ex* rights and selling for $100 when the subscription price is $80 and the number of rights needed to buy one share is 10?

b. If you should find that the price of a right is selling for $3, how do you explain the deviation from your answer to (a)?

c. If investment bankers are willing to enter a rights financing with a company, do you think that the commission they will seek will be greater if this company prefers a direct (nonrights) underwriting agreement?

Selected References

Bacon, P. W., "The Subscription Price in Rights Offerings," *Financial Management*, 1 (Summer 1972), pp. 59–64.

Beranek, W., *Common Stock Financing, Bank Values and Stock Dividends: The Theory and the Evidence.* Madison Wis.: University of Wisconsin School of Commerce, 1961.

Blume, M. E., and F. Husic, "Price, Beta and Exchange Listing," *Journal of Finance*, 28 (May 1973), pp. 273–282.

Evans, G. H., Jr., "The Theoretical Value of a Stock Right," *Journal of Finance*, 10 (Mar. 1955), pp. 55–61; and "Comment," by S. H. Archer and W. Beranek, *Journal of Finance*, 11 (Sept. 1956), pp. 363–370.

Flink, S. J., *Equity Financing for Small Business.* New York: Simmons-Boardman Books, 1962.

Furst, R. W., "Does Listing Increase the Market Price of Common Stocks?" *Journal of Business*, 43 (Apr. 1970), pp. 174–180.

Keane, S. M., "The Significance of the Issue Price in Rights Issues," *Journal of Business Finance*, 4 (Sept. 1972), pp. 40–45.

Logue, D. E., "On the Pricing of Unseasoned Equity Issues: 1965–1969," *Journal of Financial and Quantitative Analysis*, 8 (Jan. 1973), pp. 91–104.

Lynch, T. E., "Accounting for Equity Securities," *Financial Management*, 2 (Spring 1973), pp. 41–47.

McDonald, J. G., and A. K. Fisher, "New Issue Stock Price Behavior," *Journal of Finance*, 27 (Mar. 1972), pp. 97–102.

Nelson, J. R., "Price Effects in Rights Offerings," *Journal of Finance*, 20 (Dec. 1965), pp. 647–660.

Stevenson, H. W., *Common Stock Financing.* Ann Arbor, Mich.: University of Michigan Press, 1957.

Weiss, E., "Regulation A under the Securities Act of 1933—Highways and Byways," *New York Law Forum*, 8 (Mar. 1962), pp. 3–131.

part five
THEORY OF FINANCE

18

ENTERPRISE VALUATION

Determining the value of a firm is a difficult and complex matter. First, the valuation process requires estimates of future earnings, and such estimates are uncertain. Second, valuation involves estimating a capitalization rate for these future earnings. Third, valuation is undertaken for a specific purpose—for example, to determine the value of two companies to be merged or to determine the value of stock not traded in the market for estate tax purposes. In each case there are specific restraints placed on the valuation process. In this chapter our primary interest is the valuation of the securities of the firm.

USUAL INADEQUACY OF BOOK VALUE AS A MEASURE OF VALUE

The value of a firm (or of an asset) can have little relation to its cost to the present owners, although value may clearly have a relation to the cost of replacing the asset. The replacement cost will place an upper limit on the value of an asset but will not guarantee the lower limit of value. The figure —book value per share—is not the answer to value in the case of most corporations since it is not consistently related to the market value of the assets after liabilities have been paid.

For a small group of companies, book value per share has some meaning. These firms are mostly financial institutions such as banks and insurance companies whose assets are largely limited to those involving money claims that carry a fixed income and are of low default risk. The major risk to the value of such assets is a sharp change in the interest rate. In the case of banks and insurance companies many specialized accounting rules are applicable, and hence, even here book value is usually quite different from market value.

Book value is relevant when the assets of a firm carry approximately their market value and the earnings of the firm are low. In this case the liquidating value of the firm may be above the value established by capitalizing its earnings.

Volatility of Market Value

Market value is sometimes advanced as the true measure of value on the ground that it represents the current valuation (in the market place) to be placed on the future earnings of a firm at a capitalization rate that the market place finds satisfactory. But the market value of the securities of a corporation fluctuates even in a "normal" year. It is unlikely that the future earnings prospects of the company would have changed drastically in so short a time. More likely the capitalization rate changed during the year, and small absolute changes in the capitalization rate can produce large changes in the market value of a security.

VALUE AS THE CAPITALIZATION OF EXPECTED EARNINGS

In Chapter 10 we discussed discounted present value in evaluating investment opportunities. The same principle can be applied to establish the value of a firm. Initially we assume the firm to be entirely equity financed.

Capitalization of earnings consists of dividing the expected annual earnings by an annual rate, called the *capitalization rate*. The resulting quotient is the *capitalized value*, or what we consider the investment is worth. In other words, the capitalized value will then earn the annual expected earnings in perpetuity (no growth) at the rate we used; we selected that rate as satisfactory to us as a rate of return on the investment. This can be simply stated as

$$V = \frac{E}{k}$$

where V is the value of the investment, E the expected earnings, and k the capitalization rate.

It is important that the expected future earnings take proper account of "regular" earnings and nonrecurring earnings. Often the estimate of future earnings is prepared by examining historical earnings. Care must be taken to separate out nonrecurring earnings.

The capitalization rate we use in our computation is critical. A small absolute difference in this rate appears to be magnified in its effect on the absolute difference in value. Thus if a firm is expected to realize $1000 in earnings and we capitalize at 5 percent, the firm has an investment value of $20,000 (or $1000/0.05), but if we capitalize at 6 percent, this value is only $16,667 (or $1000/0.06).

THE THEORY OF THE TREND VALUE OF COMMON STOCKS

The capitalization process we have just examined is at work in the area of common stocks. It might appear, however, that when some stocks sell at a price–earnings ratio of 100 and others sell at a ratio of 5, something is wrong in the theory. The stock selling at a price–earnings ratio of 100 is being capitalized at an apparent rate of 1 percent on an earnings basis; that selling at a price–earnings ratio of 5 is being capitalized at an apparent rate of 20 percent. Both may be well-established firms. Surely the risk differences are not that great.

The explanation may lie in an assumption we have been making, that the expected earnings of the several firms would remain the same indefinitely into the future.

Many studies have demonstrated that the values of common stocks have increased over long periods of time at an annual rate averaging approximately 7 to 9 percent. Since common stocks are one way of protecting against the erosion of purchasing power due to inflation, their rate of growth in value must exceed the rate of inflation if they are to achieve this goal. But even the "real" value of common stocks has on the average increased. If the capitalization process is to be validly applied to common stocks, some adjustment is necessary to recognize the fact that earnings are not expected to remain the same in the future, as in the case of a bond or lease, but, rather, are expected to grow.

Valuation of Common Stocks

In the valuation of common stock it is customary to capitalize expected dividends, the dollars shareholders expect to receive, rather than expected earnings. Common stocks with expected dividends that will not change present no difference from our previous case of valuation. Hence, value = dividend/rate of capitalization, or $V = D/k$.

To value common stocks whose dividends are expected to grow, the valuation formula must be adjusted. Thus for a given company the dividend will grow at the annual rate g and one year from today will equal $D_1 = D_0(1 + g)$, where D_0 *and* D_1 are the dividends today and one year hence, respectively. We assume dividend payments are once a year and made at the end of the year. Thus the total of all future dividends will be

$$V_0 = \frac{D_1}{(1 + k)^1} + \frac{D_2}{(1 + k)^2} + \frac{D_3}{(1 + k)^3} + \cdots \qquad (18\text{--}1)$$

Then, since $D_1 = D_0(1 + g)$, we can substitute for $D_1, D_2, D_3, \ldots$ in Eq(18–1) and obtain

$$V_0 = \frac{D_0(1 + g)}{(1 + k)} + \frac{D_0(1 + g)^2}{(1 + k)^2} + \frac{D_0(1 + g)^3}{(1 + k)^3} + \cdots \qquad (18\text{--}2)$$

which results in

$$V_0 = \sum_{t=1}^{\infty} \frac{D_0(1 + g)^t}{(1 + k)^t} \qquad (18\text{--}3)$$

Using algebra,[1] this becomes

$$V_0 = \frac{D_0(1 + g)}{k - g} \qquad \text{or} \qquad V_0 = \frac{D_1}{k - g} \qquad (18\text{--}4)$$

To express this verbally, the present value of a common stock is equal to the expected dividend divided by the capitalization rate less the growth rate. We should point out that the no-growth case is simply a special case where the term for the growth rate is zero.

---

[1] The algebra is

$$V_0 = \frac{D_0(1 + g)}{1 + k} + \frac{D_0(1 + g)^2}{(1 + k)^2} + \frac{D_0(1 + g)^3}{(1 + k)^3} + \cdots \qquad (i)$$

We multiply by $(1 + g)/(1 + k)$;

$$V_0 \frac{1 + g}{1 + k} = \frac{D_0(1 + g)^2}{(1 + k)^2} + \frac{D_0(1 + g)^3}{(1 + k)^3} + \cdots \qquad (ii)$$

and subtract Eq. (ii) from Eq. (i):

$$V_0 - V_0 \frac{1 + g}{1 + k} = \frac{D_0(1 + g)}{1 + k} \qquad (iii)$$

$$V_0 = \frac{D_0(1 + g)}{k - g} \qquad \text{or} \qquad V_0 = \frac{D_1}{k - g} \qquad (iv)$$

Valuation of Common Stocks with Above-Average Growth Rates

Frequently certain common stocks are expected to grow at rates in excess of the average 7 to 9 percent rate of most stocks. In valuing such a security, we assume this above-average growth rate will continue for a specified period, such as five years, and then that it will revert to the average growth rate of all stocks. This has been the pattern of many new industries such as television and electronics. Sometimes the period has been somewhat longer than five years, and sometimes it has been shorter.

As a first approximation, the valuation of the above-average common stock can be broken into two periods, the above-average growth period and the mature period, represented, respectively, by the first and second terms in the following equation:

$$V_0 = \sum_{t=1}^{N} \frac{D_0(1 + g_{aa})^{t-1}}{(1 + k)^t} + \sum_{t=N+1}^{\infty} \frac{D_N(1 + g_a)^N}{(1 + k)^t} \qquad (18\text{--}5)$$

where g_{aa} is the above-average growth rate and g_a is the average rate.

We now present four examples applying the valuation formulas in four growth cases. In each case we will assume a capitalization rate of 9 percent. The current dividend is $1 per share.

Case 1: Negative Growth. The company is slowly sinking. There is an annual decline of 2 percent in the dividend. The value of the firm's stock is calculated using Eq. (18–4):

$$V_0 = \frac{D_1}{k - g}$$

$$V_0 = \frac{\$1(1 - 0.02)}{0.09 - (-0.02)} = \frac{\$0.98}{0.11} = \$8.91$$

Case 2: No Growth. The company shows no growth but is able to maintain its dividend. The formula for a perpetuity $V = D/k$ or Eq. (18–4) may be used to determine the value of the common stock:

$$V_0 = \frac{D_1}{k - g}$$

$$V_0 = \frac{\$1(1 + 0)}{0.09 - 0} = \frac{\$1}{0.09} = \$11.11$$

Case 3: Average Growth. The company grows at an average rate, which is taken to be an average annual increase in dividends of 7 percent. Using Eq. (18–4), the stock value is

$$V_0 = \frac{D_1}{k - g}$$

$$V_0 = \frac{\$1(1 + 0.07)}{0.09 - 0.07} = \frac{\$1.07}{0.02} = \$53.50$$

Case 4: Above-Average Growth. The company grows at an above-average rate, which translates to an annual increase in dividends of 20 percent for 15 years. Thereafter dividend growth returns to an average rate of 7 percent. The two-stage approach of Eq. (18–5) must be employed to determine value in this case.

For the next 15 years the dividend is expected to grow from $D_0 = \$1$ to $D_{15} = \$15.07$ for a total of \$86.44. If our discount rate is 9 percent, this 15-year stream has a present value of \$35.24. Table 18.1 shows all the necessary dividend computations.

Table 18.1. Dividend Computations

Year	Dividend $1(1.20)^t$	Discount Factor $1/(1.09)^t$	Dividend Present Value
1	$ 1.200	0.917	$ 1.100
2	1.440	0.842	1.212
3	1.728	0.772	1.334
4	2.074	0.708	1.468
5	2.488	0.650	1.617
6	2.986	0.596	1.780
7	3.583	0.547	1.960
8	4.300	0.502	2.159
9	5.160	0.460	2.374
10	6.192	0.422	2.613
11	7.430	0.388	2.883
12	8.916	0.356	3.174
13	10.699	0.326	3.488
14	12.839	0.299	3.839
15	15.407	0.275	4.237
	$86.44		$35.24

At the end of the 15-year period of above-average growth, the firm will experience average growth (as in Case 3). The value of the stock at the end of 15 years is

$$V_{15} = \frac{D_{15}(1 + 0.07)}{k - g}$$

$$V_{15} = \frac{\$15.407(1 + 0.07)}{0.09 - 0.07} = \frac{\$16.49}{0.02} = \$824.50$$

The present value of \$824.50 to be received in 15 years discounted at 9 percent is \$226.74 (\$824.50 × 0.275). Combining this value with the present value of the expected dividend stream for the next 15 years (\$35.24), an investor would be willing to pay \$261.98 per share for this stock.

It may appear necessary that $k > g$ or the stock would have an infinite price. However, note that in the above-average growth case in Table 18.1 we have a g of 20 percent and a k of 9 percent. We avoided the mechanical problem of $g > k$ by our methods of computation. A *real* problem in this regard would arise only if we assumed $g > k$ for an infinite period. Such an assumption is clearly nonsense since it would require the investment to take over the whole world in a rather short period of time.

Summary

The determination of a proper concept of value and the selection of the method and relevant data for translating this concept into a dollar figure are the two fundamental problems that underlie the valuation of any property. We are primarily interested in determining the market value of a firm via the capitalization of earnings. Required, therefore, is a reasonably accurate estimate of the future earning power of the firm and an appropriate capitalization rate. The generation of a solid earnings estimate usually proceeds from a study of the past. The earnings record is examined and the relation of the firm's earnings to major economic movements is studied. The trends in the economy and the industry are then analyzed and the earnings projected based on the movements of these major factors in the economy and the industry. The determination of an appropriate capitalization rate is more difficult. A wide variety of opinions exist regarding the appropriate rate to apply in a particular situation. In the valuation formulas presented, this capitalization rate reflects the investors' required rate of return. Appropriate adjustments to this rate are made to reflect the specific growth prospects of the company being analyzed.

Study Questions

1. What factors make valuation of a firm such a difficult task?
2. What are some of the areas in which the valuation problem appears? How does the valuation problem differ in each of these areas?
3. At one time an important measure, book value no longer is as significant as to the value of major industrial firms. What is the major determinant of the value of an industrial firm? Why is the book value figure not similarly disregarded in the valuation of financial institutions and small firms?
4. What would be the value of the Ritz Hotel built in the middle of the Sahara desert in an inaccessible location at a cost of $10 million? How do you arrive at your estimate? What are your assumptions?
5. How will the rates on U.S. government securities affect the valuation figure placed on a firm?
6. Give several examples of stable stocks and growth stocks. Why are growth stocks more difficult to value than stable stocks? Are the wider market price fluctuations for growth stocks a reflection of this greater difficulty? Support your answer.
7. What is the payout ratio? Under what conditions might a firm increase its payout ratio and thereby increase the market price of its stock?
8. Of what importance is the "growth horizon" in valuing growth stocks? How does it affect the calculated value of the stocks?

Problems

1. A woman purchases an elegant pair of leather gloves for $15.00. Upon leaving the store she loses one of them. An unscrupulous person finds the glove. Since it is brand new, he believes the glove has considerable value and decides to try to sell it "in the market."
   a. For what price do you think the glove can be sold in a normal market?
   b. The finder discovers the owner of the glove and decides to try to sell it back to her. How much do you think the owner might be willing to pay for the glove?
   c. Assuming the owner is willing to pay a good price for the glove, how do you reconcile her willingness to pay for the glove with what would normally be the market price for one glove?
2. The Mini-Machine Shop is expected to generate earnings of $1000 a year forever. Comparable firms are currently selling on a 10 percent capitalization rate basis.
   a. How much can the owners of Mini-Machine expect to receive for their firm should they decide to sell?
   b. The following year people's attitudes toward risk change. The market now is willing to buy such firms on a 5 percent capitalization rate basis. How much can the owners of Mini-Machine now expect to receive for their firm?
   c. A new product is introduced into the market and the sales of Mini-Machine plummet to zero. The equipment of Mini-Machine is still in perfect working condition, but being highly specialized, cannot be used for the manufacture of any other products. What is the market value of Mini-Machine now?

3. What is the basis of the market value of an enterprise? of the value of consumers' goods? How do your answers to these questions help to answer questions 1 and 2?

4. A manufacturing firm is currently paying a dividend of $1 a share. Earnings and dividends are expected to grow at the rate of 5 percent per year. Comparable companies with no growth are selling on a 10 percent capitalization rate basis. Management is considering a stock issue.

   a. Approximately what price per share can management expect to receive?

   b. Management is reluctant to proceed because of new developments on the horizon. Several years later the firm introduces a new product which is expected to permit dividends to grow at the rate of 10 percent a year for three years. After this period the dividends will return to the normal growth rate of 5 percent. Over the past years dividends had remained at $1 per share. The firm required all its available funds to develop this new product. The market rate of capitalization had dropped to 9 percent. Approximately what price per share can management now expect to receive should it decide to offer a new issue in the market?

   c. Management decides to proceed and sells the new issue in the market for the price determined in (b). In fact, the issue is enthusiastically received. Shortly thereafter the threat of new competition appears. It is now expected that the $1 dividend will grow at the rate of 10 percent a year for only two years, and after that time growth will be at a rate of 4 percent per year. The market rate of capitalization is still 9 percent. What is the new market price of the stock and how much did the investors lose that purchased the stock at the offering?

   d. Compare the numbers derived from the calculations in parts (b) and (c). What was the relative influence of the shortened rapid growth horizon from three to two years, and the reduced long-term growth rate from 5 to 4 percent? Did these changes tend to offset or reinforce each other?

5. Ricochet, Inc., a small measuring instrument manufacturer, is currently earning $5 a share and paying a $1 dividend. The firm acquires through merger a medical electronics firm. With the combined capability the market expects the firm to grow at the rate of 20 percent a year for 10 years and then level off to 7 percent a year. The market rate of capitalization is 9 percent.

   a. Based on these estimates, what is the current fair value of the stock?

   b. If the stock actually sells at this price, what is the price–earnings ratio?

   c. Ricochet has several projects that promise a return in excess of 20 percent. Internal funds are not available to undertake these projects. Accordingly, management plans to issue additional stock but feels the current price–earnings ratio is too low. Management feels a ratio of 45 to be appropriate. What action would you recommend to management to raise the price–earnings ratio to this level?

   d. What would be the indicated market price for the stock?

   e. Is this a sustainable market price if the firm's earnings actually grow faster than 20 percent?

   f. What will happen if the firm cannot maintain the anticipated 20 percent growth rate? Why?

Selected References

Beranek, W., *Common Stock Financing, Book Values and Stock Dividends: The Theory and the Evidence.* Madison, Wis.: University of Wisconsin, 1961.

Durand, D., "The St. Petersburg Paradox and Growth Stock Valuation," *Journal of Finance,* 12 (Sept. 1957), pp. 348–363.

Fama, E. F., and M. H. Miller, *The Theory of Finance.* New York: Holt, Rinehart and Winston, 1972.

Gordon, M. J., *The Investment, Financing and Valuation of the Corporation.* Homewood, Ill.: Richard D. Irwin, 1962.

Heidrick, H. H., "Determining Utility Market Value," *The Appraisal Journal,* 38 (Apr. 1970), pp. 253–272.

Herzog, J. P., "Investor Experience in Corporate Securities: A New Technique for Measurement," *Journal of Finance,* 19 (Mar. 1964), pp. 46–62.

Kotler, P., "Elements in a Theory of Growth Stock Valuation," *Financial Analysts Journal,* 18 (Mar. 1961), pp. 37–42.

Malkiel, B. G., "Equity Yields, Growth and the Structure of Share Prices," *American Economic Review,* 53 (Dec. 1963), pp. 467–494.

Olson, I. J., "Valuation of a Closely Held Corporation," *Journal of Accountancy,* 128 (Aug. 1969), pp. 35–47.

Walter, J. E., "Dividend Policies and Common Stock Prices," *Journal of Finance,* 11 (Mar. 1956), pp. 19–47.

19

THE COST OF CAPITAL AND CAPITAL STRUCTURE MANAGEMENT

The cost of capital is an important element in determining which projects to undertake and the composition of assets of the firm. No capital expenditure proposal should be approved that does not promise an expected return greater than the cost of capital. Hence it is important to minimize the cost of capital in order to maximize net return and growth. If the firm employs the net present value method, the cost of capital will be used as the discount rate to determine whether the project promises a positive net present value. If the internal rate of return method is employed, the internal rate will be compared with the cost of capital to determine if the internal rate of return is greater than the cost of capital.

In this chapter we explore ways in which the cost of capital may be minimized through rearrangement of the capital structure to establish the optimum mix of low-cost debt and high-cost equity. The financial manager seldom has an opportunity to build the capital structure of his firm from the beginning. He comes to a going concern that has a capital structure fashioned by those who went before. Within limits, he can slowly change the capital structure with the objective of minimizing the cost of capital to the firm.

At the outset, let us define several key concepts. *Capital structure* refers to the long-term financing of the firm, long-term debt, and net worth. *Net worth* consists of preferred stock, common stock, capital surplus, retained earnings, and net worth reserves. *Financial structure* refers to all the financial resources marshaled by the firm, short as well as long term, all forms of debt as well as equity.

THE WEIGHTED MARGINAL COST OF CAPITAL

The firm may borrow from its bank, expand its current liabilities, sell bonds or preferred or common stock, or retain a greater portion of its earnings. The cost of these funds to the firm may be determined with varying degrees of ease. The direct cost of a new bank loan or new bond issue is not difficult to calculate; the cost of foregone trade discounts due to allowing current liabilities to increase is only slightly more difficult. On the other hand, the cost of new common stock and retained earnings is surrounded by uncertainty and controversy. We are ultimately interested in calculating a weighted marginal cost of capital that includes all the sources of funds the firm employs. If we stop short of this and consider only the cost of funds from a specific source for a particular project, the cost of capital will fluctuate sharply as the firm finances one project with a bank loan, the next with an issue of common stock, and a third with a convertible debenture issue. Projects will be penalized or made to appear more favorable depending upon the source of funds tapped to finance that project at that particular time. Such a randomly fluctuating cost of capital will not lead to as good decisions as will be possible when employing the weighted marginal cost of capital. The principle we follow is that for any project to win support it must promise a return greater than the weighted marginal cost of capital.

The weighted marginal cost of capital depends on the costs of the individual sources of funds and on their proportions in the capital structure. It is current costs and not historical costs that are relevant in this calculation. Likewise, it is the intended future mix of debt and equity that provides the weights we will use. Our concern is with the cost of the new capital that the firm *will use* and not with the cost of capital that it *has used*.

The capital structure itself can influence the cost of its components. For example, the cost of debt may be higher if the firm's debt-to-equity ratio is 1:1 than if it is 0.5:1. Thus should a firm decide to change its capital structure, it is best to estimate what each component would cost under the proposed capital structure and then use these costs in determining the weighted marginal cost of capital.

As we proceed to calculate the weighted marginal cost of capital, we must first measure the costs of each component of the capital structure.

The Cost of Long-Term Debt

A $1000 bond bearing a 4 percent interest rate sold to an investor for $1000 will result in a cost to the firm of 4 percent if there are no other costs. If the flotation costs are $10 per bond, the longer the term to maturity, the closer to 4 percent will be the cost. If the bond runs for one year the cost of this debt will be 5 percent. If the bond runs infinitely long, the cost will be 4 percent. The same observations may be applied to any premium or discount.

Bond tables indicate the effective interest rate (the rate to maturity) a particular bond is yielding given the market price, the stated interest rate, and the years to maturity. Lacking such a bond table, one can make a good approximation of the effective rate by adding to or subtracting from the stated interest amount the discount or premium reduced to an annual amortized basis and dividing by the average of the current market price for the bond and the face value. The rationale is that the annual amortized amount of the discount or premium accrues to the holder and that his investment is not the current market price but, rather, the average of the market price and the face value.

The formula for approximating the effective interest rate for bonds selling at a premium or discount is

$$k_b = \frac{\text{annual interest payment} \left(\begin{array}{c} + \text{ discount years to maturity} \\ \text{or} \\ - \text{ premium years to maturity} \end{array} \right)}{(\text{par of bond} + \text{market price})/2}$$

where k_b indicates the cost of bonds.

For example, assume the $1000, 4 percent bond matured in 25 years. Now five years after the issue, due to a shift upward in interest rates, the bond is selling at $900. If the firm issued a new 4 percent bond of the same maturity as the remaining life of the old bond (20 years), it could expect to get $900 per new bond before adjusting for the cost of financing. The effective rate of interest investors currently demand on their funds is

$$k_b = \frac{\$40 + (\$100/20)}{(\$1000 + 900)/2} = 4.73 \text{ percent}$$

To adjust for flotation costs, add to the numerator the flotation costs divided by the number of years to maturity. This gives the pretax cost of debt to the firm. The number must be adjusted for taxes since the weighted marginal cost of capital is on an after-tax basis. If the corporate tax rate is 48 percent, the after-tax cost of debt, $k_b(1-t)$, is 2.5 percent. The definiteness of the cost of funds raised through bonds disappears if they are callable, convertible into stock, or include warrants to buy stock.

Cost of Short-Term Obligations

The cost of trade credit for the buyer is high if cash discounts are missed. If payment is made within the discount period, there is no explicit cost for the credit, though there may be more administrative costs to the firm in buying goods on credit rather than for cash. Also the seller may hide some of the credit costs in the price, but these ordinarily can not be ascertained or avoided.

Accrued liabilities carry no explicit cost to the firm and can be an important source of "free" capital. An example would be accrued taxes where a profitable firm may have outstanding average accrued taxes of $1 million as it moves from one quarterly tax payment to the next.

The stated interest rate on a short-term loan appears as an annual rate in the loan agreement. The true interest rate, however, varies from the stated rate, depending on whether the loan is discounted (that is, the interest is deducted in advance), whether the loan is repaid in equal installments, or whether there is a balloon payment at the end. Discounting a $1000 loan at 4 percent for one year makes available to the borrower only $960, and the effective interest rate is

$$\frac{\$40}{\$960} = 4.16 \text{ percent}$$

The $1.60 additional profit (4 percent on $40) to the banker appears to be negligible, but the $40 helps cover the reserve requirement of $160 which the banker must maintain for a $1000 loan when the reserve ratio is 16 percent. If the loan were not discounted but the principal were repaid in 12 equal installments, the interest rate would be approximately double the 4 percent stated rate, or 8 percent. Formulas are available for calculating the rate exactly, but the thinking proceeds along the following lines. The $40 interest for the year is paid for the $1000 loan, but if the principal of the loan is repaid in equal installments, the borrower really has available for his use over the entire time only one half of the funds. As in the case of long-term debt, the cost of short-term obligations should be calculated on an after-tax basis. In this illustration, assessing a 48 percent tax rate, the after-tax cost approaches 2.2 percent.

In addition, there is the compensating balance requirement by a bank. If this required balance is higher than would normally be maintained, the effect is to reduce the amount of the bank loan that can be used and to raise the effective cost of the loan. Thus if the loan is $100,000 at 4 percent, but the banker requires the borrower to keep an average of $20,000 on deposit when the normal bank balance is $15,000, the true interest rate is 4.21 percent (namely, $4000/$95,000).

Cost of Preferred Stock

The cost of noncallable preferred stock, since it carries no maturity date, is a function of the stated dividend, the current price, and flotation costs. A 5 percent preferred issued at par of $100 may at a later date sell in the market at $90. The new purchaser would receive a 5.55 percent return. The rise in this return may have resulted from a general rise in interest rates, a decline in the investment quality of the firm, or fear of inflation. The formula for determining the pretax cost of noncallable preferred stock capital is

$$k_p = \frac{\text{dividend on the preferred}}{\text{market price of the preferred} - \text{flotation costs}}$$

When we come to the cost of callable preferred, the stockholder receives a premium at the time the preferred is called. Preferred may be called when market rates of interest fall sufficiently below the issue rate to enable the firm to absorb the premium. The risk of call for the preferred stockholder complicates the computation of the rate of return—and complicates the cost for the issuer. Almost all preferreds are callable. If the preferred is convertible into common stock or participates in additional dividends after receiving its stated dividend, the cost of preferred is further complicated.

Preferred stock dividends are not deductible for corporate income tax purposes as are interest payments on debts. For this reason, no adjustment is necessary for k_p when calculating the weighted marginal cost of capital.

Cost of Common Stock

Earnings generated by the firm accrue to the stockholders who can spend or reinvest that portion of the earnings paid out in dividends. Another way a shareholder may realize a return on his investment is to sell his shares at a higher price than that at which he purchased them, thus realizing a capital gain. Excluding consideration of capital gains for the moment, since common, like noncallable preferred, has no maturity date, we might calculate the cost of common in the same way as noncallable preferred. Thus,

$$k_c = \frac{\text{dividend on the common}}{\text{market price of the common} - \text{flotation costs}}$$

If the current dividend on the common were not expected to change, this would be an adequate solution. Testing this formula in the market, we might expect to find common stocks selling on a dividend-yield basis of 8, 10, or 12 percent return, depending upon the risk involved and upon the ratio of dividends paid out to earnings (the payout ratio).

This is not what we find. Instead, we find common stocks selling at modest yields of 5 percent, at very low yields of around 1 percent, or at zero yield where the stock has never paid a dividend. Do these low yields mean that common is less costly than preferred or even debt? Not in the least! Where common stocks are selling on such a low dividend-yield basis, investors are anticipating a growth in dividends such that the combined return of current dividend yield and the annual rate of growth will exceed the yield on prior claim securities. Investors anticipate high future dividends or capital gains from currently low or nondividend-paying shares.

Since common stocks do not have a maturity date, we can either discount dividends into the far distant future, adding a growth factor, or discount those dividends for a shorter period, with a growth factor, and calculate the capital value of the shares at the end of the shorter period. The difference between the current market price and the later higher price would be the anticipated capital gain. Since that later price is itself a function of the discounted future dividends and growth, we will find it convenient to calculate common stock costs simply in terms of dividend yield and growth. Thus,

$$k_c = \frac{\text{dividend on the common}}{\text{market price of the common} - \text{flotation cost}} + \text{growth rate}$$

For example, suppose a company is paying a current annual dividend on common stock of 76 cents and it is selling at $38. Neglecting the growth factor, we see that the stock is selling on a current dividend-yield basis of 2 percent. If the firm were to accept 2 percent as its true cost of equity, sell large additional amounts of common stock at $38, and undertake projects with an expected return of around 2 percent (assume the firm has an all common stock capital structure), the price of its stock would drop from $38 to around $8 (which would be a 10 percent yield) if no further growth in dividends were expected. A market price of $38 reflects something more than the 2 percent current dividend yield, and that something is an anticipated annual growth rate of 8 percent or more.

The question is, what rate of growth is the market discounting? A starting point might be the historical growth rate. If the firm has grown at the rate of 8 percent per year for the past five years and is selling on a 2 percent dividend yield basis, it might be reasonable to conclude that the firm's cost of common equity, as determined in the market place, is 10 percent. A comparison might also be made with firms—probably in the same industry—representing a similar degree of risk. By comparing growth rates and dividend yields, an approximation may be reached regarding the firm's cost of equity. The difficulty with this approach is the absence of a definitive scale of risk classes; without such a scale it is not easy to identify the risk class to which the firm belongs. Whether easy or difficult, the financial manager must reach some conclusion regarding the cost of common equity to his firm.

Cost of Retained Earnings

Earnings not paid out in dividends are reinvested in the firm. The cost of these funds is identical with the cost of new issues of stock. Some textbooks imply that retained earnings cost less than new common stock because the firm avoids flotation costs and the stockholders avoid income tax payments on dividends. If the firm were to apply a cost less than the new issue cost to retained earnings, the cut-off point for capital investment would be lower. Investors would notice a shrinkage in the return on assets, and the stock price would decline. For this reason it is customary to apply the common stock formula to all common equity—new issues and retained earnings:[1]

$$k_e = \frac{D}{P} + g \quad \text{or} \quad k_e = \frac{\text{dividend on the common}}{\text{market price of the common}} + \text{growth rate}$$

WEIGHTED MARGINAL COST OF CAPITAL COMPUTATION

Cost of Capital Using Book Values as Weights

To this point we have developed measures for the cost of debt k_d, preferred stock k_p, and common equity k_e.

The determination of the weighted cost of capital is almost anticlimatic once the appropriate costs of debt, preferred, and common have been determined. We compute the percentage each source of capital bears to the total capital structure and multiply this percentage by the cost of that particular source of capital, as shown in Table 19.1.

The weighted cost of capital for Horizon, Inc., is 14.8 percent. These calculations are based on book values of debt, preferred stock, and common

[1] Note the switch in notation from k_c to k_e. In the previous section we were concerned with k_c, the common stock cost of capital. We are now concerned with the cost of the entire common equity.

Table 19.1. Horizon, Inc., Cost of Capital Calculation Weighted by Book Values

Capital Structure	Book Value	Percent of Total	After-Tax Cost of Capital	Weighted Cost
Debt	$ 2,000,000	20%	2%	0.4%
Preferred stock	1,000,000	10%	4%	0.4%
Common equity	7,000,000	70%	20%	14.0%
	$10,000,000	100%		14.8%

stock. While these figures may be of historical interest, the firm's capital budgeting decisions are carried on in the present, and what we need is a current cost-of-capital figure. The use of market value weights rather than book value for the capital structure components achieves this objective.

Cost of Capital Using Market Values as Weights

Assuming Horizon, Inc., is a growth company, its stock sells substantially above book value. Using market value weights rather than book values increases the importance of the high-cost equity in the capital structure and thereby increases the weighted marginal cost of capital as shown in Table 19.2.

Table 19.2. Horizon, Inc., Cost of Capital Calculation Weighted by Market Values

Capital Structure	Market Value	Percent of Total	After-Tax Cost of Capital	Weighted Cost
Debt	$ 2,000,000	10%	2%	0.2%
Preferred stock	1,000,000	5%	4%	0.2%
Common equity	17,000,000	85%	20%	17.0%
	$20,000,000	100%		17.4%

The cost of capital using market values is 17.4 percent, substantially above the 14.8 percent if we used book value figures. In slowly growing firms, book and market values may not differ greatly. Here there is little danger that the financial manager will sharply underestimate the weighted marginal cost of capital. But where a company is growing rapidly and market values are far above book values, market values must be used to calculate the weighted marginal cost of capital to guard against underestimating the cost of capital.[2]

MANAGEMENT OF THE CAPITAL STRUCTURE

Generally firms can borrow funds comparatively cheaply up to a point. Preferred, because of its junior position and the tax factor, usually costs more. Common equity seems an expensive source of funds. If nothing else entered the picture, the apparent conclusion would be the more prior claim securities in the capital structure and the less common equity the better. The best capital structure providing the lowest overall cost of capital would then be the one with the largest percentage of prior claim securities and the lowest percentage—just a few shares—of common stock. But the element of financial risk enters and with it the difficult question of determining the ideal capital structure.

Starting from an all-equity capital structure, a firm can obtain some amount of debt at comparatively low rates. As the percentage of debt moves up, the interest rate the firm must pay also rises. At first the rate rises slowly, but as the percentage of debt increases, the rate rises faster until the point is reached where the firm for all practical purposes cannot obtain any additional debt. Lenders are not available at any price. Shareholders, after a point in the process of increasing debt, will also demand a higher return on their capital to compensate for the higher financial risk.

With the introduction of low-cost debt into the capital structure, both the market value per share and the total market value of the firm will rise. As increasing amounts of debt are added, both the market price per share and total market value of the firm decline. This is caused by the higher interest rates demanded by lenders and the lower price–earnings ratios investors are willing to pay for the shares. This illustration suggests that the total market

---

[2] The weighted marginal cost of capital is the hurdle rate used in the analysis of capital investments. Cash flows have traditionally been computed on an after-tax basis; so to be consistent, the weighted marginal cost of capital is also computed net of taxes. If the firm is operating at an income level less than the tax rate assumed in this computation, then the firm's cost of capital is understated and incorrect investment decisions may follow.

The tax laws are continually being "reformed," and thus the correct tax assumption is not readily known. Recent items being considered by congressional tax committees include the elimination in whole or part of the corporate income tax and the denial of the deductibility of interest payments (*Business Week,* July 28, 1975, pp. 58–59). Aware of the dangers of using an incorrect assumption and in light of the potential changes in the tax laws, there exists a good reason to analyze potential investments on both a before- and after-tax basis.

Figure 19.1. Total market value of the firm; possible curve.

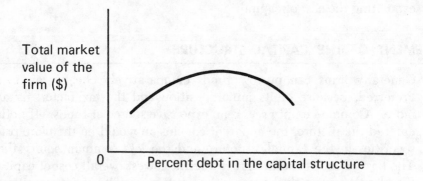

value of the firm as a function of percent of debt in the capital structures is inverted saucer-shaped, with the total market value of the firm low at the extremes of all equity and heavy debt financing, and higher with moderate prior-claim financing, as appears in Figure 19.1.

The weighted marginal cost of capital, on the other hand, would be saucer-shaped, as in Figure 19.2. The highest cost of capital would be at the

Figure 19.2. Weighted marginal cost of capital curve.

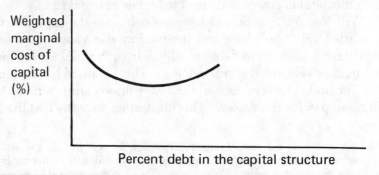

extremes of an all-common stock capital structure and heavy debt financing. Common stock normally carries the highest cost. The initial introduction of much lower cost debt will result in the cost of equity rising more slowly than the cheaper debt is pushing down the weighted marginal cost of capital. The net effect is to reduce the weighted marginal cost of capital. As we expand debt, however, the equity cost rises faster than more expensive debt can push down the weighted marginal cost of capital. At this point the subsequent introduction of additional debt causes the weighted marginal cost of capital to rise. This pattern demonstrates that every time a company borrows it "uses up" a piece of its equity base. Thus the opportunity cost of debt is greater than appears in any computation of weighted marginal cost of capital.

The Optimal Capital Structure

In a static situation, the optimum debt position would be at the point where the price–earnings ratio begins to fall faster than the earnings per share are rising from the introduction of additional debt. This situation is illustrated in Figure 19.3. Given a certain level of operating income, the price–earnings

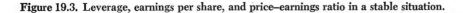

Figure 19.3. Leverage, earnings per share, and price–earnings ratio in a stable situation.

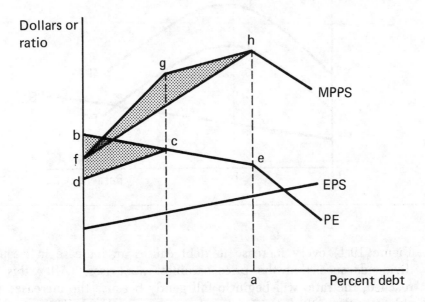

ratio (PE) may rise or fall as the first debt is introduced, reflecting the desire of the investing community to see the management use some debt financing or none. The price–earnings ratio will trace a path somewhere in the shaded area *bcd* and the market price per share (MPPS) would trace a path somewhere in the shaded area *fhg*. At *a* the price–earnings ratio would begin to turn down sharply, more than offsetting the rise in earnings per share, and the market price would fall. This would be the case for a static situation in which we postulate a fairly steady income level, and changes in the price–earnings ratio and in earnings per share (EPS) are reflections of the proportion of debt in the capital structure.

The price–earnings ratio of a growth stock is normally at a high level because of the anticipated growth in earnings and dividends. The introduction of leverage increases the rate of growth in earnings per share and dividends, as appears in Figure 19.4. Hence at least up to some point (*b* in

---

Figure 19.4. Leverage, earnings per share, and price–earnings ratio in a growth situation.

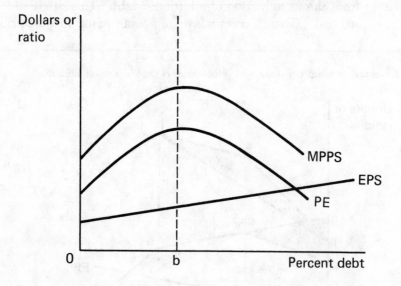

Figure 19.4) every increase in debt causes an increase in earnings and dividends such that the price–earnings ratio rises. After this point is reached, the ratio will begin to fall gently because the increased financial risk more than offsets the increased earnings per share. Then as added debt substantially increases the financial risk, the price–earnings ratio falls sharply.

The financial manager will have difficulty in setting the exact inflection points on the MPPS and PE curves, but insights may be obtained into the relationships we have here sketched by observing the practices of other companies and the market performance of their stock and studying the effects of debt financing.

Summary

The appropriate capital budgeting hurdle rate is the weighted marginal cost of capital. This chapter is devoted to measuring the weighted marginal cost of capital—debt, preferred and common stock, and retained earnings—and to determining the optimum capital structure.

The cost of debt (before income tax) is the ratio of the interest cost, taking into consideration any premium or discount and flotation costs, to the debt funds currently obtainable. The cost of noncallable preferred stock is measured by the ratio of the preferred dividend to the market price of the preferred stock less flotation costs. The measurement of the cost of common stock is more difficult. We measure cost of the common stock by dividing the current dividend by the market price, and adding the estimated dividend growth rate.

The proper hurdle rate is the weighted marginal cost of capital. A slowly growing firm might use book value weights in determining its cost of capital because book value is close to market value. Rapidly growing firms with high price–earnings ratios must calculate the weighted marginal cost of capital based on market value weights to avoid underestimating it.

Leverage is a key factor in determining the optimum debt-to-equity mix. The weighted marginal cost of capital curve is saucer-shaped, first falling as debt is increased and then rising. The introduction of increasing amounts of debt will push earnings per share upward. With the introduction of increasing amounts of debt the price–earnings ratio may either start to fall immediately, reflecting the rising risk from the increasing amounts of debt, or it may actually rise, reflecting the investment community's favorable reaction to seeing some debt in the capital structure. In either event, at first the market price per share will rise as earnings per share are rising and after some point it will fall as the price–earnings ratio falls faster than the earnings per share are rising. The turning point of the market price per share curve represents the optimum percentage of debt in that capital structure.

Study Questions

1. Would you agree that the hurdle rate in capital budgeting should be the cost of capital? Why?
2. Can it be said that any part of the funds used by a firm is free? Explain.
3. Can the historical interest rate on outstanding bonds of the issuer be used to get the cost of debt capital for current capital budgeting decisions?
4. Would you agree that the cost of common equity is the reciprocal of the price–earnings ratio? What is the reasoning behind your answer?
5. Do you agree that the price–earnings ratio will fall when an all-equity company

accepts new projects with a rate of return on assets below that presently enjoyed by the company on its assets?

6. If a company knows that its future investment opportunities will be less rewarding than its recent record but the market place does not know this, would you advise the company to sell common stock at the present time?

7. How would you reconcile the statement that earnings determine the price of a stock with the statement that dividends determine the price?

8. A company's growth rate will depend on the proportion of annual earnings together with depreciation that is reinvested and the earnings realized on these funds if no common stock is sold. Do you think this is a complete statement?

9. If financial risk did not exist, the optimal capital structure would include a minimum of common equity. Do you agree?

10. As a company increases its ratio of debt in the capital structure, it is argued that we can measure the cost of this debt by the change in the weighted marginal cost of capital. Do you agree?

Problems

1. A company sold $1000, 5 percent coupon bonds carrying no maturity date to the public several years ago at par. Interest rates have since risen, so that bonds of the quality represented by this firm are now selling on a 7 percent yield basis.
   a. Compute the current indicated market price of the bonds (ignoring the capital gains tax).
   b. Because of market imperfections the bonds now are selling at $800. If the bonds have 10 years to run to maturity, compute the approximate effective yield an investor would earn on his investment (ignoring the capital gains tax).
   c. The investment outlook for the company brightens so that the bonds are bid up to sell on a 5 percent yield basis. What is the current market price for the bonds?

2. The $7 noncallable preferred stock of F133, Inc., is selling to yield investors a 6 percent return on their money.
   a. Compute the current indicated market price of the preferred stock.
   b. Assume the $7 preferred stock of F133, which is of 6 percent yield quality, is callable at 110. Estimate the market price of the preferred and the indicated yield.
   c. Why might F133 be reluctant to refinance its outstanding preferred if the situation were as in (a) above but anxious to refinance if the situation were as in (b) above?

3. A stock is currently selling at $30 per share. The firm is paying $1 per share dividend annually and the investment community expects a growth rate of approximately 5 percent per year.
   a. Compute the firm's indicated equity cost of capital.
   b. Compute the indicated market price of the stock if the anticipated growth rate of the firm were to rise to 6 percent.
   c. Compute the indicated market price of the stock if the firm's cost of capital were 9 percent, the anticipated growth rate 5 percent, and a $1 per share dividend were being paid annually.

4. C-V, Inc., wishes to raise an additional $10 million in funds. Federal income tax rate is 50 percent. The company is considering the following mix of securities.
   1. $3 million, 10 year bonds. Coupon rate 5 percent. Net proceeds to the company $950 per bond.
   2. $2 million, 6 percent preferred stock. Net proceeds to the company $100 per share.
   3. $4 million, common stock. Current market price $45. Present earnings per share $3. Best estimate of future earnings per share without return from additional funds $4.80. The company will be able to sell common stock at a price that will net at $40 per share.
   4. $1 million, retained earnings. Stockholders of C-V, Inc., are typically in the 40 percent bracket.

Calculate
   a. The approximate after-tax unweighted cost of bonds.
   b. The after-tax unweighted cost of common stock.
   c. The after-tax unweighted cost of retained earnings.
   d. The after-tax unweighted cost of preferred stock.
   e. The weighted marginal cost of capital (after taxes).

5. Renold Corporation has the following capital structure as of May 31, 1976:

Bank notes, 8.5%	$ 900,000
Long term debt	
Straight debentures: 5¾% due May 31, 1986	3,754,000
Subordinated debentures: 6½% due Dec. 1, 1981	4,600,000
Conv.-Sub. debentures: 5% due May 31, 1998	5,840,000
4% due Dec. 1, 1996	9,600,000
Preferred stock, 3.25%, $100 par	13,000,000
Common stock, $1 par	774,923
Common surplus	5,864,077
Retained earnings	11,841,000
Total liabilities and net worth	$56,174,000

The Bank notes require a balance of $30,000 above Renold's normal transaction balances. Renold's effective income tax rate is 40 percent.

On June 1 Renold Corporation is going to issue 100,000 shares of new common stock which will reduce dividends per share from $1.96 to $1.85. Renold's investment banker feels that the effect of this issue along with the new bond issue (described below) will increase the current growth estimate in dividends from 7 to 9 percent. The spread on the new common will be $2.

The bond issue is a $2,000,000 straight-debt 30-year issue with a 7½ percent coupon for which Renold has been guaranteed $997.

Currently Renold's securities have been selling on AMEX for the following prices:

Securities	Price
5¾% debentures	$87½
6½% subordinated debentures	85½
5% convertible subordinated debentures	70
4% convertible subordinated debentures	60
Preferred	33⅞
Common	39

Compute Renold's weighted after-tax cost of capital both before and after the new issues.

6. The capital structure of Mr. Chips, Inc., on the eve of a major expansion program to be financed by the sale of new securities is as follows:

First mortgage bonds, 5% of 79	$1,000,000
Debentures, 5½% of 88	2,000,000
Preferred stock, 6%	3,000,000
Common stock, 100,000 shares	1,000,000
Retained earnings	3,000,000
Total capital structure	$10,000,000

The first mortgage bonds were sold in 1955 at 101. The firm netted 100. The bonds are currently selling in the market below par. Investment bankers estimate that a comparable new issue could currently be brought out with a 5¾ percent coupon at a price of 100 net to the firm.

The debentures were sold in 1963 at 102 and the firm netted 100. The bonds are currently selling on the market substantially below par. The investment bankers estimate a comparable new issue could currently be brought out with a 6½ percent coupon at a price of 100 net to the firm.

The preferred stock was originally sold at $107 and the firm netted $100, the par value. Comparable issues are currently selling at $87. The costs incurred in bringing out a new issue would be the same as those incurred on the previous issue.

The common stock is earning $2.40 per share, paying a $1.20 dividend, and selling at 28 times earnings. The firm has historically paid out 50 percent of its earnings in dividends and plans to continue this policy. The market estimates that the earnings of the firm will grow at the rate of 10 percent per year. Underwriting and other costs associated with bringing out a new issue of common stock are expected to total $7.20 per share and are not tax deductible. The firm is in the 50 percent tax bracket.

Compute the weighted after-tax cost of capital using market value weights.

Selected References

Arditti, F. D., "The Weighted Average Cost of Capital: Some Questions on Its Definition, Interpretation and Use," *Journal of Finance*, 28 (Sept. 1973), pp. 1001–1008.

Barges, A., *The Effect of Capital Structure on the Cost of Capital*. Englewood Cliffs, N. J.: Prentice-Hall, 1963.

Baxter, N. D., "Leverage, Risk of Ruin and the Cost of Capital," *Journal of Finance*, 22 (Sept. 1967), pp. 395–404.

Beranek, W., *The Effects of Leverage on the Market Value of Common Stocks*. Madison, Wis.: University of Wisconsin School of Commerce, 1964.

Breen, W. J., and E. M. Lerner, "Corporate Financial Strategies and Market Measures of Risk and Return," *Journal of Finance*, 28 (May 1973), pp. 339–352.

Brigham, E. F., and M. J. Gordon, "Leverage, Dividend Policy and the Cost of Capital," *Journal of Finance*, 23 (Mar. 1968), pp. 85–103.

Cragg, J. G., and B. G. Malkiel, "The Consensus and Accuracy of Some Predictions of the Growth of Corporate Earnings," *Journal of Finance*, 23 (Mar. 1968), pp. 67–84.

Durand, D., "Costs of Debt and Equity Funds for Business: Trends and Problems of Measurements," *Conference on Research in Business Finance*. New York: National Bureau of Economic Research, 1952.

Durand, D., "Growth Stocks and the Petersburg Paradox," *Journal of Finance*, 12 (Sept. 1957), pp. 348–363.

Elton, E. J., and M. J. Gruber, "The Effect of Share Repurchases on the Value of the Firm," *Journal of Finance*, 23 (Mar. 1968), pp. 135–149.

Fisher, I., *The Theory of Interest*. New York: Macmillan, 1930.

Haley, C. W., "Taxes, the Cost of Capital, and the Firm's Investment Decisions," *Journal of Finance*, 20 (Sept. 1971), pp. 901–917.

Kessel, R. A., "Inflation-Caused Wealth Redistribution: A Test of a Hypothesis," *American Economic Review*, 46 (Mar. 1956), pp. 128–141.

Lange, O., "The Rate of Interest and the Optimum Propensity to Consume," *Economica* (New Series), 5 (Feb. 1938), pp. 12–32. Reprinted in American Economic Association, *Readings in Business Cycle Theory*. Homewood, Ill.: Richard D. Irwin, 1951, pp. 169–192.

Lerner, E. M., and W. T. Carleton, *A Theory of Financial Analysis*. New York: Harcourt, Brace & Jovanovich, 1966.

Lewellen, W. G., *The Cost of Capital*. Belmont, Calif.: Wadsworth Publishing, 1969.

Lintner, J., "The Cost of Capital and Optimal Financing of Corporate Growth," *Journal of Finance*, 18 (May 1963), pp. 292–310.

Modigliani, F., and M. Miller, "The Cost of Capital, Corporation Finance, and the Theory of Investment," *American Economic Review*, 48 (June 1958), pp. 261–296.

——, "Dividend Policy, Growth and the Valuation of Shares," *Journal of Business*, 34 (Oct. 1961), pp. 411–432.

——, "Taxes and the Cost of Capital: A Correction," *American Economic Review*, 53 (June 1963), pp. 433–444.

Porterfield, J. T. S., *Investment Decisions and Capital Costs*. Englewood Cliffs, N. J.: Prentice-Hall, 1963.

Robichek, A. A., and J. G. McDonald, "The Cost of Capital Concept: Potential Use and Misuse," *Financial Executive*, 33 (June 1965).

Robichek, A. A., and S. C. Myers, *Optimal Financial Decisions*. Englewood Cliffs, N. J.: Prentice-Hall, 1965.

Rubinstein, M. E., "A Mean-Variance Synthesis of Corporate Financial Theory," *Journal of Finance*, 28 (Mar. 1973), pp. 167–181.

Schwartz, E., and J. R. Aronson, "Some Surrogate Evidence in Support of the Concept of Optimal Financial Structure," *Journal of Finance*, 22 (Mar. 1967), pp. 10–18.

Sharpe, W. F., *Portfolio Analysis and Capital Markets*. New York: McGraw-Hill, 1970.

Solomon, E., *The Theory of Financial Management*. New York: Columbia University Press, 1963.

Stiglitz, J. E., "A Re-examination of the Modigliani–Miller Theorem," *American Economic Review*, 59 (Dec. 1969), pp. 784–793.

Vickers, D., "The Cost of Capital and the Structure of the Firm," *Journal of Finance*, 25 (Mar. 1970), pp. 35–46.

Appendix 2

The Capital Asset Pricing Model and the Cost of Capital

The role of the weighted marginal cost of capital in the capital budgeting process has been modified with the recent introduction of the capital asset pricing model (CAPM).[1] To understand this model, we must begin with the concept of diversification.

If the risks of one project can be offset by the risks of another—as when the two risks are negatively correlated—the firm's cost of capital may be reduced. Successful diversification involves a mating of projects whose risks are negatively correlated.

Risk can be separated into two parts, the unsystematic risk (which can be eliminated by diversification involving negative correlation of projects) and the systematic risk (which cannot be so removed).[2] To calculate its systematic risk we must determine

1. The coefficient of correlation between the investment j and a general market index m, such as the Dow Jones Average, r_{jm}
2. The standard deviation of the returns of the proposed investment, σ_j
3. The standard deviation of the returns of the market index, σ_m

Systematic risk is the ratio of the covariance of the investment and market returns to the variance of the market returns and is called beta, β_{jm}. Statistically, beta is expressed as

$$r_{jm}\sigma_j\sigma_m/\sigma_m^2$$

If investors must be rewarded for risks they cannot diversify, then the expected rate of return of an investment R_j is equal to the risk-free rate R_f plus the excess of the expected return of the market index R_m above the risk-free rate times β_{jm}, or

$$R_j = R_f + (R_m - R_f)\beta_{jm}$$

In other words, investors can get some returns without assuming risk. This is R_f. They demand an added premium for investing in risky ventures such as the stockmarket. This is $R_m - R_f$. The magnitude of this premium depends on how risky the investment appears relative to the market in general. This is measured by β_{jm}. When this equation is generalized to all assets, it is referred to as the CAPM.

The relationship of the CAPM to the weighted marginal cost of capital is best seen through an illustration.

[1] Rubinstein, M. E., "A Mean-Variance Synthesis of Corporate Financial Theory," *Journal of Finance*, 28 (Mar. 1973), pp. 167–181.
[2] Sharpe, W. F., *Portfolio Analysis and Capital Markets*. New York: McGraw-Hill, 1970) and his earlier articles such as "Capital Asset Prices: A Theory of Market Equilibrium under Conditions of Risk," *Journal of Finance*, 19 (Sept. 1964), pp. 425–427. In turn, work in this area stems from H. Markowitz, *Portfolio Selection: Efficient Diversification of Investments*. New York: Wiley, 1959.

If the risk-free rate is 4 percent and the average market return over a long period of time is accepted as an estimate of the expected future market return and this is 9 percent, and if β_{jm} is 2, then the expected return of project j after diversifying away nonsystematic risks is

$$R_j = 0.04 + (0.09 - 0.04)2$$
$$= 14 \text{ percent}$$

Referring now to Figure 19.5, if the weighted marginal cost of capital is 14 percent, this is represented by the horizontal dotted line. The market line begins at 4 percent, the risk-free rate, and increases with the risk. Suppose that the market line is such that for a β of 2, the market requires an expected return of 14 percent. Then our project is just at the cut-off rate which is where the market line intersects the weighted marginal cost of capital.

Figure 19.5. Market line for risk compared to weighted marginal cost of capital.

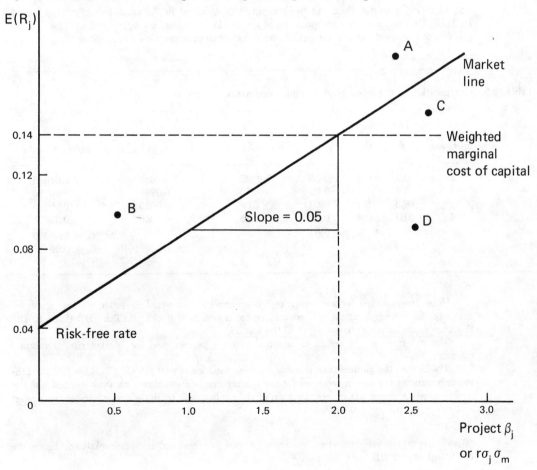

Now if we examine project A in Figure 19.5 we find it satisfies both the market line test and the weighted marginal cost of capital test. Project C satisfies the weighted marginal cost of capital test but fails the market line test, the rate of return is not adequate for the risk. Accepting this project would raise the cost of capital. Project B would be accepted even though it fails the weighted marginal cost of capital test because its low risk will bring the cost of capital down since its return is above what the market requires for such a risk. Project D fails both tests.

In Figure 19.5 notice that the slope of the market line is 0.05. For an increase in β_j from 0 to 2, there is an increase in expected return from 4 percent to 14 percent. This slope is the risk premium of 5 percent appearing in the expected return equation as the excess return of the expected market rate R_m over the risk-free rate R_f, or 9 percent less 4 percent.

The capital asset pricing model examines not only whether the project's return meets the weighted marginal cost of capital, but it also examines the effect of the risk of the project on the weighted marginal cost of capital.

An Example Applying the Capital Asset Pricing Model

The following example illustrates the computations involved in the capital asset pricing model. In Table 19.3 we show the computation of the market variance, assuming probabilities for four possible outcomes of the market, which might range from depression to prosperity.

Table 19.3. Computation of Expected Market Return and Market Variance

Situation	(1) p	(2) R_m	(3) pR_m	(4) $R_m - E(R_m)$	(5) $[R_m - E(R_m)]^2$	(6) $p[R_m - E(R_m)]^2$
1	0.2	−0.4	−0.08	−0.45	0.2025	0.04045
2	0.2	−0.1	−0.02	−0.15	0.0225	0.00450
3	0.3	0.1	0.03	0.05	0.0025	0.00075
4	0.3	0.4	0.12	0.35	0.1225	0.03675
		$E(R_m) = \overline{0.05}$				$var\ R_m = \overline{0.08245}$
						$\sigma R_m \cong 0.29$

Using the expected market return of 5 percent with a standard deviation of 29 percent, we compute the expected return and covariance for a proposed project in Table 19.4[3] faced with the same probabilities as to outcomes of the market.

The risk-free rate of return is assumed to be 4 percent and the market risk premium 5 percent.

The beta of this project then is covariance jm/variance m or $0.11955/0.08245 = 1.45$, and the measurement of the return required by the market line is $R_f + R_m B_{jm}$ or $0.04 + 0.05(1.45) = 11.25$ percent. Since the expected return of the project is 0.07, the excess return of the project is $(0.07 - 0.1125) = -0.0425$.

---

[3] This computation of covariance assumes random variates and is not normalized, hence the coefficient of correlation r is not used.

Table 19.4. Computation of Expected Return and Covariance of a Proposed Project

	(1)	(2)	(3)	(4)	(5)	(6)	(7)
						$[R_j - E(R_j)] \times$	
Situation	p	R_j	pR_j	$R_j - E(R_j)$	$R_m - E(R_m)$	$[R_m - E(R_m)]$	$p(6)$
1	0.2	−0.5	−0.10	−0.57	−0.45	0.2565	0.0513
2	0.2	−0.2	−0.04	−0.27	−0.15	0.0405	0.0081
3	0.3	0.1	0.03	0.03	0.05	0.0015	0.0045
4	0.3	0.6	0.18	0.53	0.35	0.1855	0.05565
		$E(R_j) = \overline{0.07}$				$cov\ (R_j, R_m) = \overline{0.11955}$	

The margin of the project's return over the risk-free rate, 7 percent − 4 percent, is not sufficient to meet the relatively high beta of 1.45. The market demands an extra 7.25 percent for this risk (5 percent × 1.45) but the project achieves only 3 percent toward this risk.

20

DIVIDEND POLICY

In the previous chapter we noted that both the price of common stock and the market value of the firm are influenced by the division of earnings between retention and payout. With the goal of financial management being maximization of the value of the firm, it is apparent why the dividend decision is a major element in corporate financial policy.

THE MARGINAL PRINCIPLE OF EARNINGS RETENTION

The marginal principle of earnings retention states that such earnings should be retained as can be invested at a higher rate of return, considering the risks, than that which the stockholders could obtain if the funds were paid out. Ideally, in following this principle, the capital budget should mesh with the decision on earnings retained. Dividends may mean the sale of stock or borrowing at a later date to cover what previously was paid out in dividends. Viewed in this light, is it proper that any dividends at all be paid by a firm that requires external financing? The answer to this question may be found in the marginal principle illustrated by the following example. The situation is presented first in static terms and then its application is traced over a period of years.

During the current year Swing Company has earnings of $2,500,000 which represent a 10 percent earning on assets, and has three projects promising a 20, 15, and 8 percent rate of return, respectively. Stockholders can invest their funds in other firms at the same degree of risk and earn a 10 percent return. The figures appear in Table 20.1. The marginal guide to dividend policy tells us that if we retain $1 million and invest in project A, our earnings will be lifted by $200,000 annually; a marginal rate of 20 percent will be earned. Considering the risk of the project, the stockholders, if given the funds, could not do as well investing outside the firm. With project B, retaining $500,000 more, the firm will improve its earnings by $75,000 annually, earning a marginal rate of 15 percent on the retained earnings. Again the shareholders could not do as well outside the firm. Retention of the last $1 million to finance project C produces a different picture. Project C promises only an 8 percent return, lifting earnings by $80,000 annually. Since stockholders have alternative investment opportunities of equal risk promising 10 percent, management should not retain the last $1 million to undertake project C. In the interests of shareholder

Table 20.1. Swing Company Use of Earnings of $2,500,000 for Capital Budgeting Projects, Dividend Payment, and Stockholder Returns

Project	Cost of Project	Marginal Earnings Increase from Projects	Rate of Return on Project	Dividends Paid	Cumulative Retained Earnings for Projects
A	$1,000,000	$200,000	20%	$1,500,000	$1,000,000
B	500,000	75,000	15	1,000,000	1,500,000
C	1,000,000	80,000	8	0	2,500,000

wealth, maximization of the value of the firm, and optimum allocation of economic resources, management should retain $1,500,000 of the earnings of $2,500,000 (a payout ratio of 40 percent). Retention of the last $1 million would cause a drop in the market price of the firm's stock, since the firm is currently earning 10 percent on assets. Thus total stockholder earnings would be reduced—compared to paying out $1 million on which stockholders could earn 10 percent directly. Through application of the marginal principle the firm will optimize the utilization of earnings, retaining the portion that it can reinvest more profitably than the shareholders and paying out the remainder.

The marginal principle is simply illustrated; its application is difficult. The rate of return to be expected from the various capital budgeting projects must be calculated and estimates made of the rate of return on similar risks open to shareholders generally. These alternative projects open to shareholders are the *opportunity cost* of retained earnings.

The Marginal Principle, Stockholders' Income Taxes, and Future Financing Requirements

Strict adherence to the marginal principle makes retained earnings the active variable and dividend payout the residual. This fact can be illustrated by a continuation of our example. Assume next year Swing Company has earnings of $3 million and two capital budgeting projects, one costing $2 million and the other $1 million. The anticipated returns are 25 to 20 percent, respectively. Alternative stockholder investment opportunities promise 10 percent. Following the marginal principle, no dividends would be paid this year. The third year the firm earns $3,500,000 and has only one attractive project, costing $1,500,000 and promising a return of 20 percent. The firm this year retains $1,500,000 and pays out $2 million.

With retention as the active variable, the result is an uneven dividend payout. But stability of dividends has value in the market. Also, when considering the maximization of the market price of the stock, the tradeoff between a dollar of retained earnings and a dollar of dividends may not be equal. A dollar of dividends may be valued more highly by the investor than a dollar of retained earnings.

On the other hand, we have the income tax. The investor receiving a dollar of dividends does not keep the entire amount. If he is in the 40 percent marginal tax bracket, he keeps only 60 cents of each dollar. At the margin and *for him* a 6 percent return on an equivalent investment by the corporation matches a 10 percent return earned outside the corporation. But to view the situation only through the eyes of *existing* shareholders is self-defeating. While the present stockholder in our case might prefer that the firm accept a 7 percent return project rather than pay a dividend of which he can keep only 60 percent, it is clear that by admitting 7 percent projects, the firm will no longer appear in the market place as a 10 percent firm to *prospective* stockholders and the price of the firm's stock will fall.

Even with retained earnings as the active variable, retention should not be related solely to current capital budgeting requirements but also to those of the future. The firm might not have immediate need for some of the funds retained but may see a major project on the horizon that cannot be financed from the earnings retained for a single year. The firm could accumulate the required funds over a period of years, investing them in the interval in short-term securities of risk equal to that of the forthcoming investment. The alternative would be to pay out the funds not currently needed and go to the market to raise the funds when the time comes. If the funds were to be raised through the sale of bonds, the prior dividend policy would probably have little effect on the cost of debt capital, so long as some dividends were paid, because the rule of some states requires that dividends be paid annually on the common stock if the bonds are to qualify for a legal list. Certain financial institutions in these states must select their bond investments from the legal list. Thus a bond that can qualify for the list sells at a lower yield than one that does not. But if the funds for expansion are to be raised through a stock issue, a more generous dividend policy may raise the market price of the stock, thus requiring that fewer shares of stock be sold to obtain a given amount of money.

DIVIDEND STABILITY AND PAYOUT POLICY

Total corporate dividends exhibit greater stability than earnings. Figure 20.1 and Table 20.2 show fluctuations in earnings, dividends, and retained earnings since 1929. Earnings were substantially less than dividends during the Great Depression. During this period dividends were paid out of

Table 20.2. Schedule of Earnings, Dividends and Payout Ratio for Corporations, 1930–1974
(in billions of dollars)

Period	Earnings	Dividends	Payout Ratio
1930–34	($1.3)	$21.3	—
1935–39	21.3	19.0	89.2%
1940–44	50.7	21.7	42.8
1945–49	85.9	30.7	35.7
1950–54	107.1	44.2	41.3
1955–59	131.0	57.7	44.0
1960–64	156.9	76.2	48.0
1965–69	239.7	110.0	45.9
1970–74	301.2	139.3	46.2

Source: Economic Report of the President, 1975. Washington, D.C.: Government Printing Office, Table C–74, p. 335.

past accumulated earnings (surplus). Then earnings slowly began to rise and by the latter half of the 1930s more nearly approximated dividends. With the advent of World War II earnings rose sharply and dividends continued their slow but steady rise.

These statistics, for all private corporations, cover a wide range; some firms pay no dividends at all, and never have. Others pay out a high percentage of earnings in dividends. Some firms continue to pay dividends in

Figure 20.1. Corporate earnings after tax and dividends of all corporations 1929–1974.

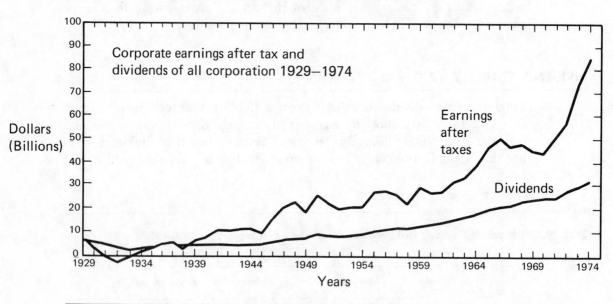

the face of declining earnings while others cut or suspend dividends immediately when earnings dip. Generally the electric utilities and telephone companies because of their steady and slowly rising earnings and access to external sources of funds pay a high and steadily increasing dividend. But rapid-growth utilities do not pay out a large percentage of earnings. The cyclical industries such as machine tools tend to pay out a high percentage of current earnings, but when earnings dip, dividends are quickly reduced. Often firms in the same industry will have widely different dividend policies, thus making generalizations about most industries difficult.

DIVIDEND POLICY IN PRACTICE

Dividend Disbursement Procedure

Customarily dividends are paid quarterly by U.S. firms. The dividend item will appear at specific intervals on the agenda of the directors' meetings, and the directors decide both the form—cash or stock—and the amount of the dividend as well as the record date and the date of payment. Those whose names appear on the stockholder list on the record date receive the dividend. The checks may be mailed on the date the dividend is payable or several days earlier so as to arrive on the payment date.

Stock is traded ex-dividend starting with the fourth business day before the record date. The purchase of the stock on or after the ex-dividend date will not carry with it the right to the dividend declared at the last directors' meeting; hence the name ex-dividend. Other things being equal, the stock should drop in price on the ex-dividend date by the amount of the dividend. But other things do not remain the same. The stock may fall more or less than the amount of the dividend or even rise in price. Everything depends on the supply and demand for the stock on the ex-dividend day, as it does on any trading day.

Dividend Policy of Business Firms

One study of dividend policy found that in the majority of firms the current dividend decision is closely related to past dividend decisions.[1] The existing payments tend to be continued until the reasons for change are strong. Management is reluctant to give the impression that it acts hastily, an impression that might arise if dividends were adjusted frequently, particularly in our economy where stability and gradual increases are *the* goal.

Common stock carries no specified dividend rate, but the strong predilection of corporate managers to favor the payment of a regular dividend generates an expectation among stockholders that the next dividend will approximate the last one. Since in practice directors start with the past dividend and continue it unless there are compelling reasons for change, this expectation among stockholders is justified. The major reason for dividend change is a shift in earnings, actual or anticipated. A drop in earnings will cause directors reluctantly to lower the dividend—usually only after the evidence of reduced earning power is overwhelming. The dividend is re-

---

[1] Lintner, J., "Distribution of Incomes of Corporations among Dividends, Retained Earnings, and Taxes," *American Economic Review*, 46 (May 1956), pp. 97–113.

duced to the level the directors believe can be maintained for a reasonable period of time.

A rise in earnings will cause directors to examine its strength and origin, and when convinced that the increased earning power will be maintained for a reasonable period, directors will raise the dividend. This is particularly true of growth companies that raise their dividend slowly in response to rising earnings. A slowing in the rate of earnings growth of these firms is usually detectable only over a longer period of time. The price–earnings ratio then would decline only slowly. A cut in a dividend previously raised to an unmaintainable level by a growth firm would be a clear signal for all to see. The price–earnings ratio and the market price of the stock would plummet. Understandably, directors cautiously adjust dividends upward.

Examination of Figure 20.1, showing corporate earnings after taxes and dividends from 1929 to the present, clearly confirms the general policy of dividend stability and the gradual adjustment to changes in earnings. Also noticeable is a steady relation between earnings and dividends. It is apparent that directors believe there is an appropriate payout ratio to be maintained over time. The most popular payout ratio runs from 40 to 60 percent.

The actual payout ratio varies from year to year depending on the current level of earnings and the dividend decisions by the corporate board of directors. With a steady rise in earnings and maintenance of the same dividend the payout ratio falls. For example, a firm is earning \$1.20 per share and paying dividends of 60 cents. If earnings slowly rise in the following years to \$1.80 per share, and dividends remain at 60 cents, the payout ratio falls from 50 percent to $33\frac{1}{3}$ percent. Directors, now convinced of the increased earning power of the firm, may belatedly increase the dividend to 90 cents. This cautious attitude results in the observable pattern of step-by-step dividend increases.

Extra Dividends

Directors, not fully convinced of the increased earning power of the firm, but feeling a responsibility to pay out some of the increased earnings, may proceed to an intermediate stage. They may declare the regular dividend of 15 cents per quarter and in the last quarter of the year declare an extra dividend of 20 cents for a total payment of 80 cents per share. The implication is that the extra dividend is added to the regular dividend in response to the increase in earnings for the current year, strictly a one-shot deal, with no suggestion that the extra will be paid again next year. Because of the implication, the market price of the stock will not increase, which in turn leads to the feeling that the money paid out has been "wasted." Hence the extra dividend is seldom used.

Dividend Policy and the Marginal Principle

Initially the corporate practice of paying regular dividends does not appear to be consistent with the marginal principle. A policy of dividend stability implies that the directors determine an appropriate level of dividends, pay out that amount each year, and retain the remainder. But the marginal principle specifies that retained earnings be the active variable and dividends the residual. The reconciling fact is that a stable dividend policy enhances the price of the stock and reduces the cost of capital. Thus both the dividend policy and the marginal principle of earnings retention are active variables.

THE LEGAL BASIS OF DIVIDENDS

When a corporation makes a dividend payment, it is distributing something it owns to its stockholders. All stockholders of a particular class must be treated equally. Cash is most frequently distributed as a dividend. Sometimes stock in another company is distributed. On occasion inventory of the firm may be distributed.[2] Cash, stock of another company, and inventory are known as *asset dividends*. The payment of these dividends has the effect of reducing the book value of the firm. Net worth, or more specifically, surplus, is reduced. It is popular to talk of a dividend being paid out of surplus, but in fact the debit is to surplus to record the portion of the stockholder's equity that has been withdrawn by the payment of the dividend. The credit is to cash, inventory, or the share of another company being held as an asset.

Directors Declare Dividends

The directors of a corporation have the discretionary power to declare dividends. The preferred or common stock contract cannot carry a provision obligating the firm to a fixed payment or face bankruptcy in the event of default. Owners assume fixed obligations to pay principal and interest on bonds or debt; they cannot meaningfully grant such obligations to themselves. Directors must vote to declare preferred and common stock divi-

---

[2] A tobacco company may distribute packages of cigarettes or a cosmetic company bottles of its newly developed after-shave lotion.

dends. But once declared, the dividend becomes a current liability. Without action by the directors no dividend can be paid. And as long as they act in good faith, no legal means exist to force a dividend where none has been declared or to increase a dividend that the shareholders consider too small.

The nonpayment of dividends, or a decision to keep dividends low when the firm has fair but not rapidly rising earnings, may have unpleasant consequences for management. Stockholders dissatisfied with the entire corporate policy will have a strong talking point and increased chances for winning a proxy fight. Directors have been known to reinstitute dividends or to increase dividends and declare stock dividends or stock splits when threatened with a takeover.

No legal rules require dividend declaration, but legal rules do exist specifying the conditions under which dividends must *not* be paid. The corporate laws of the various states differ in detail, but the general rule is clear. Dividends may be paid only from retained earnings and unimpaired capital surplus. The rationale of this rule lies in protecting creditors and encouraging people with funds to extend credit. The rule protects creditors against withdrawal from the firm of the equity cushion they had originally relied upon when extending credit.

There Must Be a Surplus

Dividends can legally be declared as long as a surplus exists. This means that dividends can be paid out of past as well as current earnings. During the early 1930s dividend payments exceeded current earnings by a wide margin. The dividends were paid against prior accumulated surplus.

Asset dividend distributions that impair capital are illegal and most state statutes provide that the approving directors be personally liable to the corporation for the amount of the illegal dividend, and in some states the firm can recover the amount from the shareholders. If the directors acted in good faith and relied on the books of the firm, they may be absolved from liability.

Contractually Assumed Dividend Restrictions

Important restrictions on the payment of dividends may be accepted by a firm when obtaining external capital either by loan agreements or by preferred stock contracts. Such restrictions may require the firm to maintain a certain current asset position or restrict surplus available for dividends to the amount existing at the time the agreement is made. The payment of a cash dividend in violation of a restriction would be an act of default in the case of a loan and the entire principal would become due and payable immediately through the inclusion of the acceleration clause in the contract.

ECONOMIC BASIS OF DIVIDEND POLICY

Earnings Availability

The level of economic activity fluctuates from year to year and causes a certain instability in the earnings stream of every firm. This instability leads directors to establish a modest dividend policy that can be maintained over a reasonable period of time, considering both the earning power of the firm and the availability of cash resources.

Retained earnings are usually invested in fixed assets and required working capital. Having become an integral part of the income-producing capital of the firm, these accumulated earnings are responsible for providing a portion of the current earnings. Directors would hesitate to reduce the firm's future earnings through liquidating a portion of its "earning" assets to pay dividends. Consequently, dividends normally represent some portion of the current earnings of the firm.

Dividends in any one year may exceed current earnings. This practice could not be continued very long without diminishing the firm's earning power and its capacity to pay dividends. Therefore, directors look ahead, anticipating future earnings, the need for capital, and the availability of funds for distribution of dividends.

Cash Availability

Dividends are normally paid with cash. A firm may be legally entitled to pay a dividend and yet be unable to do so because of a deficient cash position. It is currently profitable operations that generate the cash enabling the firm to continue the payment of dividends.

It is desirable to link dividend policy to the capital budget in order to promote the long-run profitability of the firm and to contribute to the optimum allocation of economic resources in the nation. Dividend policy must also be tied to the cash budget to provide for that dividend cash outflow. A given dollar amount of earnings generated in a period does not necessarily result in an equivalent sum of cash added to the bank balance. The dynamic firm experiencing a tight liquidity position will tend to reinvest each dollar of revenue—the profit as well as the cost portion—in the working capital stream. Without fitting the dividend payments into the cash budget the firm will continually be strained to meet this outflow, and because of their noncontractual nature, common stock dividends will be meager. Corporate management will see dividends as a diversion of funds from more productive uses and explain the low dividend on the basis of the great need of the firm for funds. Better planning of cash flows, including dividends, and the provision for a margin of liquidity would enable the firm to maintain an adequate dividend policy over time.

Reinvestment Opportunities in a Fluctuating Economy

A growing firm has many alternative uses for funds. Its major problem is to uncover sources of funds at a reasonable cost, not how to put them to work. Dividends in such firms compete with other uses of funds, and the directors must decide between making cash payments to the shareholders and employing the funds to increase the earning power of the firm.

Firms not in a long-term expansion phase will tend to find their investment opportunities fluctuate with the level of economic activity. During a recession fewer profitable opportunities for investment exist. Corporate managers applying the marginal principle to the projects generated by the capital budgeting system will find that for all projects the scale of rates of return has moved downward. But during periods of reduced economic activity not only are the firm's investment opportunities reduced, but the stockholders' alternative investment opportunities are reduced also. The reason for the higher dividend payout ratios during these periods is the better liquidity position of the firms. Reduced economic activity lowers working capital needs—cash, receivables, and inventory—and fixed assets are not replaced as rapidly as depreciation is charged. Therefore the "free" cash balance rises and dividends can remain at a high level while earnings fall. A fall in earnings to the dividend level, however, will force directors to cut the dividend.

A period of prosperity brings with it an increase in investment opportunities. Directors, anticipating the improved profitability of capital investments, will hold dividends down, reinvesting all available working capital and current earnings as they are generated. Increase in dividends will lag behind the rising earnings. The dividend is not reduced; it is just not increased as fast as earnings are rising. What is often forgotten in the rush to reinvest is that shareholders' alternative investment opportunities have also improved.

DIVIDEND POLICY AND MANAGEMENT CONSIDERATIONS

Focusing on a dividend policy rather than on a single dividend payment, we have seen that the market prefers a stable to a fluctuating dividend, that some firms can be expected to pay out a high percentage of earnings in dividends and others a low percentage, and finally, that changes in the payment influence the market price of the stock. Shareholders attach informational value to dividends, and when dividends are raised this is taken as evidence of the increased earning power of the firm. Accordingly, up to some point each dollar of dividends may be valued more highly than each dollar of retained earnings.

New Stock Issue

Management, knowing that the market will respond to changes in dividend policy, is in a position to influence the market price of the firm's stock. If the stock is selling too low and management is contemplating a stock issue in the near future, raising the dividend will call favorable attention to the stock and most likely will result in an increase in the market price, particularly if the dividend increase is unexpected. If the new dividend rate is not maintainable, the action takes on the appearance of manipulation.

Maintaining Control

In pursuing the goal of maximizing the market price of the firm's stock, dividend policy is a key variable, but sometimes management employs dividend policy as an effective instrument to maintain its position of command and control. Where an outside group is seeking to gain control of the firm, management has been known to declare stock splits and stock dividends or to increase or reinstate dividends in an effort to strengthen stockholder loyalty and raise the market price, making it more expensive for outsiders to acquire control. On the other hand, if management is securely in control, either through large holdings or through wide stock distribution and a favorable corporate image, it may seek to avoid all risk to its tenancy in office and shun debt financing, preferring retained earnings, even though the firm might advantageously substitute debt financing for retained earnings and raise the market price of its stock.

Stock Options

Sometimes the factor guiding management is gaining large stock options and protecting large stock holdings. Management would then be particularly unhappy to see the market price fall and would be inclined to maintain dividends at the same level long after it has become evident that the earning power of the firm has declined. In the short run higher prices may be maintained in this way, but where the dividend outflow significantly reduces the future expected rate of earnings, this will at some point be recognized in the market, and the price–earnings ratio will decline, reflecting the slower projected growth rate.

To Whom Is Dividend Policy Geared?

The difficulty of ascertaining the optimum split between retention and dividends is the result of diverse investment goals and alternative investment opportunities of the current and potential shareholders. Since various groups of stockholders have different objectives and desires, we might let investors gravitate to that firm that combines the mix of growth and dividends they desire.

Whether maximization of market value of the firm will result from a dividend policy designed to appeal to a segment of investors or from one geared to investors in general will depend upon dividend policies of other firms. Thus if at a given time there is a shortage of firms following a policy currently preferred by a substantial segment of investors (say, a particular mix of growth and cash dividends), the market will bid up the price of such stocks. This might, for example, happen as the result of personal income tax rate changes. A sharp increase in such rates increases the demand for high-growth no-dividend stocks.

This is similar to the question of whether a firm should specialize or diversify. No simple conclusion is possible. If many firms are specializing, it may pay to diversify. On the other hand, as the recent history of the market shows, the first firms to become conglomerates skimmed the cream while latecomers in the movement gained nothing and, indeed, lost.

Optimum economic development of society will be served by diverse dividend policies as long as investors are permitted to have differences in objectives.

Summary

The basic determinant of the market price of a company's stock, given the capital structure and degree of risk, is earning power, but the price of stock can be influenced by the division of the earnings between retention and payout. The marginal principle holds that a firm retain all the earnings that it can reinvest at a rate in excess of the investment opportunities available to its stockholders, current and prospective. The dividend policies of many firms over time can be at least roughly reconciled with this principle. During periods of economic expansion when attractive investment opportunities abound, earnings usually climb rapidly, but dividend increases are allowed to lag. The result is a declining payout ratio. When the economy levels off or begins to dip, earnings may decrease, but the dividend tends to be maintained and as a result the payout ratio rises.

Optimal dividend policy will attempt to maximize the market value of the firm's shares, but this is likely to conflict with the marginal principle because of practical aspects. Firms in a declining industry represent the greatest departure from the marginal principle of retention and payout. Many factors motivate management: industry position, prestige, and continuation in a top management position. Consequently, management of such firms is tempted to reinvest as much as possible in an effort to turn the company around. Through branching out in new fields a company can be rejuvenated. The risk is great, however, and losses by firms venturing into new areas are frequent and large. The better course of action often would be paying out a substantial portion of earnings in dividends, repurchasing shares, or gradually liquidating the firm, depending upon the circumstances. Such a course of action would be beneficial to both the stockholders and the economy.

Study Questions

1. How does the dividend policy of a firm influence the allocation of resources within the nation? What arguments can you cite to support or reject a proposal that firms be compelled to pay out all of their earnings in dividends?

2. Since the main determinant of the market price of a firm's stock is earning power, given the degree of risk, how is it possible for dividend policy to influence market price? Is setting the dividend policy to influence the market price of the stock really manipulation? How would you distinguish between constructive influence and manipulation?

3. Why do dividends exhibit a more stable pattern than earnings? What arguments can you give to support management's practice of maintaining the same dividend in the face of fluctuating earnings? Is it logical for stockholders to prefer stable to fluctuating dividends? Why or why not?

4. "A firm that pays dividends and subsequently raises equity capital through a 'rights offering' is taking back with one hand what it distributed with the other. In view of the tax bite and brokerage commissions, a firm requiring common stock financing should never pay a dividend." Discuss.

5. The management of a particular firm may not wish to set the dividend policy in

such a manner as to maximize the market value of the company's shares. How can such action be explained? What other factors may be motivating management?

6. One approach to dividend policy suggests that management set the percentage distribution at its discretion and investors will gravitate to those firms that offer the desired combination of current dividends and growth. Discuss the advantages and disadvantages of this approach.

7. Growth companies generally are justified in retaining a larger proportion of earnings in dividends than are mature companies. Why? Though supporting arguments can be marshaled, the management of a declining company is reluctant to pay out all earnings in dividends. Why?

8. Dividend declarations are usually made shortly before the date the dividend is to be paid. Since firms sometimes make earnings projections, would anything be wrong with declaring a dividend one year in advance?

9. Firms in some countries pay only one dividend annually. The practice in the United States is to pay dividends quarterly. Discuss the advantages and disadvantages of each procedure.

10. What legal restrictions exist regarding the payment of asset dividends? What contractual restrictions may a firm assume on the payment of dividends? What purpose do these restrictions serve? Are they not an infringement on management freedom? If so, how are they justified?

11. Why is it not possible for common stock to carry a meaningful fixed dividend clause? If the stock contract carried such a clause, would it still be a common stock, even if the certificate stated common stock? Why or why not?

12. Why does management raise the dividend only slowly in response to rising earnings? Why is management usually even more reluctant to cut dividends than to increase them? Is this a rational attitude? Why or why not?

Problems

1. The Henry Company, a closely held firm, has long geared its dividend policy to maximizing the market value of the firm. Accordingly, each year at dividend

Table 20.3. Henry Company

Dividends	Retain	Earnings on Retention before Taxes
—	$1,000,000	$250,000
$ 100,000	900,000	240,000
300,000	700,000	208,000
600,000	400,000	130,000
900,000	100,000	40,000
1,000,000	—	—

time the capital budget is reviewed in conjunction with the earnings for the period and the alternative investment opportunities of the shareholders. In the current year the firm reports earnings of $1 million. It is estimated that the firm can earn the indicated amounts on the retained earnings shown in Table 20.3 before taxes of 50 percent.

The stockholders have alternative investment opportunities that will yield them 10 percent.

    a. Calculate the amount that Henry should retain this year if it wishes to maximize the total earnings of the stockholders.

    b. How much should Henry pay out in dividends?

    c. What would be the payout ratio?

2. The following year Henry, which is in the glamorous medical electronics field, decides to "go public." Management holds all the present 400,000 shares and the firm sells 600,000 new shares of stock to the public at $60 per share. The estimated earnings for the year are $2 million.

    a. What is the price–earnings ratio on the estimated earnings basis at which the stock was sold?

    b. Henry announces its intention at the time of the stock issue of paying a dividend of 60 cents a share. The market rate of capitalization for this firm is 11 percent. Given the market price of $60 per share and the 60-cent dividend, what is the growth rate anticipated for this firm by the market?

    c. The capital budget is prepared for the coming period on the basis that the $2 million in earnings will actually be realized. It is estimated that thereafter the firm can earn the amounts on the retained earnings indicated in Table 20.4. The income tax rate is 50 percent.

Table 20.4. Henry Company Projection of Earnings on Retained Earnings

Dividends	Retain	Earnings on Retention before Taxes
—	$2,000,000	$560,000
$ 600,000	1,400,000	500,000
1,000,000	1,000,000	420,000
1,800,000	200,000	100,000
2,000,000	—	—

Henry decides to reinvest all funds that will produce an earnings rate at least equal to the rate of capitalization. How much would the firm retain?

    d. What is the payout ratio?

    e. What is the rate earned by Henry on its retained earnings?

3. In a few years Henry is earning $4 million, or $4 a share, and paying a dividend of $1. During these intervening years the market rate of capitalization for this firm has risen to 21 percent and the anticipated growth rate is 20 percent.
   a. What is the market price? The price–earnings ratio?
   b. Management is distressed with the low price–earnings ratio at which the stock is selling and is of the opinion it should sell at about 40 times earnings. To what amount would the dividend have to be increased to achieve a price–earnings ratio of 40? Does this make sense? What else must occur if this is to be feasible?

Selected References

Brennan, Michael, "A Note on Dividend Irrelevance and the Gordon Valuation Model," *Journal of Finance*, 26 (Dec. 1971), pp. 1115–1121.

Brittain, J. A., *Corporate Dividend Policy*. Washington, D. C.: The Brookings Institution, 1966.

Ellis, C. D., "Repurchase Stock to Revitalize Equity," *Harvard Business Review*, 43 (July–Aug. 1965), pp. 119–128.

Elton, E. J., and M. J. Gruber, "Marginal Stockholder Tax Rates and the Clientele Effect," *Review of Economics and Statistics*, 52 (Feb. 1970), pp. 68–74.

Friend, I., and M. Puckett, "Dividends and Stock Prices," *American Economic Review*, 54 Sept. 1964), pp. 656–682.

Gordon, M. J., "Dividends, Earnings and Stock Prices," *Review of Economics and Statistics*, 41 (May 1959), pp. 99–105.

Harkavy , O., "The Relation between Retained Earnings and Common Stock Prices for Large Listed Corporations," *Journal of Finance*, 8 (Sept. 1953), pp. 283–297.

Higgins, R. C., "The Corporate Dividend–Saving Decision," *Journal of Financial and Quantitative Analysis*, 7 (Mar. 1972), pp. 1527–1541.

Lerner, E. M., and W. T. Carleton, "The Integration of Capital Budgeting and Stock Valuation," *American Economic Review*, 54 (Sept. 1964), pp. 683–702.

Lintner, J., "Distribution of Incomes of Corporations among Dividends, Retained Earnings, and Taxes," *American Economic Review, Proceedings*, 46 (May 1956), pp. 97–113.

——, "Dividends, Earnings, Leverage, Stock Prices and the Supply of Capital to Corporations," *Review of Economics and Statistics*, 44 (Aug. 1962), pp. 243–269.

——, "Optimal Dividends and Corporate Growth under Uncertainty," *Quarterly Journal of Economics*, 78 (Feb. 1964), pp. 49–95.

Miller, M. H., and F. Modigliani, "Dividend Policy, Growth and the Valuation of Shares," *Journal of Business*, 34 (Oct. 1961), pp. 411–433.

Pettit, R. R., "Dividend Announcements, Security Performance, and Capital Market Efficiency," *Journal of Finance*, 27 (Dec. 1972), pp. 993–1007.

Porterfield, J. T. S., "Dividends, Dilution and Delusion," *Harvard Business Review*, 37 (Nov.–Dec. 1959), pp. 56–61.

Pye, G., "Preferential Tax Treatment of Capital Gains, Optimal Dividend Policy, and Capital Budgeting," *Quarterly Journal of Economics*, 86 (May 1972), pp. 226–242.

Van Horne, J. C., and J. G. McDonald, "Dividend Policy and New Equity Financing," *Journal of Finance*, 26 (May 1971), pp. 507–519.

Walter, J. E., "Dividend Policies and Common Stock Prices," *Journal of Finance*, 11 (Mar. 1956), pp. 19–41.

——, *Dividend Policy and Enterprise Valuation.* Belmont, Calif.: Wadsworth Publishing Company, 1967.

——, "Dividend Policy: Its Influence on the Value of the Enterprise," *Journal of Finance,* 18 (May 1963), pp. 280–291.

Whittingdon, G., "The Profitability of Retained Earnings," *Review of Economics and Statistics,* 54 (May 1972), pp. 152–160.

part six

MANAGEMENT PROBLEMS IN LONG-TERM FINANCING

21

TIMING: REFINANCING, RECAPITALIZATION, AND SHARE REPURCHASE

Refinancing involves the sale of securities of the issuer to replace existing securities. *Recapitalization* involves changing the form or the amount of outstanding securities in a voluntary exchange, or with stockholders' consent, or unilaterally by action of the board of directors. *Reorganization*, on the other hand, involves changes in the capital structure that occur because of insolvency either in the equity sense (inability to meet debts as they mature, sometimes called "technical insolvency") or in the bankruptcy sense (excess of liabilities, excluding capital account, over assets).

There are three types of refinancing, (1) funding, that is, the conversion of short-term debt into long-term debt, (2) refunding, that is, the replacement of maturing long-term debt or the calling of long-term debt for the purpose of replacement, and (3) the calling of preferred stock for replacement with new preferred bearing a lower rate or with other features different from the outstanding preferred. There is also the possibility of replacing the debt or preferred stock with common stock.

THE IMPORTANCE OF TIMING

Although timing is always important in finance, it is particularly so in refinancing and recapitalization. One factor that affects timing is whether the industry in which the company is classified leads, coincides, or lags behind the general business cycle. Another factor is that, in general, the stock market leads the business cycle of the economy. Many analysts believe this lead is about 6 months, although there are exceptions. (The stock market drop in 1962 anticipated nothing—or what it anticipated was headed off.) A third factor involved in timing is that investors or speculators shift funds from the bond market to the stock market, and vice versa, making bond or stock financing easier at different times.

Also important are the monetary and fiscal policies pursued by government to head off extreme economic conditions, namely, lower rates and easier money in recessions and higher rates and tighter money during inflationary periods. The latter was illustrated in 1969–1970 when money rates of all types reached the highest points since 1929. At the same time the stock market had steadily declined so that in May, 1970, both the bond market and the stock market were in poor condition for any new issue, with respect to both costs and the availability of funds. Despite a temporary letup in 1971, the capital markets continue in poor condition into 1975.

Both stock and bond yields are indicators of the availability of funds. High bond yields are associated with a relative scarcity of debt money. With stock the same situation is likely to exist, namely, low price–earnings ratios on stocks are an indication of a relative scarcity of equity funds.

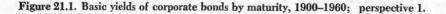

Figure 21.1. Basic yields of corporate bonds by maturity, 1900–1960; perspective 1.

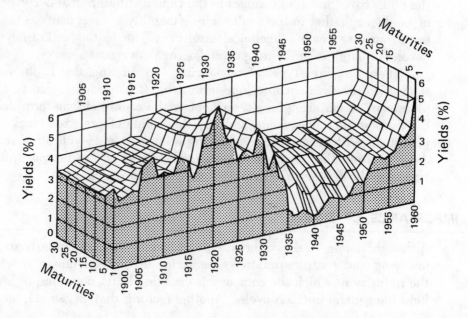

Figure 21.2. Basic yields of corporate bonds by maturity, 1900–1960; perspective 2.

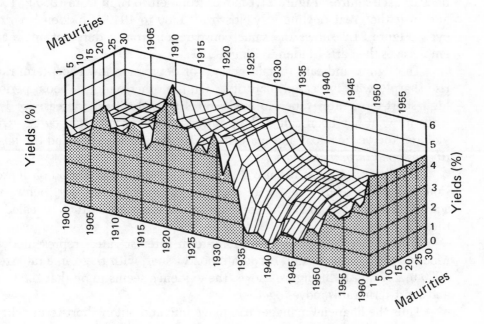

There is still another aspect of timing that we dealt with in discussing capital budgeting, that is, the internal rate of return. What the internal rate of return from a project will be depends in part on *when* the project is undertaken. If the project materializes just as demand for the product involved is strong, the early return flow of funds is higher; the rate of return is higher; and perhaps a somewhat higher cost of capital can be profitably tolerated, the differential increase in the rate of return being more than the differential in the cost of money. It is foolhardy for a financial manager to chase the lowest cost of money only to find that he has procured the funds at bargain rates when the time for their usefulness has passed.

One aspect of timing that has drawn considerable attention in recent years is the *term structure of interest rates*. By term structure is meant the increase or decrease in the interest rate for a given debtor at any point in time as the maturity of the debt is extended.

Figures 21.1 and 21.2 show two views of the same three-dimensional construction that relates three variables: the interest rate (yield), the maturity of the loan, and the time period from 1900 to 1960. The shortest maturity yields are nearest the viewer and the longest maturity yields are at the back of each figure. Figure 21.1 moves from left to right from 1900 to 1960, and in it the great decline in yields from 1930 to 1940 is hidden from the eye. Figure 21.2 shows the same construction from a different angle and emphasizes the parts hidden in Figure 21.1.

The figures indicate that in periods of depression low short-term rates rise sharply with increased maturity. On the other hand, in boom periods high short-term rates taper to lower rates as maturity is increased. This leads to what has been called the *positively sloped term yield curve* (with yield on the vertical axis and maturity on the horizontal axis) and the *negatively sloped term yield curve.*

The figures suggest the use of short-term money in a period of depression and of long-term money in a period of boom. However, before we accept that conclusion let us examine another dimension not revealed in these figures.

Figure 21.3 is a plotting of long-term interest rates, represented by Moody's yield on new AAA corporate bond issues, with the prime rate from 1960 to 1974. As this figure shows, the evidence seems to be that the long- and short-term rates move together.

Thus the financial manager can move into and out of short-term debt at appropriate times in order to optimize his situation with respect to long-term debt and equity. In fact, there is much to recommend a policy of using short-term debt this way even though short-term rates might fluctuate widely. We must remember that the high rate of interest on a short-term loan will be paid for a much shorter period of time than the saving would be on a properly timed long-term debt issue.

Finally, the financial manager is concerned with the cost of money to a particular company in a particular industry. But this cost will, in part, be determined by the overall situation with respect to capital. Consideration must be given not only to fiscal policy (taxes, budget surplus or deficit, and so on) but also to Federal Reserve bank policy as expressed in the discount rate, reserve requirements, open-market operations, and selective credits controls (such as margin requirements and real estate and consumer credit).

The financial manager must keep himself in a situation where he can change position. Flexibility, however, can be achieved only at a cost. When a financial manager achieves flexibility it means that the party on the other end of the transaction is foregoing something, and for doing this he wants a price.

The use of short-term funds is a focal point of financial strategy. Call provisions in preferred stocks, options for prepayment of long-term debt, and the purchase of firm lines of credit for short-term commitments at the cost of a standby fee are all devices for maintaining flexibility. But one can buy more flexibility than is justified by the price, since each of these devices costs something in the interest rate to be paid.

Figure 21.3. Yield on Moody's new AAA corporate bonds monthly and prime rate, 1951–1974.——— = prime rate, . . . Moody's AAA new bonds.

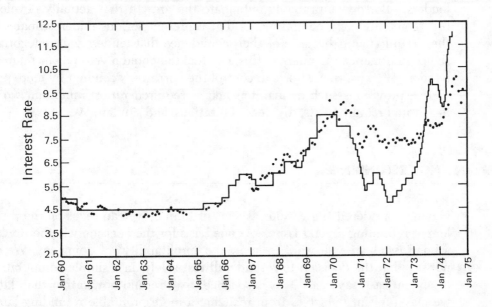

The dramatic growth of term loans is one evidence of the philosophy of using short-term funds. When a company appears to have maximized its use of short-term funds, there is an exposure to the risk that there is no margin of safety for more short-term funds. Term loans exist to meet this possibility by enabling the borrower to keep some unused short-term capacity without using long-term funds to do so.

Staggered maturities reaching into the future can present the ideal of flexibility. If it then becomes necessary to bridge temporary conditions prevailing in the longer term markets, short-term funds can be used even at high cost. But this relatively high cost will be more than compensated for by the ability of the firm to choose the advantageous point for long-term commitments.

It is a fact that currently many privately placed intermediate and long-term debt commitments are being "reset" every two years. In this resetting process the amount of the loan is frequently increased, repayment schedules are altered, interest rates revised, and protective provisions modified not to reassure the lender but to avoid strangling the borrower. This pattern suggests a failure to anticipate the growth rate of the economy or the company or both. Such resetting also indicates the greater bargaining strength of lenders. Borrowers probably anticipate the growth that actually develops but reluctantly sign commitments that represent serious underestimates of their requirements because of their confidence that lenders will renegotiate the commitments. Lenders in this way feel they hold a veto power that can be more effective than efforts to control the borrower's conduct by mere protective provisions such as maintenance of required ratios, minimum working capital requirements, dividend limitations, and similar covenants.

REFINANCING: REFUNDING

Having considered the various aspects of timing, we can focus on the problem of refunding a bond issue. As one basis for the decision whether to call a bond issue, we will want to know the "profitability" of doing so. We do not say that the decision to refund will rest solely on a simple computation of annual cash savings. This is so since if we refund now rather than later we may prevent ourselves from realizing a more profitable refunding later. There are considerable costs in each refunding that must be absorbed before we can speak of a gain from refunding. Thus refunding is essentially an investment decision and subject to analysis by capital budgeting techniques.

Let us suppose we have an issue of $1 million 6 percent 30-year bonds callable at 105 which have just ended their tenth year. There remain unamortized issuance expenses of $30,000 and an unamortized bond discount of $40,000 (the issue having been sold originally below par). The market interest rate may have fallen since the issue date or our credit may have improved so as to warrant a lower interest rate or both. We now can call and refund this issue with 4 percent bonds which are salable at a discount of 2 percent and with issue costs of $40,000. For simplicity we assume the new bonds run for the unexpired life of the old issue, namely; 20 years.[1]

In a refunding operation both issues are usually outstanding for 30 to 60 days to facilitate the transaction. There may be a delay in registration of the new issue. This duplicate interest can be reduced by investing the proceeds of the new issue in Treasury bills or other short-term securities until the funds are needed to pay off the bonds of the old issue.

Both cash and noncash aspects are involved in the proposal, as the analysis in Table 21.1 indicates.

We can summarize this analysis by stating that for an investment of $51,250 we can secure an annual cash gain of $10,750 (computed in Table

Table 21.1. Expenses for Tax Purposes and Cash Flow of Proposed Refunding

	Expenses for Tax Purposes	Cash Flow
Retirement of old bond principal		($1,000,000)
Call premium	$ 50,000	(50,000)
Issue cost of new bonds		(40,000)
Net overlapping interest (pre-tax)*	2,500	(2,500)
Unamortized bond discount, old bonds**	40,000	
Unamortized issue costs, old bonds**	30,000	
Totals	122,500	(1,092,500)
Tax savings	61,250	61,250
After-tax expense	61,250	
After-tax cash outlay		(1,031,250)
Receipts of new issue		980,000
Cash outlay to refund		($ 51,250)

* Overlapping interest is computed as follows, assuming a 30-day overlap:

Extra 30 days interest of old issue	$5,000
Offsetting 30-day Treasury bill income of 3 percent	2,500
Pre-tax cost of extra 30 days' interest	2,500

** These items can be handled in any of three ways acceptable to accountants: (1) expensed during the year of refunding, (2) amortized over the life of the new bonds, (3) amortized over what would have been the remaining life of the old bonds. We have used the first method.

[1] If the maturity date of the new issue extends beyond the maturity of the old issue, we have the case of a strict refunding combined with additional financing for the period beyond the original maturity date. This might be handled by determining the rate for a refunding due at the original maturity date and attributing the difference between that rate and the rate for the extended maturity as the cost of the additional financing.

21.2) or a return of roughly 20 percent annually for 20 years. Put in this way we see that the problem is one of capital budgeting. If our weighted marginal cost of capital is below 20 percent, the refunding decision would be viewed favorably. If our weighted marginal cost of capital is above 20 percent, we may still accept the project because of its low risk.

Table 21.2. Annual Cash Gains Resulting from Refunding

	Expenses for Tax Purposes	Cash Flow
Old bonds		
Interest on retired bonds	$60,000	$60,000
Amortization of bond discount	2,000	
Amortization of issue cost	1,500	
Total expense	63,500	
Less income taxes	31,750	31,750
After-tax expense	$31,750	
Annual cash outlay		$29,250
New bonds		
Interest on new bonds	$40,000	$40,000
Amortization of bond discount	1,000	
Amortization of issue cost	2,000	
Total expenses	43,000	
Less income taxes	21,500	21,500
After-tax expense	$21,500	
Annual cash outlay		$18,500
Annual gain in cash outlay $29,250 − $18,500 = $10,750		

Some analysts state that the refunding decision involves no risk because the annual gain of refunding is certain. Some even go so far as to argue that the savings of refunding should be discounted not at the weighted marginal cost of capital but at the *after-tax* rate of the new debt. This is wrong for several reasons. (1) The interest must be paid even if it is not earned, and in that case there is no income tax advantage to having debt, but rather, there would be "reverse" leverage. (2) Investment in refunding takes funds away from alternative investment opportunities which, after risk adjustments, may well earn more than the after-tax cost of new debt. (3) Future credit rating improvements of the firm or declines in the interest rate would offer new refunding chances and many of the current costs of refunding would be duplicated with a resulting loss.

Essentially the same approach is applicable to calling preferred stock for replacement by a new issue of preferred, except that preferred has no maturity such as a bond has.

RECAPITALIZATION

Changes in the Capital Stock Account to Reflect the New Status of the Business

Over a period of time the affairs of a firm may prosper or decline to the point where the old capitalization is no longer appropriate. In the case of declines, many companies in the Great Depression piled up sizable deficits over a number of years. The accrued deficits wiped out what earned surplus had existed. Dividends had ceased. The volume of business had been greatly reduced. To recognize the fact that the capital stock account no longer represented an existing investment value, the par value (or stated value in the case of no par shares) in many cases was reduced in an amount sufficient to eliminate the accrued deficit and perhaps by an additional amount to create a modest capital surplus.

In most states such a change requires the approval of two thirds of the stockholders in the case of par or no par stock and an amendment of the corporate charter in the case of par stock. But two additional questions are involved. There may be loans or bond indentures outstanding which forbid the reduction of capital stock. Consent of the lender or bondholders is then required. The more important point concerns the resumption of dividend payments. Some reductions in capital stock are motivated by the desire to wipe out deficits in earned surplus and thus to accelerate the day when dividend payments can be resumed. The law protects creditors in existence at the time of the reduction if resumption of dividend payments impairs the payment of their claims.

Stock Dividends and Stock Splits

The reverse situation exists when the business has grown and reached new plateaus, meanwhile developing a very large earned surplus through a policy of low dividend payout. To indicate that part of this swollen earned surplus is not a true surplus but is permanently committed to the business and to give creditors the assurance that this part will not be available for dividends, a large stock dividend may be declared by the board of directors. This would increase the number of shares without changing the par or stated value of a share and effect the transfer of surplus to the capital account. If the stock dividend is less than 25 percent, New York Stock Exchange rules require that an additional amount of earned surplus equal to the difference between the market value of the dividend shares and the par or stated value of those shares be transferred to paid-in or capital surplus. A stock dividend over 25 percent is treated as a stock split and only the amount of par or stated value is transferred to capital.

In a true stock split the par or stated value of existing shares is reduced in the amount necessary to cover the new shares issued in the split, so that the dollar amount of the new total of shares is the same as before but the unit amount of par or stated value per share is reduced. Because of the reduction in par or stated value per unit, a two-thirds stockholder consent is required.

In both the stock dividend and the stock split, the issuance of the new shares is not a taxable event to the stockholder on the theory that the ownership position of the stockholder is not changed. But a dividend in other than common stock on common stock is likely to be taxable as income to the stockholder because the ownership position of the stockholder has changed. Although a dividend of common stock on common stock is not a taxable event, the basis of the old share for income tax purposes is reduced by the percentage of the stock dividend with that percentage of the old basis assigned to the new shares.

There is a rare phenomenon called a reverse split or split-down in which the par of stated value of each share is increased and the number of shares is reduced to keep the total capital stock account the same.

In addition to the recognition of the larger commitment to capital stock that occurs in a stock dividend but not in a stock split, there is a second result in both cases, namely, the market price per share will be reduced in proportion to the increase in the number of shares. This is true if nothing else occurs at the same time such as a dividend increase.

The reduction in market value of a share pursuant to a stock dividend or stock split appears to have an additional purpose. Studies of the New York Stock Exchange have indicated that there is a tendency for the number of stockholders to increase after such a reduction in share price. This may be because more people can deal in round lots of 100 shares as a result of the lower price per share. The adjustment of the shares may also have advertising value. Attempts to measure whether there has been a permanent value to stock dividends have been fraught with difficulty and are inconclusive. The arguments advanced for the stock dividend are that (1) cash is conserved, (2) stock ownership is broadened, (3) underwriting fees are avoided, and (4) the total market value of all shares is increased. However, the costs of administering a stock dividend are ten times as large as for a cash dividend.

Recapitalization to Conserve Cash

One of the chief reasons advanced for stock dividends is the conservation of cash, yet there exists a more clear-cut way to achieve this objective. This can be done by creating two classes of common stock, one paying cash dividends and the other paying stock dividends. It may happen that this policy also serves the personal interests of stockholders. Thus the stockholders in high tax brackets seeking capital gains could buy the class that pays stock dividends. Those in lower brackets or seeking income could buy the class that pays cash dividends. Equity between the classes would be easily maintained by declaring the stock dividend that is indicated by dividing the cash dividend by the market price of the stock at the dividend declaration date. The market price of the two classes can be kept parallel by permitting the stockholders of the class that pays stock dividends to convert to the class that pays cash dividends.

Recapitalization Incident to a Sale of Securities

Often the first public offering of a corporation involves a secondary distribution by selling stockholders. Sometimes this is combined in the same offering with the procurement of additional funds for the corporation. Until the public offering such a corporation has been closely held and the matter of the value of a single share has not in itself been of concern. From the beginning days of the corporation when only a few thousand shares were outstanding, there has been no need for adjustment, particularly where growth has been achieved through the use of debt and retained earnings. Each share may now be worth thousands of dollars while it may have sold for only $100 at the time of incorporation.

At the time of going public the expected market value of the total equity of the corporation is determined by appropriate capitalization of earnings at a rate developed by comparison with similar companies. The desired price range of a single share of the offering is then determined. This price of a single share is then divided into the total value of the equity to determine the number of new shares, and the ratio of the total number of new shares to the total number of old shares determines the size of the split, which often is 400 for 1 or even more.

At the same time the selling stockholders may decide not to sell straight equity and particularly not to part with the proportionate voting rights. In this event the recapitalization might involve two classes of common stock, one with voting rights and the other without voting rights. The selling stockholders then exchange their stock for the two new classes of common, and the shares of the nonvoting class are offered to the public while the selling stockholders retain the shares of the voting class.

The technique of issuing two classes of common stock for a young company at the time of going public is frequently used to reduce cash drains. In this case the class of stock publicly offered carries cash dividends while that retained by the principal owners carries no dividends but is convertible into the class that pays cash dividends according to a timetable. Thus in the public offering of AMT Corporation in 1961 conversion of the no-dividend stock followed this schedule: 1962, none; 1963, 20 percent; 1964, 25 percent; 1965, 33⅓ percent; 1966, 50 percent, 1967, all. These percentages apply to the percentage owned each year, and this amount is a constant 20 percent per year of a stockholder's original shares if conversion is maximized each year.

The large number of possible combinations of securities that can be created prior to the sell down is limited only by the variety of objectives the selling stockholders may seek to achieve and the creativity and competence of the corporate counsel they retain to carry out their objectives.

Changes in the Capital Stock Account to Reflect New Status—Mergers

Another major category of recapitalization changes concerns companies involved in a merger or consolidation. The purposes to be achieved may vary considerably. In a very simple case the exchange might involve adjustments of the capitalization of either or both companies so that a simple one-for-one exchange of shares is the ultimate proposal submitted. A more complicated case might involve the acquisition of a small but publicly owned company with a record of rapid growth and high profitability by a larger concern with prospects of earnings drifting downward. The larger company might offer attractive terms well above the market price, but the stockholders of the smaller company might want a priority position in the larger company's capital structure. Still greater complications such as avoiding (not evading) income taxes or security registration may dictate much more elaborate recapitalization changes such as the creation of holding companies and intermediate transactions.

Recapitalization to Eliminate Accrued Preferred Dividends or to Change the Position of Preferred Stock

One interesting problem that occurred frequently as an aftermath of the Great Depression involved accrued preferred dividends. After a period of seriously reduced earnings or in a situation in which an undue amount of senior securities has been created in the capital structure or heavy sinking fund commitments have been made, a cumulative preferred stock on which dividends have not been paid for some time may have an arrearage of as much as $75 to $100 and more per $100 share. If there is an improvement in earnings, the corporation may be under pressure for dividends by common stockholders. But such dividends may well be many years away if the arrearage must first be discharged in cash.

This problem raises fundamental questions concerning the nature of the rights of preferred stock. There is no question but that a bankruptcy court can make alterations in the rights of bondholders and stockholders, but in the case of arrearages on preferred stock there is no basis for a bankruptcy court to intervene. Short of bankruptcy, the contract specifying the rights of stockholders cannot be constitutionally altered without the consent of each stockholder.[2] This rule of law threatened to stymie corporate finance until the loophole was found. Accrued preferred dividends can be altered as part of the merger process. The stockholder must have always been aware of the possibility of merger, which requires only two thirds vote of each class of stock. Thus many mergers have been brought about to lift the burden of the preferred arrearages. However, most states grant dissenters' rights in mergers. This is the right of each dissenter to a merger to be paid in cash for the appraised value of the security. Many mergers have been aborted because of the inability of companies—even large and well-known ones—to come up with the cash to meet this requirement.

Since the merger route requires cash, the corporation with accrued preferred arrearages is well advised to attempt a straightforward but tempting proposal to induce the consent and surrender of the preferred stockholders. There are myriad possibilities.

While we have presented the discussion in terms of preferred dividend

---

[2] Only one state (Wisconsin) holds to the contrary. See Nemmers, E. E., "Accrued Preferred Dividends," *Wisconsin Law Review* (May 1943), pp. 417–424.

arrearages, all of the principles apply to efforts to change the position of the preferred stock itself whether there are arrearages or not.

REPURCHASE BY A CORPORATION OF ITS OWN SHARES

The difficult but widespread problem of the repurchase by a corporation of its own shares is classified under recapitalization because this activity has many of the same consequences. For example, the cushion of the creditors is seriously reduced.

One reason the problem of repurchase is difficult is that the law on the subject is complicated and has led to many recent state statutes attempting to unravel the difficulties. In a general way the law of most states in this area can be summarized as follows:

1. In no case may repurchase jeopardize the corporation's ability to pay debts as they mature.
2. There are many repurchases that are exempt from additional restrictions: repurchase of shares sold to employees under a repurchase plan, preferred stock redemption programs, repurchase to fulfill the rights of dissenting stockholders in mergers or other activities requiring stockholder approval.
3. Also exempt from additional restriction is repurchase if the corporate charter contains specific authority on the matter or if two thirds of the stockholders, each class considered separately, consent to the repurchase.
4. In all other cases repurchase is limited to the amount of earned surplus that the company has, and each repurchase freezes earned surplus, dollar for dollar, until the shares are resold.

The reasons for the legal restrictions on repurchase are several. (1) repurchase represents a reduction in capital stock and of the protective cushion, thus posing a threat to creditors (and to preferred stock if the repurchase is of common). (2) Repurchase can be used as a preferential liquidation system through paying the withdrawing shareholder more than is due him (the question is, what repurchase price is permissible?). (3) Repurchase in the case of a closely held company with no market price to serve as a guide raises the opposite question—whether the withdrawing stockholder has been defrauded.

The subtlety of this subject is recognized by the Internal Revenue Service, which originally took the position that no gain or loss would be recognized for the corporation in any repurchase transactions whether or not any resale of these shares by the corporation occurred. This has been changed to a rule that whether gain or loss to the corporation will be recognized is dependent on an individual analysis of the "real nature of each transaction." No guidelines for such analysis are stated.

In the case of the stockholder who sells his shares back to the corporation, there is a capital gain (at lower tax rates than ordinary income). Such a selling stockholder takes out his share of surplus at advantageous rates compared to the receipt of dividends.[3] But proportionate repurchase of shares from all stockholders would clearly be recognized as, in effect, a dividend, and would be taxable as ordinary income.

If a corporation develops excess cash and has no senior securities and lacks normal earnings opportunities, it is a prime candidate to repurchase its shares. To continue the payment of dividends will merely increase income taxes for its stockholders. The corporation cannot develop the liquidating dividend exemption from income taxes for its stockholders as long as earned surplus is available. Hence repurchase is indicated. Some corporations feel that a formal call for tenders by stockholders is in order, or at least notice to all stockholders that the corporation is a buyer.

The question of repurchase also arises for the corporation with only normal earnings opportunities. In this case the corporation may find the price of its own stock such that it is a better "investment" than any other proposal available. Again repurchase is indicated. One method of testing a proposed repurchase is to develop a pro forma earnings per share after repurchase for comparison with current earnings per share.

Another reason for share repurchase is a form of leverage. When shares are repurchased, the number of outstanding shares is reduced and the market value of each share may well increase. This situation is in contrast to the use of the same amount of funds by the corporation to pay a dividend. After any dividend is paid the number of shares has not been reduced. Thus the "leverage" we are describing is in terms of the position of the stockholder who does not sell.

Other companies have used repurchase to reduce stockholder expenses in the case of small holdings which cost more to service than the dividends they receive.

Unless the company cancels the repurchased stock, its problems have

---

[3] Bierman and West have argued that the only rational basis for repurchase of shares is the tax advantage for the stockholders that the distribution of surplus via repurchase has over distribution via dividends. Assuming a tax rate of 70 percent on ordinary income and a capital gains tax rate of 25 percent, they demonstrate that with the interest rate at 4 percent an infinite flow of repurchases rather than dividends would triple the value of a firm. Bierman, H., and R. West, "The Acquisition of Common Stock by the Corporate Issuer," *Journal of Finance*, 21 (Dec. 1966), pp. 687–696.

only begun. Upon resale the SEC claims the same jurisdiction as over any issue. The law is in conflict as to whether preemptive rights are applicable to the resale of repurchased shares. There is no clear legal or accounting authority as to whether any gain or loss on the resale of the shares is to appear in earned or capital surplus, and the Internal Revenue Service will examine taxability in the light of "the real nature" of the transaction.

Disclosure of Repurchase by Corporation when Control Is at Issue

The Williams Act of 1968 authorized the SEC to make rules requiring the disclosure of pertinent information in connection with the repurchase by a corporation of its outstanding equity securities when it is involved in a battle for control of the corporation.

Summary

Timing in finance involves having the company's affairs in optimum condition when the market is in optimum condition for procurement of funds. Timing is affected by the industry in which the company functions and whether it leads, coincides with, or lags the general business cycle. Timing further involves the type of security (debt or equity, for example) being offered. Optimum conditions for debt financing seldom coincide with optimum conditions for equity financing, and either or both seldom coincide with optimum conditions in the economy as a whole.

The term structure of interest rates refers to the increase or decrease in the interest rate for a given debtor at any point in time as the maturity of the debt is extended. In depression low short-term rates taper to higher rates as maturity is increased.

The financial manager's rules must include (1) maintenance of flexibility, (2) effective use of short-term funds to achieve long-term financing goals and timing, and (3) maintenance of staggered maturities.

Refinancing involves the sale of new securities to replace existing securities. One form of refinancing is refunding a bond issue either at maturity or prematurely. In determining whether to refund prematurely the after-tax earning on the cash outlay for (or investment in) refunding costs is compared with discounted future savings due to the lower interest rate of the new issue in order to establish a rate of return on the cash outlay.

Recapitalization involves changing the form and/or the amount of outstanding securities in a voluntary exchange or with stockholder consent or unilaterally by action of the board of directors. Recapitalization may take many forms: (1) reduction of the capital stock account by a reduction of par or stated value, (2) increase in the capital stock account through a stock dividend, (3) change in the number of shares without a change in the amount of capital by a stock split, (4) reclassification of stock accounts for merger or other purposes, and (5) elimination of accrued preferred stock dividends.

Repurchase of its own shares by a corporation is frequent practice today. The reasons usually advanced for repurchase are (1) repurchase offers the best investment opportunity available to corporations with limited investment opportunities, (2) it makes possible the achievement of a leverage effect for remaining stockholders that cannot be otherwise achieved, (3) there are significant tax advantages to stockholders by distributing corporate assets in this way rather than as dividends.

Share repurchase is hedged about by legal rules designed to avoid corporate illiquidity after the purchase and to prevent reduction of the equity cushion of creditors (through limiting repurchase to the amount of earned surplus). There are some exceptions to the latter of these two rules in the case of employee stock repurchase agreements, preferred stock redemption provisions, elimination of fractional shares, compromise of corporate debts, and the statutory rights of dissenters from some corporate actions such as merger.

The Williams Act of 1968 requires disclosure of repurchases when there is a battle for control of a corporation.

Study Questions

1. With respect to timing in the field of finance, do you think it is more important that the firm be in optimum condition or that the market be in optimum condition when the time comes for new financing for the firm?

2. If a smaller company has never resorted to long-term borrowing, should it make the effort to fund as soon as possible at current market rates, wait for what is thought to be a low point in interest rates in the current short-run business cycle, or depend on what terms it can get for funding at the time it needs funds?

3. The local broker says that he likes to see stocks priced in the range of $10 to $20 a share because then the average man can buy 100 shares without as much strain on the family budget as would be required if the price per share were higher. Likewise, the commission rate is less for a round lot than for an odd lot. The broker thinks that companies should split their stock to keep the price in this range and take advantage of the strong preference by the average man for 100 shares. Do you agree?

4. A well-known text states, "It should be noted that if our objective is to lower the

market price of the stock, we could probably achieve the same result at a lower cost through a stock split [rather than through a stock dividend]." Do you agree?

5. The argument is advanced that as long as a company has cash it should repurchase its common stock whenever the market price falls below book value. Do you agree?

6. A stockholder proposes that the company reduce its cash dividends and use that amount to repurchase its own stock, thus cutting the tax bill for each stockholder. Do you agree?

7. If you were framing the provisions of a preferred stock issue would you specify that sinking fund purchases of the stock should take precedence over preferred dividends or vice versa? Would the company's position on this matter be different from that of the investor?

Problems

1. What will be the cash outlay to refund an issue of $3 million 5 percent 30-year bonds callable at $105 that have an unamortized bond discount of $60,000 and unamortized expenses of $90,000 after five years of the life of the bonds if we can replace the $3 million issue with 4 percent 25-year bonds sold at par with issue costs of $50,000, callable at $104? You may further assume an overlapping net interest cost of $5000 for 30 days. Assuming the tax rate is 50 percent, what will be the annual cash saving?

2. Compute the rate of return and the profitability index (the ratio of the present value of the annual cash gain to the present value of the cash outlay) for the refunding proposal in Problem 2. Assume the company's cost of capital is 10 percent.

3. What would be the break-even interest rate on the new issue in the case presented in Problems 2 and 3? *Hint:* If x is the break-even *amount* of interest, then the annual cash outlay on the new bonds is that amount of interest less the tax on that interest plus the amortization of issue cost:

$$x - 0.5(x + 2000) \qquad \text{or} \qquad 0.5x - 1000$$

and the annual cash gain of the new issue is equal to the annual cash outlay of the old bonds less the annual cash outlay on the new issue (defined above):

$$72,000 - (0.5x - 1000) \qquad \text{or} \qquad 73,000 - 0.5x$$

Furthermore, the break-even point is where the profitability index equals 1.0.

4. A closely held company is preparing to go public and will recapitalize in an effort to offer shares in the $20 to $30 price range. The firm's earnings in the most recent three years have been $400,000, $450,000, and $500,000. The underwriters believe the stock can be sold at a price–earnings ratio of 20 times the average of the most recent three-years' earnings. There are now 1000 shares outstanding. What stock split is indicated?

Selected References

Barker, C. A., "Effective Stock Splits," *Harvard Business Review*, 32 (Jan.–Feb. 1956), pp. 101–106.

——, "Stock Splits in a Bull Market," *Harvard Business Review*, 35 (May–June 1957), pp. 72–79.

Beranek, W., *Common Stock Financing, Book Values and Stock Dividends: The Theory and the Evidence*. Madison, Wis.: University of Wisconsin School of Commerce, 1961.

Bierman, H., and R. West, "The Acquisition of Common Stock by the Corporate Issuer," *Journal of Finance*, 21 (Dec. 1966), pp. 687–696.

Bothwell, J. C., Jr., "Period Stock Dividends," *Harvard Business Review*, 28 (Jan. 1950), pp. 89–100.

Bowlin, O. D., "The Refunding Decision: Another Special Case of Capital Budgeting," *Journal of Finance*, 21 (Mar. 1966), pp. 55–68.

Brigham, E. F., "The Profitability of a Firm's Purchase of Its Own Common Stock," *California Management Review*, 7 (Winter 1964), pp. 69–76.

Ellis, C. D., "Repurchase Stock to Revitalize Equity," *Harvard Business Review*, 43 (July–Aug. 1965), pp. 119–128.

Elton, E. J., and M. J. Gruber, "The Effect of Share Repurchases on the Value of the Firm," *Journal of Finance*, 23 (Mar. 1968), pp. 135–150.

Fergusson, D. A., "Preferred Stock Valuation in Recapitalizations," *Journal of Finance*, 13 (Mar. 1958), pp. 48–69.

Guthart, L. A., "More Companies Are Buying Back Their Stock," *Harvard Business Review*, 43 (Mar.–Apr. 1965), pp. 40–53.

Hausman, W. H., R. R. West, and J. A. Largay, "Stock Splits, Price Changes and Trading Profits, A Synthesis," *Journal of Business*, 44 (Jan. 1971), pp. 69–77.

Homer, S., *A History of Interest Rates*. New Brunswick, N. J.: Rutgers University Press, 1963.

Irving Trust Company, *The Calculation of Savings in Bond Refunding*. New York: Irving Trust Company, 1962.

Jen, F. C., and J. E. West, "The Effect of Call Risk on Corporate Bond Yields," *Journal of Finance*, 22 (Dec. 1967), pp. 637–652.

Johnson, K. B., "Stock Splits and Price Change," *Journal of Finance*, 21 (Dec. 1966), pp. 675–686.

Merrill, E. S., "A Guide to Bond Refunding," *Public Utilities Fortnightly*, 70 (Sept. 27, 1962), pp. 385–394.

Nemmers, E. E., "Accrued Preferred Dividends," *1943 Wisconsin Law Review* (May 1943), pp. 417–424.

——, "The Power of a Corporation to Purchase Its Own Stock," *1942 Wisconsin Law Review* (Mar. 1942), pp. 161–197.

Pye, G., "The Value of Call Deferment on a Bond: Some Empirical Results," *Journal of Finance*, 22 (Dec. 1967), pp. 623–636.

Spiller, E. A., Jr., "Time-Adjusted Break-even Rate for Refunding," *Financial Executive*, 31 (July 1963), pp. 32–35.

Sussman, M. R., *The Stock Dividend*. Ann Arbor, Mich.: University of Michigan Press, 1962.

Young, A., and W. Marshall, "Controlling Shareholder Servicing Costs," *Harvard Business Review*, 49 (Jan.–Feb. 1971), pp. 71–78.

22

EXTERNAL GROWTH THROUGH ACQUISITIONS: THE MERGER AND THE HOLDING COMPANY

Growth is essential to the health of a firm. It creates the opportunities that draw and challenge superior management, and makes possible the opportunities for promotion that are necessary to retain that management.

A firm can grow horizontally by enlarging its market share in the industry and by moving into related product lines and industries. A firm can also grow vertically by invading the industries that supply it and by invading the industries that supply the ultimate consumer if the firm does not presently serve them. It is also possible for a firm to grow by moving into products or processes that are unrelated to its industry or even to its industry classification; for example, a consumer goods company merging with a capital goods firm. Such mergers are called *conglomerate mergers.*

There are three formal devices for carrying out acquisitions: (1) *merger,* which involves the combining of two or more companies so that only one of the original companies survives, with the other being dissolved, (2) *consolidation,* in which a newly formed company takes over two or more companies which are then dissolved, and (3) the *holding company,* which acquires the stock of the companies being united, so that all the corporate entities continue to survive. There is a fourth category which might be recognized, namely, *affiliation,* in which firms join together to an extent by contractual arrangements, by stockholders common to the firms, by interlocking directorates, or by other ways.

ACCOUNTING RULES

Two different accounting methods are practiced in mergers. The first is the *purchase* method, which reflects the actual terms of the acquisition. If the surviving company pays more than book value for the acquired company, this increment is recognized as goodwill on the asset side of the balance sheet and as acquisition surplus on the liability-ownership side of the acquiring company. This goodwill[1] must be written off over a period of not more than 40 years and not directly against the surplus account but through the income statement.

Another alternative in purchase is that the acquired assets be appraised at more than their book value in the hands of the acquired company. Then the increase in value of these assets replaces what would have been goodwill on the books of the acquiring company. If this increase in asset values is real, the Internal Revenue Service will allow the acquiring company to use these values for depreciation.

The other method, the so-called *pooling of interests,* combines the assets and liabilities of the separate balance sheets, and any differences between the terms of the merger and book values of net worth are directly accounted for in the capital surplus of the combined companies.[2]

INTERNAL GROWTH VERSUS EXTERNAL GROWTH

The expansion of American firms has been largely carried out by internal funds: depreciation and retained earnings. However, periods of prosperity

---

[1] The handling of goodwill arising from mergers is covered by Accounting Principles Board, Opinion 17 (1970).

[2] Under the purchase method of accounting the earned surplus of the acquired company is transferred to capital surplus, but under the pooling of interests method the earned surplus of the acquired company is added to the earned surplus of the acquiring company.

Accounting Principles Board, Opinion 16 (1970), states the guidelines for corporate merger accounting. Pooling of interest is permitted only when

1. The acquired firm's stockholders continue as owners in the acquiring firm.
2. Each firm was autonomous for two years prior to the plan to combine. Ownership of more than 10 percent of either firm's stock by the other shows lack of independence.
3. The accounting basis for assets of the acquired company is continued.
4. A single transaction is involved (no contingent payouts).
5. No significant part of the two companies' assets is disposed of within two years after merger.
6. The acquiring firm issues only common stock of its voting class of common for substantially all (at least 90 percent) of the voting common of the acquired company.

Thus the use of preferred stock requires the purchase method of accounting.

in the past have been times of much external growth. Thus in the 1920s the notorious amalgamation of electric and gas companies into public utility holding company empires reflected the external growth concept. There is no question but that the failure rate of companies involved in extensive external growth efforts greatly exceeds that of companies emphasizing internal growth. In the conflict between internal and external growth, the advocates of external growth have crystallized the following arguments for merger.

Speed

The merger device increases the speed of growth. By a merger a company can acquire a going concern more quickly than it can put one together internally. It takes time to organize a production process. But two points must be remembered. The seller who put the operation together knows its value and by increasing his selling price will deprive the buyer of a good part of the advantage of entering the field by purchase as against putting together his own operation. Second, if the buyer is purchasing a "mature" operation, he has simply acquired a new problem of how to make it grow, and if he is acquiring a smaller, more rapidly growing operation that is still in its development stage, he assumes higher risks and still has the problem of continuing the development. In this case, price is the issue, not speed.

Cost or Price

Is it cheaper to acquire than to grow internally? That is *the* question and it is a matter of what price the seller seeks. In particular cases a low-priced seller can be found. However, one factor must be remembered. The time to buy a business is early in the upswing of the business cycle. No doubt many acquisitions in the period immediately following World War II have worked out advantageously to the buyer. But what of acquisitions made late in the upswing and at the peak or plateau of the cycle? Can we postulate that there will be no major downturn in the next decade?

Offsetting Cyclical or Seasonal Instability

Many companies are acutely aware of the cyclical or seasonal weaknesses of their own operations. This leads them to seek "mates" with compensating instability—match your peak with the valley of the new business, and vice versa. Offsetting seasonals is the easier objective to achieve. It is more difficult to offset cyclicals because the cycle of each business and particularly the relation of the cycles to each other are much less regular than are seasonal patterns. And in a major downturn, *all* the cycles of various businesses drop, though in differing degrees.

Economics of Diversification and Large-Scale Operation

When this argument is advanced we are no longer pursuing the question of internal versus external growth, but are examining the merits of diversification and large-scale operations, both of which can be achieved by internal or external growth.

Tax Advantages

Income tax considerations of sellers are a major factor in the sale of companies.[3] The main tax interest of stockholders of the selling corporation is to liquidate the accrued earnings of the selling corporation at capital gains tax rates rather than as ordinary income. Taxes are less frequently a motive for the buyer, although we are all aware of the notorious cases in which a company with large and recently accrued losses is picked up in order to take advantage of the loss carry-forward provisions of the income tax law. Recently the tax laws on the use of this device have been tightened considerably. Even in this case the seller knows what he has and bargains a piece of it away from the buyer.

Thus it appears that arguments for external growth rather than internal growth are reduced to the single matter of price—as is usually the case in economic questions.

Example of Antitrust Aspects

Finance discussions of merger often proceed as if the antitrust laws did not exist. Under antitrust laws, market dominance may be much more easily achieved by internal growth rather than by external growth. Consider the following case.

On March 16, 1967, the Federal Trades Commission in a consent order announced that W. R. Grace & Company was barred from acquiring any

---

[3] Butters, J. K., J. Lintner, and W. L. Cary, *Effects of Taxation: Corporate Mergers.* Boston: Harvard Graduate School of Business Administration, 1951. This study is based on 1990 mergers and consolidations between 1940 and 1947 and found that taxes were a major factor in one fourth of the mergers. More recently, in a study of 72 mergers using convertible preferred stock from 1962 through 1967, tax advantages were a consideration in 71 percent of the mergers. Sprecher, C. R., "A Note in Financing Mergers with Convertible Preferred Stock," *Journal of Finance,* 26 (June 1971), pp. 683–685.

more chocolate and cocoa products firms for ten years without prior Commission approval. On October 20, 1964, Grace, with sales in excess of $1 billion, had acquired virtually all the assets of the relatively small Ambrosia Chocolate Company for 116,000 shares of Grace common stock with a market value of $6.7 million. Grace is widely diversified in transportation, manufacturing, agriculture, banking, food products, brewing, and other areas. The firm is sixth in world chocolate companies but had no production facilities in the United States until buying Ambrosia. In 1965 there were 11 *independent* chocolate manufacturers in the United States plus even more "captive" operations. Grace had sought to acquire Fanny Farmer Candy, Inc., another relatively small company, as a market outlet for the output of Ambrosia. The Federal Trade Commission order barred this effort.

The acquisition of Fanny Farmer in addition to Ambrosia would hardly have given Grace market dominance. On the other hand, there is little doubt but that Grace will now legally enter the marketing of Ambrosia chocolate through internal expansion.

In sharp contrast, Aluminum Company of America quite legally, as the courts held, achieved by internal growth a 95 percent monopoly of basic aluminum production and fabrication in pre-World War II days. This monopoly was sharply cut down after World War II by the sale of government-owned aluminum facilities built during the war. Such sales by the government were made to companies such as Kaiser and Reynolds and at such low prices as to make certain that these firms could effectively compete against Alcoa.

These are just two instances of many that could be cited to support the proposition that under the antitrust laws market dominance is much more easily achieved by internal growth than by external growth. The reason lies in the very nature of the events. The antitrust laws are directed against two areas, (1) activity in restraint of trade and (2) activity tending to monopolize. The claim that internal growth is so directed must be proved by a *pattern* of conduct, or a series of events. The claim that external growth is so directed can be focused on a *single* event, namely, the acquisition, known to all the world. To ferret out proof of a pattern of conduct is much more of a problem, since it is difficult even to know where to look.

Many surviving companies in mergers have been forced to unscramble the legal aspects of the merger years after it has taken place. The acquiring company is often placed under legal mandate to conduct a forced sale, to say nothing of triple-damage claims it may face.

The mechanics of merger are the province of the legal expert. Enforcement of the antitrust law is not solely limited to the Federal Trade Commission, since the Justice Department and private persons (including corporations) may proceed under it, as is demonstrated by the hundreds of private cases that have arisen following the Philadelphia decision procured by the Justice Department in the electric utility equipment industry in the early 1960s.

THE MECHANICS OF EXTERNAL GROWTH: MERGERS AND CONSOLIDATIONS

A merger can be effected by the acquiring company paying cash, stock, or a combination of the two for the stock or assets of the acquired company. In some cases the merger may involve acquisition of only part of the selling company.

The statutes of many states contain a separate provision covering the sale of all assets and a separate provision covering a merger involving the trade of stock for stock. The main purpose of the state statutes is not to distinguish a merger carried out by stock for stock from one using stock for assets. Rather, the purpose of the separate statute on the sale of assets is to make it applicable not only where mergers occur but to "any sales, lease, mortgage or pledge" of all "or substantially all" of the assets "when not made in the usual and regular course of business." In brief, the sale of assets section applies to many types of transactions other than mergers.

Similarly, there is no significance as far as state statutes are concerned between merger and consolidation. The requirement is simply that the plan specify which company will survive and whether that one is to be a new one created for the purpose.

Likewise, there is little significant difference between the two methods (stock for assets, stock for stock) with respect to either the rights of creditors or the rights of dissenting stockholders to be paid in cash at the appraised value of their shares. One difference sometimes mentioned is that in the stock-for-assets purchase the buying corporation may avoid assuming the liabilities of the selling corporation, but in the stock-for-stock merger such assumption is automatic by statute. Without going into legal analysis, we can say that the avoidance of the seller's liabilities is a dubious proposition. The law is far from settled on what rights each group of creditors has in the situation. By "each group of creditors" is meant not only the creditors of the surviving corporation in contrast to those of the corporation to be dissolved, but also other groupings such as secured and unsecured creditors of each firm. This says nothing about the conflict of state laws when one corporation is incorporated in one state and the other in another state.

The Securities and Exchange Commission and the Internal Revenue Service

There are two agencies that draw distinctions between the various mechanics of mergers—the SEC and the IRS.

Sale of Assets for Stock. Under the method of sale of assets by the selling corporation for stock of the surviving corporation, the selling corporation agrees not to compete and in the case of the sale of all its assets to dissolve after distributing the survivor's stock to the stockholders of the selling corporation. If properly carried out, this is a tax-free distribution for stockholders of the selling corporation until they sell the new stock. The SEC has no registration jurisdiction, since there is no public offering of stock by the selling corporation, but it has jurisdiction to the extent of any proxy statement issued by the selling corporation in the case of reporting companies (those with 500 stockholders, assets over $1 million, and engaged in interstate commerce).

On the other hand, if the surviving corporation offers cash in whole or part for all stock of the selling corporation, there is an immediately taxable event for the selling stockholders but no SEC jurisdiction. If the surviving corporation offers cash for only some of the stock of the selling corporation but stock of the surviving corporation for the balance of the stock of the selling corporation, only the stockholders receiving cash have incurred a taxable event.

Stock for Stock. If there is a stock-for-stock transaction other than under the merger statute of the state of incorporation, then the SEC has full registration as well as proxy statement jurisdiction because a public offering is being made to the selling stockholders. But if the stock-for-stock merger is undertaken pursuant to merger statutes, Rule 133 of the SEC recognizes that no registration is required on the questionable theory that the transaction is not completely "voluntary," since any minority is not free to do otherwise. If a single individual or small group is in control of either corporation in a statutory merger, the SEC may require registration. In both cases there is a tax-free exchange if the transaction is properly executed.

There can also be different tax consequences between these methods of acquisition for the surviving corporation depending on whether the acquisition is a purchase or a pooling of interests for accounting purposes. The determining factor is the values at which assets go onto the books of the buying corporation, which, in turn, determines allowable depreciation and losses on inventory.

THE MECHANICS OF EXTERNAL GROWTH: THE HOLDING COMPANY

The term "holding company" can be used to describe a corporation that owns (1) any significant amount of stock of another company, (2) an amount of stock sufficient to constitute effective control of another corporation, or (3) nothing but stock of another corporation or corporations. It is apparent that the term presents difficulties, but we will use it generally to describe a company at least one of whose activities is holding effective *control* of at least one other company. The emphasis is on control.

Perhaps the most widely recognized advantages of the holding company are (1) minimization of the amount of money needed to get control and (2) the leverage achieved by pyramiding. Suppose, for simplicity, that there are five operating companies each with the balance sheet given in Table 22.1.

Assume that the after-tax income of each operating company is $212,-000, of which $12,000 is due the preferred stock. Assume also that the common stock can be bought at book value. Control may require buying at most 51 percent of the common. If we create a new company whose assets are the controlling stocks of the five operating companies and finance the acquisition with bonds and preferred as well as common stock, the balance sheet might be as given in Table 22.2, assuming we acquire 50 percent of the common stock of each operating company at book value. Now with $150,000 of the holding company's common stock we control $5 million in assets of the operating companies and claim $500,000 of earnings of the operating companies (assuming they pay out 100 percent of earnings). Of the $500,000 we apply $24,500 to holding company bonds and $8000 to the preferred stock (both of which carry higher rates than these securities of the operating companies because their income depends on the common stock earnings of the operating companies). If the holding company owns 80 percent or more of the operating company's voting stock, no income tax is due because the intercompany dividends are exempt. But here we own only 50 percent, and hence only 85 percent of the intercompany dividends are exempt. At a tax rate of 48 percent the effective tax rate on the holding company receipts is 0.48×0.15, or 7.2 percent. Here 15 percent of the $500,000 is taxable, or $75,000. But since the bond interest of $24,500 of

Table 22.1. Balance Sheet of Each Operating Company

Assets		Liabilities	
Operating assets	$1,000,000	Current liabilities	$ 200,000
		5 percent bonds	300,000
		6 percent nonvoting	
		preferred stock	200,000
		Common stock	100,000
		Surplus	200,000
Total assets	$1,000,000	Total liabilities and net worth	$1,000,000

Table 22.2. Balance Sheet of Holding Company

Assets		Liabilities	
Investment in operating companies		7 percent bonds	$350,000
($150,000 of common equity in each of five operating companies)	$750,000	8 percent nonvoting preferred stock	100,000
		Common stock	300,000
Total assets	$750,000	Total liabilities and net worth	$750,000

the holding company is deductible, only $50,500 is taxable.   This drives the effective tax rate to approximately 4.8 percent in this case.   While the common stock of the operating companies earns 66 percent ($200,000 on $300,-000), the common of the holding company earns 150 percent ($449,760[4] on $300,000).

We have considered the use of only one level of holding company. Above this level the leverage increases.   Holding companies have the advantages of avoiding dissenters' rights, minimizing the investment needed for control, and achieving leverage.   In addition, they might achieve (1) selective insulation of risks and (2) facility in financing.   However, these additional advantages are not clearcut.   If there are intercompany transactions

[4] Computed as $500,000 less $24,500 bond interest, $8000 preferred stock dividends, and $17,740 income taxes (22 percent on first $25,000 and 48 percent on $25,500).

in the system, the courts may easily refuse to recognize the distinction of the corporations. But if the distinction between the holding company and the operating companies is maintained, the decline of one operating company may not affect the holding company as seriously as it affects the operating company. Ease in financing may follow from the superior standing of the system compared to the lesser status the individual operating companies would have.

Abuses of the Holding Company Technique

A number of abuses have come to be identified with the holding company technique, particularly because of their frequent occurrence during the 1920s and early 1930s in the public utility area.

Excessive Use of Leverage. In the eight-layered Insull empire the leverage was so great that the Federal Trade Commission found that the West Florida Power Company was controlled by one tenth of 1 percent of its securities[5] measured at book value. In view of the leverage effect already discussed, it is easy to see how defaults in holding company bonds quickly occurred with the serious drops in operating income of the 1930s. Not only were excessive layers used but excessive debt was used in each layer.

Excessive Property Valuation. Because operating companies were the basis for building the electric company empires, competitive bidding for their common stock led to such stocks being greatly overvalued as assets in the hands of the holding company. This practice is commonly called "watering" the securities.

Excessive Charges for Expert Services and Profit on Construction Activities. The holding company system in theory made possible economies in the use of specialized services spread over a number of operating companies, but in practice this area was abused and the cost of services increased. Similarly, in the area of construction, in theory economies flow from scheduling many projects of operating companies to keep construction activity constant and to establish facilities that can be jointly used to effect savings. But in practice there is evidence that in this area, too, excessive profits were taken.

Upstream Loans. An *upstream loan* is a loan by an operating company to the parent holding company. The theory of the holding company device is

---

[5] Federal Trade Commission, *Utility Corporations* (1934), report under Senate Resolution 83, 70th Cong., 1st Sess., p. 160.

that the larger and better known parent can get funds more cheaply than smaller operating companies, and the parent can in turn pass these savings on to the operating companies by lending them funds. But because of excessive leverage, as already explained, a decline in operating company income means a magnified decline in the earnings of the common stock of the holding company. In order for the holding company to maintain its financial standing by continuing to pay dividends, the holding company caused the operating company to lend funds to the holding company to be used for such dividends. This steady drain of funds led to the situation in which the holding company was paying dividends on its common stock when the operating company had already ceased paying dividends on its stock—both that part held by the public and that part held by the holding company. Further, such intrasystem loans would not appear on the consolidated statement of the system under the accounting rule that intercompany transactions are eliminated in preparing a consolidated statement.

Remedial Legislation

The abuses just described led to the Public Utility Holding Company Act of 1935. The effect of this act may be summarized as follows.

1. The SEC was granted jurisdiction over all gas and electric holding company systems with properties in more than one state. This jurisdiction extended regulatory powers to all aspects of the business, including all financial transactions. A holding company was defined as any corporation owning 10 percent or more of the voting stock of an operating electric or gas utility.
2. Two specific provisions struck hard at key abuses. Utility systems had to be directed to a unified geographic area rather than be scattered over large regions and had to be limited in size so as not to "impair the advantages of localized management." In addition, gas and electric utility had to be divorced so that their operations could be analyzed separately. All of these provisions were summed up in the expression, the "death sentence." The other provision required that the levels of corporations in a holding company structure be no more than three. This provision was termed the "grandfather" clause, since an operating utility could have no more than a parent holding company and a grandfather holding company.

Competent administration by the SEC over a long enough period of time has resulted in an orderly dismantling of the complicated holding company structures that had been created in the 1920s.

Somewhat parallel problems in the bank holding company area led to the Bank Holding Company Act of 1956. The provisions of this act may be summarized as follows:

1. Existing bank holding companies may continue but may not own nonbanking assets. New bank holding companies owning 25 percent or more of two banks need a permit from the Board of Governors of the Federal Reserve System. Such a permit is also required for the merger of two bank holding companies.
2. Bank holding companies cannot cross state lines unless the state into which the system seeks to extend affirmatively authorizes such a move (and no state has).
3. Bank holding companies cannot borrow under "upstream loans" from subsidiaries, and "horizontal lending" by one subsidiary of the system to another is forbidden, although "downstream loans" by a parent to a subsidiary are permitted.

Abuses other than the tendency to monopoly were not widespread in the bank holding company development. The recent rapid growth in bank holding companies and in bank mergers led to the Bank Merger Act of 1960, which applies the limitations of the Bank Holding Company Act to the bank merger situation. The merger act requires consent for bank mergers from each of the Board of Governors of the Federal Reserve System, the Federal Deposit Insurance Corporation, and the Comptroller of the Currency. Both the Bank Holding Company Act and the Bank Merger Act were amended in 1966.

The existence of these two acts does not imply that banks are free of the antitrust provisions of the Sherman Act and the Clayton Act,[6] and the Department of Justice has attacked a number of bank mergers in recent years despite the blessing conferred on them by the various federal agencies under the Bank Holding Company Act and the Bank Merger Act.

Legislation in the public utility and bank area is of general interest, because such legislation may be extended to apply to all mergers.

THE TERMS OF MERGERS

Having considered merger from various aspects and having come to the conclusion that price is critical, we now consider the terms of a merger. In the case of a combination of two companies, price is expressed as the number of shares the acquiring company gives up for the shares of the acquired

---

[6] This point was settled in *U. S. vs. Philadelphia National Bank,* 374 U.S. 321 (1963), which held Section 7 (including stock acquisition as well as asset acquisition) of the Clayton Act applicable to bank mergers, and *U. S. vs. First National Bank,* 376 U.S. 665 (1964), which held Section 1 (restraint of trade) of the amended Sherman Act applicable to bank mergers.

company. There is no reasonably comprehensive information available on the percentage of merger proposals that fail to be finalized or of the reasons for the failure, but disagreement on price is certainly a major factor.

The principal financial determinants of the terms of a merger are (1) earnings, (2) market value of the firms, (3) dividends, (4) book value, and (5) net current assets.

It is clear that if we distribute securities in the new firm in proportion to any one of these bases, there will be a conflict with a distribution that uses any other of the bases except in an extremely fortuitous case. Such a conflict suggests the question of what weight is to be attributed to each of these bases of comparison.

Before we examine the interplay of the different bases of valuation of a firm at the practical level, we must emphasize that the pie to be divided is not the total of the two separate pies as they have existed. What is being divided is the pie that is *expected* from the fusion of the two separate pies, and the new pie is expected to be greater than the sum of the two old pies. This is called the *synergistic effect*. Thus in merger negotiations there is always discussion of (1) the improvement of total receipts that can be anticipated beyond the sum of the separate earnings, (2) the savings or cost reductions expected from the fusion, and (3) the impact of both of these factors on the market value of the securities that would result from the merger. To illustrate the complexity of the problem, even if there were no increase in earnings by fusion and no cost savings, it is quite possible that the merger would result in a price–earnings ratio higher than the separate price–earnings ratios of the two companies, for example, due to offsetting risks. Hence we see that *historical* earnings or price–earnings ratios are usually inadequate as the principle of merger.

It follows, then, that much of the popular analysis of mergers is based on faulty assumptions, namely, that (1) the past record and valuation of each separate entity is indicative of its separate future records and (2) the future record and valuation of the fusion is the sum of the separate (even future) records and valuation of the separate firms.

Let us assume that it is agreed that the future valuation of the fused firms is what is to be divided. We might propose that this value should be divided between the two firms in proportion to the present value of each firm (or the market value ratio). But such a proposal assumes that each firm contributes to an improvement in the total value of the new firm in proportion to its separate market value.

Actually one or the other of the merging companies may have more opportunities to merge at high values with other companies. This is some-times described as bargaining power, and it affects not only the division of the increment of the fused value over the sum of the values of the two separate firms but can extend so far as to shift part of the original value of one of the firms to the other as a result of the ratio of shares in the fused firms.

Table 22.3. Proposal to Merge Company X into Company Y

	Growth Company X	Mature Company Y	Exchange Rate (Y for X) Indicated if Only One Factor Were Considered and No Increase in Earnings or PE for Fused Firm
Total earnings	$20,000	$50,000	
Shares of common stock outstanding	10,000	10,000	
Earnings per share	$ 2.00	$ 5.00	0.4
Price–earnings ratio	20	10	
Market value per share	$40.00	$50.00	0.8
Dividends per share	$ 0.20	$ 4.00	0.05
Book value per share	$ 8.00	$20.00	0.4
Net current assets per share*	$ 0.50	$ 3.00	0.17
Expected annual growth rate of earnings	10%	5%	

* Net current assets is the term used in Moody's Manuals and is the same as net working capital, which is the Standard & Poor's term. Both terms describe current assets less current liabilities.

Table 22.4. Possible Results of One for One Merger of Company X into Company Y

Total earnings	$70,000
Shares of common stock outstanding	20,000
Earnings per share	$ 3.50
Market value per share	$45.00
Price–earnings ratio	12.8
Dividends per share	$ 2.10
Book value per share	$14.00
Net current assets per share	$ 1.75

Illustration of the Problem of Merger Terms

The quantitative data most readily available and most frequently used to evaluate merger terms in the practical world are, as already indicated, earnings, dividends, market value, book value, and net current assets.

Assume the data given in Table 22.3. It is apparent that computations on a per share basis are convenient, and this is the customary procedure. A look at the data suggests that Company X is a so-called growth company and Company Y is mature. If an exchange of one for one were to occur and if the market were to place no higher value on the fused operation than on its two separate parts and Company Y were the surviving company, the results might be those given in Table 22.4.

One thing immediately apparent is that all of the per share figures are the arithmetic means of the separate company figures, but that the new price–earnings ratio is not an average of the old price–earnings ratios, but is determined by the new price and the new earnings.

Notice also that *none* of the single-factor exchange rates is 1 or greater. The exchange rate of one for one cannot be arrived at by some weighting of the several factors set out. However, in many cases after the exchange rate is established the result can be arithmetically equated to a number of different weighting systems applied to the several factors.

By now the reader is doubtful that the proposed one for one exchange is realistic, or he infers that some factor or factors are missing from our list, although this list includes the five factors that have received the greatest emphasis in arriving at merger terms.

Before going further, notice that a one for one exchange ratio offers the acquired company more than its present market value, but the reverse is true for the acquiring company, which may lead to the problem of paying off dissenters in cash. This is basic. Unless the acquiring company is in a position to come up with the necessary cash, merger may not result.

In addition to the dissenter problem, what might account for the apparently high exchange ratio? There are a host of qualitative factors and we will mention just a few.

1. Company Y may be listed on the New York Stock Exchange and Company X traded over-the-counter, with little prospect of qualifying for the Big Board and with major holders seeking the better marketability for large blocks that the exchange offers.
2. Top management of Company X may be a dynamic young team. Executive "head hunting" has been done through mergers. However, the procurement of individual executives does not guarantee that a team will result.
3. We made one weak assumption in our case, although it is one commonly made

in analysis by those who do not have access to the information that is exchanged behind closed doors, namely, that the earnings of the fused operation will not exceed the sum of the separate earnings. Here is one problem posed by the SEC regulatory process. If we are involved with a corporation that is procuring new money, the SEC requires the prospectus to state how the new money will be used and to show the pro forma capital structure after the issuance of the securities. But in a merger speculative projections of the effect of the merger are barred from use in solicitation; yet how else can the investor evaluate the effect of the merger? A few definite items can be stated and indeed must be, such as a plan to close a plant as a result of the merger. But what is definite is seldom sufficient to form a reasonable judgment.

Thus far we have not considered the impact of the different growth rates shown in Table 22.3 for the two companies in relation to the merger terms. Figure 22.1 shows that Company Y's earnings per share will be initially reduced by the terms of the merger but that after a period of 26.4 years, Company Y's earnings will be higher than they would have been without the merger. The converse is true for Company X, but the number of years until this happens will not, except by coincidence, be the same.

Figure 22.1. Growth in earnings per share of Companies X and Y separately and after merger.

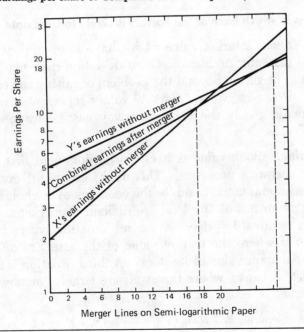

We can determine how long this time period will be by solving the following equation for N:

$$E_1(1 + g_1)^N = E_2(1 + g_2)^N$$

where E_1 and g_1 are the earnings and growth rate before merger, E_2 and g_2 are the earnings and growth rate after merger, and N is the break-even number of years. The growth rate after merger is the average of the separate growth rates, weighted by the *total* earnings of each company. In our case g_2 is $[0.10(\$20,000) + 0.05(\$50,000)]/\$70,000$, or 6.43 percent. Thus Company Y is trading a current earning of $5 per share with a growth rate of 5 percent for a current earning of $3.50 per share and a growth rate of 6.43 percent. Conversely, Company X is trading a current earning of $2 per share with a growth rate of 10 percent for a current earning of $3.50 per share and a growth rate of 6.43 percent. Substituting in this equation, N turns out to be 26.4 years for Company Y and 17 years for Company X.[7]

Figure 22.1 illustrates what the analysis of Table 22.3 makes clear: the exchange ratio of one for one appears to favor Company X—if we can extrapolate the growth rates of companies X and Y as we have done. However, if the mature Company Y cannot maintain its growth rate for long, then Company Y will recover its earnings position much sooner than 26.4 years.

Situations in which Each of the Factors Is Likely to Dominate

Market Value. Market value as we have suggested, will dominate when there are dissenter problems. Great deviation from market value threatens to result in litigation beyond the problem of raising the cash needed for dissenters. However, when "market" values represent a thin or even a supported market, only the naive company will be trapped into recognizing "market" value.

Book Value. Book value is likely to be dominant first in the case where liquidity carries a premium. This might occur, for example, at any time when the capital market and/or the economy as a whole have slowed down and new securities of any kind are difficult to market at anything approximating a reasonable price. A second situation where book value will be dominant is where the market value of the assets of one company is well above the market value of its stock. A third situation is in financial institutions, such as banks, where the assets are largely "money assets."

---

[7] In computing form, $\log E_1 + N \log (1 + g_1) = \log E_2 + N \log (1 + g_2)$.

Dividends.   Dividend rates of the two companies are not likely to influence the terms of the merger but can be expected to affect the form of securities used.   Dividends depend on earnings and policy as to payout.   But in a merger every effort will be made to use a type of security which will preserve existing cash dividends for stockholders of the acquired company. The payout policy of the fused operation cannot be readily determined in advance except where the policies of both companies have been nearly the same, thus creating an expectation that the same pattern will continue.

Earnings.   Earnings are sometimes stated to be the dominant single factor, and "earnings" in such a statement means historical earnings.   The relevant earnings, however, are expected future earnings, and these are reflected in the market value.   Variability of earnings is a factor to be considered, but this is reflected in the market value and appears in the price–earnings ratios, which reflect risk as well as growth prospects.

Earnings are inevitably a factor for discussion in a merger in connection with the use of market value in establishing the exchange ratios.   When the price–earnings ratios of the two companies are different, the result is the so-called earnings dilution for one company and an earnings accretion for the other company, which we have already described in connection with Figure 22.1.

Management: The Vital Factor Difficult to Measure

Textbooks rarely consider the effect that the quality of management has on the terms of a merger.   Management abilities of companies are difficult to measure.   Often the difference between the actual terms and those that analysis of the factors would suggest can be accounted for by the management factor.   For example, one of the companies may have a new management whose efforts have not yet appeared in improved earnings, although there may be agreement that the new management has made many substantial changes whose effects on earnings can already be estimated.   This situation merely emphasizes again that what is relevant in all valuation problems is the future or expected earnings stream and not the historical record.

Risk Differences

Another important factor to be considered in determining merger terms is the difference in the risk associated with each firm.   Of the factors that are actually weighted to set merger terms, only market value of the securities includes an estimate of risk. This, then, is one reason that market value dominates in mergers.

The Earn Out

As the merger phenomenon has grown more popular in recent years, specialized techniques have been developed. One of these is the *earn out* which is used to deal with high-risk acquisitions. For example, a small firm with attractive products under development may catch the eye of a mature firm. Both firms have considerable confidence in the new products. But the selling firm wants a price based on the potential value of the firm if the products succeed. The buying firm is willing enough to pay handsomely *if* the products succeed. This dilemma is quickly resolved by a down payment and a later second payment based on the earnings (if any) actually achieved. The down payment will be in the amount of the fair market value of the selling firm today.

Various formulas can be devised to determine the "earn out" or second payment. Most formulas involve two factors to determine the agreed-upon additional payment: the earnings *increase* in a specified period after the acquisition over the earnings at the acquisition date times a multiplier (price–earnings ratio). Then there is a fork in the road. This agreed-upon amount is to be paid either in shares of the buyer valued at the date of the acquisition or valued at the date of payment. The former denies the selling firm the "P/E play" that develops in the buyer's stock after the acquisition; the latter permits the selling firm to participate in the rise (or decline) of the buyer's price–earnings ratio after the date of the acquisition.

It is basic to an earn out that the selling firm must have autonomy during the earn out period. If the terms are set right, the selling firm has everything to gain by optimum performance. Interference by the buying firm during the earn out period can only lead to possible lawsuits. The terms of the deal must also spell out with great care the accounting practices to be followed, particularly as to expensing or capitalizing many costs such as research and development and depreciation rates.

Dissenters' Rights: The Foe of All Mergers

For every merger proposal that becomes an actual fact there are many that never come to fruition. There are no statistics in this area, but one factor that torpedoes many merger proposals is the right of any dissenting stockholder to demand payment in cash of the fair value of his stock *prior* to the proposed merger. The inability of the liquidity position of the two companies to handle this drain of cash can easily bring further maneuvers to a halt. Because it is difficult to determine the number of stockholders likely to claim dissenters' rights, the merger agreement provides that if more than a stated percentage (usually 5 percent) of the stock held by the stockholders of either corporation (with dissenters' rights) dissents, the agreement may be canceled.

Bondholders continue to hold their rights after a merger. Here it becomes important whether the bonds are secured by a mortgage; if so, then their priority in the collateral continues.

Tender Offers

In recent years the *tender offer* has been increasingly used by one corporation to "take over" another. In earlier years the classical method to achieve a takeover was a proxy fight to gain control of the board of directors. As explained in Chapter 17, the SEC has tight rules as to disclosure when proxies are solicited and special rules for the proxy fight situation. To avoid these rules, the acquisitive (and smart) corporation resorts to the tender offer, which consists of a full-page ad in major newspapers stating the price and terms upon which that corporation will acquire shares of the "victim" corporation. Usually the tender offer is stated to be not effective unless a stated percentage of the shareholders accept the offer and deliver their shares to an agent named in the offer. The tendering corporation seeks out victims with current difficulties, which in turn have caused the price of the shares of the victim corporation to decline sharply. At the extreme, a tendering corporation may be a "raider" whose purpose is to liquidate the victim for a quick profit. Another abuse of the tender offer takes the form of "short tendering." Here the tendering corporation specifies that actual stock need not be tendered if a bank or broker guarantees delivery of the shares.

The Williams Act of 1968 authorizes the SEC to make rules covering tender offers, which had up to that time been a "loophole" in SEC jurisdiction. Under the Act as amended in 1970, the SEC requires a filing in all cases where a successful tender would result in the tendering corporation acquiring more than 5 percent of any class of equity securities.

Summary

Growth is essential to the health of a firm. It can be achieved (1) by expansion of the existing firm through increasing its market share or expanding forward or backward into new products and markets (internal growth), or (2) by acquisition of other businesses (external growth). Whether the better choice is the first, called internal expansion, or the second, called external expansion, depends on the price demanded by the selling firm and environmental factors such as the antitrust laws.

External growth is effected in any of three ways: (1) merger, in which one firm takes over another and dissolves the acquired firm, (2) consolidation, in which a new firm replaces both the acquiring and the acquired firm, and (3) the holding company, which acquires the stock of another firm but does not proceed to dissolve the acquired firm. Sometimes two or more firms "affiliate" by contract, interlocking directorates, or other methods that fall short of full control.

In the case of merger, the acquiring company may use the purchase method by buying the assets of the acquired company or may follow "statutory" merger, which involves the exchange of stock of the acquiring company for stock of the acquired company.

Accounting for a merger may follow either of two methods: purchase in which "goodwill" appears on the asset side of the acquiring company to represent the payment of more than book value for the acquired company, or pooling of interests in which the assets and liabilities of the two firms are combined and any differences between the terms of the merger and the combined book net worth of the two firms is recognized directly in capital surplus of the combined companies. Use of the pooling method has recently been restricted.

Expansion by internal growth rather than external growth (mergers) offers advantages in keeping the capital structure simple, avoiding financial charges, maintaining a strong working capital position, avoiding dilution of voting control, retaining maximum financial strength to meet the business cycle, and minimizing the danger of antitrust charges.

Expansion by external growth (mergers) may offer the advantages of (1) speed in entering a given market, (2) a lower cost for entering the market area (depending on the price paid for the firm acquired), (3) economies of diversification or large-scale operation, and (4) tax advantages.

Merger raises potential antitrust problems either under the section relating to restraint of trade or under that relating to the tendency to monopoly. Merger tends to focus antitrust problems on a specific event, namely, the merger, whereas internal growth proceeds in an inch-by-inch manner and is hard to pin down.

Both the SEC and the IRS are involved in mergers. If the IRS does not declare the proposed transaction a tax-free reorganization, the merger will most likely not proceed. In the case of the sale of the assets of the selling corporation for stock of the buying corporation, the SEC has no jurisdiction over the sale because there is no public offering of securities, although it does have jurisdiction over any proxy statement used by the selling corporation.

In the case of a stock-for-stock merger under the statutes of the states of the two corporations, Rule 133 of the SEC recognizes that there is no federal jurisdiction because the transaction is not voluntary as to any minority. The rule is different if a single person or small group is in control of either corporation.

Instead of formal merger the proposed union may be carried out by the holding company technique. Then there are no dissenters' rights, the acquiring company can easily reverse the acquisition by selling the stock, the amount of money needed to acquire control is reduced, leverage is achieved, and there is selective insulation of risks and increased facility in financing. But the holding company technique is exposed to the claim that the two companies have not been kept separate.

The holding company technique lends itself to abuses, such as (1) excessive leverage, (2) excessive valuation of the properties of operating companies, (3) excessive profits on construction by operating companies and excessive charges for expert services to the holding company, and (4) "upstream loans" by the operating company to the holding company. These abuses, particularly in the case of public utility companies, led to the Public Utility Holding Company Act of 1935, giving the SEC the authority to require that holding companies be restricted to a unified geographical area and involve no more than three levels of corporations.

The use of the holding company technique has also resulted in special legislation in the area of banking.

Merger terms involve a consideration of the two companies as to (1) earnings, (2) market value of the stock, (3) dividends, (4) book value, and (5) net current assets. The earnings accretion to one company and the dilution to the other company will erode with time. The relevant question is not the values of the two companies separately considered but the division of the value of the combined firm that the union creates. Actual merger terms reflect the relative "bargaining power" of each company.

Regardless of manipulation of these quantitative measures, some qualitative factors have been omitted, such as listing of the securities of one company and the skill and age of the respective managements.

Stockholders who do not want to go along with proposed mergers are entitled to be paid in cash for the market value of their holdings. These dissenters' rights create cash requirements that defeat many merger proposals.

The tender offer is a public offer to all stockholders of a "victim" company inviting those stockholders to tender their stock pursuant to the offer made. The SEC now has jurisdiction over tender offers under the Williams Act of 1968.

Study Questions

1. It is sometimes said that a company cannot afford to merge if its price–earnings ratio is low. Do you agree?

2. A well-known text states, "A particularly difficult problem regarding business combinations has been whether to treat the new company as a purchase or as a pooling of interests." Do you think this is a problem, or do you believe accounting is a branch of history that records events but does not shape them?

3. What basis would you use to determine the terms of merger of a small, rapidly growing, high-profit company into a large company with good earnings but poor growth prospects if neither company's securities are publicly traded?

4. If you were the financial manager of a company that has determined to make some acquisitions because it has excess cash and lacks internal investment opportunities, rank the following aspects of companies to be acquired in the order you would favor:

   a. A company with sound management regardless of the industry in which the company operates
   b. A company with a record for rapid growth and good profits
   c. A company that operates in a field closely allied to your company's field
   d. A company whose seasonal swing offsets that of your company.

   Would your ranking depend on the strengths and weaknesses of your company? If so, what strengths and what weaknesses? Would you consider merger an expensive way to correct the weaknesses in your company?

5. Would you prefer to acquire another company by the use of a holding company or by a statutory merger? What would be the advantages of using a holding company and later performing the actual merger?

6. A well-known text states, "The existence of long-term debt in a company's financial structure affects its valuation for merger purposes." Do you agree?

7. It is commonly stated that a pure (nonoperating) holding company is exposed to the risk that its only asset is the stock of other companies. Is there any way of compensating for this risk? Is there any relevance in the common proverb: "bulls and bears make money but pigs don't"?

Problems

1. Using the holding company system given in Table 22.5, develop the earnings applicable to the common stock of the several companies. You may assume an income tax rate of 50 percent, with bond interest deductible, and an 85 percent exemption of intercompany dividends. Likewise, assume all earnings available to common stock are paid in dividends and that holding company acquisitions were made at book value.

Table 22.5. Holding Company System

Operating Company A Balance Sheet			
Assets	$3,000,000	6% bonds	$1,000,000
		5% nonvoting preferred stock	500,000
		Nonvoting common stock	1,000,000
		Voting common stock	500,000
Total assets	$3,000,000	Total liabilities and net worth	$3,000,000

Operating Company B Balance Sheet			
Assets	$5,000,000	5% bonds	$2,000,000
		6% nonvoting preferred stock	1,000,000
		Nonvoting common stock	1,500,000
		Voting common stock	500,000
Total assets	$5,000,000	Total liabilities and net worth	$5,000,000

Holding Company X Balance Sheet			
Voting common stock of operating Company A	$250,000	6% bonds	$200,000
		7% nonvoting preferred stock	100,000
Voting common stock of operating Company B	250,000	Nonvoting common stock	150,000
		Voting common stock	50,000
Total assets	$500,000	Total liabilities and net worth	$500,000

Holding Company Y Balance Sheet			
Voting common stock of holding Company X	$25,000	7% bonds	$10,000
		8% nonvoting preferred stock	5,000
		Nonvoting common stock	8,000
		Voting common stock	2,000
Total assets	$25,000	Total liabilities and net worth	$25,000

Operating Company A Earnings on Assets before Bond Interest and Taxes	Case 1 20%	Case 2 15%	Case 3 10%
Earnings before taxes and interest	$600,000	$450,000	$300,000
Deduct bond interest			
Taxable income			
Deduct tax			
Net income			
Paid to bonds			
Paid to preferred			
Paid to nonvoting common			

Table 22.5. Holding Company System (contd.)

Operating Company B Earnings on Assets before Bond Interest and Taxes	Case 1 15%	Case 2 10%	Case 3 5%
Earnings before taxes and interest	$750,000	$500,000	$250,000
Deduct bond interest			
Taxable income			
Deduct tax			
Net income			
Paid to bonds			
Paid to preferred			
Paid to nonvoting common			
Paid to voting common			

	Case 1	Case 2	Case 3
Holding Company X			
Earnings before taxes and interest			
Taxable dividends			
Deduct bond interest			
Taxable income			
Taxes			
Net income			
Paid to bonds			
Paid to preferred			
Paid to nonvoting common			
Paid to voting common			
Holding Company Y			
Earnings before taxes and interest			
Taxable dividends			
Deduct bond interest			
Taxable income			
Taxes			
Net income			
Paid to bonds			
Paid to preferred			
Paid to nonvoting common			
Paid to voting common			

2. The Active Corporation acquires the Passive Corporation and issues stock in the amount required by the comparative market values of the common stock of the firms before the merger. Active decides to handle the transaction by the purchase method of accounting rather than by a pooling of interests. The balance sheets of the firms are given in Table 22.6.

   Make the necessary adjusting entries and develop a pro forma balance sheet. To do this you will need to fill in the blanks in the balance sheets. What is the dilution or accretion to each company if the combined earnings continue unchanged?

Table 22.6. Balance Sheets of the Active and Passive Corporations

	Active	Passive	Adjustments Debit	Credit	Pro Forma Balance Sheet
Current assets	$600,000	$200,000	_____	_____	_____
Fixed assets	300,000	500,000	_____	_____	_____
Goodwill	_____	_____	_____	_____	_____
Total assets	900,000	700,000	_____	_____	_____
Current liabilities	200,000	100,000	_____	_____	_____
Long-term debt	200,000	100,000	_____	_____	_____
Common stock	100,000	300,000	_____	_____	_____
Capital surplus	100,000	100,000	_____	_____	_____
Retained earnings	300,000	100,000	_____	_____	_____
Total liabilities and net worth	$900,000	$700,000	_____	_____	_____
Par value of share	$10	$6			_____
Net income	100,000	50,000			_____
Current price–earnings ratio	15	12			_____
Number of shares	_____	_____			_____
Book value per share	_____	_____			_____
Earnings per share	_____	_____			_____
Market value per share	_____	_____			_____

Table 22.7. The Electric Company and the Static Company

	Electric Company	Static Company	Adjustments Debit	Credit	Pro Forma Balance Sheet
Current assets	$2,000,000	$1,000,000	_____	_____	_____
Fixed assets	3,000,000	1,000,000	_____	_____	_____
Goodwill	_____	_____	_____	_____	_____
Total assets	5,000,000	2,000,000			
Current liabilities	1,000,000	500,000	_____	_____	_____
Long-term debt (5%)	1,000,000	500,000	_____	_____	_____
Common stock, $5 par	2,000,000	800,000	_____	_____	_____
Capital surplus	500,000	0	_____	_____	_____
Earned surplus	500,000	200,000	_____	_____	_____
Total liabilities and net worth	$5,000,000	$2,000,000	_____	_____	_____
Earnings	$ 200,000	$ 100,000	_____	_____	_____
Price–earnings ratio	15	20			
Book value per share	_____	_____			_____
Earnings per share	_____	_____			_____
Market value per share	_____	_____			_____
Net current assets per share	_____	_____			_____
Dividends per share if Electric payout is 40% and Static is 80%	_____	_____			_____
Return on assets (including interest)	_____	_____			

What is the dilution or accretion if earnings of the combined operation increase 30 percent?

3. Assume the same facts as in Problem 2 except that the Active Corporation will apply pooling of interests as the method of accounting.

4. You are confronted with the proposed merger of the Electric Company and the Static Company. You may assume that the combined operation is expected to continue to perform as the sum of the separate companies. The balance sheets and earnings of the two firms are given in Table 22.7.

What exchange ratio would you recommend? What would be the dilution or appreciation for the shares of each firm in the event of merger at your calculated exchange ratio?

Selected References

Alberts, W. W., and J. E. Segall, Eds., *The Corporate Merger*. Chicago: University of Chicago Press, 1966.

Butters, J. K., and W. L. Cary, "Motives Affecting Form of Sales and Purchases of Business," *Harvard Law Review*, 64 (Mar. 1951), pp. 697–726.

Butters, J. K., J. Lintner, and W. L. Cary, *Effects of Taxation: Corporate Mergers*. Cambridge, Mass.: Harvard Graduate School of Business Administration, 1951.

Cheney, R. E., "What's New on the Corporate Takeover Scene," *Financial Executive*, 40 (Apr. 1972), pp. 18–21.

Cohen, M. F., "Takeover Bids," *Financial Analysts Journal*, 26 (Jan.–Feb. 1970), pp. 26–31.

Crowther, J. F., "Peril Point Acquisition Prices," *Harvard Business Review*, 47 (Sept.–Oct. 1969), pp. 58–62.

Gort, M., *Diversification and Integration in American Industry*. Princeton, N. J.: Princeton University Press, 1962.

Gort, M., and T. E. Hogarty, "New Evidence on Mergers," *Journal of Law and Economics*, 13 (Apr. 1970), pp. 167–184.

Hogarty, T. F., "The Profitability of Corporate Mergers," *Journal of Business*, 44 (July 1970), pp. 317–327.

Jaenicke, H. R., "Management's Choice to Purchase or Pool," *Accounting Review*, 37 (Oct. 1962), pp. 758–765.

MacDougal, G. E., and F. V. Malek, "Master Plan for Merger Negotiations," *Harvard Business Review*, 48 (Jan.–Feb. 1970), pp. 71–82.

Mace, M. L., and G. G. Montgomery, Jr., *Management Problems of Corporate Acquisitions*. Cambridge, Mass.: Harvard University Press, 1962.

McCarthy, G. D., *Acquisitions and Mergers*. New York: Ronald Press, 1963.

Melicher, R. W., and D. F. Rush, "The Performance of Conglomerate Firms: Recent Risk and Return Experience," *Journal of Finance*, 29 (May 1973), pp. 381–388.

Patton, E. J., "Tax Implications of Mergers and Acquisitions," *The Financial Executive*, 31 (Jan. 1963), pp. 33–34.

Reinhardt, V. E., *Mergers and Consolidations: A Corporate-Finance Approach*. Morristown: General Learning Press, 1972.

Reum, W. R., and T. A. Steele, III, "Contingent Payouts Cut Acquisition Risks," *Harvard Business Review*, 48 (Mar.–Apr. 1970), pp. 83–91.

Rockwell, W. F., Jr., "How to Acquire a Company," *Harvard Business Review*, 46 (May–June 1968), pp. 121–132.

Scharf, C. A., *Techniques for Buying, Selling and Merging Businesses.* Englewood Cliffs, N. J.: Prentice-Hall, 1964.

Shick, R. A., "The Analysis of Mergers and Acquisitions," *Journal of Finance,* 27 (May 1972), pp. 495–504.

Sprecher, C. R., "A Note on Financing Mergers with Convertible Preferred Stock," *Journal of Finance,* 26 (June 1971), pp. 683–685.

Weston, J. F., *Planning for Corporate Mergers.* Los Angeles, Calif.: University of California at Los Angeles, 1963.

Wyatt, A. R., "Inequities in Accounting for Business Combinations," *Financial Executive,* 40 (Dec. 1972), pp. 28–35.

23

TAX MANAGEMENT OF ENTERPRISE FINANCIAL AFFAIRS

Taxes are important considerations in almost all business decisions and particularly in the area of financing. Inventories, fixed assets, selling and credit policies, and wages are also influenced by taxes.

Today federal, state, and local taxes take an amount equal to slightly more than 25 percent of gross national product, with 58 percent of total taxes going to the federal government. These figures do not include the current federal deficit nor the federal funds transferred to state and local government, which equal 12 percent of state and local taxes.

Taxation is a vast subject. The concerns of the financial manager in this area may be outlined as follows.

1. Activities directed to avoiding multiple taxation and to shifting ordinary income into capital gains to take advantage of the tax rate differential.[1]

[1] Throughout this chapter the term "capital gains" refers to long-term capital gains, that is, when the asset has been held more than six months and is not of the type that is held by the business for generating ordinary income. Under the Tax Reform Act of 1969 as amended in 1970, long-term capital gains carry the advantage of being subject to a maximum tax rate of 25 percent (30 percent in the case of corporations) on up to $50,000 per year with the excess taxable at 35 percent. In addition, a special additional "preference" tax of 10 percent applies to the difference between the half of the long term capital gain not taxed and the capital gains tax. There is an annual specific exemption of $30,000 plus income tax paid from this last 10 percent tax. Gains on assets held for six months or less constitute short-term capital gains and are taxed at regular income tax rates.

The purpose of the new capital gains provisions is to close almost completely the gap between the tax rate on ordinary income and that on *large* capital gains.

2. Activities directed to delaying tax payment, thus creating interest-free loans by the government to the taxpayer (accelerated depreciation and sale and leaseback are examples).
3. Activities directed to averaging income over the years to offset income in one year against losses in another.
4. Inventory problems.
5. Merger and reorganization problems.
6. Foreign activities.
7. State and local taxation.
8. Tax minimization as a possible overriding consideration.

At the time of writing, Federal corporate income tax rates on ordinary income are 22 percent on the first $25,000 of annual income and 48 percent on income above $25,000 for years before and after 1975. In 1975 the rates are 20 percent on the first $25,000, 22 percent on the next $25,000, and 48 percent on income above $50,000. Tax legislation in 1975 may extend these new rates beyond 1975.

In the use of cash or accrual basis the rules are the same for a corporation and a sole proprietorship. But in a partnership a partner's share of accrued income must be included on his personal return even though not paid to him. Although in general all "ordinary and necessary expenses" are allowable as deductions from revenues in order to determine taxable income, Congress can constitutionally eliminate any and even all classes of deductions and can, in addition, change the tax rate for the year that has passed.

MULTIPLE TAXATION

Interest on debt has always been allowed as a deduction to the corporation and the individual while dividends on stock have always been denied as a deduction to the corporation. Thus corporate dividends are subject to double taxation—once as equity income of the corporation and again as personal income to the stockholder.

Intercompany Dividends: Preferred Stock

The Internal Revenue Code prevents double taxation in one case: where one taxable corporation pays dividends to another taxable corporation. Here the second corporation pays a tax on only 15 percent of the dividends so received, with 85 percent of the dividends free of tax. Another provision permits consolidated tax returns by several corporations where one corporation owns 80 percent or more of the others. In this case all intercompany dividends are tax free.

The 85 percent exemption of intercompany dividends has important consequences in the capital market. Dividends received by a corporation on the preferred stock of another corporation enjoy a tax advantage over interest similarly received on bonds. The interest is fully taxable while only 15 percent of the preferred dividends is subject to tax. Thus to an investing corporation a preferred stock with adequate provisions limiting the prior debt may be more attractive than a bond. The same exemption is applicable to common stock dividends received by a second corporation. In addition, if almost all income is paid over to the shareholders, then investment companies, savings and loan associations, and cooperatives are virtually exempt from corporate taxes. Mutual insurance companies were once in this category but now are partially taxable.

DEVICES TO AVOID MULTIPLE TAXATION OR TO RECLASSIFY INCOME TO CAPITAL GAINS

A number of other devices may be employed to avoid multiple taxation or to change the classification of income from ordinary income to capital gains income. Some of these have been classified as loopholes and have been rendered ineffective by amendments of the law. Others still survive and some are newly created.

Election of Corporation to Be Taxed as Partnership

While many loopholes have been plugged, a new method has been created for a corporation to elect treatment as a partnership, with each stockholder reporting his share of the corporation's earnings without any income tax payable by the corporation. This device is limited to a corporation with not more than ten shareholders, all of whom must be individuals or estates. Such exemption is not applicable if the corporation is foreign or if it received more than 80 percent of its receipts from foreign sources or more than 20 percent from security income or from profit on transactions in securities, rents, royalties, or annuities. This section was enacted in response to pressure to give "small businesses" the benefit of the limited liability of a corporation and all the benefits available to shareholder-employees such as pension plans and stock options. However, the device has no limit as to size of net worth or volume of sales.

Personal Holding Companies

The income tax law defines a personal holding company as one that derives at least 60 percent of its gross income from security income, profits on transactions in securities, rents, royalties, or annuities and in which over 50 percent of the stock is owned by not more than five persons. In addition to the regular (current) corporation income tax of 48 percent, a personal holding company pays a penalty tax of 70 percent on its *undistributed* income. The personal holding company was used as a device for individuals in high income tax brackets to transfer property to a corporation where the income would be taxed at only 48 percent.

Unreasonable Accumulation of Earnings

Instead of trying to get income out of a corporation without paying a corporate tax or attempting to take income out of the corporation by a sale of stock now and taxed at capital gain rates, one might resign himself to leaving the income in the corporation indefinitely, paying the corporate tax and delaying the personal capital gains tax that would ultimately be due upon the sale of the stock. To block this loophole, Section 531 of the Internal Revenue Code (still commonly referred to by its earlier number, Section 102) taxes *unreasonably* accumulated income. The first $100,000 of such accumulated surplus is exempted but the tax is 27.5 percent on the next $100,000 and 38.5 percent on any further amounts. However, this section of the law is difficult to administer, since any active corporation always has plans for retained earnings and, in view of the tax, may well entertain areas of investment that its management might otherwise reject.

Taking Dividends Out in Disguises

One basic method of removing income from a corporation to avoid the corporate income tax is to find a disguise for what is really a dividend. The word "disguise" is well chosen because the possibilities in this area are numerous. An obvious one is for members of management to take money out as excessive salaries, which are deductible by the corporation, instead of as dividends, which are not. In this case there is not only the likelihood that the Internal Revenue Service will unmask the disguise but there also exists the problem of suits by stockholders who are not participating in these "dividends." Other disguises are low-interest loans to stockholders, excessive fees for professional-type services where the value of the services performed is difficult to establish, excessive rentals or other payments for fixed property or inventory (and, conversely, selling out fixed property or inventory at excessively low prices), personal expenses run through the corporation's books as business expenses, and repurchase of shares by the corporation at excessively high prices.

Income Bonds

While preferred stock offers no tax advantage to the issuing corporation (although as we pointed out, there is a benefit to the taxable corporation that buys preferred stock), income bonds present possible tax savings to the issuing corporation. The terms of an income bond can be drawn so as to be different from preferred stock in name only. Owners of an income bond can have voting rights upon stated conditions without the Internal Revenue Service being able to pin down the issue as preferred stock. Income bonds can provide for cumulation or noncumulation of "arrearages."

DELAYING BOTH THE TAXABLE EVENT AND THE PAYMENT OF THE TAX

Another category of devices is aimed primarily at delaying the payment of the income tax. Any legal delay in payment of a tax is an interest-free loan by the government to the taxpayer. If the delay extends for 20 or 30 years, the interest saving is substantial. There is also another aspect to this subject: income tax rates change from time to time and delaying the tax may enable the taxpayer to set the "taxable event" into a low-rate year. The variation in federal income tax rates has been great. From a starting corporate rate of 1 percent in 1909 the rate increased to 12 percent in World War I, dropped back to 10 percent in the 1920s, increased to 17 percent in the 1930s, peaked at 80 percent in World War II (including the excess profits tax in this rate), varied in the 1950s between 30 and 52 percent, and stood from 1954 to 1963 at 52 percent on amounts over $25,000. The rate dropped to 50 percent in 1964 and to 48 percent for 1965 through 1967 but increased to 52 percent in 1968 and 1969, dropped to 49 percent in 1970 and to 48 percent for 1971 to 1975.

Accelerated Depreciation

One device for delaying the tax is the use of accelerated depreciation methods, which have been available since 1954 for assets with a minimum life of four years. The stated purpose of the government in recognizing accelerated depreciation was that these methods reflect more accurately the pattern of the declining economic value of fixed assets. At the same time, the government shortened the allowable life periods for various assets. There was a deeper reason, however, for the change. A niggardly depreciation allowance for tax purposes encourages business to continue to hold antiquated assets, since their early retirement involves a capital loss rather than recovery as a deduction against ordinary income. Some European countries, notably England, found their industrial plants antiquated in World War II. One of the reasons for this was a low depreciation allowance, since in England capital losses (and gains) are not recognized for income tax purposes.

In addition to these methods of accelerated depreciation, there is a category of special certificates issued by the government establishing even shorter life periods (usually five years). These apply if the proposed assets have defense significance.

It should be noted that even though the benefits of accelerated depreciation are claimed for tax purposes, the company is free to elect regular depreciation for financial reporting to stockholders. When this is done, an appropriate reserve for tax reconciliation on the right-hand side of the balance sheet offsets the higher values at which the assets appear on the left-hand side of the balance sheet. As time passes this reserve is periodically reduced, since the ordinary depreciation method arrives at the same net figure that the accelerated depreciation method had earlier established.

Sale and Leaseback: Lease Rather Than Purchase

Another method of delaying tax payment is the sale and leaseback, or the leasing of property rather than purchasing. The most important reason supporting the use of the lease technique is the tax-saving possible to the lessee, or the company using the asset, since lease payments are tax deductible. One potential disadvantage to the lessee is that the effective rate of interest implied in the lease agreement may be higher than the lessee could get on a loan to finance the purchase.

One tax advantage of the lease is that the life of the lease can be shortened compared to the depreciable life otherwise allowable if the company purchased the asset. Thus there is a delay in paying taxes and, in effect, an interest-free loan by the government to the extent of the delay in taxes. This advantage was, of course, reduced by the 1954 amendments to the Internal Revenue Code, which recognized accelerated depreciation methods. However, there is still the aspect that any loss on premature obsolescence of the asset is fully allowable against ordinary income through the continued rental payments due, whereas disposing of the asset at a loss while owned results in only a capital loss (with its lower effect because of the 25 to 35 percent tax limit on capital gains).

Another tax advantage of the lease is the opportunity to, in effect, depreciate otherwise nondepreciable assets. The principal asset of this type is land. The lease rental covers the cost of the land, which thus becomes deductible.

One possible disadvantage of the lease is that the lessee loses his right to continue to have the asset when the lease expires. However, this is easily handled by giving the lessee the option or a series of successive options to renew the lease for a much reduced rental payment. There is one caution. An option in the lessee to purchase the asset at the expiration of the lease for a small sum can be fraught with danger. The Internal Revenue Service is then in a position to argue that the lease was really an installment purchase contract, resulting in the disallowal of all prior rental payments.

OPERATING LOSS CARRY BACK AND CARRY FORWARD

The matter of averaging income over a number of years has had a checkered history with respect to taxation laws, and provisions covering this area have varied greatly over the last 50 years. Essentially the problem arises from the fact that income taxes are assessed on an annual basis, yet the ordinary income of some taxpayers fluctuates from year to year more than that of others, resulting in an inequity. Fluctuations in capital gains and losses create much less sympathy in Congress.

The most readily available device for meeting this problem is the operating loss carry back and carry forward. Since 1959 the federal tax law permits operating losses to be carried back three years and carried forward five years to be used to offset operating profits in such years and thus in effect to produce a tax on an average of the income. This type of provision, when considered in conjunction with the techniques for fusing two companies, creates substantial possibilities for avoiding taxes. Corporations that have accrued sizable losses and have no prospects for improvement have a ready value in reducing the taxes of the successful corporation. The case for denying tax benefits is easy for the tax authorities where such a "loss corporation" is acquired and dissolved promptly after the ritual has been completed. The 1954 amendments to the Internal Revenue Code also reached out to bar cases in which more than 50 percent of the stock changes hands within two years after purchase. The use of the device of a loss corporation is usually carried out by the successful corporation purchasing the stock of the loss corporation and then filing consolidated returns. The purpose is clearly to avoid contaminating the successful corporation with hidden liabilities of the loss corporations which would occur in the case of a statutory merger.

The other method of averaging income involves the manipulation of a delayed taxable event so that taxes are due on the event in a year in which the corporation would otherwise have a loss. During the period when the tax laws severely limited loss carryovers this was the more sophisticated device used.

INVENTORY PROBLEMS

The Internal Revenue Code does not require any specific form of accounting for inventory but insists that whatever method is used must clearly reflect income and must be used consistently. No change in method (except a shift to last in, first out) can be made without the commissioner's consent; and before that consent is given the commissioner must be satisfied that as a result of the change no income will escape taxation and no delay in taxation will occur. If either will occur, a tax must be paid currently to adjust for the changeover.

Differences in inventory methods can have an important effect on the profit and loss statement and on the balance sheet but do not affect cash flows before income tax payments, although the source and application of funds statement will be affected.

The principal methods of inventory accounting are (1) average cost, (2) average cost or market, whichever is lower, (3) first in, first out (FIFO), and (4) last in, first out (LIFO). The best way to observe the effects of the different methods is to follow a simple illustration. We will dispense with the second method where market is taken as the bid price on the inventory date because its effects are readily understood once we know the other three methods.

Suppose we commence a simple trading operation with the following balance sheet.

Northwestern Trading Company
Balance Sheet, January 1, 1976

Cash	$1,000	Common stock	$1,000

During the year we made purchases of goods to be resold:

January	100 units	$1.00 each
March	100 units	2.00 each
May	100 units	2.40 each

and we sold 210 units in June at $3 each.

What is our profit and what will our balance sheet look like? Under average cost we paid $540 for 300 units, or $1.80 per unit. Units sold cost $378, our profit is $252 (or $630 minus $378), and ending inventory is $162 (or $540 minus $378).

Under FIFO, the units sold cost $324 (100 at $1, 100 at $2, and 10 at $2.40), our profit is $306 (or $630 minus $324), and ending inventory is $216 (or $540 minus $324).

Under LIFO, the units sold cost $450 (100 at $2.40, 100 at $2, and 10 at $1), our profit is $180 (or $630 minus $450), and our ending inventory is $90 (or $540 minus $450).

Neither sales nor purchases were affected by the difference in accounting method but cost of sales, profit, and ending inventory all were affected. In all cases the cost of goods sold plus the value of ending inventory must equal purchases. This can be used as a check on the computation.

One proposition is clear. In a rising price level FIFO gives the higher profit and inventory values and LIFO gives the lower profit and inventory figures with average cost in between. The converse is also true: in a falling price level FIFO gives the lower profit and inventory figures and LIFO gives the higher profit and inventory figures with average cost again falling in between.

Our example was simple and reflected only changes in unit costs of "raw materials." If this had been a manufacturing operation, we would also be involved with different unit costs of labor and manufacturing overhead for each month's operations. These differences in unit costs would be handled in the same way and might have moved in the same direction or in the opposite direction from raw materials cost changes.

There are two points in our illustration to note carefully. The amount by which the earnings of FIFO are larger than LIFO exactly matches the amount by which the FIFO inventory exceeds the LIFO. The "larger" earnings finance the "larger" inventory—but this will not be true when we have to pay an income tax on the "larger" profit. Thus not only do we have an "inventory profit" as part of our total profit under FIFO, but we also have to come up with financing in the amount of the increase in our tax bill. We may be forced to cut dividends to pay the increase in taxes. This is probably why the historical dividend payout percentages for the total economy dropped from 65 percent in the period before World War II to about 50 percent in recent years.

MERGER AND REORGANIZATION PROBLEMS

It is difficult to consider the tax implications of recapitalization, mergers, consolidations, and reorganization without a full discussion of the other problems involved in these activities. Hence tax implications are considered in Chapters 21, 22, and 25 where these areas are developed.

FOREIGN ACTIVITIES

An increasing number of American businesses are becoming involved in various foreign enterprises. In general, the income of a U.S. corporation is subject to the U.S. corporate income tax regardless of where that income is earned. At the same time, individuals who are out of the country for a minimum of 18 continuous months are not taxed on income earned abroad up to $20,000 and after three years up to $25,000.

The device for reaching foreign income has been to *attribute* undistributed income and tax it to U.S. owners of controlled corporations. A foreign corporation is considered controlled if more than 50 percent of its voting stock is U.S. owned, provided at least one U.S. owner holds 10 percent of the voting stock. In an effort to get at the shuffling of funds from one foreign corporation to another, the new legislation taxes "foreign-based company income," which is defined as security income, rents, royalties, and income from sales and services acquired from other persons or corporations in another foreign country.

In an effort to deal with the multiple taxation question, all the income of the controlled foreign corporation is considered distributed if a minimum percentage of net profits, varying with the foreign tax rate, is distributed. If the foreign tax rate is less than 10 percent, 90 percent of the foreign income is considered distributed, and scaling down to no income is considered distributed if the foreign tax rate is 43 percent or more. Thus no income is to be attributed when the sum of the U.S. tax on distributed earnings and the foreign tax on total earnings is 90 percent of the tax that a domestic U.S. corporation would have paid.

In addition, the 1962 act classified any gains realized by a U.S. shareholder owning 10 percent or more of any foreign corporation as ordinary dividend income regardless of the form of the transaction. Likewise, the sale of a patent, copyright, or similar asset by a U.S. parent corporation to a subsidiary controlled by more than 50 percent U.S. ownership is ordinary income.

Finally, U.S. corporations either can deduct from their income the foreign taxes paid or can credit against U.S. taxes due on the foreign income the income tax paid to a foreign country (up to the U.S. tax due on the foreign income). For this purpose all foreign income and foreign taxes paid are lumped together. Prior to 1961 each foreign country was separately considered, thus working to the U.S. taxpayer's disadvantage in that the income of a high-tax foreign country could not be set off against the income of a low-tax foreign country.

In an effort to equate foreign subsidiaries with foreign branches of U.S. corporations, the U.S. corporation must "*gross up*" its foreign subsidiary income by using the preforeign tax income in order to claim the credit for foreign taxes paid.

Preferential treatment is accorded foreign corporations in two areas: less developed countries (except those of Western Europe and Canada, Australia, Japan, and South Africa) and Western Hemisphere Trade Corporations. U.S. corporations are not required to "gross up" income from less-developed countries. In the case of Western Hemisphere Trade Corporations, which now number about 700, the U.S. corporate tax rate is limited to 15.6 percent of the first $25,000 (instead of 22 percent) and 34 percent of the excess (instead of 48 percent). Credit for foreign income taxes paid is applicable to reduce these amounts. To qualify as a Western Hemisphere Trade Corporation, the company must be chartered in the United States, 95 percent of its gross income must originate outside the United States, and 90 percent of its gross income must come from a trade or business.

STATE AND LOCAL TAXATION

While state and local taxation adds up to 42 percent of the total of federal, state, and local taxes, state corporate income taxes are only about 2 percent of total state and local taxes. Property taxes, sales taxes, license fees, and similar monies constitute the bulk of state and local taxes. Personal state income taxes are only about 4 percent of total state and local taxes.

State corporate income taxes average 6 percent of income, but the state income tax is deductible on the federal tax, reducing the effective rate to 3 percent.

The main concern of the state corporate income tax for the financial manager lies in the matter of plant location. Prior to 1959 corporate income was generally taxed only by the state of incorporation. A few states such as Massachusetts, Wisconsin, and Minnesota had anticipated the rule that has ultimately developed and were taxing the income of out-of-state corporations under a formula allocating to the taxing state that proportion of the out-of-state corporation's income determined by the average of

1. The ratio of the sales of the company in the state to the company's total payroll,
2. The ratio of the payroll of the company in the state to the company's total payroll,
3. The ratio of the property of the company in the state to the company's total property.

In 1959 the Supreme Court ruled that states might tax the income from state sales of out-of-state corporations even though the out-of-state corporation did nothing more than send salesmen into the state. Congress promptly canceled this decision by enacting the Interstate Income Tax Law returning the situation to that prior to the court decision and requiring a warehouse, plant, or other basis more substantial than merely sending in salesmen.

The formula just given for determining the proportion of the income of an out-of-state corporation taxable by each state is not exactly the same in each state having a corporate income tax law. Hence to a limited extent there may be overlapping of income and multiple taxation or, conversely, a gap of untaxed income.

TAX MINIMIZATION AS A POSSIBLE OVERRIDING CONSIDERATION

Where tax structures reach excessively high rates, tax minimization can become *the* overriding consideration. Thus in Sweden personal income taxes are so high that individuals cannot be significant suppliers of equity to business firms. On the other hand Swedish tax policy permits businesses to write off buildings over 23 years (compared to 40 in the United States) and *all* other fixed assets over no more than five years. The result is that Swedish corporations are encouraged to adopt improvements quickly and to be risk-takers—becoming tough and effective competitors in the world market. The result also is that when ecological expenditures and benefits are considered, the Swedish standard of living may be the world's highest.

The consequence for Swedish business finance has been a heavier reliance on retained cash as the source of financing. Hence Swedish firms carefully select investments with those growth rates, rates of return, and investment mixes that offset risks and heavy capital requirements so that taxes are minimized. Volvo, for example, is estimated to pay no more than 20 percent in taxes on predepreciation income by minimizing taxable income while maximizing cash flow and turnover.

Even in the United States, firms can minimize somewhat external equity requirements by accelerated depreciation and a *sustained* growth rate. If the growth rate can be maintained indefinitely, the day of tax reckoning can be postponed indefinitely because of the heavy deductions for tax purposes in the early years of a capital-intensive investment. Dividends can be kept to a minimum and the great bulk of the profit taken out via the tax-free merger route while the securities received in the merger are liquidated gradually over time at capital gains rates, thus avoiding the new preference tax on large capital gains. Information about such planning is kept ultra secret in the United States because of the ardor of the Internal Revenue Service. There is a lack of a national policy encouraging risk-taking and new investment except in the so-called tax shelter areas of oil and real estate. The investment tax credit is being increasingly relied upon to stimulate investment. In 1975 the credit was raised to 10 percent on new plant and equipment with lives of seven years or longer.

Summary

Taxes are a vital factor in financing decisions. The main areas of taxation of interest to a financial manager are (1) avoiding multiple taxation and shifting ordinary income to capital gains, (2) delaying tax payments to secure interest-free use of funds (accelerated depreciation and sale and leaseback), (3) averaging income and losses over a period of years, (4) inventory problems, (5) merger and reorganization problems, (6) foreign activities, and (7) state and local taxation.

The exemption of 85 percent of intercompany dividends from income taxation gives particular attractiveness to preferred stock for taxable corporate investors. Corporations with no more than ten shareholders can elect to be taxed as partnerships. The use of personal holding companies and unreasonable accumulation of earnings as devices to avoid taxation are subjected to punitive taxes. The withdrawal of dividends under other disguises is difficult for tax authorities to detect.

Accelerated depreciation is one of the principal ways of delaying the date of tax payment. Another is the sale and leaseback.

Averaging income and losses over a period of years is done through the operating loss carry back (three years) and carry forward (five years).

Inventory methods affect the amount and due date of taxes by determining what income is received in what period. In a period of rising prices FIFO results in the higher profits and taxability but in a period of falling prices LIFO gives the higher profits and taxability.

Before 1962 foreign corporations controlled by U.S. individuals or corporations were taxed only when the income was repatriated, but branches of U.S. firms were fully taxed. Since 1962 legislation has attempted to equalize the tax situation for the various forms in which U.S. corporations do business abroad.

State and local taxes are particularly important in determining plant location. Taxes can reach such proportions that tax minimization reaches overriding importance.

Study Questions

1. Do you think taxation should be a factor for the financial manager to consider in making his decisions or should he permit taxation to enter his thinking only after he has made his decision and then only for the purpose of deciding how and when to execute what he has decided to do?

2. Can a financial manager assume that tax rates or tax rules will remain constant? For example, should he assume that the income tax laws will always distinguish between ordinary income and capital gains? If not, how should he proceed to deal with tax questions in planning?

3. Do you consider the limited liability aspect of a corporation more important than the avoidance of double taxation by using a noncorporate form of business? Would your attitude be influenced by whether you were a rich man or a poor man?

4. Do you think it is wise to place in the minutes of a corporation's board meetings elaborate detail of proposed activities in order to avoid any claim by the Internal Revenue Service of unreasonable accumulation of earnings?

5. Would you as a financial manager favor the use of accelerated depreciation (in any of its several forms)? Do you think the stock market recognizes the consequences of differences in depreciation policies? What evidence is there to support your answer to the preceding question?

6. As a financial manager would you be impressed with the accrued losses of any proposed acquisition because of the tax carry back and carry forward provision of the income tax law? What is the other side of the coin?

7. In view of the fact that over the long run periods of rising price levels have been of much greater duration than periods of falling price levels, what inventory-valuation principle would you recommend to a corporation? Why?

Problems

1. An individual stockholder holds $1 million of current market value of stock of a corporation (such as IBM) which he bought for $10,000 many years ago. The current dividend on this stock is $10,000, and the taxpayer is in the 50 percent

income tax bracket. The stockholder has confidence in the future of the corporation. He understands that if he sells at present he is liable for $197,925 in taxes at capital gains rates (25 percent on first $50,000, 35 percent on excess plus a preference tax of 10 percent on the excess of $495,000 over the sum of $30,000 plus capital gains tax paid of $168,250.) Further, he will be presented with the problem of how to invest the remaining $802,075 which might be placed in tax-exempt municipal bonds at a yield of 5 percent in 1972 (if he accepts a lower rating such as Moody's BAA for New York City bonds). What is your advice to the stockholder?

2. The Catalpa Corporation has a pre-tax earnings record as follows:

1964	$100,000
1965	100,000
1966	(400,000)
1967	—
1968	50,000
1969	50,000
1970	100,000
1971	75,000
1972	(75,000)

What is the total federal income tax of Catalpa for these years? Assume a tax rate of 50 percent.

3. The Western Corporation deals in wheat. The purchase and sale record during the year is set out below. What is the income tax and value of ending inventory if Western uses the FIFO inventory method? What is the tax if LIFO is used? Assume the tax rate is 22 percent on the first $25,000 and 48 percent on the excess over $25,000.

Jan. 10, bought	100,000 bushels at $1.25 a bushel
Jan. 26, bought	5,000 bushels at $1.00 a bushel
Jan. 31, sold	10,000 bushels at $1.15 a bushel
Feb. 6, bought	30,000 bushels at $0.90 a bushel
Feb. 20, bought	5,000 bushels at $1.10 a bushel
Mar. 10, sold	20,000 bushels at $1.20 a bushel
Mar. 16, sold	10,000 bushels at $1.00 a bushel
Mar. 20, sold	50,000 bushels at $1.10 a bushel

4. Gusto Enterprises has experienced unprofitable operations for several years as follows:

1970 loss of	$100,000
1971 loss of	50,000
1972 loss of	10,000 (estimated)

Bright Company has earned $500,000 per year in each of these years. The market value of the assets of Gusto is estimated at $125,000 against a depreciated cost on Gusto's books of $250,000. The total liabilities of Gusto are estimated at $60,000. Bright Company believes it can manage Gusto so as to achieve at least cash break-even operation for several years (excluding depreciation charges). Income taxes are 50 percent on corporate incomes over $25,000 and 22 percent on the first $25,000.

a. What is the maximum price that Bright Company could pay for Gusto and still break even if it buys Gusto in late 1972?

b. What is the maximum price that Small Company, with earnings of $25,000 per year (which it expects will continue), can pay for Gusto and break even, assuming all other facts are the same?

Selected References

Barboli, F. P., "United States Taxation of International Business," *Business Topics,* 12 (Summer 1964), pp. 55–62.

Brittain, J. A., "The Tax Structure and Corporate Dividend Policy," *American Economic Review,* 54 (May 1964), pp. 272–287.

Butters, J. K., J. Lintner, and W. L. Cary, *Effects of Taxation: Corporate Mergers.* Cambridge, Mass.: Harvard University Graduate School of Business Administration, 1951.

Davidson, S., and D. F. Drake, "Capital Budgeting and the 'Best' Tax Depreciation Method," *Journal of Business,* 34 (Oct. 1961), pp. 442–452; "The 'Best' Tax Depreciation Method—1964," *Journal of Business,* 37 (July 1964), pp. 258–260.

Harley, C. E., "Dealings between Closely Held Corporations and Their Stockholders," *Tax Law Review,* 25 (Jan. 1970), pp. 211–341.

Holzman, R. S., *Tax Basis for Managerial Decisions.* New York: Holt, Rinehart and Winston, 1965.

Miller, M. H., "The Corporation Income Tax and Corporate Financial Policies," in *Commission on Money and Credit Stabilization Policies.* Englewood Cliffs, N. J.: Prentice-Hall, 1968.

O'Connor, W. F., "United States Taxation of Earnings of American-Controlled Foreign Corporation," *Taxes,* 42 (Sept. 1964), pp. 588–637.

Shelton, J. P., and C. C. Holt, "The Implications of the Capital Gains Tax for Investment Decisions," *Journal of Finance,* 16 (Dec. 1961), pp. 559–580.

Smith, D. T., *Effects of Taxation on Corporation Financial Policy.* Cambridge, Mass.: Harvard Graduate School of Business Administration, 1952.

Weinrobe, M. D., "Corporate Taxes and the U. S. Balance of Trade," *National Tax Journal,* 24 (Mar. 1971), pp. 79–86.

24

EMPLOYEE STOCK PURCHASE PLANS, STOCK OPTIONS, PROFIT-SHARING, AND DEFERRED COMPENSATION

The corporation can be viewed as a stool supported by three legs: the customers, the employees, and the stockholders. Executive stock options and employee stock purchase plans, though primarily forms of compensation, are closely tied to the values of stock. A poor plan can injure stockholders while a good plan can increase profits for all stockholders.

EMPLOYEE STOCK PURCHASE PLANS

Employee stock purchase plans have a long history. At first such agreements involved isolated individual employees. The motivation of the corporation in encouraging employee purchases varies considerably. Reasons for employee stock purchase plans include stimulating thrift, protecting retirement income against inflation, promoting the free enterprise system, reducing labor turnover, increasing labor productivity, broadening stock ownership, and raising funds without underwriting costs.

A rapid growth of employee stock plans occurred in the 1920s. At the same time, a number of customer ownership plans were introduced in the public utility field. It was difficult at that time to anticipate some of the dire problems that arose with such plans in the 1930s. Typically, such stock purchase plans involved an installment purchase, sometimes over many years. As the economy slumped in the Great Depression, the employee-purchaser frequently found that he still owed more for the unpaid balance than the stock was worth in the current market. Some employees had relied on dividends to help pay for the purchase, but dividends ceased. Many of the stock plans contained various types of agreements that the company would repurchase the stock either when the employment terminated or at any time. Some repurchases were in the form of options (of either the company or the employee) and some were in the form of commitments. Such proposed repurchases by the corporation of its own stock ran afoul of the legal restrictions on share repurchase which we discussed in Chapter 21. Some sympathetic courts were able to find that the employee "purchases" were options or even agreements for "sale or return" so as to relieve the employee of the remaining indebtedness. For the employee to lose both his job and his stock was a double blow.

Today many state statutes provide special rules for employee repurchases, but no law can grant an employee-purchaser equality with creditors—much less priority—in cases of insolvency.

An employee stock plan can be implemented either by the issuance of shares by the corporation or by the purchase of shares by the corporation in the open market as agent for employees. Many plans provide for a discount to employees in the price of the stock from the going market price. Tax law permits a maximum discount of 15 percent on employee shares without depriving the employee of the later tax advantage of a capital gain rather than ordinary income. The discount furnishes a cushion against employee dissatisfaction if the market price of the stock dips.

Employee stock purchase plans expanded rapidly in the 1950s and 1960s and have achieved greatest popularity among financial institutions. Thus in 1966, 36 percent of a sample of 141 stock insurance companies with 200 or more employees had plans and 25 percent of a sample of 171 commercial banks with deposits over $100 million had plans. These two samples included slightly more than half of the insurance companies and banks of such size. In the case of companies whose securities were listed on the New York Stock Exchange, in the spring of 1966 some 251, or 21 percent, had employee stock purchase plans, representing an increase in all types of industry, as indicated in Table 24.1.

Employee stock purchase plans are more numerous among larger companies, as Table 24.2 indicates.

Another study by the exchange indicated that 21 percent of the 30.9 million shareholders in 1970 bought their first shares under an employees stock purchase plan, and that the number of shareholders making their first

Table 24.1. Percentage of Companies Listed on New York Stock Exchange Having Employeee Stock Purchase Plans in 1960 and 1966

Industry	1960	1966
Manufacturing	12%	22%
Utilities	26	41
Retail trade	9	23

Source: Meyer M., and H. Fox, *Employee Stock Purchase Plans*, Studies in Personnel Policy No. 206. New York: National Industrial Conference Board, 1967, p. 5.

purchase through their employer increased 77 percent between 1965 and 1970.[1]

Employee stock purchases have also been melded into employee savings programs. Under such plans the employer contributes to the savings fund, usually in an amount equal to the employee's contribution. The fund is invested partly in the company's stock and partly in fixed-income investments, usually government bonds. One purpose of such plans is to modify

Table 24.2. Percentage of Companies Listed on New York Stock Exchange Having Employee Stock Purchase Plans in 1966, Classified by Industry and Size of Company

Industry	1965 Sales Volume of Company	Percentage of Companies with Plan
Manufacturing	$1 billion and over	46%
	$400–$999 million	29
	$100–$399 million	22
	Under $100 million	12
	All manufacturing	22
Utilities	$200 million and over	53
	Under $200 million	32
	All utilities	41
Retail trade	$300 million and over	33
	Under $300 million	21
	All retail trade	23

Source: Meyer M., and H. Fox, *Employee Stock Purchase Plans,* Studies in Personnel Policy No. 206. New York: National Industrial Conference Board, 1967, p. 5.

[1] New York Stock Exchange, *Shareownership—1970.* New York: The Exchange, 1970, p. 3.

the effect of any fall in the market price of the stock; another achieves a reduction in labor turnover, since if the employee leaves he takes only his own contributions, which were invested in fixed-income investments.

To illustrate the importance of employee stock purchase plans to the financial manager, we can cite the stock-savings plan of Sears, Roebuck and Company which began in 1916 and today owns about 25 percent of the company's outstanding stock. The market value of the company's stock is approximately $3 billion. The Sears plan is limited to a maximum of 5 percent of the employee's salary up to $500 when he joins. On the other hand, American Telephone & Telegraph Company in recent years has permitted employees to subscribe for amounts in excess of 30 percent of their annual salary.

STOCK OPTIONS

A stock option is a right granted most often to management-level employees to buy the stock of the employing company at a set price close to the market price at the time the option is granted. The employee pays nothing for the right, which continues for a number of years and then expires. If the market value of the stock advances during the option period, the employee can exercise his right to purchase at the set price and either retain the stock or dispose of it at a profit. The motivation to the employee is that he will participate in the fruits of his work. This can also be achieved by any profit-sharing arrangement. The particular attraction of the stock option is that the gain may be taxable at the lower capital gains rate rather than the higher rates applicable to ordinary income.

The stock option is a relatively recent phenomenon compared to the stock purchase plan. The reason for the tardy development of the stock option device lies in income tax rules. Until 1939 the Internal Revenue Service regarded all employee stock options as a form of compensation subject to taxation as ordinary income. Then until 1945 the difference between the option price and the market value at the time the option was exercised was taxed as ordinary income only to the extent that this amount could be considered compensation for services. In 1945 the United States Supreme Court ruled that the recipient of an option was taxable on the "paper profits" he realized on the differences between the market price of the stock at the time the option was granted and the option price.[2] This effectively terminated the stock option as an attraction.

[2] *Commissioner vs. Smith,* 324 U.S. 177 (1945).

In 1950 Congress created the concept of a *restricted stock option*. If the option met the requirements set by Congress, no tax was due when it was created and none was due when it was exercised, and only a capital gain would result when the option stock was sold.

Without disturbing the restricted stock options already granted, Congress in 1964 tightened the rules for *qualified stock options* to allow for tax-free status when granted and to qualify for only a capital gains tax when the stock is sold. Rules now require that the option price be equal to market value at the time of the grant. The one receiving the option must exercise it within five years and must be an employee (or within three months of terminating employment), and the stock must be held until three years after the date of the grant for the ultimate gain to qualify as a capital gain. In addition, the one receiving the option must own less than 5 percent of the stock except for companies with less than $2 million in equity. Furthermore, options must be exercised (or expire) in the order in which they were granted.

The 1964 Act also requires stockholder approval of the stock option plan. This is the first time the tax law attempted to provide some protection for stockholders.

The 1969 Tax Reform Act represents the latest and most serious tightening of the tax benefits of stock options for executives. A special tax of 10 percent is imposed at the time the option is *exercised* to the extent the then-unrealized gain exceeds an annual exemption of $30,000. Finally, there will be a regular capital gains tax due at the time the stock is sold. Because the capital gains rate increases to 35 percent over $50,000 in any one year plus the 10 percent preference tax and another special tax of 1.5 percent that may then be due, the total tax on an option gain can reach 46.5 percent. On the other hand, if the executives receive a cash bonus instead of the option gain, in years after 1971 this maximum tax on such earned income (regardless of amount) is 50 percent. Furthermore, the corporation receives a deduction for the cash bonus but no deduction for the option gain.

Hence, except for smaller options where the unrealized gain at time of *exercise* is under $30,000 in that year and the employee has no long-term capital gains in that year, the 1969 Tax Reform Act has effectively terminated the tax benefits of stock options.

Many companies have moved to "phantom" stock options, which give the employees as a cash bonus the amount of gain which the employee would have had if he had a stock option. In short, this is a bonus based not on profits but on "market action" of the stock.

Performance Stock

The stock options just described depend for their value not only on the efforts of the individual receiving the option but also on (1) the efforts of other employees and (2) many events over which the holder of the option has no control. Performance stock is a device to establish a more direct relation between the effort of the employee and his reward. Thus a stated number of shares may be issued at no cost to the employee upon achievement of a specific goal such as attainment of a given level of profit over a number of years in his division. Such stock is treated as ordinary income at its market value when received and is deductible by the corporation as compensation.

This detailed treatment of stock options is warranted by their importance (until recently) in the area of executive compensation. However, it appears that the performance of the stock of companies with stock options does not differ from that of companies without stock options.[3]

Some companies, for example, Allied Chemical, have shifted away from the stock option to granting employees "dividend units," which are simply varying bonuses measured by the amount of dividends the employee would receive if he owned a given number of shares. This substitutes the lesser risk (for the employee) of a change in the dividend rate for the greater risk of a change in the market value of a share. Such bonus amounts are taxable as ordinary income to the employee but are tax deductible by the corporation, whereas ordinary dividends are not.

PROFIT-SHARING AND DEFERRED COMPENSATION

Having examined employee stock purchases and stock options, we can briefly view the principal alternative devices: profit-sharing and deferred compensation. Profit-sharing can be of two types, providing either for immediate cash payment to the employees or for a deferred payment. The immediate cash payment type is simply a bonus. We will consider the deferred payment type, which has financial implications to the corporation.

Guthmann and Dougall have described the usual profit-sharing plan as "profit-sharing without investment"[4] to point out that employee stock pur-

---

[3] Wallace, E., *Appraisal of Stock Options as an Incentive Device*, unpublished Ph.D. dissertation, Columbia University, 1961.
[4] Guthmann, H. G., and H. E. Dougall, *Corporate Financial Policy*, 4th ed. Englewood Cliffs, N. J.: Prentice-Hall, 1962, p. 433.

chase plans involve an investment by the employee. In the typical profit-sharing plan the company's contribution is stated as a percentage of profits before income taxes, since the company's contribution is itself tax deductible if the plan qualifies under the Internal Revenue Act.[5] Profit-sharing has had a rapid growth, from only 37 such plans in existence in 1940 to 3565 plans in 1950 and 33,222 plans in 1963.[6]

Since profit-sharing contributions are tax deductible, the cash drain of the corporation is only half what it would be if employees received an equal amount in dividends.

Deferred profit-sharing requires the annual payment of the shared profit to an independent trustees who administers the fund under the provisions of the plan. The trustee may invest by buying shares of the company's stock. In this case we have the same result as an employee stock purchase plan but with several added and important advantages. The corporation gets tax deductibility for the purchase price of the shares and the employee's tax payment is deferred until he receives a distribution, which may be at retirement. In addition, the earnings of the trust fund are tax free, resulting, in effect, in another deferment of tax. In fact, if the employee dies before retirement or if he terminates employment and the entire amount due him is paid within one year, the entire amount is recognized as a capital gain rather than as ordinary income.

In lieu of investment in the shares of the company the trustee may purchase property which is then leased to the corporation.[7] Here we have the company maintaining the *availability* of cash with which it parted at the time of the profit-sharing payment. The availability is not cost free, since the company will be paying for the use of these funds, but it will have had the advantage of deducting the profit-sharing payment for tax purposes, thus making the amount of available cash twice what would exist in the form of retained earnings.

---

[5] The main requirements under the Internal Revenue Act are that the plan not favor officers and highly paid employees and that there be no possibility of return of the fund to the company when the profits are not to be immediately distributed but are to accumulate in a program that provides for payment to the employee after retirement. The Internal Revenue Service limits tax deductibility by the corporation to 15 percent of the annual compensation of covered employees in the case of deferred plans. Employees have no taxable income until they receive actual distribution.

[6] Metzger, B. L., *Profit-Sharing in Perspective in American Medium-Sized and Small Business.* Evanston, Ill.: Profit Sharing Research Foundation, 1964, p. 6.

[7] The lease must be an "arm's length transaction" or the transaction will run afoul of the Internal Revenue Service, which could result in denial of the tax deductibility of the profit-sharing payments.

Deferred compensation is the term used to describe the postponement of the payment of salary that would otherwise be currently payable. Deferred profit-sharing is a form of deferred compensation but is not considered within the meaning of the term "deferred compensation." Deferred compensation is used to offer a tax advantage to one in a high tax bracket. When the deferred part of the salary is paid at a later date (often after retirement), the taxpayer expects to be in a lower bracket. However, the corporation is not allowed a current tax reduction for the amount of deferred compensation but must wait until actual payment is paid before gaining the deduction. Another reason sometimes advanced for deferred compensation is that the corporation may not be in a position currently to pay the salary requirements of a sorely needed executive.

Deferred compensation presents a number of problems to the executive recipient. First, tax rates may advance between the current year and the year in which payment is scheduled, thus wiping out part of the original tax motives. Second, the executive is deprived of the investment opportunities to which he might currently apply the after-tax salary. This can be partially remedied by adjusting the deferred compensation upward by a compound rate to the date of payment. Third, the executive is exposed to the risks of inflation as to the unpaid balance of his salary. This can be dealt with by agreement to adjust this balance by the use of a price index. Finally, the executive becomes a creditor investor of the business and assumes the risk of bankruptcy.

Summary

Special compensation methods create varying financial consequences for financial managers, since there is an effect on the value of the shares of stock.

Employee stock purchase plans have a long history. In the 1930s repurchase agreements by the corporation and unpaid installment purchases caused serious problems. Currently such plans are increasing, and in 1966 21 percent of all companies listed on the New York Stock Exchange had such plans, with larger companies showing an even higher percentage.

Stock options are used to increase the incentive to management. The particular attraction of options is that they result in capital gains for the holder rather than in ordinary income. A 1945 Supreme Court decision hindered the use of options by holding that any difference in price of the option from the market value of the shares at the date of grant was ordinary income. In 1950 Congress created the concept of a restricted stock option which negated this decision. The rules were tightened in 1964 to provide for qualified stock option plans. Then the 1969 Tax Reform Act limited the tax advantage to small amounts.

Profit-sharing involves no investment on the part of the employee, in contrast with employee stock purchase plans. The company's contribution is tax deductible if the plan meets tax standards and does not exceed 15 percent of eligible employee compensation. The number of profit-sharing plans has grown from 37 in 1940 to 33,222 in 1963.

Deferred compensation involves no current tax deduction to the employing corporation but a deferment of tax to the employee until he actually receives the compensation, which is usually after retirement, thus leveling the income of the employee over the years.

Both profit-sharing funds and deferred compensation funds may be invested in the shares of the employing corporation or may be used to purchase assets for lease to that corporation.

Study Questions

1. As an employee, would you favor a profit-sharing plan or a pension plan if the company is willing to contribute in the current year the same amount toward either plan? You may assume that in the past your company has grown in both profits and sales at a better than average rate.
2. As a company, would you favor the adoption of an employee stock purchase plan or a profit-sharing plan, assuming that the company is willing to contribute the same amount to either plan?
3. As an executive, would you favor a company's program for deferred compensation for yourself if you are 55 years old, earning a large salary, and have accumulated a substantial estate? The deferred compensation is proposed as an alternative to increasing your salary, with a provision that the deferred salary will be increased by an appropriate interest rate to the date of payment.
4. What do you think are appropriate provisions of a profit-sharing plan on the following points:
   a. Who should decide what the investments of the fund will be?
   b. When should the share of each member of the fund be subject to withdrawal?
   c. Should the provision for withdrawal of a member's share provide for a penalty, such as a provision that after one year the forfeiture should be 50 percent, after two years, 40 percent, and so on, until final "vesting" of the entire amount in the employee?
   d. What factors (salary, senority, and so on) should determine the share of each employee in the profit-sharing total?
5. As a stockholder, do you favor the use of stock options as an incentive to key employees? Would your thinking be influenced by the degree to which the employee can affect the profitability of the enterprise by his performance? Or do you think his value is already reflected in his salary?

6. It is sometimes argued that deferred compensation is to be preferred by an employee because he assumes no risk as to the amount of his deferred compensation while under profit-sharing he is exposed to the vicissitudes of the business. Would you therefore prefer deferred compensation?

7. From the point of view of the company, which type of program would you prefer: the employee stock purchase plan, the stock option, the profit-sharing plan, or the deferred compensation plan?

Problems

1. Prepare the terms that you would include in an employee stock purchase plan, covering provisions (if any) that you would include on the following subjects. Give reasons for each position you take.
   a. Whether the company or an independent party such as a bank should handle the administration of the plan.
   b. Whether shares to be purchased under the plan should be issued by the company or bought in the open market.
   c. Whether the plan should be limited to purchase of the company's shares or combined with a savings aspect involving some investment in government bonds or similar assets.
   d. Whether the company should contribute to the plan, and if so, how much and on what basis.
   e. Whether employee funds should be collected by payroll deductions or volunteered from time to time by employees.
   f. Whether there should be any provision for repurchase of the shares by the company, and if so, at what price and at what times.
   g. Whether the plan should permit purchase of shares on credit with installment payment later or should provide for accumulation of money until sufficient funds are on hand for the proposed purchase.
   h. Whether the plan should have a maximum limit per employee.
   i. Whether the plan should require that the employee continue in employment in order to obtain full right to any company contribution.
   j. Any additional provisions.

2. Prepare the terms that you would include in a qualified stock option plan, covering provisions (if any) that you would include. What provisions must be included in order to meet Internal Revenue Service requirements to qualify for delayed capital gain treatment?

3. Prepare the terms of a profit-sharing agreement, including any provisions that would be necessary for the plan to meet the requirements of the Internal Revenue Service.

Selected References

Baker, J. C., "Stock Options at the Crossroads," *Harvard Business Review,* 41 (Jan.–Feb. 1963), pp. 22–31.

Foote, G. H., "When Deferred Compensation Doesn't Pay," *Harvard Business Review*, 42 (May–June 1964), pp. 99–106.

Fox, H., "Deferred Compensation for the Executive," *Business Management Record*, 9 (July 1963), pp. 10–21. (Name of journal changed in 1964 to *Conference Board Record*, monthly, beginning with volume 1.)

———, and M. Meyer, *Employee Savings Plans in the United States*, Studies in Personnel Policy, No. 184, New York: National Industrial Conference Board, 1962.

Goldman, D., "Stock Options—Where to Now?" *Financial Executive*, 39 (Mar. 1971), pp. 51–57.

Holland, D. M., and W. G. Lewellen, "Probing the Record of Stock Options," *Harvard Business Review*, 40 (Mar.–Apr. 1962), pp. 132–150.

Lewellen, W. G., *The Ownership Income of Management*. National Bureau of Economic Research, Fiscal Studies 14. New York and London: Columbia University Press, 1971.

Meyer, M., and H. Fox, *Employee Stock Purchase Plans*, Studies in Personnel Policy No. 206. New York: National Industrial Conference Board, 1967.

Monahan, J. P., and K. B. Monahan, "Company Contributions to Discretionary Profit-Sharing Plans: A Quantitative Approach," *Journal of Finance*, 29 (June 1974), pp. 981–994.

Nemmers, E. E., "Employee Stock Repurchase Agreements," *Marquette Law Review*, 26 (June 1942), pp. 187–196; reprinted in *Current Legal Thought*, 9 (Oct. 1942), pp. 3–7.

25

BANKRUPTCY, LIQUIDATION, AND DISSOLUTION

The financial manager even of a successful company must understand the area of failure if for no other reason than because the company lives in a world where failure is a fact. Failure may involve customers of the firm and thus affect, for example, the accounts receivable. Failure may involve competing firms in the industry and thus unstabilize pricing and other aspects of business vital to the company. Failure may involve a supplier of the firm and jeopardize the flow of incoming materials. Thus there are many points at which failure of another firm may impinge on the financial manager.

It is unfortunately true that as soon as failure is suspected, the typical reaction of the financial manager and of the other executives of outside firms is to seek to withdraw and write off the situation. This in turn leads a firm confronted with financial problems to "cover up" as long as possible, since it is aware of the dire consequences of full disclosure.

A firm's financial problems can almost always be traced, to inadequate management. To proceed as if recessions do not occur, to assume that markets do not shift, to ignore the fact that there is a probability distribution associated with every decision—these are the hallmarks of inadequate management.

It has been suggested that accounting entries are the first type of remedy available to deal with financial failure in its mildest form. This may involve such entries as reducing capital stock to create capital surplus and then charging accrued losses appearing as a deficit in retained earnings against the capital surplus. These accounting entries may be associated with a writing down of asset values. The purpose of this manipulation is to accelerate the date when dividends can legally be paid.

EXTENSION AND COMPOSITION

Both extension and composition involve *voluntary* actions on the part of the firm's creditors. The essential difference between an *extension* and a *composition* is that the former involves the agreement by one or more of the creditors to delay the date of payment of their claims while the latter involves the agreement of *all* the creditors to accept partial payment in full satisfaction of their debts. If only one creditor agrees to partial payment, the arrangement is called an *accord*.

In the case of a small business where the creditors are few and have confidence in the management and the difficulties appear to be temporary, it is possible that an extension and/or composition may be worked out. The incentive to the creditors, obviously, must be that the successful liquidation of their claims plus the potential future profits of the business they expect to do with the debtor warrant the extension. This can be quickly tested. If the principal creditors feel justified in advancing sufficient funds to pay off lesser creditors in full, then the operation of revitalizing the company may be successful. If the principal creditors feel they cannot go this far, then their future activities in participating in the reorganization are self-deluding.

The analysis so far focuses on several items. First there is the need for the consolidation of smaller claims in order to avoid the threat of litigation. The channel often used to consolidate debts in this manner is a loan by a financial institution, and the creditors are paid with the proceeds of this loan. Presumably the debtor has exhausted his possibilities with banks and even with commercial credit companies who accept risks beyond the limits of banks. Presumably also the debtor has exhausted the loan possibilities of assets that can be mortgaged or pledged, such as real estate and accounts receivable. In addition, the cash account has been run down.

It is clear that even if an extension can be established or a composition agreed upon, the business will be without current funds to purchase inventory, meet its payroll, finance receivables, and so on. Unless some assets can be promptly liquidated and new credit or new funds procured on some basis, the prospects will not be encouraging.

SALE AND MERGER AS AN ALTERNATIVE

With the exception of public utilities, one answer to the problem of financial difficulty is to sell or merge the business. In the case of public utilities this answer is not feasible. First, the sale or merger would require the consent of a regulatory agency such as the Interstate Commerce Commission or state public service commissions. Second, the purchaser or surviving company in the merger usually contemplates radical surgery upon the old company such as terminating product lines or selling off facilities. Such surgery on a public utility is not possible without extensive and time-consuming proceedings before abandonment of lines or types of service is permitted.

It is not surprising, then, that most of the cases involving receivership are public utilities, especially railroads and transit companies. Usually industrial companies take the sale and merger route rather than receivership.

MODERN REORGANIZATION AND BANKRUPTCY

The Great Depression brought to a head the festering inadequacies of the law governing reorganization and bankruptcy, particularly in the case of railroads. Bankruptcy is made a matter for federal courts by the U. S. Constitution. It is true that there can be matters such as an assignment for the benefit of creditors which may be settled in state courts, but any unhappy group of three creditors with claims totaling $500 can march the proceedings over to the federal court. After four months in the state court without such a move, however, the federal law concedes jurisdiction to the state court. One important thing that no court but a federal court can grant is a discharge in bankruptcy which terminates all claims. Whatever a state court may do, the debtor's liability cannot be terminated. In the case of a corporation, this is not important, since the corporation can be abandoned.

The Bankruptcy Act of 1898 stood unamended until a hasty amendment for railroads in 1933 and the final amendment in 1938 known as the Chandler Act. In essence, there are now two channels, known as Chapter X and Chapter XI. Section 77, which applies only to railroads, largely follows the pattern of Chapter X and need not be separately discussed. Section 77 was amended in 1948 by the Mahaffie Act.

Chapter XI Proceedings

Chapter XI purports to deal with milder situations and euphemistically identifies the process as an "arrangement." The proceeding is begun only by voluntary petition of the debtor and involves only the unsecured creditors. The court may or may not appoint a trustee or receiver. The proceeding is applicable to corporate or noncorporate debtors. Hearings are held and a plan is developed which may or may not scale down claims and may or may not authorize the issuance of bonds or stock to the creditors for their claims.

Any plan requires the majority approval by number and amount of each class of creditors and binds even dissenting creditors. One principal purpose of Chapter XI is to bring to a halt all actions by creditors who are individually tearing the business apart. Hopeless cases under Chapter XI may be ordered to proceed under Chapter X.

Chapter X Proceedings

Chapter X is the traditional bankruptcy section. Proceedings may be begun voluntarily by the debtor or forced (involuntary) by petition of three or more creditors with provable claims totaling at least $500 who can prove that one of the six acts of bankruptcy occurred in the preceding four months. These acts of bankruptcy are the following:

1. Transferring or concealing assets with intent to defraud creditors.
2. Transferring property to a creditor with intent to prefer him while insolvent (excess of liabilities over assets).
3. Permitting a creditor to obtain preference in legal proceedings, such as obtaining a lien or judgment while insolvent (excess of liabilities over assets).
4. Making a general assignment for the benefit of creditors.
5. Permitting a receiver to take charge while insolvent (excess of liabilities over assets or inability to pay debts as they become due).
6. Admitting in writing inability to pay debtors and willingness to be adjudged bankrupt on that ground.

Pending the hearing on the bankruptcy petition, the court may appoint a receiver. Once court jurisdiction is established, the court appoints a disinterested party as trustee, although a person from the old business may be appointed a co-trustee. A meeting of creditors is held and all claimants are required to file and prove their claims. The trustee and any other interested party may propose reorganization plans, and hearings are held on all plans. The SEC renders an advisory report to the court on the plans.

Fair and Feasible Plan of Reorganization

The critical words are that any reorganization plan that is to be approved must be "fair and feasible." Fairness presents no problem. A plan is fair only if it meets the rule of absolute priority that we have already discussed. But what meets the standard of feasibility is a difficult question indeed. The plan, if approved by the court, requires a two-thirds vote of each class of creditors by value. Only a majority of the stockholders is required if assets exceed liabilities. If no fair and feasible plan is found, then the matter proceeds to liquidation and dissolution.

Feasibility of a reorganization plan is best handled by examining a number of cases. However, we can indicate generally some of the issues involved. A business under the control of a bankruptcy court clearly involves greater uncertainty as far as forecasting its future is concerned than would be true if the heavy hand of the law were not upon it. The statute specifying that the plan of reorganization must be "feasible" does not offer one word of explanation. By the time proceedings in the case have reached the point of considering feasibility, heavy expenses of administration have been incurred and the willingness to prolong litigation has weakened. Many plans have gone into operation despite serious doubts as to their feasibility because the exhausted parties have been unable to see much marginal value in trying to improve the feasibility of the plan.

Feasibility of a plan involves a probability distribution. The statute specifies no standard of probability, but the law falls back on the vague standard of a "reasonable" probability when the statute says nothing.

In all considerations of feasibility it is clear that forecasting the future revenues and expenses of conducting the business under the plan is a basic problem. Even if such forecasts can be made, problems remain about what type of capital structure is feasible, given the assumed future revenue and expense forecast.

The feasibility of a proposed capital structure is examined first in terms of the appropriate capitalization rate to apply to estimated income in order to establish the total of the capital structure. Then the division of the capital structure among debt, preferred stock, and common stock is considered together with some examination of the problem of annual variability in the forecast income stream.

Because of the high level of uncertainty involved in this whole process, an attempt may be made to mollify the parties and grease the plan through by using warrants to purchase future common stock. Such warrants appear attractive to the various parties because if the estimates on which the plan is based later turn out to have been pessimistic, then some kind of equity will prevail for those who were (mistakenly?) frozen out in the reorganization plan. They will have a chance to recoup their losses.

But this method of proceeding has been challenged by the SEC in its advisory reports.[1] First the SEC argues that things of value (warrants) are being given to those who have no value or position in the reorganization. Second, the SEC objects that future financing is being hampered—at least

---

[1] The SEC renders advisory reports to federal courts on proposed reorganization plans under Section 1738, Chapter X, of the Bankruptcy Act.

future common stock cannot be sold on as favorable terms as it could if no warrants were outstanding. To this extent the (future?) feasibility of the reorganization plan is being jeopardized.

The infinite variety of the question of feasibility is demonstrated in the Northeastern Steel Corporation case. Here the proposed plan involved the taking over of the defunct Northeastern Steel by Carpenter Steel, and the discussion shifted to how feasible Carpenter's capital structure might be after acquisition on the terms proposed by Carpenter.

Theory of Receivership, Reorganization, and Bankruptcy

Until recent years, little work has been done in the theory of corporate failure. Initial effort[2] has been directed at determining the variables that indicate impending corporate failure. It is important that modern theoretical work in this area begins with ratio analysis so widely used by practitioners in finance but downgraded as arbitrary rules of thumb by many theorists.

Tests of various ratios suggest[3] the most reliable ratios indicating impending failure are, in order of reliability, (1) retained earnings/total assets, (2) earnings before interest and taxes/total assets, and (3) working capital/total assets.

These results are not surprising. As a firm begins to slip, its retained earnings feel the first impact as the directors are reluctant to cut dividends. As earnings decline further, liquidity problems increase even though dividends have been terminated.

The debt-to-equity ratio (as a measure of financial leverage) and the sales-to-total-assets ratio (as a measure of asset turnover) are valuable *when used in conjunction* with the first three ratios. The higher the debt-to-equity ratio and the lower the asset turnover, the greater the risk of bankruptcy.

Further study[4] has sought to include the risk of bankruptcy in the

---

[2] Cohen, K., T. Gilmore, and F. Singer, "Bank Procedures for Analyzing Business Loan Applications," in *Analytical Methods in Banking*, K. Cohen and F. Hammer Eds. Homewood, Ill.: Richard D. Irwin, 1966, pp. 218–251; Beaver, W. H., "Financial Ratios as Predictors of Failure,"—*Empirical Research in Accounting: Selected Studies*, supplement to *Journal of Accounting Research* (1966), pp. 71–111; and Altman, E. I., "Financial Ratios, Discriminant Analysis and the Prediction of Corporate Bankruptcy," *Journal of Finance*, 23 (Sept. 1968), pp. 589–609.

[3] Altman, E. I., *op. cit.*, pp. 594–597.

[4] Altman, E. I., "Corporate Bankruptcy Potential, Stockholder Returns and Share Valuation," *Journal of Finance*, 24 (Dec. 1969), pp. 887–900. An earlier study is Fisher, L., "Determinants of Risk Premiums on Corporate Bonds," *Journal of Political Economy*, 67 (June 1959), pp. 217–237.

valuation formulas discussed in Chapters 18 and 19. Specifically, the variable measuring the stockholders' investment might be the amount they *could* have received had they sold prior to bankruptcy (or *would* have invested had they bought prior to bankruptcy). Alternatively, investors holding for a long time prior to bankruptcy might compute their return as including pre and postbankruptcy dividends.

VOLUNTARY LIQUIDATION AND DISSOLUTION
UNDER CORPORATION STATUTES

The theoretical basis for liquidating a company is that the assets of the business, when sold for cash, will yield more than the same assets employed in the business. But the legal rules of reorganization and bankruptcy protect creditors when their position is threatened. In the case of stockholders the courts have repeatedly held that a corporation that is steadily losing money cannot be forced to liquidate unless the stockholders by the required statutory vote of two thirds decide to dissolve. There is only one qualification to the rule, namely, that those in control must be proceeding in good faith, free of fraud and self-dealing. Ignorance is not evidence of bad faith. It is not enough to offer clear proof that the buildings and other assets of the firm can be sold for two and three times the amount at which they are carried on the books of the losing company. The reasoning of the law is quite simple: corporate stock is a plane ticket to wherever the majority wants to go, provided the statute permits the trip, and subject only to specific rules of the statute.

However, once the corporation has become entangled with Chapter X of the Bankruptcy Act, the court, under existing legislation, must proceed to liquidation and dissolution if no fair and feasible plan can be proposed.

Voluntary dissolution would be followed in the belief that more can be realized by a piecemeal sale of the assets by the existing management than by a sale of the entire business as a unit. The corporation laws of the various states specify how dissolution is to be carried out.[5] A resolution of dissolution is adopted first by the board of directors and then by a two-thirds vote of the stockholders present at the meeting. A plan of dissolution is then adopted, again by a two-thirds vote of the stockholders present after written notice setting forth the plan has been distributed to all stockholders. Under the statutes the plan of dissolution may provide (after payment of

---

[5] The following outline of dissolution statutes is based on the laws of Wisconsin (*Wis.Stats.* 1973, Chaps. 181.50–181.55) but is representative of modern state corporate statutes.

all liabilities or adequate provision therefor) either for the distribution of the excess to the stockholders *or* for any other distribution if the articles and bylaws do not specify return to the members.

The reason for setting out what appears to be detail is to emphasize that a corporation is a creature of the state and that its conduct must conform to statutes. Thus if two thirds of the stockholders desire to forgo the return of their money and desire to dispose of it otherwise, the remaining third has no choice in the matter. Indeed, failure to follow the statute creates liabilities. Likewise, such failure results in the forfeiture of benefits granted by the statute, such as the shortening of the period of the statute of limitations on claims.[6]

Thus finance textbooks are misleading when they recommend that voluntary dissolution be carried out by a common law assignment or a statutory assignment or an assignment with settlement, stating that such procedures are superior to bankruptcy. An assignment can never result in a discharge of the debtor's liability. The debtor can be haunted by creditors as long as the statute of limitations permits. Furthermore, it is clear that an assignment for the benefit of creditors is itself an act of bankruptcy. In an effort to avoid the expense and delay of bankruptcy, such a maneuver plays into the hand of bankruptcy. The only reason that the practice of assignment continues in the case of corporations is that no one seems to care what the liabilities of a corporation are once its assets are gone. But even here there is danger, since those who receive the assets in the case of an assignment can be forced to give them up so that a bankruptcy proceeding can examine who is entitled to them.

The state has specified a simple, direct way for a corporation to liquidate. In the case of a sole proprietorship or partnership, the use of an assignment is also to be avoided. Even when the debtor obtains a release from every creditor in such a program, claims can continue to be made until the final toll of the statute of limitations. Since the statute does not run during infancy, incapacity, or absence of the defendant from the state, that toll may be a lifetime away. In addition, in the case of a sole proprietorship or partnership, all the assets of the owners are subject to claims of the business and not just business assets. The only exceptions are the small exemptions allowed by statute in each state. Thus an assignment for the benefit

---

[6] A statute of limitations defines the period within which a claimant must act in court or lose his claim. Dissolution statutes provide for a shortening of this period (in many cases from six to two years) if the statute is followed.

of creditors which does not include every asset of the debtor is a fraudulent act and all the releases obtained are subject to being set aside.

LIQUIDATION IN BANKRUPTCY

When a Chapter X proceeding has reached the point where the court has determined that no plan of reorganization is fair and feasible, the case proceeds to liquidation. At this point all claims will have been determined and appraisals completed, both being prerequisites to the decision concerning whether a fair and feasible plan of reorganization is possible.

All that remains are the sale of assets and the distribution of proceeds. Despite the best efforts of competent appraisers, the sale of assets usually produces surprises. The assets are offered for bid individually, in various combinations, and finally as an entire unit. That set of bids will prevail which yields the greatest cash total. There may be problems when mortgaged property is involved and the proceeds of the sale of the mortgaged property are insufficient for the secured debt. If offered as part of the total business, the mortgaged property may increase the total proceeds compared to a separate offer. How should this increase be allocated between secured and unsecured creditors?

The sale must be confirmed by the court and may be set aside if the court for any reason is dissatisfied.

The order of priority of distribution of the proceeds of the sale to satisfy claims is as follows:

1. The costs of administering the proceedings and of operating the property during proceedings, including any trustee's certificates for new money granted priority by the court.
2. Unpaid wages up to $600 per person if earned within three months before the date of filing of the petition.
3. Unpaid taxes due the United States or any state or subdivision thereof.
4. Secured creditors to the extent of the proceeds of the specific property mortgaged, and as to any balance due, the secured creditors qualify as general creditors.
5. General or unsecured creditors.
6. Stockholders, with any stock having preference coming first.[7]

The sale having been confirmed and the proceeds distributed, the case is now ready for the issuance of a discharge in bankruptcy. Only one such discharge can be granted to the same person in any six-year period.

[7] In state proceedings the order of priority is generally the same except that (2) and (3) are reversed, namely, taxes come before wages and (4) comes even before (1).

Summary

Failure in finance is a matter of degree. Insolvency in the equity sense means inability to meet debts as they mature. Insolvency in the bankruptcy sense means excess of liabilities over assets.

Insolvency in the equity sense subjects the company to supervision by a court of equity. Before this occurs creditors may extend their due dates. If all creditors agree to an extension of their maturities and to acceptance of partial payment, the transaction is called a composition. In view of the great changes in American business in recent years, the prospects for a composition are slim.

In the old equity receivership the hopes of creditors rested on new funds entitled to priority and correction of management deficiencies while the court-appointed receiver managed the business. Unless a plan of reorganization could be worked out, the company was thrown into bankruptcy for liquidation.

There are two rules of priority: absolute and relative. Under absolute priority (enforced as the law since a Supreme Court decision in the 1930s) bonds must be paid in full in the order of their priority before anything is paid to stock. In short, the priorities agreed to in securities are enforced. Under relative priority each prior class must merely receive relatively more than each succeeding class, even though it is not paid in full (as provided in its security) before anything passes to the next lower level of priority.

As an alternative to reorganization, a company may consider merging before the more drastic losses of bankruptcy set in.

Milder problems are dealt with currently under Chapter XI of the Bankruptcy Act in a process called an "arrangement." This process can be begun only by voluntary petition of the debtor and involves only the unsecured creditors. A plan is developed after majority approval by creditors and it binds even dissenting creditors.

Liquidation is in order when the assets of a business are worth more when sold than when used in the business.

Legal rules govern liquidation to make certain that creditors receive their priority. But a corporation that is meeting its obligations cannot be forced to liquidate no matter what its losses unless two thirds of the stockholders at the meeting vote to liquidate. This is on the assumption that the corporation commits none of the acts of bankruptcy.

Liquidation may be ordered once the company is in bankruptcy if no fair and feasible plan of reorganization can be developed. But liquidation may be voluntarily undertaken by a two-thirds vote of the stockholders even if no losses have been suffered.

If liquidation will not yield sufficient funds to pay all debts, an individual should proceed through bankruptcy in order to obtain a discharge, which can only be granted by a *federal* court. Otherwise the individual continues to be liable for unpaid debts. In the case of a corporation there is less concern, since only the corporation (not the stockholders) continues to be liable if there is no discharge by a federal court.

The order of priority in liquidation is

1. Expenses of administration
2. Wages up to $600 per employee for the prior three months
3. Taxes
4. Secured creditors
5. Unsecured creditors

If no such plan can be developed under Chapter XI, the matter proceeds to bankruptcy under Chapter X. Or proceedings may be initially started voluntarily or involuntarily (by three or more creditors) under Chapter X upon proof of any of six acts of bankruptcy.

Under Chapter X any proposed reorganization plan must be "fair and feasible." If no plan can be had, liquidation is in order. To be "fair," a plan must follow the absolute priority principle. To be "feasible" it must offer a reasonable probability that the firm will not return to the bankruptcy court. The heart of any plan involves forecasting the future income of the reorganized company and the use of a realistic rate of capitalizing such income. Given these conditions, a financial structure can often be designed that provides reasonable coverage for any senior securities involved in the plan.

Study Questions

1. The argument supporting the prevailing practice of firms in shunning any firm involved in financial difficulty is that their time and energy are more profitably employed in pursuing their normal activities rather than in trying to improve the amount that can be salvaged from a firm in financial difficulty. Is there social waste in permitting business firms to follow this policy?

2. Would you favor a law prohibiting accounting entries that reduce the capital stock account to wipe out accrued losses so that dividend payments can be resumed as soon as earnings improve? Is there any disadvantage to the investor in permitting this practice?

3. Should a company in financial difficulty concentrate its management talent on developing favorable merger opportunities or should management focus on rehabilitating the company?

4. Considering the "efficient" view as to where to apply management's efforts when another firm is in financial difficulty, do you think that present-day management is being inefficient in pursuing the area of mergers rather than that of internal expansion, particularly when the typical merger involves one partner of the merger who is in a weak position financially?

5. Would it be possible to list criteria by which to judge the feasibility of a plan of reorganization? What do you think such criteria might be?

6. Do you believe that merging two unsuccessful companies can produce a profitable company or would it merely compound the failure? Explain your position.

7. Should the court give weight to the current market value of the several types of securities of a debtor corporation when considering proposed reorganization plans?

8. It has been said that attempting to effect a composition is like poking your finger into a balloon—it merely gives somewhere else. The metaphor refers to the fact that the last few persons to sign an agreement of composition realize that nothing will happen if they fail to sign. Realizing this, they are aware that they might demand payment in full. Does this mean that all efforts at composition are wasteful?

9. If a corporation faces a serious threat of bankruptcy, what alternatives does it have?

10. Why would any corporation be dissolved when its accrued losses are a valuable asset for tax purposes to any successful corporation?

11. Can you advance any reason why a corporation would realize more out of a liquidation sale than it could out of its earlier efforts to merge?

12. As the financial manager of a creditor, what are your reactions when you are called by other creditors who seem interested in pushing the debtor into a liquidation?

13. If you are the financial manager of a company and someone in the company proposes buying assets from a company that is liquidating, what are the considerations that enter your mind for evaluation?

14. Why do some firms not liquidate when their present assets are worth more in the market place than the values at which they are carried on the books of the firm, especially if their earnings are subnormal?

Problems

1. Swinger Enterprises landed in reorganization. Fundamentally, growth had not been controlled. In an effort to move too quickly the company acquired assets for expansion too far ahead of its ability to finance the increase. By the time the officers understood what they had done, the possibility of procuring additional equity was reduced to very unfavorable terms. The owners preferred to go through the wringer rather than dilute ownership on such unfavorable terms. The current balance sheet is given in Table 25.1.

    The building account represents a $300,000 expansion of the old building but only $200,000 of the expansion has been finished. The contractor ceased work

Table 25.1. Swinger Enterprises Balance Sheet

Assets		Liabilities	
Cash	$ 1,000	Bank loan	$300,000
Receivables	99,000	Accounts payable	120,000
Inventory	400,000	Accrued expenses	100,000
Total current assets	500,000	Accrued taxes	60,000
Prepaid expenses	10,000	Total current liabilities	580,000
Land	40,000	Net worth, 1000 shares, $100 par	100,000
Buildings, net	300,000	Retained earnings	300,000
Machinery, net	130,000	Total net worth	400,000
Total assets	$980,000	Total liabilities and net worth	$980,000

when progress payments were not maintained and threw Swinger into reorganization for the unpaid balance of $60,000 currently due him. Accrued taxes of $60,000 include $30,000 in taxes past due. The bank holds a pledge of the accounts receivable and a mortgage on the land and buildings. The mortgage is of doubtful validity, since it was taken in recent months as added security. The confused state of Swinger's finances has caused a drop in Swinger's current sales as doubt has spread regarding the firm's ability to meet delivery schedules.

The receiver has developed several proposals.

First, half of the land is held for future expansion. The receiver has procured a buyer willing to pay $20,000 for this half of the land and willing to grant an option to repurchase it at $30,000 at any time in the next two years.

Second, the receiver has procured a tenant willing to occupy the unused space in the new building for warehouse purposes at an annual rental of $7500 for the next two years payable monthly at the end of each month.

Third, the receiver has obtained an offer to buy the finished-goods inventory of $100,000 at $110,000.

Fourth, the bank has agreed that if these steps are taken it will advance $60,000 for working capital on the security of the receiver's certificates (granted priority by the court) provided all other cash realized is applied to payments, first to past due taxes and then to other accounts payable and accrued expenses.

Fifth, the contractor has agreed to accept notes due in 18 months secured by a mortgage having priority over the bank's claim. The owners have agreed that no dividends will be paid and no shares repurchased without the bank's consent. The officers have agreed to a 25 percent salary cut for the next two years, totaling $12,000, and will receive favorable options on stock in lieu thereof.

a. Evaluate the situation in view of the proposals. Assume a 50 percent income tax rate applicable to all profits.

b. What is the most important missing piece of information?

c. What motivated the bank in its agreement?

d. Which asset valuation do you consider most critical in the proposed situation?

2. Canned Foods, Inc., decided to liquidate voluntarily and consented to a receiver taking over its assets on June 21, 1972. At that time the company owed the Citizens Bank a first mortgage loan of $25,000 secured by its real estate and dated April 1, 1969, carrying 5 percent interest. Accrued interest is $3342 to date. The company also owed the bank on a loan of $44,939 dated March 15, 1969, carrying 5 percent interest, on which interest of $4841 is accrued to date. This loan was secured by a second mortgage on the real estate and warehouse receipts covering the company's inventory of 7507 cases of canned corn. The total indebtedness of the first mortgage loan to its date of payment from sale proceeds was $28,342. The total indebtedness on other loan to its date of payment was $49,780.

The company owed wages and taxes of $3127 and general claims of $26,931 on June 21, 1972. Wages totaled $540, due one man for the last two months of work.

The receiver had expenses as follows during his operation:

Receiver's fee	$ 1,600
Attorney's fee	1,500
Advertising expense	807
Auction expense	313
Real estate taxes	4,655
Personal property taxes	596
Miscellaneous	2,479
Storage charges	3,013
Cost of corn sales	3,656
Total	$18,619

The sales conducted by the receiver produced the following results:

Real estate	$ 45,000
Machinery sale	19,000
Corn sales	39,000
Warehouse rent	600
Sale of supplies	4,285
Insurance proceeds	1,835
Total	$109,720

What distribution should the receiver make?

3. Wilson Manufacturing Company was placed in bankruptcy by some of its employees who had unpaid wages due them. At that point in time the company's balance sheet was as given in Table 25.2.

Table 25.2. **Wilson Manufacturing Company Balance Sheet**

Assets			Liabilities	
Cash		$ (670)	Accounts payable	$41,282
Accounts receivable		3,450	Accrued expenses	27,620
Inventory		27,413	Accrued taxes	7,380
Total current assets		$30,193	Total current liabilities	76,282
Prepaid insurance		602	Realty mortgage loan	27,132
Fixed assets			Net worth, 200 shares,	
Building	$31,117		$100 par, common stock	20,000
Equipment	6,830		Deficit	(59,992)
	37,947			
Depreciation	5,320	32,627		
Total assets		$63,422	Total liabilities and net worth	$63,422

The accounts payable include one item of $4662 due a supplier who also owes Wilson $2815. The accrued expenses include the following:

John Starr	$ 753	Wages for last two months
Bill Oar	840	Wages, of which $520 is for last three months and $320 previously
Oscar Goodman	300	For booking service "Mail me Monday"
Marion Crost	458	Wages for last three months
Priscilla More	210	Disputed wages, claim is six months old
	$2,561	

Bankruptcy expenses to date have been $4315.

Upon sale of the assets, the proceeds given in Table 25.3 are realized (two sets of assumed figures).

Prepare the distribution of proceeds under each assumed set of facts.

Table 25.3. Wilson Manufacturing Company Proceeds upon Sale of Assets

	Assumption 1	Assumption 2
Receivables, other than the one supplier who owes Gungho $2815	$ 320	$ 0
Inventory	15,000	680
Prepaid insurance	380	380
Building	27,222	23,146
Equipment	4,500	6,000
	$47,422	$30,206

Selected References

Altman, E. I., "Financial Ratios, Discriminant Analysis and the Prediction of Corporate Bankruptcy," *Journal of Finance,* 23 (Sept. 1968), pp. 589–609.

——, "Corporate Bankruptcy Potential, Stockholder Returns and Share Valuation," *Journal of Finance,* 24 (Dec. 1969), pp. 887–900.

——, *Corporate Bankruptcy in America.* Lexington, Mass.: Heath Lexington Books, 1971.

Ballantine, H. W., *Ballantine on Corporations,* rev. ed. Chicago: Callaghan & Company, 1946.

Beaver, W. H., "Financial Ratios as Predictors of Failure," *Empirical Research in Accounting: Selected Studies,* supplement to *Journal of Accounting Research* (1966), pp. 71–111.

Calkins, F. J., "Corporate Reorganization under Chapter X—A Post Mortem," *Journal of Finance,* 3 (June 1948), pp. 19–28.

——, "Feasibility in Plans of Corporate Reorganizations under Chapter X," *Harvard Law Review,* 61 (May 1948), pp. 763–781.

Cohen, K., J. Gilmore, and F. Singer, "Bank Procedures for Analyzing Business Loan Applications," in *Analytical Methods in Banking,* K. Cohen and F. Hammer, Eds. Homewood, Ill.: Richard D. Irwin, 1966, pp. 218–251.

Edmister, R. O., "An Empirical Test of Financial Ratio Analysis for Small Business Failure Prediction," *Journal of Financial and Quantitative Analysis,* 7 (Mar. 1972), pp. 1477–1493.

Gordon, M. J., "Towards a Theory of Financial Distress," *Journal of Finance,* 26 (May 1971), pp. 347–356.

Murray, R. F., "Lessons for Financial Analysis," *Journal of Finance,* 26 (May 1971), pp. 327–332.

Van Arsdell, P. M., *Corporation Finance.* New York: Ronald Press, 1968, chaps. 48–53.

Walter, J. E., "Determination of Technical Insolvency," *Journal of Business,* 30 (Jan. 1957), pp. 30–45.

GLOSSARY
OF FINANCIAL TERMS

Absolute Priority. The right of senior creditors and stockholders to be paid in full before any junior issues receive anything. For example, if there are $500,000 in assets, $100,000 in bonds, $500,000 in preferred stock, and $500,000 in common stock, the bondholders are paid in full, the preferred stockholders get 80 cents on the dollar, and the common stockholders nothing.

Accelerated Depreciation. Depreciation at a faster rate than usual. In recent years the term has been used to refer to *tax amortization certificates,* which (upon government consent) allow writing off an asset in five years for income tax purposes regardless of its life. Also recently used to describe *sum-of-the-years' digits method of depreciation, constant percent of declining balance method of depreciation,* and *double declining balance method of depreciation.*

Account Payable. A debt, owed by an enterprise, that arises in the normal course of business dealings and has not been replaced by a note payable of a debtor. For example, bills for materials received but not yet paid.

Account Receivable. A debt, owed to an enterprise, that arises in the normal course of business dealings and is not supported by negotiable paper. For example, the charge accounts of a department store. But income due from investments (unless investments are the business itself) is not usually shown in accounts receivable.

Accrued Interest. Interest that has been earned but is not yet paid or payable.

Acquisition. A generic term covering all forms of acquiring another firm, such as *consolidation, holding company, merger,* purchase of assets by cash or stock.

After-Acquired Property Clause. A clause in a mortgage providing that any property acquired by the borrower after the date of the loan and mortgage will automatically become additional security for the loan.

After-Market. The term describing the market for a security after it has been initially sold by the issuer through *underwriters.*

Aging of Accounts. Arranging the accounts (such as receivables or payables) in chronological order and grouping the accounts by intervals, such as accounts less than 30 days old, 30 to 60 days old, and so on.

Amortization. A reduction in a debt or fund by periodic payments covering interest and part of principal, distinguished from (1) depreciation, which is an allocation of the original cost of an asset computed from physical wear and tear as well as the passage of time, and (2) depletion, which is a reduction in the book value of a resource (such as minerals) resulting from conversion into a salable product.

Annuity Bond. A bond without a maturity date, that is, perpetually paying interest.

Arrangement. In law, the term applied to the plan resulting from a *receivership* proceeding under Chapter XI of the Bankruptcy Act.

Bankruptcy. A legal method by which a debtor may be relieved of his financial obligations. A court, through a trustee, takes the debtor's property and distributes it among his creditors in proportion to their respective claims against him. Bankruptcy is subject to federal law and may be voluntary or involuntary. There are six acts, any one of which constitutes bankruptcy: (1) making a general assignment for creditors, (2) admitting in writing inability to pay debts, (3) concealing or conveying property with intent to defraud creditors; and the following three acts if done while insolvent: (4) preferring one creditor, (5) failing to discharge a lien within 30 days, or (6) permitting a receiver to take over while unable to meet debts as they mature.

Basis Point. In government securities one one hundredth of 1 percent (or of one unit) change in the yield (or price) of the security. Because government securities move less in absolute dollar amounts than other securities, though relatively the movement in their price may be more significant, the term "basis point" has come into use as a shorthand method of referring to absolute changes that would be more cumbersome to express in customary terms.

Bearer Bonds. Bonds payable to the person having possession of them. Such bonds do not require endorsement to transfer ownership but only the transfer of possession.

Bear Market. A market in which prices are falling or are expected to fall.

Big Board. A popular term referring to the board showing the current prices of securities listed on the New York Stock Exchange.

Blue Sky Laws. State laws governing securities. So called because they are designed to protect investors from purchasing a piece of the blue sky (worthless securities). Different in principle from the current federal legislation directed only at disclosure. Blue sky laws may also extend to determination of the legitimacy of the proposed financing.

Bond. (1) A written promise to pay the holder a sum of money at a certain time (more than one year after issue) at a stated rate of interest. A debt due in less than one year from the date of issue is usually called a note. (2) In suretyship the obligation of a guarantor to pay a second party upon default by a third party in the performance the third party owes to the second party.

Book Value. (1) The value of an outstanding share of stock of a corporation at any one time, determined by adding the par (or stated) value of the stock outstanding to the surplus applicable to that class of stock and dividing by the number of shares of that class outstanding. (2) The valuation at which assets are carried on the books, that is, cost less reserve for depreciation.

Break-Even Point. There are three break-even points: the *cash break-even point, the financial break-even point,* and the *profit break-even point.* When only the term "break-even point" is used, profit break-even point is the one intended. The formula is BE = FC/(1 − variable cost ratio), where FC is the fixed cost in dollars for any output, and the variable cost ratio is the ratio of variable costs in dollars to sales in dollars for any output.

Broker. An agent of a buyer or a seller who buys or sells stocks, bonds, commodities, or services, usually on a commission basis.

Bull Market. A market in which prices are rising or are expected to rise.

Business Risk. In finance, the risk of default or variability of return arising from the type of business conducted.

Call. (1) An option permitting its holder (who has paid a fee for the option) to call for a certain commodity or security at a fixed price in a stated quantity within a stated period.

The broker is paid to bring the buyer and seller together. The buyer of this right to call expects the price of the commodity or security to rise so that he can call for it at a profit. If the price falls, the option will not be exercised. The reverse transaction is a *put*. (2) A demand by a corporation for payment against stock subscribed but not fully paid. (3) Notice by a corporation that it will redeem securities on a given date.

Call Premium. The amount over *par* or *face value* payable by the issuer of the security upon calling a security in for payment or redemption.

Capital. (1) In accounting the amount invested in a business. (2) In economic theory there are several meanings. "Capital" may be used to mean (a) capital goods, that is, the tools of production, (b) the money available for investment, or invested, (c) the discounted value of the future income to be received from an investment, (d) the real or money value of total assets. (3) In law "capital" means capital stock.

Capital Budgeting. The analysis of investment projects to determine the *rate of return* of the investment and the *cost of capital* required to undertake the investment so as to compare the proposed investment with other opporunities and to decide under all the circumstances whether to make the investment commitment. Differences in risks are important in the computation.

Capital Gains Tax. A provision in the income tax that profits from the sale of capital assets are taxed at separate (lower) rates than the rate applicable to ordinary income.

Capital Market. The market for long-term investment funds. Thus primarily investment bankers, savings banks, insurance companies, pension funds, and trust companies are involved. See *money market*.

Capital Structure. In finance the total of bonds (or long-term money) and ownership interests in a corporation, that is, the stock accounts and surplus.

Figure A.   Cash and financial break-even points.

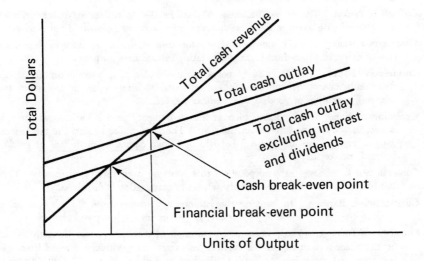

Cash Break-Even Point. Assuming a plant organized for a given ideal volume of output, if units of output are put on the x axis and total dollars on the y axis, the cash break-even point is the intersection of the total cash revenue curve with the cash outlay curve.

Cash Budget. A period-by-period statement of opening cash on hand, expected cash receipts, expected cash disbursements, and resulting expected cash balance at the end of each period.

Cash Cycle. The time lapse between purchase of materials and collection of *accounts receivable* for finished product sold.

Cash Discount. A discount allowed for payment of a debt in advance of a due date. For example, 2/10 net 30 means a 2 percent discount if paid within 10 days, the net price if paid after 10 but before 30 days.

Cash Flow. The *net profits* of a business plus the charges of the accounting period for *depreciation, depletion, amortization,* and extraordinary charges to reserves not paid in cash. This is the cash generated in a period if all other accounts do not change. In addition, decreases in assets, increases in liabilities, and new capital added are sources of cash, while increases in assets and decreases in liabilities and net worth are applications of cash.

Certificate of Participation. A certificate issued instead of shares of stock to show a proportionate interest in an unincorporated business or in the ownership of debt of a corporation.

Chattel Mortgage. A conveyance of personal property as security for the payment of a debt.

Class A and B Stock. During recent years it has been the practice of some corporations to issue common stock in two general classes, A and B, with the holders of only one class having voting power or with one class having preference. Also called classified common stock.

Clean-up Provision. In bank loans, an agreement by the borrower that at least once a year he will have repaid all bank loans and be "out of the bank" for a stated period, usually 30 days.

Closed-End Mortgage. A *mortgage* that does not permit additional borrowing.

Collateral Trust Bonds. Bonds of one corporation secured by its holdings of stocks, bonds, and/or notes of another corporation.

Collection Period. The average number of days needed to collect an *account receivable.* To compute, divide average daily credit sales into accounts receivable outstanding.

Commercial Bank. A bank, one of whose main functions is acceptance of deposits and creation of credit through short-term loans mainly for business purposes.

Commercial Paper. (1) Promissory notes, commercial drafts, trade acceptances, and similar documents issued by business firms. (2) In banking, loans arising from transactions covering purchases of goods. See *financial paper.*

Commitment Fee. The amount (such as ½ or ¼ percent) paid by a borrower to a lender for a loan in addition to interest on the loan. The fee may be against the total amount of the loan or against the unborrowed balance of a loan commitment or *line of credit* and may be paid once or annually.

Common Stock. Shares in a corporation that have no fixed rate of dividends. They are the last to secure a share in the property when the corporation is dissolved.

Compensating Balance. In banking the balance a borrower from a bank is required by the bank to keep in his account. Typically, 15 percent of the borrowed amount.

Competitive Bidding. The process of preparation of a security issue through the solicitation by the issuing company of the highest bids from competitive groups of investment banking firms and awarding the issue to the highest bidder. Since 1941 the required method for public utility holding companies and their subsidiaries unless exempted by the *SEC.*

Conditional Sale. A security transaction in which the seller retains title to the property until the buyer has made full payment.

Conglomerate. A company with widely diversified *product lines* which comes about through *merger* of many companies.

Consolidated Statements. The financial reports for a group of affiliated corporations or enterprises, eliminating intercorporation debts and profits and showing minority stockholders' interests.

Constant Percentage of Declining Balance Method of Depreciation. Taking the initial cost of a capital asset, deducting the expected salvage value, and spreading the difference by a constant percentage of the undepreciated balance, so that at the end of the expected life the undepreciated balance equals the salvage value. The percentage is determined as $1 - \sqrt[n]{s/c}$ where n is the number of periods, s the salvage value, and c the cost.

Convertible Bonds. Bonds that may be converted into stock at the option of the owner.

Convertible Stock. Preferred stock that may be converted into common stock at the option of the owner.

Corporation. An association of stockholders created under law and regarded as an artificial person by the courts. The chief characteristics are (1) limited liability of stockholders, (2) continuity in existence, and (3) easy transferability of ownership interest.

Corporation Charter. A document issued by the state or federal government giving a group of persons the right to act as a legal person in the conduct of an enterprise and specifying at least some of the conditions of operation.

Cost of Capital. In *capital budgeting* the cost to the investor of the funds to be committed to a proposed investment. This cost includes not only the "nominal" rate paid for the funds, but the net effect (plus or minus) on the investor's cost of funds compared to not making the investment.

Cost of Goods Sold. Determined for any period by subtracting the value of the ending inventory from the sum of the value of the beginning inventory plus the cost of goods bought or manufactured during that period.

Coupon Bonds. Bonds provided with coupons, one for the amount of interest due on each interest date. Upon surrender of the coupon on the maturity date the bondholder receives the interest payment.

Credit Instrument. Any written or printed paper by means of which funds are transferred from one person to another. The most common are checks, drafts, money orders, promissory notes, and letters of credit.

Cumulative Dividend. A dividend that if not paid annually (or periodically as provided in the stock certificate) will ultimately have to be paid before any common stock dividend can be paid. The arrearage is said to accumulate.

Cumulative Voting. In a corporation a method of voting for directors involving the simultaneous election of all directors, with each stockholder receiving as many votes as he has voting shares multiplied by the number of directors to be elected. This assures some representation on the board for the minority if they cast all their votes for a limited number of directors. The number of shares needed to elect one director is determined by this formula (dropping fractional shares) *provided* all stockholders vote only for the number of directors who can be elected by their shares.

$$\frac{(\text{total shares voting}) \times (\text{number of directors desired})}{\text{number of directors to be elected} + 1} + 1$$

Current Assets. Any property that will be converted into cash in the normal operation of business at an early date, usually within one year.

Current Liability. A liability that will be paid in the normal operation of a business at an early date, usually within one year.

Dealer. (1) One who purchases goods for resale to final consumers. (2) In securities one who acts for his own account rather than as an agent for another.

Debenture Bonds. Bonds not secured by any specific property but issued against the general credit of a corporation or government.

Debt Service. The interest and charges currently payable on a debt, including principal payments.

Depreciation. (1) In accounting the allocation of the cost (purchase price minus salvage) of an asset that will be used up over a long period of time by charging a portion of the cost to each period of expected life. (2) More generally, any drop in value.

Dilution. In finance, crudely used to describe the reduction in the proportion of a corporation owned by old shareholders when new shares are sold. More accurately, dilution occurs only when the proceeds of the new shares earn at a lesser rate than the earning rate just before the new shares are issued.

Direct Placement. The negotiation by a borrower, such as an industrial or utility company, directly with the lender, such as a life insurance company or group of companies, for an entire issue of securities. No *underwriter* is involved and the transaction is exempt from SEC filing.

Discount Bond. A bond sold for less than face or maturity value. No interest is paid annually, but all interest accrues to the maturity date when it is paid.

Discounted Cash Flow. In capital budgeting a method of analysis emphasizing the time factor in considering receipts and outlays and further emphasizing that receipts are to be considered as after income tax but with depreciation charges "added back." The time factor is recognized in the form of a rate of interest (or discount) applicable to both outlays and receipts. Two methods are common, the *internal rate of return* and the *present value method*.

Dissolution. As applied to a partnership or corporation, the termination of the business with the assets distributed according to priorities to the creditors and owners.

Dividend. (1) The earnings or profits that a corporation, upon the order of its board of directors, pays to its stockholders. The dividend may be in cash, property, securities, or any combination of these. Dividends can also, in some states, be declared out of non-earnings, for example, out of paid-in surplus. (2) Special types of businesses (for example, cooperatives and insurance companies) also declare dividends. In this case the "dividend" is a refund due to overpayment of the sales price or premium.

Dividend Yield. The current annual dividend divided by the market price per share.

Double Declining Balance Method of Depreciation. Spreading the initial cost of a capital asset over time by deducting in each period double the percentage recognized by the *straight-line method* and applying that double percentage to the undepreciated balance existing at the start of each period. No salvage value is used in the calculation.

Earnest Money. A sum of money paid by a buyer at the time of entering a contract to indicate the intention and ability of the buyer to carry out the contract. Often the contract provides for forfeiture of this sum if the buyer defaults.

Earnings per Share. One common measure of the value of common stock. The figure is computed by dividing the net earnings (after interest and prior dividends) by the number of shares of common stock.

Earn Out. A type of *merger* agreement in which all or a part of the price received by the acquired company is dependent upon the future earnings of that company.

Ebit. Abbreviation for "earnings before interest and taxes."

Efficient Frontier. The set of securities that minimizes the *variance* of a *portfolio*.

EPS. Abbreviation for "earnings per share."

Ex Rights. Literally, without rights. Stock sold ex rights is sold without privileged subscription rights to a current new issue by a corporation.

Face Value. The value stated on the face of a security or insurance policy. This is the value at maturity or death.

Factoring. Sale of *accounts receivable* of a firm to a *factor* at a discounted price.

Federal Reserve System. A system of 12 central banks created in 1913 and controlled by the Board of Governors of seven men in Washington, D. C. National banks must belong and state banks may. A member bank must invest 6 percent (of which only 3 percent or half has currently been called) of its own capital and surplus in the stock of its regional Federal Reserve bank and must also keep a minimum reserve of 12 percent if a country bank and 16.5 percent if a Reserve-city bank of its demand deposits in the Reserve bank or in vault cash and 4 percent of its time or savings deposits. The Board of Governors has the power to vary these percentages from a minimum of 7 for country banks and 10 for Reserve-city banks to a maximum of 14 and 22, respectively. The 12 cities in which the Federal Reserve banks are located are (1) Boston, (2) New York, (3) Philadelphia, (4) Cleveland, (5) Richmond, (6) Atlanta, (7) Chicago, (8) St. Louis, (9) Minneapolis, (10) Kansas City, Mo., (11) Dallas, and (12) San Francisco. There are also 25 branch offices.

Financial Intermediaries. Financial institutions such as *commercial banks,* insurance companies, and *investment companies* that act as an intermediary between lenders (and savers) and borrowers.

Financial Lease. Such a lease as provides for rental payments that cover the full repayment of original cost of the asset plus interest (with zero terminal value) and is noncancellable. See *operating lease.*

Financial Leverage. The use of the fact that the interest rate on debt is different from the earning rate of assets. If the rate on debt is lower than the earning rate, the leverage is favorable. See *leverage factor, operating leverage.*

Financial Paper. Accommodation paper, that is, a short-term loan not supported by a specific commercial transaction or transfer of goods. See *commercial paper.*

Financial Risk. In investments used in contradistinction to *interest rate risk* and *purchasing power risk* to refer to the risk of default in performing the obligations of a security.

Financial Statement. Any report summarizing the financial condition or financial results of an organization on any date or for any period. The two principal types of financial statements are the *balance sheet* and the *profit and loss statement.*

Financial Structure. All the financial resources of a firm, short term and long term, debt and equity. Distinguished from *capital structure,* which includes only long-term resources.

First In, First Out Method of Inventory. Under the first in, first out rule (FIFO) items of inventory issued are priced out at the purchase price of the oldest batch in stock, then the purchase price of the next oldest batch, and so on. Inventory value is thus computed by assuming that goods on hand are those most recently purchased and are valued at the successively latest purchase prices.

First, Second, or Third Mortgage. The words "first," "second," or "third" applied to a *mortgage* indicate the priority of the interest of the *mortgagee* in the property given as security for a debt. Mortgages are ranked in the time order in which they are made unless earlier mortgagees consent otherwise.

Fixed Charges. The expenses that have to be borne whether any business is done or not. The chief items are the company's interest on bonds, some taxes levied by the government, insurance payments, and depreciation due to obsolescence.

Flexible Budget. A *budget* that provides estimates for varying levels of sales and hence of cash requirements, profits, and financing needs for these several levels. Also called *variable budget*.

Float. (1) In banking practice checks and other items in the process of collection. (2) In manufacturing the amount of goods in the process of production, usually measured in terms of the number of units in process divided by the number of finished units produced per average day and expressed as, for example, "six days float." (3) In finance the unsold part of a security issue or (4) the number of shares actively traded.

Floor Planning. Any method such as a *trust receipt* by which the borrower keeps possession of goods pledged as security for a loan and is able to sell such goods.

Flotation Cost. The expenses of selling securities such as underwriting *spread*, legal and accounting fees, and printing and engraving charges.

Foreclosure. (1) The legal procedure that provides for the sale of mortgaged property when the mortgagor fails to pay the debt. The proceeds of the sale are then applied to the mortgage debt. Any excess of proceeds over the debt is refunded to the debtor; and deficiency is charged against the debtor in a *deficiency judgment* if that is asked for. (2) Strict foreclosure involves forfeiture of the mortgaged property upon default.

Fully Diluted Earnings. In accounting, the adjustment of current earnings per share to show the result if all options and conversion privileges of bonds and preferred stock were exercised.

Funded Debt. The indebtedness of a business or government that has been formally evidenced, as in a bond issue. Usually the line is drawn at debt due more than one year hence.

Going Public. A colloquial term describing the first offering of the stock of a company for purchase by the general public.

Gross Profit. The difference between sales and the *cost of goods sold* before allowance for operating expenses and income taxes

Gross Spread. In finance the difference between the price paid by an investment banker for an issue and the price paid by the buying public.

Gross up. Colloquial term in taxation of U.S. international businesses under which U.S. corporations must "gross up" any income from foreign subsidiaries, that is, include preforeign tax income in U.S. income tax returns in order to claim credit against U.S. income taxes for foreign income taxes paid.

Holding Company. A corporation that controls the voting power of other individual corporations for the purpose of united action. A holding company may also be an operating company, as the American Telephone and Telegraph Company, which operates long distance lines and controls local telephone companies.

Hurdle Rate. In *capital budgeting*, the minimum *rate of return* acceptable to a firm on an investment. Also called *cutoff rate*.

Hypothecate. To pledge something as security for a debt. Technically there is no pledging, since possession is not transferred but only the right to order sale upon default.

Impaired Capital. A negative surplus account. Hence the amount represented by the capital stock of the corporation has been reduced below what it was at the time the stock was issued.

Income Bonds. Bonds that receive interest only when it is earned during any one year. Ordinarily other fixed charges are paid first, then the income bonds, and then dividends on stocks.

Indenture. (1) Any written agreement. The term derives from the former practice of tearing the edges of two copies of a document so that later matching of the torn edges would establish the identity of the copies. (2) The contract between an apprentice and his master. (3) Historically the indentured servant contract of Colonial times, which provided for a term of personal service by a servant to his master.

Index of Profitability. The ratio of the *present value* of an asset to its purchase price.

Insider. In security regulation, anyone who has knowledge of facts not available to the general public. Specifically includes directors, officers, and holders of more than 10 percent of a corporation's stock who must report all transactions to the SEC if the stock is listed on an exchange or there are more than 500 stockholders.

Installment Equipment Financing. Buying equipment for a *down payment* with an agreement to pay installments thereafter until the account is settled.

Intercompany Dividends. Dividends from one corporation fully taxable under the income tax law paid to another fully taxable corporation are excluded up to 85 percent of such dividends from taxable income of the receiving corporation.

Interest Rate Risk. In investments used in contradistinction to *financial risk* and *purchasing power risk* to refer to the risk that the interest rate may change, thus affecting the market value of a security even though its obligations continue to be met.

Intermediate Financing. Somtimes defined in terms of length of time to maturity, such as more than one year but less than five or ten years. However, intermediate financing is not merely a matter of time to maturity but rather of the type of arrangement, namely, a *private placement*, which allows easy refinancing arrangements.

Internal Financing. Securing the funds needed by a firm from retained earnings and depreciation rather than going outside the firm to borrow or sell stock.

Internal Growth. The expansion of a firm from increased sales of its products rather than by acquiring new firms through *merger*.

Investment. (1) The purchase of stocks, bonds, and property that, upon analysis, promise safety of principal and a satisfactory return. These factors distinguish investment from speculation. (2) In economic theory investment means the acquisition of means of production (including goods for selling) with money capital.

Investment Banking. *Underwriting* and selling primarily new issues of stocks and bonds to investors.

Investment Company. A corporation or trust organized for the purpose of dealing in securities. Shares in the company are sold to the public. The supporting argument is that this device "spreads the risk" and cost of handling by pooling the investments of many people.

Investment Tax Credit. Federal legislation designed to stimulate purchase of capital goods by allowing a percentage of the purchase price as a credit against taxes due and not merely as a deduction from taxable income. The percentage is in addition to *depreciation*.

Last in, First out Method of Inventory. Under the last in, first out rule (LIFO) items of inventory used are priced out at the latest purchase prices of the goods. Inventory value is thus computed by assuming that goods on hand are those remotely purchased and are valued at the successively most remote purchase prices.

Leasehold Mortgage Bond. A bond secured by a building constructed on leased real estate. This bond is subject to the compliance by the lessee (who issues the bond) with the terms of the lease; upon default in the terms of the lease the lessor of the leased real estate has priority over the holders of the leasehold bonds.

Letter Stock. Stock not registered under the Securities Act of 1933, where the buyer gives the seller a letter stating the buyer intends to hold for investment purposes and does not contemplate reoffering the stock to others.

Leverage Factor. (1) In finance the extent to which a corporation can effect, by the use of bonds and preferred stocks, proportionate changes in return to common stock greater than the changes in operating income. If the bulk of the corporation's capital is represented by bonds and preferred stock, the corporation has a high leverage factor. The process of using the leverage factor is called trading on the equity. (2) The increase in the rate of profit that follows an increase in the volume of sales or production when fixed costs are spread over more units. Called *operating* leverage to distinguish (1), which is *financial* leverage.

Lien. A right by way of security against real estate or personal property for the satisfaction of a debt. May be created by specific act of the individual (for example, a *mortgage*) or by operation of law (for example, a mechanic's lien for work done or vendor's lien for the unpaid purchase price). A lien is lost when possession is surrendered, but a court of equity may impose an equitable lien where possession has been lost.

Limited Liability. Restriction of the liability of an investor to the amount invested. In a *limited partnership* the limited partners, and in a business corporation all the stockholders, have such limited liability. Formerly, in the case of a bank, liability of stockholders extended to double the par value of stock owned. This was double liability.

Limited Partnership. A partnership that has one or more partners whose loss is limited to the investment in the business. The name of a limited partner cannot be used in the firm name unless identified as limited. The limited partner cannot engage in business for the partnership. The limited partnership must also have one or more general partners who have unlimited personal liability for the debts of the partnership. Under the Uniform Limited Partnership Act the agreement of partnership must be publicly recorded.

Liquidation. (1) The winding up of affairs, selling assets for cash. (2) More narrowly, the termination of liabilities or the selling of assets even though there is no winding up.

Liquidity Preference Theory of Interest. An explanation of the rate of interest as the price adjusting (1) the *liquidity preferences* of individuals, which determine demand for money, and (2) banking policy, which determines the supply of money. See *loanable funds theory of interest*.

Listed Security. A security that has met the requirements of a stock exchange for listing. Such requirements include submitting financial reports, consenting to certain supervision, and so on.

Listing. (1) In real estate, the contract of an owner authorizing a broker to sell the owner's real estate. (2) In securities, the contract between a firm and a stock exchange covering the trading of that firm's securities on the stock exchange.

Loanable Funds Theory of Interest. An explanation of interest as the price adjusting the demand for and the supply of loanable funds available at any particular time, with demand determined mainly by investment opportunities and supply by savings and credit creation. See *liquidity preference theory of interest*.

Lock-Box Financing. The operation of a system of lock boxes in post offices in many cities with instruction to customers of a firm to mail payments to the nearest city in order to speed the collection funds. A bank in each city collects the contents of each box at frequent intervals.

Margin. (1) In commercial transactions the difference between the purchase price paid by a middleman or retailer and his selling price. Also called *gross margin*. (2) In trading, the purchase of a stock or commodity with payment in part in cash (called the margin) and in part by a loan. Usually the loan is made by the broker effecting the purchase.

Margin Call. A demand by a broker to put up money or securities upon purchase of a stock, or if the stock is already owned on margin, to increase the money or securities where the price of the stock has fallen since purchase. The last process is remargining.

Marginal Efficiency of Capital. The relation between the prospective yield of a capital asset and its supply price or replacement cost. Also the rate of discount that would make the present value of a series of annuities given by the returns expected from the capital asset during its life just equal to its supply price.

Market Order. An order to buy or sell on a stock or commodity exchange at the current price when the order reaches the floor of the exchange.

Market Risk. In finance, the risk of being unable to sell securities or assets at a price near the last price.

Merger. (1) In a broad sense, the combination of two or more corporations by any of several devices. (2) The acquisition by one corporation of the stock of another corporation. The acquiring corporation then retires the other corporation's stock and dissolves it.

Money Market. The institutions and practices through which short-term funds are channeled to borrowers and entrepreneurs. See *capital market.*

Mortgage. A conveyance of property as security for the payment of a debt. The mortgage may specify that the property is now conveyed subject to redemption by payment of the debt or that upon nonpayment of the debt the property is to be conveyed automatically.

Mortgage Bonds. Bonds for which real estate or personal property is pledged as security that the bond will be paid as stated in its terms. May be first, second, refunding, and so on.

National Association of Securities Dealers. An association of more than 3000 American *investment bankers* who police the *over-the-counter market.*

Negative Pledge Clause. A clause in a mortgage providing that the borrower will not pledge any of his assets or will pledge his assets only if the notes or bonds outstanding have certain protection.

Negotiable. (1) In a popular sense the term means transferable by delivery. (2) In law, however, a document is negotiable when it meets certain legal formalities (for example, it must be in order or in bearer form). Then, as a consequence, one taking such a document is relieved of certain claims that could otherwise be made against him, provided the document has been received in good faith, for value, before maturity, and without knowledge of any defect in it. The other requirements of form to make a document negotiable are (1) it must be in writing and signed by the maker or drawer, (2) it must be payable on demand or at a fixed or determinable time, (3) it must be an unconditional promise or order to pay a definite amount of money, and (4) if a bill of exchange, the drawer must be named or identified.

Net Operating Assets. The assets, net of depreciation and bad debts, employed in the ordinary course of business. Hence excludes investments in stocks and bonds owned by a manufacturing company, for example.

Net Operating Income. Income before interest and income taxes but after depreciation produced by *operating assets.*

Net Present Value. The difference between future cash inflows of an investment discounted to the present at an assumed rate and all cash outflows similarly discounted.

Net Profit. Deducting the *cost of goods sold* from sales gives the *gross profit.* Deducting the operating expenses (overhead) from gross profit gives the *operating profit.* Deducting income taxes from operating profit gives the net profit.

Net Worth. The total assets of a person or business less the total liabilities (amounts due to creditors). In the case of a corporation net worth includes both capital stock and surplus; in the case of a partnership or single proprietorship it is the original investment plus accumulated and reinvested profits.

Nominal Interest Rate. The rate of interest stated in a security as opposed to the actual interest yield that is based upon the price at which the interest-bearing property is purchased and the length of time to maturity of the obligation.

Nonnegotiable. Frequently misunderstood to mean not transferable. Correctly, nonnegotiable means wanting in one of the requirements of a *negotiable* instrument, and as a consequence not entitled to the benefits of negotiability such as freedom from many defenses that could otherwise be raised by the maker, for example, fraudulent inducement. A nonnegotiable document is transferable by assignment. To prevent transfer the label nontransferable should be used.

Nonrecourse Loan. A loan under the U.S. agricultural program to farmers on the security of surplus crops which are delivered to the government and held off the market. The loan must be liquidated as provided by the government's program, but the government has no recourse against the farmer for a deficiency if the security fails to bring the amount of the loan.

No Par Stock. Stock without par value but which represents a proportionate share of the ownership of a corporation based on the number of shares. One issue of stock in a corporation may have par value and another issue may have no par value. New York was the first state to pass a no par value law in 1912.

Odd Lot Dealers. Members of a stock exchange who handle transactions in less than the usual trading unit. The ordinary unit on the stock exchange is 100 shares, although a few inactive stocks have smaller units.

Off-Board Trading. Buying and selling a security listed on an exchange without routing the transaction over the exchange.

Open Credit. A credit established by a bank (or a business house) permitting a borrower (or customer) to make withdrawals (or buy goods) up to a stated amount without depositing security (or making payment for the goods).

Open-End Mortgage. A *mortgage* that allows the borrowing of additional sums, usually providing that at least the stated ratio of assets to the debt must be maintained.

Open-Market Operations. The purchase or sale of government bonds and bills of exchange by the Federal Reserve System for several possible objectives: (1) to support the market price of government bonds, (2) to affect member-bank reserves and thus their lending policy. In the second case purchasing by the Federal Reserve makes possible the expansion of credit through the increase of reserves, and vice versa, for selling.

Open-Market Paper. Bills of exchange or notes drawn by one with high credit standing, made payable to himself and indorsed in blank. These are sold to financial institutions other than banks.

Open-Market Rate. The interest or discount rate for *commercial paper* in the open market.

Operating Assets. The assets that contribute to the regular income from the operations of a business. Thus stocks and bonds owned, unused real estate, loans to officers, and so on, are excluded from operating assets.

Operating Costs. *Cost of goods sold* plus operating expenses.

Operating Expenses. Commercial overhead; those expenses other than direct labor, materials, and manufacturing expense and other than financing expenses and income taxes.

Operating Lease. Such a lease as provides for rental payments covering less than the full cost of an asset plus interest assuming zero value at the end of the lease. May or may not provide for the lessor to bear costs of maintenance. See *financial lease*.

Operating Leverage. The increase (or decrease) in rate of profit following any increase (or decrease) in volume of sales or production due to fixed costs. See *financial leverage*.

Operating Margin. Net *operating income* divided by sales for the period.

Operating Profit. Deducting the *cost of goods sold* from sales gives *gross profit*. Deducting the *operating expense* (overhead) from the gross profit gives the operating profit.

Oversold. (1) In securities or commodities the situation in which the amount of *selling short* is excessive in relation to the available items. (2) More generally, any businessman who has committed himself for more than he can do.

Over-the-Counter Market. Generally applied to security transactions which take place outside of an organized stock exchange whether the securities are listed on an organized exchange or not.

Paper Profits. Profits that would exist at a given moment if a person closed transactions of sale or purchase. For example, a house was purchased for $5000. The present price if it were to be sold would be $8000. There is a "paper profit" of $3000.

Partnership. An association of two or more persons who own a business jointly for profit. The chief characteristics of a partnership are (1) unlimited liability of all members (except for a limited partnership), (2) nontransferability of ownership unless the other partners consent, (3) instability of existence (death and other events can terminate the partnership).

Par Value. In the case of bonds and stock, the face value appearing on the certificate is the par value. Those stocks not containing such a statement have no par value.

Payback Period. In *capital budgeting*, the cost of an investment divided by the annual cash inflow from the investment gives the number of years to recover the cost of the investment. An alternate form computes the payback period using profit earned rather than cash return.

Payout Period. In *capital budgeting* the ratio of the original investment to the average annual cash earnings (after income taxes) plus depreciation. The result is in units of years.

Pay-out Ratio. The ratio of dividends paid to earnings in a given period.

"Pegging" Prices. Prices are spoken of as pegged when they are artificially held at a given level usually through governmental action.

Point. (1) A unit amount of money is referred to in different markets as a point. Thus in the stock market a point is one dollar, in foreign exchange a point is one hundredth of a cent, and in commodity markets a point is one one hundredth of a cent per pound. See *basis point*. (2) A change of one unit in an average such as the Dow–Jones industrial average.

Pooling of Interests. That method of accounting for a *merger* in which the asset and liability accounts of each company are combined with any difference between the merger terms and the book values of net worth accounted for in the *capital surplus* account of the combined companies. The *earned surplus* of the acquired company is added to the earned surplus of the acquiring company.

Portfolio. In investments the collective term for all the securities held by one person or institution.

Portfolio Effect. The offsetting of the risk of one project with the risk of another whose returns fluctuate in the opposite direction from the first project. Thus the combined risk (variation in return) of the portfolio is smaller than of the individual items in the portfolio.

Preferred Stock. Stock with a claim to earnings and/or assets of a corporation prior to that of some other class of stock.

Prepaying.   Paying before the date on which payment is due.

Present Value.   The sum of future payments due discounted back to the present date at an assumed rate of interest.

Price–Earnings Ratio.   The market price of a security divided by the earnings per share.

Primary Market.   In finance, the market where the initial sale by the issuer of securities occurs.

Prime Rate.   In banking, the rate of interest charged the most creditworthy customers for short-term loans.

Pro Forma.   Latin for "for the sake of form."   Used to describe accounting, financial, and other statements or conclusions based upon assumed or anticipated facts.

Prospectus.   A statement issued by a corporation at the time that securities are offered.   The prospectus gives the details of the various issues of the corporation and other financial data such as comparative balance sheets and operating statements.

Protective Covenants.   In finance, provisions in a loan arrangement designed to reduce the risk of the lender such as restrictions against increase in officers' salaries and dividends.

Purchase Method of Accounting.   That method of accounting for a *merger* in which any difference between the merger terms and the book value of the acquired company is accounted for as goodwill on the asset side of the balance sheet and as *acquired surplus* on the liability side.   The *earned surplus* of the acquired company is added to the *capital surplus* of the acquiring company.

Purchasing Power Risk.   In investments used in contradistinction to *financial risk* and *interest rate risk* to refer to the risk that the price level may move, thus affecting the market value of bonds, for example, relative to common stock.

Put.   An option permitting its holder to sell a certain commodity at a fixed price for a stated quantity and within a stated period.   Such a right is purchased for a fee paid the one who agrees to accept the goods if they are offered.   The buyer of this right to sell expects the price of the commodity to fall so that he can deliver the commodity (the put) at a profit. If the price rises, the option need not be exercised.   The reverse transaction is a *call*.

Pyramiding.   (1) In finance the narrowing of the amount of capital needed to control a business through the use of a number of *holding companies,* making use of the principle that ownership of 50 percent of the voting stock of a corporation gives control.   (2) In the stock market an increase of holdings of a particular stock financed out of the margin created by a rise in the price of shares already owned.

Qualified Stock Option Plan.   A plan for the issuance of *stock options* to key employees of a corporation.   The plan must qualify under Section 422 of the Internal Revenue Code in order for employees to gain the benefit of *capital gains* tax rates when they exercise the option, that is, hold the shares for six months and sell.   Prior to January 1, 1964, such a plan was called a restricted stock option plan under Section 424 of the Internal Revenue Code.

Ratio Analysis.   In finance, the use of various ratios (such as *asset turnover*) for comparison with the ratios of the same firm earlier in time or with those ratios of other firms to establish the progress or deterioration of a firm as to liquidity, profitability, and other aspects.

Recapitalization.   A voluntary readjustment of the bonds and stocks of a corporation.   For example, replacing debentures with mortgage bonds or replacing part of the common stock by an issue of second preferred stock.   Does not imply financial embarrassment of the corporation.

Receivership.   A legal proceeding involving the appointment by a court of a person (the receiver) to administer the affairs of a person or firm unable to meet its debts as they mature.   The receiver administers matters until a decision is made to reorganize or to liquidate. If the decision, by court or by owners, is to liquidate, the receiver carries out the liquidation, although his title is changed to trustee in bankruptcy.

"Red Herring." In finance an advance copy of the statement (prospectus) to be filed with the *SEC* preceding an issue of securities. The copy is marked in red ink, "not a solicitation, for information only."

Refunding. (1) In finance the replacement of an outstanding issue or issues of bonds by a new issue either at or before maturity. Usual purposes are the extension of the loan period or the reduction of the interest rate. (2) In general, the repayment of all or part of money paid previously.

Registered Bonds. A bond entered on the books of the issuing corporation or of its transfer agent in the name of the purchaser, whose name also appears on the face of the bonds. Either principal alone or both principal and interest may be registered.

Reorganization. The legal readjustment of bonds and stocks of a corporation, usually eliminating some of the securities which have become worthless because the value of the firm's assets has fallen.

Revolving Fund. A fund from which withdrawals are made either as loans or as disbursements, with the obligation of repaying the fund (with or without interest) to keep the fund intact.

Rights Offering. The issuance of new shares by distributing *stock rights* to existing stockholders.

Risk. The chance or possibility of gain or loss. (1) Risk may be economic, moral, physical, and so on. In finance, risk is classified as *business risk, financial risk, market risk, money rate (interest rate) risk,* and *purchasing power risk.* (2) Risk is frequently measured by the *standard deviation;* the greater the standard deviation (or variability) of a series, the greater the risk.

Round Lot. The term applied to the unit of trading on the New York Stock Exchange, namely, 100 shares in the case of stock and $1000 par value in the case of bonds except for some special instances.

Sale and Leaseback. A sale of an asset to a vendee who immediately leases back to the vendor. The usual objectives are (1) to free cash in the amount of the purchase price for other uses by the vendor, (2) for benefits not otherwise available such a deduction by the vendor of the full value of the property for income tax purposes as rental payments over a period of time shorter than would be in depreciation where the base period is the allowable depreciable life. The rental payments total the purchase price plus interest less an estimated salvage value.

Secondary Offering. The sale of a block of securities by a large stockholder.

Secured Loan. A promise to pay by a person, corporation, or government. Against the promise are pledged specific assets, usually by means of a mortgage.

Selling Short. The agreement to deliver at a future date a security or commodity the seller does not own but which he hopes to buy later at a lower price.

Serial Bonds. A serial bond issue consists of a number of bonds issued at the same time but with different maturity dates (serially due), usually with interest rates varying for the different maturity dates. To be distinguished from *series bonds.*

Series Bonds. Groups of bonds (for example, series A, series B) usually issued at different times and with different maturities but under the authority of the same indenture. To be distinguished from *serial bonds.*

Sinking Fund. (1) In general accounting segregated assets that are being accumulated for a specific purpose. (2) In governmental accounting, a fund established to accumulate resources for the retirement of bonds but not for the payment of interest, which is handled through the general fund or a special revenue fund.

Solvency. This term is used in two different primary meanings. (1) An enterprise is solvent when it is able to meet its obligations as they become due. This is the equity sense. (2) An enterprise is solvent when the total of its assets exceeds the total of its liabilities. This is the bankruptcy sense.

Source and Application of Funds Statement. A statement of the sources of funds of a business and the uses or applications of such funds during any given period. Sources of funds are (1) increases in liabilities, (2) increases in net worth, and (3) decreases in assets. Applications of funds are (1) decreases in liabilities, (2) decreases in net worth, and (3) increases in assets.

Specialist. In finance, a member of the stock exchange who handles for other brokers orders with limits above or below the current market price, and who may deal for his own account. The specialist usually confines himself to one or a few issues.

Spread. (1) In general, the difference between the total cost of production and the selling price to consumers. In this sense, the mark up. (2) In underwriting the difference between the buying price of the underwriter and the selling price to the public. (3) On exchanges the difference between present spot or cash prices and present prices for future delivery. (4) On exchanges a combination of a *call* and a *put,* so that the purchaser of the spread may at his option demand delivery from or make delivery to the seller of the spread. The *put* and the *call* are for different prices. If they are for the same price, it would be a *straddle.* (5) The difference between *ask* and *bid* prices.

Stock Dividend. Distributing stock as a dividend. If the dividend is common stock declared on common stock, the only result other than to reduce the value of each share of common and to maintain the proportionate interest of each stockholder is to transfer part of surplus to the stock account. To be distinguished from *stock split.*

Stock Option. The right to purchase shares of a corporation upon set conditions. The term "stock option" is used when the right is issued other than pro rata to all existing shareholders. When so issued to existing stockholders, the option is called a "stock right."

Stock Right. A right to purchase stock issued pro rata to existing shareholders. Sometimes issued on a "when, as, and if" basis, that is, the holder can buy the stock when it is issued, on such basis or of such kind as is issued, and if it is issued. The theoretical value of a New York right (the right that goes with one existing share) is determined by the following formula *before* the *ex* rights date:

$$\frac{\text{market price} - \text{subscription price}}{\text{number of rights needed to buy one share} + 1}$$

After the *ex* rights date the 1 is dropped from the formula. A Philadelphia right is the right to buy one share of the new issue and is worth the value of a New York right times the number of such rights needed to buy one new share.

Stock Split. The issuance of a number of shares for each share of stock now outstanding. The purpose of a stock split is to reduce the market price per share in order to make for wider trading and a larger price for the same ownership.

Straight-Line Method of Depreciation. Taking the initial cost of a capital asset, deducting the expected salvage value at the time it is expected to be discarded, and spreading the difference in equal installments per unit of time over an estimated life of the asset.

Street Name. The name of a broker or bank appearing on a corporate security with *blank endorsement* by the broker or bank. The security can then be transferred merely by delivery since the endorsement is well known. Street name is used for convenience or to shield identity of the true owner.

Subordinated Bonds or Debentures. *Bonds* or *debentures* which yield priority in liquidation to other (senior) debt of a corporation. Usually such bonds or debentures are not subordinate to general creditors but only to debt owed to a financial institution.

Sum-of-the-Years'-Digits Method of Depreciation. Taking the initial cost of a capital asset, deducting the expected salvage value at the time it is expected to be discarded, and spreading the difference over the life of the asset, deducting each year that fraction of this difference determined in the following way: Add the numbers of the number of years of life of the asset (thus for an asset of 4 years life, add 1, 2, 3, and 4 to get 10) and use each of these numbers as the numerator of fractions whose denominator is the sum of the digits (thus $\frac{1}{10}$, $\frac{2}{10}$, $\frac{3}{10}$, $\frac{4}{10}$). The fractions are then used in reverse order (the first year's depreciation would be $\frac{4}{10}$).

Tax Shield. In *capital budgeting* some expenditures that are deductible for income tax purposes (such as start-up costs for a new plant) are recognized as reducing (shielding against) income taxes that otherwise would be due. Depreciation acts similarly.

Tender Offer. In finance, an offer to purchase shares made by one company direct to the stockholders of another company, with a view to acquiring control of the second company. Used in an effort to go around the management of the second company, which is resisting acquisition.

Term Loan. A loan to a business for a term, usually 1 to 10 years, and usually repayable in installments.

Third Market. In securities, the purchase and sale of securities listed on a stock exchange without routing the transaction through the exchange. Called *off-board trading.*

Trader. One who buys or sells for his own account for a short-term profit.

Treasury Bill. An obligation of the U. S. Treasury with a maturity date less than one year from the date of issue and bearing no interest but sold at a discount. To be distinguished from a *certificate of indebtedness,* which likewise is of a maturity of one year or less but bears interest.

Treasury Stock. (1) Issued stock that has been reacquired by the corporation from stockholders. (2) Less commonly, authorized but unissued stock that is still in the "treasury" of the corporation.

Trust Receipt. A document indicating that the entruster has advanced money to the trustee for the purchase of goods, with the trustee to hold the goods in trust until the debt is paid. The trustee is authorized to sell in regular course of trade.

Underwiter. (1) Any person, banker, or syndicate that guarantees to furnish a definite sum of money by a definite date to a business or government in return for an issue of bonds or stock. (2) In insurance the one assuming a risk in return for the payment of a premium.

Working Capital (Net). (1) In accounting the difference between current assets and current liabilities. (2) In public utilities the amount of cash required by a business to carry on operations.

Yield Curve. In finance, with time to maturity plotted on the x axis and interest rate on the y axis, the curve tracing the variation in interest rate for a given security (or given quality of security) for various maturities.

TABLES

Table A.1. Present Value of One Dollar Due at the End of *N* Years

N	1%	2%	3%	4%	5%	6%	7%	8%	9%	10%	N
01	.99010	.98039	.97087	.96154	.95238	.94340	.93458	.92593	.91743	.90909	01
02	.98030	.96117	.94260	.92456	.90703	.89000	.87344	.85734	.84168	.82645	02
03	.97059	.94232	.91514	.88900	.86384	.83962	.81630	.79383	.77218	.75131	03
04	.96098	.92385	.88849	.85480	.82270	.79209	.76290	.73503	.70843	.68301	04
05	.95147	.90573	.86261	.82193	.78353	.74726	.71299	.68058	.64993	.62092	05
06	.94204	.88797	.83748	.79031	.74622	.70496	.66634	.63017	.59627	.56447	06
07	.93272	.87056	.81309	.75992	.71068	.66506	.62275	.58349	.54703	.51316	07
08	.92348	.85349	.78941	.73069	.67684	.62741	.58201	.54027	.50187	.46651	08
09	.91434	.83675	.76642	.70259	.64461	.59190	.54393	.50025	.46043	.42410	09
10	.90529	.82035	.74409	.67556	.61391	.55839	.50835	.46319	.42241	.38554	10
11	.89632	.80426	.72242	.64958	.58468	.52679	.47509	.42888	.38753	.35049	11
12	.88745	.78849	.70138	.62460	.55684	.49697	.44401	.39711	.35553	.31863	12
13	.87866	.77303	.68095	.60057	.53032	.46884	.41496	.36770	.32618	.28966	13
14	.86996	.75787	.66112	.57747	.50507	.44230	.38782	.34046	.29925	.26333	14
15	.86135	.74301	.64186	.55526	.48102	.41726	.36245	.31524	.27454	.23939	15
16	.85282	.72845	.62317	.53391	.45811	.39365	.33873	.29189	.25187	.21763	16
17	.84438	.71416	.60502	.51337	.43630	.37136	.31657	.27027	.23107	.19784	17
18	.83602	.70016	.58739	.49363	.41552	.35034	.29586	.25025	.21199	.17986	18
19	.82774	.68643	.57029	.47464	.39573	.33051	.27651	.23171	.19449	.16351	19
20	.81954	.67297	.55368	.45639	.37689	.31180	.25842	.21455	.17843	.14864	20
21	.81143	.65978	.53755	.43883	.35894	.29415	.24151	.19866	.16370	.13513	21
22	.80340	.64684	.52189	.42195	.34185	.27750	.22571	.18394	.15018	.12285	22
23	.79544	.63416	.50669	.40573	.32557	.26180	.21095	.17031	.13778	.11168	23
24	.78757	.62172	.49193	.39012	.31007	.24698	.19715	.15770	.12640	.10153	24
25	.77977	.60953	.47761	.37512	.29530	.23300	.18425	.14602	.11597	.09230	25

Reprinted with permission of The Macmillan Company from *The Management of Corporate Capital*, E. Solomon, Ed. Copyright 1959 by The Graduate School of Business, University of Chicago.

Table A.1. Present Value of One Dollar Due at the End of N Years (Continued)

N	11%	12%	13%	14%	15%	16%	17%	18%	19%	20%	N
01	.90090	.89286	.88496	.87719	.86957	.86207	.85470	.84746	.84034	.83333	01
02	.81162	.79719	.78315	.76947	.75614	.74316	.73051	.71818	.70616	.69444	02
03	.73119	.71178	.69305	.67497	.65752	.64066	.62437	.60863	.59342	.57870	03
04	.65873	.63552	.61332	.59208	.57175	.55229	.53365	.51579	.49867	.48225	04
05	.59345	.56743	.54276	.51937	.49718	.47611	.45611	.43711	.41905	.40188	05
06	.53464	.50663	.48032	.45559	.43233	.41044	.38984	.37043	.35214	.33490	06
07	.48166	.45235	.42506	.39964	.37594	.35383	.33320	.31392	.29592	.27908	07
08	.43393	.40388	.37616	.35056	.32690	.30503	.28478	.26604	.24867	.23257	08
09	.39092	.36061	.33288	.30751	.28426	.26295	.24340	.22546	.20897	.19381	09
10	.35218	.32197	.29459	.26974	.24718	.22668	.20804	.19106	.17560	.16151	10
11	.31728	.28748	.26070	.23662	.21494	.19542	.17781	.16192	.14756	.13459	11
12	.28584	.25667	.23071	.20756	.18691	.16846	.15197	.13722	.12400	.11216	12
13	.25751	.22917	.20416	.18207	.16253	.14523	.12989	.11629	.10420	.09346	13
14	.23199	.20462	.18068	.15971	.14133	.12520	.11102	.09855	.08757	.07789	14
15	.20900	.18270	.15989	.14010	.12289	.10793	.09489	.08352	.07359	.06491	15
16	.18829	.16312	.14150	.12289	.10686	.09304	.08110	.07078	.06184	.05409	16
17	.16963	.14564	.12522	.10780	.09293	.08021	.06932	.05998	.05196	.04507	17
18	.15282	.13004	.11081	.09456	.08080	.06914	.05925	.05083	.04367	.03756	18
19	.13768	.11611	.09806	.08295	.07026	.05961	.05064	.04308	.03669	.03130	19
20	.12403	.10367	.08678	.07276	.06110	.05139	.04328	.03651	.03084	.02608	20
21	.11174	.09256	.07680	.06383	.05313	.04430	.03699	.03094	.02591	.02174	21
22	.10067	.08264	.06796	.05599	.04620	.03819	.03162	.02622	.02178	.01811	22
23	.09069	.07379	.06014	.04911	.04017	.03292	.02702	.02222	.01830	.01509	23
24	.08170	.06588	.05322	.04308	.03493	.02838	.02310	.01883	.01538	.01258	24
25	.07361	.05882	.04710	.03779	.03038	.02447	.01974	.01596	.01292	.01048	25

N	21%	22%	23%	24%	25%	26%	27%	28%	29%	30%	N
01	.82645	.81967	.81301	.80645	.80000	.79365	.78740	.78125	.77519	.76923	01
02	.68301	.67186	.66098	.65036	.64000	.62988	.62000	.61035	.60093	.59172	02
03	.56447	.55071	.53738	.52449	.51200	.49991	.48819	.47684	.46583	.45517	03
04	.46651	.45140	.43690	.42297	.40960	.39675	.38440	.37253	.36111	.35013	04
05	.38554	.37000	.35520	.34111	.32768	.31488	.30268	.29104	.27993	.26933	05
06	.31863	.30328	.28878	.27509	.26214	.24991	.23833	.22737	.21700	.20718	06
07	.26333	.24859	.23478	.22184	.20972	.19834	.18766	.17764	.16822	.15937	07
08	.21763	.20376	.19088	.17891	.16777	.15741	.14776	.13878	.13040	.12259	08
09	.17986	.16702	.15519	.14428	.13422	.12493	.11635	.10842	.10109	.09430	09
10	.14864	.13690	.12617	.11635	.10737	.09915	.09161	.08470	.07836	.07254	10
11	.12285	.11221	.10258	.09383	.08590	.07869	.07214	.06617	.06075	.05580	11
12	.10153	.09198	.08339	.07567	.06872	.06245	.05680	.05170	.04709	.04292	12
13	.08391	.07539	.06780	.06103	.05498	.04957	.04472	.04039	.03650	.03302	13
14	.06934	.06180	.05512	.04921	.04398	.03934	.03522	.03155	.02830	.02540	14
15	.05731	.05065	.04481	.03969	.03518	.03122	.02773	.02465	.02194	.01954	15
16	.04736	.04152	.03643	.03201	.02815	.02478	.02183	.01926	.01700	.01503	16
17	.03914	.03403	.02962	.02581	.02252	.01967	.01719	.01505	.01318	.01156	17
18	.03235	.02789	.02408	.02082	.01801	.01561	.01354	.01175	.01022	.00889	18
19	.02673	.02286	.01958	.01679	.01441	.01239	.01066	.00918	.00792	.00684	19
20	.02209	.01874	.01592	.01354	.01153	.00983	.00839	.00717	.00614	.00526	20
21	.01826	.01536	.01294	.01092	.00922	.00780	.00661	.00561	.00476	.00405	21
22	.01509	.01259	.01052	.00880	.00738	.00619	.00520	.00438	.00369	.00311	22
23	.01247	.01032	.00855	.00710	.00590	.00491	.00410	.00342	.00286	.00239	23
24	.01031	.00846	.00695	.00573	.00472	.00390	.00323	.00267	.00222	.00184	24
25	.00852	.00693	.00565	.00462	.00378	.00310	.00254	.00209	.00172	.00142	25

Table A.1. Present Value of One Dollar Due at the End of N Years (Continued)

N	31%	32%	33%	34%	35%	36%	37%	38%	39%	40%	N
01	.76336	.75758	.75188	.74627	.74074	.73529	.72993	.72464	.71942	.71429	01
02	.58272	.57392	.56532	.55692	.54870	.54066	.53279	.52510	.51757	.51020	02
03	.44482	.43479	.42505	.41561	.40644	.39754	.38890	.38051	.37235	.36443	03
04	.33956	.32939	.31959	.31016	.30107	.29231	.28387	.27573	.26788	.26031	04
05	.25920	.24953	.24029	.23146	.22301	.21493	.20720	.19980	.19272	.18593	05
06	.19787	.18904	.18067	.17273	.16520	.15804	.15124	.14479	.13865	.13281	06
07	.15104	.14321	.13584	.12890	.12237	.11621	.11040	.10492	.09975	.09486	07
08	.11530	.10849	.10214	.09620	.09064	.08545	.08058	.07603	.07176	.06776	08
09	.08802	.08219	.07680	.07179	.06714	.06283	.05882	.05509	.05163	.04840	09
10	.06719	.06227	.05774	.05357	.04973	.04620	.04293	.03992	.03714	.03457	10
11	.05129	.04717	.04341	.03998	.03684	.03397	.03134	.02893	.02672	.02469	11
12	.03915	.03574	.03264	.02984	.02729	.02498	.02287	.02096	.01922	.01764	12
13	.02989	.02707	.02454	.02227	.02021	.01837	.01670	.01519	.01383	.01260	13
14	.02281	.02051	.01845	.01662	.01497	.01350	.01219	.01101	.00995	.00900	14
15	.01742	.01554	.01387	.01240	.01109	.00993	.00890	.00798	.00716	.00643	15
16	.01329	.01177	.01043	.00925	.00822	.00730	.00649	.00578	.00515	.00459	16
17	.01015	.00892	.00784	.00691	.00609	.00537	.00474	.00419	.00370	.00328	17
18	.00775	.00676	.00590	.00515	.00451	.00395	.00346	.00304	.00267	.00234	18
19	.00591	.00512	.00443	.00385	.00334	.00290	.00253	.00220	.00192	.00167	19
20	.00451	.00388	.00333	.00287	.00247	.00213	.00184	.00159	.00138	.00120	20
21	.00345	.00294	.00251	.00214	.00183	.00157	.00135	.00115	.00099	.00085	21
22	.00263	.00223	.00188	.00160	.00136	.00115	.00098	.00084	.00071	.00061	22
23	.00201	.00169	.00142	.00119	.00101	.00085	.00072	.00061	.00051	.00044	23
24	.00153	.00128	.00107	.00089	.00074	.00062	.00052	.00044	.00037	.00031	24
25	.00117	.00097	.00080	.00066	.00055	.00046	.00038	.00032	.00027	.00022	25

Table A.2. Present Value of One Dollar per Year, N Years at R Percent

Year	1%	2%	3%	4%	5%	6%	7%	8%	9%	10%	Year
1	.9901	.9804	.9709	.9615	.9524	.9434	.9346	.9259	.9174	.9091	1
2	1.9704	1.9416	1.9135	1.8861	1.8594	1.8334	1.8080	1.7833	1.7591	1.7355	2
3	2.9410	2.8839	2.8286	2.7751	2.7232	2.6730	2.6243	2.5771	2.5313	2.4868	3
4	3.9020	3.8077	3.7171	3.6299	3.5459	3.4651	3.3872	3.3121	3.2397	3.1699	4
5	4.8535	4.7134	4.5797	4.4518	4.3295	4.2123	4.1002	3.9927	3.8896	3.7908	5
6	5.7955	5.6014	5.4172	5.2421	5.0757	4.9173	4.7665	4.6229	4.4859	4.3553	6
7	6.7282	6.4720	6.2302	6.0020	5.7863	5.5824	5.3893	5.2064	5.0329	4.8684	7
8	7.6517	7.3254	7.0196	6.7327	6.4632	6.2098	5.9713	5.7466	5.5348	5.3349	8
9	8.5661	8.1622	7.7861	7.4353	7.1078	6.8017	6.5152	6.2469	5.9952	5.7590	9
10	9.4714	8.9825	8.5302	8.1109	7.7217	7.3601	7.0236	6.7101	6.4176	6.1446	10
11	10.3677	9.7868	9.2526	8.7604	8.3064	7.8868	7.4987	7.1389	6.8052	6.4951	11
12	11.2552	10.5753	9.9539	9.3850	8.8632	8.3838	7.9427	7.5361	7.1607	6.8137	12
13	12.1338	11.3483	10.6349	9.9856	9.3935	8.8527	8.3576	7.9038	7.4869	7.1034	13
14	13.0038	12.1062	11.2960	10.5631	9.8986	9.2950	8.7454	8.2442	7.7861	7.3667	14
15	13.8651	12.8492	11.9379	11.1183	10.3796	9.7122	9.1079	8.5595	8.0607	7.6061	15
16	14.7180	13.5777	12.5610	11.6522	10.8377	10.1059	9.4466	8.8514	8.3125	7.8237	16
17	15.5624	14.2918	13.1660	12.1656	11.2740	10.4772	9.7632	9.1216	8.5436	8.0215	17
18	16.3984	14.9920	13.7534	12.6592	11.6895	10.8276	10.0591	9.3719	8.7556	8.2014	18
19	17.2261	15.6784	14.3237	13.1339	12.0853	11.1581	10.3356	9.6036	8.9501	8.3649	19
20	18.0457	16.3514	14.8774	13.5903	12.4622	11.4699	10.5940	9.8181	9.1285	8.5136	20
21	18.8571	17.0111	15.4149	14.0291	12.8211	11.7640	10.8355	10.0168	9.2922	8.6487	21
22	19.6605	17.6580	15.9368	14.4511	13.1630	12.0416	11.0612	10.2007	9.4424	8.7715	22
23	20.4559	18.2921	16.4435	14.8568	13.4885	12.3033	11.2722	10.3710	9.5802	8.8832	23
24	21.2435	18.9139	16.9355	15.2469	13.7986	12.5503	11.4693	10.5287	9.7066	8.9847	24
25	22.0233	19.5234	17.4131	15.6220	14.0939	12.7833	11.6536	10.6748	9.8226	9.0770	25

Table A.2. Present Value of One Dollar per Year, N Years at R Percent (Continued)

Year	11%	12%	13%	14%	15%	16%	17%	18%	19%	20%	Year
1	.9009	.8929	.8850	.3772	.8696	.8621	.8547	.8475	.8403	.8333	1
2	1.7125	1.6901	1.6681	1.6467	1.6257	1.6052	1.5852	1.5656	1.5465	1.5278	2
3	2.4437	2.4018	2.3612	2.3216	2.2832	2.2459	2.2096	2.1743	2.1399	2.1065	3
4	3.1024	3.0373	2.9745	2.9137	2.8550	2.7982	2.7432	2.6901	2.6386	2.5887	4
5	3.6959	3.6048	3.5172	3.4331	3.3522	3.2743	3.1993	3.1272	3.0576	2.9906	5
6	4.2305	4.1114	3.9976	3.8887	3.7845	3.6847	3.5892	3.4976	3.4098	3.3255	6
7	4.7122	4.5638	4.4226	4.2883	4.1604	4.0386	3.9224	3.8115	3.7057	3.6046	7
8	5.1461	4.9676	4.7988	4.6389	4.4873	4.3436	4.2072	4.0776	3.9544	3.8372	8
9	5.5370	5.3282	5.1317	4.9464	4.7716	4.6065	4.4506	4.3030	4.1633	4.0310	9
10	5.8892	5.6502	5.4262	5.2161	5.0188	4.8332	4.6586	4.4941	4.3389	4.1925	10
11	6.2065	5.9377	5.6869	5.4527	5.2337	5.0286	4.8364	4.6560	4.4865	4.3271	11
12	6.4924	6.1944	5.9176	5.6603	5.4206	5.1971	4.9884	4.7932	4.6105	4.4392	12
13	6.7499	6.4235	6.1218	5.8424	5.5831	5.3423	5.1183	4.9095	4.7147	4.5327	13
14	6.9819	6.6282	6.3025	6.0021	5.7245	5.4675	5.2293	5.0081	4.8023	4.6106	14
15	7.1909	6.8109	6.4624	6.1422	5.8474	5.5755	5.3242	5.0916	4.8759	4.6755	15
16	7.3792	6.9740	6.6039	6.2651	5.9542	5.6685	5.4053	5.1624	4.9377	4.7296	16
17	7.5488	7.1196	6.7291	6.3729	6.0472	5.7487	5.4746	5.2223	4.9897	4.7746	17
18	7.7016	7.2497	6.8399	6.4674	6.1280	5.8178	5.5339	5.2732	5.0333	4.8122	18
19	7.8393	7.3658	6.9380	6.5504	6.1982	5.8775	5.5845	5.3162	5.0700	4.8435	19
20	7.9633	7.4694	7.0248	6.6231	6.2593	5.9288	5.6278	5.3527	5.1009	4.8696	20
21	8.0751	7.5620	7.1016	6.6870	6.3125	5.9731	5.6648	5.3837	5.1268	4.8913	21
22	8.1757	7.6446	7.1695	6.7429	6.3587	6.0113	5.6964	5.4099	5.1486	4.9094	22
23	8.2664	7.7184	7.2297	6.7921	6.3988	6.0442	5.7234	5.4321	5.1668	4.9245	23
24	8.3481	7.7843	7.2829	6.8351	6.4338	6.0726	5.7465	5.4509	5.1822	4.9371	24
25	8.4217	7.8431	7.3300	6.8729	6.4641	6.0971	5.7662	5.4669	5.1951	4.9476	25

Year	21%	22%	23%	24%	25%	26%	27%	28%	29%	30%	Year
1	.8264	.8197	.8130	.8065	.8000	.7937	.7874	.7813	.7752	.7692	1
2	1.5095	1.4915	1.4740	1.4568	1.4400	1.4235	1.4074	1.3916	1.3761	1.3609	2
3	2.0739	2.0422	2.0114	1.9813	1.9520	1.9234	1.8956	1.8684	1.8420	1.8161	3
4	2.5404	2.4936	2.4483	2.4043	2.3616	2.3202	2.2800	2.2410	2.2031	2.1662	4
5	2.9260	2.8636	2.8035	2.7454	2.6893	2.6351	2.5827	2.5320	2.4830	2.4356	5
6	3.2446	3.1669	3.0923	3.0205	2.9514	2.8850	2.8210	2.7594	2.7000	2.6427	6
7	3.5079	3.4155	3.3270	3.2423	3.1611	3.0833	3.0087	2.9370	2.8682	2.8021	7
8	3.7256	3.6193	3.5179	3.4212	3.3289	3.2407	3.1564	3.0758	2.9986	2.9247	8
9	3.9054	3.7863	3.6731	3.5655	3.4631	3.3657	3.2728	3.1842	3.0997	3.0190	9
10	4.0541	3.9232	3.7993	3.6819	3.5705	3.4648	3.3644	3.2689	3.1781	3.0915	10
11	4.1769	4.0354	3.9018	3.7757	3.6564	3.5435	3.4365	3.3351	3.2388	3.1473	11
12	4.2785	4.1274	3.9852	3.8514	3.7251	3.6060	3.4933	3.3868	3.2859	3.1903	12
13	4.3624	4.2028	4.0530	3.9124	3.7801	3.6555	3.6381	3.4272	3.3224	3.2233	13
14	4.4317	4.2646	4.1082	3.9616	3.8241	3.6949	3.5733	3.4587	3.3507	3.2487	14
15	4.4890	4.3152	4.1530	4.0013	3.8593	3.7261	3.6010	3.4834	3.3726	3.2682	15
16	4.5364	4.3567	4.1894	4.0333	3.8874	3.7509	3.6228	3.5026	3.3896	3.2832	16
17	4.5755	4.3908	4.2190	4.0591	3.9099	3.7705	3.6400	3.5177	3.4028	3.2948	17
18	4.6079	4.4187	4.2431	4.0799	3.9279	3.7861	3.6536	3.5294	3.4130	3.3037	18
19	4.6346	4.4415	4.2627	4.0967	3.9424	3.7985	3.6642	3.5386	3.4210	3.3105	19
20	4.6567	4.4603	4.2786	4.1103	3.9539	3.8083	3.6726	3.5458	3.4271	3.3158	20
21	4.6750	4.4756	4.2916	4.1212	3.9631	3.8161	3.6792	3.5514	3.4319	3.3198	21
22	4.6900	4.4882	4.3021	4.1300	3.9705	3.8223	3.6844	3.5558	3.4356	3.3230	22
23	4.7025	4.4985	4.3106	4.1371	3.9764	3.8273	3.6885	3.5592	3.4384	3.3254	23
24	4.7128	4.5070	4.3176	4.1428	3.9811	3.8312	3.6918	3.5619	3.4406	3.3272	24
25	4.7213	4.5139	4.3232	4.1474	3.9849	3.8342	3.6943	3.5640	3.4423	3.3286	25

Table A.2. Present Value of One Dollar per Year, N Years at R Percent (Continued)

Year	31%	32%	33%	34%	35%	36%	37%	38%	39%	40%	Year
1	.7634	.7576	.7519	.7463	.7407	.7353	.7299	.7246	.7194	.7143	1
2	1.3461	1.3315	1.3172	1.3032	1.2894	1.2760	1.2627	1.2497	1.2370	1.2245	2
3	1.7909	1.7663	1.7423	1.7188	1.6959	1.6735	1.6516	1.6302	1.6093	1.5889	3
4	2.1305	2.0957	2.0618	2.0290	1.9969	1.9658	1.9355	1.9060	1.8772	1.8492	4
5	2.3897	2.3452	2.3021	2.2604	2.2200	2.1807	2.1427	2.1058	2.0699	2.9352	5
6	2.5875	2.5342	2.4828	2.4331	2.3852	2.3388	2.2939	2.2506	2.2086	2.1680	6
7	2.7386	2.6775	2.6187	2.5620	2.5075	2.4550	2.4043	2.3555	2.3083	2.2628	7
8	2.8539	2.7860	2.7208	2.6582	2.5982	2.5404	2.4849	2.4315	2.3801	2.3306	8
9	2.9419	2.8681	2.7976	2.7300	2.6653	2.6033	2.5437	2.4866	2.4317	2.3790	9
10	3.0091	2.9304	2.8553	2.7836	2.7150	2.6495	2.5867	2.5265	2.4689	2.4136	10
11	3.0604	2.9776	2.8987	2.8236	2.7519	2.6834	2.6180	2.5555	2.4956	2.4383	11
12	3.0995	3.0133	2.9314	2.8534	2.7792	2.7084	2.6409	2.5764	2.5148	2.4559	12
13	3.1294	3.0404	2.9559	2.8757	2.7994	2.7268	2.6576	2.5916	2.5286	2.4685	13
14	3.1522	3.0609	2.9744	2.8923	2.8144	2.7403	2.6698	2.6026	2.5386	2.4775	14
15	3.1696	3.0764	2.9883	2.9047	2.8255	2.7502	2.6787	2.6106	2.5457	2.4839	15
16	3.1829	3.0882	2.9987	2.9140	2.8337	2.7575	2.6852	2.6164	2.5509	2.4885	16
17	3.1931	3.0971	3.0065	2.9209	2.8398	2.7629	2.6899	2.6206	2.5546	2.4918	17
18	3.2008	3.1039	3.0124	2.9260	2.8443	2.7668	2.6934	2.6236	2.5573	2.4941	18
19	3.2067	3.1090	3.0169	2.9299	2.8476	2.7697	2.6959	2.6258	2.5592	2.4958	19
20	3.2112	3.1129	3.0202	2.9327	2.8501	2.7718	2.6977	2.6274	2.5606	2.4970	20
21	3.2147	3.1158	3.0227	2.9349	2.8519	2.7734	2.6991	2.6285	2.5616	2.4979	21
22	3.2173	3.1180	3.0246	2.9365	2.8533	2.7746	2.7000	2.6294	2.5623	2.4985	22
23	3.2193	3.1197	3.0260	2.9377	2.8543	2.7754	2.7008	2.6300	2.5628	2.4989	23
24	3.2209	3.1210	3.0271	2.9386	2.8550	2.7760	2.7013	2.6304	2.5632	2.4992	24
25	3.2220	3.1220	3.0279	2.9392	2.8556	2.7765	2.7017	2.6307	2.5634	2.4994	25

Table A.3. Future Value of One Dollar N Years Hence

N	1%	2%	3%	4%	5%	6%	7%	8%	9%	10%	12%	14%	N
01	1.010	1.020	1.030	1.040	1.050	1.060	1.070	1.080	1.090	1.100	1.120	1.140	01
02	1.020	1.040	1.061	1.082	1.102	1.124	1.145	1.166	1.188	1.210	1.254	1.300	02
03	1.030	1.061	1.093	1.125	1.158	1.291	1.225	1.250	1.295	1.331	1.405	1.482	03
04	1.041	1.082	1.126	1.170	1.216	1.262	1.311	1.360	1.412	1.464	1.574	1.689	04
05	1.051	1.104	1.159	1.217	1.276	1.338	1.403	1.469	1.539	1.611	1.762	1.925	05
06	1.061	1.126	1.194	1.265	1.340	1.419	1.501	1.587	1.677	1.772	1.974	2.195	06
07	1.072	1.149	1.230	1.316	1.407	1.504	1.606	1.714	1.828	1.949	2.211	2.502	07
08	1.083	1.172	1.367	1.469	1.477	1.594	1.718	1.851	1.993	2.144	2.476	2.853	08
09	1.094	1.195	1.405	1.423	1.551	1.689	1.838	1.999	2.172	2.358	2.773	3.252	09
10	1.105	1.219	1.344	1.480	1.629	1.791	1.967	2.159	2.367	2.594	3.106	3.707	10
11	1.116	1.243	1.384	1.549	1.710	1.898	2.105	2.332	2.580	2.853	3.479	4.226	11
12	1.127	1.268	1.426	1.601	1.796	2.012	2.252	2.518	2.813	3.138	3.896	4.818	12
13	1.138	1.294	1.469	1.665	1.886	2.133	2.410	2.720	3.066	3.452	4.363	5.492	13
14	1.149	1.319	1.513	1.732	1.980	2.261	2.579	2.937	3.342	3.798	4.887	6.261	14
15	1.161	1.346	1.558	1.801	2.079	2.397	2.759	3.172	3.642	4.177	5.474	7.138	15
16	1.173	1.373	1.605	1.873	2.183	2.540	2.952	3.426	3.970	4.595	6.130	8.137	16
17	1.184	1.400	1.653	1.948	2.292	2.693	3.159	3.700	4.328	5.054	6.866	9.276	17
18	1.196	1.428	1.703	2.036	2.407	2.854	3.380	3.996	4.717	5.560	7.690	10.575	18
19	1.208	1.457	1.754	2.107	2.527	3.026	3.617	4.316	5.142	6.116	8.613	12.056	19
20	1.220	1.486	1.806	2.191	2.653	3.207	3.870	4.660	5.604	6.287	9.646	13.743	20
21	1.232	1.516	1.860	2.279	2.786	3.400	4.141	5.034	6.109	7.400	10.804	15.558	21
22	1.245	1.546	1.916	2.470	2.925	3.604	4.430	5.437	6.659	8.160	12.100	17.861	22
23	1.257	1.577	1.974	2.465	3.072	3.820	4.741	5.871	7.258	8.954	13.552	20.362	23
24	1.270	1.608	2.044	2.563	3.225	4.049	5.072	6.341	7.911	9.850	15.189	23.212	24
25	1.282	1.641	2.094	2.666	3.386	4.291	5.427	6.848	8.623	10.834	17.000	26.462	25

Table A.3. Future Value of One Dollar N Years Hence (Continued)

N	15%	16%	18%	20%	22%	24%	28%	30%	34%	38%	40%	N
01	1.150	1.160	1.180	1.200	1.220	1.230	1.280	1.300	1.340	1.380	1.400	01
02	1.322	1.346	1.392	1.440	1.488	1.538	1.638	1.690	1.796	1.904	1.960	02
03	1.521	1.561	1.643	1.728	1.816	1.907	2.097	2.197	2.407	2.628	2.744	03
04	1.749	1.811	1.939	2.074	2.215	2.364	2.684	2.856	3.224	3.627	3.842	04
05	2.011	2.100	2.288	2.488	2.703	2.932	3.436	3.713	4.320	5.005	5.378	05
06	2.414	2.436	2.700	2.986	3.297	3.635	4.398	4.827	5.789	6.907	7.530	06
07	2.660	2.826	3.185	3.583	4.023	4.508	5.630	6.275	7.758	9.531	10.541	07
08	3.059	3.278	3.759	4.300	4.908	5.590	7.206	8.157	10.395	13.153	14.758	08
09	3.518	3.803	4.435	5.160	5.987	6.931	9.223	10.605	13.930	18.152	20.661	09
10	4.046	4.411	5.234	6.192	7.305	8.594	11.806	13.785	18.666	25.049	28.926	10
11	4.652	5.117	6.176	7.430	8.912	10.657	15.112	17.92	25.012	34.568	40.496	11
12	5.135	5.936	7.288	8.916	10.872	13.215	19.343	23.298	33.516	47.703	56.694	12
13	6.153	6.886	8.599	10.699	13.264	16.386	24.759	30.288	44.912	65.831	79.372	13
14	7.076	7.988	10.147	12.839	16.182	20.319	31.691	39.374	60.182	90.846	111.120	14
15	8.137	9.266	11.974	15.407	19.742	25.196	40.565	51.185	80.644	125.368	155.568	15
16	9.358	10.748	14.129	18.488	24.085	31.243	51.923	66.542	108.063	173.008	217.795	16
17	10.761	12.468	16.672	22.186	29.384	38.741	66.461	86.504	144.804	238.751	304.913	17
18	12.376	14.463	19.673	26.623	35.849	48.039	85.070	112.455	194.038	329.476	426.879	18
19	14.232	16.777	23.214	31.948	43.736	59.568	108.890	146.192	260.011	454.677	597.630	19
20	16.367	19.461	27.393	38.338	53.358	73.864	139.380	190.050	348.414	627.454	836.683	20
21	18.822	22.575	32.324	47.005	65.096	91.592	178.406	247.065	466.875	865.886	1171.36	21
22	21.645	26.186	38.142	55.206	79.418	113.574	228.360	321.184	625.613	1194.92	1639.90	22
23	24.892	30.376	45.008	66.247	96.889	140.831	292.300	417.539	838.321	1648.99	2295.86	23
24	28.625	35.236	53.109	79.497	118.205	174.631	374.144	542.801	1123.35	2275.61	3214.20	24
25	32.919	40.874	62.669	95.396	144.210	216.542	478.905	705.641	1505.29	3140.34	4499.88	25

Table A.4. Future Value of One Dollar per Year N Years Hence*

N	1%	2%	3%	4%	5%	6%	7%	8%	9%	10%	12%	14%	N
01	1.000	1.000	1.000	1.000	1.000	1.000	1.000	1.000	1.000	1.000	1.000	1.000	01
02	2.010	2.020	2.030	2.040	2.050	2.060	2.070	2.080	2.090	2.100	2.120	2.140	02
03	3.030	3.060	3.091	3.122	3.153	3.184	3.215	3.246	3.278	3.310	3.374	3.440	03
04	4.060	4.122	4.184	4.246	4.310	4.375	4.440	4.506	4.573	4.641	4.779	4.921	04
05	5.101	5.204	5.309	5.416	5.526	5.637	5.751	5.867	5.985	6.105	6.353	6.610	05
06	6.152	6.308	6.468	6.468	6.802	6.975	7.153	7.336	7.523	7.716	8.115	8.536	06
07	7.214	7.434	7.662	7.662	8.142	8.394	8.654	8.923	9.200	9.487	10.089	10.731	07
08	8.286	8.583	8.892	9.214	9.549	9.897	10.250	10.637	11.029	11.436	12.300	13.233	08
09	9.369	9.755	10.159	10.583	11.027	11.491	11.978	12.488	13.021	13.580	14.776	16.085	09
10	10.462	10.950	11.464	12.006	12.578	13.181	13.816	14.487	15.193	15.937	17.549	19.337	10
11	11.567	12.169	12.808	13.486	14.207	14.972	15.784	16.646	17.560	18.531	20.655	23.045	11
12	12.683	13.412	14.192	15.026	15.917	16.870	17.889	18.977	20.141	21.384	24.133	27.271	12
13	13.819	14.680	15.618	16.628	16.613	18.882	20.141	21.495	22.953	24.523	28.029	32.089	13
14	14.957	15.974	17.086	18.292	19.599	21.015	22.551	24.215	26.019	27.975	32.393	37.581	14
15	16.106	17.293	18.599	20.029	21.579	23.276	25.129	27.152	29.361	31.773	37.280	43.842	15
16	17.258	18.639	20.157	21.825	23.658	25.673	27.888	30.324	33.003	35.950	42.753	50.980	16
17	18.430	20.012	21.762	23.698	25.840	28.213	30.840	33.750	36.964	40.545	48.884	59.118	17
18	19.614	21.412	23.414	25.645	28.143	30.906	33.999	37.450	41.301	45.599	55.750	68.394	18
19	20.810	22.841	25.117	26.561	30.539	33.760	37.379	41.446	46.019	51.159	63.440	78.969	19
20	22.019	24.297	26.870	29.778	33.066	36.786	40.996	45.762	51.160	57.275	72.052	91.025	20
21	23.249	25.783	28.677	31.969	35.719	39.993	44.865	50.423	56.765	64.003	81.699	104.768	21
22	24.571	27.299	30.537	34.248	38.505	43.392	49.006	55.457	62.873	71.403	92.503	120.436	22
23	25.716	28.845	32.453	36.618	41.431	46.996	53.436	60.893	69.532	79.543	104.60	138.297	23
24	26.973	30.422	34.427	39.083	44.502	50.816	58.177	66.765	76.790	88.497	118.16	158.659	24
25	28.243	32.030	36.459	41.646	47.727	54.865	63.249	73.106	84.701	98.347	133.33	181.871	25

* Compounding deferred for one year. To obtain the value of one dollar per year N years hence with compounding from the beginning of year 1, multiply your figure in Table A.4 by $(1+i)$ where i is the given rate of interest.

Table A.4. Future Value of One Dollar per Year *N* Years Hence (Continued)

N	15%	16%	18%	20%	22%	24%	28%	30%	34%	38%	40%	N
01	1.000	1.000	1.000	1.000	1.000	1.000	1.000	1.000	1.000	1.000	1.000	01
02	2.150	2.160	2.180	2.200	2.220	2.240	2.280	2.300	2.340	2.380	2.400	02
03	3.473	3.506	3.572	3.640	3.708	3.778	3.918	3.990	4.136	4.284	4.360	03
04	4.993	5.067	5.215	5.368	5.524	5.684	6.016	6.187	6.542	6.912	7.104	04
05	6.742	6.877	7.154	7.442	7.740	8.048	8.700	9.043	9.766	10.539	10.946	05
06	8.754	8.977	9.442	9.930	10.442	10.980	12.136	12.756	14.086	15.544	16.324	06
07	11.067	11.414	12.142	12.925	13.740	14.615	16.534	17.583	19.876	22.451	23.853	07
08	13.727	14.240	15.327	16.499	17.762	19.123	22.163	23.858	27.633	31.982	34.395	08
09	16.786	17.519	19.086	20.799	22.670	24.713	29.369	32.015	38.029	45.135	49.153	09
10	20.304	21.433	23.521	25.959	28.657	31.643	38.593	42.720	51.958	63.287	69.814	10
11	24.349	25.733	28.755	32.150	35.062	40.239	50.399	56.405	70.624	88.336	98.739	11
12	29.002	30.850	34.931	39.581	44.874	50.895	65.510	74.327	95.637	122.904	139.235	12
13	34.352	36.786	42.219	48.497	55.746	64.110	84.853	97.625	129.153	170.607	195.929	13
14	40.505	43.672	50.818	59.196	69.010	80.496	109.612	127.913	174.065	236.438	275.300	14
15	47.580	51.660	60.965	72.035	85.192	100.815	141.303	167.286	234.247	327.284	386.420	15
16	55.718	60.925	72.939	87.442	104.035	126.011	181.868	218.472	314.891	452.652	541.988	16
17	65.075	71.673	87.068	105.931	120.020	157.253	233.791	285.014	422.954	625.659	759.784	17
18	75.836	84.141	103.740	128.117	158.405	195.994	300.252	371.518	567.758	864.410	1064.70	18
19	88.212	98.603	123.414	154.740	194.254	244.033	385.323	483.973	761.796	1193.89	1491.58	19
20	102.444	115.380	146.628	186.688	237.989	303.601	494.213	630.165	1021.81	1648.56	2089.21	20
21	118.810	134.841	174.021	225.026	291.347	377.465	633.593	820.215	1370.22	2276.02	2925.89	21
22	137.632	157.415	206.345	271.031	356.443	469.056	811.999	1067.28	1837.10	3141.90	4097.24	22
23	159.276	183.601	244.487	326.337	435.861	582.630	1040.36	1388.46	2462.71	4336.83	5735.14	23
24	184.168	213.978	289.494	392.484	532.750	723.461	1332.66	1806.00	3301.03	5985.82	8033.00	24
25	212.793	249.214	342.603	471.981	650.955	868.092	1706.80	2348.80	4424.38	8261.43	1247.2	25

INDEX